Arabs and Arabists

The History of Oriental Studies

Editors

Alastair Hamilton (*University of London*)
Jan Loop (*University of Copenhagen*)

Advisory Board

Thomas Burman (*Notre Dame*)
Charles Burnett (*London*)
Bernard Heyberger (*Paris*)
Noel Malcolm (*Oxford*)
Jan Schmidt (*Leiden*)
Francis Richard (*Paris*)
Arnoud Vrolijk (*Leiden*)
Joanna Weinberg (*Oxford*)

VOLUME 7

The titles published in this series are listed at *brill.com/hos*

For Robert Jones

Cover illustration: Leiden University Library, MS Or. 241. This fifteenth-century manuscript of fragments from the Qur'an belonged to Rutger Rescius, and then to Andreas Masius, before being owned by Franciscus Raphelengius. The passage displayed is s. 33: 32–33. The numbering at the head of the page, 'Azoar 43', refers to the different sura numbering in Robert of Ketton's translation of the Qur'an edited by Theodor Bibliander and published in Basel in 1543.

Library of Congress Cataloging-in-Publication Data
Names: Hamilton, Alastair, 1941– editor.
Title: Arabs and Arabists : selected articles / by Alastair Hamilton.
Description: Leiden ; Boston : Brill, 2022. | Series: History of Oriental studies, 2405-4488 ; vol. 7 | Includes bibliographical references and index.
Identifiers: LCCN 2021043052 (print) | LCCN 2021043053 (ebook) | ISBN 9789004498198 (hardback) | ISBN 9789004498204 (ebook)
Subjects: LCSH: Arab countries—Study and teaching—Europe—History. | Islamic civilization—Study and teaching—Europe. | Arabs—Europe—History. | Arabists—Europe—History. | Middle East specialists—Europe—History. | Arabic language—Study and teaching—Europe—History. | Islam—Study and teaching—Europe—History. | Qur'an—Translating—Europe—History. | LCGFT: Essays.
Classification: LCC DS37.65 .E97 A73 2022 (print) | LCC DS37.65 .E97 (ebook) | DDC 909/.097492707104—dc23/ENG/20211022
LC record available at https://lccn.loc.gov/2021043052
LC ebook record available at https://lccn.loc.gov/2021043053

Typeface for the Latin, Greek, and Cyrillic scripts: "Brill". See and download: brill.com/brill-typeface.

ISSN 2405-4488
ISBN 978-90-04-49819-8 (hardback)
ISBN 978-90-04-49820-4 (e-book)

Copyright 2022 by Alastair Hamilton. Published by Koninklijke Brill NV, Leiden, The Netherlands. Koninklijke Brill NV incorporates the imprints Brill, Brill Nijhoff, Brill Hotei, Brill Schöningh, Brill Fink, Brill mentis, Vandenhoeck & Ruprecht, Böhlau Verlag and V&R Unipress.
Koninklijke Brill NV reserves the right to protect this publication against unauthorized use. Requests for re-use and/or translations must be addressed to Koninklijke Brill NV via brill.com or copyright.com.

This book is printed on acid-free paper and produced in a sustainable manner.

Arabs and Arabists

Selected Articles

By
Alastair Hamilton

BRILL

LEIDEN | BOSTON

Contents

Preface XI
List of Figures XIII
Abbreviations XV

PART 1
Arabs and Arabists

1 An Egyptian Traveller in the Republic of Letters
   Josephus Barbatus or Abudacnus the Copt 3

2 Michel d'Asquier, Imperial Interpreter and Bibliophile 42

3 Isaac Casaubon the Arabist
   'Video Longum Esse Iter' 50
   1 The Apprentice 52
   2 The Method 63
   3 The Centre of a Circle 68
   4 The Arabist 75
   5 Conclusion 85

4 'To Divest the East of All Its Manuscripts and All Its Rarities'
   The Unfortunate Embassy of Henri Gournay de Marcheville 87

5 From East to West
   Jansenists, Orientalists, and the Eucharistic Controversy 111
   1 The Embassy in Istanbul 113
   2 Protestant Reactions 120
   3 Eastern Beliefs 124
   4 Conclusion 127

6 Adrianus Relandus (1676–1718)
   Outstanding Orientalist 129

7 Arabists and Cartesians at Utrecht 137

8   Pilgrims, Missionaries, and Scholars
     *Western Descriptions of the Monastery of St Paul from the Late
     Fourteenth Century to the Early Twentieth Century*   149
     1   Prosperity to Destitution   151
     2   Revival and Restoration   157
     3   Continuity and Change   169
     4   Scholarly Investigation   176

9   The Metamorphoses of Georg August Wallin   191

PART 2
Arabic Studies

10   Arabic Studies in Europe   205
     1   The Motives   205
     2   The Grammars   208
     3   The Dictionaries   211
     4   The Schools   215

11   The Victims of Progress
     The Raphelengius Arabic Type and Bedwell's Arabic Lexicon   218

12   'Nam Tirones Sumus'
     Franciscus Raphelengius's Lexicon Arabico-Latinum
     (*Leiden 1613*)   229
     1   Antwerp   231
     2   Leiden   238
     3   Publication   248
     4   Raphelengius's Arabic Manuscripts   254
          Appendix: Raphelengius's Arabic Manuscripts in the Leiden
          University Library   256

13   Franciscus Raphelengius
     The Hebraist and His Manuscripts   259

14   Abraham Ecchellensis et son 'Nomenclator Arabico-Latinus'   269
     1   Introduction   269
     2   Ecchellensis lexicologue   270
     3   Les sources du 'Nomenclator'   272

CONTENTS   IX

     4   L'organisation du 'Nomenclator' 276
     5   Un vocabulaire chrétien 276
     6   Le 'Nomenclator' et le Coran 277
     7   Conclusion 279

PART 3
Islam and the Qur'an

15   The Study of Islam in Early Modern Europe 283
     1   From the Islamic Conquests to the Reformation 285
     2   Parallel Developments: the Protestant North 289
     3   Parallel Developments: the Catholic South 296
     4   Conclusion 301

16   A Lutheran Translator for the Qur'an
     A Late Seventeenth-Century Quest 303
     1   The Turkish Defeat 304
     2   Competing Translators 307
     3   The Key to Success 322

17   'To Rescue the Honour of the Germans'
     Qur'an Translations by Eighteenth- and Early Nineteenth-Century
     German Protestants 325

18   The Qur'an as Chrestomathy in Early Modern Europe 377

19   After Marracci
     The Reception of Ludovico Marracci's Edition of the Qur'an in Northern
     Europe from the Late Seventeenth to the Early Nineteenth Century 395

     Index 415

Preface

The essays collected in this volume have been written over a period of 35 years. In that time the study of cultural relations between Europe and the Arab world has made enormous progress. New information has come to light; subjects which seemed novel at the time have now received attention and questions which remained open have found answers; works which were once forthcoming have been published and what were once unpublished doctoral dissertations have been turned into books, while documents which could only be consulted as manuscripts or in early printed editions have now either been edited or are easily accessible on internet. I have therefore tried to bring the articles up to date, both in the text and in the notes, and I have also endeavoured to correct some of the more glaring mistakes. With articles such as these a certain amount of overlap is inevitable. I have kept the repetitions to a minimum by using cross references.

The central theme of all the articles is the Western acquisition of knowledge of the Arab and Ottoman world in the early modern period. I have divided the essays into three sections. The first, 'Arabs and Arabists', is concerned with Arabs who visited Europe and gave instruction to Western Arabists, and Europeans who either visited the Arab (or the Ottoman) world in search of manuscripts and information or who, like Franciscus Raphelengius, Isaac Casaubon and Adriaen Reland, studied it at a distance and remained in the West. The second section, 'Arabic Studies', contains essays on the actual study of the Arabic language in Europe, and above all on the creation of the first Arabic-Latin dictionaries. The third part, 'Islam and the Qur'an', finally, is on the European study of Islam and the Western translations of the Qur'an.

A few of the many debts I have accumulated have, I hope, been acknowledged in the notes to the articles. The recurrent mention of Jill Kraye hardly does justice to my immense gratitude to her. For much that is in these articles I relied on the library of the Warburg Institute where I benefited from the warm reception and stimulation provided by various directors – by Joe Trapp, who introduced me to the Warburg, by Nico Mann, who arranged for me to have a visiting fellowship there, and by Charles Hope, the director during the years that I taught there and for whose friendship I shall always be grateful. I would also like to thank those who encouraged and helped me to publish these pieces in a revised form – Maurits van den Boogert, Jan Loop and Hamid Jahdani, as well as Dirk Bakker for his invaluable assistance in preparing them for the press and Arnoud Vrolijk for his kindness in searching for illustrations. And I again thank Robert Jones, to whom I owe so much and to whom this book is dedicated. The publication in this Brill series, The History of Oriental Studies, in 2020 of what was once his PhD thesis (of 1988), *Learning Arabic in Renaissance Europe (1505–1624)* (quoted throughout these articles), was one of the most gratifying moments of my career.

Figures

1 Isaac Casaubon. *Icones Leidenses* 44, Collection Leiden University   51
2 Joseph Justus Scaliger. Jacob Marci and Justum a Colster, *Illustrium Hollandiae Westfrisiae ordinum alma academia Leidensis* (Leiden, 1614), Dedication   55
3 Thomas Erpenius. Engraved portrait by (studio) de Passe. Joannes Meursius, *Athenæ Batavæ. Sive, De vrbe Leidensi, & academiâ, virisque claris* (Leiden: Andries Clouck, Bonaventura en Abraham Elzevier, 1625)   72
4 Portrait of Adriaen Reland by Johan George Colasius, c. 1710. Collectie Universiteitsmuseum Utrecht, inv.nr UG-5123   130
5 General view of St Paul's Monastery from the southeast (2005). Photograph © Nicholas Warner   150
6 Claude Sicard (1677–1726), *Carte des déserts de la Basse-Thébaïde aux environs des monastères de St Antoine et de St Paul hermites avec le plan des lieux par où les Israëlites ont probablement passé en sortant d'Egypte*. 1717. Source: gallica.bnf.fr/Bibliothèque nationale de France   159
7 The Cave Church of St Paul from the northwest with the keep and the Church of St Mercurius in the background (2005). Photograph © Nicholas Warner   164
8 A dome in the Cave Church painted with Christ surrounded by the living animals of the Evangelists above a row of the 24 elders of the Coptic Church (2005). Photograph © Nicholas Warner   165
9 Richard Pococke, *A Description of the East, and Some Other Countries. Volume the First. Observations on Egypt* (London, 1743), p. 128, pl. 51   168
10 St Paul's Monastery seen from the east. Georg Schweinfurth, *Auf unbetretenen Wegen in Aegypten* (Hamburg, 1922)   178
11 St Paul's Monastery seen from the walls. Johann Georg Herzog zu Sachsen, *Neueste Streifzüge durch die Kirchen und Klöster Ägyptens* (Leipzig, 1931)   187
12 The monks of St Paul's Monastery. Johann Georg Herzog zu Sachsen, *Neueste Streifzüge durch die Kirchen und Klöster Ägyptens* (Leipzig, 1931)   188
13 Georg August Wallin. Image from Leopold Henrik Stanislaus Mechelin (ed.), *Finland in the Nineteenth Century by Finnish authors. Illustrated by Finnish artists* (Helsingfors, 1894), p. 305   192
14 The entries in Bedwell's *album amicorum* by Frans Raphelengius Jr. and Joost Raphelengius. Leiden University Library, MS BPL 2753, fols 93^v–94^r 220
15 William Bedwell's letter to Frans Raphelengius Jr. Leiden University Library, MS Pap.15   222

16   William Bedwell's Arabic edition of the Johannine Epistles, *D. Johannis Apostoli et Evangelistae Epistolae Catholicae omnes, Arabicae anti aliquot secula factae* (*Leiden, 1612*), p. 47   223
17   Franciscus Raphelengius. *Icones Leidenses* 26, Collection Leiden University   230
18   Engraving of Friedrich Eberhard Boysen by Friedrich Schlüter. Friedrich Eberhard Boysen, *Eigene Lebensbeschreibung.* Erster Theil (Quedlinburg, 1795), Frontispiece   349
19   Jacobus Golius. *Icones Leidenses* 81, Collection Leiden University   385
20   Ludovico Marracci. Portrait held in the Church of Santa Maria in Campitelli, Rione Sant'Angelo, Rome. Painter and date unknown   395

Abbreviations

BAV	Biblioteca Apostolica Vaticana
BL	British Library, London
Bodl.	Bodleian Library, Oxford
Boysen *K1*	Friedrich Eberhard Boysen, tr., *Der Koran, oder Das Gesetz für die Muselmänner, durch Mohammed den Sohn Abdall* (Halle, 1773)
Boysen *K2*	Friedrich Eberhard Boysen, tr., *Der Koran oder Das Gesetz für die Moslemer durch Muhammed den Sohn Abdall. Nebst einigen feyerlichen koranischen Gebeten, unmittelbar aus dem Arabischen übersetzt ...* (Halle, 1775)
BnF	Bibiothèque nationale de France, Paris
Cas.Ep.	Isaac Casaubon, *Epistolae*, ed. Theodor Jansz van Almeloveen (Rotterdam, 1709)
Cat.Raph.	*Catalogus Variorum Librorum e Bibliothecis Francisci Raphelengii Hebraeae linguae quondam Professoris & Academiae Leidensis Typographi, ejusque filiorum* (Leiden, 1626)
CCH	M. Steinschneider, *Catalogus Codicum Hebraeorum Bibliothecae Lugduno-Batavorum* (Leiden, 1858)
CCO	R.P.A. Dozy, P. de Jong, M.J. de Goeje and M.Th. Houtsma, *Catalogus Codicum Orientalium Bibliothecae Academiae Lugduno Batavae*, 6 vols (Leiden, 1851–1877)
CMR	D. Thomas and J. Chesworth, eds, *Christian-Muslim Relations. A Bibliographical History* (Leiden-Boston, 2009–)
CP	M. Rooses and J. Denucé, eds, *Correspondance de Christophe Plantin*, 9 vols (Antwerpen-Ghent, 1882–1918)
CUL	Cambridge University Library
Fück	J. Fück, *Die arabischen Studien in Europa bis in den Anfang des 20. Jahrhunderts* (Leipzig, 1955)
Jones	R. Jones, *Learning Arabic in Renaissance Europe (1505–1624)* (Leiden-Boston, 2020)
Lex.	Franciscus Raphelengius, *Lexicon Arabico-Latinum* (Leiden, 1613)
Marracci	Ludovico Marracci, tr., *Alcorani textus universus* (Padua, 1698) (also containing the *Prodromus* first published in Rome in 1691, indicated as Marracci, *Prodromus*)
Megerlin *tB*	David Friedrich Megerlin, tr., *Die türkische Bibel, oder des Korans allererste teutsche Uebersetzung aus der Arabischen Urschrift* (Frankfurt am Main., 1772)

MPM	Museum Plantin-Moretus, Antwerp
ODNB	H.C.G. Matthew and B. Harrison, eds, *Oxford Dictionary of National Biography* (Oxford, 2004)
ÖNB	Österreichische Nationalbibliothek, Vienna
Sale	George Sale, tr., *The Koran, Commonly called the Alcoran of Mohammed* (London, 1734)
Scal.Cor.	P. Botley and D. van Miert, eds, *The Correspondence of Joseph Justus Scaliger*, 8 vols (Geneva, 2012)
Schnurrer	Christian Fr. de Schnurrer, *Bibliotheca Arabica. Auctum nunc atque integram edidit. Tabula auctorum et rerum digessit Victor Chauvin* (Halle, 1811, repr. Amsterdam, 1968)
Toomer	G.J. Toomer, *Eastern Wisedome and Learning. The Study of Arabic in Seventeenth-Century England* (Oxford: 1996)
UBL	Universiteitsbibliotheek, Leiden

PART 1

Arabs and Arabists

CHAPTER 1

An Egyptian Traveller in the Republic of Letters

Josephus Barbatus or Abudacnus the Copt

Yūsuf ibn Abū Dhaqn (the 'father of the beard') was an Egyptian Copt. Known in Europe as Josephus Barbatus or Abudacnus, he was one of the more exotic visitors to the Republic of Letters in the early seventeenth century. Other Arabic-speaking Christians had indeed visited the West before him. A substantial number assembled in Rome in the sixteenth century, drawn by institutions such as the Maronite College founded by Pope Gregory XIII in 1584, but few ventured much further: the Jacobite Moses of Mardin went to Vienna in the mid-1550s in order to work on the publication of the Syriac New Testament.[1] Far later, in 1614, the Maronites Gabriel Sionita and Joannes Hesronita were brought from Rome to Paris by François Savary de Brèves,[2] while, in the 1640s, the Syrian Melkite Nicolaus Petri was in Europe with the German Arabist Christian Ravius and visited England, Holland and Denmark.[3] Barbatus was even more widely travelled. From Rome he made his way to France, then to England, the Southern Netherlands, Germany and Austria, supported by princes and prelates and encountering some of the most eminent intellectuals of the time. He emerges as a figure in a class of his own, free of the social distinctions and prejudices that prevailed throughout the West. Despite the accusations of fraudulence made both by his contemporaries and by later scholars,[4] his readiness to usurp academic titles and his determination to teach Oriental languages of which his knowledge was sometimes limited, he had a remarkable aptitude for collecting distinguished acquaintances. He owed his success

---

1 R.J. Wilkinson, *Orientalism, Aramaic and Kabbalah in the Catholic Reformation. The First Printing of the Syriac New Testament* (Leiden-Boston 2007), pp. 79–85.
2 G. Duverdier, 'Les impressions orientales en Europe et le Liban' in C. Aboussouan, ed., *Le livre et le Liban jusqu'à 1900* (Paris, 1982), pp. 157–254, esp. pp. 159–173.
3 See H. Kilpatrick and G.J. Toomer, 'Niqūlāwus al-Ḥalabī (c. 1611–c. 1661): A Greek Orthodox Syrian copyist and his letters to Pococke and Golius' *Lias* 43 (2016), pp. 1–159, esp. pp. 5–20.
4 One of Barbatus's earliest and most severe critics on this score was the Lutheran ecclesiastical historian Johann Lorenz Mosheim, professor of theology first at Helmstedt and then at Göttingen. In 1743 Mosheim pointed out, correctly, that Barbatus never actually held a chair either at Oxford or at Louvain. 'Veri autem simillimum est,' he concludes, 'hominem iusto, ut solent Syri et Aegyptii, arrogantiorem, Professoris Lovaniensis nomen sibi temere sumsisse.' (*Dissertationes ad historiam ecclesiasticam pertinentes* (Altona-Flensburg, 1743), vol. 2, pp. 225–8).

to his intelligence and his boldness in presenting himself as well as to a certain personal charm; and, at a time when European Arabic studies were in their infancy and there was a growing curiosity about the languages and cultures of the Near East, the versatility of Barbatus was highly prized.

On account of his somewhat unusual publications, his *Speculum hebraicum* published in 1615 and the *Historia Jacobitarum seu Coptorum*, attributed to him but first published posthumously in 1675 and reedited into the eighteenth century, Barbatus has long attracted historians and bibliographers. He became the subject of legends. The rumour that he had been a Jesuit was swiftly dispelled. Others – that he taught Arabic at Oxford for ten years, that he travelled to Prague and Warsaw – have persisted. Our knowledge of his life is still incomplete, but it is at last possible to trace his movements over a longer period and more precisely than before, and to assess his contribution to the world of learning.

As a Copt Barbatus was a member of an Arabic-speaking community which, in the late sixteenth century, is unlikely to have amounted to much more than about five per cent of the population of his birthplace, Cairo, even if the proportion was far greater in other parts of Egypt.[5] Although Coptic scholars had been remarkably productive between the ninth and the fourteenth centuries,[6] the Church of Alexandria had been depleted by waves of persecution and massive conversions to Islam. Many of the Coptic monasteries had been pillaged, abandoned, or destroyed, and the Coptic language, long replaced by Arabic, survived only in the liturgy. Under Turkish rule in the sixteenth century the Copts were still far from their later cultural renaissance. Even if there was a caste of educated and prosperous civil servants, frequently tax collectors, scribes, customs officials, chancellors and secretaries to the Muslim authorities, the Copts were generally regarded in the West as poor and ignorant.[7]

Yet the Coptic Church was the object of great interest in Europe. Ever since the early fifteenth century the Church of Rome had been making efforts to

---

5 Cf. M. Martin, S.J., 'Note sur la communauté copte entre 1650 et 1850' *Annales islamologiques* 18 (1982), pp. 193–215, esp. pp. 202–203.
6 O.F.A. Meinardus, *Two Thousands Years of Coptic Christianity* (Cairo, 1999), pp. 52–61; G. Graf, *Geschichte der christlichen arabischen Literatur* (Vatican City, 1944–53), vol. 2, pp. 294–478.
7 A. Hamilton, *The Copts and the West 1439–1822. The European Discovery of the Egyptian Church* (rev. edn. Oxford, 2014), pp. 33–39. Western visitors to Egypt tended to have little or nothing to do with the *arākhina* or *mubāshirin*, the Coptic aristocracy. See also M. 'Afīfī, *Al-Aqbāṭ fī Miṣr fī al-'aṣr al-'uthmānī* (Cairo, 1992), pp. 105–148; M. Guirguis, 'The Coptic papacy under Ottoman rule (1517–1798)' in M. Guirguis and N. van Doorn-Harder, *The Emergence of the Modern Coptic Papacy. The Egyptian Church and Its Leadership from the Ottoman Period to the Present* (Cairo-New York, 2011), pp. 1–51, esp. pp. 34–40; F. Armanios, *Coptic Christianity in Ottoman Egypt* (New York, 2011), pp. 26–40.

re-establish the ancient union with the Churches of the East. The Copts, condemned at the Council of Chalcedon in 451 for adhering to what was known as the monophysite or Jacobite heresy, which supposedly confessed a single divine nature in Christ, were invited with the other Eastern Churches to the Council of Florence in 1439. They there distinguished themselves by the Arabic manuscripts which the delegates donated to the pope, Eugenius IV, and which were to form the basis of the great Oriental collection in the Vatican Library. Although the delegates agreed to the union with Rome requested of them at the Council, they failed to have it accepted by their brethren on their return to Egypt. The popes multiplied their efforts in the next century.[8] After the troubles attending the Turkish conquest of Syria and Egypt in 1516–17 had subsided, envoys were dispatched from Rome in another attempt to win over the Copts. They were received politely and returned home with further manuscripts; expectations for the future were raised by individual Copts converting to Catholicism; the Coptic patriarchs, in their turn, sent embassies to Rome, but union was not concluded.[9]

While the papacy courted the Copts and the other Eastern communities, the Protestant Churches marvelled at the integrity with which the Oriental Christians, with a venerable and ancient tradition, had resisted the overtures of Rome. Could they not serve as models on which the national Churches produced by the Reformation might be based? Their points of community with Protestantism were stressed, not to say exaggerated – their use of the vernacular in the liturgy, the marriage of priests, the denial of purgatory, the rejection of auricular confession and extreme unction, the administration of the eucharist in both kinds. Like the nascent Protestant Churches the Eastern communities tended to be nationally defined. Their age-old hierarchy had a special appeal in the early seventeenth century for the Anglicans, some of whom argued that the Eastern Churches resembled an equally ancient, national and hierarchic Anglo-Saxon Church which they proposed to revive. The Protestants, consequently, longed for greater knowledge of them.[10]

---

8   Discussed in *ibid.*, pp. 49–103.
9   Information on the consequences of the exchange of ambassadors from the Council of Florence onwards for the Vatican Library is given in G. Levi della Vida, *Ricerche sulla formazione del più antico fondo dei manoscritti orientali della Biblioteca Vaticana* (Vatican City, 1939), pp. 29–108. See also A. Hamilton, 'Eastern Churches and Western Scholarship' in A. Grafton, ed., *Rome Reborn: The Vatican Library and Renaissance Culture* (Washington-Vatican City, 1993), pp. 225–249, 303.
10 For Protestant interest in the Arabic-speaking Christians cf. Hamilton, *The Copts and the West*, pp. 121–151, 168–192.

Josephus Barbatus was born in Cairo, probably in the mid- or late 1570s.[11] He later told Joseph Justus Scaliger that he had only received the most elementary education, learning the rudiments of reading and writing at children's schools, 'nelle scole picole di fanciulli.'[12] Yet he also knew Greek, which he could have learnt from consorting with Greek merchants or with the monks attached to the archbishopric of Mount Sinai, and he knew Turkish. Turkish was the language of the government. Those Egyptians who spoke it usually had some connection with the Ottoman administration. Barbatus almost certainly came from the higher ranks of Coptic society, from a family with connections with the Church, and he may once have planned to become a monk. By the early 1590s he was close to Ya'qūb, the *qummuṣ* or archdeacon of the monastery of St Antony near the Red Sea,[13] and he was also acquainted with the Coptic patriarch of Alexandria, Gabriel VIII. Gabriel VIII was a keen advocate of union with Rome, who professed himself a Roman Catholic in 1597 after dispatching a number of delegates to the papal court. In 1595 he entrusted Barbatus with a letter for the pope.[14]

The Rome in which Barbatus arrived was well-disposed to Christians from the East. In the twelve years of his pontificate, which ended in 1585, Gregory XIII had founded various institutions designed to attract and train Eastern visitors who might later prove valuable missionaries – a Greek college and a College of Neophytes for converts from Judaism and Islam in 1577, and a Maronite and a (short-lived) Armenian college in 1584. He had surrounded himself with Oriental scholars who assisted him in his reform of the calendar, and he supervised the foundation of the Typographia Medicea, a printing press which was to produce works in Arabic and Syriac for distribution in the East.[15]

---

11 '... io sono nato nel gran cairo d'eggito christiano jacobita overo cophto ...' Barbatus's letter to Joseph Justus Scaliger of 25 Sep. 1608, UBL, MS Or. 1365 (4). For the letter, accompanied by Erpenius's Latin translation, see *Scal.Cor.*, vol. 7, pp. 628–631.

12 See below, p. 9.

13 Hamilton, *The Copts and the West*, p. 127.

14 Cf. the 'suggestion for Abudacnus's parting testimonial, Nov. 1637' in H. de Vocht, 'Oriental Languages in Louvain in the XVIIth Century: Abudacnus and le Wyt de Luysant' *Le Muséon* 59 (1946), pp. 671–688, esp. 687: '... en lan 1595 at este recomandé a Rome par le patriarche D'alexandrie av Pape Clement huictiesme dheureuse memoire, et la de la religion Jacobiticque ov Cophthe, (Laquelle est la religion de Prestre Jean) at esté conuertis a la foy catholicque, en Laquelle depuis at tousiour vescu, et par laide de Dieu viurat.' For the Coptic patriarch Gabriel VIII see Graf, *Geschichte der christlichen arabischen Literatur*, vol. 4, pp. 120–123.

15 The Medici press is studied by Jones, pp. 126–143 and *idem*, 'The Medici Oriental Press (Rome 1584–1614) and the impact of its Arabic publications on Northern Europe' in G.A. Russell, ed., *The 'Arabick' Interest of the Natural Philosophers in Seventeenth-Century England* (Leiden, 1994), pp. 88–108; see also G.E. Saltini, 'Della Stamperia Orientale

The letter given to Barbatus by the Coptic patriarch was addressed to a pope who had more time and a still greater desire to pursue Gregory's Eastern policy than his immediate successor Sixtus V. This was Ippolito Aldobrandini who, as Clement VIII, was elected in 1592 and remained in office until 1605. Under Clement VIII the Medici press produced its largest number of publications. Missions to the East resumed. The study of Eastern tongues was encouraged: Arabic, Syriac and Aramaic were taught at the Maronite College, and instruction in Hebrew was provided for the Neophytes. Eastern visitors, such as the young Barbatus, were made particularly welcome.[16] In May 1595 he was admitted to the College of Neophytes and was promised a subsidy of 9 or 10 scudi.[17] Although it was originally intended for Jewish and Muslim converts, the Jesuit-run college, lodged opposite the church of Sta Chiara near S. Eustachio, continued to accept Eastern Christians who were neither Maronites nor Armenians. Two thirds of the students, however, were converts from Judaism.[18]

From what little we know about Barbatus's stay in Rome he appears to have responded in the most satisfactory manner to his reception: he converted to Roman Catholicism. This must have increased his popularity and his chances of preferment. We can probably assume that it was in Rome that he received a true education. Even if he had left Egypt knowing Arabic, Turkish and a little Greek, he would have acquired when he was still in Italy the knowledge of most of the other languages which he claimed to master ten years later. He learnt Italian, and by the time he arrived in France it was the one language which he wrote with fluency, albeit not always correctly. Above all he wrote it confidently, with a far firmer hand than what survives of his Arabic. In Rome too he could have studied Latin and ancient Greek. How well he knew either remains a matter of doubt. The poor quality of his Latin in his surviving letters suggests either that the Latin of his publications was always heavily corrected by some acquaintance or editor, or that his knowledge of the language improved after his stay in England. By 1605 Barbatus had joined the Discalced

---

Medicea e di Giovan Battista Raimondi' *Giornale storico degli archivi toscani*, 4 (1860), pp. 257–308; A. Tinto, 'Per una storia della tipografia orientale a Roma nell'età della Controriforma' *Accademie e biblioteche d'Italia* 41 (1973), pp. 280–303; S. Fani and M. Farina, *Le vie delle lettere. La Tipografia Medicea tra Roma e l'Oriente* (Florence, 2012).

16 Cf. L. von Pastor, *Geschichte der Päpste im Zeitalter der katholischen Reformation und Restauration*, vol. 11, *Klemens VIII 1592–1605* (Freiburg im Breisgau, 1927), pp. 483–504.

17 J. Krajcar, S.J., ed., *Cardinal Giulio Antonio Santoro and the Christian East: Santoro's Audiences and Consistorial Acts* (Rome, 1966), p. 126.

18 See C. Hoffmann, *Ursprung und Anfangstätigkeit des ersten päpstlichen Missionsinstituts. Ein Beitrag zur Geschichte der katholischen Juden- und Mohammedanermission im sechszehnten Jahrhundert* (Münster, 1923), pp. 185–190.

Carmelites under the name of Fra Macario, but he never seems to have been fully ordained and left after a couple of years.[19]

We know nothing of the events behind Barbatus's departure from Rome in about 1607. He may have been recruited as an interpreter by one of the various French diplomats who visited Rome at the time. The first evidence of Barbatus's presence in Paris dates from July 1608, when he wrote to one of the greatest scholars living in the French capital, Isaac Casaubon, introducing himself and listing the languages he claimed to know.[20] Part of a more general attempt to gain the favour of distinguished men of learning, the letter was entirely in Arabic – a comparatively rare example of written colloquial Arabic, which remains of philological interest – and may also have been intended to flatter Casaubon, who had long been intrigued by Arabic on account of his work on the early Church, by assuming his mastery of the language. In September Barbatus followed up his letter to Casaubon with one to a scholar of equal, if not greater, distinction, Joseph Justus Scaliger in Leiden.

In Paris Barbatus was employed as interpreter at the French court and gave occasional lessons in Arabic. In his capacity as interpreter he seems to have worked for Arnoult de l'Isle, also a doctor, who preceded Etienne Hubert as the occupant of the chair of Arabic at the Collège Royal.[21] De l'Isle was well acquainted with Morocco, where he stayed from 1588 to 1599 as physician to the king, Aḥmad al-Manṣūr. From 1606 to 1607 he was again in Morocco, this time as ambassador, and was responsible for renewing French relations with the country. In 1608 he was in Madrid. He is not known to have returned to North Africa, even if the letter about Barbatus serving as his interpreter in 1609 suggests that he was planning to do so.[22] Barbatus also benefited from the interest in Arabic studies. A number of the men he mentions in his letters were connected with the Collège Royal: in addition to Hubert and de L'Isle, Jean Martin, another physician, was to lecture in Arabic at the Collège. In Barbatus scholars such as Casaubon seem to have found one of the only native speakers

---

19 V. Buri, S.J., *L'unione della chiesa copta con Roma sotto Clemente VIII* (Rome, 1931), p. 136.
20 BL, MS Burney 367, fol. 200ʳ. See below, pp. 70–71.
21 Details about Etienne Hubert and Arnoult de l'Isle are to be found in H. de Castries, *Les sources inédites de l'histoire du Maroc. Première série, Dynastie Saadienne*, vol. 3 (Paris, 1911), pp. xiii–xxi, xxii–xxvii. See also J. Balagna Coustou, *Arabe et humanisme dans la France des derniers Valois* (Paris, 1989), pp. 114–118.
22 Barbatus is described as the interpreter to the French ambassador, 'planning to travel to the king of Morocco' (*muzma'an yusāfir ilā malik Marrākish*) in Thomas Erpenius's letter to William Bedwell dated 14 September 1609. See M.T. Houtsma, 'Uit de oostersche correspondentie van Th. Erpenius, Jac. Golius en Lev. Warner. Eene bijdrage tot de geschiedenis van de beoefening der oostersche letteren in Nederland' *Verhandelingen der Koninklijke Academie van Wetenschappen, Afd. Letterkunde* 17/3 (1887), p. 6.

of Arabic available in Paris, and they entertained him and used him accordingly. Casaubon, for example, asked him to transcribe (and perhaps to translate) a letter dated March 1588 (996 AH) from the ruler of Morocco, Aḥmad al-Manṣūr, to the Portuguese pretender Antonio, which he had received from the Scottish scholar James Hepburn early in 1606.[23]

In his letter to Scaliger of 25 September 1608 Barbatus was frank about his limitations as an Arabist.[24] He had heard about the scholar in Leiden from his friends in Paris and asked whether he might visit him and serve him. Besides giving Scaliger a list of the languages, ancient and modern, which he knew, he told him how poorly he had been educated in Egypt, even if he had picked up the rudiments of Arabic grammar in the course of his journeys. The letter is in Italian, but, possibly to flatter Scaliger (just as he had flattered Casaubon), Barbatus added a summary in Arabic – Scaliger's reply, if it ever existed, has not survived. He died in the following January, but it may have been owing to him as well as to Casaubon that his young pupil in Leiden, the Dutchman Thomas Erpenius, applied to Barbatus for Arabic lessons when he arrived in Paris from England early in 1609.

---

23   BL, MS Burney 367, fol. 199[r-v]. For the entire episode see below, p. 80.
24   UBL, MS Or. 1365 (4) (cf. *Scal.Cor.*, vol. 7, pp. 629–630, for the Italian version). The letter runs: 'Essendo io capitato in paris, et per poca cognitione che ó nella lingua harabica sopito fui cognosciuto da molti gintlomini francesi desiderosi della stessa lingua et fra loro dal sig[re] Casabon, et sig[re] hopert, et sig[ri] martin, et molti altri, li quali tuti mi anno narrato dalla vostra famosa sapientia, non solamente in tute le scientie ma ancora nelle lingue orientali, et altri, et perquesto grndamente desiderai fin qui che il sig[re] Dio mi facese tanta gratia di poter pagiare li mani di vostra sig[ria] Illustre et servila in tuto quello che io sarro degno, come persona molto degna di essere servita da quelli li quali sono desiderosi di imparare le virtù dal qual desiderio sono ancora io sono stato spinto, ma più per la sua gran amorevoletia che sole usare vs Illma verso li foresteri ma acio che io non capiti da lei incognito del tuto li derró come io sono nato nel gran cairo d'eggito christiano jacobita overo cophto dove si parla la lingua come vs Illma sa che questi paesi adesso sono barbari non vi si trova ne scientia ne anco studii se non quello che simpara nelle scole picole di fanciulli, cioe solamente legere et scrivere, non dimeno per la mia conversatione nel mondo per molti anni ó hauto alcuni principi di gramatica, ma non molto, et ancora poca cognitione di altri lingue, cioè nella hebrea, siriaca, turcica, et greca comone, et alcun poco di latino. ma vs Illma che e molto sapiente della lingua harabica poterra solamente giudicare quello che io so nella detta lingua legendo la lettra la quale le mando scritta secundo la ortografia, et vera forse nostra, et pero desidero grandamente di sapere se vs Ill[ma] si contenta che io mi rapresenti, mi lo significa con quatro versi per sua gratia, li quali mi sarranno grandamente gratissime et li tengo come cosa pretiosa datami dalli mani di vs Ill[ma] Vale alii vinti cique di setembre l'anno 1608. di vs Ill[ma] humilissimo servitore giosseppe barbato iacopita dal gran Cairo deggitto.' There follows a summary of the same text in Arabic.

Erpenius already knew some Arabic – he had had a few lessons from the English Arabist William Bedwell – and he soon grew aware of Barbatus's shortcomings as a teacher and could confirm the Copt's own confession to Scaliger. Barbatus, he informed Bedwell, taught him 'many Arabic words', but of the 'corrupt language' spoken at the time 'by Egyptians and others'. Nowadays, he continued, only the learned understand Arabic as it was spoken 'of old': Barbatus could hardly even read it. Nevertheless, Erpenius remained grateful for the vocabulary Barbatus had taught him.[25] He also remained fond of his Coptic friend. In the following year, however, he found a far better instructor in the Moroccan diplomat of Andalusian origin, Aḥmad ibn Qāsim al-Ḥajarī, who was on a mission to France.[26] Shortly after, in 1613, Erpenius published the Arabic grammar which was to remain unsurpassed until the nineteenth century.

In the summer of 1610 Barbatus embarked on the most glorious phase of his career. He set out for England with letters from his friends in France, including one from Erpenius to William Bedwell. Although Bedwell held the modest position of vicar of Tottenham High Cross, he was widely esteemed both in England and abroad for his skill as a mathematician, and his learning as an antiquarian and an Arabist. Educated at Cambridge, he was protected by Lancelot Andrewes, bishop of Chichester, Ely and finally of Winchester, from whom he had received his living. He had numerous connections with the ecclesiastical hierarchy, the two universities and the court. Known for his kindness to foreign visitors, he could be an influential friend.[27]

It is not clear to what extent Bedwell helped Barbatus on his arrival. Somehow Barbatus received a recommendation from Richard Bancroft, archbishop of Canterbury, for the vice-chancellor of Oxford University, John King, bishop of London.[28] He also obtained a letter from Thomas Bodley for his

---

25 Houtsma, 'Uit de oostersche correspondentie' p. 6. Cf. Gerard Vossius's words on Barbatus as a teacher of Arabic in Paris in the commemorative address he delivered after Erpenius's death: 'Interea vero temporis praeceptorem ibi nanciscitur Iosephum Barbatum Iacobitam, domo Aegyptium, virum, qui Latinas quidem literas a limine vix salutasset; sed cujus operam in addiscenda Arabum lingua minime in postremis haberet.' (Gerard Vossius, *Oratio in obitum clarissimi ac praestantissimi viri, Thomae Erpenii, orientalium linguarum in Academia Leidensi professoris*, Leiden 1623, p. 11). For Erpenius see Jones, *Learning Arabic*, pp. 144–165; A. Vrolijk and R. van Leeuwen, *Arabic Studies in the Netherlands. A Short History in Portraits, 1580–1950* (Leiden-Boston, 2014), pp. 31–40, 59; W.M.C. Juynboll, *Zeventiende-eeuwsche beoefenaars van het Arabisch in Nederland* (Utrecht, 1911), pp. 59–118.

26 Cf. G.A. Wiegers, *A learned Muslim Acquaintance of Erpenius and Golius: Aḥmad b. Ḳāsim al-Andalusī and Arabic Studies in the Netherlands* (Leiden, 1988); Jones, pp. 77–92.

27 A. Hamilton, *William Bedwell the Arabist 1563–1632* (Leiden, 1985), pp. 34–37, 136.

28 Anthony à Wood, ed., *Fasti oxonienses*, vol. 1 (London, 1721), col. 790.

librarian, Thomas James. This contains a sympathetic description of the visitor from Egypt, who 'speaketh French and Italian very readily; also Latin well enough, to explicat his minde: being likewise, as I ghesse, of a kind and honest disposition'.[29] Bodley was eager that Barbatus should teach Arabic at Oxford. 'I would be glad to vnderstand,' he went on, 'that he might be provided of a competent intertainment, to keep him in Oxon, lest Cambridge should endeuour, as I make account they would, to draw him vnto them. I pray yow vse your owne credit & mine, where yow thinke yow may preuaile (for I haue no leasure at this present, to write to more than your self) to further his desire, whome I thinke a small mater will content at the first: which may heerafter be increased, according to the profit, which his auditours may reape.'

Furnished with such support, Barbatus arrived in Oxford in the middle of August and settled down in St Mary Hall (subsequently incorporated into Oriel College). He was evidently pleased with his reception and Bodley could thank James 'hartely for Iosippo'.[30] At Oxford Barbatus gave some instruction in Arabic, but there is no record of how much or to whom. He made a brief contribution to a work of literature. The volume in which this appears, *Eidyllia in obitum fulgentissimi Henrici Walliae Principis*, printed by Joseph Barnes in 1612, was one of a number of publications lamenting the recent death of James I's eldest son.[31] It is a collection of poems, mainly in Latin and Greek. From what we know of the few contributors who actually signed their names in full, rather than with initials, it was largely the work of students, some of whom may well have had Barbatus as their teacher. The man who was probably the editor, James Martin (Jacobus Aretius), the son of a clergyman from Staffordshire, was twenty-four years old at the time. He had been a student of Broadgates Hall and had proceeded M.A. in the previous year.[32] If 'I. Parry' corresponds to James Parry, the future canon of Hereford was still studying at St Mary Hall (where he would have met Barbatus) and was to receive his B.A. in 1616.[33] An international veneer was given to the publication by Willem Beiaert,

---

29   G.W. Wheeler, ed., *Letters of Sir Thomas Bodley to Thomas James First Keeper of the Bodleian Library* (Oxford, 1926), pp. 193–194. Wheeler's attribution of the letter to 1610, evidently unknown to most later students of Barbatus, solves the problem of the year posed by Wood, *Fasti*, vol. 1, col. 790, who dated it as 1603.

30   Wheeler, ed., *Letters*, p. 196.

31   Two complete copies are to be found at the Bodl. The copy in the BL lacks a number of gatherings, including the opening one with Barbatus's contribution. The book is described in F. Madan, *The Early Oxford Press: A Bibliography of Printing and Publishing at Oxford 1468–1640* (Oxford, 1895), p. 80.

32   J. Foster, ed., *Alumni oxonienses. The Members of the University of Oxford 1500–1714*, vol. 3 (repr. Liechtenstein, 1968), p. 978.

33   *Ibid.*, p. 1120.

who described himself as 'Anglo-Belgicus'. Although he was born in London, Beiaert matriculated at the university of Leiden in 1610 at the age of fifteen. He did not come to Oxford until 1614, when he obtained his B.A. from Christ Church.[34] By far the most cosmopolitan of the contributors was Barbatus. The work gave him a chance to exhibit his linguistic versatility and it was with his contribution that it opened. His couplet, saying that he had rejoiced in the Prince of Wales's life and had died with his death, appears in four languages – Aramaic, Syriac, Arabic and Turkish. The Aramaic is printed in Hebrew characters, but the Syriac, Arabic and Turkish have been transliterated in Roman letters in a highly arbitrary manner which, together with Barbatus's neglect of grammatical rules, bestows some mystery on the meaning.[35]

The evidence suggests that Barbatus in fact spent a great deal of his time in London. It was probably there that Bedwell showed him a manuscript of the Epistles in Arabic which he was planning to publish. Barbatus copied out the Epistle to Titus. He took his transcription back to Oxford and, in 1611, gave it to the Hebrew scholar and former Brownist Matthew Slade. Slade resided in Amsterdam, where he was rector of the Latin school. He returned with the copy to Holland and had it edited in Arabic and Latin by the teacher of Arabic at Leiden University, Johannes Antonides (Jan Theunisz). It was published by the Raphelengius brothers at the Leiden branch of the Plantin press in 1612. Bedwell discovered this to his fury when he himself went to Leiden in the same year and had to limit himself to having an Arabic-Latin edition of the Johannine Epistles issued by the same publisher. Whatever the details of this obscure episode Bedwell forgave neither Antonides nor Barbatus.[36]

---

34   G. Du Rieu, ed., *Album studiosorum Academiae Lugduno Batavae MDLXXV–MDCCCLXX* (The Hague, 1875), col. 98; A. Clark, ed., *Register of the University of Oxford, ii (1571–1622), Part I* (Oxford, 1887), p. 377.

35   The Arabic (*Eidyllia in obitum fulgentissimi Henrici Walliae Principis* (Oxford, 1612), sig. A2ᵛ) runs: 'Cairoun li can idha haijoun ia Raijz surtou / Phi baudou ma touophitou gedun li amoutou.' Barbatus signs himself 'Josephus Barbatus Arabs Memphiticus Cophteus'. The first scholar to notice his contribution seems to be P.M. Holt, 'Arabic Studies in Seventeenth-Century England with Special Reference to the Life and Work of Edward Pococke', B.Phil. thesis, Oxford University, 1952, p. 32.

36   The evidence consists of two brief reports, one by Johannes Antonides and one by Bedwell. In the preface to his edition of the Epistle to Titus Antonides wrote: 'Eam ego nactus sum beneficio doctissimi viri D. Rectoris Scholae Amsterdamensis Matthaei Sladi, in eadem etiam lingua non vulgariter versati. Acceperat autem, ille Oxonia transcriptam a Iosepho Abudacno viro Aegyptio. Hoc itaque exemplar in omnibus expressum habes, nisi quod aliquoties quae deerant puncta vocalia ad normam Grammaticae supplevi.' (*D. Pauli Apostoli Epistola ad Titum, Arabice* (Leiden, 1612), p. 3). Bedwell, in his preface to his edition of the Johannine Epistles, wrote: 'Plagiarum quendam nostrum comprehendit

In the company of Bedwell Barbatus dined with Lancelot Andrewes in London. He again saw Casaubon, who settled in England at the end of 1610, and he called on Erpenius's sister Maria, married to Daniel van Hasevelt, a merchant living in Billingsgate and a deacon of the Dutch Church at Austin Friars.[37] He even provided tuition in Arabic although, he told Erpenius in July 1611, he was only approached by 'a few gentlemen'. One of them seems to have been Miles Smith, the future bishop of Gloucester.[38] Barbatus exploited his connection with Oxford to the full. In the autumn of 1612 the chaplain of Frederick V or the 'Winter King', Abraham Scultetus, who was in London for the marriage of his employer to the daughter of James I, included in the list of illustrious scholars whom he met 'Iosephus Barbatus Memphis Aegyptii natus, religione Cophita, Professor Arabicae linguae Oxoniae'.[39] On one of his many visits to London Barbatus met his next patron, Ferdinand de Boisschot, the ambassador in England of the archdukes of the Southern Netherlands. Judging from the future pattern of his academic career Barbatus may have turned to the ambassador when he realised that the Oxford authorities, who had been so eager to engage his services in 1610, were considerably less eager to retain them three years later. Boisschot, at all events, supplied him with letters for the magistrates

---

J.A. [Johannes Antonides] et publici juris fecit. Conservum eius nosipsi manumisimus; reliquos, ut publico prodesse possint, brevi, favente Numine, libertate donabimus.' (*D. Iohannis Apostoli et Evangelistae Epistolae Catholicae omnes* (Leiden, 1612), p. 6). Juynboll, *Zeventiende-eeuwsche Beoefenaars*, p. 57, concludes somewhat imaginatively that the transcription published by Antonides was made without Bedwell's consent while Barbatus was staying at his house in Tottenham and that, had Bedwell not discovered the theft when he was in Leiden, Antonides would also have published the other epistles contained in the same manuscript. What, where, and indeed whose the manuscript really was, however, remains mysterious. Bedwell had prepared a manuscript copy of the Arabic Epistle to Titus, followed by a Latin translation, which he had dedicated to Lancelot Andrewes in about 1606. (He had also prepared similar copies of the Epistles to the Colossians and to Philemon, dedicated respectively to Richard Bancroft and Francis Burley). Yet there are numerous differences between the Arabic of Bedwell's version of Titus (BL, MS Slo. 1796) and that of Antonides's edition. The two versions can thus hardly have been based on the same original manuscript, which I have been unable to find. For an account of this episode based on the probably erroneous assumption that Barbatus in fact copied the manuscript in Oxford and for Bedwell's transcriptions of the Arabic New Testament see Hamilton, *William Bedwell*, pp. 24–25, 35, 39–40, 82–83, 106–120, 126–127. For Antonides see D. van Dalen, 'Johannes Theunisz and 'Abd al-'Azīz: a friendship in Arabic studies in Amsterdam, 1609–1610' *Lias* 43 (2016), pp. 161–189.

37   Barbatus's letter to Bedwell from Oxford, dated 28 Aug. 1610, in which he describes his experiences, is written half in Arabic and half in very broken Latin. See Hamilton, *William Bedwell*, pp. 99–100.
38   Houtsma, 'Uit de oostersche correspondentie', pp. 13–16.
39   *De curricula vitae ... Abrahami Sculteti* (Emden, 1625), p. 58.

in his home country and Barbatus left England in the autumn of 1613, bound for Antwerp.[40]

Thanks to Boisschot's letters Barbatus was well received. He was soon employed by the Antwerp city council, at a reasonable salary, to teach what he sometimes referred to as 'all oriental languages' but defined as Hebrew, Syriac, Aramaic and Arabic. His lessons were intended for missionaries from the mendicant orders as well as for other members of the clergy and the laity. According to his own statements he enabled his students to attain an astonishing degree of proficiency in an amazingly short time, but he regarded the modest position of language teacher in Antwerp as beneath the dignity of the man who had once styled himself professor at Oxford. He searched for a position to which greater prestige could be attached.

Barbatus saw his first opportunity in an episode in which he was again used as an interpreter.[41] It concerned an ambassador from the Porte dispatched by the Ottoman admiral-in-chief Khalil Pasha to the Dutch Republic. The ambassador, Omar Agha, arrived in France with nineteen liberated Dutch prisoners in December 1613 and made his way overland towards Holland. On his arrival in Antwerp he was imprisoned, in violation of the Twelve Years' Truce that had existed between the Republic and the Southern Netherlands since 1609. At this point Barbatus appears to have been summoned to act as his interpreter. The Dutch States General heard of the matter in January 1614. They immediately protested to the city of Antwerp and to the archdukes in Brussels. The ambassador was released with apologies on 15 February and allowed to set off for The Hague. He did so in the company of Barbatus. Besides displaying his knowledge of Turkish, the Copt could therefore visit the Dutch Republic, where he was entertained by the States General together with Omar Agha on 16 February. The States General were most cordial. They voted that the interpreter be rewarded with 100 guilders and expenses for lodging, and they may have held out further hopes for, in June, Barbatus wrote to offer his services as a teacher of Arabic.[42] These, however, were declined. Since the previous year the Dutch had been employing Barbatus's former pupil Thomas Erpenius as professor of Arabic at the University of Leiden. With a scholar of such excellence, they had no need to seek any further.

---

40 The episode is reconstructed and documented in L. van der Essen, 'Joseph Abudacnus ou Barbatus, Arabe né au Caire, professeur de langues orientales à l'Université de Louvain (1615–1617)' *Le Muséon* 37 (1924), pp. 1–17.

41 See A.H. de Groot, *The Ottoman Empire and the Dutch Republic: A History of the Earliest Diplomatic Relations 1610–1630* (Leiden, 1978), pp. 125–129, 305–306.

42 A.T. van Deursen, ed., *Resolutiën der Staten-Generaal. Nieuwe Reeks. Tweede Deel 1613–1616* (The Hague, 1984), pp. 207, 270.

Barbatus had better luck in another quarter. It seems to have been as an interpreter that he met Albert VII, archduke of Austria and ruler of the Southern Netherlands, in whom he was to have a loyal and powerful supporter. At the same time he managed to make the acquaintance of certain scholars at the University of Louvain. Through them, on the archduke's advice, Barbatus made his next move. He had, he said, received invitations from his friends in Paris to return and teach at the Collège Royal. The only way to keep him in the Southern Netherlands, where he was making such a signal contribution to the study of Semitic languages, was, he implied, to offer him a post at Louvain.[43] Barbatus's acquaintances at the university were equal to the occasion. They urged him to remain with them and appealed to Engelbert Maes, the president of the privy council, to persuade the States of Brabant to provide the Coptic visitor with a salary and employment at the university. In the meantime the archduke agreed to pay for his upkeep. Who Barbatus's admirers in Louvain were is not specified, but they probably included Justus Lipsius's successor to the chair of humanities, Erycius Puteanus. Puteanus, who was known for his erudition but also for his lack of discernment, was to praise Barbatus some years later in terms which reveal, as we shall see, a profound esteem.[44]

The States of Brabant agreed to pay Barbatus 200 florins per semester and passed the request on to the academic senate of the university. The senate accepted, pleased with the prospect of a teacher they did not have to pay. Barbatus was duly appointed with the title of reader in Oriental languages which, as in Oxford, he was quick to transmute into that of professor. Yet in Louvain, where he arrived in October 1615, Barbatus immediately encountered difficulties. Although he had been appointed, somewhat vaguely, to teach 'Oriental languages' in general, he claimed Hebrew as his principal subject and, under the supervision of his curator, the councillor Johannes Drusius, abbot of Parc, he endeavoured to organise his lectures in the Collegium Trilingue. This offended the holder of the chair of Hebrew, Valerius Andreas, and some of his other colleagues. They arranged their timetable in such a way that there was no free hour for Barbatus to teach. After complaining to the rector and the senate, Barbatus was given a room normally used for teaching mathematics, on

---

[43] The information on Barbatus in Louvain in F. Nève ('Nouveaux renseignements sur la résidence de Joseph Barbatus en Belgique et sur les circonstances de son départ' *Annuaire de l'Université Catholique de Louvain* 29 (1865), pp. 350–9) is supplemented by Van der Essen, 'Joseph Abudacnus' and by De Vocht 'Oriental languages'. Cf. also T.-A. Druart, 'Arabic Philosophy and the Université Catholique de Louvain' in C.E. Butterworth and B.A. Kessel, eds, *The Introduction of Arabic Philosophy into Europe* (Leiden, 1993), pp. 83–97, esp. 88–92.

[44] See below, p. 21.

the first floor of the university halls. Here he seems to have attracted a number of students, mainly of divinity, the faculty to which he was attached. Again Valerius Andreas and his friends protested. Why did Barbatus insist on teaching Hebrew, a subject in which a chair already existed and which was being taught, rather than give instruction in some of the other 'Oriental languages' he had been employed to teach? The States of Brabant now tried to prohibit Barbatus from lecturing in Hebrew. Barbatus appealed to the archduke, claiming that Hebrew was essential for the knowledge of all Semitic languages and that without it the students could proceed no further. With the support of the archduke he survived, for the time being at least. He continued to lecture principally in Hebrew, but his attempts to introduce other languages into his course were unsuccessful.

How competent was Barbatus as a teacher of Eastern languages by the time he reached Louvain, and to what did he owe his various appointments? Certainly much of his success was due to his being unique. In Paris he was entertained by scholars who, eager to improve their Arabic, were in search of native instructors. He was appointed at Oxford by men who could obviously not find anyone else prepared to teach Arabic at the university and who were delighted at last to have met an Arabic-speaking Christian. We can probably assume that Barbatus was alone in his knowledge of Semitic languages in Antwerp when he started to teach there. He must also have profited from the low level of Hebrew studies at the University of Louvain. Louvain had no great tradition of Hebraists. Robert Bellarmine had indeed once taught there, but he was attached to the Jesuit College and not to the university. The list of professors of Hebrew was undistinguished. For over thirty years before the appointment of Valerius Andreas in 1612 the chair of Hebrew had been vacant. Valerius Andreas, moreover, left his mark as an antiquarian, a historian, a jurist and above all as a bibliographer, but not as a Hebraist. In such circumstances a limited knowledge of Semitic languages must have gone further than it would otherwise have done.[45]

We may doubt, however, whether Barbatus was as poor a teacher as his enemies made out. The evidence, admittedly, is scarce. For the benefit of his students 'Iosephus Barbatus, Memphiticus, Linguarum Orientalium professor

---

45   Valerius Andreas's inaugural lecture in praise of Hebrew, *Collegii Trilinguis Buslidiani, in Academia Lovaniensi, exordia ac progressus, et linguae hebraicae encomium* (Louvain, 1614), pp. 12–30, was delivered in March 1612. Andreas gives a list of his predecessors in *Fasti Academia Studii Generalis Lovaniensis* (Louvain, 1650), pp. 283–285. Two of the better known in the early sixteenth century were Englishmen, Robert Wakefield and Robert Shirwood (who succeeded the former in 1519). See G. Lloyd Jones, *The Discovery of Hebrew in Tudor England: a Third Language* (Manchester, 1983), pp. 181–190.

Lovanii' published a single book on Hebrew grammar, his *Speculum hebraicum, quo omnium omnino radicum hebraearum, praecipuorumque inde derivatorum significata, facili methodo est intueri*, printed in Louvain in 1615 by the university printer Gerardus Rivius (who had already used his Hebrew types in an earlier publication, Angelo Canini's *De locis Hebraicis* of 1600). The book was dedicated to the markgrave of Antwerp, Hendrik van Varick, and the city council, whom Barbatus thanked for the many favours he had received from them.[46]

The twenty-two leaves of the *Speculum hebraicum* consist of tables designed to instruct students in the system of radicals peculiar to Semitic languages. The work could be used as a vocabulary. It is arranged in alphabetical order, with tables made up of squares spread over every two pages. In a column on the right stands the first radical, while the entire Hebrew alphabet runs across the top of the table and down the column on the left. At the intersection of the three radicals the meaning of the word is given in Latin. However unusual the book may look when compared to other contemporary Hebrew primers it was by no means original. It was based on an almost identical work which had been published in Hamburg in 1587 by Elias Hutter, formerly professor of Hebrew at the University of Leipzig and subsequently tutor to the elector of Saxony, Augustus. Hutter had originally appended the tables, in Hebrew and German, to his controversial Hebrew Bible. The German was then translated into Latin by David Wolder, another Hebraist in Hutter's circle and the founder of the first Greek and Hebrew printing press in Hamburg. A comparison between Barbatus's table and Hutter's reveals remarkably few differences.[47] Barbatus gives slightly fewer Hebrew words but, unlike Hutter, he adds certain words with more than three radicals in the right-hand margin. Hutter's table is preceded by an extensive introduction explaining its use. Barbatus, in his brief preface, announces a further study on Hebrew grammar in which he too will give a close account of the structure of the language;[48] but this never appeared.

---

46   The *Speculum hebraicum* prompted the first 'modern' study of Barbatus, F. Nève, 'Note sur un lexique hébreu, qu'a publié à Louvain, en 1615, Joseph Abudacnus, dit Barbatus, Chrétien d'Egypte' *Messager des sciences historiques et archives des arts de Belgique* (1850), pp. 248–59. It was reprinted in the more accessible *Annuaire de l'Université catholique de Louvain* 16 (1852), pp. 234–50, to which version I shall be referring. Cf. also *idem*, *Mémoire historique et littéraire sur le Collège des Trois-Langues à l'université de Louvain* (Brussels, 1856), p. 355.
47   The similarity between Barbatus's *Speculum* and Hutter's *Cubus alphabeticus sanctae ebraeae linguae* was pointed out by Nève, 'Note sur un lexique hébreu', p. 241.
48   'Quae autem radicales, quae item serviles sive addititiae litterae sint, ex tabella Grammaticali, quam usui vestro post pauca exhibebimus, facile erit dignoscere' (sig. Al[r]).

As it stands the *Speculum hebraicum* cannot have been of much help to the student of Hebrew without the personal assistance of the author. Few copies survive and not very many can ever have been printed.[49] The book leaves us little the wiser about Barbatus's capacities as a teacher of Hebrew. It does not contain any glaring errors, but nor does it seem to answer any particular need. We should turn, rather, to another source which yields far more evidence: the archives of the Plantin press in Antwerp. There, from January 1614 to December 1616, Barbatus, like many scholars in the Netherlands, had an account. The firm was run by Plantin's grandson, Balthasar Moretus, from whom Barbatus ordered the books he required for teaching his 'Oriental languages'. For his students of Arabic he only ordered a single book, William Bedwell's 1612 edition of the Johannine Epistles (the work which would seem to have marked the end of their friendship). For his students of Hebrew he ordered far more. Besides at least seven Hebrew Bibles, he purchased several copies of Bellarmine's grammar, the *Institutiones linguae hebraicae* (five on 1 January 1614 and others on 21 January and 7 February), Sanctes Pagnini's *Lexicon latino-hebraicum* (four copies were acquired on 7 January 1614), and Johannes Buxtorf's primer, *Institutio epistolaris hebraica*.[50] These acquisitions show that Barbatus did have students – perhaps not as many as he claimed himself but certainly more than his enemies implied. And they prove that he was using the best available textbooks for studying Hebrew.

At the end of his preface to the *Speculum hebraicum* Barbatus promised further works on Syriac and Arabic. There is no evidence that he completed anything on Syriac. On the other hand, two manuscript copies survive in the National Library in Vienna of the Arabic grammar which he must have composed when he was in the Southern Netherlands, but which he seems to have prepared for the printer only in 1620 when he was in Germany.[51] The *Grammaticae arabicae compendium* had been approved by the censor of Antwerp, Laurentius Beyerlinck, and Barbatus had requested the archduke for assistance in publishing it as early as 1616. On the title-page, moreover, Barbatus still calls himself 'Linguae sanctae, ceterarumque Orientalium in Alma Lovaniensi Academia Professor'.

In view of his admissions to Scaliger in 1608 and Erpenius's dismissive comments about his inability to teach classical Arabic in the following year, Barbatus's Arabic grammar shows signs of improvement. It was indeed strongly

---

49 Copies exist in Brussels, Bibliothèque Royale Albert 1er; London, BL; and Leuven, Universiteitsbibliotheek.
50 MPM, MS Arch. 128, fols 214[a–b].
51 Both versions are contained in a single manuscript, ÖNB, MS 15161.

influenced by Erpenius's own grammar, which Barbatus had received from the author in Antwerp in 1613 and about which he had been profuse in his praise.[52] He adopted Erpenius's structure, even if he criticised him on certain points, questioning whether the twenty-two broken plural forms he gave were all in use, and providing fifteen verbal forms rather than the thirteen of Erpenius. As contemporary Arabic grammars went it was a perfectly adequate piece of work, even if it was far inferior to Erpenius's. There is no reason, in short, to think that its author could not teach Arabic.[53] Yet there is one major weakness not so much in Barbatus's treatment of Arabic grammar as in his attitude to the language. He insisted repeatedly that the study of Semitic languages should start with the study of Hebrew. In the introduction to his *Grammaticae arabicae compendium* he went still further, stating that Hebrew was the 'fons et origo' of all languages spoken in the East except for Greek and Armenian. Its main descendants were Aramaic, Syriac and Arabic, and from Arabic descended, 'quasi filiae a matre prodeunt', Turkish, Persian, Tartar and Ethiopic.[54]

The idea that Arabic was subservient to Hebrew and that the two languages should be learnt together persisted, although formulated in a more sophisticated manner, until well into the eighteenth century.[55] Yet Barbatus showed that he had no notion of the turn which the advanced study of Arabic was

---

52   Barbatus's letter to Erpenius from Antwerp, dated 1 Oct. 1613, is published in Houtsma 'Uit de oostersche correspondentie', pp. 17–18.
53   The only scholar to have studied Barbatus's Arabic grammar is Jones, pp. 167–169.
54   Barbatus's preface runs: 'In primis te admoneo (Benigne Lector) in hoc quod praecipuum est, ne ad Linguas Orientales accedendum putes, antequam (saltem mediocriter) in Lingua Sancta (scilicet Hebraica) fundatus fueris, quippe quae est fons et Origo omnium Linguarum, (si Graecam et Armenicam excipias) quae praecipue in usu sunt, per totum Orientem, et quasi riuoli ab ipso fonte deriuantur, inter has quae magis accedent ad ipsam linguam Hebraicam et maiorem affinitatem cum ipsa habent, sunt Caldaica, Syriaca et Arabica. De duabus prioribus non multa dicenda sunt, nam hae hodiernis temporibus, certe parum sunt in usu: ab hac vero nostra Arabica, Linguae omnes quae in Oriente communiter in usu sunt, Turcica, Persica, Tartarica, Aethiopica, et siquae aliae, quasi filiae a matre prodeunt. Ipsae etiam Nationes quae totam Asiam et Africam inhabitant, si non vulgariter loqui velint, Arabicam intelligere debent et loqui. Non tantum de Christianis Haereticis Schismaticisque Orientalibus loquor, sed de Turcis, Mohamedanis, Judaeis et aliis Infidelibus, qui nullam praeterea linguam tam familiarem habent quam nostram Arabicam. Et quod maxime hanc linguam commendat, est, quod eius notitia plurimum conducat, ad intelligentiam planiorem Linguae sanctae, et utilissima eis praecipue, qui literis sacris dant operam. Huius igitur linguae (Benevole Lector) hic breuiter habes fundamenta, et hoc nostro Opusculo feliciter utere, et fruere. Si quid ad Complimentum et omnimodam perfectionem desit, ex Lexicis id colligere potes, et maxime ex nostro quam citissime, ut speramus edendo, Deo fauente. Vale.' ÖNB, MS 15161, fols 99^v, 83^v.
55   See the discussion in J. Loop, *Johann Heinrich Hottinger. Arabic and Islamic Studies in the Seventeenth Century* (Oxford, 2013), pp. 61–80.

taking in certain learned circles under the influence of Scaliger and Erpenius. For the more far-sighted Arabists were aware that the future of Arabic studies actually lay in dissociating Arabic from Hebrew, in studying it on its own terms, in connection with the Qur'an and Islamic texts and, if anything, with the other main languages spoken in the Islamic world, Turkish and Persian. Scaliger had expressed this enlightened view in his letters. His advice was followed by Erpenius, who learnt Turkish in order to use Arabic-Turkish dictionaries, and by Erpenius's successor to the chair of Arabic in Leiden, Jacobus Golius, who employed both Arabic-Turkish and Arabic-Persian dictionaries to compile his own great Arabic dictionary of 1653.[56]

To begin with Barbatus was confident that he would be able to publish his Arabic grammar as well as a number of other works. In November 1616 he wrote to Archduke Albert begging his support in doing so and providing a list of the further writings he hoped to send to the press: an Arabic translation of *De procuranda omnium gentium salute* by the Discalced Carmelite Thomas a Jesu; an Arabic dictionary; a polyglot psalter in Hebrew, Arabic, Greek and Latin; and a book on mathematics he had translated into Arabic. The archduke responded generously with a subsidy of 250 florins, but this was of no avail.[57] Barbatus found himself sharing the predicament of so many contemporary Arabists. In the Southern Netherlands there was a lack of Arabic types. Thomas Erpenius was distressed by the decision of the Leiden branch of the Plantin press, which had produced his grammar, to cease printing in Arabic after publishing the collection of Arabic proverbs prepared by Scaliger and Casaubon and completed by himself in 1614. As a result he had other types cast and set up his own Arabic press in Leiden in 1615, but he could hardly have been expected to print the work of a rival which was also of a quality far inferior to his own. By 1616 the Leiden Officina Plantiniana run by the Raphelengius brothers, the most obvious publishers of Arabic in the Low Countries, was trying to get rid of its Arabic equipment. Franciscus and Justus Raphelengius had managed to sell some of their types to William Bedwell in 1614, but he could do nothing with them. At the same time they were negotiating the sale of the recently recast types, together with the punches and matrices, to their cousin Balthasar Moretus in Antwerp. It was not until 1621, however, that the terms were agreed upon.[58]

Quite apart from the practical difficulty of finding a printer, Barbatus was facing increasing hostility in Louvain. He survived 1616, but in the following year his enemies at last triumphed. Certainly Barbatus exposed himself

---

56   Cf. Fück, pp. 47–53, 59–73, 79–84; and below, pp. 248–249, 251–254.
57   Cf. Nève, 'Nouveaux renseignements', pp. 352–353.
58   Cf. below, pp. 218–228.

to criticism. He was discovered to be living with a concubine. To this he confessed and had to perform a penance imposed by the rector of the university, Johannes Wiggers. But what was even more serious was the doubt cast on the orthodoxy of his Catholicism. His uncertain beliefs, and above all his very limited theological training, his enemies claimed, meant that he was incapable of teaching, or of commenting on, biblical texts. An attempt was consequently made to bring about his dismissal.[59] The university was divided. In the summer of 1617 Puteanus wrote to the court almoner, Pedro de Toledo, in order to enlist his support in favour of a man whose teaching, he said, did such credit to the university.[60] And indeed Barbatus, however undeservedly, had by then acquired something of an international reputation. In October the German Arabist Johann Melchior Maderus mentioned 'Barbatus, Maurus, Lovaniensis professor arabs' among the 'Illustres et Clarissimi eruditione Viri' promoting Arabic studies.[61] The archduke, too, intervened on behalf of his protégé, and the university senate decided to allow him to continue. Barbatus himself, however, ultimately admitted defeat. His curator, Johannes Drusius, informed the privy council that the money paid him would be better spent on more necessary lectureships, in medicine for example. Hebrew, he reminded the council, was already taught in Louvain and Barbatus had not succeeded in lecturing on any of the other Eastern tongues he claimed to know since he had been unable to attract students. As for having types cut in which to print his works in Arabic, there was no one able to do it.[62] Barbatus was persuaded to resign. This enabled him to avoid the ignominy of a dismissal and to approach future patrons as a former professor at Oxford and Louvain who had tired of his previous posts. He could still count on the friendship of the archduke. Albert supplied him with a letter for the Holy Roman Emperor in Prague, Matthias I, requesting that he either be employed at a university or be dispatched to the Turkish sultan so that he might proceed to Istanbul and thence return to his

---

59   Nève, 'Nouveaux renseignements', pp. 353-354.
60   E. Puteanus, *Epistolarum selectarum apparatus ... centuria prima* (Amsterdam, 1646), pp. 73-74: 'Omnibus modis Humanitati tuae obstrictus sum, illustrissime Vir, quae et in alios mea se caussa extendit. Josephum Barbatum, sic amari, virum Orientalium linguarum peritum, Academiae vero nostrae, adeoque Reipublicae utilem, quidni gaudeam? Laudo hominem; ut tuum sic magis beneficium aestimem, extollam favorem, quo neglectas artes linguasque ipse extollis. Nam profecto quorsum doctrina, nisi cultus ille varii atque eruditi sermonis accedat? quorsum, multa scire, nec posse eloqui? Quamplurima etiam alieno et exotico idiomate sepulta iacent, quae aut Barbati, aut fortassis nullius opera vitam et vigorem accipient; sed si ipse vivendi et vigendi fomenta. Bene spero: accipiet, et sic Benignitati tuae magis debebit.'
61   J.M. Maderus, *Oratio pro lingua arabica* (Augsburg, 1617), sig. D2^r.
62   Nève, 'Nouveaux renseignements', pp. 354-6.

native country. The archduke also listed the languages which Barbatus knew: Spanish and English could now be added. At the same time he was given 500 florins for his travel expenses, a substantial reward for services which had not been entirely satisfactory.[63]

Unabashed by his failure Barbatus took other measures to ensure his future. He wrote from Louvain to the bishop of Würzburg and Bamberg, Johann Gottfried von Aschhausen, requesting a recommendation for the duke of Bavaria, Maximilian I. To the bishop he expatiated on his success as a teacher of Hebrew at Louvain. Within two or three weeks, he said, his students had made such progress that they could not only understand Hebrew, but could read the entire Bible in it. But, he added, he had now decided to leave Louvain and to proceed to another university, either Munich or Ingolstadt.[64]

Although he had originally intended to travel to Prague the political unrest attending the outbreak of the Thirty Years War had made Barbatus abandon his plan and, in the late summer of 1618, he set off for the Bavarian court. On his way he passed through Altdorf where, in September, he matriculated at the academy (due to become a university five years later).[65] He also did some teaching, and appears to have given Arabic lessons to Daniel Schwenter, professor of Hebrew at the academy since 1606.[66] Schwenter, who made his name as an inventor and a mathematician, would be appointed professor of Oriental languages in 1625 and obtained the chair of mathematics in 1628.

From Altdorf Barbatus went to Munich. The bishop of Würzburg and Bamberg must have given him the necessary recommendations, and he was made welcome at the court library. The librarian at the time was Esaias Leuker, Maximilian's garrulous but diligent privy secretary who also served the duke on numerous diplomatic missions. Yet the most inspiring figure connected with the library seems still to have been its former director and superintendent, Johann Georg Herwarth zu Hohenburg. Once a privy councillor, he was among the more learned members of the ducal court. A mathematician, astronomer,

---

63   *Ibid.*, pp. 357–358; De Vocht, 'Oriental languages', pp. 681–682, 687.
64   L. Scherman, 'Abudacnus (Barbatus), ein koptischer Orientalist aus dem siebzehnten Jahrhundert, und seine Beziehungen zu München' *Jahrbuch für Münchener Geschichte* 2 (1888), pp. 341–54. This article, one of the best to have been written on Barbatus, documents his plans for leaving for Bavaria and his activity in Munich. For the letter to the bishop see p. 353. Scherman, however, gives no information about the court library or its librarians.
65   G.A. Will, *Geschichte und Beschreibung der Nürnbergischen Universität Altdorf* (Altdorf, 1795), p. 141. 'In indice civium academicorum Altdorf. deprehenditur "1618. d. 18. Sept. Josephus Abuzacno, Arabs, natus Memphi, seu Alcayri Aegypti".'
66   Asaph Ben-Tov, *Johann Ernst Gerhard (1621–1688). The Life and Work of a Seventeenth-Century Orientalist* (Leiden-Boston, 2021), p. 101.

philologist and archaeologist, in correspondence with a vast circle of scholars, he was interested in Egyptology and for this reason may have extended his protection to the Coptic visitor. Barbatus was appointed to assist the librarian in translating the titles of Eastern manuscripts, a considerable number of which were in languages he knew – Arabic, Turkish, Syriac and Hebrew. The library had a large oriental section, thanks to the collection assembled by the Syriac scholar Johann Albrecht Widmanstetter and purchased in 1558, and the Hebrew manuscripts in the collection donated by Johann Jakob Fugger in 1571, as well as more recent acquisitions.[67]

Later in 1618 Barbatus begged the Bavarian ruler for permission to continue to work for him, or alternatively for a further letter to the Holy Roman Emperor. He was promptly rewarded for his work in the library with forty florins. Shortly after he presented another petition: would the duke provide him with a letter for the king of Poland who might employ him as an interpreter of Turkish and other Eastern tongues, or for some other sovereign who could assist him in travelling to Istanbul? Once more Maximilian complied, sending Barbatus a letter for Sigismund III in Warsaw in which he confirmed that the Copt had worked in his library.[68]

Barbatus never used the letter to the Polish king. He remained in Bavaria, probably because of the deteriorating military situation. As he had done in France, England and the Low Countries, he ingratiated himself with the most exalted circles. In 1620 we find him as a guest staying with Count Johann Fugger the Younger at the family castle of Kirchheim near Augsburg. He inscribed his host's *album amicorum* with a quotation in Hebrew (Eccles 7.1, 'A good name is better than precious ointment'), and expressed his appreciation of what he had been given to drink.[69] Also in 1620 he prepared his Arabic grammar for publication, evidently still hoping to have it printed at the university where he

---

67 On the Bavarian court library see R. Hacker, 'Die Münchener Hofbibliothek unter Maximilian I' in H. Glaser, ed., *Wittelsbach und Bayern*, ii.1, *Um Glauben und Reich. Kurfürst Maximilian I. Beiträge zur Bayerischen Geschichte und Kunst 1573–1657* (Munich, 1980), pp. 353–63. For Herwarth zu Hohenburg and Leuker see R. Heydenreuter, *Der landesherrliche Hofrat unter Herzog und Kurfürst Maximilan I. von Bayern (1598–1651)* (Munich, 1981), pp. 335–336, 343.
68 Scherman, 'Abudacnus', pp. 347, 353–354.
69 'In gratia III. Dni. Johannis Fuggeri bibit, ac bibit totumque exausit.' Cf. G. Lilli, 'Das Willkommbuch des Grafen Markus Fugger d. J. zu Kirchheim' *Festgabe Hermann Grauert zur Vollendung des 60. Lebensjahres gewidmet von seiner Schülern* (Freiburg im Breisgau, 1910), pp. 260–283, esp. 266. See also Graf, *Geschichte*, vol. 4, p. 132, who corrects the reading of the Hebrew but confuses Markus Fugger with his heir Johannes d. J. With unusual modesty Barbatus signed himself 'Josephus barbatus Arabs linguarum orientis medii studiosus'.

had once taught. For the time being, however, the manuscript accompanied him on his travels.

The next we hear of Barbatus is in May 1622. Possibly as a consequence of the death of Herwarth zu Hohenburg in January, he had at last decided to leave Bavaria and was making his way to the imperial court in Vienna. In the course of his journey he stopped at Linz and managed to meet a distinguished friend of Herwarth zu Hohenburg, the astronomer Johann Kepler. Like Thomas Bodley before him, Kepler was beguiled by the affable visitor who had taught Arabic and Hebrew 'per Academias Europae'. He gave him a warm recommendation for the imperial librarian Sebastian Tengnagel, whom he urged to be kind to a man so far from his homeland, with such an agreeable personality and of such moral integrity.[70]

When he arrived in Vienna Barbatus had the very best credentials, a letter from Archduke Albert of the Southern Netherlands for the emperor (who was, however, no longer Matthias I in Prague, to whom the document was originally addressed, but Ferdinand II) and a letter from Kepler for Tengnagel. A Dutchman by birth, a friend of his compatriot Thomas Erpenius and of most of the European Arabists, Tengnagel, a keen Orientalist, was eager to employ someone who might help him expand both his own private library and the imperial collection.[71] Barbatus was sufficiently well educated to be of use, not in Vienna itself, Tengnagel seems to have realised, but as an agent in the Ottoman empire. Thanks to his letter for the emperor and to Tengnagel's own support, Barbatus was employed by the imperial war council as dragoman or interpreter. This meant translating into Italian the various languages spoken in Istanbul – chiefly Turkish, but probably also Arabic and Greek.[72]

---

70 J. Kepler, *Gesammelte Werke*, vol. 18 (Munich, 1959), p. 88: 'Etsi nuper ad te scripsi, Cl: Vir, nec quicquam occurrit; cum expectem responsum tuum cum Plutarchij libello: praesens tamen Aegyptius, Josephus Abudakan, professionibus Arabicae et Hebreae linguae per Academias Europae obitis clarus factus, a me literulas ad te commendatitias impetravit. Dignus equidem videtur, cui si quid potes, impertiaris, humanitatisque officijs eum adjuves. Nam et patria longe dissita nos hospitalitatis admonet, et morum suavitas, vitaeque integritas omnium favorem meretur: et communis utrique vestrum professio Linguae Arabicae notitiam inter vos mutuam suadere videtur. Plura amoris argumenta invenies ipse, ubi propius hominem cognoveris.'

71 For Tengnagel see F. Unterkircher, 'Sebastian Tengnagel (1610–1636)' in J. Stummvoll, ed., *Geschichte der Österreichischen Nationalbibliothek, Erster Teil: Die Hofbibliothek (1368–1922)* (Vienna, 1968), pp. 129–145. Cf. also N. Mout, *Bohemen en de Nederlanden in de zestiende eeuw* (Leiden, 1975), pp. 63, 92, 111, 115–116.

72 Barbatus's career from his arrival in Vienna onwards is described in a report submitted to the imperial war council by Michel d'Asquier in 1641. Vienna, Haus-, Hof- und Staatsarchiv, MS Türkei 1/115, D'Asquier 1641, fol. 194^r.

Barbatus's stay in Vienna was brief. Nevertheless he had time to make a number of acquaintances and may have entrusted Tengnagel with the manuscript of his Arabic grammar. Besides taking a spiritual adviser, a 'spiritual Padre', the Jesuit Kasper Bichler who may have seen to the improvement of his orthodoxy, Barbatus was introduced to some of the leading figures in imperial politics – the future vice-president of the war council Gerard von Questenberg, the vice-chancellor Otto von Nostiz, and the first imperial chancellor Johann Baptista Verda von Werdenberg.[73] Above all, Barbatus met the man who was to be his last patron and who was to support him loyally for over twenty years, Michel d'Asquier.

D'Asquier was born in Marseilles in 1598. It must have been on the French coast, possibly from merchants, that he learned Turkish and started to cultivate the extraordinary talent for languages which he placed at the service of the Habsburg court in the reign of the emperor Matthias some time before 1618.[74] Like Tengnagel, a close friend, he was an ardent bibliophile and collected a library of exceptional splendour. Three of the books he is known to have possessed and which found their way into the Schönborn-Buchheim library in the eighteenth century, have magnificent fanfare bindings executed in France.[75]

---

73   In his letter to Tengnagel from Istanbul dated 3 January 1625 Barbatus mentions 'Padre Casparo mio spiritual Padre' (ÖNB, MS 9737.t, fol. l^v). Kasper Bichler was chaplain to Petrus Lubitsch, the confessor of the imperial ambassador to the Porte Hans Ludwig von Kuefstein, whom both priests accompanied to Istanbul in 1628. Cf. K. Teply, *Die kaiserliche Grossbotschaft an Sultan Murad IV. 1628. Des Freiherrn Hans Ludwig von Kuefsteins Fahrt zur Hohen Pforte* (Vienna, 1976), p. 23. In his letter of 29 July 1627 he sends his greetings 'alli Illustrissimi Signori di Nostiz, Questenberg, Vereda ...' (*ibid.*, fol. 264^v). For Nostiz and Verda von Werdenberg see H.E. Schwarz, *The Imperial Privy Council in the Seventeenth Century* (Cambridge, Mass., 1943), pp. 314–315, 383–385. For Questenberg see I. Hiller, *Palatin Nikolaus Esterházy. Die ungarische Rolle in der Habsburgerdiplomatie 1625–1645* (Vienna – Cologne – Weimar, 1992), pp. 26–86.

74   Invaluable information on d'Asquier is provided on the tablet erected by his friends under his tomb in the Stephansdom in Vienna and in the record of his death, Vienna, Wiener Stadt- und Landesarchiv, Totenbeschauprotokolle, s.v. d'Asquier, 28-7-1664. See below, p. 43. For d'Asquier's dealings with the imperial court and his career as dragoman see P. Meienberger, *Johann Rudolf Schmid zum Schwarzenhorn als kaiserlicher Resident in Konstantinopel in den Jahren 1629–1643. Ein Beitrag zur Geschichte der diplomatischen Beziehungen zwischen Österreich und der Türkei in der ersten Hälfte des 17. Jahrhunderts* (Bern-Frankfurt 1973), pp. 80–82; Hiller, *Palatin Nikolaus Esterházy*, pp. 71–75.

75   See, for example, ÖNB, MSS 9737.s, fol. 313^{r–v}; 9737.t, fol. 1^r. They are illustrated and discussed by A. Hobson, 'Three bindings *à la fanfare* and the origins of the fanfare style' in G. Mandelbrote and W. de Bruijn, eds, *The Arcadian Library: Bindings and Provenance* (London-Oxford, 2014), pp. 177–190, plates 1–3. See also A. Hamilton, 'Princes, ministers and scholars: some foreign provenances in the Arcadian Library,' *ibid.*, pp. 81–144, esp. pp. 108–110.

In the early 1620s d'Asquier was appointed imperial dragoman. His function was to interpret for delegates from the Turkish sultan, to translate correspondence from Turkish and Hungarian, to put German texts into Latin, Spanish and Italian, as well as to receive, and on occasion to provide, reports from the Ottoman empire. In 1624/5 he was himself in Ottoman territory, serving the imperial delegate at the peace negotiations of Szőny and Gyarmath, visiting Buda and Istanbul, and sending reports to Tengnagel from the border fortress of Komárom. Principally, however, d'Asquier was stationed in Vienna, occupying a post of importance in which he was succeeded by the great Turcologist from Lorraine, Franz von Mesgnien Meninski.

Barbatus's first task in his new employment was to interpret for the imperial ambassador Johann Jakob Kurz von Senftenau, who was sent by Ferdinand II in 1623 to congratulate the new sultan, Murad IV, on his accession to the throne. To begin with Barbatus was under the wing of d'Asquier who had evidently grown fond of 'il S. Giuseppe Barbato'. Together with d'Asquier he also served Tengnagel in his hunt for Oriental manuscripts. Istanbul was one of the most attractive cities for European Orientalists wishing to expand their manuscript collections, for Arabic, Turkish and Persian works could be acquired with facility. Thomas Erpenius thus had an agent in Istanbul, while others went in person. Tengnagel was in the habit of sending his agents lists, often based on the catalogues of other European libraries. After Erpenius's death in 1624 he sent d'Asquier a copy of the catalogue Erpenius had himself drawn up (and which was subsequently published) of his own collection, and asked the dragoman to collect as many of the titles as he could. D'Asquier passed the list on to Barbatus.[76]

Kurz von Senftenau went back to Vienna after a relatively brief stay in the Ottoman empire. Shortly after his return to the imperial court he joined the Society of Jesus and established his reputation as a preacher.[77] Barbatus remained in Istanbul. He was now instructed to serve a different diplomatic representative, the imperial resident Sebastian Lustrier von Liebenstein, a canon of Olomouc who was protected by his bishop, the governor of Moravia Cardinal Franz von Dietrichstein. Lustrier had accompanied Kurz von

---

76 In a letter from Komárom to Tengnagel dated 26 Sep. 1624 d'Asquier wrote: 'Il S. Giuseppe Barbato (del quale VS desidera sapere) e rimaso a Costantinopoli appresso il Sig. Residente. Non ha potuto ricuperar gran cosa, ritrovandosi con pochi danari. Gli ho lasciato il Catalogo che V.S. mi diede. col tempo potrà forse trovar qualche cosa.' ÖNB, MS 9737.s, fol. 313^{r-v}.

77 Cf. B. Spuler, 'Die europäische Diplomatie in Konstantinopel bis zum Frieden von Belgrad (1739)' *Jahrbücher für Kultur und Geschichte der Slaven* 11 (1935), p. 332.

Senftenau on his visit to Turkey in 1623 and received his appointment as resident in the following year.[78]

The period in which Barbatus served Lustrier, from 1624 to 1629, was one of unhappiness. Two of his letters to Tengnagel survive, the first dated 3 January 1625 and the other 29 July 1627.[79] They both tell a story of woe. Barbatus's main complaint was lack of money. In the second letter he said that he had been paid no more than 200 ducats of his salary since 15 June 1623 and he implored Tengnagel to make sure that if a proper ambassador were sent to the Porte he would give him what he was owed. But that was not all that grieved him. He had wished, he wrote, to come to Turkey in order to improve his knowledge of 'qualche vertu o scientia', but he regretted his decision and wished only to leave.[80] He had been treated scandalously, insulted and menaced by the Turks and handled by Lustrier, whom he had grown to hate, as little more than a lackey. He was asked to wear livery. He was hardly even allowed time to eat, let alone to acquire the manuscripts Tengnagel desired. He appeared as a pauper beside the dragomans of other nations. His requests to relinquish the imperial service were invariably rejected. Barbatus still looked back fondly on the countries of the West where he had been so well received for almost twenty years and, in what seems to be his last surviving letter to the imperial librarian, he laments the death of Erpenius, one of his earliest acquaintances in the Republic of Letters, of which he had been told some two years after it had occurred by 'certain Flemings' in Istanbul.[81]

There is no reason to doubt the accuracy of Barbatus's description of his predicament. As an Egyptian Copt he was an Ottoman subject who was not entitled to any sort of diplomatic immunity. The representatives of the Habsburg emperor, moreover, were still treated with some contempt in Istanbul in the early seventeenth century. The 'King of Vienna', as the emperor

---

[78] For Lustrier see R. Bireley, S.J., *Religion and Politics in the Age of the Counterreformation: Emperor Ferdinand II, William Lamormaini, S.J., and the Formation of Imperial Policy* (Chapel Hill, 1981), pp. 206, 277.

[79] The first letter is ÖNB, MS 9737.t, fols 1^r–2^v. The second, mistakenly split, is *ibid.*, fols 263^r–64^v, 152^r.

[80] '… ho voluto restare nella porta ottomana (del che mi sono molto pentito) per imparare qualche vertu o scientia, il che si po benissimo per merito di Arabi tanto di Eggitto quanto di Barbaria, persone dottissimi, et peritssimi in tute le scientie.' *Ibid.*, fol. 263^r.

[81] 'Questi giorni passati,' he wrote on 29 July 1627, 'ho recevuto una gravissima sua nella quale mi significa la morte del Signor Erpenio, la quale seppi l'anno passato da certi fiamenghi non senza dolore et lacrime, per conversazione di molti anni havuta con lui, et ancora per havere perso tanto dotto e amico, con tuto questo, detto o indetto, tuti havemo da passare per questo camino, ancora nella sua humanissima parla che io habbi imparato molte cose et veramente questo era il mio antichissimo desiderio …' *Ibid.*, fol. 263^{r-v}.

was dismissively known at the Porte, was officially a tributary of the Turks who had earned his treatment by his military inferiority. Although he occasionally dispatched ambassadors – Kurz von Senftenau in 1623, Hans Ludwig von Kuefstein in 1628, Johann Rudolf von Puchheim in 1634 – these were only allowed to stay briefly in Istanbul, for a few weeks or months, and, under constant surveillance, had to limit their activities to visits to the grand vizier and a couple of senior officials. The emperor's other representative, the resident, was an innovation dating from the second decade of the century.[82] Drawn from a class inferior to that of the ambassadors, the residents lived in Istanbul and had regular dealings with a wide variety of Ottoman officials and other members of the local population. In the diplomatic hierarchy, however, the imperial resident ranked well below the ambassadors of France, England, Venice and the Dutch Republic. Shortage of money was chronic among foreign diplomats in Turkey, but the funds at the disposal of the imperial resident were always far smaller that those provided for the other representatives: hence Barbatus's lamentations about his unpaid salary.

With little money, the resident had to content himself with a small household of which the dragoman was part. But the importance of the post for imperial politics meant also that the interpreter was kept busy. Besides translating for the resident in his day-to-day dealings with the Turks, he had to represent his employer at official meetings with government ministers. He also performed missions of his own to Turkish dignitaries and drew up confidential reports about politics and other developments. He was involved in every action the resident might take, and one of the most significant episodes in which Barbatus must have played his part as interpreter from the late 1620s onwards was the fall of the Greek Orthodox patriarch of Constantinople, Cyril Lucaris.[83] In his struggle to defend the autonomy of the Greek Church against the encroachments of Rome and the creation of a Uniate Church at the Synod of Brest-Litovsk in 1596, Lucaris turned for help to the Reformed Churches of Northern Europe for whose doctrine he had some sympathy. He supported the Ottoman government in a policy of aggression to the Catholic powers, particularly to Poland. Although incapable of acting in unison, the Catholics responded, and Ferdinand II became one of Lucaris's fiercest opponents.

---

82 The situation is well described by Meienberger, *Johann Rudolf Schmid*, pp. 9–99.
83 Cf. G. Hering, *Ökumenisches Patriarchal und europäische Politik 1620–1638* (Wiesbaden, 1968), pp. 115–130, 256–259, 266–270, 274–321. See also S. Runciman, *The Great Church in Captivity. A Study of the Patriarchate of Constantinople from theEve of the Turkish Conquest to theGreek War of Independence* (Cambridge, 1968), pp. 259–288.

In 1628/9 the imperial ambassador Kuefstein had tried vainly to work against Lucaris, while Lustrier, in the last year of his office, had endeavoured equally vainly to win the patriarch over to the idea of union with the Church of Rome. Lustrier was not a successful resident. He seems to have left a poor impression in Istanbul and did little to increase the emperor's prestige, even if he returned to the imperial court in 1629 to pursue a good diplomatic career elsewhere, as resident in Paris and later as chancellor and representative in Rome of Cardinal von Dietrichstein. He was succeeded in Istanbul by a far more enterprising man, Johann Rudolf Schmid.

Born in Stein am Rhein near Schaffhausen in 1590 from a Protestant family, Schmid appears, in his youth, to have travelled in Italy and Hungary and to have been involved in the military skirmishes against the Turks.[84] He was then taken prisoner and spent some twenty years in Turkish captivity. He was a slave, but a privileged one, living in Istanbul where he learnt excellent Turkish, both spoken and written, and occasionally serving the Ottoman authorities as interpreter. In 1623 he met the ambassador Kurz von Senftenau, who probably ransomed him. In his company he must also have encountered Barbatus and d'Asquier. Soon after his arrival in Vienna, where he had hastened from Istanbul, Schmid started to work for the war council. He owed his swift preferment to the influence of d'Asquier who was to remain his friend. After visiting Lustrier in Istanbul in the winter of 1626–7 and performing various diplomatic missions, he was appointed imperial resident himself.

Schmid served his masters well. He created an impressive network of informers and had a hand in a number of events. He made every effort to prevent further Turkish intervention in Europe (which was encouraged by the Swedes). He did his utmost to deter the Turks from invading Poland. The best hope for Catholic Europe, he believed, was to further the Ottoman war with Persia. Determined to obliterate any suspicion that might be attached to his Lutheran origins, he exerted himself in the interests of the Church of Rome. He intrigued more actively against Cyril Lucaris than his predecessors, endeavouring to have him replaced by the philo-Catholic Cyril Contares, the man responsible for the patriarch's assassination in 1638. He also tried to protect imperial interests against the ambitions of the French. After his return to Austria in 1643 Schmid was rewarded by being created Freiherr zum Schwarzenhorn.

In his activities Schmid was well served, in his turn, by Barbatus. What the Copt thought of his impetuous and sometimes brutal employer (whose misdemeanours included the attempted murder, concocted together with d'Asquier,

---

84   Meienberger, *Johann Rudolf Schmid*, pp. 101–13.

of a rival interpreter) we do not know, but it is probably safe to conclude that in Schmid, as in d'Asquier, Barbatus had a friend and protector. In 1634 the imperial ambassador Johann Rudolf von Puchheim submitted a report in which he recommended that Barbatus be dismissed.[85] Although Puchheim praised his energy, industry and trustworthiness, he said that an Ottoman subject could never be counted upon for complete fidelity to the emperor. Yet Barbatus survived. His salary was paid irregularly, and it was low – about a quarter of what the Venetian dragoman was getting at the same time[86] – but throughout Schmid's term of office Barbatus could count on d'Asquier's support in Vienna. Certainly the former 'professor of oriental languages' at Oxford and Louvain, the protégé of princes and the friend of some of the greatest scholars of his time, had fallen a considerable distance. He was now referred to somewhat cavalierly as 'l'interprete Barbato' by d'Asquier and 'der Josefo' by Schmid,[87] but he had a job which, he had assured both Archduke Albert and Maximilian of Bavaria many years earlier, he keenly desired.

Barbatus was not immune to the blows of fortune. He lived at Schmid's house in the Greek quarter of Phanar, on the southern side of the Golden Horn. Schmid had chosen his residence, in preference to the official building intended for the imperial representatives closer to the bazaars, because of its proximity to the water and the possibility of crossing to Pera in the event of fire. And on two occasions, in the fires of August 1633 and the summer of 1640, the resident and his interpreter lost most of their property.[88] But the greatest blow came when, in 1643, after fourteen years of service, Schmid was recalled, largely as a result of the intrigues of the Hungarian palatine Miklós Esterházy. He was replaced by Alexander Greiffenklau von Vollrats. There was a strong

---

85   Vienna, Haus-, Hof- und Staatsarchiv, MS Türkei I/113, Finalrelation Puchheim, fol. 368ᵛ. For the attempted murder of the Ragusan Vicenzo Brattuti, see I. Hiller, 'A tolmácsper: A bécsi Haditanács működése és a Habsburgok tolmácsai a 17. század első felében' *Történelmi szemle* 33 (1991), pp. 203–214.

86   Meienberger, *Johann Rudolf Schmid*, p. 97.

87   *Ibid.*, p. 173. In one of his requests that the resident be given more money by the war council, d'Asquier added: 'L'istesso per l'Interprete Barbato, che patisce anch'egli molta necessità' (Vienna, Haus-, Hof- und Staatsarchiv, MS Türkei I/115, d'Asquier 1640, fol. 19ʳ).

88   In a petition concerning Barbatus addressed to the war council in 1641, d'Asquier wrote: 'Viene pero a supplicare humilmente le Signorie Vostre Illustrissime (alli quali crede sia ben nota la sua lunga e penosa servitù) restar servite aggratiarlo della loro benigna interpositione accio possa conseguire qualche Aiuto di Costa, e rifarsi del danno patito due volte dall'incendio in Constantinopoli.' Vienna, Haus-, Hof- und Staatsarchiv, MS Türkei I/115. D'Asquier 1641, fol. 194ʳ.

feeling of antipathy between Schmid and his successor, and Barbatus was dismissed for good.[89]

Although we have little information about Barbatus's life in Istanbul, particularly after his last letter to Tengnagel of 1627, he is unlikely to have severed his connections with the Republic of Letters. Because of the availability of Oriental manuscripts, the Ottoman capital was, as we have seen, an attractive goal for European Arabists. Some of the most distinguished visited the city while Barbatus was in imperial employment, and they stayed with their respective ambassadors. Barbatus's allusion in his last letter to Tengnagel to 'certain Flemings' who informed him of Erpenius's death, proves that he was in touch with the other foreign communities. The Dutch colony, to which he was referring, was centred around Cornelis Haga, the ambassador of the Dutch Republic from 1612 to 1639. Besides about thirty residents of various origins, it included a number of visitors connected with the University of Leiden. The most eminent was Jacobus Golius, Erpenius's pupil and successor to the chair of Arabic, who spent most of 1628 staying with Haga and occasionally serving him as chancellor and interpreter. Two years later Golius's brother Pieter, a Discalced Carmelite who also made his name as an Arabist, was staying at the Dutch embassy. Some ten years after that two pupils of Golius, both of German origin, Georgius Gentius and Christian Ravius, came to Istanbul. In 1645, two years after Barbatus's dismissal as interpreter, the best of Golius's German students, Levinus Warner, settled in the city where he remained, acting as Dutch diplomatic representative, until his death in 1665.[90]

Besides the Leiden Arabists who would have reminded Barbatus of his former friendships, there were two scholars from Oxford who reached Istanbul in 1637: the Arabist Edward Pococke in the company of the mathematician and astronomer John Greaves. Both men had been friends of William Bedwell.[91] Pococke received Arabic lessons from him in 1626 and owed to him his introduction to William Laud. In 1629 Pococke was appointed chaplain to the merchants of the Levant Company in Aleppo and in 1636, thanks to Laud who had been created archbishop of Canterbury in 1633 and was chancellor of the University of Oxford, he was given the newly founded chair of Arabic. He thus

---

[89] Meienberger, *Johann Rudolf Schmid*, pp. 94, 112; Hiller, *Palatin Nikolaus Esterházy*, pp. 87–88.

[90] Cf. De Groot, *The Ottoman Empire*, pp. 190–207, 217–229; A. Vrolijk, J. Schmidt and K. Scheper, *Turcksche boucken. De oosterse verzameling van Levinus Warner, Nederlands diplomaat in zeventiende-eeuws Istanbul* (The Hague, 2012), pp. 42–45; Juynboll, *Zeventiende eeuwsche Beoefenaars*, pp. 132–135, 215–222.

[91] Cf. Hamilton, *William Bedwell*, pp. 46–47, 52–53.

had the professorship to which Barbatus had laid a specious claim over twenty years earlier. After a few months in Turkey Greaves proceeded to Egypt, but Pococke remained, staying at the English embassy until August 1640.[92] The visitors from Leiden and Oxford must have come across Barbatus in the relatively small foreign colony in Istanbul, even if they are unlikely to have approved of his part in the machinations against Cyril Lucaris. For the English and Dutch embassies provided the patriarch with constant support in his struggle for independence from Rome. Pococke, particularly, felt committed to his cause. He became a close acquaintance of Lucaris and sent Archbishop Laud a detailed account of his assassination.[93]

The remaining pieces of evidence concerning Barbatus after his dismissal in 1643 are puzzling. One is an Arabic psalter in the Österreichische Nationalbibliothek in Vienna, copied in Jerusalem in 1620. The first page bears an inscription in Barbatus's own hand: 'pertinet ad Josephuin Barbatum S.C.M. Int.' and below, in a different ink, 'Emptus A. 1664'.[94] This could mean that Barbatus shared the longevity of his last employer, Schmid zum Schwarzenhorn, who lived well into his seventies. He may even have returned to Vienna where the imperial library might have purchased his manuscript after his death. Another possibility is that he bequeathed his papers to d'Asquier. D'Asquier himself retained his post as imperial dragoman for a remarkably long time, serving under three successive emperors. Under Leopold I, however, he fell into disgrace. Accused of various misdemeanours, including negligence, he was dismissed and tried in 1663.[95] The following year he died of dropsy and, despite his fall, was buried in the Stephansdom in Vienna. His heirs might at that point have sold Barbatus's manuscript to the new imperial librarian, Peter Lambeck.

The year 1664 brings us closer to an event even more puzzling than the arrival of Barbatus's psalter in the imperial library: the publication by Oxford University in 1675 of the work which was to ensure Barbatus's reputation over the centuries, the *Historia Jacobitarum, seu Coptorum, In Aegypto, Lybia, Nubia, Aethiopia tota, et parte Cypri Insulae habitantium*. The book raises

---

92 Cf. P.M. Holt, *Studies in the History of the Near East* (London, 1973), pp. 7–9; Toomer, *Eastern Wisedome*, pp. 127–146.

93 Cf. H. Trevor-Roper, 'The Church of England and the Greek Church in the time of Charles I' in D. Baker, ed., *Religious Motivations and Social Problems for the Church Historians* (Oxford, 1978), pp. 213–240.

94 The codex (ÖNB, MS A.F 398) is described in G. Flügel, *Die arabischen, persischen und türkischen Handschriften der Kaiserlich-Königlichen Hofbibliothek zu Wien* (Vienna, 1865–7), vol. 3, pp. 4–5, no. 1542.

95 Meienberger, *Johann Rudolf Schmid*, p. 81.

various questions: who edited it and added the unsigned preface? When and where was the work written? How did the editor obtain it? And was it really by Barbatus? The traditional answer is that the book was edited by Thomas Marshall of Lincoln College who had found the manuscript in Oxford where it had been written by Barbatus during his stay there between 1610 and 1613.[96]

First, Thomas Marshall.[97] He had not been long in Oxford in 1675. He had fled from England after the surrender of the university town to the parliamentary forces in 1647 and had settled in the Low Countries where he acted as chaplain to the Company of Merchant Adventurers, first in Rotterdam and then in Dordrecht. He did not return to Oxford until about 1672 to take up his post as rector of Lincoln College. Marshall had for some time been interested in the Copts and, when in Holland, he had been encouraged and assisted in his study of their language and culture by various scholars at Leiden – the younger Franciscus Junius, Isaac Vossius and Jacobus Golius. He was aware of the progress in Coptic studies. Through Robert Huntington, the chaplain of the Levant Company in Aleppo, he was in touch with the German Johann Michael Wansleben, who had been dispatched to Egypt in order to collect manuscripts and antiquities (and to proceed to Ethiopia, which he never did) by the French minister Jean Baptiste Colbert and who produced a far more substantial study of the Copts than the one by Barbatus. The French version of Wansleben's work, *Histoire de l'église d'Alexandrie*, appeared in 1677, but Marshall owned an autograph of the Italian original finished in 1674.[98] Marshall also assembled a fine collection of Coptic manuscripts which is now in the Bodleian Library, and looked forward, when he was still in Dordrecht, to publishing some of them.[99]

John Fell, the bishop of Oxford who played such an important part in the publications of the university, had Coptic types cut for Marshall, and the last sentence of the preface to the *Historia Jacobitarum* refers to manuscripts owned by Marshall: 'With the help of God our press will soon issue a most ancient version of the Gospels in the Coptic language and characters, as well as of the authentic liturgy of this same Church, which, we trust, will not displease

---

96 The idea that the *Historia* was written at Oxford gained currency in the late 17th century when it was realised that Barbatus had taught at Oxford (see below, p. 37). The attribution of the 1675 edition to Thomas Marshall, however, seems to start in the late nineteenth century with Miss B. Porter's article on Marshall in the *Dictionary of National Biography* which appeared in 1893.
97 For Thomas Marshall see V. Green, *The Commonwealth of Lincoln College* (Oxford, 1979), pp. 275–280, 680–681, and K. Dekker, 'Marshall, Thomas' ODNB.
98 Bodl., MS Marshall 18.
99 Cf. his letter to the astronomer and orientalist Edward Bernard written from Dordrecht in 1669 in which he refers to his plans. Bodl., MS Smith 45, fol. 109^r.

our learned readers.'[100] Yet Marshall never completed his plan to publish his Coptic manuscripts. The types cut for him only came into their own in 1713 when Oxford University published the Coptic New Testament edited by the Prussian convert to Anglicanism David Wilkins, based on various manuscripts (including Marshall's) in the Bodleian and collated with codices in Paris and at the Vatican.[101]

With his interest in Coptic and his close association with the Oxford press and John Fell, Marshall would certainly seem a likely editor. Yet there is no sign of Barbatus's manuscript in Marshall's collection or any reference to it in his surviving correspondence. None of his contemporaries seem to have attributed its publication to him, and no later editor of the work suggests that he was behind the first edition. The only attempt by a seventeenth-century scholar to identify the author of the anonymous preface seems to be that of Leibniz's versatile friend, the historian Wilhelm Ernst Tentzel. He suggests John Fell, a candidate just as likely as Marshall and whom he had known some years earlier.[102]

The identity of the editor of the *Historia Jacobitarum* thus remains in doubt. If it was not Marshall or Fell it was someone close to them, and the next question is how he obtained the manuscript. Did Barbatus really write the work when he was in Oxford? And did it remain there for sixty-three years to await the upsurge of interest in the Copts of the mid-seventeenth century? This is most implausible. Although individual scholars had had plans for studying Coptic at an earlier stage, the true interest in Coptic culture only really started in the late 1620s and the 1630s, particularly in Rome after the Italian scholar Pietro Della Valle had returned from the East with a collection of Coptic manuscripts and the German Jesuit Athanasius Kircher had settled there and begun to publish his works on hieroglyphs.[103] This was long after Barbatus had left Oxford. Barbatus himself, who was always eager to supply potential patrons with an impressive *curriculum vitae* and a list of the books he hoped to have

---

100 'Prodibunt brevi, bono cum Deo, ex Typographeo nostro Evangelii versio antiquissima lingua et Characteribus Copticis, nec non authenticae ejusdem Ecclesiae Liturgiae, quae lectoribus eruditis non ingrata fore confidimus.' J. Abudacnus, *Historia Jacobitarum* ... (Oxford, 1675), sig. a2ᵛ.

101 H. Hart, *Notes on a Century of Typography at the Oxford University Press*, ed. H. Carter (Oxford, 1970), pp. 32, 166, 182. For Marshall, Wilkins, and Coptic studies see Hamilton, *The Copts and the West*, pp. 262–265.

102 W.E. Tentzel, *Monatliche Unterredungen einiger guten Freunde von allerhand Büchern und andern annehmlichen Geschichten* ... (Leipzig, 1693), p. 202.

103 See N.-C. Fabri de Peiresc, *Lettres à Claude Saumaise et à son entourage (1620–1637)*, ed. A. Bresson (Florence, 1992), pp. xxii–xxxiii, 27–133, for a survey of Coptic studies at the time, and Peiresc's comments on Kircher's progress. See also Hamilton, *The Copts and the West*, pp. 195–228.

published, never mentions, in his surviving letters, the *Historia Jacobitarum*, the one book which was to ensure his reputation after his death. Nor did he display any interest in the Church of Alexandria. The Oxford editor, moreover, seems to be unaware that Barbatus had ever been associated with the university. Indeed, he knows curiously little about Barbatus, and only describes him as 'Josephus Abudacnus, born in Cairo, a man of little learning but of blameless character and a reliable witness of matters occurring in his country'. What the editor does say, however, is that Barbatus 'had *recently* composed a brief commentary on the religion and customs of his countrymen'.[104] Could this not mean that Barbatus had actually written his book in Istanbul and that it had recently been brought to Oxford, perhaps by one of the many foreigners whom the dragoman must have met when he was in Turkey? And finally the question remains of whether Barbatus was indeed the author. One fact which suggests that he was is that he was far too little known for his name to be an attractive pseudonym.

The *Historia Jacobitarum* is, as the editor says, a brief work, the twenty-three short chapters covering some thirty pages of the small quarto first edition. It opens with a chapter on the name of the Copts, at the time still known as Jacobites, the term indiscriminately applied to all the monophysite Churches. Information is then given on the early history of the Church of Alexandria, the election and consecration of its clergy, the shape of its churches, its ritual and sacred vestments, its sacraments, cult of images and relics, monastic rules, fasts, pilgrimages, diet, education and, finally, the place of the Copts in contemporary Ottoman society. While the description of Coptic beliefs and customs is largely accurate, the author is far less reliable in his account of the origins of the Church of Alexandria. It was above all on this point that he was to be criticised by his eighteenth-century commentators. Refusing to accept the widely approved view that the Jacobites owed their name to the sixth-century monophysite Jacob Baradaeus, he attributes the name and the origin of his people to Jacob the Hebrew patriarch.[105]

Contemporary reactions to the publication varied. That it was expected to have a certain commercial success is shown by the existence of a pirate edition, in a far smaller 16° format, printed in Amsterdam and giving the same

---

104 'Cum ergo Josephus Abudacnus in ipsa Cairo natus, vir quidem parum literatus, sed inculpatis moribus, et rerum in patria sua gestarum testis locuples, brevem commentarium, de cultu et moribus Popularium suorum nuper contexuerit: non abs re futurum judicavimus si publica luce donaremus; praesertim, cum sine magna temporis aut impensarum factura, et imprimi et perlegi potuerit.' Abudacnus, *Historia*, sig. a2^{r-v}.
105 *Ibid.*, pp. 1–2. For a further discussion of the book see Hamilton, *The Copts and the West*, pp. 134–136.

year (and publisher) as the English quarto edition.[106] The work was reviewed respectfully in the *Journal des Savants* and elsewhere. Yet there were also criticisms. The Orientalist Humphrey Prideaux, then a student at Christ Church and already close to John Fell, described the *Historia Jacobitarum* in 1675 to John Ellis as one of the 'pidleing things printeing here'.[107] A century later Edward Gibbon referred to it as a 'slight' work,[108] and indeed, it could not be compared in thoroughness to Wansleben's book which covered the very same ground in far greater depth and also used some of the most important Arabic sources, which Barbatus entirely neglected. The *Historia*, rather, is exceptional in that it is by a Copt. Its publication must be seen as a result of the interest in the Copts, their culture, religion and language, which was gaining ground throughout Europe.

At first it seemed that the future of the *Historia* was to lie in the hands of eccentrics. It was translated from Latin into English in 1692 by Sir Edwin Sadleir, Bart., of Temple Dinsley in Hertfordshire, a 'person of quality' who laid no claims to scholarship but was intrigued by the title of the Latin original since it brought to his mind the Jacobites in contemporary England. In 1693 Sadleir had a second edition printed in order to rectify the misprints in the first.[109] In the early eighteenth century, however, it became clear that the survival of Barbatus's reputation was ensured by a combination between the increasing interest in bibliography and the quest for knowledge of the Copts manifested particularly by Lutheran scholars, Hebraists and historians, in the German-speaking areas.

Mentioned by the professor of Hebrew at Copenhagen, Thomas Bang, in his *Coelum orientis* of 1657, Barbatus's *Speculum hebraicum* soon found its way into bibliographies. Both historians and bibliographers were intrigued by the summary description of Barbatus's *Grammatica arabica* in the first volume of the *Commentarii* on the imperial library in Vienna, published by the librarian Peter Lambeck in 1665. There remained some confusion about Barbatus's

---

106 See F. Madan, *Oxford Books. A Bibliography of Printed Books Relating to the University and City of Oxford or Printed or Published There*, vol. 3, *Oxford Literature 1651–1680* (Oxford, 1931), p. 309. The 16° pirate edition is rare. Copies exist at the Bodl. and the BnF.
107 Quoted by Madan, *Oxford Books*, p. 309.
108 Edward Gibbon, *The Decline and Fall of the Roman Empire*, ed. D. Womersley (London, 1995), vol. 2, p. 997.
109 J. Abudacnus, *The True History of the Jacobites, Of Aegypt, Lybia, Nubia, etc. and their Origine, Religion, Ceremonies, Lawes, and Customes whereby you may se how they differ from the Jacobites of Great Britain* (London, 1692), was followed by *The History of the Copths, Commonly called Jacobites, Under the Dominion of the Turk and Abyssin Emperor* (London, 1693). For Sadleir see R. Clutterbuck, *The History and Antiquities of the County of Hertford*, vol. 3 (London, 1827), p. 27.

identity. That Barbatus, the professor at Louvain and author of the *Speculum hebraicum* and the manuscript Arabic grammar was the same person as the 'Abudacnus seu Barbatus' who wrote the *Historia Jacobitarum* was suggested by the knowledgeable Tentzel in 1693, but not by many other bibliographers. Referring to Abraham Scultetus's description of his meeting with Barbatus in London in 1612 and to Puteanus's letter to Pedro de Toledo of 1617, Tentzel also concluded that he had taught at Oxford – a fact confirmed in Anthony à Wood's *Fasti oxonienses* of 1691 – and that he had written his work on the Copts during his stay there.[110]

The original edition of the *Historia Jacobitarum* soon became something of a rarity. This provided the German scholars with an excuse to republish it. Were they, one wonders, using the work in order to make a Lutheran contribution to the history of the Copts in deliberate contrast to the studies by Catholics – Wansleben's *Histoire* of 1677 and Eusèbe Renaudot's even more important *Historia Jacobitarum Patriarcharum Alexandrinorum* of 1713? The Lutherans could indeed point to a certain tradition of their own.[111] In 1666, at the University of Jena, Frans Wilhelm von Ramshausen had submitted his *Exercitatio theologica Ecclesiae Copticae* to Johann Ernst Gerhard, the professor of theology to whom the work is sometimes attributed.[112] Here we see the influence of Athanasius Kircher's ideas on the affinity between Coptic and ancient Egyptian together with a Protestant determination to confute the faith of Catholic theologians like Baronius who had claimed that the union between the Churches of Rome and Alexandria was imminent. Besides such minor works as this, there were the monumental publications on the greatest of the Coptic nations, the Abyssinians, produced by Gerhard's friend Hiob Ludolf after 1660. Ludolf presented himself as an objective and eirenic scholar, weary of religious conflict and a friend of simple piety wherever he might find it, as ready to use Catholic sources, if he considered them reliable, as Protestant ones.[113] Yet, for all his claims to impartiality and his loyalty to the Habsburg emperor, when he was living in Erfurt and corresponding with August Hermann Francke in 1703 Ludolf was a keen advocate of an essentially

---

110 Tentzel, *Monatliche Unterredungen*, pp. 203–204.
111 For the Lutherans and Coptic studies see Hamilton, *The Copts and the West*, pp. 139–151.
112 The work is discussed by A. Ben-Tov, *Johann Ernst Gerhard*, pp. 171–174.
113 H. Ludolf, *Historia Aethiopica* (Frankfurt am Main, 1681), sig. a3^r: 'Erunt, credo, qui putabunt, me in causa Religionis plus dicere potuisse; erunt, qui minus: ego certe maluissem, nihil omnino. tam ingratae mihi sunt Christianorum inter se de Religione altercationes; maxime ubi vim et arma intervenire video. Qui enim putant charitatem et dilectionem mutuam suae tantum sectae hominibus deberi, nae illi a scopo perfectionis Christianae, secundum Christi ejusque Apostolorum praecepta, procul aberrant.'

Lutheran missionary activity,[114] and Eusèbe Renaudot accused him of describing the Copts as Lutherans.[115]

Few of the writers on the Church of Alexandria were free of confessional prejudice. The Lutheran editors of the *Historia*, although they too quoted Catholic authors, were strikingly reticent in their use of Wansleben.[116] This can perhaps be explained by Hiob Ludolf's dislike of a man who had once been a Lutheran himself, a pupil and a close friend. Wansleben had seen to the publication of Ludolf's Ethiopic-Latin dictionary in London in 1661. Yet not only had he proved an unsatisfactory editor but he had betrayed the trust of the duke of Saxe-Gotha who had sent him to Ethiopia. He had remained for some time in Egypt and then, rather than pursuing his journey to Ethiopia or returning to Gotha, had gone to Rome where he converted to Catholicism and became a Dominican. Changing masters, he worked for Colbert. In the epistle dedicatory of his *Histoire* he joined in the chorus of Roman Catholic missionaries. 'Le premier dessein que j'ai eu en donnant cette Histoire au public,' he wrote, 'est de contribuer à ce que cette Eglise, qui est une des premières du monde, revienne à l'obeïssance du Saint Siège'.[117] Ludolf and his circle seem never to have forgiven him.

The reaction to Wansleben is especially evident among those Lutherans who made use of the *Historia*. Already in 1685 Johann Balthasar Jacobi, a minister in Leipzig who had studied in Wittenberg, published his *Dissertatio historica de secta Jacobitarum*. Compared with some later Lutheran works on the Copts this is a level-headed study which cites some of the best and most reliable books on the subject, irrespective of the authors' confession. Jacobi quotes the Anglican Edward Brerewood, the Calvinist Hottinger and the Catholic Kircher besides Lutherans such as Ludolf. Above all he quotes the *Historia*. Although he criticises the assertion that the Jacobites owed their name to Jacob the patriarch, Jacobi takes the *Historia* as his main source for the Coptic teaching on the sacraments. Here for the first time we can discern a Lutheran tendency

---

114 Cf. O. Podczek, 'Die Arbeit am Alten Testament in Halle zur Zeit des Pietismus: Das Collegium Orientale theologicum A.H. Franckes' *Wissenschaftliche Zeitschrift der Martin-Luther-Universität Halle-Wittenberg* 7 (1958), pp. 1059–1078, esp. pp. 1062–1066.

115 E. Renaudot, *Historia Patriarcharum Alexandrinorum Jacobitarum* (Paris, 1713), sig. o4^v: 'Nihil non molitur Ludolfus, ut eos Lutheranos esse demonstret.'

116 For the rivalry between Wansleben's work and that of Barbatus see Hamilton, *The Copts and the West*, pp. 170–177. For Wansleben and Ludolf see *idem, Johann Michael Wansleben's Travels in the Levant 1671–1674. An Annotated Edition of His Italian Report* (Leiden-Boston, 2018), pp. 4–7, 17, 40–43.

117 J.M. Wansleben, *Histoire de l'église d'Alexandrie* (Paris, 1677), sig. aiii^v.

to value Barbatus as a primarily Coptic authority, of equal value to far earlier Egyptian chroniclers. Nowhere, however, does Jacobi mention Wansleben.[118]

The first Lutheran scholar to republish the *Historia* in the eighteenth century was the rector of the grammar school in Lübeck, Johann Heinrich von Seelen. A theologian, Hebraist and antiquarian, Seelen had his edition of the *Historia* printed in Lübeck by Jonas Schmidt in 1713. In a long introduction he lists all the bibliographers and historians who had ever mentioned Barbatus and gives a thoroughly documented survey of the current speculations concerning him. Barbatus now emerges as a lecturer at two universities and the author of three books. Both in his introduction and his notes Seelen corrects errors and discusses points in Barbatus's text, basing himself on numerous more recent works. Although he only refers once to Wansleben, and then to his *Voyage fait en Egypte* rather than to his *Histoire de l'église d'Alexandrie*, he makes slightly more use of Renaudot. His main sources are Hiob Ludolf and, above all, Giuseppe Simone Assemani, the Maronite librarian at the Vatican. While lamenting Assemani's anti-Protestant prejudice,[119] he makes ample use of the documentation contained in his *Bibliotheca orientalis*, which started to appear in 1719, and he quotes a sizeable excerpt on Jacob Baradaeus to show that he was the true founder of the Jacobite Church.

Seven years later, in 1740, another edition of the *Historia* appeared. It was published in Leiden, edited by the professor of Greek, rhetoric and history at the university, Sigebert Havercamp, and dedicated to the professor of Arabic Albert Schultens, but the substance of this edition too was the work of a German. The first twelve chapters of Barbatus's text are swamped by the notes compiled by the Lutheran Johannes Nicolai, the professor of classical studies at Tübingen. Nicolai's notes, interrupted by his death in 1708, display an erudition even more impressive than that of Johann Heinrich von Seelen. Not having lived long enough to consult the works of Renaudot or Assemani, Nicolai used Ludolf and a vast assortment of patristic and other sources to exhibit his knowledge of the early Church. Like Seelen he attributes the foundation of the Church of Alexandria to Jacob Baradaeus. He argues at some length against the statement in the *Historia* that the Copts only celebrated prime, terce and none, objecting that the early custom was to celebrate terce, sext and none. Here, however, his discussion suffers from his failure to use Wansleben's *Histoire*, which he only quotes on a single occasion but where the complicated matter of the Coptic offices is examined in detail and the conclusions reached

---

118 J.B. Jacobi, *Dissertatio historica de secta Jacobitarum* (Leipzig, 1685), pp. 7–9, 30–40. Copies of this rare publication are at the library of the Franckesche Stiftungen in Halle.
119 J. Abudacnus, *Historia Iacobitarum seu Coptorum*, ed. L.H. a Seelen (Lübeck, 1733), p. xxv.

are entirely different from his own.[120] Nicolai also introduces a touch of anti-Catholic polemics in his discussion of the sacramental value of confirmation, which he denies.

The *Historia* was no longer republished after 1740 but, as Gibbon and other historians show, the 'slight' work continued to be read. It was even praised more highly than ever before. The twenty-four-year old Karl Heinrich Tromler, a future Lutheran pastor who was to have a lifelong interest in the Oriental Churches, expressed little short of veneration for Barbatus in his *Abbildung der Jacobitischen oder Coptischen Kirche* which appeared in Jena, where he was studying, in 1749. Delighted by the words about the Copt's 'blameless character' in the preface to the Oxford edition of the *Historia*, Tromler claimed that Barbatus was a particularly reliable witness of the Church of Alexandria since he was such a 'good, honest and sincere man' from whom no lies could be expected. Tromler was even ready to excuse his attribution of the name 'Jacobite' to the Hebrew patriarch as a legend which he had piously believed in his youth. Barbatus, a candid observer with direct experience of the Church he was describing, should thus be preferred, Tromler implied, to the Arabic sources cited by Wansleben and to later European writers on the subject – above all to the ever partial Catholics whose misleading prognostications of union with the Copts Tromler deplored.[121]

Barbatus's career and fortunes in Europe illustrate the curiosity, the benevolence, and sometimes the ingenuousness of his hosts as well as the scholarly shortcomings and confessional obstinacy of certain of his later admirers. By Western standards the position he acquired in the history of scholarship was modest. By Coptic standards, on the other hand, his contribution was immense. He remains one of the only Coptic authors between 1500 and 1700, and his list of writings far exceeds that of any of the others.[122] For justice to be done to him he should be judged as a Copt, a member of a community whose intellectual tradition had dwindled sadly over the centuries, and as an individual with the enterprise and courage to make his way in a very different world.

---

120 J. Abudacnus, *Historia Jacobitarum, seu Coptorum, cum annotationibus Joannis Nicolai*, ed. S. Havercamp (Leiden, 1740), pp. 130–2, 184–185. Cf. Wansleben, *Histoire*, pp. 64–8.

121 K.H. Tromler, *Abbildung der Jacobitischen oder Coptischen Kirche* (Jena, 1749), sigs. b3ᵛ–b4ʳ: 'Von so einem Mann, der den Zustand seiner Kirche, in der er erzogen und gebohren ist, kennet, kann man nicht so leichte Unwahrheiten erwarten. Wir mögen auf alle Blätter sehen, so leuchtet überall eine ungemeine Redlichkeit hervor, und wir getrauen uns in seinem ganzen Aufsatz keine Ausnahme zu machen … Was wir also noch etwa vollständiges von den Copten besitzen, das haben wir gröstentheils diesem zu danken'. On Tromler see F.A. Weiz, *Das gelehrte Sachsen* (Leipzig, 1780), pp. 256–257.

122 See the survey in Graf, *Geschichte*, vol. 4, pp. 114–168. Graf's entry for Barbatus, pp. 131–133, also contains the most complete bibliography to date.

Acknowledgements

This article originally appeared in the *Journal of the Warburg and Courtauld Institutes* 57 (1994), pp. 123–150. My greatest debt in writing it was to Gerald Toomer who commented on a first draft and generously allowed me to use the results of his own research. I am also most grateful for the information kindly given me by Alexander de Groot and Robert Jones. I would like to thank Hermann Hauke, Maurice Martin, Francine de Nave, Ernst Petritsch, Nicholas Poole-Wilson, Marcus de Schepper, Rijk Smitskamp, and Jan Just Witkam. My thanks are due, finally, to Johannes den Heijer, Jill Kraye and Joanna Weinberg.

CHAPTER 2

Michel d'Asquier, Imperial Interpreter and Bibliophile

In most European countries in the first half of the seventeenth century speakers of Oriental languages were employed incidentally as interpreters. They generally had other occupations – in the Church or at the universities. In Habsburg Austria the situation was different. On the western borders of the Ottoman Empire, in a more or less permanent state of war with its Turkish neighbour, Austria offered abundant opportunities for interpreters, just as it did for soldiers of fortune. The post of imperial interpreter in Vienna was both influential and demanding. It was attended by political and administrative responsibilities which left no time for an academic or ecclesiastical career. Although the Austrians set up an interpreters' school, the Orientalische Akademie, only in 1754, long after the Venetians and the French had done so,[1] linguists from all over Europe had found employment by the *Hofkriegsrat* or war council in Vienna, the body of officials and generals responsible for Habsburg military dispositions and, above all, for the administration of areas bordering on Ottoman territory and the settlement of frontier disputes.[2] Like the later products of the Orientalische Akademie, the interpreters included highly educated men with refined scholarly tastes.[3] One was Michel d'Asquier, a book collector, an antiquarian, and a citizen of the Republic of Letters, who has hardly received the attention he deserves.

---

1 For the Venetian school, first set up in Istanbul in 1551, see I. Palumbo Fossati Casa, 'L'école vénitienne des "giovani di lingua"' in F. Hitzel, ed., *Istanbul et les langues orientales (actes du colloque, Istanbul 1995)* (Paris, 1997), pp. 109–122. For the French school, finally established in Paris in 1770 (after various abortive attempts from the late 17th century), see A. Ter Minassian, 'Les "Arméniens" du roi de France', *ibid.*, pp. 215–234; and Fück, pp. 126–128.
2 I. Hiller, *Palatin Nikolaus Esterházy: Die ungarische Rolle in der Habsburgerdiplomatie 1625 bis 1645* (Vienna-Cologne, 1992), pp. 31–32; R.J.W. Evans, *The Making of the Habsburg Monarchy 1550–1700* (Oxford, 1985), pp. 149–150. See also O. Regele, *Der österreichische Hofkriegsrat 1556–1848* (Vienna, 1948).
3 For a survey of the early interpreters see E.D. Petritsch, 'Die Wiener Turkologie vom 16. bis zum 18. Jahrhundert' in *Germano-Turcica. Zur Geschichte der Türkisch-Lernens in den deutschsprachigen Ländern*, exhib. cat. (Bamberg, 1987), pp. 25–39, esp. pp. 25–27.

Michel Asquier was born in Marseilles in about 1598.[4] The family, of Piedmontese origin, seems to have had two branches, one which produced jurists and the other which produced merchants.[5] It is tempting to assume that Michel came from the merchant branch. This, certainly, would explain his mastery of languages. That he should later have decided to call himself d'Asquier de Ialion, moreover, reflects a widespread tendency among the merchants in seventeenth-century Provence to lay claim to a frequently imaginary noble descent.[6] D'Asquier must have started to exploit his extraordinary gift for languages at an early stage. How he first learned Turkish remains a mystery, but there are various possibilities. The likeliest is that he had relatives who traded with the Ottoman Empire, and he may well have accompanied them to the Levant himself. He may also have sought instruction from one of the official interpreters in Marseilles,[7] and it is possible, although less probable, that he picked up some Turkish there by consorting with Ottoman merchants, or perhaps even with galley slaves.

When he arrived at the court of the Habsburg emperor Matthias, some time before 1618, Michel d'Asquier was equipped with a good knowledge of Turkish. As a linguist he seems to have been formidable, a star even in the cosmopolitan world of the Habsburgs. To Turkish, Arabic, Latin, French, Italian, Spanish, Hungarian and German, he could probably add Czech (still widely spoken at

---

4   Much of what we know about Michel d'Asquier is contained in an inscription below his tomb in the Stephansdom in Vienna: 'D. O. M. / MICHAEL D. ASQVIER / GENERI NOBILIS NATIONE GALLVS PATRIA MASSILIENSIS // NOTVM NOMEN ORIENTI OCCIDVOQVE ORBI QVORVM LINGVAS TAM PERFECTE / CALLVIT VT CVIVSLIBET PATRIAE CIVEM LOQVENDO REFERRET / VITAE SVAE STVDIVM / MATHIAE FERDINANDIS SECVNDO ET TERTIO NEC NON LEOPOLDO / FIDELISSIME DICAVIT / QVORVM CONSILIARIVS ET LINGVARVM ORIENTALIVM PRIMARIVS INTERPRES EXTITIT / LEGATIONE VOCE CALAMO / PACIS CVM TVRCA PACTAE COLENDAEQVE PERPETVVS ASSERTOR / SEPTVAGENARIVS OCCVBVIT LIBENS / NE PERFIDIAE TVRCARVM SVPERSTES / RVPTAS FOEDERVM TABVLAS FLAGRANTEM BELLO AVSTRIAM / DIVTIVS SPECTARET / AETERNITATI TAMEN VT VIVAT MONVMENTVM HOC AMICI / QVIBVS ET IPSE STVDIOSISSIME VIXIT / MOESTISSIMI POSVERE / DIE XXII IVLII ANNO MDCLXIIII'. Some caution should be exercised with regard to his age, however, since it emerges from his death certificate that he died at the age of 66 (Vienna, Wiener Stadt- und Landesarchiv, Totenbeschauprotokolle, s.v. Dasquier, 28 July 1664, fol. 54ʳ).
5   I owe this information to the kindness of Wolfgang Kaiser.
6   W. Kaiser, 'Une aristocratie urbaine entre la plume et l'épée: les "nobles marchands" de Marseille, XVIᵉ–XVIIᵉ siècles' in C. Grell and A. Ramière de Fortanier, eds, *Le second ordre: l'idéal nobiliaire. Hommage à Ellery Schalk* (Paris, 1999), pp. 264–73.
7   P. Masson, *Les Compagnies du Corail. Étude historique sur le commerce de Marseille du XVI siècle et les origines de la colonisation française en Algérie-Tunisie* (Paris-Marseilles, 1908), pp. 7–8, lists the official interpreters of the governor of Provence up to the appointment of Honoré Suffin in 1600 and emphasizes how low their salaries were.

the imperial court),[8] Persian, and possibly Greek. There can hardly have been much exaggeration in his epitaph which states that he learned languages so well that he could pass for a citizen of any country whatsoever.[9] He was immediately employed as a translator, and in 1625 the war council entrusted him with the newly established post of chief interpreter at the court of Ferdinand II in Vienna.[10] He would also be made an imperial councillor.

With his appointment Michel d'Asquier found himself at the centre of an intricate diplomatic and political network. Responsible for appointing and training younger interpreters, he translated from and into Turkish whenever delegates from the sultan visited the emperor. He was in charge of the secret correspondence between the Habsburg capital and Istanbul, and saw to its coding and decoding. Acting as the main adviser on Ottoman matters, he received, and wrote, reports from the Porte – his surviving letters and dispatches in the Österreichische Nationalbibliothek and the Österreichisches Staatsarchiv remain of fundamental importance for the study of Austro-Ottoman relations.[11] He thus held a pivotal position in the reception and the transmission of information from the Ottoman Empire. His official source was the imperial resident in Istanbul, but he also had at least one other, an unidentified 'amico' who informed him about the resident himself.[12]

D'Asquier, who travelled frequently to Buda and Istanbul, was well acquainted with the northern Ottoman territories. In 1618 he had participated in the peace negotiations at Komárom,[13] and in 1624–25 he served the imperial delegates at the peace negotiations of Szőny-Gyarmat.[14] In December 1627 the Habsburg resident at the Porte, Sebastian Lustrier von Liebenstein, named d'Asquier and two other men as the best people to succeed him.[15] D'Asquier, however, remained in Vienna, and Lustrier was replaced by Johann Rudolf Schmid, one of his other recommendations. In 1642 d'Asquier played an important part in

---

8   Evans, *The Making of the Habsburg Monarchy*, p. xiv.
9   See above, p. 43.
10 D. Kerekes, 'A császári tolmacsok a Magyarországi visszafoglaló háborúk idején' *Századok* 48 (2004), pp. 1189–1228, esp. p. 1199.
11 For his duties see P. Meienberger, *Johann Rudolf Schmid zum Schwarzenhorn als kaiserlicher Resident in Konstantinopel in den Jahren 1629–1643. Ein Beitrag zur Geschichte der diplomatishcen Beziehungen zwischen Oesterreich und der Türken in der ersten Hälfte des 17. Jahrhundert* (Bern-Frankfurt, 1973), p. 81; Kerekes, 'A császári tolmacsok', pp. 1199–1200.
12 Hiller, *Palatin Nikolaus Esterházy*, pp. 73–74.
13 Ibid., pp. 75, 120.
14 Meinberger, *Johann Rudolf Schmid*, p. 81.
15 Brno, Moravský Zemský Archiv, Collalto family archive (G 169), MS I-1774, fol. 43ᵛ. I owe this reference to Noel Malcolm.

the second peace negotiations of Szőny-Gyarmat.[16] An active and enterprising employee of the inert and conservative war council, he occupied a post of increasing importance in the emperor's dealings with his most dangerous neighbour, the sultan whose territory extended to within a hundred miles of Vienna and who, aware of his military superiority, still treated the Habsburg ruler, or the 'king of Vienna' as he was mockingly known at the Porte, with contempt.[17]

D'Asquier seems to have been trusted by the Turks, and he could indeed be a loyal friend. He proved so in his relationship with Schmid, and with Schmid's Coptic interpreter in Istanbul, Josephus Barbatus or Abudacnus.[18] But he could also be a redoubtable enemy. Together with Schmid he was accused of planning the murder of a rival dragoman, the Ragusan Vincenzo Brattuti, who had in fact been spying on d'Asquier.[19] D'Asquier was hated, moreover, by the powerful Hungarian palatine Miklós Esterházy, who deplored both his atheism, due, Esterházy implied, to the fact that he was French, and his outspoken criticisms of the emperor.[20] Yet, although Esterházy managed to have Schmid ousted from Istanbul, he never seems to have got the better of d'Asquier.

Despite his enemies d'Asquier survived for an astonishingly long time, a beneficiary of the immobility of the war council. He served four emperors, Matthias, Ferdinand II, Ferdinand III and Leopold I. Under Leopold, however, he fell into disgrace. Possibly held responsible for the revival of Turkish aggression against the Habsburgs in 1663, he was accused of various misdemeanours including negligence. He was consequently dismissed and legal proceedings were opened against him.[21] By then in his mid-sixties, d'Asquier was not only in bad health but he had also proved replaceable. Leopold I had summoned to Vienna a man from Lorraine, François de Mesgnien, generally known in the Polish form of Meninski, who had been serving as interpreter

---

16 B. Majláth, *Az 1642-ik évi szőnyi békektötés története* (Budapest, 1885), pp. 87–92, 106–110.
17 Meienberger, *Johann Rudolf Schmid*, p. 16.
18 See above, pp. 3–40.
19 The evidence is by no means conclusive, although d'Asquier attended the lunch at Schmid's residence in Istanbul on 7 February 1633 when Brattuti was supposed to have been given a glass of poisoned wine. See Z. Šundrica, 'Poisons and poisoning in the Republic of Dubrovnik' *Dubrovnik Annals* 4 (2000), pp. 7–79, esp. pp. 44–48.
20 See I. Hiller, 'A tolmácsper: a bécsi Haditanács működése és a Habsburgok tolmácsai a 17. század első felében' *Történelmi Szemle* 33 (1991), pp. 203–14, esp. 212. Esterházy declared: 'personam vero domini D'Ascquirii sibi omnino suspectam esse, utpote qui et Gallus esset natione et ita atheus, insuper male contentum [cum Sua Majestate]. Ex cuius ore ipse dominus palatinus haec verba audivisset: "In mundo non esse maiorem ingratitudinem, quam domus Austriacae, ego vix non fame pereo."'
21 Meienberger, *Johann Rudolf Schmid*, p. 81.

to the Polish ambassador in Istanbul. In January 1662 the emperor appointed him to share d'Asquier's duties. Meninski was probably an even better linguist than d'Asquier. With his great Turkish-Arabic-Persian-Latin dictionary and grammar, the *Thesaurus linguarum orientalium* which appeared in 1680, he certainly made a more enduring contribution to Oriental studies. As soon as d'Asquier fell Meninski replaced him for good.[22] Notwithstanding the legal proceedings against him, d'Asquier died of dropsy in his bed in Vienna, at the sign of the White Rose in the Riemerstrasse, on 28 July 1664. He was allowed the privilege of burial in the Stephansdom.

Although most of his time was taken up with administrative duties d'Asquier also indulged in more scholarly pursuits. One of his closest friends was Sebastian Tengnagel, the imperial librarian of Dutch origin, who occupied a prominent position in the Republic of Letters.[23] With a strong interest in antiquarianism, d'Asquier wrote in July 1655 to the man regarded as the greatest antiquarian in the Roman Catholic world, the Jesuit Athanasius Kircher in Rome.[24] He declared himself at Kircher's service and enclosed a note from another acquaintance of his, Panaiotis Nicousios.[25] Nicousios, who had been

---

22   Petritsch, 'Die Wiener Turkologie', pp. 26–30. See also R.F. Kreutel and E. Prokosch, *Im Reiche des Goldenen Apfels: Des türkischen Weltenbummlers Evliyâ Çelebi denkwürdige Reise in das Giaurenland und in die Stadt und Festung Wien anno 1665* (Graz-Vienna-Cologne, 1987), p. 276.

23   On Tengnagel see F. Unterkircher, 'Sebastian Tengnagel (1608–1636)' in J. Stummvoll, ed., *Geschichte der Österreichischen Nationalbibliothek. Erster Teil. Die Hofbibliothek (1368–1922)* (Vienna, 1968), pp. 129–45.

24   On Kircher see Paula Findlen, 'The last man who knew everything ... or did he: Athanasius Kircher, S.J. (1602–1680) and his world' in P. Findlen, ed., *Athanasius Kircher: The Last Man who Knew Everything* (London, 2004), pp. 1–48. The many aspects of Kircher are studied in the other articles in this collection.

25   Rome, Archivio Pontificia Università Gregoriana, MS 555, fol. 207: 'Molto Reverendo Padre mio signore Osservatissimo, Se io non fussi trattenuto in Vienna dal servitio dell'Imperatore mio signore clementissimo verrei più volentieri a Roma per visitare Vostra Paternità Molto Reverenda che non vi vennero già quegli habitanti delle Gadi per vedere Tito Livio, Ornamento del suo tempo di cotesta eterna Città, come è Vostra Paternità nel nostro secolo. Ma impedito da causa tanto legitima, si compiacerà gradire ch'io la riverischi con queste righe, e me le dedichi servitore di molta osservanza. Per insinuarmi maggiormente, mi vaglio dell'annesso Pieghetto raccomandatomi dal signore Panaioti Nicussio Interprete Cesario in Costantinopoli, molto servitore (come intendo) di Vostra Reverenza La quale compiacendosi farli risposta, restarà servita mandarmela col latore di questa (molto mio Amico) o con altra occasione più pronta, che gli è la farò capitare sicura. E se Vostra Reverenza mi conosce habile in altro in queste parti, mi commandi che restarà servita con ogni prontezza. Mentre baciandole con ogni affetto la mano, le prego dal Signore quella maggiore contentezza che brama, e resto Di Vostra Paternità molto Reverendissima Devotissimo servitore, Michele d'Asquier. Vienna 19 luglio 1655.'

educated by the Jesuits in his birthplace, Chios, and who studied at the patriarchal academy at Istanbul before becoming a student of medicine at the university of Padua, had a high reputation as a man of letters in the Ottoman world. He had assembled a library the fame of which had reached Louis XIV's minister Colbert in Paris. On his return to Istanbul from Italy he taught at the patriarchal academy himself. He served as interpreter to the imperial and other foreign embassies and was appointed chief physician to the grand vizir, Fazıl Ahmet Pasha Köprülü, and subsequently imperial interpreter. From 1669 until his death in 1673, he acted as grand dragoman, an office which was especially created for him and which would then become the prerogative of the Phanariots, the members of the prosperous Greek community living in the Phanar quarter in Istanbul.[26] As eager as d'Asquier to be numbered among Kircher's correspondents, Panaiotis had written to him in June 1654 with expressions of admiration for his learning and enclosing a copy of the hieroglyphs on the column of Theodosius and an Arabic treatise on divination.[27]

Like Tengnagel, who vastly increased the Oriental holdings of the imperial collection as well as assembling a sizeable private library, d'Asquier was a bibliophile. When he was in the Ottoman Empire he assisted Tengnagel in his quest for manuscripts,[28] and he is now known to have had a fine collection of books of his own, mainly, but by no means exclusively, on history, travel, antiquities, art and architecture. Some of his books were of considerable rarity – Antoine Le Pois's *Discours sur les medalles* [sic] *et graveures antiques* (Paris, 1579), Szymon Okolski's *Orbis Polonus* (Cracow, 1641–45), Michele Mercati's *Degli obelischi di Roma* (Rome, 1589), Paul Boyer's *Dictionaire, servant de bibliothèque universelle* (Paris, 1649), and the fine first edition of the works of Arnald of Villanova (Lyons, 1504). Others were of singular splendour, such as the Italian translation of Ovid's *Metamorphoses* (Venice, 1584) and the works in three elaborate bindings 'à la fanfare' – the French translation of Zonaras's chronicles (Lyons, 1560); the *Chronique de Flandres* (Lyons, 1562) bound with *Les mémoires d'Olivier de la Marche* (Lyons, 1562); and a French translation of

---

26 D. Janos, 'Panaiotis Nicousios and Alexander Mavrocordatos: The rise of the Phanariots and the office of Grand Dragoman in the Ottoman administration in the second half of the seventeenth century' *Archivum Ottomanicum* 23 (2005/6), pp. 177–196. See also Antoine Galland, *Voyage à Constantinople (1672–1673)*, ed. C.H.A. Schefer (Paris, 2002), part 1, p. 18 and, for Colbert's interest in his library, p. 274. On the Phanariots see S. Runciman, *The Great Church in Captivity: A Study of the Patriarchate of Constantinople from the Eve of the Turkish Conquest to the Greek War of Independence* (Cambridge, 1968), pp. 360–384 (and on Panaiotis Nicousios in particular pp. 363–364); G. Koutzakiotis, *Attendre la fin du monde au XVIIe siècle. Le messie juif et le grand drogman* (Paris, 2014), pp. 125–174.
27 Rome, Archivio Pontificia Università Gregoriana, S 568, fol. 257^{r-v}.
28 See, for example, ÖNB, MSS 9737.s, fol. 313^{r-v}; 9737.t, fol. 1^r.

Antonio de Guevara's *Reloj de principes*, entitled *Histoire de Marc Aurèle*, bound with Appian of Alexandria's *Des guerres des Romains* (Paris, 1569). They are now among the finest items in the Arcadian Library in London.[29] After Tengnagel's death, moreover, d'Asquier acquired some of his books – the attractive copy of Joinville's *Histoire et chronique du ... roy Saint Louis* (Paris, 1595) now also in the Arcadian Library, Martin Du Bellay's *Mémoires* (Paris, 1572), and Giovanni Villani's *Historie universali* (Venice, 1559).[30] Sold first to the Schönborn family in Vienna in the late eighteenth century,[31] d'Asquier's books were auctioned, together with the rest of the Schönborn-Buchheim library, in Germany in 1993 and 1994.

The figure of d'Asquier pales beside that of his successor Meninski and some of the later students of the Orientalische Akademie. Yet d'Asquier helped to form the tradition of learning which made the academy in Vienna so unique. In contrast to the other interpreters' schools in Europe which limited themselves to supplying able translators, the students of the Orientalische Akademie obtained the best education Austria had to offer. Besides mastering social accomplishments such as drawing, dancing, fencing and riding, they studied philosophy, logic, mathematics, physics, law, French, Italian, Latin, Greek, history and geography in addition to Eastern languages (Turkish, Persian and Arabic). They could aspire to patents of nobility and to be ambassadors and statesmen,[32] and the careers of Bernhard von Jenisch, the prefect of the imperial library, Franz Maria de Paula von Thugut (who became minister of foreign

---

29   They are illustrated and discussed by A. Hobson, 'Three bindings *à la fanfare* and the origins of the fanfare style' in G. Mandelbrote and W. de Bruijn, *The Arcadian Library: Bindings and Provenance* (London-Oxford, 2014), pp. 177–190, plates 1–3. See also A. Hamilton, 'Princes, ministers and scholars: some foreign provenances in the Arcadian Library', *ibid.*, pp. 81–144, esp. pp. 108–110.

30   An idea of D'Asquier's library can be obtained from *Bibliothek der Grafen von Schönborn-Buchheim, Teil 1, Atlanten. Reisen. Geographie* [Reiss & Auvermann Auction Catalogue no. 50] (Königstein-im-Taunus, 1993), nos 215, 342, 625, 723; Teil 3, *Alte Drücke. Geschichte. Naturwissenschaften. Varia.* [Reiss & Auvermann Auction Catalogue no. 53] (Königstein-im-Taunus, 1994), nos 7, 39, 61, 64, 80, 92, 109, 135, 141, 151, 155, 177–79, 235, 325, 361, 484, 491, 502, 600, 621, 636, 655–56, 713, 747, 764, 818, 992, 1002, 1070, 1072.

31   Vienna, Wiener Stadt- und Landesarchiv, Totenbeschauprotokolle, s.v. Dasquierin, Theresia, 5 January 1781.

32   Fück, p. 129: 'Ein wesentlicher Unterschied war jedoch der, daß den Zöglingen der Orientalischen Akademie alle Stellen des konsularischen und diplomatischen Dienstes offenstanden.' See also Petritsch, 'Die Wiener Turkologie', pp. 30–31; *idem*, 'Erziehung in *gutten Sitten, Andacht und Gehorsam*: Die 1754 gegründete Orientalische Akademie in Wien' in M. Kurz *et al.*, eds, *Das Osmanische Reich und die Habsburgermonarchie. Akten des internationalen Kongresses zum 150-jährigen Bestehen des Instituts für Österreichische Geschichtsforschung. Wien, 22.–25. September 2004* (Vienna, 2005), pp. 491–501.

affairs), Josef von Preindl, imperial chargé d'affaires in Sweden and Denmark, the imperial councillor Thomas von Chabert, Franz von Dombay, the author of the first grammar of the Moroccan dialect, Josef von Hammer-Purgstall, the finest Turcologist of the nineteenth century, and many others testify to the high standards of the academy.

Acknowledgements

This article was originally published in the *Journal of the Warburg and Courtauld Institutes* 72 (2009), pp. 237–241. I am particularly grateful for the advice of Noel Malcolm, and I would also like to thank J.N. Adams, Wolfgang Kaiser, Jill Kraye, Ernst Petritsch, Cornelia Plieger and Ivan Zmertych.

CHAPTER 3

Isaac Casaubon the Arabist

'Video Longum Esse Iter'

The Huguenot scholar Isaac Casaubon (1559–1614; Fig. 1) owed his reputation to many achievements – his unparalleled knowledge of Greek, his editions of classical texts with their erudite philological annotations, his attack on Baronius which included an accurate dating of the writings attributed to Hermes Trismegistus and entailed the destruction of the myth of their antiquity.[1] Arabic plays a small part in his publications, but its presence is all the more striking. The large, and somewhat ungainly, Arabic types of Guillaume Le Bé in Paris which, on small pages such as those in Casaubon's edition of Gregory of Nyssa's third epistle, occupy anything up to three lines, give the Arabic words a far greater prominence than the passages in Hebrew and Greek. The relevance of these words to Casaubon's profound textual analyses is sometimes slightly mystifying and leaves the impression of a man revelling in his own discovery of a language which was still little known in Europe. Yet Casaubon also displayed a remarkable insight into the culture of the Arabs; the language occupies an important place in his correspondence and his unpublished notebooks; and it was to the promotion of Arabic studies in the West that he made a significant contribution.

Casaubon was a close witness of the greatest revolution ever to have affected the study of Arabic in Europe. When he started to learn the language there existed no truly satisfactory Arabic grammar or dictionary in print. By the time of his death in 1614 a grammar had been published which would remain unsurpassed for over two hundred years and a dictionary had been printed with an appendix which would influence Arabic lexicography in Europe for just as long. Both the grammar and the appendix were the work of one of his closest friends, the young Dutchman Thomas Erpenius, and, in his letters to Causaubon, for whose help and encouragement he was to remain deeply grateful, Erpenius recorded every stage of his progress. Casaubon can hardly be said to have taken a direct part in this revolution, but the mere fact that Erpenius

---

1 A. Grafton, *Defenders of the Text: The Traditions of Scholarship in an Age of Science, 1450–1800* (Cambridge, MA, 1991), pp. 145–161.

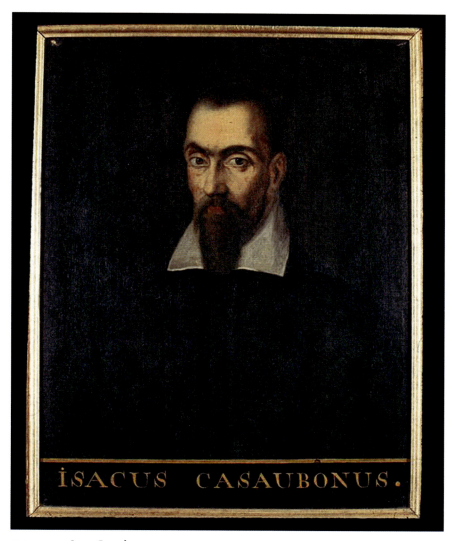

FIGURE 1   Isaac Casaubon
ICONES LEIDENSES 44, COLLECTION LEIDEN UNIVERSITY

should have owed him so much and informed him of his advance in such detail shows that he had an unusual understanding of the problems involved, while his immense reputation as a scholar made him a focal point among European Arabists who consulted him and sent him their works. So what do we know about Casaubon's own efforts to learn Arabic and his accomplishments as an Arabist in his own right?

1 The Apprentice

In a letter to Philippe de La Canaye de Fresnes of August 1592 Casaubon, who was still living in Geneva, said he was preparing to study Arabic, the language used by so many great philosophers, by reading Hebrew.[2] Because of his voracious appetite for information, however, his reasons most probably corresponded to those listed by Guillaume Postel some time earlier, or, as Roger Bacon had put it earlier still, 'for the absolute acquisition of knowledge' ('propter studium sapientiae absolutum').[3] To the benefits of Arabic given by Bacon and other apologists, its use for philosophers, physicians, astronomers, geographers, theologians, missionaries and historians, Postel had added another one. Arabic, he maintained, was spoken throughout Asia and Africa, from the Fortunate Isles to the Moluccas, from the Atlantic to the eastern shores of the Indian Ocean.[4] It was consequently invaluable for travellers, and Casaubon, whose study of antiquity embraced the eastern Mediterranean, suggested in his letter to De Fresnes that he too would like to travel in the Middle East where he would practise his rabbinic Hebrew and devote himself seriously to learning Arabic.

In 1596 Casaubon moved to Montpellier and, when he left Montpellier for Paris three years later, he owned at least some of the books he used subsequently for his Arabic studies. These included an *Alphabetum arabicum* and an unspecified Arabic grammar.[5] But it was only after he had settled in Paris in 1600 that Casaubon, aged just over forty, really began to get to grips with the language. Delighted by the quantity and variety of Arabic material he discovered in the French capital[6] – he immediately had the run of the rich collection of his

---

2   *Cas.Ep.*, p. 569: 'Veruntamen, quod uni tibi dictum sit, fatebor, quod res est; non eo animo tantum studii ponerem in linguis his, ut Hebraeos Rabbinos intelligam; non est, inquam, id ἀρχιτεκτονικὸν meum τέλος. Sed ut harum ope Arabicam intelligere queam; qua usi sunt plerique summi Philosophi, quorum scripta in omni sapientiae parte praestantissima, linguae illius imperitia hodie vel ignorantur, vel nulla, certe parva cum utilitate leguntur. Igitur, quod Deus Opt. Max. bene vertat, constitui tantisper in Rabbinicis scriptis me exercere, donec facultas detur isthuc eundi. Isthuc enim ire mihi necesse est, si studium meum Arabicae linguae serio applicare velim.' For Casaubon's early study of Hebrew see Grafton and Weinberg, *"I have always loved the Holy Tongue"*, pp. 60–102.
3   Roger Bacon, *Opus majus*, ed. J.H. Bridges (Oxford, 1897), vol. 1, p. 92. On Casaubon's inexhaustible quest for knowledge see M. Pattison, *Isaac Casaubon 1559–1614* (Oxford, 1892), p. 54: 'Casaubon is always ill at ease, unless he is acquiring, and acquisition does but give him a glimpse of the untravelled world beyond.'
4   Guillaume Postel, *Linguarum duodecim characteribus differentium alphabetum introductio* (Paris, 1538), sigs D1r–2v; idem, *Grammatica arabica* (Paris c. 1538), sigs D1v, D2r–3r.
5   Bodl., MS Casaubon 22, fols 43v, 46r.
6   For Casaubon's impressions of Paris see Pattison, *Isaac Casaubon*, pp. 115–21.

intellectual patron Jacques-Auguste de Thou besides limited access to the royal library (of which he would become custodian in 1605) – Casaubon proudly reported his swift progress in Arabic to Jacques Lect in December 1600.[7] And in Paris, in addition to the books and the manuscripts, he found other scholars, some of them lecturers in oriental languages at the Collège Royal and most of them members of the medical profession, who would encourage and help him. One was Étienne Hubert, who had served for a year as physician to the ruler of Morocco, Aḥmad al-Manṣūr, and had subsequently been appointed physician to the French king and nominated professor of Arabic in 1600.[8] It seems to have been Hubert who gave Casaubon his first lessons.[9] Another French Arabist was Hubert's predecessor at the Collège Royal, Arnoult de L'Isle, once the physician of Henri III and later of Aḥmad al-Manṣūr. Returning to Paris in 1599, de l'Isle left again for Morocco, this time as French ambassador, in 1606.[10] And a third was Jean Martin, yet another doctor who probably lectured in Arabic at the

---

[7] *Cas.Ep.*, p. 113: 'Quid dicam de optimis et rarissimis libris, quibus hic fruimur? Censen' potuisse me alibi trimestri spatio tantos in Arabica Lingua facere progressus, ut jam ingentem sylvam observationum eo spectantium habeamus?' On Casaubon's relations with De Thou see Pattison, *Isaac Casaubon*, pp. 114–120.

[8] His competence as an Arabist was called in doubt by François Savary de Brèves: 'Il y a un médecin du roi nommé Monsieur Hubert, qui a été à Fez et Maroc qui sait quelque chose de cette langue mais bien peu', Savary de Brèves wrote to Jacques-Auguste de Thou in 1613. 'Il m'a écrit être maintenant légiste en cette langue. A dire le vrai c'est abuser le public, mais n'en faites pas semblant.' Quoted in G. Duverdier, 'Les impressions orientales en Europe et le Liban' in C. Aboussouan, ed., *Le livre et le Liban jusqu'à 1900* (Paris, 1982), pp. 157–280, esp. p. 165. Contemporary Arabists, as we shall see, were notoriously damning about one another. It is not clear on what Savary de Brèves based his opinion since Hubert never wrote anything concerning Arabic. Brèves's judgement, however, is to some degree confirmed by another episode. In 1611 Hubert asked the Moroccan envoy in France, the Andalusian Aḥmad ibn Qāsim al-Ḥajarī who would assist Erpenius in his studies, to help him read the manuscripts he collected when he was in Marrakesh, hoping 'that you will explain some of their contents to me'. For their relations see Aḥmad ibn Qāsim al-Ḥajarī, *Kitāb naṣir al-dīn 'ala'l-qawm al-kafirīn (The Supporter of Religion against the Infidels)*, ed. and tr. P.S. van Koningsveld, Q. Al-Samarrai and G.A. Wiegers (Madrid, 1987), pp. 31–32, 109.

[9] *Scal.Cor.*, vol. 4, pp. 130–133, esp. pp. 131–132: 'Nacti enim ducem ad studia Arabica', Casaubon wrote to Scaliger on 8 December 1601, 'incredibili quadam cum voluptate paucos menses illis literis impendimus. Dux ille fuit Hubertus, medicus, qui Arabicam linguam jussus a Rege in hac schola profiteri, cum a quaestoribus nummum adhuc nullum potuerit extorquere, et Scholae et urbi coactus est valedicere. Vir est optimus, et qui in Africa linguae principia edoctus, alterum jam annum non infeliciter in eo studio est versatus. Ingratus sim, nisi me plurimum illi debere agnoscam.'

[10] On Hubert and Arnoult de l'Isle see J. Balagna Coustou, *Arabe et humanistes dans la France des derniers Valois* (Paris, 1989), pp. 114–117. For the Arabists in Paris see Toomer, pp. 26–35.

Collège Royal.[11] Then, outside the academic world, there was Étienne Fleury, the distinguished councillor who was also interested in Arabic.[12] Casaubon's scholarly reputation was high enough to draw these men to him, and the protection of De Thou was a valuable asset.

Casaubon's main source of inspiration, however, was Joseph Justus Scaliger (Fig. 2), who had left Paris for Leiden in 1593 and with whom Casaubon first corresponded in 1594. Scaliger never returned to France. His correspondence with Casaubon intensified over the years and continued until his death in 1609. Scaliger, who was taught Arabic by Guillaume Postel in 1562,[13] owed his fame as an orientalist above all to his work on chronology, *De emendatione temporum*, first published in 1583. By the time he was corresponding with Casaubon, he was engaged in the compilation of an Arabic dictionary, the 'Thesaurus linguae arabicae', which he completed in April 1597.[14] An accomplished Arabist – he produced a remarkably good Arabic translation of a letter of safe-conduct from Maurice of Nassau[15] – he imparted to Casaubon his perceptive ideas about how the language should be studied.[16]

Late in September 1601 Casaubon was taking Arabic lessons,[17] and on 8 December he told Scaliger that he was drawing up a word list.[18] From then on, for some five years, Arabic became one of the subjects he and Scaliger discussed most frequently. From then on, too, Casaubon began to scour his books

11   A. Lefranc, *Histoire du Collège de France depuis ses origines jusqu'à la fin du Premier Empire* (Paris, 1893), p. 383.
12   Isaac Casaubon, *Ephemerides*, ed. J. Russell (Oxford, 1850) (hereafter *Ephemerides*), vol. 1, p. 374: 'Studia parum promovimus: sed virum magnum Florum, Curiae Parisiensis amplissimum Senatorem, cognitione literarum Arabicarum insignem, adiimus, et cum eo multas horas fuimus.'
13   C.M. Bruehl, 'Josef Justus Scaliger. Ein Beitrag zur geistesgeschichtlichen Bedeutung der Altertumswissenschaft' *Zeitschrift für Religions- und Geistesgeschichte* 12 (1960), pp. 201–18, esp. 209–14; A. Grafton, *Joseph Scaliger: A Study in the History of Classical Scholarship*, vol. 1, *Textual Criticsm and Exegesis* (Oxford, 1983), p. 104.
14   UBL, MS Or. 212. A. Vrolijk and K. van Ommen, eds, *'All my Books in Foreign Tongues': Scaliger's Oriental Legacy in Leiden 1609–2009* (Leiden, 2009), pp. 61–63, no. 24.
15   Discussed by A. Vrolijk, 'Scaliger and the Dutch expansion in Asia: An Arabic translation for an early voyage to the East Indies (1600)' *Journal of the Warburg and Courtauld Institutes* 78 (2015), pp. 277–309, esp. pp. 277–286, 295–309.
16   The safe-conduct is in UBL, MS Or. 1365 (3). For an appreciation of Scaliger as an Orientalist see Fück, pp. 47–53.
17   *Ephemerides*, 1, pp. 372–374. On 25 September he noted: 'Magnum vero ἑρμαῖον hoc die contigit nobis, ex communicatione cum professore Arabicae linguae.' Four days later we read: 'Mane in Arabicis studiis fuimus: a prandio per amicos librum inspicere non licuit. Etiam lucubratio tota in Arabicis studiis.' Cf. also p. 376.
18   *Scal.Cor.*, vol. 4, p. 132: 'Ausi sumus συναγωγὴν vocum Arabicarum in usum nostrum tentare: jamque crescebat moles, cum incepto desistere sumus coacti ...'

FIGURE 2   Joseph Justus Scaliger
JACOB MARCI AND JUSTUM A COLSTER, *ILLUSTRIUM HOLLANDIAE WESTFRISIAE ORDINUM ALMA ACADEMIA LEIDENSIS* (LEIDEN, 1614), DEDICATION

for Arabic words,[19] and Marcus Welser, the classical scholar from Augsburg, expressed the fear that his commitment to Arabic might distract him from his other studies.[20] But, Casaubon informed Scaliger on 27 March 1602, he, like Scaliger himself, had no illusions about the difficulties involved in acquiring even a limited knowledge of the language. It would be 'a long journey'.[21]

What characterises Casaubon's study of the Arabic language is his dependency on his teachers. First it was Etienne Hubert, and when Hubert absented himself from Paris, Casaubon, who was trying to complete his edition of the *Historiae Augustae scriptores*, temporarily abandoned Arabic.[22] He did not do so for long. In March 1602 Adriaen Willemsz arrived in France with a letter from Scaliger.[23] Born in Flushing, Adriaen had matriculated at the Faculty of Arts at Leiden University in April 1595 at the age of eighteen,[24] and had subsequently turned to medicine. He may well have benefited from the appointment to the chair of Arabic in August 1599 of the converted Polish Jew Philippus Ferdinandus, who was greatly admired by Scaliger but died some four months after his nomination.[25] He certainly had lessons from Peter Kirsten

---

19 See, for example, his notes on the flyleaf of his copy of Johannes Stoeffler's *Elucidatio fabricae ususque astrolabii* (Paris, 1585), BL, shelf-mark 531.f.14.

20 *Cas.Ep.*, p. 146. 'Desine, Vir praestantissime,' Casaubon wrote to Welser in April 1602, 'Musas Arabicas incusare, quasi illae a prioribus studiis nos avocent.' On Marcus Welser see *Allgemeine Deutsche Biographie*, vol. 41 (Leipzig, 1896), pp. 687–90.

21 *Scal.Cor.*, vol. 4, p. 237: 'Video longum esse iter, non dicam, ad cognitionem ejus linguae perfectam, sed vel mediocrem notitiam. Nam quod venuste sic, ut nihil possit magis, scriptum a te, in aditu blandiri hanc linguam; cum vero intus admissus fuerit aliquis, commendatitiis esse opus; id, inquam, experti reapse nos sumus. Initio cum huic curae primum adjecimus animum, comparationem quandam institueramus Hebraicae Arabicaeque linguae: quo incepto, fatebor enim ingenue, visi sumus nobis per dies aliquammultos belli homines, qui eramus saperdae meri. Fruantur illi sane opinione sua, qui ex aliquot pagellarum intuitu, non enim lectione, satis scio, repente prodierunt Arabes.' Cf. Scaliger's letter of 22 January 1602, p. 180: 'Ego, mi Casaubone, multa volumina Arabica versavi: magnam silvam verborum mihi ea illa lectione comparavi. Nihil tamen aut parum me praestitisse sentio. Adhuc tyro sum. Et tamen videas, qui ex lectione unius libri nihil sibi putant reliquum esse ad absolutam illius sermonis cognitionem.'

22 *Ibid.*, p. 237: 'Conatus nostros in Arabicis literis non tam rei difficultas, quam Huberti mei discessio, et instituta editio Spartiani ac reliquorum hactenus interruperunt, ne dicam, abruperunt.'

23 *Ibid.*, pp. 231–233; Pattison, *Isaac Casaubon*, pp. 237–238.

24 G. Du Rieu, *Album Studiosorum Academiae Lugduno Batavae MDLXXV–MDCCCLXX* (The Hague, 1875), col. 42. For what little was previously known about Adriaen Willemsz see F. Natglas, *Levensberichten van Zeeuwen*, (Middelburg, 1890), vol. 1, pp. 310–11, but see now A. Hamilton and A. Vrolijk, 'Hadrianus Guilielmi Flessingensis. The Brief Career of the Arabist Adriaen Willemsz' *Oriens* 39 (2011), pp. 1–15.

25 A. Hamilton, 'Ferdinand, Philip (1556–1599)' *ODNB*.

from Breslau, a physician who had been touring Europe in an endeavour to learn enough Arabic to read the medical works of Avicenna.[26] In the course of his travels Kirsten met an Arabic-speaking Christian who gave him some tuition, and his tour included a visit to the Low Countries and a meeting with Scaliger, who assured him that 'the true doctor of medicine' could better dispense with Latin than with Greek or Arabic: 'verus medicus, potius lingua latina carere posset, quam vel Arabica, vel Graeca'.[27] Erpenius thought Kirsten worthless as an Arabist,[28] but in a letter to Casaubon Kirsten would claim some credit for the extraordinary progress made by Adriaen Willemsz and propose that he should edit Adriaen's posthumous papers himself.[29] Adriaen, therefore, arrived in France with what would seem to have been a solid grounding in the language. Not only did Casaubon become devoted to Adriaen – he and his wife would consider him an adopted son – but Casaubon used him as his Arabic teacher and relied on him for reading the Arabic texts in his possession.[30] Adriaen, for his part, availed himself of the manuscripts owned by Casaubon and his friends. We still have his marginal notes to al-Ḥasanī's *al-Durra 'l-naḥwiyya*, a grammatical text in a manuscript belonging to Etienne Hubert,[31] and Casaubon kept the autograph list of words Adriaen drew up when he was reading the codex of the Arabic Dioscorides in the royal library in October 1603.[32]

In March 1603 Casaubon noted in his journal that he was beginning to study Matthew's Gospel in Arabic 'with the utmost delight' ('cum summa

---

26 For Kirsten as an Arabist see Fück, pp. 57–59.

27 Peter Kirsten, *Grammatices arabicae, Liber I* (Breslau, 1608), pp. 5, 7.

28 See below, pp. 81, 379–380.

29 BL, MS Burney 364, fol. 332^{r-v}: 'Anno enim CIƆIƆCII praeterito, cum ad te adducerem Juvenem doctissimum, linguarumque studiosissimum Adrianum Wilhelmi Flüssingem, de quo summam spem conceperam, eum fore qui literas Arabicas, Europae nostrae communicaturus esset, ideoque et ego tunc multo remissius id studii tractabam. Eo enim eum jam perduxeram, ut, quod dicitur, sine cortice fere natare posset ...'

30 Another example of Casaubon's enthusiasm for a younger scholar who could assist him in his quest for knowledge is his relationship with Jacob Barnet at Oxford in 1613. See Pattison, *Isaac Casaubon*, pp. 368–370.

31 BnF, MS Arabe 4127, p. 26. The manuscript was discovered by Jones, pp. 147–148, 149–150 (where the marginalia are illustrated).

32 Bodl., MS Casaubon 27, fols 148^r–151^v. Cf. *Cas.Ep.*, p. 194. The Dioscorides manuscripts in the BnF are discussed by L. Leclerc, 'De la traduction arabe de Dioscorides et des traductions arabes en général: Études philologiques pour faire suite à celles sur Ebn Beithâr' *Journal Asiatique*, sér. 6, 9 (1867), pp. 5–38, esp. pp. 6–8; and C.E. Dubler and E. Terés, *La 'Materia médica' de Dioscórides: transmisión medieval y renacentista* (Barcelona, 1953–59), vol. 2, pp. IX–XII. Cf. also B. de Slane, *Catalogue des manuscrits arabes [à la Bibliothèque nationale]* (Paris, 1883–95), pp. 513–514, nos 2849–2850.

voluptate' – the same phrase he used when he was reading the Hebrew version), and he accordingly compiled a wordlist.[33] Sometime earlier, late in 1601, he had acquired the edition of the Arabic Gospels published in 1591 by the Typographia Medicea, the Oriental printing press in Rome founded in 1584 with the encouragement of Cardinal Ferdinando de' Medici, the future grand duke of Tuscany.[34] Casaubon's copy – but not all copies – had an interlinear Latin translation. Originally Casaubon had written on the flyleaf, triumphantly in red ink, that he had started to consult the work on the Ides of November 1601, but he subsequently added another two digits in black ink, and, below, stated that he had taken it up again later.[35] The splendour of the Roman edition, with its woodcuts by Antonio Tempesta, made it an attractive text on which to practise, but it was also an obvious one since all the publications on Arabic grammar and the Arabic alphabet available to Casaubon provided Arabic versions of scriptural passages as exercises.[36] Scaliger, with characteristic perceptiveness, warned Casaubon against this particular manner of studying the language. He had always had misgivings about learning Arabic from the New Testament.[37] 'You can no more master Arabic without the Qur'an than Hebrew without the Bible', he told Casaubon in April 1603,[38] and,

---

33   Bodl., MS Casaubon 23, fol. 128ʳ. For Casaubon's comment see *Ephemerides*, vol. 1, p. 473 (13 March): 'In instituto pergebamus, et partem bonam εὐαγγελίου κατὰ Matthaeum ex interpretatione Arabica legimus cum summa voluptate ...'; and the next day, 'In Novi Testamenti Arabici lectione diem fere egimus ...' Cf. p. 478: 'Fuimus hodie in lectione Hieronymi et Nov. Test. Arabici horas aliquot'. See also p. 300 for his comment on the Hebrew version.

34   R. Jones, 'The Medici Oriental Press (Rome 1584–1614) and the Impact of its Arabic Publications on Northern Europe' in G.A. Russell, ed., *The 'Arabick' Interest of the Natural Philosophers in Seventeenth-Century England* (Leiden, 1994), pp. 88–108.

35   BL, shelf-mark Or.72.a5.

36   A. Hamilton, *William Bedwell the Arabist 1563–1632* (Leiden, 1985), pp. 80–81, on the various uses to which Arabic versions of the Bible were put at the time.

37   *Scal.Cor.*, vol. 4, p. 318: 'Qui tantum thesaurum Arabismi mihi paravi καὶ ἐταμιευσάμην, adhuc profiteor inopiam meam. Hoc non facerent, qui trihorio prodierunt doctores Arabismi, et quum quaedam ex novo Testamento interpretarentur, quia nihil aliud praeter illa pauca legerant, et fieri non poterat, ut lectione tam paucorum verborum, tam brevi tempore omnem Arabismum ediscerent, sed occurrebant multa verba, quae nunquam viderant, eorum verborum ex Lexico Munsteri Chaldaico interpretationem petebant.' Cf. also pp. 180–181.

38   *Ibid.*, vol. 5, pp. 29–30, esp. p. 30: 'Si serio Arabismi studiosus es, quem non magis sine Alcorano perfecte discere potes, quam Hebraismum sine Bibliis. Nihil enim possunt loqui Arabes, quod non ad aliquod comma aut sententiam Alcorani alludat. Si quid boni inde expiscari poteris, candidus imperti. Ego sane diligenter totum Alcoranum legi. Tamen non sum ex illis gloriosulis, qui nihil ignorant. Quare non ignorem, quae et doctiores Muhammedani fatentur se nescire?'

by May, Casaubon had procured himself a copy of the Qur'an.[39] In August he said he had embarked on an Arabic lexicon – one of the many plans he would never complete.[40] In the summer of the following year Scaliger expressed his amazement at how a man with so many other activities could have made such progress and write Arabic in so fluent a hand.[41]

For two years, from the summer of 1602 to the summer of 1604, Casaubon studied Arabic with Adriaen Willemsz. On 23 September 1602 he informed Scaliger that he was already reading, with Adriaen's help, the *Kitāb nuzhat al-mushtāq*.[42] This was an abridgement, printed by the Typographia Medicea in Rome, of the work on geography by the twelfth-century topographer al-Idrīsī. But al-Idrīsī, Hispano-Arab by origin, Moroccan by birth, and Sicilian by adoption, had not been identified, and was still generally known in Europe as 'geographus Arabs' or 'Nubiensis'.[43] Casaubon and Adriaen also read the Qur'an together. Adriaen made marginal annotations in one of Casaubon's manuscripts and added an index of the suras at the end.[44] The most intriguing Qur'anic manuscript on which they worked, however, was a bilingual fragment, on the left-hand page the Arabic, and on the right a Latin translation, which is now in the Cambridge University Library, MS Mm v 26. Thomas Burman has shown that the Latin translation was made in Spain by Johannes Gabriel Terrolensis or Juan Gabriel from Teruel, a Muslim convert to Christianity, for the Italian scholar Cardinal Egidio da Viterbo who was dispatched by the pope, Leo X, on a mission to the Spanish king in 1518 in order to discuss the possibility of a crusade against the Turks.[45] The manuscript is covered with notes, both interlinear and beside the Latin translation from sura 2:46 to 2:231, which Anthony Grafton identified as being in the hand of Casaubon.[46] Burman had already studied the notes in

---

39 *Ephemerides*, vol. 1, pp. 481–482: 'Hadriano Guilielmo a nobis Aureliam discedenti Alcoranum dedimus utendum triplex Arabicum cum interpretatione Latina: omnia manuscripta.' By the end of his life Casaubon owned various manuscript copies of the Qur'an. See Bodl., MS Casaubon 22, fols 44ʳ, 82ᵛ.
40 See below, pp. 66–68.
41 *Scal.Cor.*, vol. 5, p. 121: 'Non possum satis mirari, te hominem in aliis occupatissimum, tam brevi tempore tantum in Arabismo profecisse, quod mihi licet ea charactere perspicere.'
42 *Ibid.*, vol. 4, p. 413: 'Legebamus hodie, ego, et eruditissimus atque optimus ille Φιλάραψ, juvenis Flessingensis, quem ante menses aliquot mihi commendasti, in Arabe Geographo v. Climatis Sectionem secundam.' See also *Ephemerides*, vol. 1, pp. 481–82, 509, 510, 525.
43 For contemporary speculation over his identity see below, pp. 75–76.
44 *Cas.Ep.*, p. 214. The Qur'an, which Casaubon subsequently gave to Erpenius, is Bodl., MS Marsh 358 (see below,). For an example of Adriaen's marginalia see p. 69.
45 New information about Juan Gabriel is provided by Katarzyna K. Starczewska, *Latin Translation of the Qur'ān (1518/1621) Commissioned by Egidio da Viterbo. Critical Edition and Case Study* (Wiesbaden, 2018), pp. xxx–lxxxiii.
46 Grafton and Weinberg, *"I have always loved the Holy Tongue"*, p. 306.

the utmost detail and had concluded that their author 'had a very impressive knowledge of Arabic.'[47] The marginalia show that the two scholars were trying to correct Terrolensis's translation and to convey a more literal meaning of the text. Even if they were not all of the same quality, the notes testify to Casaubon's command of Arabic as long as he was working with Adriaen.

It was with Adriaen, moreover, that Casaubon returned to his copy of the Medici Gospels, and they started on Avicenna's *Qānūn*, also printed by the Typographia Medicea.[48] The two men planned a joint publication. In 1602 David Rivault de Fleurance, the future tutor of Louis XIII who was travelling in Italy, sent Casaubon, who had always had an interest in proverbs as we see from his editions of Theophrastus,[49] an Arabic manuscript containing two hundred proverbs. They were attributed mainly to Abū ʿUbayd, the philologist born in Herat in the eighth century, but were in fact of various origin, partly Muslim and partly Christian.[50] Rivault had had the text translated into Latin by a Maronite in Rome, but Casaubon, drawn by the idea of editing the proverbs, found the translation unsatisfactory. He copied out the entire text, as well as the Maronite's translation, and added a few notes of his own.[51] He also had Adriaen transcribe the first 176 proverbs,[52] which he sent to Scaliger in Leiden at the end of 1602,[53] suggesting that he elucidate some passages. Scaliger did so, and dispatched his translation to Casaubon in May 1603.[54]

---

47 T.E. Burman, *Reading the Qurʾān in Latin Christendom (1140–1560)* (Philadelphia, 2007), p. 169. For his discussion of the notes and the manuscripts see pp. 166–173.

48 *Scal.Cor.*, vol. 5, p. 174.

49 See both the copy of the Paris edition of 1592 with his own marginalia, BL shelf-mark 525. A. 10, and the later edition of 1612. His Hebrew and Greek proverbs are collected in Bodl., MS Casaubon 17.

50 Abraham Ecchellensis, *De origine nominis papae, nec non de illius proprietate in Romano pontifice adeoque de eiusdem primatu* (Rome, 1660), pp. 362–77; H. Zotenberg, 'Les sentences symboliques de Théodore, patriarche d'Antioche' *Journal asiatique*, ser. 7, 8 (1876), pp. 425–476; C. Brockelmann, *Geschichte der arabischen Literatur*, 2nd edn (Leiden, 1943), vol. 1, pp. 105–107; R. Sellheim, *Die klassisch-arabischen Sprichwörterversammlungen, insbesondere die des Abū ʿUbayd* (The Hague, 1954), pp. 56–89.

51 Bodl., MS Casaubon 30. In the published edition Erpenius included four notes by Casaubon, to proverbs 1.67, 1.82, 11.24 and 11.55.

52 Adriaen Willemsz's transcription of the first 176 proverbs with Scaliger's marginalia is in UBL, shelf-mark 874 D 7:3. The discovery was made by Arnoud Vrolijk; see Vrolijk and Van Ommen, eds, *'All my Books in Foreign Tongues'*, pp. 98–99.

53 *Scal.Cor.*, vol. 4, p. 531. Cf. the account in Casaubon's preface to Joseph Justus Scaliger, *Opuscula varia antehac non edita* (Paris, 1610), sigs 13ᵛ–4ʳ.

54 *Scal.Cor.*, vol. 4, p. 484. Cf. pp. 318, 445.

Adriaen subsequently copied the rest of the manuscript,[55] but Scaliger never completed his work on it.

Having begun under such good auspices, Casaubon's Arabic studies met with a major setback in the summer of 1604. Adriaen Willemsz died, unexpectedly after a brief illness, in July. Casaubon was heart-broken. In an emotional letter to Scaliger, in which he described his frantic ride to Adriaen's lodgings and the scene at his deathbed, he expressed to the full the affection he had for him, his admiration for his learning, and the depth of his grief.[56] As a result of Adriaen's death Casaubon's commitment to Arabic underwent a long interruption.[57] Even if he told Scaliger in March 1605 that he was still translating the Arabic *Geographia* into Latin,[58] and in November that he was reading more of Avicenna's *Qānūn*,[59] he had in fact turned his attention almost entirely to his edition of Polybius and, as he informed Sebastian Tengnagel, the Dutch imperial librarian in Vienna, in March 1607, he had all but abandoned Arabic.[60] He mentioned it less and less in his letters to Scaliger, and not until January 1609,

---

55 UBL, MS Or. 4726.
56 *Scal.Cor.*, vol. 5, p. 363–367, esp. p. 364–365: 'Itaque ea coaluerat inter nos amicitia, ut cum ego illum filii charitate complecterer, ille et me et uxorem non aliter quam parentum loco amaret et coleret … Sed me non tam privata amicitia movet, quam respectus publicae rei literariae; quae in hujus adolescentis morte incredibilem, si quid judico, fecit jacturam … Nam in Arabicis literis quantum profecisset, sine lacrymis recordari non possum. Tantum affirmo tibi, magne Scaliger, eam ἕξιν fuisse adeptum, ut pauca legeret, quorum mentem non caperet, ubi paululum attendisset. Avicennam usu contriverat: Alcoranum ita familiarem habebat, ut cum a te discessi, neminem Europaeorum fuisse illi putem secundum. Sed quoque maxime sum admiratus, praeceptiones grammaticas ejus linguae eximie callebat …'
57 *Ibid.*, p. 408. On 11 September 1604 he wrote to Scaliger: 'Ego, mi Scaliger, amisi socium ac ducem studiorum meorum in literis Arabicis.' Cf. Pattison, *Isaac Casaubon*, p. 238: 'Casaubon's arabic reading was discontinued when the instructor and the stimulus were withdrawn.'
58 *Scal.Cor.*, vol. 5, p. 563: 'Ego his diebus cum longo admodum intervallo Arabicos libros revisissem, impetum cepi, exercendi mei caussa, transferendi in Latinum sermonem Geographum Arabem; et statim operi manum admovi. Itaque totum ferme primum clima absolvi; nisi quod vacua multis locis spatia sunt relicta, ignorantiae meae μηνύματα. Quam tu solus potes sanare, velis modo: quod si per te licet, de nonnullis tecum proximis literis agam; doceri enim cupio, et doceri a te.' All that he would seem to have done of the translation is in Bodl., MS Casaubon 17, fols 81ʳ–96ʳ.
59 *Scal.Cor.*, vol. 6, p. 210. His notes on Avicenna are in Bodl., MSS Casaubon 23, fols 136ʳ–138ᵛ; Casaubon 31, fols 14ᵛ–29ᵛ.
60 *Cas.Ep.*, p. 286: 'Coepimus Lexicon nobis conficere. Ausi et eramus Geographiam Arabicam, Romae editam, facere Latinam. Posuimus et in Avicenna aliquid temporis. Sed ubi socium laborum istorum amisimus, adolescentem Flessingensem, ad miraculum usque in his literis versatum, spes nostrae retro coeperunt labi; neque adhuc opportunum tempus indipisci potuimus, sitis hujus nostrae ex plendae. Utinam propius abessemus,

the month of Scaliger's death, did his interest in the language revive with the arrival in Paris of another of Scaliger's protégés, Thomas Erpenius (Fig. 3).

By this time, however, Casaubon seems to have assumed above all the role of an adviser, an assistant and a spectator. As Erpenius made his gigantic strides forward, it was to Casaubon that he confided the details of his advance, what he read, whom he met, and his opinion of other Arabists. Thanks to Erpenius Casaubon himself returned to the proverbs he had planned to publish with Adriaen Willemsz but had put aside after his death.[61] In October 1609 he entrusted the manuscript in Adriaen's transcription with Scaliger's translation, and annotations by both Scaliger and himself, to Erpenius, asking him to retranslate the text, edit and publish it.[62]

Casaubon's renewed determination to proceed with Arabic was relatively brief. Just as he had depended on Etienne Hubert and on Adriaen Willemsz, so he depended on Erpenius, and when Erpenius left Paris at the end of the year Casaubon's Arabic studies came to a standstill.[63] He already referred to them in a letter to Johannes Buxtorf in February 1610 as a thing of the past.[64] A little later he told Erpenius that his own days as an Arabist had ended when he moved to England at the end of 1610. He had left nearly all his Arabic material in Paris – he would subsequently recover much of it – and in England he found himself engaged in controversy with Baronius and concerned with his own conversion to Anglicanism.[65] Despite his close friendship with the

---

haberes me discipulum, ut quondam ὁ μακαρίτης juvenis Flessingensis, cujus meminisse absque suspiritibus non possum, neque unquam potero.'

61 Bodl., MS Casaubon 30, fols 98ᵛ–144ᵛ.
62 *Ephemerides*, vol. 2, p. 694. On 22 October 1609 he noted in his journal: 'Preste a M. Arpennius Proverbia Arab. Cum interpr. Scal....'. Cf. *Cas.Ep.*, p. 339. The edition is analysed by A. Vrolijk, 'The Prince of Arabists and his many errors: Thomas Erpenius's image of Joseph Scaliger and the edition of the *Proverbia arabica* (1614)' *Journal of the Warburg and Courtauld Institutes* 73 (2010), pp. 297–325.
63 *Cas.Ep.*, p. 339: 'Mea studia Arabica post tuum discessum frigent.'
64 Basel, Öffentliche Bibliothek, MS GT 62, fol. 99ᵛ: 'Simul inflammabat me cupiditas Arabicae linguae cognoscendae cuius multa vocabula in libris Rabbinicis passim legi exposita noram. Sed me aliae curae ab illo incepto mox revocaverunt ...' I owe this reference to Joanna Weinberg.
65 *Cas.Ep.*, p. 477: 'Sed nostros', he wrote to Erpenius from London in July 1612, 'in eo genere conatus, postquam huc venimus, multa retardarunt. Nam et libri nostri fere omnes Lutetiae adhuc haerent; et nos alia studia mire occupatos habent. Habemus in manibus, mi Erpeni, opus arduum, cujus finem si dederit Deus videre, fructum, ut spero, non mediocrem e vigiliis nostris Ecclesia Dei percipiet. Animadversiones enim scribimus in Annales Baronii, et fraudes illius atque imperitiam stupendam orbi patefacimus. Non tamen a studiis linguarum Orientalium ita sumus alieni, ut non aliquando de illis quoque cogitemus. In Rabbinis praesertim succisiva temporum nostrorum, quoties licet, collocamus. Sed de his rebus brevi, ut spero, una agemus ...'

English Arabist William Bedwell, Casaubon had had to give preference to his rabbinic studies.

Nevertheless, it would be wrong to say that Casaubon had entirely abandoned his intention of studying Arabic himself. His marginal notes to the fragment of Avicenna's *Qānūn* in Arabic and Latin, prepared by Peter Kirsten and published in 1609, show that he was still reading Arabic texts,[66] and we shall return to the use he made of Arabic material in his attack on Baronius. He followed Erpenius's studies closely. In 1613 he could admire Erpenius's additions to Franciscus Raphelengius's Arabic lexicon.[67] A little later he received an inscribed copy of Erpenius's grammar, 'Clarissimo doctissimoque Viro Isaaco Casaubono, Domino et amico suo plurimum colendo Auctor D.D.'[68] And in March 1614, a few months before his death, he was sent the *Kitāb al-amthāl seu Proverbiorum arabicorum centuriae duae*, the edition of the proverbs printed at the Leiden Officina Plantiniana, edited and retranslated by Erpenius with his own notes added to those of Scaliger and Casaubon, and dedicated to Casaubon himself.[69] The little book remains a monument to the collaboration between the four friends, Casaubon, Scaliger, Adriaen Willemsz and Erpenius, and in his preface Erpenius described its genesis and gave credit to Adriaen's talents as an Arabist.[70]

2 The Method

Owing to his diary, his letters, his notebooks (the *Adversaria* now at the Bodleian Library) and his marginalia, we are comparatively well informed about how Casaubon proceeded with the study of Arabic. The knowledge of Hebrew he shared with nearly all the other early European Arabists was an

---

66 BL, shelf-mark C.82.h.12. Cf. Schnurrer, pp. 451–452.
67 *Cas.Ep.*, p. 537.
68 BL, shelf-mark 622.h.5(2).
69 *Cas.Ep.*, p. 556: 'Gavisus sum esse a te perfectum adeo feliciter, quod ante aliquot annos quum scripsissem te effecturum, multi non crediderunt posse a te praestari. Liberasti eadem opera fidem meam, et decus tibi apud vere eruditos immortale peperisti. Mihi in primis illud placuit (percurri enim statim, licet πύρεττων) quod magnum Scaligerum saepe errantem sic revocasti in viam, ut nihil propterea ejus existimationi sit decessurum. Fecisti quod virum bonum decebat, et doctum … Quod voluisti opus elegantissimum in publicum prodire meo nomine inscriptum, ago tibi eo nomine et habeo grates gratissimas, quantas possum, maximas …' For Erpenius's criticisms of Scaliger's Arabic see below,
70 Thomas Erpenius, ed., *Kitāb al-amthāl seu Proverbiorum arabicorum* (Leiden, 1614), sig. *4ʳ: 'iuvenis cum propter insignem probitatem, et omnigenam eruditionem; tum propter admirandos in Arabismo progressus, et laudabiles conatus, longiori vita dignissimi.'

advantage and does much to account for his progress in the first stages. He was already acquainted with the morphology of a Semitic language and would have been familiar with certain Arabic words. Yet he also soon realised that the assistance provided by Hebrew was limited. Postel had attributed his own swift mastery of Arabic to his command of Hebrew,[71] but Casaubon, who had initially read Hebrew in order to pass on to Arabic, discovered that the proximity between the two languages had been vastly exaggerated, and wondered how Postel could possibly imagine that the two years which he said it might take the Hebraist to learn Arabic was a short time. He dismissed Postel's claim that Arabic was spoken across Asia.[72]

Casaubon appears to have acquired most of the available material on Arabic, and his collection of Arabic printed books, one of the many fruits of his own form of bibliophilia so memorably described by Mark Pattison,[73] would, when presented to the British Museum many years later, become the basis of the Arabic collection in what is now the British Library.[74] The books he is known to have owned include four works on the Arabic alphabet.[75] One is the *Alphabetum arabicum* by the professor at Heidelberg Jacob Christmann.[76] Christmann's brief book, published in Neustadt an der Hardt, had come out in 1582, and its treatment of the different elements of the alphabet, such as the number, name, shape and phonetic value of the consonants in separate sections with separate headings, was indeed innovative,[77] while the exercises it provides are the Lord's Prayer in Arabic intended as an improvement on the version given by Guillaume Postel in his Arabic grammar of 1538, and a passage (2:6–11) from the Arabic version of the Epistle to the Philippians which Christmann had copied from a manuscript deposited by Postel in the library in Heidelberg. The second work was the *Specimen characterum arabicorum* by

---

71 Postel, *Linguarum duodecim ... introductio*, sig. D2ʳ; *idem*, *Grammatica arabica*, sig. D3ʳ.
72 Bodl., MS Casaubon 60, fol. 283ʳ⁻ᵛ.
73 Pattison, *Isaac Casaubon*, p. 38: 'Pinched everywhere else, he spent all he could save on books. Book-buying was to him not the indulgence of a taste or a passion, it was the acquisition of tools.' Cf. p. 429.
74 T.A. Birrell, 'The reconstruction of the library of Isaac Casaubon' in A.R.A. Croiset van Uchelen, ed., *Hellinga Festschrift: Forty-Three Studies in Bibliography presented to Prof. Dr. Wytze Hellinga on the Occasion of his Retirement from the Chair of Neophilology in the University of Amsterdam at the End of the Year 1978* (Amsterdam, 1980), pp. 59–68, esp. p. 64: 'Until Panizzi's policy began to bear fruit in the late 19th century, Casaubon's little nucleus of orientalia was virtually all that was available to scholars working in the British Museum.'
75 A number of Casaubon's Arabic books are mentioned in *ibid.*, pp. 59, 63–64.
76 BL, shelf-mark 622.h.2(4).
77 Jones, pp. 122–125. See also Fück, pp. 43–44.

Franciscus Raphelengius.[78] It was published in 1592 and was intended primarily as a specimen to exhibit the Arabic types Raphelengius had had cut for the Officina Plantiniana, the Leiden branch of the printing firm belonging to his father-in-law, Christophe Plantin, in Antwerp. It simply contains the Arabic alphabet (with no further elucidation) and an Arabic version of Psalm 50 (51).

The third work, also dated 1592, is the *Introductio in linguam arabicam* by Bartholomeus Radtmann, professor in Frankfurt an der Oder. Despite the title this again is solely concerned with the Arabic alphabet and gives the Arabic text of Psalm 145 (146):1–7.[79] Casaubon's surviving copy in the British Library lacks the preliminary matter as well as Radtmann's long introduction, which is in fact the most interesting part of his work. Assisted as he was by a Turk, he provides the Turkish terminology for the vowel signs, and he also gives the *abjad* or numerical order of the alphabet besides the standard *hijā'* order.[80] Although he does endeavour to display variations and alternatives, his work is less satisfactory than Christmann's, and the lack of Arabic types in Frankfurt an der Oder meant that the Arabic words had to be written in by hand. The fourth work, finally, was the best, even if that too was restricted to the alphabet. This was the *Alphabetum arabicum* of 1592 by Giambattista Raimondi, the director of the Typographia Medicea in Rome.[81] Although Raimondi followed Christmann in his treatment of the different elements of the alphabet in separate sections, he wrote his little book on the basis of his own immense experience of Arabic manuscripts and relied exclusively on the classification provided by Arabs writing about the phonetic value of the consonants. He also introduced further Arabic terminology for the vowel and phonetic signs.[82] As sample texts he gave the Lord's Prayer, the Ave Maria, Psalms 112 (113) and 116 (117), and the first nine verses of the Gospel of John, and added a vast syllabary illustrating the vocalisation.

Of the other Arabic grammars in circulation, Casaubon owned Ruthger Spey's *Compendium grammatices arabicae* of 1583,[83] the grammatical instructions appended to an edition of the Arabic version of the Epistle to the Galatians taken from another manuscript in Heidelberg which had once belonged to Postel. This would have provided him with more information

---

78 BL, shelf-mark 622.h.2(3).
79 Casaubon's copy, BL, shelf-mark 622.h.2(2*), lacks the title-page and was identified by Robert Jones. For the identification and a discussion of the text see Jones, pp. 54–56, 126–127, 251–252.
80 See below, pp. 67–68.
81 BL, shelf-mark 622.h.2(2).
82 For an extensive discussion of Raimondi's work see Jones, pp. 126–130, 184–198.
83 Bodl., MS Casaubon 22, fol. 119ʳ. For Spey see Jones, pp. 124–126.

about Arabic grammar than any of the texts on the alphabet, and he undoubtedly consulted – although I can find no evidence that he owned – Spey's main source, Guillaume Postel's earlier *Grammatica arabica*, the first to assimilate the information provided in the monolingual grammars by the Arabs themselves.[84] Thanks to the Typographia Medicea, moreover, Casaubon was able to obtain a copy of one such grammar, the *Ajurrūmiyya* by the fourteenth-century Moroccan grammarian Muḥammad ibn Muḥammad ibn Dāwūd-al-Ṣanhājī. It came out in 1592.[85] The *Ajurrūmiyya* was solely in Arabic, and it says much for Casaubon's progress that, with the help of Adriaen Willemsz, he was able to translate it and to make use of it. But the use he made of it can only have been of limited value to him. The *Ajurrūmiyya* is primarily concerned with inflection and government, thus with the external form of the language rather than with grammatical function.[86]

As for vocabulary, Casaubon followed the same path as his contemporaries – Scaliger in Leiden, Raphelengius in Antwerp, Bedwell in London and many others. He drew up wordlists of his own based on all the Arabic sources he could procure. He did so, as we saw, with the Medici press edition of Matthew's Gospel, diligently noting the words and, in the case of the verbs, giving the correct root and form.[87] He also started to do so with the 1593 edition of Avicenna's *Qānūn*.[88] And he tried to extract the Arabic words from Maimonides's *Moreh Nevukhim*.[89] One result of his efforts was the wordlist, which can probably be dated around 1603,[90] in his interleaved copy of the *Dittionario novo hebraico*, the Hebrew-Italian-Latin dictionary by the Italian Jewish scholar David De' Pomi which came out in 1587.[91] On the flyleaf of the dictionary Casaubon listed his sources. Most of them are the publications of the Typographia Medicea – the Gospels, the *Ajurrūmiyya*, the *Kitāb nuzhat al-mushtāq*, Nāṣir al-Dīn al-Ṭūsī's Arabic version of Euclid's *Elements* of 1594 and Avicenna's *Qānūn*. With the exception of the Gospels, all these works were entirely in Arabic.

---

84 Jones, pp. 113–120. Casaubon discusses Postel's *Linguarum duodecim characteribus differentium introductio* at length in Bodl., MS Casaubon 30, fols 281ʳ–292ʳ; cf. also *ibid.*, fol. 65ʳ and Bodl., MS Casaubon 50, fols 281ff.
85 BL, shelf-mark 14593.b.31.
86 Jones, pp. 199–212.
87 Bodl., MS Casaubon 23, fol. 128ʳ.
88 *Ibid.*, fol. 136ʳ.
89 Bodl., MS Casaubon 30, fol. 74ᵛ.
90 *Ephemerides*, vol. 1, p. 510, where, in August 1603 he notes: 'Τὰ ἐγκύκλια id est, Lexicon institutum', and on the following day, 'Τὰ ἐγκύκλια et auctum nostrum Lexicon Arabicum.' Five years later, in August 1608, he records lending his lexicon to Jean Martin (*Ephemerides*, vol. 2, p. 624).
91 BL, shelf-mark C.79.d.6.

To these Casaubon added the polyglot Psalter (in Latin, Greek, Hebrew, Aramaic and Arabic) published by Agostino Giustiniani in Genoa in 1516; two manuscripts, the one of the Qur'an and the one of the proverbs attributed to Abū 'Ubayd; and, finally, the Arabic passages in the 1598 edition of Scaliger's *De emendatione temporum*.[92]

To bring an Arabic vocabulary into line with a Hebrew dictionary entails one great difficulty, the alphabetical order. A number of Arabic letters are missing in Hebrew. When Casaubon was at work a few European Arabists, such as Bedwell and Scaliger, preferred the so-called *abjad* order, or variants of it, closer to the Hebrew than that of the *hijā'* alphabet customary today in which the characters are ordered by shape. The *abjad* was the earliest Arabic alphabetical order and is sometimes known as the Aramaic or numerical order since the letters are arranged according to their numerical value. Two versions of it exist, an eastern one and a western one – the change in the two occurs after the fourteenth character (the *nūn*). The European Arabists tended to choose the eastern version, in which the characters with no Hebrew equivalent are placed, in numerical order, at the end of the alphabet, ending with the *ghain* (غ), with the numerical value of 1000.[93] This was the order used by Avicenna in his list of medicaments in the *Qānūn*. While all the works on the Arabic alphabet owned by Casaubon give the *hijā'* order, Radtmann alone also discussed the *abjad* at some length.[94]

The *abjad* was in fact well known in Europe. Postel had given it in his Arabic grammar,[95] and Theodore Bibliander in his *De ratione communi omnium linguarum et literarum commentarius* of 1548,[96] simply in order to illustrate its numerical function. Yet neither Casaubon nor any of the other European Arabists followed the *abjad* arrangement, whether western or eastern, in full. Postel was the most faithful, following the eastern system for twenty-three

---

92   For the Giustiniani Psalter see R. Smitskamp, *Philologia Orientalis: A Description of Books Illustrating the Study and Printing of Oriental Languages in 16th- and 17th-Century Europe* (Leiden, 1992), pp. 231–34. For the proverbs see above. Casaubon's third entry on the flyleaf of De' Pomi is 'Computus apud Jos. Scaligerum et eius libris.' This refers to Joseph Justus Scaliger, *De emendatione temporum* (Leiden, 1598), pp. 664–673, 716–729.

93   The two versions are reproduced in F. Maddison and E. Savage-Smith, eds, *Science, Tools and Magic* (London-Oxford, 1997), vol. 1, p. 199.

94   Bartholomeus Radtmann, *Introductio in linguam arabicam* (Frankfurt an der Oder, 1592), pp. 3–4. He seems to have relied on his Turkish informant for much of his information. 'Ordo duplex est. Alio enim ordine alphabeti Arabes utuntur, quando primum pueros docere incipiunt. Alio quando illum priorem norunt.'

95   Postel, *Grammatica arabica*, sig. D5ᵛ.

96   Theodor Bibliander, *De ratione communi omnium linguarum et literarum commentarius* (Zurich, 1548), p. 65.

characters, but ending with the *ẓā'* (ظ), *ghain* (غ), *ḍād* (ض); Bibliander and Radtmann followed the same order as far as the *thā'* (ث) and omitted the last six characters; Scaliger, in his Arabic glossary, the unpublished 'Thesaurus linguae arabicae',[97] compromised with the *hijā'* order and arranged some of the letters according to their shape, placing the *dhāl* (ذ) after the *dāl* (د), the *khā'* (خ) after the *ḥā'* (ح), the *ẓā'* (ظ) after the *ṭā'* (ط), the *ghain* (غ) after the *'ain* (ع), and the *ḍād* (ض) after the *ṣād* (ص), and ending with the *thā'* (ث). Bedwell, in his Arabic-Latin dictionary in Cambridge University Library,[98] did something similar, but treated the *dāl* and the *dhāl* as if they were the same letter, as he did the *ḥā'* and the *khā'*, the *ṭā'* and the *ẓā'*, the *'ain* and the *ghain*, the *tā'* and the *thā'*, and the *ṣād* and the *ḍād* (with which he ended). Even Franciscus Raphelengius, who followed Postel and the majority of Western Arabists in using the traditional *hijā'* order in his *Lexicon Arabico-Latinum*, published posthumously in 1613, treated those characters only differentiated by diacritical points – the *jīm* (ج), the *ḥā'* (ح) and the *khā'* (خ); the *thā'* (ث) and the *tā'* (ت); the *dāl* (د) and the *dhāl* (ذ); the *shīn* (ش) and the *sīn* (س); the *ḍād* (ض) and the *ṣād* (ص); the *ṭā'* (ط) and the *ẓā'* (ظ); and the *'ain* (ع) and the *ghain* (غ) – as though they were the same character.[99]

In his own interleaved dictionary Casaubon seems to have been influenced by Scaliger, following the Hebrew order wherever possible but grouping, according to their shape, the characters with no Hebrew equivalent together with the ones that corresponded to the Hebrew. In Casaubon's case, as, indeed, in the case of both Bedwell and Raphelengius, this meant implicitly denying their value as independent letters. We thus find the *dāl* joined to the *dhāl* under the Hebrew *daleth* (ד), the *khā'* and the *ḥā'* under the *ḥet* (ח), the *ṭā'* and the *ẓā'* under the *ṭeth* (ט), the *'ain* and the *ghain* under the *'ayin* (ע), the *ṣād* and the *ḍād* under the *ṣadeh* (צ), the *sīn* and the *shīn* under the *sin* (שׂ), and the *tā'* and the *thā'* under the *taw* (ת).

3 The Centre of a Circle

Word soon spread that Casaubon was interested in Arabic and he gradually established relations with other scholars in the same field. The first was Scaliger, and it was to Casaubon that Scaliger imparted some of his most important

---

97   UBL, MS Or. 212.
98   CUL, MSS Hh.5.1–7.
99   Cf. below, p. 243.

insights. He warned him against positing too close a relationship between Arabic and Hebrew and, as we saw, against studying Arabic on the basis of excerpts from the New Testament. He discussed with him numerous aspects of the language, including the peculiarities of Moroccan Arabic and its influence on Spanish.[100] In February 1602 Casaubon was asking Scaliger about the Arabic version of Maimonides's *Moreh nevukhim*, Arabic paraphrases of the Old Testament, and the Arabic name of Alexander the Great.[101] He informed Scaliger about manuscripts which might interest him. He told him about a French-Arabic-Turkish lexicon he had discovered,[102] and he sent him some notes on the Qur'an by a 'Dominican'[103] and a specimen of the Arabic types owned by Guillaume Le Bé in Paris (which he had used in his own publications and would use again in his edition of Scaliger's posthumous *Opuscula*).[104]

In July 1603 Casaubon entered into correspondence with William Bedwell, known as the founder of Arabic studies in England.[105] Casaubon had heard about Bedwell from Lauge Christensen, a well-connected Dane from Ribe who, after studying in Copenhagen and Franeker, had proceeded to Oxford.[106] A friend of Daniel Rogers and William Camden, with an interest in Semitic languages, Christensen had met Bedwell in 1597. From England he had gone to Germany and the Netherlands, and then to France. He had contributed to the spread of Bedwell's reputation as an Arabist on the European continent, and in Paris he sought out Casaubon.

Casaubon made the first approaches to Bedwell, addressing him with the modesty of a student calling on a master.[107] When Casaubon first wrote to him Bedwell, who had studied at Cambridge, was rector of the church of St Ethelburgha in Bishopsgate and lived in London. Diffident and retiring, he nevertheless had powerful friends, such as Lancelot Andrewes, once master of Pembroke Hall at Cambridge, where he and Bedwell probably first met,

---

100   *Scal.Cor.*, vol. 4, pp. 317–318.
101   *Ibid.*, vol. 4, p. 205.
102   *Ibid.*, p. 238.
103   *Ibid.*, pp. 535–536; vol. 5, pp. 30, 109, 112.
104   *Ibid.*, vol. 4, p. 577. For Le Bé's Arabic types see Schnurrer, pp. 506–12; Toomer, pp. 29–30; Smitskamp, *Philologia Orentalis*, pp. 259, 281, 312.
105   Their correspondence is collected in Hamilton, *William Bedwell*, pp. 97–101 (*Cas.Ep.*, pp. 183–184).
106   Hamilton, *William Bedwell*, pp. 14–15, 20–21, 97, 122–23.
107   *Ibid.*, p. 97: 'Ignotus fortasse tibi etiam de nomine, te appello, Vir doctissime. At tu non ignotus nobis: tuum enim nomen auditione pridem accepimus; cum multi viri docti isthinc venientes, et de caeteris tuis virtutibus, et de peritia atque usu, quem habes linguae Arabicae, eximia quaedam et rara praedicarent. Atque hanc famam confirmavit non mediocriter eruditissimus hic Lago, tibi probe notus ...'

and subsequently dean of Westminster (1601), bishop of Chichester (1605), bishop of Ely (1609), and finally bishop of Winchester (1619). Andrewes presented Bedwell with the vicarage of Tottenham High Cross in 1607 and would subsidise his trip to Leiden in 1612. Bedwell seems to have introduced him to Casaubon. Like Scaliger and Erpenius, Bedwell informed Casaubon about his various discoveries. He told him of his efforts to find an Arabic printer, listed the Arabic texts in his possession, and commented on the Arabic versions of the New Testament.

Casaubon corresponded with all the main European Arabists. In September 1608 Jacob Christmann, in Heidelberg, made a copy for his benefit of the first two chapters of the Arabic version of the Epistle to the Romans which had been acquired by Postel;[108] and in 1611 he was referring to mathematical terms in Arabic and asking Casaubon about the Mozarabic Latin-Arabic glossary in Leiden.[109] Etienne Hubert also discussed Arabic terminology with Casaubon.[110] Christophe Dupuy, Cardinal Du Perron's secretary and subsequently royal chaplain, informed him, early in 1604, of the Arabic books and manuscripts he had brought back from Rome, and communicated further bibliographical discoveries in Rome to him two years later.[111] Other scholars sent him their works. Kirsten, besides telling him about his studies and enquiring about manuscripts in the royal library, sent him his Arabic grammar, his edition of Avicenna and his notes on the Matthew Gospel,[112] while Georg Michael Lingelsheim, councillor of the Elector Palatine, lent Casaubon the manuscript of an Arabic medical lexicon from the Heidelberg library.[113]

In 1608 Casaubon was approached by Yūsuf ibn Abū Dhaqn, known in Europe as Josephus Barbatus or Abudacnus, a Copt who had recently arrived in Paris and, impelled by a thirst for knowledge and curiosity about the West, was in search of celebrities.[114] Barbatus, from Cairo, had come to Rome in 1595 with a letter to the pope, Clement VIII, from the patriarch of Alexandria, Gabriel VIII.

---

108   UBL, MS Or. 2083/Ar. 1129.
109   BL, MS Burney 363, fol. 224ʳ. See pp. 232–233 below.
110   BL, MS Burney 364, fols 299ʳ–303ʳ.
111   Bodl., MS Casaubon 30, fol. 99ʳ. Cf. *Scal.Cor.*, vol. 5, p. 450, 531.
112   BL, MS Burney 364, fols 334ʳ, 336ʳ⁻ᵛ. Cf. Bodl., MS Casaubon 22, fols 63ʳ, 69ʳ, 85ᵛ. Casaubon's copy of Kirsten's Avicenna is BL, shelf-mark C.82.h.12.
113   BL, MS Burney 365, fol. 106ʳ. Although this marked the beginning of a long epistolary friendship, Lingelsheim may have regretted his decision. He sent Casaubon the manuscript in 1604 (*Cas.Ep.*, pp. 210, 217, 233). When Casaubon moved to London he left the manuscript behind in Paris and was still searching for it in 1613 (*Cas.Ep.*, pp. 454, 462, 540). Lingelsheim displayed commendable patience (BL, MS Burney 365, fol. 123ʳ). For Casaubon's use of the manuscript see below, p. 76.
114   On Barbatus see above, pp. 3–40.

He had converted to Catholicism and joined the Discalced Carmelites, but he seems never to have been fully ordained and left Rome for Paris in about 1607. Once he was in France he managed to enter the circle of professors of Arabic at the Collège Royal, thanks to whom he was appointed interpreter royal and occasionally employed as a teacher of Arabic. On 9 July 1608 he wrote Casaubon a letter introducing himself and listing the many languages he claimed to know.[115] His eagerness to get in touch with Casaubon, and the fact that his letter was entirely in Arabic, is evidence of the reputation Casaubon had acquired. A few months later, in September, Barbatus wrote a similar letter to Scaliger in Leiden, but he wrote it in Italian and added an Arabic summary.[116]

Casaubon's last mainstay in Arabic studies was, as we saw, Thomas Erpenius (Fig. 3) who arrived in Paris in January 1609. Erpenius had studied in Leiden.[117] He had there mastered Hebrew, and his decision to proceed to Arabic seems to have been due to the influence of Scaliger. Scaliger had given him a letter of introduction to English scholars, and Erpenius had travelled from Leiden to England in order to attend the universities of Oxford and Cambridge. Once in England, in September 1608, he made the acquaintance of William Bedwell. In December Bedwell began to teach him the rudiments of Arabic.[118] Erpenius stayed in Paris from January to November 1609. It was there that he started to make the rapid progress in Arabic which enabled him to compile his grammar, and this progress, as Erpenius always admitted with passionate gratitude,[119]

---

115   BL, MS Burney 367, fol. 200ʳ.
116   *Scal.Cor.*, vol. 7, pp. 628–631.
117   For Erpenius's life see W.M.C. Juynboll, *Zeventiende-eeuwsche Beoefenaars van het Arabisch in Nederland* (Utrecht, 1931), pp. 59–118; A. Vrolijk and R. van Leeuwen, *Arabic Studies in the Netherlands. A Short History in Portraits* (Leiden-Boston, 2014), pp. 31–40; Jones, pp. 144–165.
118   Hamilton, *William Bedwell*, p. 31.
119   For example, in the epistle to Casaubon's son in the second edition of the book of Arabic proverbs, Thomas Erpenius, ed., *Kitāb al-amthāl. Proverbiorum arabicorum centuriae duae* (Leiden, 1623), sig. *2ʳ⁻ᵛ: 'Is [sc.Casaubon] autem simul ac me vidit, et Linguarum Orientalium studiosissimum esse cognovit, vehementer et me amare, et studiis meis favere caepit, ita quidem ut, cum Arabicae linguae desiderio, magni Scaligeri hortatu, jam totum me flagrare, et libris omnibus destitui animadverteret, supellectilem suam Arabicam, quam satis habebat luculentam, ultro mihi offerret, et concederet. quod quidem beneficium tanto me gaudio affecit, ut me beatiorem crederem vivere neminem: et tantum Arabismi studium in me excitavit, ut majori cum ardore atque animi alacritate neminem unquam illas literas aggressum esse persuasum habeam.' Cf. also his oration on Hebrew delivered at Leiden university on 27 September 1620 (Thomas Erpenius, *Orationes tres de linguarum ebraeae, atque arabicae dignitate* (Leiden, 1621), p. 129): '… hoc tantum dico Clarissimum virum Ishacum Casaubonum seculi hujus insigne ornamentum, et cui plurimum debent studia mea orientalia …'

FIGURE 3   Thomas Erpenius. Engraved portrait by (studio) de Passe
JOANNES MEURSIUS, *ATHENÆ BATAVÆ. SIVE, DE VRBE LEIDENSI, & ACADEMIÂ, VIRISQUE CLARIS* (LEIDEN: ANDRIES CLOUCK, BONAVENTURA EN ABRAHAM ELZEVIER, 1625)

was due in part to Casaubon. To begin with, Casaubon encouraged him with his expressions of admiration;[120] he lent him his Arabic material and introduced him to Barbatus who gave him further tuition. Neither Bedwell nor Barbatus, however, proved particularly good teachers. In November 1609 Erpenius left Paris for Saumur, where he spent much of 1610 before returning again to Paris. He continued to work on his Arabic grammar and was attracted by Casaubon's proposal that he should have it published, together with the proverbs, by Le Bé in Paris.[121] In March 1611, however, Casaubon had to inform him that Le Bé now refused to publish works by 'heretics'.[122] Casaubon gave him his manuscript Qur'an with Adriaen Willemsz's marginalia by way of consolation.[123]

On his second visit to Paris Erpenius made a further advance in Arabic thanks to the lessons he received from the Moroccan envoy, Aḥmad ibn Qāsim al-Ḥajarī, whom he met in Conflans – an episode which he recounted to Casaubon in detail.[124] At this point, too, apparently again thanks to Casaubon who approached them through William Bedwell,[125] the surviving sons of Franciscus Raphelengius in charge of the Officina Plantiniana in Leiden asked Erpenius to correct their father's Arabic-Latin lexicon which they had at last decided to publish and wished to issue together with Erpenius's own Arabic grammar. Hoping to improve his Arabic, Erpenius left France for the south in an attempt to sail from Venice to Istanbul. No ships were sailing, and he had to content himself with the Venetian bookshops and the European libraries – Milan, Basel, Geneva and, above all, Heidelberg – before he made his way back to Leiden. He arrived in July 1612 and took up the professorship of Arabic at the university in the following year. Here again Casaubon had done his utmost to help him, enlisting the support of Hugo Grotius and Daniel Heinsius in Holland.[126] Throughout this period Erpenius kept in touch with him. From his letters we can follow his improvement, his expeditions to the various European collections of Arabic manuscripts, and his revolutionary discovery of the

---

120   *Cas.Ep.*, p. 346: 'Tu unus es omnium, qui futuri, volente Deo, aedificii fundamenta jecisti firma et solida. Noli spem nostram fallere; neque dubita, vel alibi terrarum oblatum iri aliquam occasionem cum publica utilitate et tua, haec nobilissima studia excolendi.'
121   *Ibid.*, pp. 345, 355–356.
122   *Ibid.*, p. 375.
123   *Ibid.*; the manuscript is Bodl., MS Marsh 358. A note by Etienne Hubert in the manuscript suggests that it had remained in Paris after Casaubon's departure for London and that it was he who gave it to Erpenius at Casaubon's request.
124   *Cas.Ep.*, pp. 660–662; Juynboll, *Zeventiende-eeuwsche Beoefenaars*, p. 71; Jones, p. 148; G. Wiegers, *A Learned Muslim Acquaintance of Erpenius and Golius: Ahmad b. Kāsim al-Andalusī and Arabic Studies in the Netherlands* (The Hague, 1991), pp. 45–63.
125   Juynboll, *Zeventiende-eeuwsche Beoefenaars*, p. 72.
126   *Cas.Ep.*, pp. 478–79; Juynboll, *Zeventiende-eeuwsche Beoefenaars*, p. 74.

Arabic-Turkish glossaries and of the monolingual Arabic dictionaries which enabled him to correct countless errors in Raphelengius's lexicon.[127]

Casaubon left France at the end of 1610 and settled in London. Here he found himself again in the company of Arabists. His arrival coincided with Barbatus's stay in England, and they met in London, where Barbatus's collection of celebrities grew by the day. Casaubon could also at last meet his English friends with whom he had corresponded for so long. One was Lancelot Andrewes, who had been elevated to the see of Ely, and the other was Bedwell. Bedwell introduced him to the publisher and bookdealer John Bill, who would furnish him with books throughout his stay in London and publish his critique of Baronius.[128] When he visited Leiden in 1612 Bedwell carried with him letters from Casaubon to his Dutch friends.[129] He sent Casaubon an account of his experiences and his meetings, and when the two men were both in London Bedwell showed him his Arabic lexicon.[130] However little time he had for his Arabic studies in England, Casaubon continued to encourage other Arabists, urging Etienne Hubert, for example, to publish something on Arabic with the collaboration of Le Bé.[131] Casaubon was still believed to be one of the foremost scholars studying Arabic, and Bedwell transcribed a letter written to Casaubon in July 1613 by the Arabic-speaking Christian Murqus al-Duʿābilī al-Kurdī or Marco Dobelo, who had lectured in Arabic in Rome, moved to Spain, and was searching for employment in England.[132]

Quite apart from the services which Bedwell and Andrewes rendered to Casaubon, they were loyal and affectionate friends who did much to mitigate the xenophobia he detected in the streets of London and the resentment of his achievements he believed he found at the court and universities.[133] In a querulous letter to Étienne Hubert from London Casaubon said he had never encountered such hostility in any other country. The only two men who were constantly generous and kind were Andrewes and Bedwell.[134]

---

127 For Erpenius's letters to Casaubon see *Cas.Ep.*, pp. 343–46, 660–63, 665–167; BL, MS Burney 364, fol. 24. Cf. Jones, pp. 144–151, for the genesis of Erpenius's grammar and his reports to Casaubon.

128 Hamilton, *William Bedwell*, pp. 33–34. For Casaubon's critique of Baronius see Grafton and Weinberg, *"I have always loved the Holy Tongue"*, pp. 164–230.

129 Hamilton, *William Bedwell*, pp. 37–38.

130 *Cas.Ep.*, p. 485.

131 *Ibid.*, p. 485.

132 Bodl., MS Bodl. Or. 298.3. See G. Levi della Vida, *Ricerche sulla formazione del più antico fondo dei manoscritti orientali della Biblioteca Vaticana* (Vatican City, 1939), p. 282.

133 Pattison, *Isaac Casaubon*, pp. 373–384.

134 Hamilton, *William Bedwell*, p. 54.

4   The Arabist

Casaubon started to quote Arabic in his works shortly after he began to study it, and, from his application of Arabic over the years, we can identify various fields of interest which he shared with other contemporary antiquarians – topography, the technical terminology to be found in Avicenna, etymology and vocabulary, and the New Testament.[135] In the case of Casaubon, however, we encounter some highly original features. Aware though he was of the limitations of his knowledge of the Arabic language, he approached his sources in the same critical spirit we find in so much of his work.[136] We shall see that he was critical of the Medici press edition of Avicenna and, where he could, corrected misprints and other inaccuracies. He was even more critical of the Roman edition of the Gospels. In his approach to certain aspects of Arab culture, moreover, he was well ahead of most of his contemporaries. His efforts to publish the proverbs attributed to Abū 'Ubayd make of him one of the very first Arabists to plan to edit an Arabic literary text, and he was amongst the first European scholars to propose a discussion of Arabic poetry.

Casaubon was writing at a time when the topography of the Arab world claimed increasing attention. This was partly due to scholars who were endeavouring to locate classical sites and establish the Arabic name to which they might correspond. That this was one of Casaubon's concerns is shown by his providing two Arabic spellings of the city of Libyan Tripoli in connection with the birthplace of Britannicus in his notes to the *Historiae Augustae scriptores*.[137] But the widespread interest in topography was also owing to merchants and navigators who were trying to draw up ever more reliable charts and maps. The work of al-Idrīsī, with its details of distances, consequently came to be regarded as an important source. It was some time, however, before the author of the *Nuzhat al-mushtāq* was identified. We saw that he was known as the Nubian, 'Nubiensis', or as 'geographus Arabs', and he remained an object of speculation until 1646, when he was at last recognised by John Selden.[138] The Maronites Joannes Hesronita and Gabriel Sionita, who translated part of the *Nuzhat* into Latin in 1619, were unaware of his identity, and so was Casaubon. For Casaubon he was an Egyptian, since he called Egypt 'our country', and he

---

135   He was also interested in Arabic (and Turkish) inscriptions on coins and medallions. See Bodl., MSS Casaubon 11, fol. 150ʳ, and Casaubon 60, fols 109ʳ–112ʳ.
136   Grafton, *Defenders of the Text*, pp. 145–161.
137   Isaac Casaubon, *In Aelium Spartianum, Iulium Capitolinum, Aelium Lampridium, Vulcatium Gallicanum, Trebellium Pollionem, et Flaminium Vopiscum Emendationes ac notae* (Paris, 1604), p. 266. The spellings he gives are طرابلس and اطرابلس
138   Toomer, pp. 23, 65, 68; idem, *John Selden: A Life in Scholarship*, (Oxford, 2009), vol. 2, p. 619.

lived 'over four hundred years ago', thus in the twelfth or thirteenth century.[139] But Casaubon was also struck by the respect with which the 'geographus Arabs', although clearly a Muslim, referred to Christ, and he made particular use of his description of the Holy Land. In his edition of Gregory of Nyssa of 1606 he quoted the geographer's passage on Bethlehem and his descriptions of the gates of Jerusalem and the Holy Sepulchre,[140] while in his attack on Baronius, *De rebus sacris et ecclesiasticis exercitationes* of 1614, he cited him on the distance from Bethlehem to Jerusalem.[141]

The terminology of Avicenna attracted special attention in medical circles, and the quest for reliable manuscripts of Avicenna's writings on medicine induced many doctors to study Arabic. On a couple of occasions Casaubon corrected the Arabic in the Medici press edition of Avicenna's *Qānūn*. In the notes to the *Historiae Augustae scriptores* of 1604 he pointed out an error in Avicenna's use of the term *conditum*, a pharmaceutical 'preparation'.[142] Two years later, in *De satyrica Graecorum poesi*, he quoted Avicenna in Arabic on priapism and again corrected an error in the Medici press version;[143] and in his edition of Persius of the same year, when discussing the herb *ocimum* (basil), he recommended the use of the Arabic medical lexicon in the Heidelberg library lent him by Lingelsheim for elucidating a vocabulary which had so often been misinterpreted.[144]

---

139 See Casaubon's comment in his edition of Gregory of Nyssa, *Ad Eustathiam, Ambrosiam et Basilissam epistola* (Paris, 1606), pp. 66–67: 'Eximius ille scriptor professione Muhammedanus, ut satis declarant varia eius operis loca, de Christo ubique honorificam mentionem habet: hoc vero capite veteres historias quibus fides Christiana firmatur, non minore studio persequitur, quantum ratio instituti ferebat, quam si ex fidelium numero esset. patria fuisse Aegyptium ex eo coniicimus, quod parte IV. climatis primi de Aegyptiaco Nilo (nam alterum facit Africanum: qui est Niger amnis) loquens, Aegyptum appellat ارضنا *terram nostram*. Vixit ante quadringentos et quod excurrit annos ...'
140 *Ibid.*, pp. 66–71, 103.
141 Isaac Casaubon, *De rebus sacris et ecclesiasticis exercitationes XVI* (London, 1614), p. 162.
142 Casaubon, *In Aelium Spartianum*, p. 337: '... et apud Avicennam, qui sumsit a Graecis, ut fere omnia, sed in Arabica eius editione ita scriptum hoc nomen quasi legisset apud Graecos, χόνδιτον pro κόνδιτον duplici errore. Quorum prior ipsius est Avicennae, qui solens talia passim in peccato admittit. Alter error non est auctoris, sed librarii, qui ق pro ت perperam scripsit: prono lapsus, et quem saepe deprehendere licet in libris Arabicis, Romae nuper magro Reip. literariae bono, editis.'
143 Isaac Casaubon, *De satyrica Graecorum poesi, et Romanorum satira libri duo* (Paris, 1605), p. 99: فريسيموس, he writes, should be فرياڢيسموس.
144 Persius, *Satirarum liber*, ed. Isaac Casaubon (Paris, 1605), pp. 335–337. Here Casaubon's treatment of the Arab physicians Serapion and Avicenna seems to be based on the Latin translations. In discussing the divergent spellings *phelengemischki* and *pherengemischki* he observes (pp. 336–337): '... l et r in omnibus linguis facile invicem commutantur. Fuisse autem utramque scriptionem Arabibus in usu diserte observat Arabs auctor qui medicum

Only once did Casaubon refer to his collection of Arabic proverbs – in his notes to the *Historiae Augustae scriptores* where he compared one of them to a Latin equivalent.[145] He made, on the other hand, a somewhat catholic use of his acquaintance with Arabic vocabulary. In his analysis of the word *caesa*, defined in the same text as the 'Moorish' for elephant, he pointed out that the Arabic, like the Hebrew, is *fīl* (of which he gave only the Hebrew transcription, in a smaller typeface better suited to the rest of his book).[146] Like a number of his contemporaries, such as William Bedwell, he speculated on etymology. He had corresponded with Scaliger about the etymology of the name 'Heliogabalus' and advanced the words for 'God', *Allah* and for 'mountain', *jabal*, which he printed in Arabic.[147]

One of the sources Casaubon quoted in this connection is of particular interest: the Mozarabic Latin-Arabic manuscript glossary in Leiden, dating from the twelfth century, about which Christmann enquired in 1611.[148] Originally owned by Postel, who had given Franciscus Raphelengius his first Arabic lessons, it had been lent, by way of Andreas Masius, to Christophe Plantin's firm in Antwerp for use by Masius's pupil Guy Le Fèvre de la Boderie when he was preparing the Syriac text for the Antwerp Polyglot Bible. Postel subsequently allowed Raphelengius to keep it. It would form the basis of the Arabic-Latin lexicon on which Raphelengius was still working in Leiden when he died in 1597, and it was also used by Scaliger as one of the main sources for his own Arabic-Latin 'Thesaurus'. As long as he lived, Scaliger appears to have had it on permanent loan from its true owners, Raphelengius's sons and heirs, to whom it returned after Scaliger's death.[149] The manuscript, therefore, always remained in Leiden, but Casaubon nevertheless cited it as though he had seen it himself. How can this be explained?

Scaliger had copied out extracts from the glossary, and the Latin words from the extracts, but not the Arabic ones, had been published by Bonaventura

---

Lexicon scripsit, quod in illustrissimi Electoris Palatini Heidelbergensi bibliotheca servatus. Is liber utilissimus fuerit ad corrigendas mendas illas quibus Arabica editio Avicenae, et omnes Arabum interpretes passim scatent. Nec pauca in eo genere nobis observata, cum superioribus mensibus beneficio Georgii Michaelis Lingelsheimii, viri nobilissimi, illius libri usum ab optimo principe impetrassemus. Sed de his volente Deo alias.'

145 Casaubon, *In Aelium Spartianum*, p. 401.
146 *Ibid.*, p. 97.
147 *Ibid.*, p. 316. Cf. *Scal.Cor.*, vol. 4, p. 132. For Bedwell's use of Arabic for etymological purposes see Hamilton, *William Bedwell*, p. 75.
148 UBL MS Or. 231. The glossary was published by C.F. Seybold, *Glossarium latino-arabicum ex unico qui exstat codice Leidensi undecimo seculo in Hispania conscripto* (Berlin, 1900).
149 See below, pp. 254–255.

Vulcanius in his *Thesaurus utriusque linguae* of 1600.[150] On the first of the two occasions on which Casaubon cited the Mozarabic glossary, when referring to a jewelled clasp, he was clearly quoting from Vulcanius.[151] The second reference concerns the gender of the word 'moon'.[152] Casaubon pointed out that قمر (*qamr*) was masculine, but added that هلالة (*hilāla*), which he claimed to have seen in the Mozarabic dictionary, was feminine. *Hilāla*, however, does not exist. It is not to be found either in the Mozarabic glossary or in Scaliger's 'Thesaurus'. Both the glossary[153] and the 'Thesaurus'[154] give the correct form, هلال (*hilāl*), which is masculine. Nevertheless, there can be no doubt that Scaliger was Casaubon's source. In the last, separately paginated, section of the 1598 edition of his *De emendatione temporum*, the 'Veterum Graecorum fragmenta selecta', Scaliger gave *hilāla* and said he found it in the Mozarabic glossary.[155] The mistake, therefore, is Scaliger's, who may have confused the singular with the plural (اهلة, *ahilla*), which is indeed in the glossary.[156]

By far the most frequent references to Arabic in Casaubon's publications are to the New Testament. These are mainly to the Gospels – but not exclusively so. In his notes to Gregory of Nyssa he cited an Arabic version of the Epistle to the Galatians.[157] The passage he discussed is Galatians 6:16, and the word to which he referred is στοιχήσουσιν. He preferred the Arabic *tabi'a* (which he transliterated in Hebrew), 'to follow', to the Latin translation *incedere*. In many of his references to the Gospels Casaubon simply confirmed a reading in Syriac as he found it in Tremellius's 1569 edition of the Peshitta (printed in Hebrew characters).[158] Otherwise he was critical of the Medici press

---

150   P.S. van Koningsveld, *The Latin-Arabic Glossary of the Leiden University Library* (Leiden, 1977), pp. 5–6.
151   Casaubon, *In Aelium Spartianum*, p. 46: 'clusor, qui gemmas auro concludit', p. 46. Cf. Bonaventura Vulcanius, *Thesaurus utriusque linguae, Hoc est Philoxeni, aliorumque veterum authorum Glossaria Latino-graeca et Graeco-Latina* ... (Paris, 1600), col. 703.
152   Casaubon, *In Aelium Spartianum*, p. 293. For John Selden's objections in connection with his work on the bisexuality of the gods, see J.P. Rosenblatt, *Renaissance England's Chief Rabbi: John Selden* (New York, 2006), p. 58.
153   Seybold, *Glossarium*, p. 338. Cf. UBL, MS Or. 231, fol. 87ᵛ.
154   UBL, MS Or. 212, fol. 48ʳ.
155   Scaliger, *De emendatione temporum*, p. xxv: 'Nam etiam hodie هلالة ἀλιλάτ τὸ φεγγάριον, id est, Lunam μηνοειδῆ et nascentem vocant, cum secundo die a coitu visionis suae potestatem facit, ut loquitur Vitruvius. Itaque in pervetusto Glossario Latino Arabico legimus هلالة Lunula, et هلال Noctiluca.' I owe this reference to Gerald Toomer.
156   Seybold, *Glossarium*, p. 299.
157   Gregory of Nyssa, *Ad Eustathiam*, p. 140. Casaubon is presumably quoting a manuscript since the version of Galatians published by Ruthger Spey gives an entirely different term (يوافقون): *Epistola Pauli ad Galatas* (Heidelberg, 1583), sig. F2ᵛ.
158   Casaubon, *De rebus sacris*, pp. 178, 250, 288, 289, 624, 714.

publication. Although we do not know for sure on what manuscript the Arabic text of the Gospels was based, it corresponds largely to what is now known as the 'Alexandrian Vulgate', the origin of which can be traced back to the thirteenth century when a Coptic (Bohairic) version was supplemented by passages from Syriac and Greek versions. The result was to be the basis of all the published editions of the Gospels in Arabic from 1591 to the twentieth century and has 'very little value for critical purposes'.[159] Casaubon can hardly have been aware of the complex genealogy of the version he was dealing with, but he certainly knew it should be treated with caution and that the Roman edition, published under the aegis of the Church, showed markedly Catholic tendencies. The passage about which he expressed the greatest perplexity – and where his Protestantism emerges in full – was Matthew 16.18, the ideological foundation of the papacy, 'Thou art Peter, and upon this rock I will build my church.' The Arabic of the Roman edition runs انت الصخر (*anta al-ṣakhr*), 'Thou art the rock', which was even better suited to the Roman interpretation than the Greek or the Vulgate.[160]

For Casaubon's command of Arabic the evidence is contradictory. Hardly any of the references to Arabic in his publications can be advanced as proof of a deeper knowledge of the language, any more than his citations of the Syriac New Testament suggest a mastery of Syriac. Casaubon's letters, notebooks and marginalia provide far more information, but we are also faced with a problem. He relied, as we saw, on the help of Adriaen Willemsz.[161] The very fact of their collaboration makes it hard to judge Casaubon individually. The heavily annotated copy of the *Ajurrūmiyya*, for example, is almost certainly a result of their working together. But what about the translation of al-Idrīsī?[162] We know that Casaubon started reading the *Nuzhat* together with Adriaen, but we also know that he continued to translate it after Adriaen's death,[163] so the question remains of how much Casaubon did on his own. The surviving translation covers little more than twenty-five pages of the original (which is over 320 pages long). It comprises the prologue, and the first five sections and the

---

159   B.M. Metzger, *The Early Versions of the New Testament: Their Origin, Transmission, and Limitations* (Oxford, 1977), p. 265.
160   Casaubon, *De rebus sacris*, p. 388: 'Sed nos tirones horum studiorum semel volumus monitos; illam Arabicam paraphrasin, quae magno alioquin bono literarum Roma prodiit, recentem esse admodum, et multo meliores illa alibi reperiri: hanc vero nuper ῥωμαίζειν: quod nunquam tamen certius deprehendi potest, quam hoc loco.' He was also critical on p. 638.
161   *Cas.Ep.*, pp. 185, 216; *Ephemerides*, vol. 1, pp. 481–482, 509, 510, 525.
162   Bodl., MS Casaubon 17, fols 81ʳ–96ʳ.
163   See above, p. 79.

beginning of the sixth of the first chapter or 'region', mainly concerning the Nile and the eastern part of Africa. Initially the translation is hesitant. Arabic words are given in brackets, and sometimes more than one possible meaning is suggested. As it progresses, however, it becomes more fluent and testifies to an ability to cope with what is generally a clear, and not particularly challenging, printed text.

Yet Casaubon never seems to have been altogether confident about his Arabic. We see this from his decision to ask Erpenius to translate the proverbs attributed to Abū 'Ubayd rather than to do so himself. When he was on his own, moreover, Casaubon had difficulty in reading certain Arabic manuscripts. Early in 1606 the Scottish scholar James Hepburn showed him a letter dated March 1588 (996 AH) from the ruler of Morocco, Aḥmad al-Manṣūr, to the Portuguese pretender Antonio.[164] Antonio, prior of Crato, the bastard son of the Infant Luis, had reigned briefly in 1580 but was ousted by the Spanish forces at Alcántara. He subsequently withdrew to the Azores and from there tried to enlist the assistance of the queen of England and Aḥmad al-Manṣūr against Spain. That is the context of the somewhat obscure letter filled with the rhetorical flourishes characteristic of official documents. Casaubon dispatched a copy to Scaliger in order to obtain the correct Christian dating,[165] but the only copy that appears to survive is the one made by Barbatus, probably in about 1608. The Arabic of the letter is poor and the spelling inconsistent. 'Sultan' is spelt in two different ways, correctly with a *sīn* (سلطان) and incorrectly with a *ṣād* and a *wāw* (صولطان). The meaning is often unclear. Barbatus's somewhat clumsy Arabic hand is not too difficult to read, but the original may have been more so. Although Casaubon described the Arabic as 'degenerate' since it is in 'Moroccan dialect,' he could not always decipher it and failed to understand *fuṣūlhā wāabuwābhā* (فصولها وابوابها), meaning 'the parts and sections' [of the agreement]. He thought that the second *bā* in *abuwābhā* was a *lām* and read the word as *abwāl* (ابوال), the plural of *bawl* (بول), 'urine'.[166]

The most complex case of all is the collection of Arabic proverbs, a text which, in its published form, tells us much about the advance of Arabic studies in general. When Casaubon first sent him the work with Scaliger's Latin translation, in 1609, Erpenius was in Saumur and already aware of having made

---

164   BL, MS Burney 367, fol. 199[r-v].
165   *Scal.Cor.*, vol. 6, pp. 293–295, 313, 355–357. Scaliger replied (p. 313): 'Illud diploma, praeterquam quod litera tum Africana, quae deterrima omnium, tum cursiva, ut vocant, quae impeditissima est, descriptum est, pessime ab eo qui descripsit, repraesentatum est. Praeterea maior pars verborum est stilo, ut vocant, Cancellariae. Quem ne nos quidem, ut concipitur ab hominibus nostratis aut Latinae linguae, intelligimus ...'
166   Bodl., MS Casaubon 11, fol. 85[r].

greater and faster progress in Arabic than any of his contemporaries. He tended to be excoriating about his fellow-Arabists. He accused Kirsten of knowing no Arabic at all.[167] He had told Casaubon that Barbatus was unsatisfactory as a teacher,[168] and he lamented Bedwell's slowness and his reliance on a limited number of sources.[169] He was dismissive of the Mennonite Jan Theunisz, who taught Arabic in Leiden before he himself was given the chair.[170] And in the marginalia which he, too, added to Hubert's al-Ḥasanī manuscript once used by Adriaen Willemsz, he made it clear that a number of the corrections which Adriaen had proposed to the original were completely wrong.[171] He even had reservations about his early master Aḥmad ibn Qāsim al-Ḥajarī; and al-Ḥajarī, who called on Erpenius in Leiden, was amused at his former pupil's Arabic, so classical and inflected. He pointed out that he did not observe the *jazm*, the vowellessness of certain consonants,[172] and, he might have added, spoke a language quite unlike anything spoken by the Arabs themselves.

Erpenius wrote a cordial letter to Casaubon about the proverbs. Nevertheless he observed that Scaliger's notes and translation required much improvement. Indeed, he felt that Scaliger's version was far inferior to the much criticised Maronite translation which Casaubon had been sent from Rome. The Arabic itself, he said, was so full of mistakes in the vocalisation as to be virtually incomprehensible. He admitted that this must have been due to the intervention of colloquial forms and the copyist's ignorance of the classical language, but the implication of his criticisms was that none of the scholars involved – Casaubon, Scaliger and Adriaen Willemsz – had fully appreciated the defects of the text.[173]

---

167   Cas.Ep., p. 356: 'Vidi nuper initium secundi libri Avicennae, cum versione Latina et notis Kirstenii. Quam iste homo est nugator! Quam parum peritus Arabismi, et coeptis suis impar!' Cf. p. 662: 'Petrus autem Kirstenius nuper reliquos duos Grammaticae suae libros evulgavit; qui quales sint, vis uno verbo dicam? Non merentur legi. O inscitiam hominis et audaciam!'
168   See above, p. 10.
169   Hamilton, *William Bedwell*, p. 31.
170   Cas.Ep., p. 666.
171   BnF, MS Arabe 4127, p. 26.
172   Al-Ḥajarī, *Kitāb naṣir al-dīn*, p. 263: '… tenia muchos livros aravigos y savia la gramatica araviga rrazonablemente y hablava comigo de la manera que la gramatica dispone: declinando los nombres sin poner en ellos chazme y conjugando los bervos.' Cf. pp. 195, 268–269 and, for a slightly different version in Arabic, p. 140: الفعل يعرب الاسما ويصرف ('he declines the nouns and conjugates the verbs').
173   Cas.Ep., p. 355: 'De Proverbiis Arabicis nuper serio coepi cogitare, quo ea, quam fieri poterit, explicatissima et politissima propediem tibi queam offerre, ut facias iis כאשר טוב בעיניך. Multa omnino occurrunt in iis mutanda et corrigenda, tum in textu Arabico, tum in translatione Latina et notis Domini Scaligeri. Nam textus Arabicus pessime est

Erpenius was right in observing that the rules of classical Arabic were violated repeatedly in the manuscript he received, but was he right in calling these violations mistakes? If we look closely at the transcriptions of the original, by Casaubon and Adriaen Willemsz, the matter appears in a different light. The text is one of many examples of what is now known as Middle Arabic, a state of the Arabic language heavily influenced by colloquial usage which is of increasing interest to linguists at the moment.[174] Like many editors to this day, Erpenius believed that, in order to be published, an Arabic text should necessarily be in the classical language, and he used his publications for teaching it to his Leiden students. So he improved and purified the Arabic of the proverbs. He corrected the plurals, turning, for example, the oblique *al-sayyādīn* ('huntsmen') of the original into the correct nominative, *al-sayyādūn* (1:12), and changing the nominative *al-khāṭifūn* ('robbers') into the oblique *al-khāṭifīn* (1:18). He supplied the vowel and other orthographic signs he had learnt from the Arab grammarians. He added an *aliph* with the *tanwīn* or 'nunation' to undefined substantives in the accusative case. In proverb 1:37 he preferred the construct state *fū* (فو) to *fam* (فم), 'mouth'. By classicising the text and turning it into Qur'anic Arabic he had transformed it.

However Erpenius may have judged his transcription, Casaubon's plan to publish the proverbs is another example of his originality as a scholar. When he received the manuscript hardly any text of Arabic literature existed in print. Works in Arabic had indeed appeared – on history, topography, medicine, mathematics and grammar. There were devotional writings and, above all, parts of the New Testament, so frequently used as linguistic exercises. The proverbs, on the other hand, belonged to an entirely different genre. In 1591 Johannes Drusius, the former professor of oriental languages at Oxford, who had subsequently been given the chair of Hebrew at the University of Franeker,

---

punctatus, ac ita quidem, ut in compluribus proverbiis tot errata sint, quot syllabae. Rationem ejus esse puto, quod is, qui puncta apposuit, literalem Arabicam non novit, sed vulgarem tantum, secundum quam ea punctavit; etsi subinde paulo ulterius progredi voluerit, et doctorum punctationem adhibere, quam tamen infeliciter, aut non, didicerat. Itaque omnino statui etiam exacte secundum Grammaticam, et rationem Alcorani punctare (ita tamen, ut ea puncta, quibus mutatis sensus aliquomodo mutari queat, intacta relinquam) quo libellus iste commodus queat esse praelectioni; nihil enim tale hactenus impressum est: scelestissimus autem Alcoranus id non meretur, nec ejus etiam exemplar quilibet habere potest. Translationem Domini Scaligeri quod attinet, vix alteram partem bene videtur vertisse: interdum ab unius et alterius verbi; interdum a totius proverbii sensu aberravit; et certe quaedam sunt, quorum ne unum quidem verbum bene transtulit; cujus causa est proculdubio, quod pessime scriptum exemplar habuerit, et festinando et aliud agendo ea verterit ...' See the analysis by Vrolijk, 'The Prince of Arabists'.

174 K. Versteegh, *The Arabic Language* (Edinburgh, 1997), pp. 114–129.

had indeed included some Arabic proverbs (transliterated in Hebrew) in his *Apophtegmata Ebraeorum ac Arabum*,[175] but Casaubon, Scaliger and Erpenius made a still greater contribution. After their publication Erpenius himself edited further collections of Arabic sayings, while later European Arabists also advanced to different works of literature – to the poets, to the authors of the *Maqāmāt* in rhyming prose, and to the tales which would at last give the culture of the Arabs a more popular appeal.

Casaubon was equally original in his approach to other aspects of Arab culture. In his edition of the satires of Persius, which came out in 1605, he announced his intention of discussing Arabic poetry,[176] his interest in which is further confirmed by the passages he underlined and commented on in his copy of the 1566 Antwerp edition of *De totius Africae descriptione* by Leo Africanus.[177] That he never carried out his plan could be attributed in part to shortage of time, but also to the lack of texts available in the West at that moment. The project itself, however, is yet another indication that he was in the vanguard of students of Arabic. Bedwell had no such insight and, in his various apologies of Arabic, never refers to its poetry. Erpenius, on the other hand, would present a stirring defence of Arabic poetry in his orations of 1613 and 1620.[178]

Casaubon had started to read the Qur'an in 1602, and although he often dismissed it in the traditional terminology of anti-Islamic rhetoric, referring to its 'many absurdities and abominations'[179] and 'insane figments' (charges which he also applied to the writings of the rabbis),[180] he had a genuine interest in

---

175 N. Malcolm, 'The study of Islam in early modern Europe: obstacles and missed opportunities' in P.N. Miller and F. Louis, eds, *Antiquarianism and Intellectual Life in Europe and China, 1500–1800* (Ann Arbor, 2012), pp. 265–288, esp. pp. 266–267. For an interesting study of the future of the Arabic proverbs in New England see A. Whiting, 'Thomas van Erpe at Harvard. Samuel Whiting's use of three Arabic proverbs in *Oratio quam comitijs Cantabrigiensibus Americanis peroravit* (1689)' *Early American Literature* 53 (2018), pp. 851–876.

176 See his edition of Persius, pp. 133–134: 'De Arabum rhythmica poesi, qua fere contextum est Muhammedis Alcoranum, si clementissimo Deo fuerit visum, alias disseremus.'

177 BL, shelf-mark 793.d.2, fols 19ʳ–20ᵛ, 42ᵛ, 132ʳ.

178 Erpenius, *Orationes*, p. 33; R. Jones, 'Thomas Erpenius (1584–1624) on the Value of the Arabic Language' *Manuscripts of the Middle East* 1 (1986), pp. 15–25, esp. p. 19.

179 Gregory of Nyssa, *Ad Eustathiam*, p. 132: 'ridicula multa et abominanda'.

180 Casaubon, *De rebus sacris*, p. 100: 'Nam si valet haec ratio, ut credi omnia debeant, quae aliquis haereticus aut fanaticus finxerit, quia Deus illa potest facere: quid est cur deliria Rabbinorum, aut etiam Mahometis, respuamus? etsi enim stupenda sunt, et insana figmenta, quae in libris Rabbinorum aut in Alcorano recitantur, nihil tamen est adeo portentose excogitatum, quod, si omnipotentiam Dei respicimus, fieri a Deo non posse credi debeat.' See also p. 211.

it. He transmitted to Scaliger some notes on it by 'a Dominican', of which he was himself critical.[181] Erpenius discussed with him the meaning of certain Qur'anic terms.[182] The various lists of his books show that he owned at least three copies of the Qur'an in Arabic, a Latin translation which must have been the Bibliander edition of 1543, and the so-called *Epitome Alcorani*,[183] an anonymous Latin abridgment of the text edited in 1543, together with medieval material and other pieces of his own, by Johann Albrecht von Widmanstetter.[184]

Casaubon's immense interest in all aspects of the Arab world, in its topography, its history and its religions, as much as in its language, is attested not only by his translation of al-Idrīsī but also by the marginalia in his copy of Leo Africanus. When Leo wrote his *Descrittione dell'Africa* in Italian in 1526 he had converted to Christianity. That was the price of his release from Castel S. Angelo, where he had been held ever since the pirates who had captured him off the island of Djerba had presented him as a gift to the pope, Leo X. But he was born a Muslim and had served the ruler of Morocco, and he would seem to have reverted to Islam after his departure from Italy.[185] His religious sympathies thus remain something of a mystery, and Casaubon speculates on them on the flyleaf of his copy. But Leo's work contains a wealth of details about the institutions of Islamic Africa, and particularly of Morocco, and his accounts of Arab learning and Arabic literature would be exploited by European apologists of Arabic such as Erpenius.[186] These items of information too were underlined by Casaubon, who seems to have been especially interested by what Leo had to say about Egypt.

Another work to which Casaubon provided abundant marginalia was the Maronite confession of faith published entirely in Arabic by the Typographia Medicea in 1595,[187] probably a relatively late acquisition, which he might

---

181 *Scal.Cor.*, vol. 5, p. 112: 'De notis Dominicani Alcoranicis, quia oblitus sum in epistola, his accipe. Chartae sunt paucae, eaeque solutae ac semiputridae. Continentur iis aliquot scharath versae, nescio qua fide, certe non ad verbum.' Cf. also pp. 39, 122, 137, 143, 150, 159–160.
182 *Ibid.*, p. 666.
183 Bodl., MS Casaubon 22, fols 44ʳ (nos 51, 53 and 55), 60ᵛ, 69ʳ.
184 Discussed by H. Bobzin, *Der Koran im Zeitalter der Reformation. Studien zur Frühgeschichte der Arabistik und Islamkunde in Europa* (Beirut, 1995), pp. 348–359; Burman, *Reading the Qurʾān*, pp. 103–110, 248–252.
185 N. Zemon Davis, *Trickster Travels: In Search of Leo Africanus, a Sixteenth-Century Muslim between Worlds* (London, 2007), pp. 55–69, 153–90, 245–260.
186 Jones, 'Thomas Erpenius', p. 18.
187 Casaubon's copy of the *Brevis orthodoxae fidei professio* (Rome, 1595), is BL, shelf-mark 753.G.72(2). Judging from Bodl., MS Casaubon 22, fol. 121ʳ, he owned the work when he was in London.

have read on his own. He marked those points which a Protestant would have regarded as contentious, such as the Catholic claim that the Maronites believed both in the seven sacraments and in purgatory, and he underlined the passages concerning the Church councils in which the Eastern Churches played an important part – Nicaea, Chalcedon, Constantinople and Florence. He could have intended to use the information in his *De libertate ecclesiastica* of 1607, or, more probably, in the continuation of his critique of Baronius, in answer to Baronius's statements about the Eastern Churches and their imminent unity with Rome.

Interest in the Christians of the East was widespread in the circle of scholars surrounding Casaubon. Their Churches, generally regarded as a more faithful reflection of the early Church than the Catholic one, were admired by Protestants for their resistance to the overtures of the papacy. This same concern with the Eastern Christians also led Casaubon to expand his knowledge of their languages. His curiosity was by no means limited to Hebrew, Aramaic, Syriac and Arabic. He owned material in Ethiopic[188] and in Armenian,[189] although he never actually studied them. When he was in Paris he came across a bilingual version of the New Testament in Arabic and Coptic, as well, it would seem, as a trilingual manuscript, in Coptic, Arabic and Greek, of the Epistle to Philemon, belonging to Cardinal Du Perron. He consequently tackled Coptic.[190] Even if he does not appear to have gone much further than the alphabet, his efforts, made some twenty years before Athanasius Kircher truly introduced Coptic into the West,[191] do credit to Casaubon's intuition of its importance.

5   Conclusion

As a practitioner of the Arabic language Casaubon may have had his shortcomings, and his competence probably fluctuated according to the presence (or absence) of his teachers, but as a student of Arab culture he often displayed extraordinary foresight. His criticism of the Arabic New Testament and his interest in Arabic literature are some of the first signs of developments that would come into their own later in the century. The enthusiasm with which

---

[188]   Bodl., MS Casaubon 22, fols 34ʳ, 120ʳ. See also the list of Ethiopic words, transcribed and taken from Francisco Alvares's account of the quest for Prester John, in MS Casaubon 30, fols 75ʳ–78ʳ, and his comments on the Ethiopic liturgy in MS Casaubon 60, fols 62ʳ–63ᵛ.
[189]   Bodl., MS Casaubon 22, fol. 44ʳ.
[190]   Bodl., MS Casaubon 11, fols 51ʳ–52ᵛ.
[191]   On the early history of Coptic studies see A. Hamilton, *The Copts and the West 1439–1822. The European Discovery of the Egyptian Church* (rev. edn. Oxford, 2014), pp. 197–199.

he tackled the language infected others. The better contemporary Arabists – Kirsten, Christmann, Tengnagel, Hubert, Scaliger, Bedwell, and the best of all, Erpenius – regarded him as an equal who could understand their problems and appreciate their discoveries. Befriended by the foremost scholars in Europe, Casaubon was also one of the great letter writers of his day. Even if he owed his reputation to his activity in fields other than Arabic, it was as an Arabist, too, that he assumed a pivotal position in the Republic of Letters. His writing desk, like those of Erasmus, Nicolas Fabri de Peiresc, Jean Le Clerc, Mathurin Veyssière de La Croze and Gottfried Wilhelm Leibniz, became one of its ephemeral capitals. We are indebted to his letters for much of what we know of the development of Arabic studies in Europe in the early seventeenth century, and he played a central part in the reception and transmission of ideas about the subject.

Acknowledgements

I owe the idea of this article, originally published in the *Journal of the Warburg and Courtauld Institutes* 72 (2009), pp. 143–168, to Joanna Weinberg and Anthony Grafton, for whose encouragement and cooperation I am deeply grateful. Their research bore fruit in A. Grafton and J. Weinberg, *"I have always loved the Holy Tongue". Isaac Casaubon, the Jews, and a Forgotten Chapter in Renaissance Scholarship* (Cambridge, Mass., 2011) and my contribution was a brief appendix, 'The long apprenticeship: Casaubon and Arabic', pp. 293–306. My thanks also go to Paul Botley, Jenny Boyle, Charles Burnett, Johannes den Heijer, Jill Kraye, Christopher Ligota, Gerald Toomer, Arnoud Vrolijk, and Colin Wakefield for their invaluable advice.

CHAPTER 4

'To Divest the East of All Its Manuscripts and All Its Rarities'

The Unfortunate Embassy of Henri Gournay de Marcheville

Seldom has a French embassy to the Ottoman Empire been planned with such intellectual ambitions and ended in such failure as the one led by Henri de Gournay, comte de Marcheville, in 1631. It was originally intended to be a scientific expedition which would surpass in magnificence and in the standard of the scholars accompanying it anything organized previously. Its object, according to Joseph Bougerel, the biographer of Pierre Gassendi, was 'rien moins que d'enlever à l'Orient tous ses manuscrits et toutes ses raretez'.[1] Yet it ended with Marcheville's being enticed onto a vessel and sent back to France on the orders of the sultan, Murad IV, who had narrowly failed to have him murdered. Historians have consequently been hard on Marcheville.[2] Their judgement, although by no means incorrect, is based largely on reports written by his fiercest enemy, Philippe de Harlay, comte de Césy, the ambassador whom Marcheville was supposed to replace and whose blunders he was supposed to repair. This article proposes to reassess Marcheville, whom some of his contemporaries seemed readier to forgive than posterity and who, in his efforts to bring the most brilliant members of the Republic of Letters to the Levant, met with particular favour among scholars.

Henri de Gournay de Marcheville was baptised in Lunéville in the duchy of Lorraine in 1585. He was the second son of Regnaut de Gournay, bailiff of Nancy and head of the Council of State of Lorraine, by his second wife, Louise d'Apremont, who brought the estate of Marcheville near Verdun into the family. Henri himself married Philiberte de Châtillon, whose first husband, Robert de Ravenel de Sablonnières, died in 1609.[3] Their marriage was childless and seems

---

1 J. Bougerel, *Vie de Pierre Gassendi* (Paris, 1737), p. 91.
2 G. Tongas, *Les relations de la France avec l'empire ottoman durant la première moitié du XVIIe siècle et l'ambassade à Constantinople de Philippe de Harlay, Comte de Césy (1619–1640)* (Toulouse, 1942), p. 23: 'Son caractère extravagant, sa conduite insensée transformèrent son séjour en Turquie en une série ininterrompue d'insuccès et d'aventures indignes de sa qualité d'ambassadeur de France'. Tongas seems to have been dazzled by his admiration for Harlay de Césy.
3 F.A. Aubert de la Chenaye-Desbois, ed., *Dictionnaire de la noblesse* (Paris, 1863–76), vol. 9, p. 551; vol. 16, p. 802. Various mistaken ideas about Marcheville have been perpetuated by

to have ended in 1630 when Philiberte decided to join a religious order.[4] Henri de Marcheville's first appointment was as tutor to the future duke of Lorraine, Charles IV, and in 1622 the reigning duke, Henri II, turned the Marcheville estate into a county. Marcheville's next nomination was as first chamberlain to Gaston d'Orléans, Louis XIII's brother and heir apparent to the French throne.

Throughout his career Marcheville displayed some of the contradictions characteristic of many French statesmen and diplomats who had a connection with the Levant in the early seventeenth century. They manoeuvred their way between the religious aspirations of the *dévots* and the practical policy traditionally pursued by the French government. The *dévots*, the more uncompromising French Catholics, were the spiritual heirs of the anti-Huguenot *Ligue* of the previous century. They tended to disapprove of the alliance with the Turkish sultan which had been a more or less constant feature of French policy ever since François I had received a capitulation or trading privilege in 1535 and had turned to the Turks for military assistance against his great European rivals, the Habsburgs. The *dévots*, attracted by an anti-Islamic crusade, often preferred the prospect of an agreement with the Habsburg rulers of Austria and Spain and, sometimes, of an anti-Ottoman alliance with the shah of Persia, who, they thought, might be converted to Christianity. A majority of Frenchmen, on the other hand, undoubtedly shared many of the persuasions of the sixteenth-century *politiques*, agreeing that religious compromise was preferable to civil unrest and that much was to be gained from good relations with the Porte – commercial advantages and the prospects of holding in check the ambitions of the Habsburg emperor. On the extreme edge of this second category we have the so-called *libertins érudits*, a loose group of intellectuals – philosophers, scientists, novelists, poets and playwrights – suspected, sometimes rightly, of a very considerable freedom of thought, with powerful

---

historians. He is said to have had a German mother. In fact it was his father's first wife, Agnes von Esch, who was German. By her Regnaut de Gournay had his first son, Charles, comte de Gournay, bailiff of Nancy and seneschal of Lorraine, who died in 1632. Marcheville is also said to have acted as tutor to the duc d'Orléans, and to have had a son with him in Istanbul who was arrested on the sultan's orders for assisting in the escape of a slave. Saint-Priest, *Mémoires sur l'ambassade de France en Turquie et sur le commerce des Français dans le Levant* (Paris, 1877), p. 212.

4 According to Peiresc, in a letter to the Capuchin missionary Gilles de Loches of 22 July 1634, this was why Marcheville was able to accept the cross of the Knights of Malta on his way back from Turkey. A. de Valence, ed., *Correspondance de Peiresc avec plusieurs missionnaires et religieux de l'Ordre des Capucins 1631–1637* (Paris, 1891), pp. 74–5: '… le dict Sr de Marcheville a prins la croix de l'ordre, ayant fait voir que sa femme estoit entrée en religion dez que luy fut declaré ambassadeur pour le Roy à Constantinople'.

protectors (who included Marcheville's employer Gaston d'Orléans), but also with relentless enemies.

Despite his many free-thinking friends Marcheville often approached the position of the *dévots*. He was one of the very first members of the crusading militia founded by Charles de Gonzague, duc de Nevers, in 1617, with the ultimate object of reconquering Jerusalem where the duke hoped to have himself proclaimed king.[5] Marcheville also became a protégé of Cardinal Richelieu, and above all of Richelieu's *éminence grise* revered among the *dévots*, the Capuchin Joseph Leclerc du Tremblay. Père Joseph entrusted him with his first diplomatic missions. In 1625 he was dispatched to Germany to negotiate with Archduke Leopold V, the younger brother of the emperor Ferdinand II, about concessions to the French in the Valtelline. In the following year he held talks with Maximilian, duke of Bavaria, and subsequently approached other German princes – the electors of Saxony, Mainz and Trier – in an attempt to win them over to the French sphere of influence.[6] Although he was ultimately unsuccessful, Marcheville gained a reputation as an expert on German affairs.[7] Bailiff of Saint-Mihiel and a member of the royal council, he was an experienced diplomat by the time he was appointed ambassador to Istanbul in 1630.[8]

One of Marcheville's oldest and closest friends was a central figure in the Republic of Letters, the antiquarian with a life-long interest in the East, Nicolas Fabri de Peiresc.[9] A frequent guest of Peiresc in his summer house of Beaugency near Aix-en-Provence, Marcheville turned to Peiresc when he started to plan his embassy to Turkey in the summer of 1630 and Peiresc was only too pleased

---

5 BnF, MS Français 1054, fol. 15ʳ. He joined on 28 September 1617.
6 G. Fagniez, *Le Père Joseph et Richelieu (1577–1638)* (Paris, 1894), vol. 1, pp. 256, 266–273. See also G. d'Avenel, ed., *Lettres, instructions diplomatiques et papiers d'état du Cardinal de Richelieu*, vol. 7 (Paris, 1874), pp. 584–585, 641, 978.
7 In April 1627 Fabri de Peiresc referred to him as 'Mr de Marcheville qui cognoit l'humeur de cette nation là [sc. the Germans], comme la nostre'. P. Tamizey de Larroque, ed., *Lettres de Peiresc aux frères Dupuy* (hereafter *Lettres de Peiresc*) (Paris, 1888–98), vol. 1 (Paris, 1888), p. 195.
8 For a bibliography see A.H. de Groot, *The Ottoman Empire and the Dutch Republic. A History of the Earliest Diplomatic Relations 1610–1630* (Leiden-Istanbul, 1978), p. 328.
9 *Lettres de Peiresc*, vol. 2, p. 259. 'Au reste Mr de Marcheville desire bien d'estre agrégé à vostre Academie avant que de s'en aller en Constantinople, et m'a dict qu'il vous iroit voir,' Peiresc wrote to Jacques Dupuy in July 1630. 'Il y a vingt ans que je le cognois, et que j'ay veu en luy de tres belles et recommandables parties de probité, de curiosité, et de courtoisie; vous aurez du contentement à le gouverner, et je participeray à ses obligations'. For Peiresc's position and influence in the Republic of Letters see P.N. Miller, *Peiresc's Europe: Learning and Virtue in the Seventeenth Century* (New Haven-London, 2000).

to cooperate.[10] A year later Peiresc would tell Marcheville that he himself would have been delighted to accompany him to Turkey but no longer felt that his health allowed him to do so.[11] It was through Peiresc that Marcheville sent out his invitations to other intellectuals of distinction – above all to the mathematician Pierre Gassendi and the antiquarian Lucas Holstenius.[12]

Gassendi had just returned from a journey to the Low Countries, where he had met some of the leading scholars. He had established a friendship with Jacobus Golius, the professor of Arabic and of mathematics at Leiden, and his letters to him testify to his own interest in Arabic. By August 1630 Gassendi had been invited to join Marcheville's embassy which was supposed to leave France in November. Both Gassendi and his rich friend and patron, the treasurer François Luillier, planned to accept.[13] Gassendi was determined to make the most of the expedition, culturally and scientifically. He consequently returned to the study of Homer and of Strabo.[14] Assured by Marcheville that he would also be able to visit Alexandria, he looked forward to checking Ptolemy's astronomical observations.[15] He wrote to the astronomer and mathematician

---

10 P.N. Miller, 'Peiresc, the Levant and the Mediterranean' in A. Hamilton, M.H. van den Boogert and B. Westerweel, eds, *The Republic of Letters and the Levant* (Leiden-Boston, 2005), pp. 103–122, esp. pp. 108, 115.

11 Bibliothèque Inguimbertine, Carpentras, MS 1874, fol. 602^r.: 'Je me suis marry que de ne pouvoir assez promettre de santé pour un si long voyage …'.

12 *Lettres de Peiresc*, vol. 2, pp. 257–258, Peiresc wrote to his friend Jacques Dupuy on 26 July 1630 about: '… Mr de Marcheville, qui est pressé de passer oultre et m'a donné avec un peu de peine le temps qu'il a fallu pour escrire à Mr Holstenius par le susdict courrier et à Mr Gassendy, pour les inviter à faire quant et luy le voyage de Constantinople, où il a grand envie de les mener. Et j'estime que l'occasion est si belle pour leur curiosité qu'ils ne la debvront pas laisser perdre, et qu'ils y proffiteront grandement pour le public, et saulveront de bons livres, et aultres singularitez, s'ils veullent'.

13 Gassendi's eagerness is confirmed in a letter from Jacques Dupuy to Peiresc. *Lettres de Peiresc*, vol. 2, p. 703: 'Les belles offres de Mr de Marcheville à Mr Gassendi l'ont comme vaincu et crois asseurement qu'il fera le voyage de Levant avec luy. Mr Lhuillier le consent, ne pouvant pour luy presentement le faire à cause de la caducité de son père, et de l'incertitude où les officiers sont touchant le droit annuel, mais ces deux obstacles ostez, je vous assure qu'il fera ce voyage pour contenter son esprit, et cette absence ne diminuera en rien l'affection qu'il porte au dit sieur Gassendi'.

14 Bougerel, *Vie de Pierre Gassendi*, p. 92: 'Gassendi qui pensoit sérieusement à ce voyage, se mit de nouveau à la lecture d'Homere, parcequ'il vouloit porter avec lui Strabon qui a pris à tâche d'éclaircir ce poëte …'.

15 *Lettres de Peiresc*, vol. 5, pp. 354–5. 'Monsr Gassendi', Peiresc wrote to Holstenius, 'qui estoit à Paris trez bien logé, a obtenu la mesme permission de son patron pour ne perdre une si belle commodité et s'en va fourny comme il fault de grands instruments de mathematiques faire de belles observations celestes et terrestres, avec promesse que luy a

Wilhelm Schickard in Tübingen on 27 August, expressing his excitement about the journey and assuring both him and Johann Kepler that he would be delighted to be of service to them in the East.[16] Three days later he repeated his offer to Galileo Galilei in Florence.[17] He announced his plans to the historians Erycius Puteanus in Louvain and Aubert Le Mire in Antwerp and to the philosopher Hendrik Reneri in Utrecht.[18] He told Golius that he awaited an Arabic dictionary and proposed to study the language further in the course of his travels.[19]

---

faicte Mr le Comte de Marcheville de l'envoyer en Alexandrie pour aller examiner et faire la comparaison de ce qu'il y pourra observer avec ce que Ptolemée en a laissé par escript afin de pouvoir tirer de plus exactes consequances de ce qui s'y trouvera de conformité ou de différence, car c'est un homme des plus curieux et des plus exactes qui se soient encores meslez de ces sciences là'.

16 Pierre Gassendi, *Opera omnia*, vol. 6 (Stuttgart-Bad Cannstatt, 1964), p. 36: 'Caeterum si fortuna volet, potero fortassis et ipse brevi tempore te ex Oriente adiutare. Cogito enim Constantinopolim, Alexandriam et alia illa celebria loca eo fine invisere, ut prae caeteris organis instructus Quadrante aurichalcico, quem (Radio duobus Pedibus longiore) Willebrordus ille Snellius amicus meus singularis, dum esset in vivis, confici mihi curaverat, insigneis quasdam Observationes, quantum licebit, perficiam. Discedere spero proximo Novembri, una cum viro illustri, meique impense amante Comite Marchavillaeo, qui eo tempore ad eas oras est Orator nomine Regis Christianissimi concessurus. Id perscribere, si videbitur, ad Keplerum poteris (oblitus sum enim literis ad illum hoc inserere) ut si fortassis illinc gentium opellam meam uti velit, significare valeat. Tu vero mihi praecipue manda, si quid meam egeas industriam: ac si quis forte apparatus faciendus esse videbitur, cura ante finem Octobris Literas tuas accipiam'.

17 *Ibid.*, p. 37.

18 *Ibid.*, pp. 39–40, 42.

19 *Ibid.*, pp. 38–9: 'Mea illa Arabica intermissa potius, quam dimissa sunt, exspectatione Dictionarij, quod neque prece, neque pretio comparare hactenus licuit ... Superavi iampridem omneis Grammaticae molestias; si Dictionarium habuero, en quid mihi iam incidat, quod Arabismi maiorem spem faciat. Habemus hinc virum illustrem Comitem Marchaevillaeum, qui Regius Orator proximo Novembri Constantinopolim discessurus est. Is cum me amet et nescio quid de studiis meis conceperit, testatur sibi esse in votis, ut ego illunc una concedam ad peragendum Observationes, quascumque lubuerit, et licuerit. Itaque iam pene constitui, sic generose invitatus, et virum sequi, et cumprimum ad eas oras appulero Arabicam linguam ita colere, ut ad qualecumque Grammatices studium conversationem adiiciens, sperem me tandem aliquid eruditionis consequuuturum. Tu seu illinc opellam mea fortassis indigueris, seu gnarus locorum, et rerum illarum directorium mihi quoddam impertiri haud grave habueris; poteris aut ante Novembrim hunc rescribere, aut cum illunc pervenero, apud illustrem Oratorem literas ad me destinare'. Schickard replied on 4 October expressing his anxiety about Gassendi's departure and his excitement about the plans he and 'illustris Comes Marchaevillaeus' hoped to carry out. W. Schickard, *Briefwechsel, Band I, 1616–1632*, ed. F. Seck (Stuttgart-Bad Cannstatt, 2002), p. 582.

Lucas Holstenius, from Hamburg, was planning to produce an edition of the writings on historical geography by the minor Greek authors.[20] The future librarian of the Vatican, at the time of Marcheville's invitation he was employed in Rome by Cardinal Francesco Barberini (the nephew of the pope, Urban VIII). Peiresc wrote to him on 27 July 1630 in the most flattering terms, stressing the immense admiration which Marcheville had for him.[21] And to Holstenius Marcheville was even more lavish in his promises than to Gassendi. Not only would Holstenius be spared any expense, but the ambassador would actually bring a printing press which would be at his disposal all the time he cared to spend in Istanbul and which would enable him to produce anything he might like to have printed on a larger scale in Paris or elsewhere. Marcheville promised to accompany him personally on the sultan's own ships to visit the ruins of Athens and other Greek sites, to inspect the libraries of Mount Athos, and to travel throughout the Holy Land.[22]

Holstenius was tempted to accept. He was not ready to leave in November 1630, but nor, as it turned out, was Marcheville. On 12 February of the following year, however, Holstenius told Peiresc that the very uncertainty of Marcheville's plans was an obstacle. Nobody seemed to know for sure either when he would travel or what route he would take. Some said he would make the whole journey by sea, others that he would sail from Venice to Ragusa and then proceed by land. Besides, Holstenius had affairs of his own which he had to settle in Germany. The best solution, he suggested, would be if he could make his own

---

20   For a survey of Holstenius's career see A. Mirto, *Lucas Holstenius e la corte medicea. Carteggio (1629–1660)* (Florence, 1999), pp. 7–36; P. Rietbergen, *Power and Religion in Baroque Rome. Barberini Cultural Policies* (Leiden-Boston, 2006), pp. 256–295.

21   *Lettres de Peiresc*, vol. 5, p. 352: '... il a ouy parler de vous, et de vostre eminente doctrine et piété, et desireroit avec une passion extreme de vous pouvoir mener en Constantinople, et m'a fort conjuré de vous en escrire et de vous en supplier ...'.

22   *Ibid.*, p. 351: 'Il m'a dict que si vous vous y resolvez il vous donnera rendez vous à Malte pour vous y prendre en passant ..., il m'a dict de plus qu'il fera porter une imprimerie pour vous servir d'entretien si vous vouliez faire quelque sesjour en Constantinople, et y faire tirer au net ce que vous vouldrez envoyer reimprimer plus copieusement à Paris ou ailleurs. Mais ce que j'y trouve de plus considerable est qu'il faict estat d'aller pour l'amour d'un homme de lettres comme vous en personne avec des galeres du grand seigneur ou autrement pour aller visiter et faire fouiller dans les ruines d'Athenes et autres lieux plus celebres de la Grece, et surtout dans la bibliothèque du Mont Athos, ne voulant rien espargner pour la descouverte et acqusition des bons livres et autres notables singularitez et monuments de l'Antiquité. Il faict mesmes estat de passer en Terre Saincte et de voir en passant par l'Asie Mineur tout ce qui s'y pourra recognoistre de plus recommandable. Voyez si ce party sc peult honnestement refuser. Il ne vous astraindra poinct à plus de sesjour que vous ne vouldrez, et vous donnera toutes sortes de bonnes adresses et supports pour voyager par tout le Levant où vous vouldrez ...'.

way to Istanbul overland, and join Marcheville there.[23] But in June 1631 he was still unable to leave Rome, because Barberini was in particular need of him.[24]

As Peiresc tried to persuade Holstenius to be part of Marcheville's train, so he endeavoured to urge the brilliant young Jean-Jacques Bouchard, who was also working for Francesco Barberini in Rome, to make the journey.[25] Another intellectual whom Marcheville hoped to recruit was Descartes, who had settled in Holland in 1628. Descartes himself had been interested in Arabic work on mathematics. His decision to study at the University of Leiden owed much to the presence there of Golius, and the copy Golius had made in Aleppo of the Arabic version of the *Conica* of Apollonius of Perga, which contained Books V–VII, previously unknown in the West.[26] In his turn Golius became a supporter of Descartes.[27] Yet, for all his interest in Arabic, Descartes was by no means as eager to accept Marcheville's offer as Gassendi, Holstenius or Bouchard. He received the invitation from the instrument-maker Jean Ferrier in Paris in October 1630, and, at first, did not take it seriously. He had never met Marcheville, he told Marin Mersenne, and saw no reason why Marcheville should ever have heard of him. When he realised that the invitation was indeed authentic he was sorry that it had not been made four or five years earlier, when he would have accepted with alacrity. As it was he had neither the time nor the desire to travel.[28] Marcheville continued to postpone his departure. First he

---

23   L. Holstenius, *Epistolae ad diversos*, ed. J.F. Boissonade (Paris, 1818), pp. 197–198, 202–203, 214–215, 219.
24   Bibliothèque Inguimbertine, Carpentras, MS 1874, fol. 601ᵛ.
25   *Lettres de Peiresc*, vol. 4, pp. 66, 71. On Bouchard see R. Pintard, *Le libertinage érudit dans la première moitié du XVIIᵉ siècle* (Paris, 1943), vol. 1, pp. 200–203, 209–214, 231–245. On his dealings with Marcheville see pp. 202, 239, 610.
26   T. Verbeek and E.-J. Bos, *Descartes en Leiden. Vrienden en vijanden, bewonderaars en bestrijders. Catalogus bij een tentoonstelling in de Universiteitsbibliotheek Leiden, 30 januari–9 maart 2003* (Leiden, 2003), pp. 9, 40–42; T. Verbeek, 'A Philosopher's life' in T.M. Lennon, ed., *Cartesian Views. Papers presented to Richard A. Watson* (Leiden, 2003), pp. 53–69, esp. pp. 57–61. On Golius and Apollonius see also Toomer, pp. 50, 122, 183–185.
27   C.L. Thijssen-Schoute, *Nederlands Cartesianisme* (Amsterdam, 1954), pp. 74–79; T. Verbeek, *Descartes and the Dutch. Early Reactions to Cartesian Philosophy, 1637–1650* (Carbondale-Edwardsville, 1992), pp. 34, 39, 95.
28   Mme P. Tannery and C. de Waard, eds, *Correspondance du P. Marin Mersenne, religieux minime*, vol. 2 (Paris, 1645), p. 545. 'J'ay receu une lettre du mesme [Ferrier] il y a huit jours,' Descartes wrote to Mersenne from Amsterdam on 4 November 1630, 'par laquelle il me convie, comme de la part de Mr. de Marcheville, à faire le voyage de Constantinople. Je me suis mocqué de cela; car outre que je suis maintenant fort éloigné du dessein de voyager, j'ay plustost crû que c'estoit une feinte de mon homme, pour m'obliger à luy répondre, que non pas que Mr. de Marcheville, de qui je n'ay point du tout l'honneur d'estre connu, luy en eust donné charge, comme il me mande. Toutesfois, si par hazard cela estoit vray, ce que vous pourrez, je croy, sçavoir de Mr. Gassendy, qui doit faire le voyage avec luy, je seray

waited for the king to recover from an indisposition. Then, in March 1631, he accompanied Louis XIII to Dijon to confer with the duc d'Orléans.[29] When he finally set sail in July neither Gassendi nor Holstenius were ready, even if they still hoped to join him at a later stage. Yet Marcheville had indeed managed to assemble a small number of intellectuals. One of his secretaries was Jacques Angusse, another friend of Peiresc who had served earlier ambassadors and who, with a sound knowledge of Turkish and Persian, was a keen collector of Eastern manuscripts. Angusse brought with him his son, the younger Jacques Angusse.

As his interpreter and councillor Marcheville chose André Du Ryer. Between 1623 and 1626 Du Ryer had acted somewhat unsuccessfully as French viceconsul in Egypt, an appointment he owed to his first patron, the ambassador to Istanbul François Savary de Brèves to whom the consulate had been entrusted. He then returned to France and, in 1630, published a Turkish grammar, widely (but wrongly) regarded as the first of its kind, and established his reputation as an Orientalist. Later, in 1634, he would bring out a French translation of part of Saʿdī's *Gulistān*, thereby introducing the European reading public to Persian literature, and later still, in 1647, he would produce his French translation of the Qurʾan, the first complete translation into a European vernacular made directly from the Arabic to appear in print, and so influential as to be published, in its turn, in English, Dutch, German and Russian.[30]

Most of the intellectuals whom Marcheville wished to recruit had some connection with the world of the *libertins érudits*. According to the malicious Tallemant des Réaux, who himself sympathised strongly with the libertines, François Luillier, to whose bastard son Gassendi acted as tutor, was notoriously dissipated.[31] It was in his household, moreover, that Jean-Jacques Bouchard, a self-proclaimed atheist, sought refuge after a scandal resulting from his attempts to seduce his mother's chambermaids. Some of Marcheville's other travelling companions, although befriended by Peiresc, tended more towards the position of the *dévots*. When he returned to France in 1634 Marcheville was

---

bien aise qu'il sçache que je me ressens extremement obligé à le servir pour les honnestes offres qu'il me fait, et que j'eusse chery une telle occasion il y a quatre ou cing ans, comme l'une des meilleures fortunes qui m'eussent pu arriver, mais que pour maintenant je suis occupé en des desseins, qui ne me la peuvent permettre, ..'. Cf. also [A. Baillet], *La vie de Monsieur Descartes* (Paris, 1691), vol. 1, pp. 226–227.

29 *Lettres de Peiresc*, vol. 4, pp. 246–247.
30 Du Ryer's career and achievements are examined in A. Hamilton and F. Richard, *André Du Ryer and Oriental Studies in Seventeenth-Century France* (London-Oxford, 2004).
31 Tallemant des Réaux, *Historiettes*, ed. Antoine Adam (Paris, 1960–1961), vol. 2, pp. 87–90.

accompanied by the son of the typographer royal Antoine Vitré,[32] the printer of Du Ryer's Turkish grammar and already engaged in the preparation of the 'Paris' polyglot bible. Antoine Vitré has been described as 'le libraire du parti dévot'.[33]

Another of Marcheville's travelling companions in 1631 was the Minim Théophile Minuti. A protégé of Peiresc whom he supplied with manuscripts and antiquities, Minuti had already spent some years in the Levant. In 1629 he had sent Peiresc a copy of the Pentateuch in Samaritan, Hebrew, Syriac and Arabic characters (one of Peiresc's most cherished possessions which is now at the Vatican), two copies of the New Testament in Syriac, and a number of Arabic manuscripts. When he came back to France in 1630 he also brought with him some Coptic manuscripts, two mummies and a collection of coins and medallions from Cyprus.[34] Having savoured his value as an agent, Peiresc was most eager that he should avail himself of Marcheville's expedition to assemble further 'rarities'. And with Minuti travelled a second scholar from Provence, François Gallaup, sieur de Chasteuil.

Gallaup de Chasteuil had once been a mathematician with a pronounced interest in astrology. He was also an accomplished biblical scholar, with excellent Greek, Hebrew and Aramaic. Staying at Peiresc's house at Beaugency in 1629 he worked with Peiresc and Minuti on the copy of the Samaritan Pentateuch and came to the conclusion that the Samaritan version was far later than was generally believed. At the same time he was drawn more and more to asceticism. According to one of his hagiographers, Louis XIV's court preacher Gaspard Augeri, Gallaup was attracted by various features of the Levant.[35] He hoped to visit the Holy Places, to follow in the footsteps of Christ and relive his sufferings; he wished, as a missionary, to confute the local heretics, and most particularly the Jews and the Muslims; he was drawn by the solitude and the biblical associations of the Lebanese mountains; and he wanted to increase his acquaintance with the Bible and to improve his knowledge of the biblical languages. Since Gallaup never seems to have made the pilgrimage to Jerusalem, the first of these reasons seems unconvincing. His chief incentive was, rather, his desire to settle in the Lebanon and combine an ascetic existence with an

---

32 *Lettres de Peiresc*, vol. 3, pp. 152, 155.
33 A. Adam, *Théophile de Viau et la libre pensée française en 1620*, repr. (Geneva, 1966), p. 386.
34 S.H. Aufrère, *La momie et la tempête. Nicolas-Claude Fabri de Peiresc et la curiosité égyptienne en Provence au début du XVIIe siècle* (Avignon, 1990), pp. 109–112, 171–181; N.-C. Fabri de Peircsc, *Lettres à Claude Saumaise et à son entourage (1620–1637)*, ed. Agnès Bresson (Florence, 1992), p. 83.
35 G. Augeri, *Le Provençal solitaire au Mont Liban, ou la vie de Monsieur François de Gallaup, Sr. de Chasteuil, Gentil-homme de la Ville d'Aix* (Aix-en-Provence, 1671), pp. 88–97.

intensive study of Arabic, and above all of Syriac in an area where it was still a living language.[36] Marcheville's embassy provided him with the chance to do so. Gallaup burnt his notes on astrology in order to free himself from any temptation and, together with Minuti and four large chests full of books, he joined Marcheville when the ambassador called on Peiresc on his way to Marseilles.[37]

Marcheville set sail on 20 July 1631. The vessel which carried him and his immense suite was of such splendour – in a later report to the king Marcheville attributed the extravagance and magnificence of his embassy to his desire to defend the honour of his country[38] – that it would draw crowds of admiring Turks when it at last arrived in Istanbul.[39] On the way Marcheville stopped in Malta. On 1 August he was at Kythera in the Greek Archipelago. He disembarked on the island of Miconos, from where he visited the ruins in Delos, and then made for Chios. While he was in Chios a group of his officers seem to have attacked a Turk and were only saved from the wrath of the local inhabitants by the good sense of the cadi. Marcheville also met the Ottoman grand admiral (*kapudan paşa*), Cambulat Mustafa Paşa, who, we know from Gallaup de Chasteuil and his biographer, entertained him courteously.[40]

A detailed list of instructions for Marcheville had been drawn up in Paris on 6 March 1631.[41] One of the main objects of his embassy was to see to the welfare of the Catholics in the Ottoman Empire. The missionaries were to be his

---

36 In a letter written in December 1632 Peiresc stressed Gallaup's interest in Arabic: 'Un gentilhomme de ceste ville que j'avois introduit chez Mr l'Ambassadeur a eu tant d'envie d'apprendre la langue Arabique qu'il s'en est allé exprez au Mont Liban'. He then added that he had heard from Gallaup in the Lebanon: 'il nous mande aussy que le peuple de ce lieu là parle plus correctement le Syrique qu'en aulcun aultre lieu de Levant ...'. *Lettres de Peiresc*, vol. 2, p. 399.
37 The part of Minuti and Gallaup in Marcheville's expedition and their dealings with Peiresc are described in F. Marchety, *La vie de Monsieur de Chasteüil solitaire du Mont-Liban* (Paris, 1666), pp. 17–59. See also Augeri, *Le Provençal solitaire*, pp. 94–101; G. de Vaumas, *L'Éveil missionnaire de la France (d'Henri IV à la fondation du Séminaire des Missions Etrangères)* (Lyons, 1942), pp. 322–323.
38 Archive du Ministère des Affaires Etrangères, Paris, Correspondance politique Turquie 4, fols 409^v–410^r.
39 BnF, MS Fonds français 16173, fols 60^r, 66^v.
40 Marchety, *La vie de Monsieur de Chasteüil*, p. 43: 'Avant que de partir de cette Isle; ils rendirent visite au Capitan Bassa qui les receut avec toute la pompe et toute la magnificence d'un homme de sa condition puissant en autorité et en richesses'. Augeri, *Le Provençal solitaire*, pp. 102–109. The courteous encounter between Marcheville and the grand admiral is described p. 106.
41 For Marcheville's instructions see Tongas, *Les relations*, pp. 258–260; BnF, MS Fonds français 16173, fols 14^v–40^v.

particular concern, and he was to report regularly to the pope.[42] The Capuchins were recommended to him and he was told to keep an eye on the Jesuits, both to protect them and to monitor their behaviour. He was to ensure the safety of pilgrims to Jerusalem. He was also to secure the privileges of the French merchants, to act against piracy, and to assist in the liberation of Christian slaves. Where his foreign colleagues were concerned, he was advised to have a good relationship with the Venetians, the English and the Dutch, but to be wary of the Habsburgs. He should guard French interests from the intrigues of the Spaniards, suspected of trying to forge an alliance against France with a Muslim power, and he was to insist that traditional French precedence over the Austrian diplomatic representatives be observed. Not only was he to replace Harlay de Césy as ambassador, but he was to remedy his financial blunders. He was advised to cultivate the Ottoman officials and to be tactful in his behaviour towards them.

The standard of French ambassadors to the Porte had been declining steadily ever since the departure of François Savary de Brèves in 1606. One ambassador after the other had fallen ever deeper into debt, but Césy, who had run through a fortune while he was still in France, had been one of the very worst, and the French merchants in the Levant had suffered accordingly. Although Césy would beg the king in March 1632 to allow him to return to France,[43] his numerous financial commitments in Istanbul obliged him to stay. He claimed that he was prepared to allow Marcheville to profit from his experience and his magnanimous advice, but it was clear from the outset that he was doing his utmost to cross and frustrate Marcheville and to blacken his name in the reports he sent back to France.

Marcheville's arrival in Pera on 13 September 1631 was consequently far less agreeable than it might have been. In a letter written on the day of his arrival he complained to the secretary of state Claude Bouthillier about premises which were quite uninhabitable, falling to pieces and fit only for rats.[44] Marcheville, who also lamented the absence of any form of chapel in the embassy, was initially obliged to lodge with a French merchant.[45] Although Césy made a show of friendship he immediately started his defamatory campaign, stressing

---

42   The assiduous manner in which he did so, his correspondence with the pope, his cardinals, and the direction of the principal missionary organisation, the *Congregatio de Propaganda Fide* in Rome, as well as with the convents in the Ottoman Empire, is amply documented in BnF, MS Italien 519.
43   Archive du Ministère des Affaires Etrangères, Paris, Correspondance politique Turquie 4, fols 259^r; 261^r.
44   BnF, MS Fonds français 16173, fols 64^r–65^r.
45   *Ibid.*, fol. 71^v.

Marcheville's brutality, tactlessness and ignorance of local customs. According to Césy Marcheville wished to assume his position and functions as ambassador as soon as he arrived, thus before the traditional presentation of his credentials to the sultan and the leave-taking of his predecessor.[46] Here, however, Marcheville was simply following his instructions.[47] Where Marcheville seems to have acted on his own initiative was in calling on the sultan's ministers before he had been officially presented to the sultan himself. But the instructions were ambivalent. It was assumed that Marcheville would be presented to the sultan immediately after his arrival in September, whereas it was impossible for the presentation to take place before the middle of December.

And finally there was the quarrel with the Ottoman grand admiral, Cambulat Mustafa Paşa. What would seem to have happened is that, on his departure from Chios for Istanbul on 13 September, the French ambassador fired across the bows of the grand admiral's ship when he was asked to lower his flag to the sultan. Césy's report of the events is somewhat confusing. Marcheville, said Césy, complained to the grand vizir, to the grand mufti, and even to the sultan himself, about the grand admiral's conduct and engineered his dismissal on 17 December,[48] but this last detail is wrong. Ottoman sources show that Cambulat Mustafa Paşa remained in office until 1 July 1632.[49] The comte de Saint-Priest, who also reports the clash in his far later description of Marcheville's embassy, says nothing about the *kapudan paşa*'s dismissal,[50] and a more contemporary observer, Paul Rycaut, the English consul in Izmir who reconstructed the events with the help of information supplied by the English ambassador at the time, Sir Paul Wyche, wrote that 'Marcheville being arrived at Constantinople did greatly complain of the affront and violence he received from the Captain-Pasha; which though the Grand Signior and other Ministers seemed not to approve, yet the Ambassadour received little other satisfaction than fair words and promises, that his Honour should be again repaired'.[51]

---

46   Tongas, *Les relations*, pp. 261–269.
47   BnF, MS Fonds français 16173, fol. 37r. If Césy were still in Istanbul when he arrived, Marcheville was told, 'Sa Majesté entend que le dict Sieur de Marcheville … prenne dès lors le soin et maniement de ses affaires et jouisse des appointements de l'ambassadeur du jour de son arrivée'.
48   Tongas, *Les relation*, p. 26.
49   İ.H. Danişmend, *Osmanlı Devlet Erkânı* (Istanbul, 1971), p. 189. The appointment in July 1632 seems also to be confirmed in a letter written in that month by Marcheville to Stefano Giustiniani, the consul in Chios, where he refers to 'il Cap. Bassà novo di nome Regip' (BnF, MS Italien 519, fol. 30r).
50   Saint-Priest, *Mémoires*, p. 212.
51   Paul Rycaut, *The History of the Turkish Empire from the Year 1623, to the Year 1677* (London, 1680), p. 50.

Neither do Gallaup de Chasteuil's *dévot* biographer, François Marchety, nor Gallaup himself in a letter to his brother, say anything about the matter, but then they seem to have travelled on a different ship. The episode remains obscure. What is certain is that Marcheville soon found himself on the worst of terms with one of the most powerful Ottoman officials.

Advised principally by Du Ryer, Marcheville set about cultivating those Ottoman dignitaries with whom he had not yet managed to quarrel. He was particularly pleased, he said, with the appointment on 25 October of Müezzinzade Hafız Ahmed Paşa as grand vizir,[52] and he made the acquaintance of the grand mufti, Zekeriyyazade Yahya Efendi. The official introduction of Marcheville to the sultan, Murad IV, and the leave-taking of Césy, took place on 16 December 1631, with Du Ryer acting as interpreter and pronouncing the official address in Turkish. This was probably a very small part of the text which Du Ryer would later append to the manuscript of his Turkish dictionary in both Turkish and French and which contains a eulogy of Louis XIII suggesting the influence of Guez de Balzac's *Le Prince*.[53]

Persuaded that Marcheville and most of his staff were conspiring against him, Césy first blamed Marcheville's unorthodox behaviour on his secretary Jacques Angusse, and then shifted the blame onto Du Ryer.[54] Despite Césy's ceaseless intrigues, Marcheville does not seem to have realised immediately what Césy was up to. Indeed, his unceasing endeavours to persuade Peiresc's intellectual friends to join him suggests a sense of security. For most of 1632 and 1633 Gassendi and Luillier continued to plan their journey. Gassendi again

---

52   BnF, MS Fonds français 16173, fol. 71ᵛ.
53   Hamilton and Richard, *André Du Ryer* pp. 30–9. For the text of the 'Harangue' see *ibid.*, pp. 145–150. Besides this version, based on an appendix to Du Ryer's unpublished Turkish-Latin dictionary (BnF, MS Supplément turc 465, fols 335ʳ–340ᵛ), see also MS Fonds français 16173, fols 45ᵛ.–56ᵛ.
54   On 9 November 1631 Césy had already written about Marcheville that 'son intention estoit de m'aneantir à son arrivée s'il eust peu ... J'apprends par les discours des Marchands de Marseille residents icy qu'il a promis aux Marseillois de me fere sentir qu'il estoit plus leur amy que le mien ...' (BnF, MS Fonds français 15584, fol. 108ʳ). On 21 December he continued (Tongas, *Les relations*, p. 262): 'Nous continuasmes donc en bonne intelligence quelques jours et ne me scandalizay poinct de ce que Monsieur de Marcheville pour contenter son secrétaire Angusse faisoit toutes les expeditions de la Chancellerie et des vaisseaux, ce qui ne s'est jamais fait qu'apres le baisemains par les Ambassadeurs de toutes les Nations ...'. He referred in the same letter (p. 263) to 'le secretaire Angusse seul cause de tout ce mal, et dont la personne m'est sy suspecte que j'avois fait prier Monsieur l'Ambassadeur par le Pere Archange de Fossez de ne me l'envoyer jamais, car ses mauvais comportements durant qu'il esoit a mon service m'obligerent à le chastier par mes propres mains et à le congedier'. For his relations with Du Ryer, see Hamilton and Richard, *André Du Ryer*, p. 35.

wrote about it to Golius in March 1632 and in July 1633 he told Gabriel Naudé that, even if he and Luillier had had to abandon the project for the time being, they still hoped to travel either in November or in the spring of the following year.[55] The death of Luillier's father that autumn, however, proved an insuperable obstacle. Peiresc, who had initially urged Bouchard to join Marcheville, had grown more hesitant and now warned him against the dangers of the journey. Nevertheless, in August 1633 the ambassador was still asking Peiresc about Gassendi and told him to remind him of his promises.[56]

Marcheville was all the more eager for intellectual companionship after the departure of some of the original members of his suite. André Du Ryer was appointed the ambassador extraordinary of the sultan in July 1632 and left Turkey in the same month. Marcheville's warm words about him to the papal nuntio in France, his praise of his intelligence and ability, show how much he missed him.[57] And Marcheville was even more upset by the departure of Gallaup de Chasteuil. The increasingly ascetic Gallaup had insisted on living on his own in Istanbul in order to avoid the mundane distractions of embassy life. The fame of his learning spread, and he was soon being visited and consulted by Jews, Muslims, Greeks, Armenians and Arabic-speaking Christians, as well as by the Protestant minister of the Dutch embassy. But he was determined to make better use of his time in the Levant. He told Peiresc that he was unable to find satisfactory teachers either of Syriac or of Arabic in the Ottoman capital,[58] and, after consulting Minuti, informed the ambassador of his intention to settle on Mount Lebanon. He and Minuti left Istanbul on 26 July 1632. They set sail for Rhodes, where they spent three weeks, and then proceeded by way of Cyprus to Sidon. On 11 September, having adopted Maronite dress, Gallaup de Chasteuil, still accompanied by Minuti, set out for the Lebanese interior. To begin with he stayed with Jirjis 'Amīra, a member of the powerful Dūwayhī family, close to the centre of his bishopric, Ehden. This choice confirms Gallaup's scholarly intentions, for Jirjis 'Amīra, a former student at the Maronite College in Rome, had published a Syriac grammar in 1596, and it

---

55   Gassendi, *Opera omnia*, vol. 6, pp. 47, 58. Cf. also Gassendi's letter to Luillier on 3 March 1633 (Pierre Gassendi, *Lettres familières à François Luillier pendant l'hiver 1632–1633*, ed. Bernard Rochot (Paris, 1944), p. 93): 'J'oubliay dernièrement de vous dire que nous sommes bien obligé à Monsieur de Marcheville du grand soin qu'il prend desja de nous recevoir, mais que selon mon advis nous ne serons pas sitost prest de l'aller trouver ...'.

56   *Lettres de Peiresc*, vol. 4, p. 350.

57   BnF, MS Italien 519, fol. 30ᵛ: '... avenga, che al perspicace ingegno et nobil genio, che seco ha, vi sono in compagnia la pratica, et il maneggio: sicome n'ho visto l'esperienza; mentre è contentato d'essere meco da che venni qua . .'

58   Bibliothèque Inguimbertine, Carpentras, MS 1874, fol. 603ʳ.

was under his supervision that Gallaup pursued his Syriac studies and learnt Arabic.[59] Later, in December 1633, Jirjis 'Amīra was appointed Maronite patriarch, and Gallaup de Chasteuil stayed in other convents near Ehden, setting an example of ascetic devotion to the Maronites until his death in May 1644, a few days before that of Jirjis 'Amīra.[60] Minuti, on the other hand, travelled further, visiting Damascus and Aleppo before he was reunited with Marcheville in Istanbul.

Although Gallaup de Chasteuil was a man of few words – 'Mon Dieu', Minuti is reported to have exclaimed, 'faut-il que cet homme qui a de si belles lumieres parle si peu?'[61] – Marcheville, like most of those who knew him, was devoted to him. So distressed was the ambassador by his departure that he told Peiresc of his plan to follow him to the Holy Land and bring him back to Istanbul by any means.[62] Yet this was one of the many plans that Marcheville would never carry out. Instead, he had to cope with difficulties of increasing magnitude in the Ottoman capital. By May 1632 he was fully aware of Césy's hostility, and lamented it in a letter to the king.[63] In the same month a major change occurred in the sultan's policy and of this Marcheville would seem to have been one of the victims.

Murad IV had succeeded to the throne in 1623 at the age of twelve and, throughout his minority, he had been dominated by his ministers and his mother. The older he grew the more he resented this dependence. Between

---

59 On Jirjis 'Amīra see G. Graf, *Geschichte der christlichen arabischen Literatur*, vol. 3, *Die Schriftsteller von der mitte des 15. bis zum Ende des 19. Jahrhunderts: Melchiten, Maroniten* (Vatican City, 1949), pp. 338–339. On 'Amīra as Gallaup's teacher see *Lettres de Peiresc*, vol. 2, p. 399.

60 Vaumas, *L'Éveil missionnaire de la France*, pp. 322–323.

61 Augeri, *Le Provençal solitaire*, p. 52.

62 On 16 September 1632 Marcheville wrote to Peiresc: 'Je me plaigne de la desolation, où m'a laissé Mons.r de Chastueil par son esloignement d'icy. Je vous advoüe que je n'estois pas digne de l'y arrester, mais qu'il est vray qu'il n'y a rien que je n'eusse faict pour cela, s'il eust eu agreable d'en entrer en composition avec moy. Je n'ay pour ressource de ma consolation à cest esgard que le dessein d'aller tout le plustost que je pouray en la terre Saincte, et si je le trouve encor en ces cartiers là de l'enlever à quelque prix que ce soit, et de le ramener' (Bibliothèque Inguimbertine, Carpentras, MS 9542, fol. 165ʳ). Peiresc reported Marcheville's reactions to Bouchard on 2 December (*Lettres de Peiresc*, vol. 4, p. 80), and told Bouchard how delighted Marcheville would be if he could join him: 'Je m'asseure qu'il sera infiniment aise de vous y tenir, si vous continuez en ce dessain, auquel je ne suis pas neangmoins resolu de vous induire, au contraire je vous en desmouvroys trez volontiers si je pouvoys, pour les grands perils qu'il y fault passer et les incommoditez inevitables, qu'il ne fault point esprouver tant qu'on s'en peut deffendre'.

63 BnF, MS Fonds français 16173, fol. 77ʳ⁻ᵛ, where he refers to 'les amis de Monsieur de Cesy qui en lieu de m'assister sont les suelz qui me traversent le plus en toutes choses.'

November 1631 and February 1632 he was faced with a military rebellion organised by his former grand vizir Husrev Paşa. This was followed by an even more menacing revolt of the janissaries which broke out in March 1632 and was instigated by the new grand vizir, Topal Receb Paşa. Insurrections such as these were so many reminders of the sultan's vulnerability. Towards the end of May, however, Murad triumphed.[64] He had Topal Receb Paşa put to death. Having at last gained full control of the state, he endeavoured to implement a policy of military and financial reform. His savagery in doing so was notorious, and Marcheville soon felt its effects. In December 1633 he wrote to the king describing Murad's arbitrary brutality,[65] his lust for power, the terror he inspired in his subjects whom he would murder casually in the street and none of whom dared contradict him. Marcheville, moreover, may have been compromised by his friendship with Murad's earlier ministers, with the former grand vizir Müezzinzade Hafiz Ahmed Paşa, who was killed in the janissary revolt, and with the grand mufti Ahizade Hüseyn Efendi whose disgrace was imminent. For in January 1634 the grand mufti was unjustly accused of taking part in a conspiracy to overthrow the sultan and was deposed, exiled and executed, to be replaced by his predecessor, Zekeriyyazade Yahya Efendi.[66]

Yet there can be little doubt that Marcheville owed much, if not most, of his misfortune to his own foolishness. As early as 3 January 1632 the Dutch ambassador, Cornelis Haga, lamented the blunders due to the 'great and blind' faith in the papacy of a man 'always surrounded by priests and monks'. Later in the same month, he referred to Marcheville as 'the new *dévot* ambassador

---

64   J. von Hammer [-Purgstall], *Geschichte des Osmanischen Reiches, grossentheils aus bisher unbenützten Handschriften und Archiven*, vol. 5, *Vom Regierungsantritte Murad des Vierten bis zur Ernennung Mohammed Köprili's zum Grosswesir 1623–1656* (Budapest, 1829), pp. 132–192.

65   BnF, MS Fonds français 16173, fol. 94ʳ: 'Sire, ce Seigneur a depuis quinze ou seize mois pour object une severité sans exemple, et d'executer sans autre forme de justice tout ce que sa passion luy suggere aux despens de qui que ce soit ...'. The Swedish envoy, Paul Strassburg, reached a similar conclusion (Paul Strassburg, *Relatio de Byzantino itinere at negotiis in Ottomamica aula peraclis, necnon de statu ac facie Orientalis Imperii, qualis erat circa anni* MDCXXXIII in *Monumenta pietatis et literaria virorum in re publica et literaria illustrium selecta* (Frankfurt am Main, 1701), vol. 2, 213: 'Praeterea animosus, insolens, crudelis, vindictae cupidus et in affectus praeceps, foemineo sexui plus aequo addictus, pertinax, ambitiosus, dissimulator, avarus, memoria pollens, rectaque ratione et profundo judicio, qui collapsum imperii statum sub avi, parentis et fratrum regimine modis omnibus restaurare et ad priscam dignitatem potentiamque extollere inprimis conatur'.

66   Danişmend, *Osmanlı Devlet Erkanı*, pp. 122–123. For a more detailed and colourful account of the events see Hammer[-Purgstall], *Geschichte desOsmanischen Reiches*, vol. 5, pp. 167–169.

of France'.[67] According to the Swedish envoy, Paul Strassburg, he was not only in the thrall of the Jesuits but was also vain and incompetent.[68] The Austrian diplomatic representative, Johann Rudolf Schmid, was struck by Marcheville's energy, but also by his impulsive and irrational behaviour and his readiness to take offense on his own account and on that of the king of France.[69] These judgements are borne out by Jacques Dupuy, one of Peiresc's closest friends and most assiduous correspondents. Nobody felt sorry for Marcheville, he wrote to Peiresc on 9 April 1634, less than a month before the ambassador's ignominious ejection. His interference with the Orthodox patriarch was the result of his affected bigotry, and his unbounded vanity had led him to antagonise the most influential Ottoman officials. It was just as well for Gassendi, Dupuy added, that he did not join him.[70]

Not even Césy exaggerated Marcheville's tactlessness. Marcheville clearly succeeded in arousing the hostility of both the old grand admiral and his successor, Bostanci Cafer Paşa appointed in July 1632. He quarrelled needlessly with the Greek Orthodox patriarch of Constantinople, Cyril Lucaris, noted for his attraction to Calvinism. Although France, like the other Catholic powers, wished to have Lucaris replaced by a patriarch who might unite the Greek

---

[67] K. Heeringa (ed.), *Bronnen tot de geschiedenis van het levantschen handel. Eerste deel 1590–1660* (The Hague, 1910), p. 370: '... den heer ambassadeur, die van een grooten ende blinden ijver tot het pausdom gedreven wert ende altijt met papen ende munnicken omcingelt is ...'; p. 373: '... den nieuwen devotigen ambassadeur van Vranckrijck ...'.

[68] P. Strassburg, *Relatio de Byzantino itinere*, p. 213: 'Galliae Regis Orator tunc in Porta erat Henricus Gorne Comes de Marcheville, Vir externi splendoris aulicaeque comitatis ultra modum studiosus, in agendis rebus et negotiis parum versatus. Unde cum Romano cultui superstitiose addictus esset, ac Jesuitarum consilia pro oraculis haberet, saepius imprudenter et praepostere multa admittebat'.

[69] P. Meienberger, *Johann Rudolf Schmid zum Schwarzenhorn als kaiserlicher Resident in Konstantinopel 1629–1643* (Bern-Frankfurt, 1973), pp. 223–224: 'Diser war ein betagter, aber noch frischer und unruhiger mann, in seinem thuen furiosisch und unbedachtsamb, ein mensch, der umb ein leichte sach sich und seines königs reputation impegnierte'.

[70] *Lettres de Peiresc*, vol. 3, p. 703: 'Le moins mal qui puisse arriver à mon dit sieur de Marcheville est de s'en revenir. Personne ne le plaint sachant avec quelle imprudence et temerité il s'est gouverné en cette Cour; il a une vanité si estrange qu'il a creu effacer le lustre de tous les autres ambassadeurs qui l'avoient precedé, publiant tout haut devant son partement qu'ils trahissoient l'honneur de la Nation et de leur maistre, que luy alloyt restablir tres puissamment. Il affecte aussy une cagoterie extraordinaire et c'est ce qui l'a fait bander contre ce Patriarche Cyrille qui a esté restably en dépit de luy et luy a suscité une partie des indignitez qu'il souffre maintenant. Il est aussy fort mal avec Mr de Cesis qu'il méprisa d'abord, pensant, à son avènement, avoir assez de credit en cette Porte pour s'y pouvoir conduire sans ses conseils. Je trouve le bon Mr Gassendi bien heureux de ne s'estre point embarqué avec un esprit si extravagant, car tous ceux de sa maison courent grande fortune d'estre malmenez ...'.

Church with that of Rome, Marcheville had been specifically instructed not to intrigue against Lucaris during his embassy in Istanbul since the patriarch had powerful support. Only after his death, Marcheville was told in his instructions, should he try to arrange for a sympathiser with Roman Catholicism to succeed him.[71] Shortly after his arrival in Istanbul, on 22 December 1631, Marcheville had a cordial meeting with the patriarch. Within weeks of this meeting, however, despite his promises to the Dutch ambassador and the warnings of the Venetians, and despite his lack of any backing among the other members of the Orthodox Church, Marcheville decided to act contrary to his instructions and to proceed against Lucaris.[72] He promised vast sums to the Ottoman authorities (which the impoverished French embassy could ill afford), but achieved nothing. A little later he approached both the grand vizir Topal Receb Paşa, who had succeeded Müezzinzade Hafiz Ahmed Paşa in February 1632 and who was himself favourably disposed towards Lucaris, and the grand mufti Ahizade Hüseyn Efendi, with a document purportedly proving Lucaris's treachery to the Porte. The two men passed the document on to Lucaris. Such evidence of manifest intrigue did Marcheville's reputation little good at the sultan's court when Lucaris was regaining favour, and the patriarch prepared his revenge.[73]

Marcheville also made himself more disagreeable than was necessary to the diplomatic representatives of other nations. In accordance with his instructions he was particularly eager to damage the imperial cause, and regarded this as one of the main purposes of his embassy. He tried to have the Austrian missionaries replaced by French ones in the Krim, but he also attacked the imperial representative, Johann Rudolf Schmid, on a more personal level. Schmid liked to wear Hungarian dress. This, Marcheville told the Ottoman authorities, showed that he did not represent the emperor but simply the king of Hungary. He endeavoured to have the emperor's name replaced by that of the king of France in prayers for the protector of the Roman Catholic Church, and he claimed to take precedence over the imperial representative in the Catholic churches of Istanbul.[74] Césy reported with glee that on Easter Day of 1634 Marcheville made himself ridiculous by planning to prevent the imperial ambassador, Johann Rudolf von Puchheim, from attending mass. In the end, however, it was the members of Puchheim's suite, backed up by a body of

---

71 Marcheville's dealings with Lucaris are described in detail by G. Hering, *Ökumenisches Patriarchat und europäische Politik 1620–1638* (Wiesbaden, 1968), pp. 25–26.
72 For Haga's irate report to the Dutch States General in January see Heeringa (ed.), *Bronnen*, pp. 369–373.
73 BnF, MS Fonds français 16173, fol. 117r.
74 Hering, *Ökumenisches Patriarchat*, pp. 267–268; Meienberger, *Johann Rudolf Schmid*, p. 224.

janissaries, who drove the French out of the church.[75] It is little wonder that Marcheville, who was always ready to blame his mishaps on others, should have informed the French king that he had been the victim of his colleagues – of the Dutch, the Venetians, the Austrians, and Césy.[76]

The Ottoman authorities were ever more irritated by Marcheville's conduct. Determined to repair, expand and improve the embassy buildings, Marcheville had both a public chapel built and a private one erected in his residence.[77] Not only was this an added strain on the finances of the embassy,[78] but, in view of Ottoman regulations concerning the building of Christian churches, it was a dangerous and foolhardy move. The first reaction of the Ottoman authorities (informed, according to Marcheville, by the Venetian ambassador) was to impose an *avania* or fine in March 1633.[79] In January 1634 the grand admiral ordered the public chapel to be destroyed; Murad IV had all the Christian churches sealed and the foreign merchants' houses searched for weapons.[80] His next step was to confiscate the arms of the foreign ambassadors.[81] Marcheville, now blamed by his colleagues for all their mishaps, ended by having to pull down his private chapel as well.[82] Late in 1633, acting on the sultan's orders but probably at the instigation of the grand admiral, the sultan's officers hanged the ambassador's Armenian interpreter, Balthasar Motto, when it was suspected that he had been instructed by Marcheville to

---

75   Tongas, *Les relations*, pp. 281–282.
76   Archive du Ministère des Affaires Etrangères, Paris, Correspondance politique Turquie 4, fol. 409^r.
77   *Ibid.*, fols 109^v–110^r.
78   Marcheville's building expenses were one of the reasons behind the comments, almost certainly made by Sir Peter Wyche, in the appendix to R. Knolles, *Generall Historie of the Turkes, A Continuation of the Turkish Historie, from the Yeare of Our Lord 1628, to the end of the yeare 1637 Collected out of the Dispatches of Sr Peter Wyche, Knight, Embasadour at Constantinople, and others*, 5th ed. (London, 1638), pp. 23–24. The deputies from Marseilles are said to have arrived in Istanbul with 36,000 dollars which were to be used towards defraying the debts of some 300,000 dollars incurred by Césy. 'Which mony the new Embassador, Count de Marchevilles seized upon, and converted to his owne use, without any regard to cleer the old Embassador away: some of which perhaps was emploied in his new buildings.' For Césy's version of the events in a letter to Bouthillier dated 5 May 1634 see Tongas, *Les relations*, pp. 280–292.
79   Archive du Ministère des Affaires Etrangères, Paris, Correspondance politique Turquie 4, fol. 307^r.
80   BnF, MS Fonds français 16173, fol. 108^v. The episode is also reconstructed in some detail in Saint-Priest, *Mémoires*, p. 213.
81   BnF, MS Fonds français 16173, fol. 130^v.
82   *Ibid.*, fol. 126^r.

arrange for the escape of some Spanish and Italian slaves.[83] Shortly after, the sultan even tried to have the ambassador assassinated, and rumours reached France that he had succeeded.[84]

But if it turned out that Marcheville was paying a high price for ignoring the recommendation of tact in his instructions and perhaps for having backed the wrong political faction at the Ottoman court, what about Césy? Césy, it would seem, had managed to keep on the right side of the sultan. When the foreign ambassadors were disarmed, Césy was allowed to keep his weapons. Marcheville consequently saw the hand of Césy in his final disgrace.[85] On 2 May 1634 the sultan had Marcheville hoodwinked by the grand admiral into boarding a ship in the harbour of Istanbul and ordered him straight back to France.[86] As the ship rode at anchor Marcheville was joined by his belongings and the members of his staff. Césy was triumphant. He was at last free to resume his previous functions as French ambassador even if he was denied the official title.

Although Marcheville claimed to have been deeply insulted, the return journey was not as shaming as the manner of his departure. On 27 May he stopped off in Malta, where he was welcomed by the grand master of the Knights and given the cross of the order. He then went to Rome where he reported to Urban VIII and his cardinals.[87] By the end of July he was in France. His first stage on his way from Marseilles to Paris was Aix-en-Provence where he could confer with his old friend Peiresc.[88]

Despite the detraction of Césy, some of Marcheville's other contemporaries continued to speak highly of him. The French merchants in Istanbul signed

---

83   BnF, MS Fonds français 16173, fol. 90^v. See also Saint-Priest, *Mémoires*, p. 214; Tongas, *Les relations*, pp. 21–32.
84   Tongas, *Les relations*, p. 30; *Lettres de Peiresc*, vol. 3, pp. 69, 77.
85   Marcheville's suspicions are confirmed in a report by the Austrian envoy Schmid (Meienberger, *Johann Rudolf Schmid*, p. 225): 'Hierunder hat der verschlagene Conte de Cesy für sein persohn so gewusst zu spihlen, dass endtlichen durch des Sultan Murath bevelch man (anno 1634, Mai) mit gewalt den Conte di Marcheville auf ein Französisch schiff imbarchiert und gar spötisch wider nach Frankreich geschickt.'
86   BnF, MS Fonds français 16173, fol. 141^v. 'Je vous diray Monsieur,' Marcheville wrote to Bouthillier, 'qu'il n'y a rien jusques à cette heure que ie ne fasse presentement et à l'advenir pour donner moien à Monsieur de Cesy de s'en retourner. Mais Monsieur permettez moy que ie vous die que c'est un Demon, qui sans consideration de l'honneur et de l'interest du service du Roy et service de ses sujetz, met tous les jours tout autant qu'il peut mon honneur et ma vie en compromis ..'.
87   Marcheville's return journey is described in a letter to Antoine Vitré, BnF, MS Fonds français 16173, fols 212^v–217^r.
88   *Lettres de Peiresc*, vol. 3, pp. 152–5.

a letter in his favour in May 1634.[89] The members of his staff remained loyal. His secretary Jacques Angusse sent an emotional report back to France deploring the ambassador's appalling treatment at the hands of the grand admiral.[90] André Du Ryer remembered him affectionately.[91] Tallemant des Réaux, in his vignette of Harlay de Césy of whom he disapproved, implicitly contrasted his irresponsible extravagance with the good intentions of Marcheville.[92] And if Tallemant des Réaux was writing from a libertine perspective, Gallaup de Chasteuil's *dévot* hagiographer Marchety was equally benign in his description of Marcheville's embassy. Adrien Baillet, finally, Descartes's biographer at the end of the century with allegedly Jansenist inclinations, referred to Marcheville respectfully as a patron of learning.[93] Nor does Marcheville seem to have fallen into disgrace. On his return to France he went to Paris, and spent most of the following years between the capital and his estate in Lorraine. Judging from the letters Peiresc continued to write to him, he had a certain influence at court and remained close to his first protector, Père Joseph. In 1644 he was with the troops commanded by his former employer, the duc d'Orléans, in Spanish Flanders and, at the time of the siege of Gravelines, he acted as a liaison officer between the duke and the captain general of the Dutch Republic, Frederick Henry of Nassau, prince of Orange.[94] By the end of 1651 he was living at Marcheville.[95]

But what did Marcheville's embassy achieve from a cultural point of view? Marcheville himself was delighted to receive specific requests from Peiresc who corresponded with him throughout his embassy. In April 1633, for example, Peiresc enquired about ancient decorated bronze vases, wondering if drawings, measurements, and even moulds, could be made of the vases in

---

89   BnF, MS Fonds français 16173, fols 150^r–151^v.
90   *Ibid.*, 148^v–149^v.
91   In 1651 Du Ryer received an attestation both from Marcheville and, more surprisingly, from Harlay de Césy, about his good conduct in Istanbul. Hamilton and Richard, *André Du Ryer*, pp. 56, 136.
92   Tallemant des Réaux's comment (*Historiettes*, vol. 1, p. 63): 'Cesy fit tant de sortes de friponneries que tout le commerce cessa, et il fallut, au bout de dix-huit ans, y envoyer M.de Marcheville, qui eut bien de la peine à le tirer de là'.
93   [Baillet A.], *Vie de Descartes*, p. 226: 'Ce Comte qui n'avoit pas moins de générosité pour avancer les sciences songeoit à rendre son ambassade remarquable sur tout par le nombre et le mérite des Sçavans qu'il prétendoit mener à Constantinople et dans le Levant'.
94   C. Saumaise and A. Rivet, *Correspondance échangée entre 1632 et 1648*, ed. P. Leroy and H. Bots (Amsterdam-Maarssen, 1987), pp. 371–372. It is just possible that Marcheville was accompanied by Du Ryer, for this would explain Du Ryer's reference in the 1650s to 'wounds' he had received at war (Hamilton and Richard, *André Du Ryer*, pp. 53–54, 143).
95   *Ibid.*, p. 136.

the sultan's collection.[96] In March 1634 he asked Marcheville for information about musical instruments,[97] and when he returned to France the ambassador brought Peiresc the skin of a gazelle, the so-called *alzaron*, on which Peiresc could continue to pursue his zoological investigations.[98] But it was above all for collecting manuscripts that the expedition based in a city renowned for the richness and variety (as well as the high prices) of its bookshops proved fruitful. Not only did Marcheville himself send manuscripts back from Istanbul to Europe – he sent Peiresc a work on the Muslim sects in 1633[99] – but at least two members of his staff expanded collections of their own.

Jacques Angusse and his son returned from Istanbul in 1634 with one of the earliest collections of Persian, Turkish and Arabic manuscripts to enter France. Peiresc said he had seen 'five or six different dictionaries' and his correspondent, the philologist Claude Saumaise in Leiden, referred to 'three or four large Persian lexicons'.[100] A number of these and other texts acquired by Angusse have found their way into the Bibliotheque nationale de France – Sa'dī's *Gulistān*, the *Maqāṣid* (a Persian-Turkish vocabulary), the *Danistān*, and the dictionaries of Ḥalīmī and Shāhidī.[101]

Where André Du Ryer is concerned it is more difficult to identify what he acquired in Istanbul. He had spent over ten years in Egypt and the Levant before his appointment as Marcheville's interpreter and councillor, and had certainly bought some of his manuscripts in those years. But it is also probable that he added to his collection when he was with Marcheville, and acquired manuscripts which included Aḥmad ibn Isma'īl's account of the adventures of Seyyid Battal Gazi and Shāhidī's Persian-Turkish dictionary, *Tuhfe-i Shāhidī*.

---

96   Fabri de Peiresc, *Lettres à ... Saumaise*, p. 47.
97   *Ibid.*, p. 87.
98   Gassendi, *De viri illustris Nicolai Claudii Fabricii de Peiresc*, vol. 5, p. 319; Aufrère, *La momie el la tempête*, pp. 308–313.
99   Gassendi, *De ... Peiresc ... vita* in *Opera omnia*, vol. 5, p. 314: 'Fuit etiam Comes Marchaevilla, a quo accepit Librum de variis Muhammedanorum Sectis, et ad quem praescripsit cuius notae esse deberent caelaturae, camei, numismata, et id genus caetera, ex Oriente expetita'.
100 Fabri de Peiresc, *Lettres à ... Saumaise*, p. 221: 'Monsr de Marcheville', Peiresc told Saumaise on 20 November 1635, 'auroit mené en Constantinople le sr d'Angusse qui est encores à Marseille, mais qui a un fils à Paris, lequel a emporté quelques volumes en ces langues orientales, entre lesquels j'ay veu cinq ou six dictionnaires differants, qui vous pourroient bien servir, je m'asseure, car il y a bien du turc aussi bien que du persan interpreté en arabe ...'. A little later Saumaise wrote to the German physician and Arabist Johann Elichman about 'trois ou quatre lexicons persans fort amples.'
101 BnF, MS Latin 9340, fol. 302ʳ.

This last work would be of use to him in performing his translation of part of Saʿdī's *Gulistān* which appeared in 1634.[102]

It may well have been in Istanbul, moreover, that Du Ryer began to compile the Turkish-Latin dictionary on which he worked until his death in 1672, but which remained in manuscript. At the time of Marcheville's embassy, Turkish studies were being pursued actively by the European community in the Ottoman capital.[103] In the Capuchin convent in the embassy grounds, Bernard de Paris, particularly attached to Césy (to whose son he taught Latin), was already preparing his own French-Turkish dictionary. Translated into Italian by another Capuchin, Pierre d'Abbeville, the *Vocabolario italiano-turchesco* would be published in Rome in 1665 and would be regarded as being of the greatest use to missionaries. At the same time a Venetian, Giovanni Molino, was working in Istanbul as interpreter to various diplomats. Not only did Marcheville use him frequently, but he asked him to judge the quality of the Arabic of a translation of Scriptural and other edifying texts which the ambassador tried to distribute in Aleppo and in Cairo for the *Congregatio de Propaganda Fide*.[104] Molino, too, was preparing a Turkish dictionary, accompanied by a brief grammar, his *Dittionario della lingua italiana-turchesca* which came out in Rome in 1641.

In the course of his travels in Lebanon and Syria, as well as during his stay in Istanbul, Théophile Minuti was also active in his search for objects which might interest Peiresc. Besides sending him tuberose bulbs, he obtained an Egyptian scroll designed to accompany the dead which Peiresc described enthusiastically in a letter to his friend Samuel Petit.[105] Yet, for an expedition which set out with such high ambitions, this may seem a meagre harvest. In retrospect one of the most important features of Marcheville's embassy is the interest which it aroused among so many intellectuals of distinction. It testifies to the profound curiosity about the Ottoman Empire that prevailed in the Republic of Letters and which had a variety of reasons. Antiquarians, mathematicians, astronomers and archaeologists joined forces with Orientalists in their desire to record observations and return with trophies. Peiresc, Gassendi, Holstenius, Bouchard, even Descartes, were all intrigued by the possibilities the expedition had to offer, and Gassendi's letters and messages to Reneri, Golius, Puteanus, Le Mire, Schickard, Kepler and Galilei gives us an idea of how wide was the circle of sympathetic observers.

---

102   Hamilton and Richard, *André Du Ryer*, pp. 39–40, 159–170.
103   *Ibid.*, 59–71.
104   BnF, MS italien 519, fols 46ʳ–47ᵛ.
105   Fabri de Peiresc, *Lettres à ... Saumaise*, pp. 42–43, 83.

Acknowledgements

This article first appeared in Alastair Hamilton, Maurits H. van den Boogert and Bart Westerweel, eds, *The Republic of Letters and the Levant* [= Intersections 5] (Leiden: E.J. Brill, 2005), pp. 123–150. I am particularly grateful to Peter Miller for supplying me with copies of Peiresc's letters in the Bibliothèque Inguimbertine, Carpentras.

CHAPTER 5

From East to West

Jansenists, Orientalists, and the Eucharistic Controversy

Few movements were further removed from Oriental studies than Jansenism when it started in the 1630s with the abbé de Saint-Cyran's efforts to reform the convent of Port-Royal in Paris. Its teaching was based on that of a Church Father who met with particular favour in the West, St Augustine.[1] Even as its ideals expanded, they were essentially confined to the Western Church and Western problems – to combating the Jesuits, to arguing against Molinism and probabilism, and, ultimately, to bringing about a fundamental reform of the Church itself. And this is equally true of the origins of the eucharistic controversy. To start with it was an exclusively Western concern, prompted by the publications, in the late 1620s and early 1630s, by Huguenot ministers such as Edme Aubertin, in defence of the Calvinist teaching on the eucharist, which denied that the bread and wine underwent any transformation at the consecration.[2] In 1659 the two Jansenist leaders, Antoine Arnauld and Pierre Nicole, replied by restating the Catholic belief in transubstantiation in a brief preface to the eucharistic liturgy for use by the nuns of Port-Royal. Although they were still mainly concerned with the Church of the West, they added a long section with passages from the Fathers, many of whom were Greek, and wrote that the teaching of transubstantiation 'was so universally established, not only in the entire Church of Rome but also in all the communities which were separated from it, such as those of the Greeks and the Armenians, that no trace or memory suggests that there had ever been a different view.'[3]

Jean Claude, the Huguenot minister of Charenton, responded. He claimed that the current Catholic teaching could not be traced back any earlier than the tenth or eleventh centuries, 'the darkest and most polluted centuries, the most lacking in men of piety and learning, which Christianity has ever known.'[4]

---

1 As nobody knows better than Burcht Pranger. See, for example, his 'Augustinianism and drama: Jansenius' refutation of the concept of *natura pura*' in M. Lamberigts, ed., *L'augustinisme à l'ancienne faculté de théologie de Louvain* (Leuven, 1994), pp. 299–308.
2 J.-L. Quantin, *Le Catholicisme classique et les Pères de l'Eglise: Un retour aux sources (1669–1713)* (Paris, 1991), pp. 291–239.
3 *L'Office du S. Sacrement pour le jour de la feste, et toute l'octave ...* (Paris, 1659) sig. a4ʳ.
4 Jean Claude, *Réponse aux deux traitez intitulez la Perpétuité de la foy de l'Eglise Catholique touchant l'Eucharistie*, 7th ed. (Paris, 1668), p. 9.

Claude, moreover, denied that the Greeks had had a consistent belief in transubstantiation and expressed grave doubts about whether the other Christians of the East had either. To Claude's somewhat questionable sources for this claim we shall return. Arnauld and Nicole took up the challenge with enthusiasm. For this there were many reasons. First of all it allowed them to indulge in their favourite pursuit – polemic. This, their refusal to let any argument drop, to continue discussions way beyond their point of exhaustion, was to be one of the causes of their undoing.[5] But in this case the polemic was different from the ones to which they were accustomed. They normally devoted their energy to contesting the teaching of the Jesuits or to replying to the strictures of the papacy. Now, however, they could attack Protestantism. This had immense advantages. It meant that they could prove their own orthodoxy and spring to the defence of a teaching shared by the Roman Catholic Church as a whole. Rather than defending themselves against charges of heresy, they could appear as champions of the Church to which they never ceased to profess their devotion. And besides, defence of the eucharist could also serve as an answer to those of their enemies incensed by the publication in 1643 of *De la fréquente communion*, the work in which Arnauld rejected the widespread view, greatly encouraged among the Jesuits, that communion should be taken as frequently as possible. Arnauld justified his opposition by his deep veneration for the eucharist and his insistence on the need of a particular preparation before the faithful could partake of it. His enemies had noted with horror that the number of communicants had dropped appreciably as a result of his publication, and that he was encouraging not respect, but contempt, for the sacrament.

In their first edition of *La perpetuité de la foy de l'Eglise catholique touchant l'eucharistie* of 1664 the Jansenist leaders still concentrated all but entirely on the Western tradition. Only at the very end did they turn briefly to the Eastern Churches, criticising Claude's sources and maintaining again that there was no doubt that 'all the schismatic communions of the East are in agreement with the Church of Rome on the matter of transubstantiation.'[6] In order to bear out this last point, however, they would require assistance. Fine scholars, they were sufficiently acquainted with the Greek Fathers to fend for themselves,[7] but they also wished to prove that the Christians of the East in their entirety had always believed in transubstantiation and still did so. Jean Claude had already

---

5 This is justly emphasised in A. Adam, *Du mysticisme à la révolte: les Jansénistes du XVIIe siècle* (Paris, 1968), p. 157.
6 Antoine Arnauld and Pierre Nicole, *La perpetuité de la foy de l'Eglise catholique touchant l'eucharistie* (Paris, 1664), p. 495.
7 See the analysis of the controversy in Quantin, *Le Catholicisme classique et les Pères de l'Eglise*, pp. 321–356.

suggested that 'every Greek on the face of the earth' be interrogated about whether he recognise any general law in his Church establishing the teaching of transubstantiation.[8] Arnauld and Nicole followed his advice. They set about collecting attestations. Among the first men to be approached was Arnauld's nephew, Simon Arnauld, marquis de Pomponne, who had been dispatched on an embassy to Stockholm, where he arrived in 1666. It was there, in 1667, that he assembled information about the Russians and their unswerving belief in transubstantiation.[9] In the following year a declaration was also submitted by the Greek archbishop of Cyprus,[10] and, in 1669, by the Nestorian community in Diarbekir.[11] But Arnauld and Nicole spread their net considerably further. Through the French ambassadors, consuls and missionaries posted throughout the Levant they requested attestations, signed by the various priests and prelates of all the Eastern Churches, and they consequently needed a scholar who could translate the material collected.[12]

1   The Embassy in Istanbul

Their choice fell on a young man who was going to become one of the greatest Arabists of his generation, Antoine Galland. Born in Rollo in Picardy in 1646, Galland had received his early education, which included the rudiments of Hebrew, in Noyon, and, in 1661, was sent to Paris to continue his studies. After attending the Collège Duplessis, he decided to satisfy his interest in antiquity at the Collège Royal where he seems to have been taught some Arabic by Pierre Vattier, the translator of Avicenna and al-Makīn, and to have improved his Hebrew under Valérien de Flavigny. Thanks to the vice-principal of the Collège Duplessis, Nicolas Bouthillier, he was introduced to Nicolas Petitpied, a specialist in canon law who occupied various ecclesiastical and juridical posts and who became Galland's first advisor and patron. Through him Galland obtained access to the library of the Sorbonne and took part in compiling the inventory of the oriental manuscripts in Richelieu's collection. He also made the acquaintance of numerous scholars and found his way into the circle of Port-Royal in which members of the Petitpied family would play an increasingly prominent

---

8   Claude, *Réponse*, p. 442.
9   His declaration would be included in Antoine Arnauld and Pierre Nicole, *La perpétuité de la foy catholique* (Paris, 1669–74), vol. 1, pp. 423–541.
10 BNF MS Armenien 145, fols 21–22.
11 *Ibid.*, fols 26–27.
12 A. Hamilton, *The Copts and the West 1439–1822. The European Discovery of the Egyptian Church* (rev. edn., Oxford, 2014), pp. 152–159.

part. What recommended Galland particularly to Nicole and Arnauld was his competence as a Latinist and his knowledge of Greek and Arabic, for an embassy was preparing to leave for Istanbul led by another fervent Jansenist, Charles Olier, marquis de Nointel, who had agreed to collect the professions of faith of the Eastern Churches.

Nointel, whose mother had sought spiritual guidance from the *solitaires* of Port-Royal des Champs and whose three sisters were nuns at the Abbaye du Bois, was a learned man, but he required a secretary who knew some of the Eastern languages.[13] This was to be Galland. Nointel's embassy set out in August 1670.[14] For Arnauld and Nicole it was something of a triumph since their plan of sounding out the Eastern Churches had the full support of the king and the French Church. For Galland it was a decisive experience. He spent three years in Istanbul on the first of what were to be a number of visits to the Near East. Besides learning Turkish, Persian and modern Greek, he improved his Arabic by frequenting the teacher of th*e jeunes de langues*, the young interpreters for whom Colbert was endeavouring to set up a school. He also acquired the taste for Eastern tales which paved the way to the achievement on which his reputation largely rests – the introduction into Europe, and the translation, of the so-called *Arabian Nights* nearly thirty years later. Galland and Nointel were tireless in their service to the Jansenists. Just as Arnauld had approached his nephew in Sweden, so the ambassador and his secretary asked the opinion as to the Greek view of the eucharist of numerous European diplomats and residents in Istanbul. The attestations they assembled included those of the Polish ambassador Casimir de Visocha;[15] the apostolic vicar Andrea Ridolfi;[16] the members of a Ragusan embassy who arrived in the Ottoman capital in October 1671;[17] the Genoese resident Sinibaldo Fieschi;[18] the Venetian bailo Giacomo Quirino;[19] and the community of Western merchants and interpreters living in Pera.[20] They also obtained support from less expected quarters. A German Calvinist merchant assured the ambassador repeatedly that the Greeks did indeed believe in transubstantiation and that Jean Claude had no

---

13 M. Abdel-Halim, *Antoine Galland, sa vie et son oeuvre* (Paris, 1964), pp. 11–28.
14 The best study of the embassy as a whole remains H. Omont, *Missions archéologiques françaises en Orient aux XVIIe et XVIIIe siècles* (Paris, 1902), vol. 1, pp. 175–221.
15 BnF MS Arménien 145, fol. 24.
16 *Ibid.*, fol. 41.
17 *Ibid.*, fol. 47.
18 *Ibid.*, fol. 43.
19 *Ibid.*, fol. 57.
20 *Ibid.*, fol. 50.

business to doubt it.[21] He would, he said, have attested it himself in writing were it not for his fear of being excommunicated if he ever went to Charenton. The Austrian diplomatic representative, Giambattista Casanova, on the other hand, was far less cooperative. Described by Galland as being 'de basse naissance et originaire de Milan,'[22] he refused to provide a signed document, thereby confirming the traditional hostility between the Habsburgs and the French.

But Nointel and Galland relied above all on the missionaries and the French consuls. The ambassador appears to have sent out a letter which informed the heads of the various Christian communities what the Protestants thought they believed about the eucharist, specified the Catholic teaching, and asked them to state their true belief. In Egypt the learned Capuchin Elzéar de Sanxay (who compiled a catalogue of the Eastern manuscripts collected by the French chancellor Pierre Séguier) persuaded the Greek patriarch of Alexandria to submit a confession of faith contradicting Claude's assertions.[23] Also in Egypt the French consul in Cairo, Ambroise de Tiger, obtained statements from the Coptic patriarch of Alexandria, Matthew IV,[24] and the head of the Armenian church in Cairo Gaspar.[25] They were witnessed by what seems to have been the entire Roman Catholic community in the city – the merchants of the French Levant Company, the missionaries, and the consular staff. In Persia the distinguished representative of France and French interests, the Capuchin missionary Raphaël du Mans, invited the Armenian community at New Julfa, just outside Isfahan, to provide a confession of faith which he witnessed.[26] In Mingrelia it was the Theatine missionary Giuseppe Maria Zampio who wrested an attestation from the Georgians which he himself translated into Latin.[27] Other French consuls obtained confessions of faith from the Greek communities in the islands.[28] Declarations were also submitted by the Greek archbishop of Milos;[29] the Greek bishop of Chios;[30] the Greek and the Jacobite patriarchs

---

21   Antoine Galland, *Voyage à Constantinople (1672–1673)* (Paris, 2002), vol. 1, pp. 34, 44.
22   *Ibid.*, vol. 2, p. 2.
23   *Ibid.*, vol. 1, p. 19.
24   BnF, MS Arabe 226.
25   BnF, MS Arabe 227; Galland, *Voyage*, vol. 1, pp. 111, 235.
26   *Ibid.*, 167. See also F. Richard, *Raphaël Du Mans, missionnaire en Perse au XVII*ème *siècle* (Paris, 1995), vol. 1, pp. 81–91; BnF MS Or. Arménien 141.
27   BnF, MS Arménien 145, fols 71–75. Cf. Galland, *Voyage*, vol. 2, p. 126.
28   BnF, MS Arménien 145, fols 38, 34, 36, 45, 78.
29   *Ibid.*, fol. 55.
30   Galland, *Voyage*, vol. 1, p. 60.

of Antioch;[31] Cruciador, the Armenian patriarch of Sis;[32] the Greek archbishop of Mount Sinai;[33] the Greek metropolitan of Izmir;[34] and many others.

Nointel and Galland themselves scoured the area around Istanbul and exploited their trips to nearby cities such as Adrianople (Edirne).[35] Nointel proudly reported his visit to the monastery of St George in Büyükada, the largest of the Princes' Isles in the Sea of Marmara, where he interrogated systematically 'the abbots and the monks' about their belief in 'the mystery of the eucharist.'[36] In a dispatch to Louis XIV he insisted still further on the thoroughness of his researches. He had followed Claude's advice to the letter, and had not only attended every possible religious service but had questioned 'patriarchs, archbishops, bishops, priests, gentlemen and private individuals, even the popes and people in the country.' They all expressed their abhorrence of the Calvinist accusations and affirmed their faith in transubstantiation.[37]

Galland too was personally engaged in canvassing Greek ecclesiastics. In a village close to Istanbul, for example, he went up to the local Greek priest and asked him about his views on the eucharist.[38] His main task, however, was to translate into French the attestations in Greek[39] and to write in the ambassador's name to the Greek patriarchs and metropolitans. The attestations produced by the Greeks in Istanbul were the most important of all. Galland and Nointel could count on the assistance of Panaiotis Nicousios from Chios, from 1669 to his death in 1673 the grand dragoman, or interpreter, to the sultan. A man of letters of the greatest distinction, Nicousios, educated by the Jesuits, had assembled an important library and had formerly acted as personal physician to the grand vizir and interpreter to the imperial and other foreign

---

31   Ibid., pp. 146, 177.
32   Ibid., p. 214.
33   Ibid., p. 235.
34   Ibid., vol. 2, p. 105.
35   Ibid., vol. 1, pp. 29–50.
36   BnF, MS Arménien 145, fol. 29.
37   Ibid., fol. 85^v: 'J'ay assisté a leur ceremonies, et a leurs liturgies, ou cette Verité paroist dans un éclat Invincible; Et les Patriarches, Archevesques, evesques, prestres, les gentilhommes, et les particuliers, mesme les Papas, et le peuple a la campagne, me l'ont certifié avec execration contre ceux qui Leurs Imputaient Une autre croyance, les traittans de calomniateurs et d'heretiques.' Cf. Omont, *Missions archéologiques françaises*, vol. 1, p. 180.
38   Galland, *Journal*, vol. 1, p. 104: 'Je vis le papas du village auquel je demanday, dela part de S.E., ce qu'il croyoit de l'Eucharistie. Il me dit que c'estoit le corps et le sang de Jésus Christ, et luy ayant demandé s'il resoit encore du pain, il me respondit qu'il n'en restoit pas et que la substance du pain estoit changée en la substance du corps de Jésus Christ, et la substance du vin en celle de son sang.'
39   Ibid., p. 58.

embassies.[40] It was Panaiotis who procured for the French ambassador a letter from Nektarios, former Orthodox patriarch of Jerusalem, to Paisios, the patriarch of Alexandria, confirming his belief in transubstantiation.[41] More significant still was the declaration the ambassador and his secretary received from Parthenius IV, the patriarch of Constantinople and head of the Greek Church,[42] and the important attack on the Calvinist position by Dositheos II, the learned patriarch of Jerusalem who was one of the foremost Greek theologians of his day and who would clash with Nointel over the rights of the Custodians of the Holy Land.[43]

Nointel and his secretary had every reason to be pleased with their achievements in the Ottoman Empire. Not only had they obtained an astonishing number of declarations, but some of them were documents of extraordinary beauty. The attestation of the Coptic patriarch of Alexandria, for example, is a magnificent illuminated scroll of paper on green silk.[44] The illuminated confession of faith of the Armenian catholicos, Hagop IV, is an even more splendid document.[45] Galland wrote at length about the splendour of the attestation provided by the Greek metropolitans of Athens and Adrianople,[46] and of the

---

40 D. Janos, 'Panaiotis Nicousios and Alexander Mavrocordatos: the rise of the Phanariots and the office of Grand Dragoman in the Ottoman administration in the second half of the seventeenth century' *Archivum Ottomanicum* 23 (2005/6), pp. 177–196; G. Koutzakiotis, *Attendre la fin du monde au XVIIe siècle. Le messie juif et le grand drogman* (Paris, 2014), pp. 125–174; and S. Runciman, *The Great Church in Captivity: A Study of the Patriarchate of Constantinople from the Eve of the Turkish Conquest to the Greek War of Independence* (Cambridge, 1968), pp. 363–364. See also Galland, *Voyage*, vol. 1, p. 18.
41 BnF, MS Arménien 145, fols 67–8.
42 *Ibid.*, fols 13–16; Galland, *Voyage*, vol. 1, p. 19.
43 Arnauld and Nicole, *La perpetuité de la foy*, vol. 3, pp. 690–711. Dositheos's confession is discussed and analysed by V. Kontouma, 'La *Confession de foy de Dosithée de Jérusalem: les versions de 1672 et de 1690*' in M.-H. Blanchet and F. Gabriel, *L'Union à l'épreuve du formulaire* (Paris, 2016), pp. 341–372.
44 BnF, MS Arabe 226; G. Troupeau, *Catalogue des manuscrits arabes. Première partie. Manuscrits chrétiens. Tome I. Nos. 1–323* (Paris, 1972), pp. 193–194.
45 BnF, MS Arménien 145, fol. 7. Cf. A. Vernay-Nouri, *Livres d'Arménie. Collections de la Bibliothèque nationale de France* (Paris, 2007), pp. 16–17.
46 BnF, MS Grec 431; Galland, *Voyage*, vol. 1, pp. 54–55: 'Elle estoit écrit sur un grand papier de soye collé sur de taffetas orné de peintures et principalement d'une lettre initiale qui représentoit d'un costé St Chrysostôme et St Basile de l'autre, en acte d'adoration envers un petit Jésus couché sur une patène couvert d'un voile à demy corps et un calice avec trois Chérubins qui estoient représentés au dessus. Signée du Patriarche lui-même, de trois autres ses prédécesseurs et de celuy d'Alexandrie et d'un grand nombre de Mètropolites et bullée d'un grand sceau d'argent doré … Ce bulle pesoit quarante cinq dragmes.'

profession from the Armenians of New Julfa, both lavishly illuminated.[47] They were later to become some of the most prized possessions of the Bibliothèque nationale de France.

Galland returned to Paris in 1673 and would make two other extensive journeys to the Near East before settling in France for good, ending his career as professor of Arabic at the Collège Royal, venerated in the French *salons* for his translation of the *Arabian Nights*, and admired in the world of learning for his many translations from Turkish, Persian and Arabic and his discoveries as an antiquarian and numismatist. He was, above all, a scholar, an exemplary citizen of the Republic of Letters for whom confessional allegiance was only of secondary importance when compared to the standard of a man's learning. He was not a theologian and he never indulged in confessional polemic. His friends had different religions. The scholar to whom he was closest, Jacob Spon, was a Huguenot. He had cordial relations with Anglican residents in the Ottoman Empire who, as we shall see, argued against the Greek belief in transubstantiation. He corresponded affectionately with Dutch members of the Reformed Church, and he included among his friends a number of Danish Lutherans.[48] He took employment wherever he could find it. Some of his patrons, such as the members of the Bignon family, were committed Jansenists, but others were not.[49] He himself said that he was sceptical by nature in every field except for religion,[50] but his own piety, deep though it ran, remained an essentially private matter.

The attestations which Nointel had gathered in Istanbul were sent back to France,[51] and Antoine Arnauld made instant use of them. In 1669 he had

---

47 BnF, MS Arménien 141; Vernay-Nouri, *Livres d'Arménie*, pp. 18–19; Galland, *Voyage*, p. 167: 'Elle estoit addressée à Sa Majesté en forme de lettre et on y avoit peint un Prestre à l'autel, levant le pain consacré devant le peuple à genoux avec beaucoup de dévotion, et les premières lettres représentoient en miniature assez délicate plusieurs figures d'animaux. La marge estoit ornée d'une belle vignette diversifiée fort industrieusement d'or et de couleurs fort proprement appliqués.'
48 For his friends see Abdel-Halim, *Antoine Galland*, pp. 34–35, 54–57, 106, 111–113, and for his tolerance, pp. 424–425.
49 *Ibid.*, pp. 81–97.
50 *Ibid.*, p. 113. He described himself as being 'sans fard, cherchant la droiture, aimant la vérité, et la soustenant lorsque je puis la connoistre, scepticien (je mets la religion à part) dans les choses où elle ne m'est pas apparente, et cela pour me conserver dans une tranquillité d'esprit dont j'ai grand besoin, estant né Picard, je veux dire avec la teste chaude.'
51 The most important collection is now at the BnF, MS Arménien 145 and others. These manuscripts, used by Arnauld and Nicole, were then passed on to Eusèbe Renaudot. At his death they entered the library of Saint-Germain-des-Prés, and, after the French Revolution, the BnF. Nointel, however, also had a copy made of most of the papers in MS Arménien 145 which is now in the library of Rouen. BnF Arménien 145 is described by H. Omont, 'Confessions de foi des églises orientales' *Bibliothèque de l'Ecole des Chartes* 55

started to issue a new edition of the *Perpétuité de la foy*. The small single volume of 1664 turned into three volumes. In the first he had already made use of the work of the Maronite Abraham Ecchellensis to confirm the belief in transubstantiation of the Nestorians,[52] and in the third, which came out in 1674, he included all the attestations assembled in Istanbul (and elsewhere). A more thorough exploitation of the new material, however, was due to Eusèbe Renaudot. The grandson of the Protestant physician Théophraste Renaudot, Eusèbe was a man of letters, a friend of Boileau, Racine, La Bruyère and Bossuet, but he was also a theologian, once a member of the Paris Oratory, an institution that had proved strongly sympathetic to Jansenism. His own commitment to the movement cost him the appointment as custodian of the royal library.[53] In Renaudot the Jansenist leaders had at last found someone who was both an Orientalist and a theologian, and who was ready to document their theory about the ubiquity and antiquity of the Catholic teaching on the eucharist. Opinionated and argumentative, he was, like Nicole and Arnauld, always prepared to polemicise, and in his hands the three volumes of the *Perpétuité de la foy* turned, many years later, into six.

Renaudot's additional volumes started to appear in 1711, well after the deaths of Nicole and Arnauld, and even if his first objective was to prove that all the Eastern Churches shared the belief in transubstantiation, he in fact produced a study of Eastern Christianity in its entirety – of the Melkites, the Nestorians, the Jacobites, the Copts and the Ethiopians. This was a fundamental contribution to the subject, and its importance was heightened by Renaudot's critical approach to other earlier and contemporary studies. In 1709 Renaudot had already published the homilies on the eucharist by Gennadius I, patriarch of Constantinople when the city fell to the Turks. In 1713 he made a further contribution to Oriental studies with his *Historia Patriarcharum Alexandrinorum Jacobitarum a D. Marco usque ad finem saeculi XIII*, the first extensive history of the Coptic patriarchs of Alexandria based entirely on Arabic sources, and in 1716 he published the first volume of his *Liturgiarum orientalium collectio*, containing the liturgies of the Coptic and Ethiopian Churches. The second volume would follow ten years later with the liturgies of the Jacobites and the Nestorians.

(1894), pp. 567–570, and the Rouen manuscript, also by Omont, 'Confessions de foi des églises orientales' *Bibliothèque de l'Ecole des Chartes* 45 (1884), pp. 235–236.

52 L. Khayati, 'Usages de l'oeuvre d'Abraham Ecchellensis dans la seconde moitié du XVIIe siècle: controverses religieuses et histoire critique' in B. Heyberger, ed., *Orientalisme, science et controverse: Abraham Ecchellensis (1605–1664)* (Turnhout, 2010), pp. 192–203.

53 A. Villien, *L'Abbé Eusèbe Renaudot: Essai sur sa vie et son oeuvre liturgique* (Paris, 1904), pp. 29–33.

2   Protestant Reactions

By the time Renaudot was writing the eucharistic controversy had spread far outside the French borders. But to follow it we must go back in time – to Jean Claude's original attack on the Jansenists and his assertions about the Eastern Churches. When he maintained that the Eastern Christians did not believe in transubstantiation his position was decidedly weak. For his description of the observances of the Abyssinians Claude drew on Damião de Goes (who claimed that they never exposed the eucharist),[54] but for information on most of the other Eastern Churches he seems to have relied on Edward Brerewood's *Enquiries touching the Diversity of Languages, and Religions, through the Chiefe Parts of the World*, published posthumously in 1622. In fact Brerewood had little to say about the beliefs in the eucharist, but when he came to the Armenians he stated that 'they deny the true body of Christ to be really in the sacrament of the Eucharist under the Species of bread and wine.'[55] As his source he gave the fourteenth-century Carmelite Guido Terrena, also known as Guy de Perpignan, whose inquisitorial activities as bishop first of Elna and then of Majorca bore fruit in his *Summa de haeresibus*. His long section on the Armenians is most interesting,[56] but, as Arnauld and Nicole pointed out, he was altogether alone in denying their belief in transubstantiation.[57]

For the Greek Church, on the other hand, Jean Claude advanced evidence which, at first sight, was more convincing. This was the confession of faith by Cyril Lucaris, five times patriarch of Constantinople. As the head of the Orthodox Church, Lucaris seemed a reliable spokesman of Greek views. Born in Crete, educated, like a number of promising young Cretans, in Venice and later in Padua, well acquainted with Northern Europe, he had been sent as the deputy of the patriarch of Constantinople to the Synod of Brest-Litovsk in 1595 to defend the interests of the Greek Orthodox community in Poland menaced by the advance of the Church of Rome. In the course of his travels he had had much to do with Protestants, and, as patriarch of Alexandria but resident in Istanbul, he had been befriended by Protestant diplomats and scholars.[58] One of Lucaris's main concerns was to block the many attempts of

---

54   Claude, *Réponse*, pp. 297–298.
55   Edward Brerewood, *Enquiries touching the Diversity of Languages, and Religions, through the Chiefe Parts of the World* (London, 1622), p. 173.
56   Guy de Perpignan, *Summa de haeresibus, et earum confutationibus* (Paris, 1518), fols 29ᵛ–42ʳ. For the eucharist, fols 38ᵛ–39ʳ.
57   Arnauld and Nicole, *Perpétuité de la foy* (1664), p. 494.
58   Runciman, *The Great Church in Captivity*, pp. 259–288; G. Podskalsky, *Griechische Theologie in der Zeit der Türkenherrschaft 1453–1821* (Munich, 1988), pp. 162–180.

the Catholic Church to win the Greeks over to union with Rome, and it was this that made his friendship with the European Protestants ever firmer. The outcome was a confession of faith published in 1629. Both here,[59] and in his letters to his Protestant friends,[60] Lucaris stated that the Greek Church did not accept the doctrine of transubstantiation.

Lucaris was strangled on the sultan's orders in 1638. He had a small number of disciples who continued to defend his views, and the Greeks who travelled in Northern Europe were usually prepared to please their Protestant hosts by saying that they did not share the Roman Catholic view of the eucharist.[61] Otherwise, Lucaris's confession of faith was all but unanimously rejected by the Greeks in the East. Nointel, we saw, had little difficulty in eliciting statements which clearly contradicted those of Lucaris, but the document which suited his purpose best was earlier. This was the so-called confession of Moghila, the *Orthodoxa Confessio Fidei* named after Petrus Moghila, the Paris-educated Moldavian metropolitan of Kiev who contributed, in 1640, to a slight revision of an existing confession which would be endorsed at the Orthodox councils of Kiev in 1640 and Jassy in 1642. Published in Amsterdam in 1666, again thanks to Panaiotis Nicousios,[62] it was transmitted to Nointel in a bilingual, Latin and Greek, manuscript by Nicousios himself, in 1671.[63] The statement about the eucharist could hardly have been less equivocal. 'The holy Eucharist,' it runs in the eighteenth-century English translation attributed to Philip Lodvel, 'or the Body and Blood of our Lord Jesus Christ, under the visible Species of Bread and Wine: Wherein, really and properly, and according to the Thing itself, Jesus Christ is present.'[64]

---

59 *La Confession de foy de Cyrille patriarche de Constantinople* (Sedan, 1629), p. 12. Of the eucharist he wrote 'nous confessons et faisons profession de recognostre une vraye et reelle presence de Iesus Christ nostre Seigneur. Mais telle que la foy nous la presente, et non pas celle que nous enseigne la controuvée Transubstantiation. Car nous croyons que les fideles mangent le corps de Iesus Christ en la Cene du Seigneur, non point en la brisant de la dent materielle, mais en le percevant par le sens de l'ame, veu que le corps de Iesus Christ n'est pas ce qui se presente à nos yeux au Sacrement, mais ce que nostre foy apprehende spirituellement, et qu'elle nous baille: D'où s'ensuit qu'il est veritable que si nous croyons, nous mangeons et participons, et si nous ne croyons pas, nous sommes destituez de tout fruict.'
60 Jean Aymon, *Monumens authentiques de la religion des Grecs ...* (The Hague, 1708), p. 118.
61 Runciman, *The Great Church in Captivity*, pp. 289–309.
62 Podskalsky, *Griechische Theologie*, pp. 229–236.
63 Galland, *Journal*, vol. 1, p. 19. The manuscript is now BnF, MS Grec 1265.
64 J.J. Overbeck, ed., *The Orthodox Confession of the Catholic and Apostolic Eastern Church from the version of Peter Mogila* (London, 1898), pp. 79–80.

Despite such apparently obvious evidence about the Eastern belief in transubstantiation the Protestants refused to give in. The material contained in the third volume of the new edition of the *Perpétuité de la foy* in 1674 prompted Claude to undertake the very same research, and he drew up a questionnaire, which was dispatched to Protestant chaplains in the Ottoman Empire, intended to determine the views of the Greeks and other Eastern Christians. The questionnaire is reproduced in full in *Some Account of the Present Greek Church* published by John Covel in 1722. Covel spent many years in Istanbul, acting as chaplain to the English ambassador from 1670 to 1677 and, like most of his colleagues, he had a low opinion of the education of the Greek clergy. In the case of Claude's questionnaire he was particularly sceptical. Claude, he wrote, 'supposed by his Queries, that the Greeks and Easterlings were learned and well versed in this Controversy; whereas I never met with one amongst them who ever pretended fully to understand, much less ever offer'd clearly to answer any of them.'[65] And indeed, Claude's text, steeped in scholasticism, would have been totally incomprehensible to anyone without a Western theological training. The Protestants with more experience of Eastern Christianity, in other words the Englishmen who had been posted, or who had travelled, in the Ottoman Empire, chose a different approach.[66]

Thomas Smith, Covel's predecessor as chaplain at the English embassy in Istanbul where he stayed from 1668 to 1671 and who played an important role in the idealisation of Cyril Lucaris that occurred in the Protestant world, denied the antiquity of the Greek belief in transubstantiation on philological and terminological grounds. He claimed that the term μετουσίωσις was a recent novelty, whereas the words to be found in the ancient liturgies of Basil and Chrysostom, such as μεταποίησις and μεταστοιχείωσις 'do not infer such a substantial Change, that is, that the Elements notwithstanding their Conservation retain their essence and nature, though they are, as they are justly said to be, the Body and Bloud of Christ, is clear.'[67] He also insisted that, in Greek services, the eucharist was not consecrated by the words of the priest, but by the descent of the Holy Ghost on the elements on the altar.[68]

Paul Rycaut spent over fifteen years in the Ottoman Empire, first attached to the English embassy in Istanbul and then, from 1667 to 1678, as consul in Izmir. Few Europeans knew the Ottoman world better than he did, and his *Present*

---

65   John Covel, *Some Account of the Greek Church* (Cambridge, 1722), p. vi.
66   Runciman, *The Great Church in Captivity*, pp. 306–310.
67   Thomas Smith, *An Account of the Greek Church, as to Its Doctrine and Rites of Worship* (London, 1680), p. 147.
68   *Ibid.*, p. 144.

State of the Greek and Armenian Churches, Anno Christi 1678 was published shortly after his return to England.[69] On many points he agreed with Smith and Covel. Like Smith he emphasized the novelty of the term μετουσίωσις, but he also made it quite clear that 'the Greeks detest that Confession of Faith, supposed to be wrote by Cyrillus, their Patriarch of Constantinople.'[70] Like Covel he had some contempt for the piety of the Greeks.[71] And he had even more contempt for the Armenians, 'being in most things of a dull and stupid apprehension, unless in Merchandise and matters of gain.'[72] Where the belief in transubstantiation was concerned Rycaut was hesitant to reach a definite conclusion. The Armenians, he wrote, 'hold Transubstantiation as do the Papists from whom the Priests readily accepted of such a Doctrine as tends to their Honour and Profit … Howsoever this Tenet of Transubstantiation is held as discussed but of late years amongst them and is not altogether Universally accepted; some of them will pretend to maintain, and others to deny it.'[73] Nor had it been much discussed by the Greeks. 'The question about Transubstantiation hath not been long controverted in the Greek Church, but like other abstruse notions, not necessary to be determined, hath lain quiet and disentangled, wound upon the bottom of its own Thread, until Faction, and Malice, and the Schools, have so twisted and ravelled the twine, that the end will never be found.'[74] Even if the Greeks did at least seem to accept transubstantiation, Rycaut, like Claude before him, pointed out that their devotion to the eucharist was very different from that of the Church of Rome: there were no eucharistic processions, no feast days devoted to it, no prostrations at its appearance, and no exposition in public.[75]

Where the English participants in the eucharistic controversy agreed was on the widespread theological ignorance of the Eastern Christians, and particularly of the Greeks. This was a point stressed by John Covel, who reported his urbane discussions with Nointel in the halls of the English embassy. Having studied the attestations gathered by the French ambassador, Covel concluded that, in many cases, the signatories were making no more than a gesture of obeisance to the powerful emissary of a powerful monarch, and had certainly

---

69 S.P. Anderson, *An English Consul in Turkey. Paul Rycaut at Smyrna, 1667–1678* (Oxford, 1989), pp. 216–229.
70 Paul Rycaut, *Present State of the Greek and Armenian Churches, Anno Christi 1678* (London, 1679), sig. a5r.
71 Ibid., sig. a1r.–v.
72 Ibid., p. 387.
73 Ibid., pp. 433–434.
74 Ibid., 181.
75 Ibid., pp. 182–183. Cf. Claude, *Réponse*, pp. 444–445.

not understood the theological niceties of the questions put to them. The members of the higher clergy who signed, on the other hand, had, according to Covel, all been educated in Italy. Some – like Lucaris – had benefited from the ancient links with Venice, and had studied there and in Padua. Others had been trained at the Greek College in Rome founded by Gregory XIII in 1577, where, in marked contrast to the Maronites, they benefited from the best teachers the Society of Jesus had to offer.[76] There they had been imbued with Roman Catholic teaching.

3 Eastern Beliefs

But was Covel right? And what did the Eastern Christians really believe? On one point the Anglicans were indisputably correct. The Eastern Churches had always been reluctant to discuss the consecration of the eucharist. It was a mystery, a part of the liturgy, and, as such, was never an object of theological speculation as it was in the West. The Greeks, admittedly, had devoted more attention to it since the Reformation, largely because of their links with Europe.[77] Where those Churches situated in areas which had fallen to the Arabs in the seventh century were concerned, namely Syria and Egypt, theological discussion had been largely limited to subjects about which the Christians were in particular disagreement with the Muslims. These did not include the eucharist, and the few works in which the eucharist was discussed before the eighteenth century tend to be mainly concerned with the manufacture of the bread involved.[78] Yet, we see from the rubrics of the early fifteenth century that, in contrast to what certain Protestants might claim, the Coptic congregations not only believed in transubstantiation, but worshipped the elevated eucharist with just as much veneration as the Roman Catholics, prostrating themselves and begging for the remission of their sins by striking their breasts and 'with tears and supplications.'[79]

---

76 Covel, *Some Account*, pp. xi–xxii.
77 For Greek discussions see Podskalsky, *Griechische Theologie*, pp. 82–83, 121–122, 132–133, 155, 158, 187–188, 191, 197–198, 212–213, 226–227, 235, 240–241, 272–273, 281, 289–292, 329.
78 The Coptic belief in transubstantiation is clearly stated in a tract dating from the late fourteenth century, A. 'Abdallah, O.F.M., *Un trattato inedito sulla SS. Eucaristia (MS. Vat. Ar. 123, 1396 A.D.). Testo originale e traduzione* (Cairo, 1967), pp. 345–464. For the use of unleavened bread see the extensive section pp. 389–397, 448–459. For the best general discussion see G. Giamberardini, O.F.M., *La consacrazione eucaristica nella Chiesa Copta* (Cairo, 1957), pp. 11–123.
79 A. 'Abdallah, *L'ordinamento liturgico di Gabriele V – 88° patriarca copto, 1409–1427* (Cairo, 1962), pp. 194, 379.

The shortage of disquisitions on the eucharist in the East meant that there was always room for a case against belief in transubstantiation. The answers given by the members of the Eastern Churches to the question of whether they shared the Catholic belief depended to a large extent on the way in which the question was put. The antiquarian George Wheeler encountered a young monk in a monastery in Levadhia in Boeotia. Although he was from Zante, the monk had left his birthplace when he was too young to have had any traffic with Roman Catholicism. 'When I asked him, Whether they believed that the Bread and Wine was changed into the Body and Blood of Christ? He answered me, Whether I thought them so much Beasts, as to believe such an Absurdity?'[80] Although he 'could not find, that transubstantiation hath been heard of, except among those that have conversed with the Roman Church,'[81] Wheeler, who regarded the entire debate as disruptive of Christian unity, preferred to suspend judgement.[82] The German Lutheran Hiob Ludolf had a similar experience some years earlier. Ludolf, who had devoted himself to the study of Ethiopic under the protection of the duke of Saxe-Gotha, Ernest 'the Pious,' had managed to invite to Gotha an Ethiopian monk, Abba Gregorius, whose help he enlisted in compiling an Ethiopic dictionary. When he asked Gregorius about the real presence in the eucharist, Gregorius said he knew about the teaching, but that it concerned an abstruse mystery. Questioned more closely about the Catholic doctrine of transubstantiation, Gregorius added that it was unknown to the Abyssinians, but that his compatriots would never dream of unravelling the intricate problems involved in so mysterious a process. He himself believed that the elements were purely representative of the body and blood of Christ.[83] Another testimony of particular interest is supplied by Jean Chardin. Chardin, a jeweller from Paris, was a Huguenot who emigrated to England in 1681 in order to avoid persecution in France, obtained a knighthood from Charles II, and became known as Sir John Chardin. In 1672, however, he was still a loyal subject of Louis XIV and, on his way to Persia to trade in jewels, he stopped off in Istanbul and accompanied Nointel to Adrianople to confer with the grand vizir about the renewal of the capitulations or trading agreements between France and the Porte. He then pursued his journey east. When he arrived in Mingrelia, in the western part of Georgia, he questioned various priests about the consecration of the eucharist, but only one of them could explain it. Chardin went on to ask him whether the bread and the wine were

---

80   George Wheeler, *A Journey into Greece* (London, 1682), pp. 198–199.
81   *Ibid.*, p. 197.
82   Runciman, *The Great Church in Captivity*, pp. 309–310.
83   Hiob Ludolf, *Historia Aethiopica* (Frankfurt, 1681), sigs Aa4^{r-v}.

'substantially' the body and blood of Christ. The priest burst into laughter and asked who would place Jesus Christ in the bread, how would he do it, and why would Jesus Christ want to leave heaven and come down to earth?[84]

But however vague Eastern ideas on the eucharist may have been, was there any substance to Covel's persuasion that confessions were submitted solely to please the Catholic powers? There is no doubt that in certain cases this was so. We saw that the splendour of some of the manuscripts brought back to France is striking. The Armenians in Persia had clearly taken infinite pains to produce a document which not only affirmed their belief in transubstantiation, but which was also an object of beauty. There had long been conflicting currents in the Armenian Church, some strictly orthodox, and some tending towards Roman Catholicism. The signatories of the attestations were, by and large, sympathetic to the Church of Rome, and the community of New Julfa drew up the confession of faith in a manifest effort to please Louis XIV at a time when they needed his protection. The Armenians in Persia, who had once benefited from the tolerance of Shah Abbas, had been in danger, ever since 1654, of being expelled from Persian territory, and it was their ejection from Isfahan which had led them to settle in a suburb. Taxes had increased under Shah Suleyman, Armenians had been imprisoned, and in 1672 the entire city of Isfahan was closed to them.[85] The French king, whose recent military victories had led to his being respected by the Turks, had always presented himself as the protector of the Christians in the Ottoman Empire, and even if his help never materialised, he could still raise the hopes of persecuted communities. Another fine document is the illuminated scroll containing the attestation of the Copts of Egypt and signed by the patriarch of Alexandria, Matthew IV. The head of the Coptic Church had little to expect from the king of France and the Copts owed Rome no favours, but Matthew had strong intellectual sympathies for the Roman Catholic Church – it was, after all, partly at his instigation that the German Lutheran scholar Johann Michael Wansleben, dispatched by Ernest the Pious to explore Ethiopia, converted to Catholicism in 1665.[86] But to suggest that all the attestations were signed to curry favour with the Catholics of the West is wrong. One of the best pieces of evidence is the confession of faith submitted by Parthenius IV, the patriarch of Constantinople

---

84   Jean Chardin, *Journal du voyage du Chevalier Chardin en Perse et aux Indes Orientales*, vol. 1 (Amsterdam, 1686), p. 142.
85   Richard, *Raphaël du Mans*, vol. 1, pp. 40–41, 55–57, 81–91.
86   Hamilton, *The Copts and the West*, pp. 143–144; idem, *Johann Michael Wansleben's Travels in the Levant, 1671–1674. An Annotated Edtion of His Italian Report* (Leiden-Boston, 2018), pp. 15–16.

himself.[87] Far from being an attempt to prove the proximity between Orthodox and Catholic beliefs, the patriarch started his attestation by listing those tenets which his Church did not share with Rome. When he came to the question of transubstantiation, however, he fully accepted the Catholic position. This is equally true of the confession of Dositheos, patriarch of Jerusalem. He was notoriously hostile to the Church of Rome, but shared the belief in transubstantiation.[88]

4 Conclusion

The eucharistic controversy sustained by the Jansenists continued for some thirty years after the deaths of Arnauld and Nicole and petered out, on the Protestant side, in a spirit of uncertainty, in the third decade of the eighteenth century.[89] Yet it made a deep impression on Oriental studies in the West. It drew scholars of every confession all over Europe. Anglicans, Calvinists and Lutherans joined the debate in the North, while Catholics who could hardly be considered Jansenists, such as Richard Simon,[90] did so in France. The eucharistic controversy, however, also helped to forge a connection between Oriental studies and Jansenism. It gave Antoine Galland his first taste of the East. Renaudot, a more committed Jansenist, was immensely influential. One of the foremost students of Coptic at the time, the Augustinian Guillaume Bonjour, was close to him and, in Rome, encountered patrons and scholars who also had Jansenist leanings. Bonjour himself established a tradition of Coptic studies in the Augustinian Order which can be traced down to the twentieth century.[91] Nor did the Jansenists limit themselves to interest in the Churches of the East. The section of the immense academy planned by Colbert which was to include Orientalists such as Barthélemy d'Herbelot (whose *Bibliothèque orientale* was edited by Galland) and the elder François Pétis de la Croix, collapsed, partly because it was rumoured to have Jansenist sympathies.[92] However difficult such sympathies may be to document, there is little doubt that Jansenism left its mark, for many years to come, on a number of scholars studying different aspects of the East, some of the greatest of whom, born into

---

87 BnF, MS Arménien 145, fols 13–16.
88 See Runciman, *The Great Church in Captivity*, pp. 347–353.
89 For a general survey of the controversy see Podskalsky, *Griechische Theologie*, pp. 392–396.
90 Richard Simon, *Fides ecclesiae orientalis seu Gabrielis Metropolitae Philadelphiensis opuscula* (Paris, 1671; repr. Amsterdam, 1970), pp. 84–143.
91 Hamilton, *The Copts and the West*, pp. 229–232.
92 N. Dew, *Orientalism in Louis XIV's France* (Oxford, 2009), pp. 57–58.

a family of Jansenists, were Isaac Sylvestre de Sacy and his pupils Etienne-Marc Quatremère and Joseph-Héliodore Garcin de Tassy.[93]

Acknowledgements

This article was first published in Willemien Otten, Arjo Vanderjagt and Hent de Vries, eds, *How the West was Won: Essays on Literary Imagination, the Canon, and the Christian Middle Ages for Burcht Pranger* (Leiden: Brill, 2010), pp. 83–100.

93   S. Larzul, 'Silvestre de Sacy' in F. Pouillon, ed., *Dictionnaire des orientalistes de langue française* (rev. edn., Paris, 2012), pp. 953–955, esp. p. 953. A. Messaoudi, *Les arabisants et la France coloniale 1780–1930* (Lyon, 2015), pp. 28, 43, 47; *idem*, 'Quatremère Etienne-Marc' in F. Pouillon, ed., *Dictionnaire des orientalistes*, pp. 840–841, esp. p. 840.

CHAPTER 6

Adrianus Relandus (1676–1718)
Outstanding Orientalist

By 1700 the academic study of Arabic in the Netherlands had entered a phase of decline. That the situation should have been temporarily remedied by Adriaen Reland (Adrianus Relandus; Fig. 4), who was appointed professor of Oriental languages at the University of Utrecht in the following year, is surprising for various reasons. Utrecht did not have a tradition as a school of Eastern languages comparable to that of Leiden. In the course of the seventeenth century it had indeed had competent Hebraists: one was the great theologian Gisbertus Voetius, and Voetius had also started to study Arabic. The erudite Anna Maria van Schurman, too, was known for her talents as an Orientalist and had drawn the German expert on Ethiopic, Hiob Ludolf, to Utrecht in 1647. Otherwise the only Orientalist of note to contribute to Eastern studies at the university was Christianus Ravius from Berlin who lectured there for eighteen months between 1644 and 1645. It was to him that the university library owed the half dozen Arabic manuscripts it possessed by the end of the seventeenth century.

Reland, like many members of the first generation of academic Arabists in the early seventeenth century, never set foot in the East. This was in contrast to younger scholars in the second half of the century, such as Jacobus Golius, the professor of Arabic at Leiden who had spent time in Morocco, Syria and Istanbul, and his German pupil Levinus Warner who, as Dutch diplomatic representative in Istanbul, greatly expanded the Leiden collection of Eastern manuscripts. Reland, furthermore, was in certain respects a conservative Orientalist. He was a Hebraist in the old-fashioned tradition, and he regarded the Arabic language as no more than a descendant of the 'mother of languages', Hebrew, which it should serve to elucidate. Such an attitude tended to belie the insights into the study of Arabic expressed by Scaliger, acted upon by Thomas Erpenius and Golius in Leiden, and carried to unprecedented heights by the German Johann Jacob Reiske in the eighteenth century, who all believed that Arabic should be studied independently of Hebrew.

Adriaen Reland was born in De Rijp in 1676. His father was a Reformed minister in a village still known at the time for its tolerance to the Mennonites. Subsequently he moved first to Alkmaar, and then to Amsterdam, and in this last city Adriaen, a precocious boy, was sent to the academy when he was barely eleven years old. In Amsterdam Reland was taught Latin by Petrus Francius, a

FIGURE 4   Portrait of Adriaen Reland by Johan George Colasius, c. 1710
© COLLECTIE UNIVERSITEITSMUSEUM UTRECHT, INV.NR UG-5123

notoriously elegant Latinist, and it was probably with his encouragement that he developed his interest in Latin poetry. He was taught Hebrew by two scholars of distinction: Everard van der Hooght, who produced a highly acclaimed edition of the Hebrew bible, and Willem Surenhuys, known for his edition of the Mishna and his profound knowledge of rabbinic literature, a subject on which Reland himself was later to publish extensively and sympathetically.

Reland's progress in both Hebrew and Aramaic seems to have astonished Van der Hooght, and when he was thirteen he was sent to the University of Utrecht.

In Utrecht Reland again benefited from accomplished teachers. He studied Latin and Greek under the Saxon scholar Johann Georg Graevius, appreciated for his editions of Cicero and for the immensity of his erudition. He was taught Hebrew by Johan Leusden, one of the foremost Hebraists of his day. In contrast to Graevius, a convinced Cartesian, Leusden, like many of his colleagues at Utrecht, was a loyal follower of Voetius, sharing the strictness of his orthodoxy, his neo-scholasticism, and his fierce opposition to both Arminius and Descartes. Melchior Leydekker, who lectured in theology, was equally rigorous in his orthodoxy, while the other theologian, Herman Witsius (later to become professor at Leiden) was more moderate, despite his opposition to Cartesianism. Reland's teacher of philosophy, finally, Gerard de Vries, had left Leiden because of the hostility of the Cartesians. So although Utrecht was no longer the stronghold of Voetianism which it had been some thirty years earlier, Reland received much of his theological training under the shadow of the great theologian who had died in 1676. At the same time he could study mathematics and physics with the astronomer Johan Luyts, and he obtained Arabic lessons from a fellow-student, Heinrich Siecke from Bremen (or Henry Sike as he was known in England), a learned but tragic figure who was later to be appointed regius professor of Hebrew at Cambridge where he committed suicide.

After six years in Utrecht, in September 1697, Reland proceeded to Leiden. Here the men he heard lecture in theology were also conservatives, albeit not always outspoken Voetians, and he attended the course taught by Wolferd Senguerd in experimental physics, a subject in which he was becoming increasingly interested. While Reland was at Leiden he already attracted attention to himself as a scholar. In 1698 he was briefly employed as tutor to Hendrik Bentinck, the son of Hans Willem Bentinck, earl of Portland, the friend and advisor of the stadhouder William III of Orange, and thus spent most of his time in The Hague, but he refused to accompany Bentinck to Windsor. He was offered the chair of philosophy and Eastern languages at Lingen, but his reluctance to leave his ailing father in Amsterdam caused him to reject it. What he did accept, after receiving his doctorate in Utrecht in February 1699, was a chair in physics and metaphysics at the University of Harderwijk, sufficiently close to Amsterdam for him to remain in touch with his family.

Reland delivered his inaugural address at Harderwijk in the late summer of 1700, revealing traces of his training as well as a certain independence of mind in the slightly qualified praise he bestowed on Descartes. Before the year was out, however, the earl of Portland and the stadhouder had recommended that he be appointed professor of Oriental languages at Utrecht. He took up his appointment with an inaugural address in the following year and remained there for the rest of his life, living with his wife Johanna Catharina (the daughter of Johan Teelinck, the former mayor of Zierikzee) from whom he had a son and two daughters, and travelling as little as possible. During that time he was tempted with other posts. In 1712 he was offered a chair in Franeker. As a reward for his refusal the Utrecht University raised his salary and, in the following year, gave him a chair in Jewish antiquities. In 1716 he was called to Leiden to succeed the classical philologist and historian Johann Friederich Gronovius. Again he declined and again his salary in Utrecht was raised. In 1718, at the age of forty-one, he died of smallpox.

By the time of his appointment in Utrecht Reland had given full evidence of his versatility. He had demonstrated his expertise as a scientist in his inaugural address at Harderwijk. In his student days in Utrecht he had defended a dissertation on philosophy and had already published on the subjects of Islam and Judaism. With the publication of his *Galatea* in 1701, moreover, he confirmed his reputation as one of the best neo-Latin poets of his day. But Reland's most important publications were written during the seventeen years of his career at the Utrecht University.

A clear sign of Reland's future development as an Orientalist can be seen in the inaugural address he delivered on the study of Persian. On the one hand this was a conservative lecture. Reland, perhaps more for rhetorical reasons than because of any genuine conviction, dwelt on the importance of Persian for missionary purposes. He displayed a somewhat anachronistic attitude to the language itself, laying a disproportionate emphasis on its use for an improved knowledge of Hebrew and for the understanding of certain passages in the Old Testament. He insisted, too, that the location of the Garden of Eden should be sought in the Persian-speaking area. Yet, with his inaugural address and certain other writings, Reland ranks as one of the only Dutch Arabists in the eighteenth century to defend the study of Persian, thereby continuing a tradition launched in Leiden many years earlier. This, in itself, suggests considerable perceptiveness. He dwelt not only on the utility of Persian historians and geographers for the knowledge of the Middle East, but also on the necessity of knowing Persian in order to obtain a better understanding of Islam. Already in his inaugural address he lamented the many absurdities that had been attributed to the Muslims and argued for a closer, more objective study of their faith.

Throughout his life Reland was fascinated by languages. Besides writing about Persian, ancient, modern and rabbinic, he composed a brief introduction to Hebrew grammar. He produced dissertations on Malay, Urdu and Hindi, Chinese, Japanese and the languages spoken by the American Indians. Yet, partly because of his conviction that all tongues descended from Hebrew, this was not a domain in which he made any very original contribution to learning. If we look back on his achievements we see that his main accomplishments lay in other fields, and in the astonishingly imaginative use which he made of material gathered by other scholars.

Although he never stirred outside the Netherlands Reland was an active cartographer. The countries which he charted included Palestine, Persia, Java and Japan. His map of Persia was considered particularly important and had an immense influence, while his maps of ancient Palestine were by far the best up to that time. They are contained in his *Palestina ex monumentibus veteribus illustrata*, his study on the Holy Land as illustrated by its ancient monuments which first appeared in Utrecht in 1714 and was published in a Dutch translation five years later. This work contributed in no small manner to the development of biblical archaeology. Here, as well as in his various dissertations on Hebrew and Samaritan coins, he made an unprecedented use of inscriptions and numismatics as archaeological evidence. Together with his impressive assembly of ancient documents and his critical treatment of other sources, both ancient and contemporary, this method revolutionised the approach to ancient Palestine. Although many of the travellers who visited the Holy Land in the course of the eighteenth century and scrupulously recorded the inscriptions they came across were to some extent following the technique recommended by Reland, it was not until the nineteenth century that his work was properly appreciated and, ultimately, surpassed. In 1864 the American Edward Robinson, who is generally regarded as the father of modern biblical archaeology, could still say that 'the notices of Ancient Palestine by Greek and Roman writers are found best collected in the still classic work' of Reland.

However sedentary Reland himself may have been, he encouraged learned travellers in the East. He thus had the greatest admiration and sense of friendship for the French Arabist Antoine Galland, known now mainly for having imported the *Arabian Nights* into Europe. Reland was also a friend of the Swedish Orientalist Michael Eneman. When Eneman returned from his tour of the Levant to take up a professorship at Uppsala he called on Reland in Utrecht and presented him with a copy of a Turkish representation of the great mosque in Mecca. It was on this that Reland based the first informed drawing of the building to be published in Europe, one of the illustrations adorning the second edition of his supreme contribution to the Enlightenment, *De religione mohammedica*.

De religione mohammedica appeared in 1705 and was translated into Dutch, French, English, German and Spanish. A second, considerably expanded, Latin edition appeared in 1717. The enlightened approach of Reland already emerges in the epistle dedicatory and the preface. In the epistle addressed to his brother Pieter, a lawyer in Amsterdam, he begins by observing that Islam has spread over an immense geographical area. How would this have been possible, he wonders, if it was as absurd a religion as its enemies made it out to be? Was so large a proportion of the earth populated by fools? The literature produced by the Muslims does not warrant such a conclusion: if anything it suggests the opposite, and shows that just as much intelligence and understanding can be found among other cultures as in those of the West. In the Middle Ages, moreover, the Arabs were far in advance of Europe both scientifically and philosophically. Islam should therefore be studied in the light of reason. This is what he has done and it has drawn him to conclusions very different from those current at the time.

On the face of it Reland's preface is more conservative. He starts by stating that religions have always attacked one another. They have all been the targets of misleading propaganda campaigns which have endeavoured to give an entirely false impression of them. Although he does not intend to defend Islam – indeed, he deplores it and declares that it must be detestable to a Christian – he stresses the importance of understanding the Qur'an in any discussion with Muslims which might lead to their conversion. And although he admits that few have ever gone over to Christianity of their own free will, he denies the widespread notion that they refuse to debate about their faith. If there have been so few conversions this can probably be ascribed, he suggests, to the abominable impression Christians make on the Muslims whom they encounter. The Christians who go the East tend to do so only for the sake of financial gain. Once there, they distinguish themselves by their dissipation, their lies and their deceit. These were clearly not the sort of men who could be entrusted with the conversion of the Infidel.

Another conservative idea which Reland repeats in his preface is the importance of Arabic for the better understanding of Hebrew and the Bible. Yet, despite such concessions to tradition, Reland also points to the future. The ultimate emphasis in the preface is on the importance of understanding Islam. Common sense, *bona mens*, he concedes following Descartes, is equally distributed throughout the world. We have every reason to try, at least, to understand the religion of the Prophet which is in no way more ridiculous than Roman Catholicism. It is a faith that has been unjustly maligned and gravely misunderstood. Is the duty of the enlightened scholar not to seek to reveal the truth wherever it might be? And however far the Islamic lands are from certain parts of Europe, they are close to others. The Islamic area is one with which Europeans have ever more to do. It is of immense importance for trade. This alone is a reason for studying its doctrine with due objectivity.

The actual text of Reland's work is in two sections. First he provides a compendium of Muslim beliefs contained in a manuscript in his possession. He gives the original Arabic opposite a Latin translation and provides abundant elucidatory notes. Then, in the second section of his book, he embarks on a systematic confutation of the numerous legends and misapprehensions concerning Islam. Some, such as the legend of the dove feeding out of the Prophet's ear, the idea that Muḥammad is buried in Mecca or the belief that Muslim ablutions are intended to wash away sins, could be easily contradicted. Others, such as the charge that the Muslims believe in universal salvation and in a plurality of worlds, are due to a subtle misunderstanding of passages in the Qur'an and these Reland analyses and corrects.

The scholar Reland mentions most frequently in the preface to the second edition (but not the first) of his work is the Italian Ludovico Marracci who, in Padua in 1698, produced the earliest complete bilingual (Arabic-Latin) edition of the Qur'an. He accompanied it with an extensive commentary. Despite the apologetic tone – Marracci, former confessor to Pope Innocent XI, emphasized the importance of his edition for Christian missionaries – this was the first commentary to exploit and to quote some of the foremost Muslim commentators on the Qur'an and was consequently an unprecedented contribution to the knowledge of Islam in the West. In the second part of Reland's book Marracci too, although treated with esteem, comes in for his share of criticism as the transmitter of certain anti-Islamic legends. On the whole, however, Reland attacks the Byzantine historians who concocted, or transmitted, most of the unfavourable fables about the life of the Prophet and whose writings were eagerly plundered by Western polemicists.

Ultimately Reland's statements about Islam, like those in most similar works which appeared in the course of the early Enlightenment, show a mixture of old and new. Reland never dared openly express a sympathy with the Muslim faith, any more than did other Islamologists of the time. His arguments for the study of Arabic show little sign of progressing beyond the standard apologies which had been appearing since the Renaissance. What was new was the determination to submit Islam to an objective examination, to dispel the offensive legends of the past, to let an Islamic text speak for itself, and to base as much of the examination as possible on Islamic sources, a technique which he repeated shortly before his death in his well-informed treatise on the Islamic law of war.

Together with some of the more distinguished products of the Enlightenment *De religione mohammedica* was placed on the Catholic Index. Only many years after its publication was it possible to provide a truly sympathetic image of the Prophet and his followers. When this did occur, for example in the greatest historical work of the second part of the eighteenth century, Edward Gibbon's

Decline and Fall of the Roman Empire completed in 1788, full acknowledgement was given to the writings of Adriaen Reland. Reland is praised by Gibbon as 'a judicious student' who 'had travelled over the East in his closet at Utrecht'. This makes Reland's achievement the more remarkable.

Acknowledgements

This article was first published in Hervé Jamin, ed., *Zes keer zestig: 360 jaar universitaire geschiedenis in zes biografieën* (Utrecht: Universiteit Utrecht, 1996), pp. 23–31.

CHAPTER 7

Arabists and Cartesians at Utrecht

Was there a connection between the increasingly informed approach to Islam which can be perceived in Holland in the seventeenth and early eighteenth centuries and the ideas of René Descartes? Louise Thijssen-Schoute implies that there was and refers to Johannes Bouwmeester's Dutch translation of Ibn al-Tufayl's *Hayy ben Yaqdhan* (1701), to Adriaen Reland's *De religione mohammedica* (1705), and to Glazemaker's Dutch version of André Du Ryer's French translation of the Qur'an (which ran through eight editions between 1658 and 1734).[1] The purpose of this article is to show that the connection went even deeper than she may have suspected. The growing persuasion that the non-Christian peoples should be studied without prejudice was indeed indebted to the new philosophical method which was an object of such intense discussion in the Low Countries.

Descartes himself had been interested in Arabic work on mathematics. His decision to study at the University of Leiden owed much to the presence there of the greatest Arabist of the period, Jacobus Golius, and the copy Golius had made in Aleppo of the Arabic version of the *Conica* of Apollonius of Perga, which contained Books V–VII previously unknown in the West.[2] In his turn Golius, who was the Leiden professor of mathematics as well as of Arabic, became a supporter of Descartes.[3] When the French ambassador Henri Gournay de Marcheville was planning what he hoped would be a scientific expedition to the Ottoman Empire in 1630, Descartes was invited, even if he did not accept.[4]

But let us examine the situation at the University of Utrecht between about 1690 and 1715. For it was there that Adriaen Reland taught for most of his

---

1 C.L. Thijssen-Schoute, *Nederlands Cartesianisme* (Amsterdam, 1954; repr. Utrecht, 1989), pp. 417–419.
2 T. Verbeek and E.-J. Bos, *Descartes en Leiden. Vrienden en vijanden, bewonderaars en bestrijders. Catalogus bij een tentoonstelling in de Universiteitsbibliotheek Leiden, 30 januari–9 maart 2003* (Leiden, 2003), pp. 9, 40–42; T. Verbeek, 'A Philosopher's Life' in T.M. Lennon, ed., *Cartesian Views. Papers Presented to Richard A. Watson* (Leiden, 2003), pp. 53–69, esp. 57–61. On Golius and Apollonius see also Toomer, pp. 50, 122, 183–185.
3 Thijssen-Schoute, *Nederlands Cartesianisme*, pp. 74–79; T. Verbeek, *Descartes and the Dutch. Early Reactions to Cartesian Philosophy, 1637–1650* (Carbondale-Edwardsville, 1992), pp. 34, 39, 95.
4 A. Hamilton and F. Richard, *André Du Ryer and Oriental Studies in Seventeenth-Century France* (London-Oxford, 2004), p. 30, and above, p. 93.

© ALASTAIR HAMILTON, 2022 | DOI:10.1163/9789004498204_008

peculiarly sedentary adult life, becoming the centre of an international network of scholars.[5] He there made his enduring contributions to the fields of linguistics, cartography and archaeology, and wrote his *De religione mohammedica*, justifiably regarded as one of the earliest impartial studies of Islam. Translated into Dutch, French, German, English and Spanish, it heralded a series of developments in the course of the eighteenth century which bore fruit in the influential sections on the Prophet Muhammad and his followers in the last volumes of Edward Gibbon's *Decline and Fall of the Roman Empire* over eighty years later.

In about 1690 the university at which Reland had arrived when he was thirteen years old after studying at the academy of Amsterdam was still known as a bastion of anti-Cartesianism. This was largely thanks to the lingering influence of Gisbertus Voetius, who had been appointed professor of theology in 1634. He distinguished himself by his allegiance to Aristotelianism, the rigidity of his Calvinism, his opposition to Arminianism, and his violent conflict with his Leiden counterpart, the moderate Johannes Coccejus. Until long after Voetius's death in 1676 his followers prevailed in the faculties of theology and philosophy. At the faculty of theology Voetius had been joined in 1650 by the like-minded Johan Leusden, professor of Hebrew until 1699, and, in 1653, by Andreas Essenius who taught church history until 1677. Voetius's successor was the equally loyal Pieter van Maastricht, and in 1678 Essenius was succeeded by the passionately anti-Cartesian Melchior Leydekker, who died in 1721. By the late 1670s the faculty of philosophy had among its professors Gerard de Vries, who had left Leiden in distress in 1674 because of the 'persecution, abuse, and injury' he had suffered from the admirers of Descartes,[6] and Johannes Luyts who, from his appointment in 1677 to his death in 1721, fulminated against Copernicus and those who accepted his theories.[7]

Yet, despite the strongly anti-Cartesian reaction following the murder of the pensionary of Holland Johan de Witt in 1672 and the French occupation

---

5   For a survey of Reland's career see A.J. van der Aa, *Biographisch Woordenboek der Nederlanden*, vol. 16 (Haarlem, 1874), pp. 145–150; J. Nat, *De studie van de oostersche talen in Nederland in de 18e en de 19e eeuw* (Purmerend, 1929), pp. 11–21; H.J. van Rinsum, 'Adriaan Reland (1676–1718) and his formative years. A prelude to *De religione mohammedica*' in B. Jaski, C. Lange, A. Pytlowany, H.J. van Rinsum, eds, *The Orient in Utrecht. Adriaan Reland (1676–1718), Arabist, Cartographer, Antiquarian and Scholar of Comparative Religion* (Leiden-Boston, 2021), pp. 17–43; and above, pp. 129–132.
6   C. De Pater, 'Experimental Physics' in Th. H. Lunsingh Scheurleer and G.H.M. Posthumus Meyjes, eds, *Leiden University in the Seventeenth Century. An Exchange of Learning* (Leiden, 1975), pp. 309–327, esp. p. 314.
7   For a survey of the situation at Utrecht from 1673 to1715 see G.W. Kernkamp, *De Utrechtse Academie 1636–1815* (Utrecht, 1936), pp. 272–297.

of Utrecht in the same year,[8] the city magistrates remained reluctant to allow any one faculty at the University to fall entirely into the hands of the Voetians, partly because of the danger of repelling the more open-minded students. They tried to retain a balance and Cartesians continued to be appointed, forming a small but compact group who ensured the survival of a scientific and philosophic tradition. At the medical faculty, where the most controversial of the Utrecht Cartesians, Henricus Regius, had been appointed in 1638, the conservative Jacobus Vallan, nominated in 1675, was balanced by the more progressive Johannes Munnicks, whose extraordinary professorship of 1678 was turned into a full one in 1680, the year after Regius's death. The theological faculty had had to accept the appointment of Descartes's admirer Frans Burman in 1662. At his death in 1679, he was succeeded by Hermannus Witsius, certainly no fully fledged Cartesian but nevertheless a moderate Coccejan. The Voetians had also had to accept the appointment as professor of church history of the Cartesian Ludwig Wolzogen in 1664 (even if he left for Amsterdam six years later). At the faculty of philosophy the Cartesians had been represented by the Saxon scholar Johann Georg Graevius since 1661, by Regnerus van Mansfelt, who was appointed in 1664, and by Johannes de Bruyn, appointed in 1652. Mansfelt, however, died in 1671 (to be succeeded by Gerard de Vries) and De Bruyn died four years later (to be succeeded by Luyts), so Graevius remained a somewhat isolated defender of the ideas of Descartes.

Graevius had aired Cartesian views in his oration on comets in 1665.[9] He had been close to Frans Burman and was supposed to have formed part of Burman's so-called *Collegie der sçavanten*, a group of friends who hoped to propagate the philosophy of Descartes. It was made up of the leading Utrecht Cartesians, the professors De Bruyn, Mansfelt and Wolzogen, the physician Nicolas van Solingen, and the far bolder and better known regent Lambert van Velthuysen, and its correspondents were rumoured to include some of the most distinguished figures of the Dutch Enlightenment such as Abraham Heydanus in Leiden, Jacobus Perizonius in Deventer, Christophorus Wittichius in Nijmegen

---

8 For the efforts of the secular authorities to maintain 'civic concord' see B. Forclaz, '"Rather French than subject to the Prince of Orange". The conflicting loyalties of the Utrecht Catholics during the French occupation (1672–73)' *Church History and Religious Culture* 87 (2007), pp. 509–533, esp. p. 527–528.
9 Thijssen-Schoute, *Nederlands Cartesianisme*, pp. 445–446. See also H. de Waardt, 'Academic Careers and Scholarly Networks' in W. van Bunge, ed., *The Early Enlightenment in the Dutch Republic, 1650–1750. Selected Papers of a Conference Held at the Herzog August Bibliothek, Wolfenbüttel, 22–25 March 2001* (Leiden, 2003), pp. 19–37, esp. pp. 31–36; and A. Fix, 'Comets in the Early Dutch Enlightenment' *ibid.*, pp. 157–172, esp. pp. 162, 171.

and Balthasar Bekker in Franeker.[10] Graevius also displayed his loyalty to his Cartesian friends by pronouncing the funeral addresses of De Bruyn in 1675 and of Burman and Regius in 1679.[11]

By the last decade of the seventeenth century the violent polemics of the earlier period had abated and the Voetians were entering a period of decline. One sign of a changing climate was the dissertation with which Reland graduated at the faculty of philosophy on 25 September 1694 after being taught by Graevius, but also by Graevius's anti-Cartesian colleagues: the *De libertate philosophandi*. Remarkably enough it does not appear to have done the slightest damage to Reland's reputation. He studied for another two years at the theological faculty, dominated by Voetians who all seem to have had for him a respect which was apparently reciprocated and who would welcome him to the chair of Oriental languages in 1701.

Although not quite as outspoken as his inaugural address at the University of Harderwijk in 1700, *De libertate philosophandi* is a statement of unmitigated anti-Aristotelianism which rings with admiration for Descartes. There is a constant stress on the need for personal observation free of the prejudices of tradition. The main upholders of the 'new philosophy' are quoted with approval – Nicolas Malebranche, Hugo Grotius, Robert Boyle, Pierre Gassendi, and above all Descartes – but even where Descartes is concerned there is an element of hesitation. The authority of a single master, Reland insists, must always be judged with diffidence.[12] The once flourishing school of Aristotle had been discredited by Petrus Ramus and his followers. The school of Descartes had swept away that of Ramus. We should therefore be wary of an excessive devotion even to Descartes.

At the academy of Amsterdam Reland was taught Hebrew by two acclaimed scholars, Everard van der Hooght, the editor of a widely respected edition of the Hebrew bible, and Willem Surenhuys, known for his familiarity with rabbinic literature and for his edition of the Mishna. When he was at Utrecht Reland decided to learn Arabic. Utrecht, however, had no true tradition

---

10   The *Collegie der Sçavanten* was first studied by J. Hartog, 'Het Collegie der Sçavanten te Utrecht' *De Gids* 40 (1876), pp. 77–114, esp. pp. 109–112. See also M.J.A. de Vrijer, *Henricus Regius. Een 'cartesiaansch' hoogleeraar aan de Utrechtsche Hoogeschool* (The Hague, 1917), pp. 84–85; Kernkamp, *De Utrechtse Academie*, p. 262; Thijssen-Schoute, *Nederlands Cartesianisme*, pp. 444–445; Verbeek, *Descartes and the Dutch*, pp. 75, 131–132.
11   De Vrijer, *Henricus Regius*, pp. 88–89.
12   Adriaen Reland, *Disputatio philosophica inauguralis, de libertate philosophandi* [...] (Utrecht, 1694), p. 6: 'Infirma itaque basi praeclarum nitetur Philosophiae palatium, si solius Praeceptoris mens attendatur. Quamvis enim plurimum in scientiis profecerit, tuum tamen est proprio ingenio, non alieno, sapere [...].'

of Arabic studies. For eighteen months, from 1644 to 1645, one of the better Arabists of the time, Christianus Ravius from Berlin who had studied in Leiden under Golius, had taught at Utrecht, and half a dozen of his Arabic manuscripts would find their way into the library. But this was a short-lived episode. Nevertheless there were occasional signs of an interest in Islam among Utrecht's more conservative professors. In 1648 Gisbertus Voetius himself had presented a *Disputatio de Mohammedanismo*, which he manipulated for publication in 1655. With Christian missionaries in the East in mind, Voetius argued eloquently for a greater knowledge of Islam and the Islamic world. He condemned the 'crassa rerum Muhammedicarum ignorantia' which prevailed in the West. He recommended an 'apparatus eruditionis artium seu Philosophiae, linguarum praecipue Arabicae', and stressed the use of collecting and publishing Arabic manuscripts which would make it possible for missionaries to debate with, and ultimately convert, the Muslims.[13]

When Reland was studying at Utrecht none of the university staff were equipped to teach Arabic. He consequently relied on the tuition of a German who was still inscribed as a student at Leiden, Heinrich Siecke (later known as Henry Sike). Sike, born in Bremen in 1668, had had a chequered and somewhat mysterious career before he came to Holland.[14] He completed his education at the Bremen Gymnasium Illustre, where he learned Hebrew and gained the favour of the professor of mathematics, Leibniz's friend Gerhard Meier, who would later refer to him as 'amicus et discipulus meus'.[15] He then seems to have enlisted in the Danish army and to have served as a soldier in the Levant. We know nothing about where he actually went. He matriculated as a student of theology at Leiden on 11 September 1693. Even if Syriac and Aramaic were being taught, there was no professor of Arabic at the university and it must have been on his own that Sike learnt his Arabic and some of the other Oriental languages which he mastered – Persian, Turkish and Armenian. By 1695 Sike had established a reputation as an Orientalist. Gerhard Meier wrote to Leibniz on 22 September telling him that the most promising natives of Bremen included

---

13 J. van Amersfoort and W.J. van Asselt, eds, *Liever Turks dan Paaps? De visies van Johannes Coccejus, Gisbertus Voetius en Adrianus Relandus op de Islam* (Zoetermeer, 1997), p. 149. The book also includes a text by Coccejus and Reland's preface to *De religione mohammedica* (in Latin and in a Dutch translation).

14 On Sike see L. Forster, 'Henry Sike of Bremen (1669–1712), Regius Professor of Hebrew and Fellow of Trinity' *Transactions of the Cambridge Bibliographical Society*, 10 (1991–95), pp. 249–177; A. Hamilton, 'Henry Sike (1668–1712). A German Orientalist in Holland and England' *Journal of the Warburg and Courtauld Institutes* 84 (2021), pp. 127–159.

15 G.W. Leibniz, *Allgemeiner politischer und historischer Briefwechsel*, vol. 13 (Berlin, 1987), p. 492.

'quidam Sikius Linguarum orientalium callentissimus'.[16] In June of the following year Meier informed Leibniz of Sike's plan to translate the Qur'an[17] and from then on Leibniz was to follow his career with the utmost interest.[18]

While he was a student at Leiden Sike made the acquaintance of Reland, probably on a visit to Utrecht. By 1696 Reland had developed a decided interest in Islam, and in May he defended two dissertations on the subject, thus proving that, thanks to Sike, he had acquired a sound basis in Arabic. The first, supervised by Witsius, the *Exercitatio philologico-theologica de symbolo Mohammedico (Non est Deus nisi Unus) adversus quod SS Trinitas defenditur*, was on the Prophet's treatment of the Trinity, and the second, supervised by Leydekker and dedicated to Graevius and the Voetian members of the theological faculty, the *Exercitatio philologico-theologica de consensu Mohammedanismi et Judaismi*, was on the Jewish origins of Islam and the points of community between Islam and Judaism. Although they were manifestly anti-Islamic in tone, Reland displayed a certain freedom of judgement by criticizing, albeit implicitly, some of the myths and errors circulated by adverse propaganda.[19] In *De symbolo Mohammedico* he argued that the Muslims did not believe in universal salvation (despite the Western persuasion to the contrary). In *De consensu Mohammedanismi et Judaismi* he devoted a section to Jewish and Muslim ritual ablutions from which it emerges that, again contrary to a widespread belief in the West, they were never intended to wash away sin. He would return to both these themes in his *De religione mohammedica*. Reland's two dissertations end with poems by Heinrich Sike, the one in *De symbolo* in Latin, and the one in *De consensu* in Arabic.

On 16 October 1696 Sike and Reland attended the sale in Leiden of Golius's private collection of manuscripts.[20] They both bought a number of items, and Sike acquired an Arabic codex which Golius had bought in Turkey in about 1628, an Egyptian adaptation of the so-called Arabic Infancy Gospel.[21] The

---

16   Leibniz, *Briefwechsel*, vol. 10 (Berlin, 1979), p. 683.
17   Leibniz, *Briefwechsel*, vol. 12 (Berlin, 1990), p. 614.
18   *Ibid.*, p. 615.
19   For a discussion of Reland's development see A. Hamilton, 'From a "Closet at Utrecht": Adriaan Reland and Islam' *Nederlands archief voor kerkgeschiedenis* 78 (1998), pp. 243–250.
20   On the sale see J.J. Witkam, *Jacobus Golius (1596–1667) en zijn handschriften* (Leiden, 1980), pp. 61, 67–70. On Reland's library see B. Jaski, 'The manuscript collection of Adriaan Reland in the University Library of Utrecht and beyond' in Jaski et al., eds, *The Orient in Utrecht*, pp. 321–361; *idem*, 'The manuscript collection of Adriaan Reland' in *ibid.*, pp. 434–484; A. Vrolijk, 'The Adriaan Reland collection at Leiden University Library. Antoine Galland autographs, oriental manuscripts and the enigmas of the 1761 auction catalogue' in *ibid.*, pp. 362–398.
21   The manuscript is now Bodl., MS Bodl. Or. 350.

Arabic version, which was in circulation by the ninth century, was based on an apocryphal Syriac text probably dating from the fifth or sixth century.[22] Sike's interest in it should be seen as part of the growing attention paid to the early Church, the writings of the Apostolic Fathers, and the late biblical apocrypha in general, clearly perceptible from the early 1680s on, and which would have considerable consequences not only for the dating of certain Scriptural texts, but also for the attempt to place and assess the birth of Christianity in a historical context independent of revelation.[23]

Sike's edition of the Infancy Gospel, *Evangelium Infantiae. Vel Liber apocryphus de Infantia Servatoris*, was published in Utrecht in 1697. Gerhard Meier wrote to Leibniz about it in January,[24] and Leibniz, who read the work with enthusiasm, praised the 'juvenis Bremensis pereruditus' to other friends.[25] An established citizen of the Republic of Letters, Sike was now invited to Utrecht by two Germans, the young classicist Ludolf Küster, from Blomberg in Westphalia, and the far older professor of rhetoric, statecraft and history, the Cartesian Johann Georg Graevius.

Although neither officially a student nor a member of the teaching staff of Utrecht University, Sike evidently formed part of the Cartesian group and was regarded with suspicion by the more orthodox Calvinists. The opponents of Cartesianism were quick to accuse the followers of Descartes of admiration for Spinoza. Graevius, like a number of other members of the *Collegie der sçavanten*, would express his aversion to Spinoza's teaching, but he had nevertheless been in touch with him, as we know from the letter Spinoza wrote in December 1673 about an account of the death of Descartes. And accusations of Spinozism were also levelled against his protégé Heinrich Sike. In May 1700 Sike wrote to his publisher, the university printer François Halma, denying the rumours which, he heard, Halma had been circulating about him – that he had not taken communion for over twenty years, that he had expressed the most unorthodox views about religion, and that he had made statements which savoured of 'Spinozism'.[26]

---

22   For a survey see C. Genequand's study and translation, 'Vie de Jésus en arabe' in F. Bovon and P. Geoltrain, eds, *Ecrits apocryphes chrétiens*, vol. I (Paris, 1997), pp. 207–238.
23   Cf. A. Hamilton, *The Apocryphal Apocalypse: The Reception of the Second Book of Esdras (4 Ezra) from the Renaissance to the Enlightenment* (Oxford, 1999), pp. 227–228, 235–240, 245–248.
24   Leibniz, *Briefwechsel*, vol. 13 (Berlin, 1987), p. 492.
25   Leibniz, *Briefwechsel*, vol. 14 (Berlin, 1993), pp. 225, 522, 544.
26   UBL, MS Pap. 15: 'Voici en peu de mots la raison, pourquoi je prens la liberté de vous écrire ce mot de lettre. Il court ici un un bruit, que l'apres dinée du même jour, que je vous ai parlé la derniere fois le matin chez Msr van de Water, vous ayez dit a quelque Professeur d'ici, non seulement, que je n' avois point communié il y a plus de vingt ans, mais aussi

At Utrecht Sike developed a close friendship with Frans Burman's sons, especially with Pieter, and he sealed his friendship with Reland who returned to Utrecht to take up the professorship of Oriental languages in 1701. In view of the severe limitations of the Utrecht library, Reland was partly dependent for his *De religione mohammedica* on the Arabic manuscripts in Sike's own small collection.[27] In the spring of 1703 Sike went to Austria and Italy as the travelling companion of the earl of Huntingdon, and finally left Utrecht in 1705 for Cambridge. Both Graevius and Küster had written about him to Richard Bentley, master of Trinity College, and, after the formalities of arranging for Sike to obtain a degree at Utrecht and an honorary doctorate in law at Cambridge, Bentley had him appointed Regius professor of Hebrew. In England Sike continued to correspond with his Utrecht friends.

When he was working at the Bodleian Library at Oxford Sike came across one of the manuscripts which Edward Pococke had brought back from the East and which contained the *Muʿallaqāt*, a collection, assembled in the eighth century, of works by the sixth-century 'pre-Islamic' poets. Sike clearly realized its significance and decided to edit it.[28] Had he completed his project he would have anticipated Johann Jakob Reiske's edition of 1742 which was of revolutionary importance for the dating of early Arabic literature and for the linguistic assessment of the Qurʾan.[29] All he managed to do, however, was to transcribe the odes of Imrūʾ al-Qays and Ṭarāfa. Apparently subject to fits of 'melancholy', he committed suicide in his rooms in Trinity on 20 May 1712. Shortly before, he had proclaimed the deepest admiration for the Qurʾan as the expression of a supremely rational faith, 'not only the elegantest but the most rational book in the world.'[30]

---

  que vous saviez, que j'eusse de méchants sentiments touchant la religon, que vous en aviés de preuves, et que vous aviés entendu de ma bouche des discours, qui sentient le Spinozisme [...].'

27 Adriaen Reland, *De religione mohammedica libri duo*, 2nd edn, (Utrecht, 1717), sigs 2N2ᵛ–2N3ᵛ.

28 Sike's transcription survives in manuscript, Bodl., MS Bodl. Or. 248.

29 For Reiske and the *Muʿallaqāt* see J. Loop, 'Language of Paradise: Protestant Oriental Scholarship and the Discovery of Arabic Poetry' in N. Hardy and D. Levitin, eds, *Confessionalisation and Erudition in Early Modern Europe. An Episode in the History of the Humanities* (Oxford, 2019), pp. 395–415, esp. pp. 407–11; Fück, pp. 108–124. Reiske was altogether unaware of Sike's discovery and knew no more about him than that he was the editor of the Arabic Infancy Gospel. R. Forester, ed., *Johann Jacob Reiske's Briefe* (Leipzig, 1897), p. 267 (letter dated 24 May 1748 to Johann Jacob Schultens).

30 Thomas Hearne, *Remarks and Collections*, ed. C.E. Doble et al. (Oxford, 1885–1921), vol. 3, p. 368.

If Sike can be said to have formed part of the Cartesian core at Utrecht, so, of course, can Reland. Between finishing his studies at Utrecht in 1696 and his appointment as professor of physics and metaphysics at Harderwijk in 1700, Reland studied at Leiden where he matriculated in September 1697.[31] He had there attended the course of Wolferd Sengeurd in experimental physics,[32] and it may well have been partly from Sengeurd that he derived some of the qualifications in the admiration for Descartes which he expressed in his inaugural address at Harderwijk. Like his *De libertate philosophandi* of 1694, the *Oratio de incremento, quod Philosophia cepit hoc saeculo* testifies to his strong opposition to Aristotelianism. He displayed the utmost veneration for Ramus, the first man to 'break' the authority of Aristotle and consequently to point the way to conclusions solely based on the observation of nature.[33] In a tone reminiscent of his earlier thesis, he went on to praise the various protagonists of the Scientific Revolution – Francis Bacon, Johann Kepler, Galileo Galilei, Evangelista Torricelli, William Harvey, Kenelm Digby, Robert Boyle and Pierre Gassendi – and he ended with Descartes, 'illustre saeculi nostri ornamentum'. Yet, however much he admired Descartes's ideas on the natural sciences, he said, without any further specification, that he did not approve of the whole of his philosophy.[34]

Reland's appointment to the Utrecht chair of Oriental languages was yet another indication of a growing change of climate at the university. Despite the appointment in 1699 as extraordinary professor of theology of the Voetian

---

31 G. Du Rieu, *Album Studiosorum Academiae Lugduno Batavae* MDLXXV–MDCCCLXXV (The Hague, 1875), col. 747.

32 On Sengeurd see De Pater, 'Experimental physics', pp. 319–323.

33 Adriaen Reland, *Oratio de incremento, quod Philosophia cepit hoc saeculo* [...] (Amsterdam, 1700), pp. 8–9: '[...] donec elapso saeculo, primus frangere quodammodo auctoritatem Aristotelis et doctrinam ejus labefactare Petrus Ramus sustinuit, et ad lumen illud Sapientiae, quo fruimur hodie, viam fecit. Hunc secuti ducem, quibus de meliore luto Titan praecordia finxerat, non Libros Aristotelis, sed ipsam rerum naturam, ingenii acumine investigare et explicare aggressi sunt, certissime persuasi hac sola ratione comparari posse certam cognitionem rerum naturalium et promoveri.'

34 *Ibid.*, pp. 15–16: 'Huic aetati suppar fuit quem praeterii hactenus, ut illustriori Coronide designatutn Sapientum ordinem nobilitarem, illustre saeculi nostri ornamentum, Renatus Cartesius. Hujus ego Philosophi placita licet omnia non probem, quod ob famam tanti Viri invita hoc loco fatetur oratio, id tamen affirmemus necesse est, nisi in clarissima luce caecutire velimus, summa ilium ingenii subtilitate, Mathematico, id est, accuratissimo ordine, ingenua et omnibus imitanda libertate, scientiam rerum naturalium ulterius, quam ante ejus tempora factum erat, promovisse. Qui si vel id solum praestitisset, quod aliis viae dux fuit et calcar subdidit ad Naturae inquisitionem et novum Philosophiae Systema concinnandum, dignus foret omnium laudibus et existimatione, quam talem, qualem rari ante Philosophi, est consecutus [...]'

Hendrik Pontanus, who only died in 1714, in the last decade of the seventeenth century and the years thereafter Cartesianism, as we saw, seemed to be gaining prestige. Graevius, who died in 1703, was only just in time to witness this development. When Witsius had left Utrecht for Leiden in 1698 an attempt had been made to attract the notorious Coccejan Campegius Vitringa from Franeker, but this had failed and Pontanus had been appointed to a full professorship in his stead. In 1701, however, Reland was nominated. Frans Burman's son Pieter, who had been given an extraordinary chair in history in 1696 and was known for his outspoken contempt for the Voetians, obtained a full professorship in 1703 as Graevius's successor. In the following year (when Reland was rector) Hermann Alexander Roëll was called from Franeker and given a chair in philosophy, to the horror of Leydekker, Pontanus and Pieter van Maastricht.[35] Two years later, in 1706, both Pieter van Maastricht and Gerard de Vries died, the latter to be succeeded by the renowned Cartesian Joseph Serrurier – an appointment which Pieter Burman greeted with exultation.[36] And in 1715 Pieter Burman's brother Frans the Younger obtained the professorship of theology.

In Utrecht Reland gave further evidence of his approval of the new philosophy. He had a hand in the second edition of the Dutch translation of Ibn al-Tufail's *Hayy ben Yaqdhân, De natuurlyke wysgeer, of het leven van Hai Ebn Jokdan*. The celebrated account of how sensory experience and reason could lead to the discovery not only of the natural world but also of God had originally been translated from Arabic into Latin by Edward Pococke's son, Edward the Younger, and appeared, in a bilingual edition, in Oxford in 1671. Popular in Spinozist circles, it was turned from Latin into Dutch by Johannes Bouwmeester, a close friend of Spinoza's devoted follower Ludwig Meyer, and it was even suggested that the translator, his initials given in reverse order, S.D.B., was Spinoza himself. The first edition of the Dutch translation, simply entitled *Het leven van Hai ebn Yokdhan*, had appeared early in 1701, printed by Willem Lamsveld in Amsterdam. The Rotterdam printer Pieter van der Veer then decided to produce a new edition, also in 1701, and called on Reland to check the translation against the Arabic original and to add explanatory notes of his own.[37] In the same year Reland composed a Latin ode to accompany the translation of Lucretius by the Cartesian doctor and philosopher Jan de

---

35 J. van Sluis, *Herman Alexander Roëll* (Leeuwarden, 1988), pp. 34–38.
36 Thijssen-Schoute, *Nederlands Cartesianisme*, p. 451.
37 *Ibid.*, p. 415. See R. Kruk and A. Vrolijk, 'The first Dutch translation of *Ḥayy ibn Yaqẓān*, Reland's annotated version and the mysterious translator S.D.B.' in Jaski et al., eds., *The Orient in Utrecht*, pp. 109–145. On the translation see also J.I. Israel, *Radical Enlightenment. Philosophy and the Making of Modernity 1650–1750* (Oxford, 2001), p. 198, and for Bouwmeester, p. 309.

Witt,[38] and in 1706 he joined Roëll's son in writing a eulogy to go with the inaugural address of Joseph Serrurier.[39] It was Serrurier, finally, who delivered the address at Reland's funeral on 7 March 1718.

But what of Reland's main work on Islam? Although it contains a number of traditional – and not always correct – ideas, such as the importance of the study of Arabic for the understanding of Hebrew and the Bible, his *De religione mohammedica*, foreshadowed by the work of Golius and Pocock, reveals a new approach.[40] The animosity against Islam apparent in his early dissertations has diminished. Reland now stresses the need to understand the Muslim faith. It is in this context that he again refutes a number of the more common misconceptions about Islam – the legend, for example, that the Prophet had trained a dove to pick seeds out of his ear in order to simulate divine inspiration (already denied by Pocock), the belief that Muslim ablutions were intended to wash away sins and the idea that the Muslims believed in universal salvation (the two themes he had touched on in his Utrecht dissertations). In *De religione mohammedica* Reland treats the faith of the Muslims in a different spirit from that of Voetius or of Ludovico Marracci, the pious confessor of Pope Innocent XI whose bilingual, Latin and Arabic edition of the Qurʾan, frequently quoted by Reland in the second (but not in the first) edition of his *De religione* on account of its extensive excerpts from Qurʾanic commentaries, had been published in its complete form in 1698.

Reland's eagerness to confute erroneous legends and to eliminate prejudices stems from the scepticism towards accepted views associated with the method of Descartes. The statement in his preface, 'veritas ubicunque est indagari debet',[41] which is in fact the justification of his entire investigation, refers to a truth which is neither that of Voetius, who was writing with an eye to Protestant missionaries, nor that of Marracci, who was writing with an eye to Catholic ones. And his conviction that 'bona mens aequaliter distributa est',[42]

---

38   Thijssen-Schoute, *Nederlands Cartesianisme*, pp. 432–433.
39   *Ibid.*, p. 453.
40   Reland's attitude to Islam is discussed, albeit somewhat controversially, by A. Gunny, *Images of Islam in Eighteenth-Century Writings* (London, 1996), pp. 54–57. See also L. Brouwer, 'Adriaan Reland's legacy as a scholar of Islam' in Jaski *et al.*, eds, *The Orient in Utrecht*, pp. 44–64.
41   Reland, *De religione mohammedica* (1705), **2ᵛ.
42   *Ibid.*, sig. ***2ᵛ. The Latin translation is Reland's own. Cf. Reland, *De libertate philosophandi*, p. 14: 'Et profecto, nisi Cartesius bonam mentem aequaliter esse distributam novisset, ad illud, quo pervenisse creditur, sapientiae fastigium nunquam adspirasset, verum, ut alii inter Scholasticos, ratione excussa, praeceptorum se mancipasset opinionibus, nec Aristotelis, nec illorum transgressus limites, quorum iras propterea toties expertus est.'

a transparent allusion to the opening sentence of the *Discours de la méthode*, is a far cry from Marracci's implication that non-Christians were fools. Reland may not have been a follower of Descartes in every respect – and indeed, how many Dutch Cartesians were? – but the influence of the new philosophy is evident in the novelty of his approach to many of the subjects which he studied.

Acknowledgements

This article first appeared in Paul Hoftijzer and Theo Verbeek, eds, *Leven na Descartes. Zeven opstellen over ideeëngeschiedenis in Nederland in de tweede helft van de zeventiende eeuw* (Hilversum: Uitgeverij Verloren, 2005), pp. 97–105. I am most indebted to the advice of Theo Verbeek and Jill Kraye.

CHAPTER 8

Pilgrims, Missionaries, and Scholars

Western Descriptions of the Monastery of St Paul from the Late Fourteenth Century to the Early Twentieth Century

In the late Middle Ages and the early modern period the Monastery of St Paul near the Red Sea coast of Egypt (Fig. 5) was comparatively neglected by Western travellers.[1] Regarded as a remote appendage of the Monastery of St Antony, it seldom shared the attraction of the older and larger foundation. By the time Europeans had embarked on their long hunt for Coptic and Coptic-Arabic manuscripts in the seventeenth century, St Paul's had long been abandoned. It consequently lacked the library which drew collectors to St Antony's and the monasteries of the Wādī al-Naṭrūn. Nevertheless, because of its connection with St Antony's, and the legendary friendship between Antony and Paul so evocatively recounted by Jerome, it sometimes benefited from the glory of the larger monastery, while its spectacular setting would, in due course, become a goal in itself.[2]

The statements of those few travellers who recorded their visit to St Paul's have been amply exploited by modern scholars. For anyone trying to reconstruct the history, as well as the appearance, of the monastery, they provide invaluable pieces in an intricate puzzle. But the reports and the visitors themselves also reflect various stages in European relations with Egypt. They illustrate the growing European acquaintance with the Coptic community and changing perceptions of the Copts, as well as the shifts in missionary policy, the quest for manuscripts and antiquities, and the scientific exploration of the country.

---

1 This is borne out by the remarkably small amount of graffiti that has been detected on the monastery walls. See D. von Kraack, *Monumentale Zeugnisse der spätmittelalterlichen Adelsreise: Inschriften und Graffiti des 14.–16. Jahrhunderts* (Göttingen, 1997), pp. 267–268.
2 The standard survey of travellers to St Paul's remains O.F.A. Meinardus, *Monks and Monasteries of the Egyptian Desert* (Cairo, 1992), pp. 35–43. Since the visitors to St Paul's

FIGURE 5   General view of St Paul's Monastery from the southeast (2005)
PHOTOGRAPH © NICHOLAS WARNER

1 Prosperity to Destitution

One of the first medieval travellers to leave an account of the Monastery of St Paul was Ogier d'Anglure from Champagne, who passed through Egypt on his way to the Holy Land in 1395. Like most of his contemporaries, he was stimulated to visit the monasteries on the Red Sea coast by what he knew of the lives of Antony and Paul. He was fascinated by the legend of the raven providing them with bread and of the lions helping to dig Paul's grave, and he introduced an element popular in late medieval iconography of St Antony – the pig, which he describes as Antony's guide in his quest for Paul.[3] But while many medieval pilgrims regarded the Copts simply as guardians of the holy places, worthy of no more than a cursory glance, Ogier showed a greater interest in them. They were, he wrote, 'Jacobite Christians', who were first circumcised and then baptized. They crossed themselves with the index finger of their right hand. Their liturgical rites differed from those in the West but resembled those of the 'Christians of the land of Prester John.'[4]

Such was the view of the Egyptian members of the Church of Alexandria at the time.[5] The term 'Copt' was hardly ever used. It only started to gain currency in the mid-sixteenth century, and even then did so slowly. 'Jacobite', on the other hand, was used widely. This led to a certain confusion, since no distinction was made between the Egyptian members of the Church of Alexandria, the Ethiopian members of the same Church, and the Syrian members of the Church of Antioch who rejected the Council of Chalcedon and were accused of monophysitism or belief in a single nature in Christ. The legend of Prester John, which emerged from one of the great literary hoaxes of the twelfth

---

usually visited St Antony's too, further information is to be found in G. Gabra, 'Perspectives on the Monastery of St. Antony: Medieval and later inhabitants and visitors' in E.S. Bolman, ed., *Monastic Visions: Wall Paintings in the Monastery of St. Antony at the Red Sea* (New Haven, 2002), pp. 173–183. A still more detailed list of visitors is given in the unpublished 'History of the Monasteries of St. Anthony and St. Paul', produced by the Whittemore expedition team (but above all by Alexandre Piankoff), ca. 1930–1940. The manuscript is in Dumbarton Oaks, Byzantine Photograph and Fieldwork Archives, Washington, D.C.

3 Ogier d'Anglure, *Le saint voyage de Jherusalem du seigneur d'Anglure*, ed. F. Bonnardot and A. Longnon (Paris, 1878), p. 71. Ogier's source remains unspecified, and we can only assume that he had contemporary depictions in mind. The origin of the pig as Antony's companion is obscure. For the possibility that it might indeed be derived not only from Antony's alleged patronage of domestic animals but also from Athanasius's biography of the saint where, in chapter 29, he mentions the legend that devils do not even have power over pigs, see H. Trebbin, *Sankt Antonius: Geschichte, Kult und Kunst* (Frankfurt a.M., 1994), pp. 26, 35.
4 D'Anglure, *Le saint voyage*, pp. 70–73.
5 A. Hamilton, *The Copts and the West 1439–1822. The European Discovery of the Egyptian Church*, rev. edn (Oxford, 2014), pp. 107–115.

century, a letter supposedly addressed by a mysterious Eastern potentate to the Byzantine emperor, made the issue still more complicated. The fictitious author, Prester John, who vaunted his power and his riches as well as his Christianity, claimed to be the ruler of the 'three Indias'. These were what is now the subcontinent of India, the East Indies, and Ethiopia. On contemporary maps, however, Ethiopia was represented as stretching eastward from Africa, parallel to Mesopotamia and Persia. The land of Prester John was thus situated in the East rather than in the South, and even after cartographers had allowed Ethiopia to drop south into Eastern Africa in the course of the fourteenth century, an association with India persisted, and the origin of the Copts was frequently sought in Asia.[6]

Despite the obvious differences between the Copts and the Christians of the West, Ogier d'Anglure was charmed by his reception at St Paul's, where he proceeded after staying at St Antony's, arriving on 3 December 1395. The monastery, he wrote, contained over sixty monks, and they welcomed him and his companions, getting up at midnight to let them in and providing them with an excellent hot meal. He admired 'the fine walls, high and thick' and liked the 'beautiful little chapel.'[7] Of the medieval pilgrims Ogier provided by far the most detailed description of the monastery. The Burgundian diplomat and soldier Ghillebert de Lannoy, who visited it in 1422, was far more cursory, referring simply to the site of the building at the foot of the mountains, the spring issuing from the rock, its fortified appearance, its subjection to St Antony's, and its garden of palm trees.[8]

More than two hundred years elapsed before another visitor from the West described the Monastery of St Paul. By this time not only had the monastery been abandoned since the late sixteenth century, but European attitudes to the Copts had undergone deep changes. At the Council of Florence, held between 1438 and 1445, the papacy had endeavoured to bring all the Eastern Christian Churches into communion with Rome. These included the Copts, who were represented by a small delegation led by the prior of the Monastery of St Antony. The agreement reached by the Eastern Churches with Rome, however, was never ratified – in the eighteenth century Edward Gibbon would describe the Eastern delegates as 'unknown in the countries which they presumed to represent' – and the result was the gradual organization of a mis-

---

6   For a discussion of where Prester John was thought to be, see G. Zaganelli, ed., *La lettera del Prete Gianni* (Parma, 1990), pp. 30–31.
7   D'Anglure, *Le saint voyage*, p. 72.
8   C. Potvin and J.-C. Houzeau, eds, *Oeuvres de Ghillebert de Lannoy, voyageur, diplomate et moraliste* (Louvain, 1878), p. 70.

sionary movement whose members would pursue the delegates and their successors in a quest that extended over the centuries.[9]

The first true mission to the Copts was composed of Jesuits who set off in 1561.[10] Although the mission never achieved its purpose, it marked the beginning of a Western interest in the Church of Alexandria, and the publication of the missionaries' reports, which appeared in the early years of the seventeenth century, served to familiarize Europeans with Egyptian Christianity. In 1622 Pope Gregory XV founded the *Congregatio de Propaganda Fide*, which would remain the principal coordinator of the Roman missionaries. In the seventeenth century, however, Egypt was no longer as interesting to the missionaries as it had once been. Ethiopia was considered of far greater importance. It was reportedly sympathetic to Catholicism – the emperors had been converted by the Jesuits in 1603 and 1620 – but it was difficult to reach and would become increasingly dangerous after the rejection of Catholicism in 1632. Yet its inhabitants held mysterious beliefs which the Europeans, Protestants as well as Catholics, were eager to explore. As a result, many of the missions stopped only briefly in Egypt on their way south, but they availed themselves of their stay to try to convert the Copts.[11]

By the late 1630s there was a growing Western interest in the Coptic language and in Coptic manuscripts. This was centred around the French antiquarian Nicolas Fabri de Peiresc, who was eager to obtain Coptic versions of the Bible that could be included in the great polyglot edition of the Scriptures being prepared in Paris at the time.[12] But the study of Coptic also received a strong impulse from the appearance in 1636 of the first study of the language, the *Prodromus coptus sive aegyptiacus* by Peiresc's former protégé, the Jesuit Athanasius Kircher. Kircher presented Coptic as the key to the hieroglyphs and thus to an ancient Egyptian wisdom that was the source of all learning, and however harshly criticized Kircher may have been by fellow scholars, his ideas, often outrageous, sometimes correct, and frequently original, exercised a formidable fascination throughout Europe.[13]

---

9   Edward Gibbon, *The History of the Decline and Fall of the Roman Empire*, ed. D. Womersley (London, 1994), vol. 3, p. 893.
10 C. Libois, ed., *Monumenta Proximi-Orientis. Vol. 2. Egypte (1547–1563)* (Rome, 1993), pp. 111*–120*.
11 C. Libois, ed., *Monumenta Proximi-Orientis. Vol. 5. Egypte (1591–1699)* (Rome, 2002), pp. xli–lxii.
12 P. Miller, 'Copts and scholars: Athanasius Kircher in Peiresc's Republic of Letters' in P. Findlen, ed., *Athanasius Kircher: The Last Man to Know Everything* (London, 2004), pp. 133–148.
13 Hamilton, *The Copts and the West*, pp. 195–208.

Jean Coppin, the first traveller in the seventeenth century to publish an account of his visit to the Monastery of St Paul, had served as a cavalry officer in the early stages of what would later be known as the Thirty Years War, fighting in the French army against the Habsburgs. He then decided to travel and to become acquainted with the Ottoman Empire. He arrived in Egypt early in 1638 and, in March, made the pilgrimage to the Red Sea monasteries. He set off from Cairo with eight companions.[14] Four were laymen: three European merchants, one of whom spoke Arabic, Turkish, and Greek and served as interpreter – and an Arab guide. The four others were clerics: two Franciscan Recollects, one from Aix-en-Provence and the other from Naples, and two Capuchin missionaries, Pierre from Brittany, and Agathange de Vendôme. The man about whom we are best informed is Agathange de Vendôme. He, like so many other missionaries, was on his way to Ethiopia where, together with Cassien de Nantes, he would be executed shortly after his last meeting with Coppin. While he was in Egypt Agathange also acted as an agent for Peiresc, and one of the reasons for his eagerness to visit St Antony's was to inspect its collection of manuscripts.[15] Yet it was above all as a missionary that he travelled, and his principal aspiration was to win converts for Rome.

Agathange de Vendôme was one of the more enlightened missionaries.[16] He rejected the obtuse instructions of the *Propaganda Fide*, according to which Catholics were forbidden to consort with heretics. He wrote at length to the prefect of the *Propaganda*, Cardinal Antonio Barberini, pointing out the impossibility of imposing such measures on the members of a monastic community, and he was one of many missionaries to have doubts about the actual heresy of the Copts. The only error he could detect in their liturgy, he wrote, was the invocation of two of the founders of monophysitism, Dioscorus, the patriarch of the Church of Alexandria at the time of the Council of Chalcedon, and the slightly later Severus of Antioch, who held a more moderate view of the doctrine of the single nature in Christ. It would take little, he claimed somewhat optimistically, to win over the Copts and persuade them to drop the two

---

14 Jean Coppin, *Le bouclier de l'Europe, ou la Guerre Sainte* (Lyon, 1686), pp. 291–305.

15 In A. de Valence, ed., *Correspondance de Peiresc avec plusieurs missionnaires et religieux de l'Ordre des Capucins, 1631–1637* (Paris, 1891), p. 313, Peiresc mentions Agathange's visit to St Paul's in a letter to another Capuchin, Gilles de Loches, dated 9 February 1637: 'Il a esté a l'hermitage de S. Paul pour Ar ..., où il ne trouva plus d'habitans.' Elsewhere (p. 270) Peiresc says that Agathange was at St Antony's together with yet another Capuchin, Benoît de Dijon.

16 Hamilton, *The Copts and the West*, pp. 78–79.

names at divine service.[17] Agathange de Vendôme's hagiographers delighted in his success at converting the monks of St Antony's to Catholicism, but in fact it seems most unlikely that more than a couple were so much as interested in his arguments, and even Coppin admitted that none of them abandoned the Church of Alexandria.[18]

Coppin and his companions sailed from Cairo to Beni Suef. This took four days, and, having collected camels and a Bedouin guide on the east bank of the Nile, they arrived at St Antony's three days later.[19] After spending three days exploring the monastery and the surrounding sites, Coppin decided to travel on to St Paul's with six of his companions. The others joined Coppin. Although they were offered the chance of taking the relatively brief route on foot straight over the mountains, the travellers, with bread in their pockets and two bottles of wine, preferred to keep their camels and to take the longer way, even if they left their camels shortly before St Paul's and crossed the remaining sandstone hills on foot. The monastery they discovered was abandoned. Coppin gave a detailed description of the walls with a large breach in them, of the subterranean vault once leading to the spring but almost entirely demolished, of the keep, which retained its brickwork, and above all of the Cave Church, some twelve feet underground and with twenty-three steps leading to it. In the church, and by the side of the steps, the visitors could just distinguish a number of wall paintings which the Bedouin had disfigured with their spears.[20]

Despite its state of abandonment, the Cave Church seemed evocative enough for Agathange de Vendôme to celebrate mass and for Coppin to take communion. The travellers then visited the orchard – Coppin plucked a branch from an incense tree, which he used as a stick. They drank from the spring in the grotto, had a 'sober repast' of bread in memory of the loaf given by a raven to the 'two Solitary Saints,' and admired the view of the Red Sea and the Sinai mountains. On their way back to St Antony's they recollected scenes from Jerome's *Life of Paul* as they observed the plain where Antony encountered two 'monsters', a centaur and a satyr, and where the satyr, with a human voice, testified to his knowledge of God. At St Antony's, Coppin and Agathange de Vendôme left each other, the Capuchin preferring to remain and proselytize. They would meet in Cairo the following month.[21]

---

17 Ignazio da Seggiano, 'Documenti inediti sull'apostolato dei Minori Capuccini nel Vicino Oriente (1623–1684)' *Collectanea Francescana* 18 (1948), pp. 118–244, esp. pp. 144–145.
18 Coppin, *Le bouclier*, p. 320: 'Environ un mois aprs nostre retour le Pere Agatange revint avec beaucoup de regret de n'avoir rien avancé sur l'esprit des Religieux Cophites.'
19 *Ibid.*, pp. 294–305.
20 *Ibid.*, pp. 313–317.
21 *Ibid.*, p. 320.

It was many years later that Coppin actually wrote the account of his travels, and even longer before it appeared in print. He returned to France in 1639 and travelled in Tunisia, Palestine, and Syria before going back to Egypt in 1643. In this time he gathered political and military information about the Ottoman Empire. When he was again in Egypt he acted for three years as French (and English) consul in Damietta. Once back in France, however, he entered a monastic order, joining the recently founded hermits of St John the Baptist in Chaumont near Le Puy. In 1665 he left his monastery to present his notes on the strengths and the weaknesses of the Ottoman Empire to Louis XIV's secretary of state, the marquis de Louvois, and he went on to Rome in order to persuade the pope, Alexander VII, to lead a new crusade against the Ottomans.[22] He stayed there for two and a half years before returning once more to Chaumont, where he completed the work containing his description of Egypt, *Le Bouclier de l'Europe, ou la Guerre Sainte, contenant des avis politiques et Chrétiens, qui peuvent servir de lumière aux Rois et aux Souverains de la Chrêtienté, pour garantir leurs Estats des incursions des Turcs, et reprendre ceux qu'ils ont usurpé sur eux. Avec une relation de Voyages faits dans la Turquie, la Thébaide et la Barbarie*. It was published in Lyons in 1686, some four years before Coppin's death.[23]

Coppin's work was an appeal to the rulers of Christian Europe to unite in a war against the Turks. In the course of his travels he had observed what he regarded as the more vulnerable aspects of the Ottoman defences, and he was convinced that, if the Western princes could overcome their political and confessional disagreements, they would have little difficulty in regaining the territory the Christians had once lost to the Muslims.[24] Appeals of this kind were by no means uncommon. The Arabist Pierre Vattier had repeatedly urged the French king to 'create a new France in those beautiful countries of the East' and, in 1666, strongly recommended the invasion and colonisation of Egypt. The same desire was expressed by Leibniz six years later.[25] Coppin's book, however, appeared when his hopes seemed well on the way to being fulfilled. Three years earlier, in 1683, the Turks had suffered a decisive defeat at the gates of Vienna, and the Christian armies were at last advancing into the Ottoman Empire.

---

22 J.-M. Carré, *Voyageurs et écrivains français en Egypte* (Cairo, 1956), vol. 1, pp. 18–19.
23 *Ibid.*, vol. 1, p. 19.
24 Coppin, *Le bouclier*, pp. 3–4.
25 See A. Hamilton and F. Richard, *André Du Ryer and Oriental Studies in Seventeenth-Century France* (London-Oxford, 2004), pp. 56–57.

By the time Coppin wrote his book he was evidently ill-disposed toward the Copts. He described their religion as the 'coarsest and most absurd of all those of the Christians separated from the Church of Rome and living under Turkish rule.' They retained, he continued, numerous Judaic ceremonies, and they had adopted the heresies of Dioscorus and Eutyches. It was this same faith, he added, which had drawn the subjects of Prester John, whose patriarch resided in Ethiopia.[26] From a man who had spent more than five years in Egypt, who had liked the Copts he had met, and who had known Agathange de Vendôme, such misinformation is surprising. Living in his monastery, imbued with the precepts of orthodoxy, Coppin seems to have been pandering to traditional Catholic prejudices and to have adopted age-old Western misconceptions, in circulation ever since the Church Councils of the fifth century, such as the identification of the Coptic doctrine with the teaching of Eutyches. But Coppin's account of the Church of Alexandria, coming as late as it did, had little effect on European perceptions of the Copts, since it had been preceded – and implicitly discredited – by Johann Michael Wansleben's *Histoire de l'Eglise d'Alexandrie* (1677), with its far more reliable description of Coptic beliefs and practices.[27]

2   Revival and Restoration

Deserted, partly in ruins, and difficult to reach, the Monastery of St Paul still attracted few visitors, and no other Europeans seem to have recorded their impressions until efforts were being made to repopulate and restore the monastery in the early eighteenth century. In 1716 one of the most interesting foreign residents in Egypt, the Jesuit Claude Sicard, paid a visit to St Paul's. Like Agathange de Vendôme, Sicard, who had arrived in Egypt in 1712 after spending six years in Syria, had originally hoped to travel on to Ethiopia, but the impossibility of doing so, proved by the fate of Agathange and later missionaries, led

---

26   Coppin, *Le bouclier*, p. 307: 'Nous nous entretinmes quelque tems entre nous de la grande compassion que nous sentions de voir des Religieux qui menoient une vie si austere et si bonne en apparence, croupir miserablement dans une infinité d'erreurs, car ils sont de la secte des Cophites, qui est la plus grossiere et la plus absurde de toute celle des Chretiens separez de l'Eglise Romaine qui vivent sous la domination du Turc. Ils retiennent beaucoup de ceremonies Judaïques, ils sont dans les heresies de Dioscore, et d'Eutichés, et n'admettent qu'une nature et qu'une volonté en Jesus Christ, et il n'est pas croyable combien, depuis qu'ils sont separez de l'Eglise Romaine, ils ont rassemblé de faux dogmes, et d'usages abusifs. C'est pourtant cette Religion que suivent une grande partie des sujets du Prete-Jan, et le Patriarche de ces Cophites reside d'ordinaire en Ethiopie.'
27   Hamilton, *The Copts and the West*, pp. 148–151.

him to settle in Egypt and concentrate on studying and educating the Copts as well as on exploring the country.[28] The fruits of Sicard's activities included maps (Fig. 6) of the Eastern Desert and of Cairo that were of unprecedented accuracy, and descriptions of ancient sites which are of value to archaeologists to this day. Also like Agathange de Vendôme, Sicard was in disagreement with the instructions issued by the *Propaganda Fide* in Rome. He wrote eloquently against the idea that Catholics should shun heretics, and for this the *Propaganda* never forgave him.[29] He was regarded, both in Rome and by the Reformed Franciscan missionaries in Egypt, as lax in his doctrine and following 'la strada larga', the broad path.[30]

Yet a missionary Sicard remained, and he had a true contempt for the Coptic Church and its beliefs.[31] He was astounded by the ignorance, hypocrisy, and superstition of the monks. He despised their xenophobia, and he was appalled by their incessant use of charms and their love of magical practices. At the same time, however, his more flexible attitude toward conversion, together with his intelligence and affability, meant that he was far more successful in converting individual Copts to Catholicism than were his predecessors. His technique was exhibited at Dayr al-Suryān in the Wādī al-Naṭrūn. He there informed the monks that he was a Copt – indeed, that he was a far better Copt than they were – but, he added, a Copt who followed the true teaching of the Church of Alexandria, the pre-Chalcedonian doctrines of Church Fathers such as Cyril and Athanasius. He drew their attention to the orthodox statements contained in many of their manuscripts and tried to show how their Church had been led astray since Chalcedon.[32] This was what convinced his most dis-

---

28 For a survey of Sicard's life by Maurice Martin, see Claude Sicard, *Oeuvres. Vol. 1: Lettres et relations inédites* (Cairo, 1982), ed. M. Martin, pp. v–vii.

29 G.D. Mansi *et al.*, eds, *Sacrorum conciliorum nova, et amplissima collectio*, vol. 46 (Paris, 1911), cols. 170–176.

30 Libois, ed., *Monumenta Proximi-Orientis. Vol. 6. Egypte (1700–1773)* (Rome, 2003), p. 392.

31 Sicard's comments on the monks of St Antony's provide sufficient evidence of this: 'Toucherai-je à l'intérieur? Quel spectacle dégoûtant! L'erreur du monothélisme et monophysisme, une ignorance crasse, une indolence pour la recherche de la vérité qui va jusques à l'abrutissement, l'horreur pour les Francs, l'hypocrisie, la superstition, chercher la pierre philosophale, se mêler de sortilèges, d'écrire des billets préservatifs, d'enchanter les serpents, voilà généralement le caractère des moines coptes. Sont-ce là, dira-t-on, les successeurs de ces astres lumineux qui éclairaient la Thébaide et le monde entier? Qu'est-ce donc devenu ce fameux désert, le paradis de la pénitence, cette portion si précieuse de l'Eglise de Jésus-Christ? Le Seigneur l'a abandonné, il a renversé ces autels vivants.' Sicard, *Oeuvres*, vol. 1, p. 26.

32 *Ibid.*, p. 19.

FIGURE 6 Claude Sicard (1677–1726), *Carte des déserts de la Basse-Thébaïde aux environs des monastères de St Antoine et de St Paul hermites avec le plan des lieux par où les Israëlites ont probablement passé en sortant d'Egypte*, 1717
SOURCE: GALLICA.BNF.FR/BIBLIOTHÈQUE NATIONALE DE FRANCE

tinguished convert in Upper Egypt, Rafael Tuki from Girgā, who would later settle in Rome and, with his many editions of Coptic liturgical texts as well as his Coptic grammar, make an immense contribution to Coptic studies.[33]

One of Sicard's many advantages as a missionary was his command of Arabic. When he visited St Antony's and St Paul's, moreover, he was accompanied by a native speaker of the language, the Maronite Yūsuf ibn Simʿān al-Simʿānī, known in Italy as Giuseppe Simonio Assemani. If the first Jesuit mission to Egypt in the sixteenth century had been marred by an almost complete lack of communication between the missionaries and the Copts, this was no obstacle as far as Sicard was concerned. Yet there was one aspect of his mission to the Red Sea monasteries that reflected the oddly uninformed policy of the *Propaganda*, and this was the very presence of Assemani.

Giuseppe Simonio Assemani was born in Ḥaṣrūn on Mount Lebanon. Thanks to his uncle, the bishop of Tripoli, he had been sent to Rome in 1695 at the age of eight to study at the Maronite College founded in 1585 by Gregory XIII. When he finished his studies Assemani was appointed scriptor of the Vatican Library for Syriac and Arabic literature, and in 1715 the pope, Clement XI, dispatched him to Egypt to collect manuscripts, and also to approach and report on the Copts. He stayed from the summer of 1715 until January 1717. On his return he was nominated librarian of the Vatican. He was sent as papal legate to Mount Lebanon in 1735, and he paid a second visit to Egypt on his journey back to Rome in 1738. In Italy Assemani founded a dynasty. He was joined in Rome by other members of his numerous family, cousins and nephews who rose to distinguished posts in the scholarly and ecclesiastical hierarchy. He himself has gone down to history as the compiler of the first great catalogue of Oriental manuscripts in the Vatican that contained invaluable information about Eastern Christianity in general, but his literary output, which included translations, editions, and a variety of historical and theological works, was immense.[34]

For all his qualities as a scholar, Assemani was not an ideal emissary to the Copts. The idea, cherished in Rome, that Eastern Christians might help to convert to Catholicism other Eastern Christians from different Churches, almost invariably proved mistaken, and took no account of the traditional rivalry between the Churches of the East. It would emerge in the course of the eighteenth century that the various members of the Assemani family were far from

---

33   Hamilton, *The Copts and the West*, pp. 95–101.
34   For a survey of Assemani's life and work, see G. Graf, *Geschichte der christlichen arabischen Literatur* (Vatican City, 1944–53), vol. 2, pp. 444–455.

being universally popular. Sicard's convert Tuki would inveigh against them and never failed to advise against their being used in missions to Egypt.[35] And even if the superiors of certain monasteries were prepared to sell him manuscripts behind the backs of the monks, Giuseppe Simonio Assemani was fast gaining a reputation among the Copts as an unscrupulous raider of monastic libraries.[36] So it may well have been Assemani's presence that prevented Sicard from making much headway with the monks of St Paul's.

Sicard, as able a writer and a stylist as he was an antiquarian, produced a memorable description of the monastery. He set out from Old Cairo on 23 May 1716, with various objects in mind. One was to tread in the footsteps of Antony and Paul, and his entire account is filled with references to their lives. Another was to study Egyptian antiquities in the lower Thebaid. And a third was, as he said, to convert the principal monks to Catholicism in the hope that they would soon be emulated by other Copts. Yet he was urgently begged by the Coptic patriarch, John XVI, as well as by his Coptic friends and even by the Jesuit Maronite Elia and by Assemani, not to broach any controversial points.[37]

The party, consisting of Sicard, Assemani, a Coptic priest, and a Coptic layman, followed the traditional route, sailing to Beni Suef (which they reached after two days), and then assembling guides and camels on the east bank of the Nile to pursue the three-day journey to St Antony's. Sicard, an indefatigable traveller, decided to set off for St Paul's the morning after his arrival. The prior of St Antony's, Synnodius, tried to dissuade him, assuring him that no Frank had ever dared undertake the journey, that it was full of dangers, and that the local Bedouin had just massacred some forty travellers from Beni Suef. Sicard, however, insisted, telling Synnodius that God would protect him and his travelling companions as they followed the 'sacred footsteps of the holy Fathers.' Synnodius yielded. He loaded Sicard's camels with bread, water, onions, a jar of sesame oil, a large fishing net, cooking utensils, and two sacks of flour with which the travellers could buy off the Arabs, and accompanied the party himself with two of his monks.[38]

Sicard and his companions left St Antony's on 29 May. Sicard described in detail the geological formations and the colours of the route.[39] He chose the longer way, skirting the mountains with his camels, and pointed out that

---

35 A. Colombo, 'La nascita della chiesa copto-cattolica nella prima metà del 1700' *Orientalia Christiana Analecta* 250 (1996), pp. 249–253.
36 O.E. Volkoff, *A la recherche de manuscrits en Egypte* (Cairo, 1970), pp. 93–94.
37 Sicard, *Oeuvres*, vol. 1, pp. 19, 41.
38 *Ibid.*, p. 28.
39 *Ibid.*, pp. 28–32.

the direct path straight over the mountains could be covered in less than ten hours, while the more circuitous one took fifteen. Sicard also relived Jerome's description of the toil of Antony in search of his companion, marvelling that it should have taken Antony ten and a half days to discover the hermit who was separated from him only by 'the thickness of a rock.'[40] As soon as they reached the coast, Sicard and Assemani washed their hands and faces in the sea, recited the *Te Deum*, and set about collecting shells. At two o'clock in the afternoon Sicard, Assemani, and the two Copts who had accompanied them from Cairo left Synnodius and his monks on the beach and proceeded to St Paul's, where they arrived between six and seven.[41]

The travellers found that the access to the monastery was the same as that to St Antony's. They were hoisted by a pulley issuing from a trapdoor and welcomed by a dozen monks to whom Sicard seems to have taken an instant dislike.[42] The visitors were immediately submitted to the customary ceremony of being led to the church after being draped in a cloak and entrusted with a candle. When Sicard started to talk to one of the monks from Upper Egypt whose relatives he had met, the inhabitants of St Paul's could hardly conceal their anxiety. Nevertheless, despite their promises to the patriarch, Sicard and Assemani were allowed to catechize the monks in public, and the monks pretended to agree with them and courteously praised their rhetorical gifts. As soon as their backs were turned, however, the monks warned each other to have nothing to do with the 'thieving wolves,' the subversive 'enchanters' who had made their way into their monastery.[43] At this point Sicard and Assemani asked them if they would submit to the Church and to describe what the Church actually was. Their answers to the second question varied. Some said it was the Holy Virgin, others the New Jerusalem, still others baptism, the eucharist or the elect, or even their own bishops and doctors. Sicard reported their statements to demonstrate the boundless ignorance of the members of the Church of Alexandria.[44] On the next day, Whitsun, the visitors attended mat-

---

40   Ibid., p. 30.
41   Ibid., pp. 38–39.
42   Ibid., p. 40: 'Une douzaine de religieux d'une ignorance à faire pitié, d'une antipathie contre les latins à indigner, matant leur corps par le jeûne, nourrissant leur esprit de la plus opiniâtre présomption, en un mot du caractère des autres religieux coptes, c'est ce qui se présenta à nous.'
43   Ibid., p. 40.
44   Ibid., p. 41.

ins, mass at dawn, and a further religious service, after which, at about two in the afternoon, they left the monastery and returned to the coast.[45]

The monastery Sicard visited had been all but entirely restored after its period of abandonment (Fig. 7). The Cave Church had been repaired and the walls decorated with 'sacred stories coarsely painted' (Fig. 8) Sicard met the painter – could he, one wonders, have been the future patriarch John XVII?[46] – and was informed that he had never been trained to paint, a fact, Sicard added, that was all too apparent from his work. The painter also told him that he had obtained his colours from the minerals on the surrounding heights.[47] Sicard described the monastery and made a sketch that was subsequently turned into an illustration by an Armenian artist.[48] It was, he wrote, a square building with a garden a third of the size of that of St Antony's and containing the same plants. A vault seventy yards long led to the spring – Sicard recalled Jerome's description of Paul, 'that new Elias,' having his thirst quenched there. The grotto where Paul and Antony first saw each other, recognizing one another miraculously and calling each other by name, was now part of the church and was furnished with a single altar, but the 'tears of devotion which its sight should produce,' he observed, 'are stopped by the sad reflections which the present objects naturally call to mind.'[49] Sicard and Assemani were shown the library, but, Sicard lamented, 'the good books and the manuscripts have all been removed.'[50]

Sicard's hostile attitude to the Copts seems to have softened with the passage of time. It was two years after his visit to St Paul's, in 1718, that he first started to make converts in Upper Egypt and thus laid the basis of the Coptic Catholic

---

45 Ibid., pp. 41–42.
46 See W. Lyster, 'Reviving a lost tradition: the eighteenth-century paintings in the Cave Church, context and iconography' in W. Lyster, ed., *The Cave Church of Paul the Hermit at the Monastery of St. Paul, Egypt* (New Haven, 2008), pp. 209–232; *idem*, 'Reshaping a lost tradition; the eighteenth-century paintings in the Cave Church, style and technique' in *ibid.*, pp. 233–274.
47 Sicard, *Oeuvres*, vol. 1, p. 41: 'Ses murailles, qui ont été réparées nouvellement, sont chargées depuis la voûte jusqu'au bas d'histoires sacrées grossièrement peintes, parmi lesquelles on n'a pas oublié celle des tigres qui creusèrent la fosse du Saint. Le peintre auteur de ces dévotes figures se présenta à nous. C'était un moine du couvent. Il nous dit qu'il n'avait jamais appris à peindre, il y parassait à son ouvrage. Il ajouta que les coteaux voisins lui avaient fourni les différentes terres minérales, le vert, le jaune, le rouge, le brun, le noir et les autres couleurs employées dans son dessin.'
48 Ibid., p. 18, for M. Martin's introductory discussion of the illustration of the Red Sea monasteries and its fate.
49 Ibid., p. 40.
50 Ibid., pp. 122–200, esp. pp. 175–176.

FIGURE 7   The Cave Church of St Paul from the northwest with the keep and the Church of St Mercurius in the background (2005)
PHOTOGRAPH © NICHOLAS WARNER

FIGURE 8 A dome in the Cave Church painted with Christ surrounded by the living animals of the Evangelists above a row of the 24 elders of the Coptic Church (2005)
PHOTOGRAPH © NICHOLAS WARNER

Church, which, from the 1730s on, would be organized mainly by the Reformed Franciscans.[51] Both Sicard and another Jesuit, Guillaume Dubernat, became increasingly sensitive to the problems of dealing with a Church whose members had never received the scholastic training that would have been expected in Europe. This accounted for their inability to define 'the Church', as well as for a somewhat nebulous idea about what the sacraments were. Dubernat pointed out that if they were told what the sacraments were by a Roman Catholic, the Copts would agree that they too believed in them, but if simply asked to define the sacraments, they were incapable of doing so. Dubernat, however, decided that they should be given the benefit of the doubt and that their agreement with the Catholic definition should be accepted as a sign of orthodoxy.[52]

Sicard's description of the Red Sea monasteries, addressed to his fellow Jesuit Thomas Charles Fleuriau d'Armenonville in Brussels, was published in the fifth volume of the *Nouveaux mémoires des missions de la Compagnie de Jésus dans le Levant*, which came out in 1725. Because of his fine style, his immense knowledge, and the accuracy of his descriptions, his writings on Egypt remained unsurpassed for many years, and to them other travellers, such as Claude Granger and Richard Pococke, were profoundly indebted. Claude Tourtechot, who wrote under the name of Claude Granger, was no missionary. By training he was a surgeon, and it was in that capacity that he first visited North Africa, sent by the Trinitarians to work in Tunis in 1721. In Tunis he met Pierre-Jean Pignon, the French consul, who became a close friend.[53] Granger returned to Paris, and there, working in the Jardin du Roi, he acquired some experience in chemistry, botany, and zoology. The decision to send Granger to Egypt together with Pignon, who had been appointed consul in Cairo at the end of 1729, was due to the influential secretary of state for naval affairs, Jean-Frédéric Phélypeaux de Pontchartrain, comte de Maurepas, and his cousin, the royal librarian Jean-Paul Bignon who was notoriously sympathetic to the libertines and the ideas of the Enlightenment. They both wished to organize a scientific expedition that would 'examine in Egypt those plants, animals and other things which could be of service to natural history,'[54] and Granger seemed perfectly equipped to lead it.

---

51   Colombo, 'La nascita', pp. 91–160.
52   Guillaume Dubernat, 'Lettre d'un missionnaire en Egypte, à Son Altesse Sérénissime Monseigneur le Comte de Toulouse' in *Nouveaux mémoires des missions de la Compagnie de Jésus dans le Levant*, vol. 2 (Paris, 1717), pp. 1–125, esp. pp. 43–45.
53   On Pignon, see A. Mézin, *Les consuls de France au siècle des lumières (1715–1792)* (Paris, 1997), pp. 493–494.
54   See A. Riottot, 'Claude Granger: voyageur-naturaliste (1730–1737)' Ph.D. diss., Université de Paris 7-Denis Diderot 2003. For Maurepas's orders to 'rechercher en Egypte les plantes,

Granger arrived in Alexandria on 18 July 1730. On 6 August he was in Cairo, and on 29 January of the following year he set off for Upper Egypt. One of the most original aspects of his journey to the Red Sea monasteries was that he approached them from the south, facing an eight-day trek from Akhmīm. First he went to the Monastery of St Antony, and then he proceeded to St Paul's (known by the Copts, he said, as the Monastery of the Tigers after Jerome's account of Paul's grave). He arrived on 11 April and stayed for one night. In the monastery he found fourteen monks – five priests, six clerics, and three lay brothers. He inspected the Cave Church and took measurements (32 feet long by 14 wide), commented adversely on the wall paintings, and copied the Coptic inscription on the framing arch leading to the haykal of the Twenty-Four Elders. Granger, however, took the Sahidic Coptic to be Greek.[55] Although he would admit that St Antony's and St Paul's were the 'least ugly' of the Egyptian monasteries,[56] he was displeased by his visit, finding that there was nothing there 'to satisfy anybody's curiosity, let alone a man of piety.'[57] From St Paul's he made his way back to Akhmīm. After Egypt he explored Cyrenaica, Syria, and Mesopotamia, where he died in July 1737 on his way to Bassora. His notes were collected by Pignon and published in 1745.[58]

Granger helped himself freely to the work of Sicard. He had been shown his reports on Egypt by Pignon, who had been given them by Maurepas, and Granger's account of St Antony's, as well as much of his report on St Paul's, are taken almost verbatim from Sicard, even if Granger never mentions him by name.[59] To a large extent this is also true of the English traveller Richard Pococke, who was in Egypt in 1737 and 1738. Pococke never went to the Red Sea monasteries, but, in the first volume of his popular *Description of the East*, which appeared in 1743, he felt bound to describe them, and even to provide

---

les animaux et autres choses qui peuvent servir l'histoire naturelle,' see p. ii, and for the combined plans of Maurepas and Bignon, see pp. 25, 41. For Granger and Egypt more generally see *idem*, *Voyage dans l'Empire Ottoman du naturaliste Claude Granger 1733–1737* (Paris, 2006), pp. 81–125.

55   Claude Granger, *Relation du voyage fait en Egypte par le Sieur Granger, en l'année 1730* (Paris, 1745), p. 118. For a reproduction of the inscription, see P. van Moorsel, *Les peintures du monastère de Saint-Paul près de la mer Rouge* (Cairo, 2002), p. 65.
56   Granger, *Relation*, p. 93: 'Ce Monastère est le moins vilain de tous ceux qu'il y a dans la haute Egypte, après ceux de saint Antoine et de saint Paul.'
57   *Ibid.*, p. 120: 'Le douze à midi je pris congé de ces Moines, très-peu satisfait de ce que j'avois vû chez eux, n'y ayant rien qui puisse satisfaire un curieux et encore moins un dévot.'
58   M. Martin, 'Granger est-il le rédacteur de son voyage en Egypte?' *Annales islamologiques* 19 (1983), pp. 53–58.
59   *Ibid.*, p. 54; *idem*, 'Sicard et Granger (suite et fin)' *Annales islamologiques* 22 (1986), pp. 175–180.

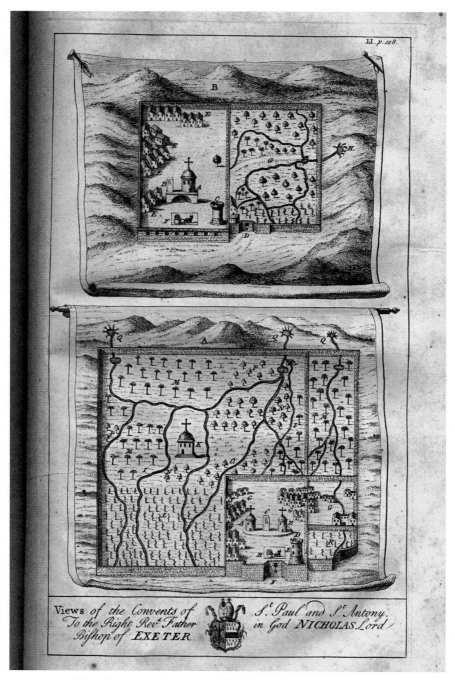

FIGURE 9　Richard Pococke, *A Description of the East, and Some Other Countries. Volume the First. Observations on Egypt* (London, 1743), p. 128, pl. 51

an illustration. The illustration (Fig. 9) is taken from the one made by the Armenian artist for Sicard, a copy of which seems to have been available in Cairo, while Pococke's description – he claimed that the monastery contained twenty-five monks who followed a rule of particular austerity – is based on the observations of other contemporaries.[60]

3   Continuity and Change

The gradual accumulation of visitors to the Monastery of St Paul in the nineteenth and twentieth centuries gives some idea of the extent to which it had been revived – artists, manuscript collectors, art historians, photographers, missionaries, and scientists all testified to its growing reputation as a site of interest and beauty, and, as time went by, they could profit from ever more practical and commodious means of transport. Yet their object frequently remained a quest for antiquity, a desire to follow Antony through the desert and to savour the atmosphere of a place that had once been frequented by Paul the Hermit.

Relations between Egypt and the West had been altered deeply by the Napoleonic invasion of 1798 and by the subsequent occupation of the country, and they changed still more after 1811 under the rule of Muhammad ʿAli Pasha. Muhammad ʿAli was particularly eager to appoint Western technicians.[61] Ever larger numbers of Europeans settled in Cairo and explored the country; travel was safer than it had been in the past; and the Coptic monasteries became an increasingly popular goal. In March 1823 an English surveyor and geologist in the pasha's service, James Burton, called on St Paul's in the course of his systematic investigation of the Eastern Desert. He was accompanied by one of his closest friends, with whom he shared lodgings in Cairo – John Gardner Wilkinson, who had arrived two years earlier in Egypt, where he would spend some twenty years and distinguish himself as an Egyptologist.[62] The two men, who had just been to St Antony's and approached the Monastery of St Paul from Zaʿfarāna on the coast, spent nine days there, arriving on the 17th and leaving on the 26th, and using the monastery as a base from which to explore

---

60 Richard Pococke, *A Description of the East, and Some Other Countries. Volume the First. Observations on Egypt* (London, 1743), p. 128, pl. 51.
61 K. Fahmy, 'The era of Muhammad ʿAli Pasha, 1805–1848' in M.W. Daly, ed., *The Cambridge History of Egypt. Vol. 2: Modern Egypt, from 1517 to the End of the Twentieth Century* (Cambridge, 1998), pp. 139–179.
62 For their friendship, see J. Thompson, *Sir Gardner Wilkinson and His Circle* (Austin, 1992), pp. 45–47.

the outlying area. Burton took notes (which have remained unpublished),[63] and made a number of interesting sketches and paintings of the surrounding landscape, the walls, the streets, and the church,[64] while Wilkinson published his own record of their visit in 1832 in the second number of the *Journal of the Royal Geographical Society*.

The two accounts are almost identical. Wilkinson seems to have copied Burton's notes with no acknowledgement and thus confirmed contemporary fears that Burton's research might be exploited by him.[65] The visitors were lavishly received. 'They spread us carpets on a large Cairo map,' wrote Wilkinson of the monks, 'and the coffee, scented with cloves, was brought in handsome cups on silver stands. Pipes, too, of no inferior quality, were given us.'[66] In the monastery churches Burton and Wilkinson observed 'some pictures – one of St Mark and another of St Athanasius (which seems to be of the Italian school), are the only two of any merit; the rest are grotesque representations of saints, dragons, miracles, and madonnas, painted on board by artists of Alexandria.'[67] As for the Cave Church, 'the walls are adorned with stiff old frescos.'[68] The visitors were struck, moreover, by the presence of church bells (which they had also discovered at St Antony's). At the time of their visit there were twenty-one inhabitants of the monastery, eighteen laymen and three brothers.[69] 'The monks,' wrote Wilkinson, 'are Ichthyophagi, and go down in small parties to the sea, where a two days' fishing suffices to load a donkey, which they keep within their walls; rice, lentils, and bread, are their principal, if not their only other food.'[70] But the two men did not take to the monks. The monastery, Wilkinson admitted, 'is situated in a more picturesque spot than that of

---

63 James Burton's notes, diaries, and drawings were given to the British Museum by his nephew, the architect Decimus Burton, and are now in the BL, MSS Add. 25,613–625,675. His description of St Paul's is in MS Add. 25,625, ff. 15–16. Substantial extracts are quoted by A. Piankoff *et al.*, 'History of the Monasteries of St. Anthony and St. Paul', pp. 97–104. For Burton, see N. Cooke, 'The forgotten Egyptologist: James Burton' in P. Starkey and J. Starkey, eds, *Travellers in Egypt* (London, 1998), pp. 85–94; for their tour of the Eastern Desert, see pp. 56–58.

64 London, British Library, MS Add. 25,628, ff. 106–112.

65 Thompson, *Sir Gardner Wilkinson*, pp. 90–91.

66 John Gardner Wilkinson, 'Notes on a part of the Eastern Desert of Upper Egypt' *Journal of the Royal Geographical Society of London* 2 (1832), pp. 28–60, esp. p. 34.

67 *Ibid.*, p. 35. For Burton's almost identical account, see Piankoff *et al.*, 'History of the Monasteries', p. 102. The monks of St Paul's still display the European oil paintings of St Mark and St Athanasius as icons in the two eighteenth-century churches at the monastery. For the painting of St Mark, see W. Lyster, *Monastery of St Paul* (Cairo, 1999), p. 72.

68 Wilkinson, 'Notes', p. 35.

69 *Ibid.*, p. 35.

70 *Ibid.*, p. 36.

St Antony, and has a much cleaner and neater appearance, owing to its having been recently repaired. The streets and houses are also laid out with some degree of regularity and order.... The monks, too, appear leaner and richer, – are better dressed and lodged, and possess more luxuries; in this alone, however, [they are] superior to the brothers of the other convent; being uncouth and even inhospitable, – ignorant, and consequently suspicious, and scarcely condescending to answer the usual questions of the traveller.'[71] They were, Burton added, 'more cunning than those of D. Antonios,'[72] but he and Wilkinson noted that, thanks to Muhammad 'Ali, caravans to the monastery were no longer attacked and the local Bedouin no longer had the right to exact a tribute from the monks.[73]

A little later the artist Joseph Bonomi, a friend of both Burton and Wilkinson (some of whose works he would illustrate), visited the monastery. A pupil of John Flaxman and the son-in-law of John Martin, Bonomi had a lifelong interest in Egypt and Egyptology. He was in Egypt twice. He first went as a salaried artist in the expedition led by Robert Hay, which set out in 1825 and travelled up the Nile to Abu Simbel. On this occasion Bonomi stayed until about 1834. His next visit was as a member of the even more important expedition of the Egyptologist Karl Richard Lepsius. He then remained in the country from 1842 to 1844.[74] It is not entirely clear when he was at St Paul's, but his friend Samuel Sharpe included in the illustrated edition of his *History of Egypt* two woodcuts by him, one of the walls of the monastery and one of the interior of the Church of St Michael the Archangel and St John the Baptist, with the monks performing penitential prostrations.[75]

More than ten years after the exploration of the Monastery of St Paul by Burton and Wilkinson, on 23 December 1834, the monks received what was probably the largest group of visitors they had ever seen, led by Marshal Auguste-Frédéric-Louis Visse de Marmont, duc de Raguse. Marmont had been one of the men closest to Napoleon. Once his aide-de-camp, he had served in nearly all his major campaigns – in Italy, Egypt, Germany, the Low Countries,

---

71 *Ibid.*, p. 34.
72 BL, MS Add. 25,625, f. 16.
73 Wilkinson, 'Notes', p. 36.
74 For Bonomi's life, see the entry s.v. by Peter Meadows in *ODNB*.
75 S. Sharpe, *The History of Egypt from the Earliest Times till the Conquest of the Arabs AD 640* (London, 1876), vol. 2, pp. 350–351 (figs. 132–133). The second of the two illustrations, of the interior of the church with the monks, is reproduced and discussed by L. Keimer, 'Les prosternations pénitentiaires des moines du couvent de St. Paul dans le désert de l'Est' *Cahiers coptes* 11 (1956), pp. 20–21. The drawing reproduced bears the caption 'about 1840,' but, as Keimer points out, this cannot be right.

Austria, Bohemia, Spain, and Dalmatia (where he was rewarded with the dukedom of Ragusa). But, inveigled by Talleyrand into negotiating with the emperor's enemies in 1814, he contributed to his fall, thereby winning the favour of the restored Bourbons. The Bourbons too turned against him in 1830, however, and accused him, unjustly, of treachery. Marmont consequently settled in Austria. He spent most of the remaining years of his life writing, defending his own reputation and blackening that of his numerous enemies.[76] But he also travelled, and on 12 October 1834, he landed in Alexandria to arrive in Cairo on the 27th. He was welcomed by Muhammad 'Ali and, above all, by his host, his former comrade at arms Colonel Joseph Sève, now known as Sulayman Pasha. Like Marmont, Sève had fought with Napoleon in Egypt. He returned there after the emperor's fall, converted to Islam, and was placed in charge of the instruction of Muhammad 'Ali's troops. Over the years he rose to become one of the most powerful men in the country, taking part in the Syrian campaign and holding the rank of second in command of the Egyptian army directly under the ruler's son Ibrāhīm. He was a pillar of the French colony in Cairo, and it was in his splendid mansion on the Nile that Marmont was invited to stay.[77]

Marmont went to the Monastery of St Paul as he was returning from an expedition to Upper Egypt. He hoped to find a boat on the Red Sea coast and proceed to Suez, and consequently turned in to the desert at al-Minyā. His travelling companions included two men who had been with him since his departure from Vienna, Burun, a French friend, and the Italian count Savorgnan di Brazzà, an amateur painter, whose family would produce illustrious explorers later in the century.[78] He was also accompanied by a number of men he met in Cairo – Lapi, the dragoman or interpreter of the Austrian consulate, a Bavarian doctor named Koch, and Yūsuf Kiachef, another veteran of the Egyptian campaign who had converted to Islam and was responsible for mediating with local officials.[79] They were joined by an escort of fourteen Bedouin and forty-

---

76 For Marmont's life, see the entry by A. Du Casse, in L.-G. Michaud, ed., *Biographie universelle ancienne et moderne* (Paris-Leipzig, 1854–1865), vol. 27, pp. 18–31. For Marmont in Egypt, see Carré, *Voyageurs*, vol. 1, pp. 279–284.

77 See Fahmy, 'The era of Muhammad 'Ali Pasha', p. 154; Carré, *Voyageurs*, vol. 1, pp. 208–209, 257, 270; 2: 56, 90, 101, 109, 251; and the description in A.-F.-L. Visse de Marmont, *Voyage du Maréchal Duc de Raguse en Hongrie, en Transylvanie, dans la Russie Méridionale, en Crimée, et sur les bords de la Mer d'Azoff, à Constantinople, dans quelques parties d'Asie Mineure, en Syrie, en Palestine et en Egypte* (Paris, 1837), vol. 3, pp. 260–268, 290–295.

78 *Ibid.*, vol. 1, p. 5, vol. 4, pp. 3–4.

79 *Ibid.*, vol. 4, pp. 3–4.

five camels, and the journey from the Nile took twelve days.[80] At the monastery Marmont found thirty-five monks. Ten of them were priests, and only four of the ten were literate. The monastery, he wrote, was shabby; the library contained only thirteen books; and the monks amazed him by the ingenuousness of their questions.[81] Did the Europeans, they asked him, celebrate mass in the same way as they did? Were laymen allowed several legitimate wives at the same time whom they could divorce with no difficulty? Was the year divided into months and weeks consisting of seven days? And had the visitors read any prophecies about Christians being freed from Muslim rule?[82]

What was still more indicative of the revival of the monastery was that it should at last have started to draw manuscript collectors, even if the English archaeologist Greville Chester said he declined visiting St Paul's when he was at St Antony's, 'as I was assured that not a single fragment of any ancient MS had escaped the wreck of the eighty years of abandonment.'[83] The Monastery of St Paul was visited in 1838 by Henry Tattam, the greatest expert on Coptic in England and, at the time, rector of St Cuthbert's in Bedford and Great Woolstone in Buckinghamshire. Tattam travelled with his niece, Miss Platt, and it was she who described the journey. They set out from Cairo on 6 March, and, with six camels, two dromedaries, an Arab interpreter, five Bedouin guides, and two servants, they took the unusual measure of crossing the desert directly from Cairo to the Red Sea and avoiding the passage up the Nile. The journey took a week. After stopping briefly at the Monastery of St Antony, which Tattam visited, they pitched their tents on the coast. Tattam then left his niece and went inland to St Paul's with his interpreter and two of the guides on 14 March.

The description of the monastery by Tattam's niece, who did not see it for herself, is cursory. The buildings, we are told, were in better repair than those of St Antony's, but the monks more isolated, even if they appeared 'to have more comfort' and could occasionally obtain fish from the Red Sea. The library was what interested Tattam most, and that he visited it proves that word was spreading that it might contain something worth seeing, however new it actually was. But Tattam was disappointed: 'The monks here possess but few

---

80   Ibid., vol. 4, p. 132.
81   Ibid., vol. 4, p. 183: 'Les églises, quoique assez ornées, sont fort sales et très-mal tenues; rien, en entrant dans ce monastère, n'inspire de respect pour ses habitants. On conçoit qu'avec de tels gens la bibliothèque, ou la réunion de livres que l'on nomme ainsi, ne soit pas considérable. Elle se compose de treize volumes, écrits en cophte.'
82   Ibid., vol. 4, pp. 186–187.
83   G.J. Chester, 'Notes on the Coptic Dayrs of the Wadi Natrun and on Dayr Antonios in the Eastern Desert' *Archaeological Journal* 30, no. 18 (1873), pp. 105–116, esp. p. 116.

religious books, or did not choose to show more. They brought out a copy of St John's Gospel in Coptic, and a copy of the Scriptures printed in Latin and Arabic, 4 vols folio.'[84] This last work is the 1671 *Propaganda Fide* edition of the *Biblia Sacra Arabica*. In three volumes rather than four, it is still in the library. After seeing the books Tattam went straight back to the coast, to St Antony's, and then to Suez.[85]

If Granger's inclusion of the Monastery of St Paul in what was essentially a scientific expedition to Egypt can be seen as an effect of the European Enlightenment and Tattam's visit as yet another incident in the increasingly fashionable hunt for Coptic manuscripts, the visitors to the monastery in the nineteenth century also exemplified the changing face of Western policies and of Egypt itself. One of the novelties of the nineteenth century was the vast expansion of the religious missions. From the sixteenth to the late eighteenth centuries the missionaries in Egypt had nearly all been Roman Catholic. The Protestant Moravian Brethren who came between 1752 and 1800 left little mark.[86] Since the Catholic missionaries provided extensive reports and had a far longer and more direct experience of the Copts than did most other residents in Egypt, the Copts, in both Catholic and Protestant Europe, were seen through their eyes, and Protestant writers were largely reliant on Catholic sources. In the nineteenth century this changed. The entire area of the Near and Middle East was infiltrated by missions from the whole of Western Christendom. The Roman Catholic missions, in decline in the eighteenth century, were vigorously revived, with a quantity of new orders. And they were joined by Protestant missions – Anglicans, Evangelicals, and Presbyterians from England, Evangelicals and Presbyterians from America, Lutherans from Germany[87] – and by the Russian Orthodox.

By the end of the eighteenth century the Russians had made themselves out to be the protectors of the Greek Orthodox Church in the Ottoman Empire, fragile though their credentials were.[88] Their ambitions increased in

---

84 Miss Platt, *Journal of a Tour Through Egypt, the Peninsula of Sinai, and the Holy Land in 1838, 1839* (London, 1841), vol. 1, pp. 97–98.
85 For a colourful description of Tattam's vicissitudes collecting manuscripts in Egypt, see Volkoff, *A la recherche de manuscrits*, pp. 177–183.
86 A. Watson, *The American Mission in Egypt, 1854 to 1896* (Pittsburgh, 1898), pp. 20–31.
87 For the missions in the entire area, see M.E. Yapp, *The Making of the Modern Near East, 1792–1823* (London, 1987), pp. 132, 144, 166, 197, 201–202. For the missions in Egypt, see A. Elli, *Storia della chiesa copta* (Cairo, 2003), vol. 2, pp. 348–353; vol. 3, pp. 35–54; H. Weir, 'Anglican Church in Egypt' in A.S. Atiya, ed., *The Coptic Encyclopedia* (New York, 1991), vol. 1, p. 133; S. Habib, 'Coptic Evangelical Church', *ibid.*, vol. 2, pp. 603–604.
88 Discussed and documented by R.H. Davison, *Essays in Ottoman and Turkish History, 1774–1923: The Impact of the West* (Austin, 1990), pp. 29–50.

the nineteenth century, and, like the Catholics and Protestants of an earlier period, they were eager to have a foothold in Ethiopia and in the Holy Land. In 1847, therefore, the archimandrite Porphyrios Uspensky set off for Jerusalem as head of the Russian mission,[89] but the objective of establishing a Russian presence in the city failed. Uspensky, nevertheless, retained a strong interest in the Eastern Christians, and he was attracted by the idea of union with the great monophysite Churches, notably the Jacobites of Syria and the Copts, having concluded that the Copts could hardly be regarded as heretical, and that their beliefs were perfectly compatible with those of the Russian Church. At the same time he was keen to collect and inspect manuscripts – he was one of the first scholars to consult and describe the Codex Sinaiticus at the Monastery of St Catherine, and the first to find the Euchologium Sinaiticum, two leaves of which he took back to Russia.[90] He paid a couple of visits to Egypt. In 1850 he called on the Monastery of St Antony, whose prior, Dāwūd, then accompanied him to St Paul's. Four years later Dāwūd would become Cyril IV, the most enterprising and enlightened Coptic patriarch of the nineteenth century, known as a pioneer of ecumenicism and for his readiness to open a dialogue with other Churches. His official discussions with Uspensky, however, which started in 1860, were interrupted by his death in January of the following year.[91]

Uspensky was an observant visitor. In his account of St Paul's he first described the relatively recent Church of St Michael the Archangel and St John the Baptist, with an inscription recording its construction on the orders of the patriarch John XVII in 1727 by the architect Abū Yūsuf.[92] Its best decoration, he wrote, was an 'icon of the Evangelist Mark, painted in Europe. The preacher of salvation in the land of Egypt is represented seated and in meditation. At his feet are two books in parchment bindings. In the background is a pyramid.'[93] He then turned to the Cave Church. He copied the Coptic and Arabic inscriptions and transcribed the Coptic inscription around the base of the Dome of the Martyrs in the narthex, but was struck by the incapacity of the monks to understand it. Above the inscription, he continued, 'are the names of the

---

89   Cf. S. Bolshakoff, *The Foreign Missions of the Russian Orthodox Church* (London, 1943), p. 99.
90   On Uspensky as a manuscript collector, see Volkoff, *A la recherche*, pp. 221–222.
91   Elli, *Storia della chesa copta*, vol. 2, pp. 346–351.
92   There are, however, a number of errors in Uspensky's reading of the inscription, which is above the door of the central haykal screen. It records the construction of the church in 1732 (AM 1448) during the patriarchate of John XVII, but identifies Jirjis Abū Yūsuf al-Surūjī, the greatest archon of the period, as the patron, not the architect.
93   Burton and Wilkinson admired this same large oil painting in 1823. It currently hangs in the Church of St Michael the Archangel and St John the Baptist.

martyrs in Arabic.... The martyrs themselves are painted very badly.' Most of the representations were so covered in soot as to be almost invisible. Uspensky could just distinguish the figures of saints on the stone iconostasis separating the sanctuary from the church, and, 'behind the consecration table, high up on the wall ... a full-size representation of the Saviour.'[94] On the eastern wall of the chapel containing Paul's tomb he found a full-length representation of St Paul, wearing a brown *chiton*, his arms uplifted, the raven bringing him a loaf and two lions licking his feet.[95] 'The paintings on the walls of the Apocalyptic Church,' he concluded, 'are bad; the faces are ugly and even terrible.'[96]

4 Scholarly Investigation

Another novelty of the nineteenth century was the network of railways established in Egypt from the 1850s on. To the first line, from Cairo to Alexandria, was added a line from Cairo to Suez, and, in the 1860s under Khedive Isma'il, the journey to the monasteries of St Antony and St Paul was conveniently abridged by the railway from Cairo to Beni Suef. Nevertheless, despite the facilitations for tourism after the opening of the Suez Canal in 1869, the trek across the desert remained as challenging as it had ever been, and the explorer and naturalist Georg August Schweinfurth, who first visited St Paul's in 1876, observed how few Europeans had in fact ventured to the Red Sea monasteries.[97] Schweinfurth's view is vindicated by the treatment of St Paul's monastery in the increasingly popular guidebooks of Egypt. The standard English guide, later to be known as 'Murray's guide' but first issued in 1847 as the *Hand-book for Travellers in Egypt*, was by John Gardner Wilkinson. Although he had visited it with Burton, Wilkinson mentions the monastery only briefly, and in the same breath as that of St Antony, but gives no details

---

[94] These figures must be the icons at the top of the two haykal screens donated to the Cave Church in 1705 by John XVI and the great archon Jirjis al-Tūkhī. Both screens are made of wood, not stone, as reported by Uspensky.

[95] No wall painting of Paul survives in the saint's shrine. Uspensky perhaps described an icon of the hermit, such as the eighteenth-century example in the monastic collection, reproduced in Lyster, ed., *The Cave Church*, p. xx.

[96] The relevant extracts from Uspensky's description have been translated by A. Piankoff, 'Two descriptions by Russian travellers of the Monasteries of St. Anthony and St. Paul in the Eastern Desert' *Bulletin de la Société royale de géographie d'Egypte* 21 (1943), pp. 61–66, esp. pp. 65–66.

[97] Georg Schweinfurth, *Auf unbetretenen Wegen in Aegypten* (Hamburg, 1922), p. 163.

about it.[98] And the German equivalent, by Karl Baedeker, was equally parsimonious in its information.[99]

By the time he went to St Paul's himself Schweinfurth had established his reputation as one of the greatest explorers of his day. He had travelled over much of Egypt and the Sudan, and, in the African interior, he had made his most important discoveries – the river Welle and the Akka pygmies northwest of Lake Albert – besides gathering an abundance of new information about the Mangbetu cannibals. He had also founded the Egyptian Geographical Society in Cairo, where he had settled in 1875 and would stay intermittently until 1889.[100]

The description of the monasteries, by a man with a thorough knowledge of geology and natural history, is highly evocative, surpassing, for the first time, that of Sicard. Like his predecessors, Schweinfurth tells of the alternative routes from St Antony's to St Paul's – the shortcut, 'accessible only to pedestrians and donkeys,' over the mountains, which took nine hours, and the more circuitous way, which took sixteen.[101] The setting of the monastery made a unique impression on him – the barren rocks, uniformly grey but framed by white precipices, the palm trees in the deep ravines, the dark walls, and the deathly silence of the menacing cliffs.[102] He made an accurate sketch of St Paul's seen from the east, showing the walls which, he said, had not been restored for many years, measuring some 455 metres and surrounding an area of one and a half hectares (Fig. 10).[103] On his first visit in 1876 Schweinfurth found twenty-three inhabitants living in two parallel rows of buildings along the southern wall. The keep was in good condition, and the garden, which took up about a quarter of the monastic space, was rich in palm trees and other plants also found at St Antony's. The Cave Church seemed to Schweinfurth to have been restored some two centuries earlier. The paintings, he commented, were primitive, 'grotesque caricatures,' but it was clear to him that they covered far earlier decorations which it would be well worth restoring 'with the aid of modern technique.'[104] He remarked on the graffiti in the cave and added

---

98   John Gardner Wilkinson, *Hand-book for Travellers in Egypt* (London, 1847), pp. 268–269.
99   Karl Baedeker, *Aegypten: Handbuch für Reisende* (Leipzig, 1877), p. 491.
100 Schweinfurth, *Auf unbetretenen Wegen*, pp. XIII–XXVI, for Schweinfurth's autobiographical sketch.
101 *Ibid.*, p. 186.
102 *Ibid.*, pp. 189–190.
103 *Ibid.*, p. 162.
104 *Ibid.*, p. 198: 'Die alte Kirche mit dem Grabe des Heiligen Paulus scheint vor etwa zweihundert Jahren renoviert zu sein, nach den äusserst rohen und barbarischen mit koptisch und arabisch geschriebenen Bibelsprüchen versehenen Wandgemälden zu urteilen, die den Kuppelraum am Eingange zieren. Alle Wände dieses uralten Heiligtums sind mit fratzenhaften Karikaturen bedeckt. Die Köpfe der Heiligen und Apostel sind, wie

FIGURE 10   St Paul's Monastery seen from the east
GEORG SCHWEINFURTH, *AUF UNBETRETENEN WEGEN IN AEGYPTEN* (HAMBURG, 1922)

information about the administration and wealth of the monastery. It had, he said, lost much of its land when the predecessor of the current bishop at Būsh converted to Islam and sold some of its property to the government. Efforts, he added, were being made to retrieve it.

On later visits to St Paul's, between 1876 and 1878, Schweinfurth counted twenty-eight monks, most of whom were very old. On the whole he liked them. He observed, however, that, in emulation of the great Antony, the monks seemed most reluctant ever to wash, and that their cells were extraordinarily untidy (a feature already remarked upon by Uspensky and one that would strike Michel Jullien).[105] But, in the spirit of the critical scepticism with which he recounted the lives of Antony and Paul, he also thought the monks had little future. They had long ceased to have either a political or a religious significance, and they remained isolated from the rest of the world and in the same state of torpor and immobility that had characterized spiritual matters in Egypt for centuries.[106]

ihre Nimbusscheiben, mit Hilfe des Zirkels entworfen und Augen, Nase und Mund mit geometrischer Regelmässigkeit eingetragen. Reiterbilder machen auch hier den Hauptgegenstand der Darstellung aus. Unter dem jetzigen, bereits stark geschwärzten Bewurf erkennt man die alte Kalkdecke der Mauer mit uralter Ornamentik, und es würde sich wohl der Mühe verlohnen, diese letztere durch die Hilfsmittel der heutigen Technik wieder herzustellen.'

105 *Ibid.*, pp. 204–205: 'Im profanen Leben, in ihrem gegenseitigen Verkehr und in ihren Gesprächen miteinander geben diese Mönche nicht den geringsten Unterschied von dem einfachen ägyptischen Landmann, überhaupt durchaus keinen Anstrich eines exklusiv kirchlichen, der Welt abgestorbenen Charakters zu erkennen. Verträglich im Umgang, gemütlich und ohne jeden lärmenden Wortwechsel in ihren Plaudereien zeichnen sie sich vor den Übrigen vorteilhaft aus; im allgemeinen lässt sich wenig Nachteiliges über ihr äusseres Leben sagen, nur im Punkte der Reinlichkeit lassen sie viel zu wünschen übrig. Sie ahmen das Beispiel ihres grossen Stifters und Vorbildes nach, diese modernen Anachoreten. Von Antonius wird uns berichtet, dass er sich nie wusch, dass er über sein Haupt und Barthaar nie eine Schere kommen liess, dass er nie seine Kleidung wechselte und aus Scham vor sich selber sich ihrer nie entledigte. In den Mönchzellen herrscht eine unglaubliche Unordnung, die verschiedensten Dinge liegen da bunt durcheinander: Bücher und Ölsamen von Saflor, Leisten und Schuhleder, angefangene Dattelkörbe und Oliven, Tabakblätter, Decken und Küchengeschirr, das alles fand sich am Boden ein und derselben Wohnzelle vor, die kaum zehn Schritte im Gevierte mass.' See also Piankoff, 'Two descriptions', p. 63, for Uspensky's reference to 'the narrow, gloomy and untidy cells of the monks scattered without order' at St Anthony's.

106 Schweinfurth, *Auf unbetretenen Wegen*, p. 209: 'Hier hatten die Klöster längst, schon vor der Invasion des Islams, aufgehört, zu dem politischen wie zu dem religiösen Leben ihrer Zeit in Beziehung zu treten, und heute erblicken wir sie in derselben Erstarrung, wie sie seit vielen Jahrhunderten allen geistigen Dingen im Lande anhaftet, immer noch grundsätzlich entfernt von dem Treiben der Welt, als Klöster in der abstraktesten Bedeutung des Worts.'

The revival of Roman Catholic missionary activity in the nineteenth century also affected the Society of Jesus. Nearly all the members of the Society in Egypt in the eighteenth century had died of the plague, and the house in Cairo was closed with the dissolution of the order in 1773.[107] It was not until 1879 that the Jesuits returned to Egypt, and when they arrived they founded an educational establishment, the Collège de la Sainte Famille. The next visitor who wrote about the Monastery of St Paul was Michel Jullien from Lyons, who had arrived in Egypt in 1881 and had purchased the ground on which the Collège de la Sainte Famille stands to this day.[108] Treading most deliberately in the steps of his great predecessor in Egypt, Claude Sicard, and with Jerome's *Life of Paul* forever in mind, he set off from Cairo on 11 November 1883, just over a year after British troops had put an end to the 'Urābī revolution and occupied the country. Jullien took the train to Beni Suef. He was accompanied by François Sogaro, the apostolic vicar for Central Africa appointed for the Egyptian Sudan; Antūn Morcos, the apostolic visitor of the Catholic Copts; Luigi Korrat, a coadjutor; and Sante Bonavia, an Italian architect who lived in Cairo.[109]

The train journey from Cairo to Beni Suef lasted three hours, but then the visitors had to mount camels after obtaining permits from the bishops of St Antony's and St Paul's at Būsh (for whom Jullien had a letter from the patriarch Cyril V). The permits were granted, and Jullien wrote a picturesque account of the journey across the desert. From the Monastery of St Antony to that of St Paul the company preferred the more circuitous road, and they were finally hoisted by ropes and greeted with the traditional procession and religious service. Jullien found that the monastery was inhabited by twenty-five monks – nine lay brothers and sixteen hiero-monks – one of whom was aged ninety. Antūn Morcos managed to deliver a sermon in which he urged the inmates of the monastery to unite with the Church of Rome. According to Jullien the monks were impressed by his arguments. Some of them tried to speak to him alone, and he spent much of the night talking to them, but there is no evidence to suggest that any of them converted. Indeed, Jullien retained a low opinion of the Copts, who, he wrote, had no idea of mental prayer, were deaf to any exhortation, hardly ever took communion, and had hearts as empty, cold, and dilapidated as their churches.[110] Nevertheless, Jullien was generally

---

107 Libois, *Monumenta Proximi Orientis*, vol. 6, pp. lviii–lx.
108 On Jullien, see C. Mayeur-Jaouen, 'Un jésuite français en Egypte: le père Jullien' in C. Décobert, ed., *Itinéraires d'Egypte: Mélanges offerts au père Maurice Martin S.J.* (Cairo, 1992), pp. 213–247.
109 M. Jullien, *L'Egypte, souvenirs bibliques et chrétiens* (Lille, 1889), p. 59.
110 *Ibid.*, p. 54: 'Ils n'ont aucune idée de l'oraison mentale; ils n'entendent aucune exhortation spirituelle; ils communient rarement et ne conservent jamais le Saint-Sacrement dans

pleased by St Paul's – after failing to sleep in his cell he found that he slept very well in the open air. He drew a plan of the monastery, took measurements of the Cave Church, which he estimated at 9 square metres, but was disappointed by the coarseness of the wall paintings.[111] On the day after their arrival the visitors attended mass and set off on their return journey at noon. Jullien's account of the Red Sea monasteries was influential in the French-speaking world and was followed closely by Charles Beaugé, a French traveller who spent some twenty years in Asyūṭ in Upper Egypt and who published an account of his experiences in 1923.[112]

Over twenty years after Jullien's expedition, in March 1908, St Paul's received yet another party of missionaries. It was organized by Fortunato Vignozzi da Seano, the head of the Franciscan mission in Beni Suef, and by Gottfried Schilling, who was then the president of the Church of St Joseph in Ismāʿīliya in Cairo and would subsequently represent the Custodians of the Holy Land in Washington. They were accompanied by another Franciscan missionary, Teodosio Somigli (who recorded their experiences in his biography of Vignozzi), and by a young archaeologist from Munich, August Schuler. Equipped with a camera, the travellers photographed Vignozzi being hoisted into the 'only remaining monastery ... without a gate.'[113] The Franciscans made further efforts to win the inmates over to Rome, and, as on the occasion of Jullien's visit, discussions were held with the monks for an entire night. In the end they were just as unsuccessful as the Jesuits, even if Somigli believed that the monks of St Paul's seemed better disposed toward them than did those of St Antony's.[114]

Despite the railway line to Beni Suef, the Monastery of St Paul remained a challenge, and as such it was taken up by two exceptional English women

---

leur église. Le chapelet d'ambre ou d'ivoire qu'ils tournent sans cesse dans leurs doigts, comme les bons musulmans, n'est qu'un ornement auquel ils n'attachent aucune prière. Je me figure leur cœur vide, froid, délabré comme leurs églises: le schisme, c'est la mort!' See also Mayeur-Jaouen, 'Un jésuite français', p. 234.

111   Jullien, *L'Egypte*, pp. 90–97, esp. p. 94: 'Les murailles et les voûtes de la chapelle sont couvertes de peintures grossières.'
112   C. Beaugé, *A travers la Haute-Egypte; Vingt ans de souvenirs* (Alençon, 1923), pp. 175–179.
113   T. Somigli di S. Detole O.F.M., *Il P. Fortunato Vignozzi da Seano O.F.M. Missionario apostolico nell'Alto Egitto (1857–1912)* (Florence, 1913), opposite p. 80, for the photograph of 'l'unico monastero che sia rimasto, come tutti una volta erano i monasteri nel deserto, senza porta.'
114   *Ibid.*, p. 86: 'Le discussioni non erano di breve durata. Mi ricordo che a S. Antonio e più a S. Paolo, ove le speranze parevano più fondate, esse si prolungarono per tutta una notte ... Sebbene confusi, i monaci pure si stringevano riverenti e affettuosi quasi intorno all'Abuna Fortunato; e nei commiati notavo qualche cosa, che poteva anche essere commozione.'

in the first decade of the twentieth century. Agnes Smith Lewis and Margaret Dunlop Gibson were twins, identical and inseparable but with gifts that complemented one another – Smith Lewis excelled in Syriac and Aramaic, and Gibson in Arabic. Frequent travellers to Egypt and the Middle East, they were rich and eccentric, known in Cambridge, where they lived in a neo-Gothic mansion, for their garden parties at which a piper would play on the lawn, and for owning one of the first motorcars in the city. As scholars they were highly respected. Smith Lewis, who had once tried her hand as a novelist, had discovered the Syriac Codex Sinaiticus at St Catherine's; she had acquired an interesting early Aramaic manuscript in Cairo which she gave to Cambridge University; and both sisters published valuable scholarly editions of early texts.[115] Yet even for these intrepid travellers, aged sixty at the time, St Paul's posed a problem: it had never been entered by a woman. Well-connected and ready to take advantage of the British occupation of Egypt, they obtained a recommendation from the British consul general, Lord Cromer, and from the prime minister, Buṭrus Ghālī Pasha, for the patriarch, Cyril v, who, in his turn, gave them letters for the bishops at Būsh. They set out on 18 February 1904, and reached Būsh by train. While they had no difficulties in obtaining a permit from the bishop of St Antony's, they had more trouble in convincing Bishop Arsāniyūs of St Paul's. Finally, however, he agreed, and wrote that any of the monks who objected to their visit should be locked up together in one room.[116]

The twins set off across the desert with a Muslim cook, a Coptic waiter, and two Bedouin guides, and they reached the Monastery of St Antony on the 23rd. On the 26th they made for St Paul's. They were at first appalled by the wall, which was fifty feet high, and by the windlass that would hoist them into the monastery, but, with the help of their travelling equipment, they managed to furnish a large padded basket and were pulled up in a decorous manner. They found thirty monks eagerly awaiting them, and, after the traditional procession and religious service, they were addressed by the prior in terms that stirred their patriotism. 'Next came a eulogium on our beloved sovereign Queen Victoria,' wrote Smith Lewis, 'and a lament over her death; then an expression of gratitude to Lord Cromer, and to the noble English nation, for their deliverance of

---

115 For their lives, see the respective entries s.v. by C. Müller-Kessler, *ODNB*. For their activities as manuscript collectors, see Volkoff, *A la recherche*, pp. 265–284, 292–304, and for their scholarship, R.J.W. Jefferson, 'Sisters of Semitics: A fresh appreciation of the scholarship of Agnes Smith Lewis and Margaret Dunlop Gibson' *Medieval Feminist Forum* 45 (2009), pp. 23–49.

116 A. Lewis, 'Hidden Egypt: the first visit by women to the Coptic monasteries of Egypt and Nitria, with an account of the condition and reasons for the decadence of an ancient Church' *Century Magazine* 68 (1904), pp. 745–758, esp. p. 746.

the Egyptians from Ahmed Arabi Pasha, for the works of irrigation, and for the establishment of schools, etc.'[117] The two ladies inspected the bakery; Gibson took photographs of the monks; and they 'examined their small store of manuscripts, which were similar in character to those at Deyr Antonius, only that one containing the sermons of St Simeon the Stylite was on vellum.' They had lunch prepared by their own cook, and were lowered down from the trapdoor.

The Smith twins, nicknamed the Giblews by their contemporaries, were scholars rather than missionaries. Nevertheless, they were committed Presbyterians. Their parents had been Presbyterians, Gibson's husband had once been a Presbyterian minister, and they contributed to the foundation of Westminster College in Cambridge, the Presbyterian theological college opened in 1897. They consequently took a strong interest in the primitive Coptic church and the remarkably successful efforts of the American Presbyterians to convert its members, even if they might have hoped for a more substantial English contribution. 'The Coptic Church,' wrote Smith Lewis, 'is now in a very critical position. To those who, like myself, have cherished the hope that she would rouse herself to feel the need of an educated ministry, well grounded in the Scriptures, and apt to teach, thus assimilating herself perhaps to the Protestant Church of England, it is a staggering reflection, and well-nigh a shattering of hope, to learn that all her bishops must be chosen from four of the monasteries which we visited.'[118] Not only did Smith Lewis regard the experience of the prospective bishops as far too limited to assist the Church in any development, but she believed that the Copts themselves, self-indulgent, lazy, and excessively corpulent, were ill-equipped to guide it. 'A change is impending,' she concluded ominously. 'Whether it will be in the direction of the Coptic Church embracing in its own bosom the ideas of modern progress and assimilating itself more nearly to the pattern of the infant church which existed in the days of St Mark, or whether it will become a mere empty shell of officialism and traditional ritual, the influences which affect it in the twentieth century will irrevocably decide.'[119]

With his practical recommendations about the restoration of the wall paintings in the Cave Church, Schweinfurth can be regarded as the first visitor to encourage research into the artistic significance of the monastery itself. In February 1901 a group of eminent German scholars – the Byzantinist Josef Strzygowski; Bernhard Moritz, the Arabist and director of the Khedival

---

117   Ibid., p. 753.
118   Besides St Antony's and St Paul's, Lewis included the monasteries of St Macarius and al-Barāmūs in the Wādī al-Naṭrūn as sources of future Coptic bishops. *Ibid.*, p. 756.
119   Ibid., p. 758.

Library in Cairo; and Carl Heinrich Becker, once professor of Semitic philology at Heidelberg and future minister of education and the arts in the Prussian cabinet – arrived at the Monastery of St Paul to examine the wall paintings and inscriptions.[120] Strzygowski was particularly interested in the equestrian martyrs for a study he was making on the iconography of St George. Reproducing a photograph of the cupola over the narthex in the Cave Church taken by Becker, he gave a detailed description of every one of the martyrs – not only on the main cupola but also by the entrance and on the walls – in the *Zeitschrift für Ägyptische Sprache und Altertumskunde* of 1902–1903.[121] He also transmitted his copy of the inscription in the cupola, which dated the restoration of the church in 1713, to the Egyptologist Walter Wreszinski. Wreszinski published it, together with the names of the equestrians in Coptic and Arabic given him by Becker, in the same number of the same journal.[122]

Many years later another distinguished group of experts visited the monastery, its members availing themselves of an altogether new means of transport, the motorcar. In 1930 the American archaeologist Thomas Whittemore, the founder of the Byzantine Institute of America in Washington, D.C., led an expedition to the Red Sea monasteries and drove to St Antony's in a convoy of Fords, accompanied by the epigraphist Alexandre Piankoff, the architect Oliver Barker, the Armenian photographer Kazazian, and the painter Vladimir Netchetailov.[123] The reason for Whittemore's interest in the Red Sea monasteries was his desire to investigate Coptic art of the Middle Ages. He had found plenty of objects from an earlier period elsewhere, but in no other sites in Egypt had he discovered such a rich selection of paintings made between the twelfth and the fourteenth centuries. The meticulousness with which he and his collaborators examined the monasteries was unprecedented. Netchetailov made copies of the paintings, and Kazazian took photographs. 'It is only now, for the first time,' Whittemore wrote, 'that these monasteries have been carefully examined. No excavations have been undertaken, since they would involve damage to conventual buildings actually in use.'[124] Whittemore spent most of

---

120 Piankoff *et al.*, 'History of the Monasteries', p. 119.
121 J. Strzygowski, 'Der koptische Reiterheilige und der hl. Georg' *Zeitschrift für Ägyptische Sprache und Altertumskunde* 40 (1902–1903), pp. 49–60. Becker's photograph is opposite p. 48, and the passage on the paintings is pp. 50–52.
122 W. Wreszinski, 'Zwei koptische Bauurkunden' *Zeitschrift für Ägyptische Sprache und Altertumskunde* 40 (1902–1903), pp. 62–55, esp. pp. 62–64.
123 On Whittemore at St Antony's, see Gabra, 'Perspectives', p. 182, and Piankoff *et al.*, 'History of the Monasteries,' pp. 119–124, esp. p. 119.
124 T. Whittemore, 'New light on Byzantine art: early Egyptian monasteries and their wall-paintings dating from the 12th to the 15th centuries' *The Illustrated London News* (4 July 1931), pp. 14–15, esp. p. 15.

his time in 1930 and 1931 at St Antony's, so much richer in works of medieval art than St Paul's. But he also worked at St Paul's, which he reached by camel. Hardly any of the results of his expedition were actually printed. Nevertheless, seven of Kazazian's splendid photographs – views of the walls, gardens, the keep, a cell-lined street, the monks in their vestments after a religious service, and the equestrian saints in the dome of the Cave Church – were indeed published, on pages 14 and 15 of *The Illustrated London News* of 4 July 1931.

At 10 o'clock in the morning on 25 March 1930, after a two-day stay at St Paul's, as he was leaving the monastery in a small caravan and in the company of another 'gentleman in European dress' (probably Kazazian), Whittemore first met Johann Georg Herzog zu Sachsen.[125] The second son of the Saxon King George, and the brother of the last king of Saxony, Frederick Augustus III (who abdicated in 1918), Johann Georg, like the other members of his branch of the family, was a Roman Catholic. He and his slightly younger brother Maximilian had received a good education, first at the University of Freiburg, and then at Leipzig, where Maximilian obtained a doctorate in 1892. Both brothers had always had a pronounced interest in Eastern Christianity. Maximilian, who had joined the priesthood, was committed to the idea of a union of the Churches, and he would boldly maintain that the Churches of the East had nothing heretical about them. He mastered Church Slavonic, Armenian, and Syriac and made a serious study of the liturgy, a subject in which he would hold a professorship at the Catholic University of Fribourg in Switzerland. Johann Georg was less single-minded. He was above all a collector of manuscripts, antiquities, and curios, with a good eye and some knowledge of art history, and he travelled to satisfy his somewhat eclectic curiosity. His main contributions to scholarship were his studies on the iconography of St Spiridion, undertaken mainly in Corfu. Despite his occasionally inaccurate attributions, particularly where dating was concerned, the energy and enthusiasm with which he studied the Copts, along with his many publications, contributed to his reputation in the German world of learning and earned him an honorary doctorate at Leipzig and a *Festschrift* from the University of Freiburg.[126]

Johann Georg first visited Egypt in 1910 and then returned repeatedly – in 1912, 1927, 1928, and 1930 – visiting, and describing, nearly all the Coptic sites. He had already planned to go to the Red Sea monasteries in 1927 but had given

---

125   Johann Georg Herzog zu Sachsen, *Neueste Streifzüge durch die Kirchen und Klöster Ägyptens* (Leipzig, 1931), p. 19.
126   For a description and an assessment of his activities, see I. Bauer, 'Das sächsische Königshaus und die Ostkirchen: Die Prinzen Johann Georg (1869–1938) und Max (1870–1951) als Forscher, Sammler und Schriftsteller' *Oriens Christianus* 80 (1996), pp. 201–227.

up the idea since nobody could give him any information about the journey. Nevertheless, in the following year he succeeded in driving to the Monastery of St Antony.[127] It was not until two years later, however, that he went to St Paul's.[128] Accompanied by a priest, the church and art historian Joseph Sauer from Freiburg, and furnished with a letter from the patriarch, John XIX, the duke left Cairo at 3 o'clock in the afternoon on 24 March in a car belonging to, and driven by, the owner of a travel agency. Travelling at almost 60 kilometres per hour, it took them two hours and twenty-three minutes to reach the Hotel Belair in Suez – Johann Georg, who had had a career in the army, always made observations with military precision. At 9:30 that evening the duke and Sauer, with a butler and an interpreter, took another car to Port Tawfik, at Suez, and boarded a steamer. The duke spent an uncomfortable night on a sofa in the saloon and, on the following morning, disembarked in Za'farāna, to be met by the coast guards, who provided the party with camels and two Sudanese non-commissioned officers as guides. They left the coast at 7:45, and at 12:15 they were at the monastery. Johann Georg noted a little petulantly that he could easily have made the journey in an hour by car and saved 'strength and energy,' but he did admit that it would have been impossible to drive the car into the monastery itself.[129]

After waiting outside the walls (Fig. 11), the visitors were finally admitted through the low gate which, the duke wrote, had been made in 1927. They were then welcomed with a toll of bells and warmly received by the monks – the duke counted twenty of them (Fig. 12) – and the hegumenos, to whom the duke gave the patriarch's letter. Although the hegumenos wanted to prolong the reception ceremony, the duke prevailed on him to show them around the monastery without further ado. The library, the duke concluded, was hardly worthy of the name, for none of the manuscripts in it was more than a hundred years old.[130] Johann Georg followed Schweinfurth in ascribing the eighteenth-century Church of St Michael and St John the Baptist to the seventeenth century and remarked on two icons, one representing Paul and Antony with staffs in their hands – he dated it between 1600 and 1650 – and one of the Madonna which he thought might be fifty years earlier. The duke took the Cave Church to date from the sixth or, at the latest, the seventh century, but he realized

---

127 Johann Georg Herzog zu Sachsen, *Neue Streifzüge durch die Kirchen und Klöster Ägyptens* (Leipzig, 1930), pp. 33–43.
128 The visit to St Paul's is described in Johann Georg, *Neueste Streifzüge*, pp. 15–25.
129 *Ibid.*, p. 21.
130 *Ibid.*, p. 18: 'Es ist auch keine Bibliothek mehr vorhanden, denn die wenigen Manuskripte, die sie für den Gottesdienst benutzen, und die meistens nicht einmal 100 Jahre alt sind, kann man kaum als solche bezeichnen.'

PILGRIMS, MISSIONARIES, AND SCHOLARS 187

FIGURE 11 St Paul's Monastery seen from the walls
JOHANN GEORG HERZOG ZU SACHSEN, *NEUESTE STREIFZÜGE DURCH DIE KIRCHEN UND KLÖSTER ÄGYPTENS* (LEIPZIG, 1931)

FIGURE 12 The monks of St Paul's Monastery
JOHANN GEORG HERZOG ZU SACHSEN, *NEUESTE STREIFZÜGE DURCH DIE KIRCHEN UND KLÖSTER ÄGYPTENS* (LEIPZIG, 1931)

that it had undergone severe renovation, the worst of which was in the eighteenth century when a 'large part of the ceiling and the walls were daubed with truly hideous frescos.'[131] He quoted Schweinfurth but added that the frescos of the equestrian saints in the front cupola were about a hundred years earlier and of superior craftsmanship. There was another wall painting, he even said, which was outstanding, representing St Paul with a long robe and a staff. He inspected it with a torch and dated it before 1000, possibly as early as the seventh century.[132]

Johann Georg was equally impressed by two icons, one of the Madonna and child, which he dated to about 1500, and one of Mary with Paul and Antony, which he found particularly well painted and of unique iconographical importance.[133] He also mentioned a bronze lectern in a dark corner near the entrance, perhaps of the fourteenth or fifteenth century, resembling another he had seen in the Coptic Museum in Cairo. He was less pleased by the Church of St Mercurius. After visiting the orchard and appreciating the general state of the monastery, but only seeing the keep from the outside, the visitors withdrew to the recently built rest house, where they ate a lunch they had brought with them and drank coffee prepared by the monks. As they were leaving, the duke was given ten candles as a present, and Sauer took a number of photographs of both the monks and the monastery. When he arrived at the coast, the duke, who was well over sixty, found his legs were so stiff that he could hardly walk, and when he boarded the boat he had to be hoisted in by his shoulders.[134]

The monastery Johann Georg visited was already changing. The new gate, rather than the traditional windlass, made it far easier to enter. The rest house, the extension of which would be completed in 1948, entailed greater comfort for pilgrims and other visitors.[135] And Johann Georg's regrets about not having had a car heralded the coast road built in 1946 and the road inland to the monastery laid in the 1980s. His conclusions, however, echoed those of travellers over the centuries. He wrote that St Paul's was by no means the most

---

131   Ibid., p. 22: 'Am schlimmsten ist es, dass man im XVIII. Jahrhundert einen grossen Teil der Decke und der Wände mit recht hässlichen Fresken überschmiert hat.'
132   Judging from Johann Georg's description, the image with a long robe and a staff was probably the painting of Murquṣ al-Anṭūnī on the eastern wall of the nave. The same eighteenth-century team responsible for the 'truly hideous frescos' in the church also produced the paintings of Murquṣ and the equestrian saints so admired by the duke.
133   The monastic collection currently contains a number of icons of Mary with Antony and Paul, and considerably more icons of the Madonna and child. None can be dated confidently before the eighteenth century. For an illustrated selection of both types, see Lyster, Monastery of St. Paul, pp. 72–79.
134   Johann Georg, Neueste Streifzüge, p. 24.
135   Meinardus, Monks and Monasteries, p. 43.

interesting of the monasteries, but the site was so spectacular and the monastery so suggestive that to visit it was one of the most exciting moments of his many journeys in Egypt.[136]

Acknowledgements

This article was first published in William Lyster, ed., *The Cave Church of Paul the Hermit at the Monastery of St. Paul, Egypt* (New Haven-London: American Research Center in Egypt, Inc.-Yale University Press, 2008), pp. 74–93, 333–336. The original version is accompanied by illustrations many of which have here been omitted.

---

136   Johann Georg, *Neueste Streifzüge*, pp. 24–25: 'Es ist sicher nicht eines der bedeutendsten. Aber in seiner unvergleichlichen Lage in den wilden Berge übertrifft es alle anderen. Es wirkt insofern fast wie ein phantastischer Traum. Künstlerisch bietet es viel weniger als das Antoniuskloster oder gar Deir-es-Suriani … Ich möchte zusammenfassend sagen, dass trotz der grossen Hitze und ziemlich bedeutenden Anstrengungen, die uns der Ausflug gebracht hat, der Besuch des Klosters sich sehr gelohnt hat. Die Lage desselben in der wilden Gegend und das Kloster selbst mit seiner uralten Pauluskirche gehören sicher zu den grössten Eindrücken, die mir auf meinen Streifzügen durch die Kirchen und Klöster Ägyptens zuteil geworden sind.'

CHAPTER 9

The Metamorphoses of Georg August Wallin

Georg August Wallin (Fig. 13) has received hardly any attention from historians of Arabic studies.[1] He was known as the first European to explore northern Arabia and as one of the few to have performed the pilgrimage to Mecca. 'All agree,' wrote Robin Bidwell, 'that he ranks as one of the greatest of all Arabian explorers.'[2] But he published little. The first reports of his journeys appeared in English in the *Journal of the Royal Geographical Society* and, posthumously, in Swedish, but his most important studies as an Arabist came out, mainly posthumously, in German in the *Zeitschrift der Deutschen Morgenländischen Gesellschaft* between 1851 and 1858. They showed that he was an expert in the dialects of the northern part of the Arabian peninsula and in Bedouin poetry. Between 1864 and 1866 Sven Gabriel Elmgren published a four-volume edition of Wallin's diary in Helsinki, but it was heavily bowdlerized. Now, at last, we have the magnificent seven-volume edition of his writings edited by Kaj Öhrnberg, Patricia Berg, and Kira Pihlflyckt, and issued by the Svenska Literatursällskapet i Finland in Helsinki between 2010 and 2016. Containing personal impressions of his journeys to and from Egypt, his travels throughout the Middle East, and daily life in Cairo, the diary is something of a *journal intime*, but it holds its own against the far more formal works of Johann Ludwig Burckhardt and Edward William Lane, both of whom Wallin admired.

Wallin was born in 1811 in the Finnish archipelago of Åland, between Finland and Sweden at the entrance of the Gulf of Bothnia. Finland had been taken by Russia from the Swedes in 1809, so Wallin was a Russian subject, but his language, like that of his educated contemporaries in Finland and all the inhabitants of Åland, was Swedish. There is no evidence that he knew much Finnish, even if he does refer to Finnish forms of pronunciation in his work on Arabic phonetics.[3] He was educated at the cathedral school in Åbo (the former capital, now Turku), on the mainland coast of Finland opposite Åland, and later, further north, in Rauma. In the meantime his family had moved to

---

1 In Fück, p. 198, he gets no more than a footnote: 'Georg August Wallin (1811–1852) war auf zwei Reisen 1845 und 1848 bis nach Ḥāyil vorgedrungen. Er brachte die ersten Proben neuarabischer Beduinendichtung nach Europa und veröffentlichte sie *zdmg* 5, 1ff.; 6, 190ff.; und 66off.'
2 R. Bidwell, *Travellers in Arabia* (Reading, 1995), pp. 140–142.
3 Georg August Wallin, 'Über die Laute des Arabischen und ihre Bezeichnung' *Zeitschrift der Deutschen Morgenländischen Gesellschaft* 9 (1855), pp. 1–69, esp. pp. 42, 54.

FIGURE 13   Georg August Wallin
IMAGE FROM LEOPOLD HENRIK STANISLAUS MECHELIN (ED.), *FINLAND IN THE NINETEENTH CENTURY BY FINNISH AUTHORS. ILLUSTRATED BY FINNISH ARTISTS* (HELSINGFORS, 1894), P. 305

the new capital, Helsinki, and Wallin, after hoping to imitate his elder brother who became a sailor, matriculated at the university in 1829 in order to study classical and Oriental languages. He there mastered a number of modern languages – German, French, English and Russian. He revealed an uncanny facility for picking them up, and, playing various musical instruments, including the guitar, the flute, the cello, and the piano, he proved to have an excellent ear which would stand him in good stead when he studied the Bedouin dialects and Arab music. At the same time he started to learn Arabic and Persian, and developed a lasting friendship with the newly-appointed professor of Oriental literature at the University of Helsinki, Gabriel Geitlin. Under Geitlin's supervision he completed his studies in 1839 with a dissertation on the differences between ancient and modern Arabic.[4]

Wallin's true progress in Oriental languages occurred in the following year when he went to St Petersburg. He described his more intimate experiences, such as visits to the opera and the ballet, and having a tooth drawn by his travelling companion, in letters to his mother, his sister, and to Geitlin.[5] Attending the lectures on Oriental languages at the university, he learnt Turkish and improved his Persian thanks to the teaching of Mirza Ismail. Within months he was able to correspond in Arabic with Muḥammad ʿAyyād al-Ṭanṭawī.[6] A distinguished Egyptian intellectual employed at the Russian university, al-Ṭanṭawī inspired Wallin with a love of Islamic culture, and gave him invaluable advice and assistance when he planned to travel to Cairo. It was largely thanks to him that Wallin applied for, and obtained, a grant to spend five years in the Arab world.

On his return to Finland from St Petersburg, Wallin made preparations for his journey by studying medicine. Like so many European travellers in the East, he intended to present himself as a doctor. His journey to Egypt, through Germany and France to Marseilles, and then to Istanbul and Izmir, is described in the first volume of his diary – the horrors of travelling by coach, the relative comfort of the new railway, the overcrowded steamers on the French rivers, the encounter in Paris with one of the greatest French Orientalists, Etienne Quatremère, the excitement of meeting Arabs in France to whom he could make himself understood in Arabic, the slave market of Istanbul, and the charm of Izmir. He disembarked in Alexandria on 14 December 1843.

---

4   *De praecipua inter hodiernam Arabum linguam et antiquam differentia dissertatio* (*Skrifter*, vol. 1, pp. 293–310).
5   *Skrifter*, vol. 1, pp. 195–261.
6   *Ibid.*, vol. 1, pp. 231–240.

The diary Wallin kept in Egypt is an enthralling record not only of everyday life in Cairo, but also of his own metamorphosis. Preparing for his journey to Arabia and the pilgrimage to Mecca, Wallin immersed himself in Islamic culture. His new name became Sheikh Wali.[7] The physical transformation required the acquisition of local clothes. In Alexandria he bought a *tarbush*.[8] Once he was in Cairo he had a Turkish *damir* or jacket made.[9] Speaking, reading, and writing – he also studied calligraphy – almost nothing but Arabic, taking daily lessons from a local teacher, ʿAlī Nidā al-Barrānī, who became an intimate friend, Wallin made increasing progress in his mastery of the language and his knowledge of the Qurʾan. He was frank about the effect the constant use of Arabic had on his other languages; it interfered with his Russian and with his German, and he had increasing difficulty with Turkish and Persian, which he had never studied for very long. This was inconvenient when he pretended to be a Muslim from the Turkish- and Persian-speaking areas.

Soon, too, Wallin adopted Muslim habits. As he told Geitlin in a letter dated 3 September 1844, he made a point of praying five times a day.[10] But he was also aware of the fragility of his disguise. 'I am convinced,' he wrote, 'that many, perhaps most, people, strongly suspect my Islam and the purity of my doctrine, but they say nothing to me and I say nothing to them, and so it goes on day after day.'[11] Whether he actually converted to Islam is something we are unlikely ever to know. As long as he was in the Arab world he was determined to pass as a Muslim, and usually succeeded. When he returned to Europe, he seems to have shed all traces of his Muslim identity. He also informed Geitlin that his fluency in Arabic meant that his Egyptian acquaintances spoke to him with an openness which they would never otherwise display before a foreigner, expressing their full hatred and contempt for Christians and Europeans.

Wallin's natural mimetism enabled him to fit into the local world of Cairo. He was assisted by his knowledge and practice of medicine, however limited it might have been, in a place where doctors were in particular demand. A certain indolence, which had already been evident before he left Finland, meant that he enjoyed the daily life of Cairo, the narguilehs, the coffee, and the leisurely conversations with friends. There were, however, limits to communication with the members of the world he had just discovered. He always

---

7   *Ibid.*, vol. 2, p. 97.
8   *Ibid.*, vol. 2, p. 111.
9   *Ibid.*, vol. 2, p. 130.
10 *Ibid.*, vol. 2, p. 337.
11 *Ibid.*: 'Jag är öfvertygad om att flere kanske större delen storligen misstänker min Islam och min läras renhet; men man säger mig ingenting och jag säger dem ingenting och så går det dag för dag.'

regretted the impossibility of sharing certain aesthetic pleasures with his Egyptian acquaintances. He would go for frequent walks in Cairo and its outskirts, and was profoundly moved by the view of the old city and the pyramids from the Muqaṭṭam Heights. When he tried to convey this to his friends, he met with complete incomprehension.[12]

Another of Wallin's disappointments in Cairo was his failure to meet Edward William Lane. According to Kaj Öhrnberg, Lane, who lived together with his sister Sophia, disapproved of what he had heard about Wallin's somewhat disreputable private life. And indeed, Wallin, in his diaries, makes no secret of his encounters with those to whom he once refers, with uncustomary coyness, as 'the worst servants of Venus'.[13] Wallin describes these frequent meetings in detail, but first in English and later in Arabic in order not to shock his mother and his sister. At the time his English, which would improve after a stay of six months in London and the need not only to correspond with English scholars but also to publish in English, was decidedly odd: 'Meeted with a girl in the street and passed with her in a house, in which I rested in her embracings the whole night. She as all her sisters here was extremely prostituted although not seeming to be of the lowest order'.[14]

But even if Wallin spent most of his time in Egyptian circles and failed to meet Lane, he had to pay regular visits to the Russian consulate in order to receive his travel allowance, and he encountered a number of the European residents in Egypt. He was charmed, for example, by the French surgeon who introduced modern medicine into Egypt – Antoine Barthélemy, known as Clot Bey. In October 1844 he sailed with a group of friends as far south as Wadi Halfa to inspect the monuments.[15] His travelling companions were August Schledehaus, the German physician of the Egyptian ruler Muhammad 'Ali, and

---

12   *Ibid.*, vol. 3, pp. 87–88: 'Här var verkeligen en plats lämplig för bön och andakt; ock dock förundrade jag mig att en muslim valt det dertil. Jag har ännu aldrig här sett en muslim som vid betraktandet af naturskönhet känt sig röras till andakt …'; p. 90: 'Sedan jag slutat mitt mål blefvo vi efter vanligheten sittande vid vårt kaffe och våra pipor och som jag kände verkeligen behof af att berätta det förunderliga jag sett i dag och so lämnat stort intryck på mig talade jag om för min Shekh hvar jag varit. Jag fann dock hos honom aldeles ingen anklang och då jag frågade om han alldrig stigit upp på berget svarade han helt kallt och litet snäsigt: hvad skulle jag hämta deri från? raiḥ agib eh min hinak. Jag sökte förklara honom att man ingenstädes så kunde se Herrens allmakt som här in i den herrliga Nildalen och det konstigt formade berget och medelbarligen i menniskors storverk som syntes härifrån. Han svarade väl ej annat än att det var sannt; men kände ingen lust röras i sig att besöka det.'
13   *Ibid.*, vol. 2, p. 240.: 'der Veneris sämsta tjenarinnor'.
14   *Ibid.*, vol. 3, p. 78.
15   *Ibid.*, vol. 3, pp. 129–259.

the Austrian landscape painter Hubert Sattler. In Luxor he made the acquaintance of the greatest contemporary Egyptologist, Richard Lepsius.

On 11 April 1845 Wallin at last left Cairo in order to explore the Arabian desert and its tribes. Originally intending to travel to the Arabian peninsula by way of ʿAqaba, he was advised to approach it from the north, and thus made for Maʿān and then for al-Jauf where he spent three months. After that he proceeded to Ḥāʾil, which he was the first European to visit. In the middle of November he joined the Persian *hajj* caravan. He first visited Medina and then Mecca, which he reached on 7 December and where he spent a week before going on to Jedda. He was back in Cairo on 14 March 1846. His description of the holy places, Mecca and Medina, is cursory, in letters to his sister and to Geitlin.[16] Repelled by religious enthusiasm, he liked neither town. He lost his heart, on the other hand, to the Bedouin tribes in the north. He told Geitlin that they were free of any kind of fanaticism. Endowed with 'a natural simplicity', they were of exemplary tolerance, incapable of saying five prayers a day or of reading the Qurʾan.[17] On his later travels, and after his return to Europe, he would long for their company and pine for the desert.

In December 1846 Wallin travelled east once more. This time he visited St Catherine's monastery in the Sinai peninsula, Jerusalem, Bethlehem, and Damascus. He disliked Jerusalem as much as he did Mecca and Medina, and for many of the same reasons.[18] And a year later, in December 1847, he set out on his third and last desert journey. This time he explored northern Arabia more thoroughly than ever before, travelling from Muwayliḥ on the west coast

---

16   *Ibid.*, vol. 4, pp. 257–258, 300–304.
17   *Ibid.*, vol. 4, p. 217: 'Beduinerne sjelfva äro, så vidt jag hittills lärt känna dem, ett folk, som man af hjertat måste älska. De hafva en naturlig enkelhet, utan allt slags krus eller complimenter och ett ända fram väsende, som fullkomligen öfverensstämmer med mitt lynne.'; p. 218–219: 'Man kunde säga, att Beduinen är ett fullkomligt barn, som ännu icke lärt sin cateches, ej heller något annat religions-kram. Han är hvarken muslim, eller christen, eller afgudadyrkare, eller något annat. Han har platt ingen religion, så till vida, att han hör till ingen sect. Detta gäller åtminstone om alla, dem jag hittils träffat. Af de femton män, som tillhöra den stam, der jag nu vistas, är ingen i stand att läsa någon af de fem dagliga bönerne, ingen som vet, att Koran är en gudomlig uppenbarelse genom propheten, o.s.v. eller med ett ord ingen, som känner de första hufvudstyckena af deras religion ... Äfven här, liksom i städerne, är Nasrani (Nazaréer, d.v.s. christna) ett öknamn, och man kan icke tala nog mycket ondt om dem. Dock måste jag erkänna, att Beduinend fördragsamhet är vida större, vida noblare ...'; cf. also p. 280. For an interesting study of the comparable attitude towards the Bedouin of Johann Ludwig Burckhardt see M. Kurpershoek, 'Burckhardt's quest for Bedouin poetry: Arabic antecedents and European followers' in L. Burckhardt, L. Burkart, J. Loop and R. Stucky, eds, *Johann Ludwig Burckhardt Sheikh Ibrahim. Entdeckungen im Orient um 1800* (Basel, 2019), pp. 101–109.
18   *Skrifter*, vol. 5, pp. 104–105.

to Tabūk and Taymāʾ, and then once more to Ḥāʾil. He was the first European explorer to describe the area, and his description earned him honorary awards from the Royal Geographical Society in London and the Société de Géographie in Paris. On this occasion, too, he recorded the Bedouin poems which he published in Europe. In September 1848 he left the Bedouin and made first for Baghdad, where he met the British consul, Henry Rawlinson, who would later become one of his main supporters in London. He then went on to Persia. He stayed in Kirmanshah, Shiraz and Isfahan, and described his experiences in letters to Geitlin. Although he had claimed to be a Persian speaker when he visited St Catherine's, his Persian, as we saw, had suffered from his practice of Arabic, and he never felt fully at ease in the language, even if he made considerable progress during the four months he spent in the country. Nor did he particularly like the people. The Persians were far too close to the Europeans. Their overdecorated mosques had nothing to do with the pure religion which could only be found in the Arabian desert. Their music was far more European than that of the Arabs.[19] The Persians, he concluded, were incapable of the frankness and openness he had found amongst the Bedouin.[20]

Wallin was again in Cairo in June 1849 and, on 9 August, having exhausted his allowance, he set sail for Europe from Alexandria. At this point his diary, apparently interrupted by his travels, is resumed. On his way back to Finland he disembarked in Trieste and then made his way through the north of Italy, Switzerland, and Germany to Belgium, where he took a ship from Antwerp to England. His stay in London, which lasted from the end of September 1849 until May of the following year, marked his return to the European world of learning.

Although he had long wanted to visit England, London was clearly less agreeable than he had hoped. He spent much of his time in the library of the British Museum, but otherwise he felt let down. He was disappointed by Macready's performance of Hamlet and by the English stage more generally. It compared unfavourably with what he had seen in Paris. He found the English women ungainly and the English men both affected and coarse.[21] He visited Madame Tussaud's and noted with distaste that the only room that drew constant crowds was the Chamber of Horrors.[22] Above all, however, he missed

---

19   Ibid., vol. 5, p. 367.
20   Ibid., vol. 5, p. 279: 'Det är ingen öppenhet ingen redlighet i deras ansigten och såsom de i sitt uppförande dölja sin charakter och sin natur under artigheter och complimenter så höljas deras egentligen vackra drag af ett moln af de elementer som äro en följd af en förvrängdt bildad natur.'.
21   Ibid., vol. 6, p. 183.
22   Ibid., vol. 6, p. 209.

the East. 'How human, how humane and cultivated are Orientals compared to these people,' he wrote.[23] 'You beloved East, how shall I ever return to you and to that wonderful natural life!'[24]

In London Wallin started to take measures to embark on an academic career in Finland. Needing to provide a 'professorial dissertation', he decided to present a Latin translation of the poetry of Ibn al-Fāriḍ (1181–1235) with the commentary of ʿAbd al-Ghanī al-Nābulusī (1641–1731) based on two manuscripts, one in London and the other in St Petersburg.[25] He also prepared a report in English on his third excursion into the desert, and read it to the Royal Geographical Society on 22 April 1850. He assisted the East India Company in improving its map of Arabia, and prepared a German translation and commentary of Bedouin songs which he dispatched to one of the most distinguished Arabists in Germany, Heinrich Leberecht Fleischer, for publication in his *Zeitschrift der Deutschen Morgenländischen Gesellschaft*.

Once back in Helsinki, Wallin defended his professorial thesis in October 1850. He was rewarded, on 1 January 1851, with the professorship of Oriental literature at the university[26] and started to make plans to travel again to the East. He approached both the English and the Russians in order to obtain a subsidy. His plans, however, ended with his sudden and altogether unexpected death on 23 October 1852. Its cause has been much disputed. It was said at the time to have been due to a ruptured aorta. It was subsequently suggested that it might have been the result of syphilis, but as Kai Öhrnberg shows in his highly informative introduction, more recent research and reports by contemporaries point to a liver disease.[27]

Wallin's merits as an explorer were recognized while he was still alive, but what about his achievements as an Arabist? Ever since the late seventeenth century it had become increasingly apparent that a European university was no place at which to learn Arabic. By and large Arabic, which was indeed taught widely, especially in the schools and universities of Protestant Germany, was studied mainly by theologians and in conjunction with Hebrew. After the death of the great Arabists, Jacobus Golius in Leiden and Edward Pococke at Oxford, hardly any teacher of the language had set foot in the Arab world. Arabic was taught as a dead language, and even if some students acquired the

---

23   *Ibid.*, vol. 6, p. 181: 'Huru mensklig huru human o. bildad är dock Orientalern i jämnförelse till detta folk'.
24   *Ibid.*, vol. 6, p. 185: 'O du kära Orient! huru skall jag kunna komma tillbaka till Dig o. ditt härliga naturliga lif?'
25   *Ibid.*, vol. 7, pp. 306–328.
26   For the documentation see *ibid.*, vol. 7, pp. 377–389.
27   *Ibid.*, vol. 1, p. 64.

rudiments of grammar and could make their way through relatively simple texts, few of them could speak it. This situation coincided with the decline of the universities in the eighteenth century and the rise of alternative institutions. Where Arabic was concerned, the most important of these were the interpreters' schools, intended to train translators and diplomats. The idea was first put into practice by the Venetians in Istanbul in 1551. It was subsequently imitated, above all, by the Austrians and the French and, far later, by the British. Although the Russians had set up an interpreters' school of their own in Orenburg in 1744, they lagged behind. Not until the first decade of the nineteenth century were chairs established at the University of Kazan. Persian and Arabic were taught at the University of Moscow between 1811 and 1837, and in 1816 Oriental languages were first taught in a pedagogical institute in St Petersburg. The institute turned into a university three years later, and to the chairs in Arabic and Persian was added a chair in Turkish in 1822.[28] In that year the chairs of Arabic and Turkish were occupied by Ossip Ivanovich Senkovski, a close friend of the German numismatist Christian Martin Joachim Frähn, the professor of Oriental languages in Kazan who had such a strong influence on Oriental studies throughout Russia. Senkovski would soon be followed by native speakers and, by the time Wallin was studying at the university, it was one of the best schools of Eastern languages in Europe.

The subject of Wallin's dissertation when he completed his studies at the University of Helsinki – the differences between ancient and modern Arabic – was indicative of his interests. With his ear for music, he was always particularly interested in the sounds of languages. He once quoted Luther on the importance of hearing people talk in the street,[29] and it was to this that he devoted so much of his time in Egypt and in the Arabian peninsula.

Wallin's first contribution to Fleischer's *Zeitschrift der Deutschen Morgenländischen Gesellschaft* was his 'Probe aus einer Anthologie neuarabischer Gesänge, in der Wüste gesammelt', which appeared in two issues, 5 (1851) and 6 (1852). This was not the first introduction to the West of Bedouin poetry. In 1830 Burckardt's *Notes on the Bedouin and Wahaby* had appeared, and contained a couple of examples of Bedouin verse given in English translation and with annotations explaining certain Arabic words. Wallin, on the other hand, gave the poems in Arabic followed by a transliteration and a German translation. In his notes he provided a detailed analysis of the linguistic and

---

28   For a survey see R.N. Frye, 'Oriental studies in Russia' in W.S. Vucinich, ed., *Russia and Asia. Essays on the Influence of Russia on the Asian Peoples* (Stanford, ca. 1972), pp. 30–51, esp. pp. 37–46.
29   *Skrifter*, vol. 5, p. 196.

grammatical structures, and laid strong emphasis on the phonetic aspects of Bedouin Arabic.

The 'Probe' was followed by Wallin's most important contribution to the study of Arabic phonetics: his 'Über die Laute des Arabischen und ihre Bezeichnung', published posthumously in two parts in volumes 9 (1855) and 12 (1858) of the *Zeitschrift der Deutschen Morgenländischen Gesellschaft*. Wallin had, in fact, been preceded by Lane, who had also published an article on the same subject in the fourth number of Fleischer's journal, which appeared in 1850, and Wallin's 'Bemerkungen über die Sprache der Beduinen' – published posthumously in *ZDMG* 12 (1858) – was intended to supplement Lane's study. Wallin's far longer 'Über die Laute' is the work most quoted by Wilhelm Spitta, a pupil of Fleischer and director of the Khedival Library in Cairo, in his *Grammatik des arabischen Vulgärdialectes von Aegypten* which appeared in 1880. Even if it has now long been surpassed, Spitta's was the first serious analysis of Egyptian Arabic.[30] He regarded the work of Wallin and Lane as by far the best early studies of Arabic phonetics,[31] and both men – Wallin perhaps even more than Lane – can be regarded as pioneers of a science which has made immeasurable advances in recent years.

Although Wallin's articles in the *Zeitschrift der Deutschen Morgenländischen Gesellschaft* have to be consulted separately, the new seven-volume edition of his writings contains far more than his diary and includes much of his output. First, there is his correspondence. The majority of the letters are to Geitlin and to Wallin's mother and sister, but there are also exchanges with his scholarly acquaintances – with al-Ṭanṭāwī and ʿAlī Nidā al-Barrānī (in Arabic), with Heinrich Leberecht Fleischer and Emil Rödiger (in German), with Norton Shaw, the secretary of the Royal Geographical Society (in Swedish), with Frederick Ayrton (in English), with members of the Russian Geographical Society (in French), and with various Swedish colleagues. The letters in languages other than Swedish are followed by Swedish translations. We also have lists of daily expenses in Egypt: the notes, mainly on the weather, made by Wallin during his travels, in Swedish but in Arabic characters; Wallin's description of his first visit to the Arabian peninsula in 1845, written on his return to Helsinki in 1850; and material related to Wallin's dealings with the University of Helsinki (such as his professorial dissertation). While the notes and most of the introductions are by Kai Öhrnberg, the various volumes are also accompanied by

---

30 Fück, pp. 239–40.
31 Wilhelm Spitta, *Grammatik des arabischen Vulgärdialectes von Aegypten* (Leipzig, 1880), p. vi: 'Was hiervon wirklich wissenschaftlichen Werth hat, wie die Arbeiten Lane's und Wallin's, ist an den betreffenden Stellen gewissenhaft angeführt.'

essays by experts in different fields. Jason Thompson has provided a piece on nineteenth-century travellers in Egypt, Patricia Berg a survey of contemporary Egyptologists, Jaakko Hämeen-Antilla an enlightening essay on Persian studies; Heikki Palva has examined Wallin's achievements in the field of linguistics. Some of these essays are more relevant than others, but the edition, together with the companion volume *Dolce far niente in Arabia. George August Wallin and his Travels in the 1840s* (with articles by Patricia Berg, Sofia Häggman, Kaj Öhrnberg, and Jaakko Hämeen-Anttila), are an outstanding contribution to the study of one of the most interesting Orientalists of his day.

Acknowledgements

This article was originally published in *Erudition and the Republic of Letters* 3 (2018), pp. 349–358 as a review of the seven-volume edition of the diaries and letters of George August Wallin, edited by K. Öhrnberg, P. Berg, and K. Pihlflyckt, Georg August Wallin, *Skrifter* (Helsinki 2010–2016) together with *Dolce far niente in Arabia. George August Wallin and his Travels in the 1840s* (Helsinki, 2014). My particular thanks are due to Fredrik Thomasson and Patricia Berg.

PART 2

Arabic Studies

∴

CHAPTER 10

Arabic Studies in Europe

1 The Motives

The study of Arabic in Europe can be traced back to the Middle Ages, and by the eighteenth century a variety of arguments had been assembled in its support. Frequently intended to attract an uninformed patron, not all of them stand up to critical scrutiny today, but they came to form a standard litany without which no apology of Arabic would be complete.[1]

The first reason, which proved remarkably resilient, was the use of Arabic for missionaries.[2] The possibility of converting the Muslims to Christianity and of combating Islam had once raised the highest hopes. These suffered a major setback in the fourteenth century when the Mongols converted to Islam, yet, if Arabic continued to be studied throughout the later Middle Ages, it was still partly due to the dream of converting Muslims by peaceful methods and partly to pastoral objectives in previously Muslim areas which had been conquered by the Christians. The establishment of chairs in Arabic, as well as in Greek, Hebrew, and Syriac, at the universities of Paris, Oxford, Bologna, Salamanca, and Avignon (the seat of the papacy), was consequently proposed at the Council of Vienne in 1312 and at the Council of Basel in 1434, but it was not carried out. At the same time the determination to win over the Muslims with rational arguments derived from a sound knowledge of Islam induced European scholars to tackle the translation of the Qurʾan from the twelfth century onwards.

At the Council of Florence, which lasted from 1438 to 1445, a further incentive to teach Arabic to missionaries emerged: the union of the Churches and the wish to convert the Arabic-speaking Christians to Roman Catholicism. In view of the difficulty of converting Muslims this second objective seemed far more practicable. It was to form a significant part of the policy behind the main missionary organization of the seventeenth century, the *Congregatio de Propaganda Fide* founded by Pope Gregory XV in 1622.

Another reason given for the study of Arabic was the need to read the works of the great medieval scientists. In view of the products in Arabic of physicians,

---

1   A. Hamilton, *William Bedwell the Arabist 1563–1632* (Leiden, 1985), pp. 66–96.
2   K.H. Dannenfeldt, 'The Renaissance humanists and the knowledge of Arabic' *Studies in the Renaissance* 2 (1955), pp. 96–117.

astronomers, and mathematicians between the eighth and twelfth centuries, and the translations of Greek scientific texts in ʿAbbasid Baghdad, this had once been a valid argument. It was in order to translate from the Arabic that an international group of scholars travelled to Toledo in the course of the twelfth century. Robert of Ketton, Hermann of Carinthia, Gerard of Cremona, John of Seville, and many others assembled in the city, which, in 1085, had at last been reconquered from the Muslims by the Christian forces. They set about turning some of the main Arabic scientific texts into Latin.[3] In the centuries that followed, their versions came under increasing criticism and later scientistslearnt Arabic in order to improve on them. But, although certain texts in the fields of mathematics and astrology which were only available in Arabic continued to fascinate the world of learning until well into the eighteenth century, even by the mid-seventeenth century the Arabic contribution to science was itself being reassessed. The discovery by the humanists of Greek manuscripts of texts previously only known in Arabic translation had confirmed the suspicion that the Arabic translations were not always reliable, and the growing tendency in the seventeenth century to question traditional knowledge, to experiment and to base scientific conclusions on personal observation, diminished the demand for the scientific works both of the Ancients and of their Arabic-writing successors.[4]

Then there was the proximity of Arabic to Hebrew and its use for students of the Bible. Throughout the early modern period the majority of academic students of Arabic were theologians, and Hebrew was the first Semitic language they encountered. Hebrew, it was generally believed in Christian Europe, was the original language from which all others descended. In the genealogical trees of languages, Arabic, together with Syriac and Aramaic, occupied a privileged place as its immediate descendants. If students learnt Arabic, it was consequently argued, they would expand their acquaintance with the kindred tongues and gain a deeper knowledge of Hebrew. Many dictionaries of the seventeenth century, such as the Arabic-Latin one of William Bedwell in England which remained in manuscript[5] and the 'polyglot' *Lexicon pentaglotton* compiled by Valentin Schindler and published in Hanau in 1612, bore out this persuasion and contained countless comparisons between the various Semitic languages which were supposed to be of use to biblical students. They led up to the largest of the polyglot dictionaries, Edmund Castell's *Lexicon heptaglotton*

---

3 C.H. Haskins, *Studies in the History of Medieval Science* (Cambridge, Mass., 1924), pp. 12–19.
4 F. Klein-Franke, *Die klassische Antike in der Tradition des Islam* (Darmstadt, 1980).
5 Hamilton, *William Bedwell*, pp. 85–94.

(London 1669), much praised at the time but of little assistance to the progress of Arabic studies.[6]

There also existed a belief among Bible students, which persisted into the eighteenth century, that the Book of Job, one of the earliest in the Old Testament, had originally been written in Arabic and that a knowledge of that language would be of assistance in solving some of the linguistic obscurities which it contained. Where the study of the New Testament was concerned, on the other hand, scholars all over Europe felt that the Arabic renderings might reflect a far earlier Syriac version and contain interesting variants which would enable them to improve on the standard Latin translation, the Vulgate attributed to St Jerome in the late fourth and early fifth centuries. This belief brought about the inclusion of Arabic versions of the Scriptures in the two principal polyglot Bibles of the seventeenth century, the Paris Polyglot (1629–1645) and the London Polyglot (1653–1657).[7]

In fact the advisability of associating Arabic with Hebrew and using it for biblical studies was soon questioned. In the first years of the seventeenth century the French scholar Joseph Justus Scaliger expressed his regret that so many people were studying Arabic in conjunction with Hebrew and limiting themselves almost entirely to biblical texts. Arabic, he pointed out, was above all an Islamic language. It could not be approached profitably without a thorough knowledge of the Qurʾan, and should then continue to be studied on the basis of a wide selection of Islamic texts. If anything, he suggested, Arabic should be learnt in association not with Hebrew but with other Islamic languages, notably with Turkish and Persian.[8]

One of the more practical reasons given for studying Arabic was the need of mercantile exchange which had been stressed intermittently ever since the thirteenth century. This objective grew in significance as the Arab world became of increasing commercial and political importance in the early modern period. The best French Arabist of the sixteenth century, Guillaume Postel, said that the knowledge of Arabic would enable a traveller to make his way from Morocco to the Moluccas without an interpreter – an attractive prospect for a merchant – and it was very largely for the sake of trade that the curators

---

6 Toomer, pp. 255–265.
7 A. Hamilton, 'The study of tongues: the Semitic languages and the Bible in the Renaissance' in E. Cameron, ed., *The New Cambridge History of the Bible, Volume 3. From 1450 to 1750* (Cambridge, 2016), pp. 17–36, esp. pp. 29–34; *idem*, 'In search of the most perfect text: The early modern printed Polyglot Bibles from Alcalá (1510–1520) to Brian Walton (1654–1658)' in *ibid.*, pp. 138–156, esp. pp. 150–155.
8 See below, pp. 248–249.

of Leiden University decided to found a chair of Arabic at the end of the sixteenth century.[9]

To the commercial importance of the Arabic-speaking world was added the fascination entailed by its antiquity, its vastity, and its comparative remoteness. In the age of both geographical and intellectual exploration it contained countless facets that intrigued scholars. Cartographers wanted to chart the area and to discover the modern Arabic names of sites only known from the geographers of Antiquity. Physicians, botanists, zoologists, and geologists were eager to assemble material concerning flora, fauna, and geological formations unknown in the West. Historians and chronologists wanted information about the Arabs which would enable them to acquire a more complete idea of the history of the world and its various civilizations. This, in its turn, ultimately led to the revision of the traditional biblical chronology hallowed in Christian Europe.

The comparison of religions which got underway in the seventeenth century led to a pronounced interest in Islam and an ever greater curiosity about Arabic religious texts, while the collections of Arabic manuscripts, brought back from the East by Jacobus Golius, Edward Pococke, Levinus Warner, and others, stimulated an interest in Arabic literature. It was only well after Antoine Galland had introduced the European reading public to the *Arabian Nights* in the first years of the eighteenth century and Johann Jakob Reiske had published some of the odes in the *Muʿallaqāt* in 1742, however, that scholars started to learn Arabic in order to gain a more direct acquaintance with literary, rather than scientific, texts. An early example of one who did so, in the 1760s, was the future Sanskrit scholar, William Jones.[10]

2 The Grammars

The first steps toward compiling an Arabic grammar in Christian Europe depended on the availability of teachers. The Christian Arabists who arrived in Toledo in the twelfth century had a wide choice, above all amongst the resident Jews (both orthodox and converted) and Mozarabs (Christians once living under Muslim rule), who knew Arabic and Spanish.[11] Outside Spain it was

---

9   W.M.C. Juynboll, *Zeventiende-eeuwsche Beoefenaars van het Arabisch in Nederland* (Utrecht, 1931), pp. 10–11.
10 Fück, p. 130.
11 C. Burnett, 'The institutional context of Arabic-Latin translations of the Middle Ages: A reassessment of the "school of Toledo"' in O. Weijers, ed., *Vocabulary of Teaching and*

considerably less easy to engage an Arabic-speaker as a teacher. In the mid-fifteenth century it took John of Segovia, who had retired to a monastery in Savoy, two years to find a copy of the Qur'an and an Arabic-speaking Muslim ready to help him translate it. He finally found a jurist from Salamanca, but the jurist was only prepared to spend a few months with him and, after his departure, John of Segovia could find nobody else.[12]

Spain at first seemed a good place in which to study Arabic, and it was there that the first printed grammar, the *Arte para ligeramente saber la lengua araviga*, appeared in Granada in 1505. The author, Pedro de Alcalá, the confessor of the archbishop of Granada Fernando de Talavera, was working in Andalusia in the years after the Christian *Reconquista* of 1492. His grammar, as well as his dictionary, were intended above all for missionaries working in the south of Spain who needed the language of the less educated people in order to converse with them, preach to them, and take their confessions. This required a particular terminology. It also meant that the Arabic he used, transliterated in the Roman alphabet and according to Castilian pronunciation, was chiefly the Arabic of al-Andalus. His main models for his grammar were the Latin and Spanish grammars by his fellow-countryman Antonio de Nebrija, and this explains the Latin structure which he imposed. At the same time, however, his Muslim informants, the 'learned faqihs' to whom he refers in his dictionary (but whose educated use of the language he rejected), obviously introduced him to the Classical Arabic grammatical tradition, and one of the infelicities of the grammar as a whole is that no distinction is made between Classical Arabic rules and those of the Andalusian dialect.[13]

As a result of Christian pressure on the Muslims to convert and the hostility that this aroused, it became increasingly hard to find either a Muslim scholar ready to impart tuition or texts with which to work in Spain. Nicolaus Clenardus, from the Southern Netherlands, taught in Salamanca in the 1530s, and there, in the library of Hernán Núñez, the professor of Hebrew, came across the manuscript of a standard Arabic manual on grammar which was to revolutionize the compilation of Arabic grammars in Europe, the thirteenth-century *Ajurrūmiyya*. Núñez proved unable to teach him how to use it, so Clenardus proceeded to Granada and, thanks to the governor of the city, was provided with a tutor in Arabic. Yet, the difficulty of obtaining Arabic

---

Research between Middle Ages and Renaissance. Proceedings of the Colloquium London, Warburg Institute, 11–12 March 1994 (Turnhout, 1995), pp. 214–235.

12 R.W. Southern, *Western Views of Islam in the Middle Ages* (Cambridge, Mass., 1962), pp. 86–92.

13 Jones, pp. 101–109. See also O. Zwartjes, 'More on "Arabic linguistic terminology in Pedro de Alcalá"' *Historiographia Linguistica* 41 (2014), pp. 247–297.

manuscripts induced him to leave for Morocco in 1640 in order to progress with his studies.[14]

To begin with, European grammarians had to rely on the combination of Arabic texts such as the *Ajurrūmiyya* and the advice of a native speaker. In the course of the sixteenth and seventeenth centuries we find Turkish prisoners-of-war and Arabic-speaking Christians being employed as teachers and copyists. The standard of their knowledge, however, varied greatly and there was seldom a guarantee of quality. By the middle of the sixteenth century scholars wishing to study Arabic consequently tried to make their way to the Arab or Ottoman worlds.

The French were among the first to avail themselves of permanent diplomatic representation at the Porte, and Guillaume Postel set out for the Levant in 1535 with the king's first ambassador to the sultan. He then devoted himself to the study of Arabic in Istanbul under the tuition of an Ottoman Christian.[15] He already knew Hebrew, and his progress in the new language was rapid. He became acquainted with the *Ajurrūmiyya* and another standard grammatical work of the thirteenth century, al-Zanjānī's *Taṣrīf*. Basing himself on these, he made the first major contribution to the knowledge of Arabic grammar in Europe. His early effort, the *Linguarum characterum differentium alphabetum introductio*, was published on his return to Paris in 1538, and he followed it up with his far more important *Grammatica arabica*, published in 1543. The *Grammatica arabica*, the first of its kind to be printed and to make use of Arabic types, was revolutionary in establishing 'the method of incorporating the information contained in Arabic grammatical tracts into Western-style grammar books about Classical Arabic'.[16]

The next step in introducing Europeans to Arabic grammar was the publication of the Arabic grammars themselves, and this was undertaken in the last decade of the sixteenth century by Giambattista Raimondi and the Typografia Medicea, the printing press which he ran in Rome. In 1592 he produced the *Ajurrūmiyya* and another work on grammar of the thirteenth century, Ibn al-Ḥājib's *Kāfiyya*, both solely in unvocalized Arabic. Almost twenty years later, in 1610, he added the *Taṣrīf*, this time in vocalized Arabic accompanied by a Latin translation.[17]

Such, together with the far less interesting European Arabic grammars by Jakob Christmann, Rutger Spey, and Bartholomaeus Radtmann, was the printed

---

14   Jones, pp. 111–112, 202–204.
15   J. Balagna Coustou, *Arabe et humanisme dans la France des derniers Valois* (Paris, 1989).
16   Jones, pp. 113–120.
17   *Ibid.*, pp. 126–136, 177–235.

material at hand when the young Thomas Erpenius decided to study Arabic.[18] Erpenius had proved himself an excellent Hebraist at Leiden University, and one of his professors was Joseph Justus Scaliger, who had himself studied Arabic under Postel in Paris. But although Scaliger advised Erpenius on how to tackle the language, he actually started learning it outside the Netherlands. He was taught the rudiments by William Bedwell in London, and received some more, but not very reliable, instruction from the itinerant Egyptian Copt Josephus Barbatus or Abudacnus in Paris.[19] It was also in France that Erpenius met Aḥmad ibn Qāsim al-Ḥajarī, an emigrant from Spain in the service of the ruler of Morocco, who was in France on a diplomatic errand in 1611. Despite the uncertain quality of his own Arabic – his first language was Spanish – al-Ḥajarī appears to have provided Erpenius with some of the information which, in combination with the Arabic grammars, enabled him to compile his own *Grammatica arabica*. It was published in Leiden in 1613, the year in which he took up the professorship of Arabic at the university.

Like Postel, Erpenius reconciled the Classical Arabic grammatical tradition with the Latin one, but he did so far more successfully and exhaustively. Postel's grammar is short, and one wonders how far a student would have progressed had he only had that on which to rely. Erpenius's work is far longer and more accurate. He gives numerous examples where Postel simply announces a general rule, and at last produced a grammar from which students could, and did, learn Arabic. Not only did Erpenius's grammar, to which he himself added in the course of his career in Leiden, remain the standard European work on the subject for almost two hundred years, but even when it was at last surpassed by Isaac Sylvestre de Sacy's *Grammaire arabe* in 1810, it had a profound influence on Sacy himself and continued to affect later grammarians such as Karl Paul Caspari and William Wright.[20]

3   The Dictionaries

An early dictionary, which was to be of crucial importance for the compilation of the first Arabic – Latin lexicon to be printed, was the Mozarabic Latin-Arabic glossary acquired by Postel in 1532 and now at the Leiden University Library.[21]

---

18   For Erpenius see A. Vrolijk and R. van Leeuwen, *Arabic Studies in the Netherlands. A Short History in Portraits, 1580–1950* (Leiden-Boston, 2014), pp. 31–40, 59; W.M.C. Juynboll, *Zeventiende-eeuwsche Beoefenaars*, pp. 59–118; Jones, pp. 144–165.
19   See above, pp. 3–40.
20   Jones, pp. 144–165.
21   The text was published by C.F. Seybold, *Glossarium Latino – Arabicum* (Berlin, 1900).

In a clear hand and with most of the Arabic words vocalized, it was compiled in Toledo shortly before 1175 by an Arabic-speaking Christian who wanted to instruct his countrymen in Latin in the period immediately before the Mozarabic community adopted Castilian as its main language. It is consequently in the Arabic spoken in Spain and had among its sources the Arabic translations of the Scriptures known to the compiler.[22]

The next dictionary to play an important role in the development of Arabic lexicography in Europe was the *Vocabulista aravigo en letra castellana*, the Spanish-Arabic wordlist compiled by Pedro de Alcalá and published in Granada in 1505 in the same year as his Arabic grammar. Like the grammar it was intended for Spanish missionaries preaching to the converts from Islam in Andalusia – thus for students of Arabic – and it was modelled after Antonio de Nebrija's Spanish-Latin dictionary. Also like the grammar, it was transliterated in the Roman alphabet for Spaniards wishing to speak the dialect of al-Andalus, and not for readers or writers of Classical Arabic.

These two dictionaries were consulted exhaustively by Franciscus Raphelengius, the son-in-law of the printer Christophe Plantin. Just as Scaliger had done, Raphelengius too studied Arabic under Postel in Paris. After working with the team of scholars who produced the Antwerp Polyglot Bible published by Plantin between 1569 and 1572, he moved in 1586 from Antwerp to Leiden and was given the chair of Hebrew at the university. He also ran the printing press established in the university town by his father-in-law. Having had Arabic types cut, he and his sons became the main printers of Arabic in northern Europe.

While he was still in Antwerp Raphelengius had come into possession of the Mozarabic Latin-Arabic glossary once belonging to Postel, as well as of Pedro de Alcalá's *Vocabulista*. It was on these that he drew when he started to compile an Arabic-Latin vocabulary. Encouraged by his colleagues in Leiden, he continued his lexicographical studies, albeit with a relatively limited number of sources. These included the Pentateuch printed in Istanbul by Gerson Soncino in 1546 with Saadia Gaon's Judaeo-Arabic paraphrase, the medieval translation of the Qur'an published by Bibliander in 1543, the few available works printed in Arabic, and a small collection of Arabic manuscripts. After 1593, the year in which Scaliger arrived in Leiden, Raphelengius also used Scaliger's own 'Thesaurus linguae arabicae', the Latin-Arabic glossary which would never be published, but to which Scaliger added in Leiden largely on the basis of the two

---

22   The standard study remains P.S. van Koningsveld, *The Latin-Arabic Glossary of the Leiden University Library* (Leiden, 1977).

Spanish dictionaries belonging to Raphelengius. The extent to which the two men used one another's material shows how closely they collaborated.[23]

Raphelengius's *Lexicon arabico-latinum* testifies to a considerable ability in turning the contents of the Mozarabic Latin-Arabic glossary and the Spanish-Arabic *Vocabulista* into an Arabic-Latin dictionary, sometimes rectifying mistakes in the original text and generally providing a correct version in Arabic characters. Certainly, the very nature of Raphelengius's two main sources occasionally led to mistakes – to forms which were exclusively Andalusian and to a number of grammatical errors – but, despite the mistakes, the object of his lexicon was strikingly modern. Admittedly, the wordlists in Greek, Hebrew, and Aramaic at the end, as well as the Hebrew equivalents in the text of the dictionary, were for the assistance of theologians and Hebraists. But the Latin wordlist, and the statements in the preface, indicate that he wanted his dictionary to serve scholars working in a variety of fields besides merchants, navigators, and diplomats who required the language for more practical purposes.

Raphelengius died in 1597. His dictionary was unfinished and, probably owing to Scaliger who was aware of its imperfections, it remained in manuscript. Only after Scaliger's death in 1609 did Raphelengius's sons, now running the family firm, consider having it completed and published. By 1611 it was in the press, but at the last moment the Raphelengius brothers turned to the young Thomas Erpenius in the hope of adding his Arabic grammar to the dictionary and of having the dictionary corrected. As Erpenius drew up his immense list of corrections he spotted the key to Arabic lexicography.

Just as the key to the European Arabic grammars consisted in the grammars by the Arabs themselves, so the key to Arabic lexicography in Europe was to be found in the monolingual Arabic dictionaries. These Erpenius was unable to obtain, but, when he stopped in Venice in his unsuccessful attempt to sail to the East, he acquired some Arabic-Turkish dictionaries which were based on the monolingual Arabic ones. 'As I once started to learn Arabic in order to improve my understanding of Hebrew,' he wrote in May 1612, 'now I study Turkish in order to know better Arabic.'[24] It was thanks to the Arabic-Turkish lexicon *al-Akhtarī*, compiled in 1545 and based on some of the finest monolingual Arabic dictionaries, including the tenth-century *Ṣiḥāḥ* and *Mujmal* and the thirteenth-century *Mughrib*, that Erpenius managed to correct so many

---

23 See below, pp. 241–242.
24 'Ut linguam Hebraeam solidius intelligerem, coepi olim Arabicam discere; ut Arabicam melius, nunc Turcicam.' BL, MS Burney 364, fol. 24ʳ. I am most grateful to Robert Jones for supplying me with a transcription of this letter.

of Raphelengius's mistakes. His corrections were added in an appendix to the published version of the dictionary which appeared in 1613 with his grammar issued separately by the same publishers.[25]

Erpenius had only just had time to catch a glimpse of the most important monolingual Arabic dictionary of all, the *Qāmūs* compiled in the late fourteenth century, before Raphelengius's *Lexicon arabico-latinum* appeared in print. Although he subsequently acquired a copy, he could make little use of it. Yet, it was the *Qāmūs* which, together with the *Ṣiḥāḥ*, would be the main source of the next Arabic-Latin dictionary, the *Thesaurus linguae arabicae* published in Milan in 1632 and compiled in the course of eighteen years by Antonio Giggei. Giggei had consulted the very considerable collection of Arabic manuscripts assembled for the Ambrosian Library by his patron, the archbishop of Milan, Cardinal Federico Borromeo, and his vast work in four volumes was indeed an improvement on Raphelengius, lacking comparisons with other Semitic languages or with Greek, and providing a far greater range of words.

Giggei's work, however, was to be superseded by that of Erpenius's successor as professor of Arabic at Leiden, Jacobus Golius. In the introduction to his *Lexicon arabico-latinum* (Leiden 1653), Golius admittted that Giggei had preceded him in the use of the monolingual dictionaries, but he himself consulted a far wider range, which included the main Arabic-Turkish and Arabic-Persian lexicons. If Giggei had freed Arabic of the assocation with Hebrew, Golius, with his Persian and Turkish sources, connected it with the other main Islamic languages.[26]

Golius's dictionary, like Erpenius's grammar, remained unsurpassed until the nineteenth century, when Georg Wilhelm Freytag, and above all Edward Lane, improved on it.[27] Yet, in contrast to that of Raphelengius and his predecessors, Golius's dictionary was solely of Classical Arabic, with no attempt to include current or dialectal forms. Invaluable for readers, particularly of poetry and early Islamic texts, it was of little use to merchants or travellers who needed to speak the language of the streets. Not until 1881 were the Mozarabic lexicon and Pedro de Alcalá's *Vocabulista* appreciated as guides to a particular form of spoken Arabic, when R.P.A. Dozy, in his *Supplément aux dictionnaires arabes*, perceived their full value and, implicitly, rendered homage to the work of Raphelengius.

---

25   See above, pp. 250–254.
26   Fück, pp. 79–84.
27   *Ibid.*, pp. 166–170.

4 The Schools

Some form of translators' school seems to have existed in Toledo since the mid-12th century, and was followed by other foundations in medieval Spain.[28] The growing interest in Arabic in the early modern period, however, is more clearly documented by the creation of academic chairs. The French king François I established a chair in Arabic for Guillaume Postel at his own humanist foundation, the Collège royal in Paris, in 1538. Very gradually other European academies followed suit. Leiden University took the decision to set up a chair in 1599.[29] A chair was endowed at Cambridge in 1632 and one at Oxford in 1636.[30] But while Arabic was being studied at the European universities and academies mainly by theologians, alternative forms of instruction were also being organized for those students who wanted to have a more practical knowledge of the Eastern languages.

Arabic was taught, interruptedly and to varying standards, in the schools and seminaries intended for missionaries. The first was probably the Dominican school in Tunis founded some time before 1250. It was succeeded by schools in Barcelona, Murcia, Valencia, and Játiva, while the Franciscan Raymond Llull set up a school at Miramar in 1276.[31] By the end of the sixteenth century Arabic could be learnt by prospective missionaries in Rome not only in some of the houses of the various religious orders and at the Collegio Romano, but also at the foundations of Pope Gregory XIII, the Neophyte College (established in 1577 for converts from Judaism and Islam) and the Maronite College (founded in 1584). It would later be taught, too, at the Collegio Urbano, set up by Pope Urban VIII in 1627. One of the main purposes of the colleges was to attract young Eastern Christians, particularly Maronites, who had been in formal communion with Rome since 1182, but also Jacobites, Copts, Nestorians, Melkites, Armenians, and, in the eighteenth century, Greek Catholics and other members of the Uniate churches. Generally aged between 9 and 15, they had received hardly any formal education in the East, and it was in Rome that they obtained intensive instruction, in Italian and Latin, but also in Classical Arabic, Syriac, and Hebrew. Having converted to Roman Catholicism, they might either remain in Europe where they often acted as librarians

---

28   Burnett, 'The institutional context of Arabic-Latin translations.'
29   Vrolijk and Van Leeuwen, *Arabic Studies in the Netherlands*, p. 30.
30   Toomer, pp. 111–114.
31   A. Cortabarria Beitia, 'L'étude des langues au moyen âge chez les Dominicains: Espagne, Orient, Raymond Martin' *Mélanges de l'Institut Dominicain d'Etudes Orientales du Caire* 10 (1970), pp. 89–248.

and as language teachers, or return to their home country to propagate the Catholic faith.[32]

The other institutions for teaching a more practical type of Arabic than was to be obtained at a university were the interpreters' schools. In the early modern period they were originally devised by the Venetians who, in 1551, sent two of their young citizens to Istanbul to study the spoken languages of the Middle East.[33] Although the project was not immediately successful, it would be imitated. In 1669, thanks to Louis XIV's minister Jean-Baptiste Colbert, the French organized a school in Istanbul for the teaching of Arabic, Turkish, and Persian.[34] Sixty years later the French emulated the Roman system by introducing a school which was to train Eastern Christians as missionaries at the Jesuit Collège de Louis-le-Grand in Paris. Such practical endeavours would lead, after many vicissitudes, to the creation in Paris of the Ecole spéciale des langues orientales vivantes in 1795.[35] The Venetians set up a similar institution in Padua in 1699, and other European countries followed them, the Austrians with the Orientalische Akademie in Vienna in 1745 and the English with the College of Fort William in Calcutta in 1800.

Yet, despite the growing number of institutions at which Arabic was learnt from the early seventeenth century onwards, most of the best Arabists were largely self-taught. They studied the language independently of any institution and often on the spot. By the first decades of the seventeenth century both Holland and England had permanent diplomatic representation in Istanbul and consulates scattered over the Arabic-speaking world. The greatest of the Dutch Arabists, Golius, had indeed been a pupil of Erpenius (who had himself learnt his Arabic from Arab travellers in France), but his true progress in the language was made when he accompanied a diplomatic mission to Morocco, and when he spent a far longer period first at the Dutch consulate in Aleppo and then at the embassy in Istanbul.[36] In England Edward Pococke, who occupied the first chair of Arabic at Oxford in 1636, had had some tuition from

---

32   B. Heyberger, *Les chrétiens du Proche-Orient au temps de la réforme catholique (Syrie, Liban, Palestine, XVIIe–XVIIIe siècles)* (Rome, 1994), pp. 408–423.

33   I. Palumbo Fossati Casa, 'L'école vénitienne des "giovani di lingua"' in F. Hitzel, ed., *Istanbul et les langues orientales. Actes du colloque organisé par l'IFÉA et l'INALCO à l'occasion du bicentenaire de l'Ecole des langues orientales, Istanbul 29–31 mai 1995* (Paris, 1997), pp. 109–122.

34   A. Pippidi, 'Drogmans et enfants de langue: La France de Constantinople au XVIIe siècle' in Hitzel, ed., *Istanbul et les langues orientales*, pp. 131–140.

35   A. Messaoudi, *Les arabisants et la France coloniale, Savants, conseillers, médiateurs 1780–1930* (Lyon, 2015), pp. 23–54.

36   Juynboll, *Zeventiende-eeuwsche Beoefenaars*, pp. 119–183; Vrolijk and Van Leeuwen, *Arabic Studies in the Netherlands*, pp. 41–48.

William Bedwell in London, but he perfected his knowledge of Arabic when he acted as chaplain to the Levant Company at the English consulate in Aleppo and, later, at the English embassy in the Ottoman capital.[37] And the Italian Ludovico Marracci, who published an edition of the Qur'an in Arabic and Latin in 1698 infinitely superior to all previous efforts, never set foot outside Italy. He learnt Arabic mainly on his own but with the occasional advice of Maronites in Rome.[38] This tendency was to become increasingly marked with the decline of the academic teaching of Arabic in the eighteenth and nineteenth centuries.

Acknowledgements

This article was originally published in Kees Versteegh, ed., *Encyclopedia of Arabic Language and Linguistics, Volume 1: A-Ed* (Leiden: E.J. Brill, 2006), pp. 166–172.

[37] Toomer, pp. 116–126.
[38] G. Levi della Vida, *Aneddoti e svaghi arabi e non arabi* (Milan-Naples, 1959), p. 196.

CHAPTER 11

The Victims of Progress
The Raphelengius Arabic Type and Bedwell's Arabic Lexicon

By 1595 the elder Franciscus Raphelengius had had Arabic characters designed for his press in Leiden, and in that year he published his *Specimen Characterum Arabicorum*, illustrating the two different type-faces in his possession – the *Maghribi* one, decidedly unelegant and apparently incomplete, and the *Naschi* one.[1] It is the fate of the latter type that I shall discuss in this essay.

My starting point is the summer of 1612. The elder Raphelengius had been dead for fifteen years; his firm was now in the hands of his youngest sons, Frans and Joost;[2] and the *Naschi* type, first used in 1595, had been employed comparatively seldom, for the odd Arabic word in such books as Joseph Justus Scaliger's *Opus de emendatione temporum* of 1598, Georgius Dousa's *De itinere suo Constantinopolitano* of 1599, Scaliger's edition of Manilius's *Astronomicon* and Hugo Grotius's *Syntagma Arateorum*, both of 1600, and Carolus Clusius's *Exoticarum Libri decem* of 1605. Although they had started to set their father's Arabic dictionary in 1611,[3] the owners of the Leiden firm had decided to put a part of their equipment up for sale, and this included the Arabic material. Such was the position in the middle of 1612, when William Bedwell, the English Arabist, resolved to pay a visit to Leiden.

Bedwell was fifty years old and, despite his interest in Oriental languages, in topography and in the art of navigation, he had never before travelled outside England. There were three main reasons for his trip to Leiden: he wished to consult the Arabic manuscripts which Scaliger had left to the university, and above all the Arabic word list which the great scholar had compiled; he wanted

---

1 They are reproduced in H.D.L. Vervliet, *Sixteenth-century Printing Types of the Low Countries* (Amsterdam, 1968–9), p. 316. On Raphelengius's Arabic type see E. Braches, 'Raphelengius's Naschi and Maghribi. Some reflections on the origin of Arabic typography in the Low Countries' *Quaestiones Leidenses. Twelve Studies on Leiden University Library and its Holdings Published on the Occasion of the Quarter-century of the University by 'Quaerendo'* (Leiden, 1975), pp. 24–34.
2 Cf. L. Voet, *The Golden Compasses. A History and Evaluation of the Printing and Publishing Activities of the Officina Plantiniana at Antwerp* (London-Amsterdam, 1969–1972), vol. 1, pp. 172–177.
3 See below, pp. 250–251.

to publish the Arabic version of the Johannine Epistles which he had copied from a codex in Oxford; and he hoped to purchase, at the expense of his patron Lancelot Andrewes, then bishop of Ely, Arabic type with which to print the immense Arabic-Latin lexicon on which he had been working ever since he first encountered Andrewes at Cambridge in the 1580s.[4]

Bedwell had been seeking a printer of Arabic for many years. He had completed a specimen of his dictionary in 1596,[5] and he had been trying to attract patrons to subsidise the printing of it since 1603 at the latest.[6] In 1606 he told his friend Isaac Casaubon that he would gladly turn to the Medici press in Rome for the publication of the Arabic version of the New Testament he had discovered in Oxford.[7] But not until 1612 did he actually find the patronage necessary for the fulfilment of his plans. He and Andrewes had toyed with the idea of applying to Guillaume Le Bé in Paris with a view to buying his Arabic type, but Le Bé was not ready to sell.[8] Leiden remained, and here Bedwell arrived in August 1612 to be welcomed by the young man to whom he had taught the rudiments of Arabic three and a half years earlier – the future professor of Arabic at the university, Thomas Erpenius.[9]

Erpenius asked the Raphelengius brothers about their plans for their Arabic material and, on 24 August, Bedwell wrote to Casaubon in London:[10]

> Raphelengii dictionarium Arabicum post mensem unum aut alterum publicum fiet. Qui hunc librum excudit filius illius docti viri fuit. Interrogatus autem ab Erpenio an velit Grammaticam suam et Proverbia illa Arabica excudere, respondit se nolle, neque alios omnium ullos: Sed postquam paternum illud opus, quod sub praelo est, fuerit abso[lutum] se statuisse Matrices, Ponsones et reliqua illa instrumenta, divendere alii[s], Hoc valde nobis placuit. placebit, scio, R.D. Episcopo [sc. Lancelot Andrewes]. Sed hoc ego in mandatis nu[nc ha]beo. Agas quaeso cum illo hac de re. Statui enim tam diu hic manere, dum resp[onsum] habuero.

---

4   A. Hamilton, *William Bedwell the Arabist 1563–1632* (Leiden, 1985), pp. 37–47.
5   Bodl., MS Bodl. Or. 372.
6   See, for example, the dedicatory epistle of his Arabic version of the Epistle to the Colossians, addressed to Richard Bancroft, then bishop of London, published in Hamilton, *William Bedwell*, pp. 106–108.
7   Hamilton, *William Bedwell*, pp. 97–98.
8   Cas.Ep., p. 485.
9   For Erpenius see Jones, pp. 144–165; A. Vrolijk and R. van Leeuwen, *Arabic Studies in the Netherlands. A Short History in Portraits, 1580–1950* (Leiden-Boston, 2014), pp. 31–40, 59; W.M.C. Juynboll, *Zeventiende-eeuwsche Beoefenaars van het Arabisch in Nederland* (Utrecht, 1931), pp. 59–118.
10 Hamilton, *William Bedwell*, pp. 100–101.

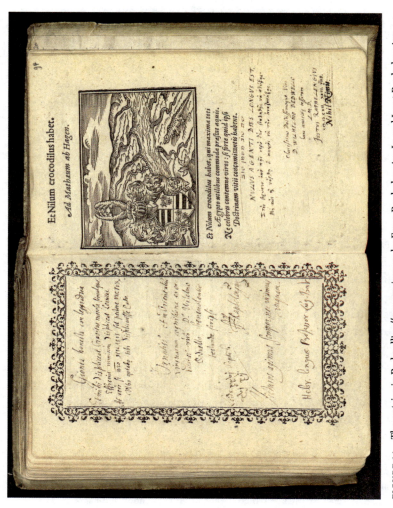

FIGURE 14 The entries in Bedwell's *album amicorum* by Frans Raphelengius Jr. and Joost Raphelengius. The information about Frans Raphelengius, added by a later owner of Bedwell's album, is incorrect and refers to Frans's father
LEIDEN UNIVERSITY LIBRARY, MS BPL 2753, FOLS 93ᵛ–94ᴿ

Bedwell had thus reached a provisional agreement to buy the Raphelengius material, but the completion of the transaction depended on Lancelot Andrewes's answer and on the money the bishop was ready to provide. About Andrewes's role in the purchase, however, we hear no more. All we know is that, by the time he left Leiden, Bedwell was regarded as the rightful owner of the characters. But there was no question of Bedwell's entering into possession of the material immediately, because the Arabic type was in greater demand than it had ever been since 1600. At the time of Bedwell's letter to Casaubon the Raphelengius brothers were still preparing their father's Arabic dictionary, which was to contain additions by Erpenius; they were still setting, or had just set, the Arabic version of the Epistle to Titus edited by the current lecturer in Arabic at Leiden university, Jan Theunisz (Johannes Antonides); and, within a few weeks of his letter, Bedwell himself, after collating it with a codex in Scaliger's collection,[11] submitted for publication the Arabic version of the Johannine Epistles.

Bedwell remained in Leiden until the end of September. The many signatures he collected in his *album amicorum*[12] – and these included the signatures of Frans and Joost Raphelengius (Fig. 14) – testify to the distinction of the scholars with whom he consorted, while the letters which men such as Johannes Meursius, Daniel Heinsius and Hugo Grotius wrote to Isaac Casaubon prove how well Bedwell was liked by his Dutch acquaintances. Early in October, after staying in The Hague and Middelburg, Bedwell set sail for England, leaving behind the Arabic material he had arranged to buy from the Raphelengius firm. Not long after his return he received a letter from Erpenius, begging him to authorise the Raphelengius brothers to retain the type in order to complete Raphelengius's lexicon and to set Erpenius's own Arabic grammar. Bedwell agreed, and wrote to Frans Raphelengius (whom he confused with his dead brother Christoffel)[13] on 18 November (Fig. 15):

> Petiit a me per literas D. Erpenius ut ill[ius] causa tibi per aliquot septimanas usum typorum Arabicorum conced[erem]. Scito, me nihil posse huic homini denegare. Lexicon tuum Arab[icum] cum Epistolis D. Joannis frustra diu expectavimus. Forte una e[t ea] dem opera cupit D.V. simul etiam grammaticam Erpenii dare. [Hoc] pergratum erit.

---

11 Bodl., MS Laud. Or. 58, fol. 71ᵛ., where Bedwell states that he collated his version with the Leiden codex (UBL, MS Or.217).
12 UBL, MS BPL 2753.
13 Hamilton, *William Bedwell*, p. 101.

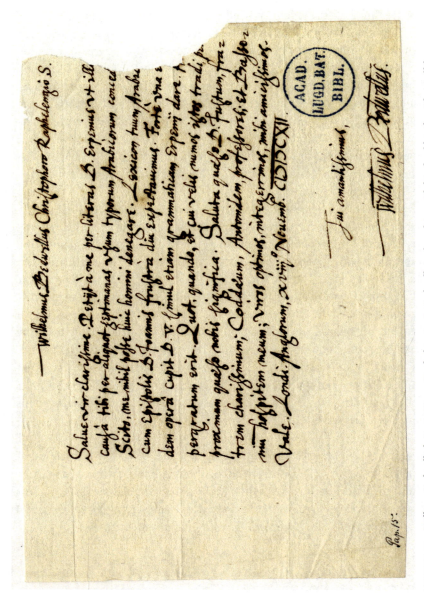

FIGURE 15   William Bedwell's letter to Frans Raphelengius Jr. Bedwell confuses him with his dead brother Christoffel.
LEIDEN UNIVERSITY LIBRARY, MS PAP.15

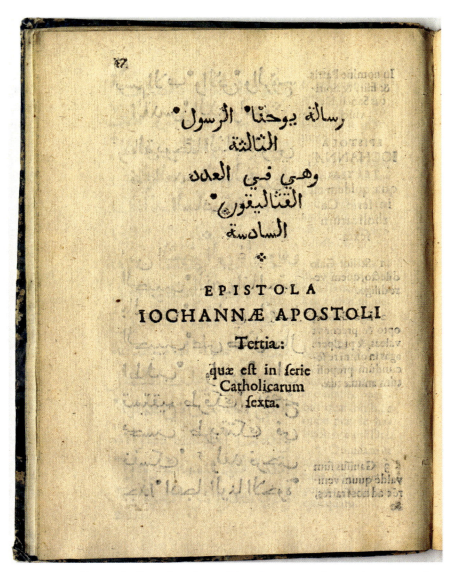

FIGURE 16   William Bedwell's Arabic edition of the Johannine Epistles, *D. Johannis Apostoli et Evangelistae Epistolae Catholicae omnes, Arabicae anti aliquot secula factae* (Leiden, 1612), p. 47

Bedwell had given his permission to Raphelengius to keep the material for a few more weeks. But the weeks turned into months, and never before had the Leiden press produced so many books with its Arabic type as in those months – Bedwell's own Johannine Epistles (Fig. 16), the elder Raphelengius's lexicon, Erpenius's Arabic grammar and Erpenius's edition of the Arabic version of the Passion from the Gospel of St Matthew.[14] In this last work, for what appears to be the first time since the *Specimen Characterum Arabicorum* of 1595, the press also made a limited use of the *Maghribi* type-face. Then, towards the end of 1613, the Raphelengius brothers decided to honour their agreement. Before dispatching the material to Bedwell, however, they again used their punches and matrices in order to have a new set of characters cast which would enable them to continue to print in Arabic.[15] And continue to print they did, for it was with the newly cast characters that they composed the collection of Arabic proverbs originally planned by Scaliger and Casaubon, and completed by Erpenius.[16]

The material does not appear to have reached Bedwell until the spring of 1614. And, at about the same time, the Raphelengius firm was struck by one of the worst disasters that could befall printers of Arabic: their one compositor capable of setting Arabic type died. Erpenius was in despair. On 26 May he wrote to Casaubon:[17]

> ... nec typos Arabicos sufficientes, nec Typographum hic nunc habeamus. Compositor enim noster obiit; et D. Raphelengius characteres suos Arabicos fere omnes iam istuc transmisit ad D. Bedwellum ...

We thus have a picture of the Raphelengius press without a compositor, 'nearly all' its Arabic characters sold to Bedwell – a press, in short, no longer in a position to print Arabic. And indeed, the Raphelengius brothers never used their Arabic type again. Erpenius himself, aware of the impossibility of having any further Arabic works published by them, had his own Arabic type made and founded his own printing press in 1615.[18] His type, inspired by one of the smaller

---

14   On the attribution of this edition to Erpenius see H.J. de Jonge, 'The Study of the New Testament' in Th.H. Lunsingh Scheurleer and G.H.M. Posthumus Meyjes, eds, *Leiden University in the Seventeenth Century. An Exchange of Learning*, pp. 65–109, esp. 70, 103.
15   MPM, Arch.92, pp. 204, 243.
16   A. Vrolijk, 'The Prince of Arabists and his many errors: Thomas Erpenius's image of Joseph Scaliger and the edition of the *Proverbia Arabica* (1614)' *Journal of the Warburg and Courtauld Institutes* 73 (2010), pp. 297–325.
17   BL, MS Burn.364, fol. 27ʳ.
18   Cf. Juynboll, *Zeventiende-eeuwsche Beoefenaars*, pp. 78–84.

type-faces of the Medici press in Rome,[19] was far more economical and practicable than the Raphelengius characters which had been inspired by the largest Medici type-face, and, as time went by, it appeared that Erpenius, rather than having suffered from the inability of his first publishers to produce any further works in Arabic, had in fact benefited from the situation.

But what became of the Raphelengius characters, recast in 1613 and used on a single occasion – so large, so clumsy and, if compared to those made for Erpenius, so obsolete? What became of all the Arabic material which had not been sent to Bedwell in England? Shortly before the characters were recast, in June 1613, Frans Raphelengius assured his cousin Balthasar Moretus in Antwerp that he wanted to keep as much of his equipment as possible in the family:[20]

> De conditie van coop van poinçoenen ende matricen accepteren wij, ende zijn blij dat die in 't geslacht blijven sullen. Is 't dat wij niewe Arabiqs doen steken, sullen die niet quijt maeken of sullen u.l. die voor presentatie doen : of verkoopen, sullen een afslag voor ons en u.l. bedingen.

We next hear of the Arabic material from the Raphelengius brothers in 1619. On 15 January Frans informed Balthasar Moretus that he was prepared to sell 'the Arabic letters' to him 'cheaply',[21] and on 18 October Joost added that the material was, to all intents and purposes, brand new and had only been used to print the Arabic proverbs.[22] In February 1620 Frans provided further details about the casting of the new letters, offering Balthasar his Arabic and his Double Median Hebrew characters for the price of 120 guilders.[23] Moretus

---

19   Erpenius describes the criteria of his press in *Locmani Sapientia Fabulae* (Leiden, 1615), fols A2ᵛ–3ᵛ. Cf. also D.W. Davies, 'The provenance of the Oriental types of Thomas Erpenius' *Het Boek* 30 (1949–51), pp. 117–122.
20   MPM, Arch. 92, p. 149.
21   *Ibid.*, p. 189: 'Onse Arabische letteren sullen wij u.l. overlaeten goeden koop. Sullen eerst sien hoe veel der is: want ons dunkt niet gescheiden dienen.'
22   *Ibid.*, p. 243: 'De Arabische is noch heel nieu: de afdrucksels daer van en zijn hier niet bij: dan u.l. machse sien in de *Proverbia Arabica* van den selven D. Erpenius: want daer en is anders niet mede gedruct.'
23   *Ibid.*, pp. 205–206: 'Aengaende de dobbel Mediaen Hebreewsch ende het Arabisch, sullen wij voor u.l. bewaeren, ende u.l. seinden beneffens de copij van Clusius gedresseert naar sijn begeeren, volgens dat wij u.l. weg segt hebben. Voor de voors. Dobbel Mediaen Hebreewsch, ende Arabisch, souden wij niet min begeeren als hondert en twintig guldens: 't welk 't uyterste is daer wij se te saemen voor laeten souden. Het Arabisch alleen kost ons ruym over de hondert en tachtig guldens: ende is maer eens gebesigt, teweten in *Proverbiis Arabicis*: welke besinge meer gedijt heeft tot uyt roeyinge vande quaede of misgotene letters, als tot slijtinge ... De Arabische letter is gegoten op de hoogde van vijf Coronellen. De letteren self zijn meest al op de Coronel gegoten, heel weinig op de Augustijn. De puncten (om onder en boven te voegen) zijn meest Augustijn, heel weinig

agreed to the purchase and, in March 1621, Frans Raphelengius asked him whether they should continue to be stored in Leiden, or how and when they should be transferred to Antwerp.[24] This seems to be the last reference to the Raphelengius Arabic type in the surviving correspondence between the cousins in Leiden and Antwerp. If the material was indeed conveyed to the Southern Netherlands – and there is no reason to think that it was not – it has since disappeared from the Plantin-Moretus Museum. Not only did Balthasar Moretus never use it, but he appears to have found it unsatisfactory, for, in June 1624, he wrote to the Raphelengius brothers announcing his intention of reprinting the *Biblia Regia* and of replacing the Aramaic paraphrase by an Arabic one. Could his cousins advise him, he asked, about having new Arabic punches made or acquiring new matrices?[25]

If Balthasar Moretus was dissatisfied with his purchase, William Bedwell was even more displeased when he got round to examining the material sent to him from Leiden. In 1638, six years after Bedwell's death, John Greaves, the Orientalist and mathematician who had been such a close friend of Bedwell's in the last years of his life, wrote from Gresham College to Peter Turner at Oxford. Oxford University was itself acquiring Arabic type[26] and Greaves warned Turner that 'Mr Bedwell when he bought Raphelengius his Arabicke press, found some characters defective, which he desired to have perfited, and

---

        Coronel. Hier van zijnder vijfthien pagien in klein quarto opgeset, wegende ruym 101 pond. De defecten of overblijfsel vande Casse ende Bak (daer men wel twee, drij of meer pagien goet schrift van soude konnen maeken) zijn ook opgeset in tien 1/3 pagien als 8º wegende 50 ponden ruym. Tot het selfde schrift is noch een pagie gesneden Arabische Cijfers. Alle dese 200 ponden et quod excurrit, Hebrewsch ende Arabisch, mach u.l. hebben (ut dictum est) te saemen voor hondert twintich guldens ten uyterste.' Cf. the comments on this letter by L. Willems, 'De herkomst van het typografisch materiaal van T. Erpenius' *De Gulden Passer*, N.R. 9 (1931), p. 89.

24   MPM, Arch. 92, p. 211: 'Voorts is mijn vraage of u.l. de Arabiksche letteren met de dobbel. Mediaen of parangon (non enim bene memini) Hebreews die u.l. van ons gekocht heeft, noch alhier bewaert wilt hebben, of hoe ende wanneer gesonden: alsoo sommige meenen dat de Trefves gecontinueert sullen worden, sommige ter contrarie. Dies sal u.l. gelieven mij te belasten wat ik daer mede doen sal.'

25   MPM, Arch. 139, p. 158: 'Item u.l. sal believen mij over te schrijven, off D. Erpenius de geheele *Biblia Arabica* sal wtgheven, ende off hij eenighe goede exemplaria manuscripta *Bibliorum Arabicorum* heeft, off hij eenighe exemplar soude willen vercoopen, off ten minsten leenen voor eenighen tydt. Waer in mij ende mijnen goeden vriendt, die de selve soude gebruijcken, vriendtschap soude geschieden. De *Bibliis* enim *Regiis* aliquando recudendis cogito, et textu Arabico *Paraphraseos* Chaldicae loco reponendo. Tegen den selven tydt soude moeten sien, goede Arabische matrijsen te hebben die schoon souden wesen ende niet te groot. u.l. raedt ende hulpe is mij hier in noodigh, off om nieuwe pinsonen te doen maecken off om eenighe matrijsen te bekomen.'

26   Cf. S. Morison, *John Fell. The University Press and the 'Fell' Types* (Oxford, 1967), p. 22.

made suitable to the rest, but was never able to effect it.'[27] How hard Bedwell had tried to 'perfit' his Arabic characters we will never know. Certainly he never used them, but the reason would seem to be as much connected with the history of his Arabic lexicon as with any deficiency in the characters.[28]

By the time Bedwell died in 1632 the lexicon, which he had originally hoped to have published some thirty years earlier, had grown into a work so vast that it defeated all those functional purposes to which he put his shorter books, his translations of texts on mathematics and other subjects intended for the use of travellers, merchants, navigators, engineers and students. In contrast to those handy short-cuts to learning which Bedwell excelled in producing, so cheap, so simple, so eminently pocketable, his Arabic lexicon ran into nine manuscript volumes (quite apart from specimens and other subsidiary glossaries) – nine volumes of learned comparisons with Greek, Hebrew and Aramaic which, if published, would never have been cheap, simple or pocketable. And what would have been the point in printing Bedwell's work after the appearance of Raphelengius's shorter and more convenient dictionary in 1613?

Bedwell's lexicon, to which he added until his death, was indeed a monument of scholarship; it was indeed of inestimable value to students of Semitic languages, some of whom were duly to make their way to the Cambridge library in order to consult it; but it could not hope to compete on a market that could offer the dictionaries of Raphelengius and, after 1632, of Antonio Giggei. Before his visit to Leiden in 1612 Bedwell had been sure that his would be the first major Arabic lexicon to be printed,[29] an enduring honour to its sponsors and patrons. The publication of Raphelengius's dictionary put paid to that hope, for Raphelengius's was a dictionary attractive to, and largely intended for, the merchant and the traveller. It followed the accepted Arabic alphabetical order while Bedwell (and Scaliger) had followed the Hebrew one,[30] and it made Bedwell's lexicon seem almost as impracticable as the Arabic characters he had purchased in order to print it.

Nevertheless, undeterred by the poor quality of the characters, Bedwell appears to have hoped to have his dictionary printed until the last. At his death he left both the lexicon and the type to the University of Cambridge,[31] and his son-in-law John Clarke, writing in the name of Bedwell's widow and executrix, insistently urged Abraham Wheelock and Barnabas Oley at the university[32] 'to acquainte the Heades what hee hath given namelye his Lexicon with the types

---

27 The National Archives, London, State Papers Domestic, SP 16. 381.* 75.
28 For Bedwell and his dictionary see Toomer, pp. 56–64.
29 Bodl., MS Laud.Or.58, p. 2.
30 See above, pp. 67–68.
31 C. Sayle, *Annals of Cambridge University Library* (Cambridge, 1916), pp. 71–72.
32 CUL, MSS Dd.3.12, fols 75^r–77^v; Oo.6.113, fols 1^r–2^r.

to print it and if they will not undertake to print it that they would accept of a booke when it is printed and let them have it that will print it.'[33] Neither 'the Heades' nor anyone else ever did have Bedwell's lexicon printed, however. The Cambridge University Library kept – and still keeps[34] – the dictionary well, and, shortly after Bedwell's death, 'the Heades' allowed Edmund Castell to consult it and put it to the best possible use in his *Lexicon Heptaglotton*. What the university does not seem to have kept, on the other hand, is the Arabic type. And yet the university received it. Bedwell's will shows that, at the time of his death, the set of Raphelengius types was complete, including punches, matrices and moulds. '[I] bequeath my great Arabick dixionarie with my types, ponsons, matrices and moulde all unto the universitiy of Cambridge.'[35] The types also reappeared – 'odd characters ... occasionally used together in a smaller fount' in Spencer's *De legibus Hebraeorum* published in Cambridge in 1683.[36] After that, however, they vanish.

Acknowledgements

This article was first published in Francine de Nave, ed., *Liber Amicorum Léon Voet* (Antwerpen: Vereeniging der Antwerpsche Bibliophielen, 1985 = *De Gulden Passer* 61–63 (1983–85)), pp. 97–108. I would like to express my gratitude to the late Ronald Breugelmans, Henk Jan de Jonge, and the late Rijk Smitskamp for the patience with which they answered my questions and gave their advice about the problems arising in this study.

---

33   CUL, MS Dd.3.12, fol. 75ʳ.
34   CUL, MSS Hh.6.1–2; Hh.5.1–7.
35   London Metropolitan Archive: OL/C/362: X19/16 fol. 154ʳ⁻ᵛ; A. Hamilton, 'Bedwell, William' ODNB.
36   R. Smitskamp, *Philologia Orientalis. A description of books illustrating the study and printing of Oriental languages in 16th- and 17th-Century Europe* (Leiden 1992), p. 276 (no. 280d).

CHAPTER 12

'Nam Tirones Sumus'

Franciscus Raphelengius's Lexicon Arabico-Latinum *(Leiden 1613)*

Franciscus Raphelengius the Elder's (Fig. 17) *Lexicon Arabico-Latinum*, the first Arabic-Latin dictionary ever to be printed, was an untidy publication by any standards when it appeared in 1613, over fifteen years after the author's death. It opens with an introduction by his two younger sons, Frans and Joost. There follows the main part of the work – 536 pages containing some ten thousand entries. To this is added a supplement of twenty pages with about a thousand further entries based on notes by Raphelengius which his sons discovered after the main part had gone to press, followed by three wordlists, the first in Hebrew and Aramaic, the second in Greek, and the third in Latin, with references to the equivalent Arabic words in the body of the dictionary. Then we have the sixty-eight-page appendix added by Thomas Erpenius very shortly before the actual publication of the book – his 'Observationes', a list of corrections, additions, and elucidations to the work of Raphelengius – and, finally, an errata leaf by the publishers.

Because of this hybrid composition the dictionary is one of the most valuable indications of the state of Arabic studies in Europe at a crucial moment of their development. The introduction by Raphelengius's sons, together with the catalogue of the sale of their, and their father's, library in 1626,[1] enable us to reconstruct Raphelengius's collection of Arabic manuscripts now in the Leiden University Library and to reassess the contribution of a scholar sentenced by posterity to stand in the shadow of Joseph Justus Scaliger. As for Erpenius's additions, they reveal the early progress of a young man who revolutionized the study of Arabic in Europe. 'Nam tirones sumus', Scaliger used to

---

1   *Catalogus Variorum Librorum e Bibliothecis Francisci Raphelengii Hebraeae linguae quondam Professoris & Academiae Leidensis Typographi, ejusque filiorum ...* (Leiden, 1626) (*Cat.Raph.*). The catalogue, which had long been known to exist, was located by Bert van Selm (cf. his *Een menighte treffelijcke Boecken. Nederlandse boekhandelscatalogi in het begin van de zeventiende eeuw* (Utrecht, 1987), p. 307), and has been studied by R. Breugelmans, 'Twee veilingen van boeken uit het bezit der Raphelengii'in F. de Nave, ed., *Liber Amicorum Leon Voet* (Antwerpen, 1985) (= *De Gulden Passer*, 61–63, 1983–85), pp. 39–47, esp. pp. 40–43. My thanks are due to Jan Just Witkam for supplying me with a photocopy of the catalogue. In identifying the manuscripts in the Leiden University Library I also relied on *CCO*. For a full list see the Appendix to this article.

FIGURE 17 Franciscus Raphelengius
ICONES LEIDENSES 26, COLLECTION LEIDEN UNIVERSITY

say of himself as an Arabist.[2] It is this apprenticeship in the new field of Arabic lexicography that I propose to examine in this article.

1 Antwerp

By 1570, when he was working for, and living with, his father-in-law Christophe Plantin in Antwerp, Franciscus Raphelengius had properly embarked on the study of Arabic, and in 1575 he sent a part of his dictionary to Benito Arias Montano in Rome.[3] The dispatch of samples – either complete wordlists or excerpts from them – was a far from uncommon phenomenon amongst contemporary Arabists. They normally distributed them in the hope of attracting patrons, and this seems to have been one of the objectives of Raphelengius just as it was of William Bedwell in England twenty years later.[4]

While some of the specimens of Bedwell's dictionary have survived, Raphelengius's samples do not appear to have come to light in the intervening years. Raphelengius's sons later described their father's early system of providing the roots and then the derivates, as he did in his printed dictionary, but also of adding entire passages illustrating the use of the words,[5] something which would have made his printed work far too long and ungainly for the purpose he intended. If we assume that this was what the early specimens contained, we are still faced with the problem of his first sources and of differentiating between material accessible to him when he was still in Antwerp and material which he first encountered after settling in Leiden in 1585 in order to run the new branch of the Officina Plantiniana.

---

2   The phrase appears in the preface to his 'Thesaurus Linguae Arabicae', UBL, MS Or. 212, fol. 1ʳ. He repeated it in his correspondence with Isaac Casaubon. Cf. *Scal.Cor.*, vol. 4, p. 532: 'Hoc si mihi accidit (et vero accidere potuit, quid ni?) ignoscendum est nobis, tum propter multiplicem idomatis usum, tum quia tirones sumus.'
3   On Raphelengius's early Arabic studies and the dispatch of samples to Arias Montano see F. de Nave, 'Franciscus I Raphelengius (1539–1597), grondlegger van de Arabische studiën in de Nederlanden' in M. de Schepper and F. de Nave, eds, *Ex Officina Plantiniana. Studia in memoriam Christophori Plantini (ca. 1520–1589)* (Antwerpen, 1989 = *De Gulden Passer*, 66–67, 1988–89), pp. 523–555.
4   Cf. A. Hamilton, *William Bedwell the Arabist 1563–1632* (Leiden, 1985), pp. 12–26.
5   *Lex.*, sig. 4*ᵛ: '... themata omnia, seu radices, ut loquuntur, in ordinem digessit alphabeticum, singulis derivata sua adiiciens, annotatis ubique locis unde petita erant, phrasibusque innumeris. Verum cum in molem maiorem opus suum excrevisse animadverteret, quam ut mediocribus sumptibus, (quos incertus de successu consilii sui facere tantum constituerat) excudi posset, visum ei fuit compendio studere, et ex magno illo thesauro maxime necessaria cum iudicio excerpere, eaque in mediocre volumen congesta typis Arabicis, quos in hunc finem sculpi curaverat, in gratiam et commodum studiosorum huius linguae evulgare.'

Raphelengius's main lexicographical source was the Mozarabic 'Latin-Arabic glossary of the Leiden University Library' (UBL MS Or. 231).[6] It almost certainly furnished the greater part of the words in the specimen sent to Arias Montano and it remains the work quoted with greater frequency than any other, on over two thousand occasions, in the published dictionary. The manuscript was originally owned by Raphelengius's Arabic teacher, the French Orientalist Guillaume Postel, who acquired it in 1532.[7] Through the intermediary of Andreas Masius it was lent to Plantin's establishment in 1569 for the use of Guy Le Fèvre de la Boderie when he was working on the Polyglot Bible, and in Plantin's offices in Antwerp it seems to have remained, Postel subsequently allowing Raphelengius to keep it.[8] It was thus one of a number of presents Postel was to make to his former pupil. The glossary itself was compiled in a scholarly circle of Mozarabs in Toledo shortly before about 1175 when the manuscript in Postel's possession was copied by Jībriyān ibn 'Īsā ibn Abī Ḥujāj. The compiler was an Arabic-speaking Christian who wanted to increase his countrymen's knowledge of Latin in the period immediately before Castilian became the prevalent language of the Mozarabic community. His sources included the various Arabic translations of the Scriptures in circulation at the time,[9] but, as later lexicographers were to establish, the glossary remained particularly valuable as an indication of the type of Arabic spoken by the Mozarabs. For Raphelengius, working when European Arabic lexicography was still in its infancy, the glossary had other advantages: it was written with considerable clarity, the Arabic words were largely vocalized, and it was one of the very few bilingual Arabic dictionaries accessible to him.

What did Raphelengius know about this dictionary? Like Postel he misdated it, judging it to be eight hundred years old and thus compiled in the eighth century rather than in the twelfth. Otherwise he was surprisingly well informed. He recognized the Visigothic script and the manuscript's Western provenance.[10] He knew more – he knew something about the manuscript

---

6   See the thorough study by P.S. van Koningsveld, *The Latin-Arabic Glossary of the Leiden University Library* (Leiden, 1977). The dictionary was published by C.F. Seybold, *Glossarium Latino-Arabicum* (Berlin, 1900).

7   Van Koningsveld, *The Latin-Arabic Glossary*, p. 43; on the owners of the manuscript see also Seybold, Glossarium, pp. viii–ix.

8   Raphelengius's ownership is recorded [fol. 7ᵛ]: 'Postea fuit Francisci Raphelengii ex dono Postelli'.

9   Van Koningsveld, *The Latin-Arabic Glossary*, pp. 40–65.

10 *Lex.*, sig. 3*ᵛ: 'Glossarium Latino-Arabicum ante annos octingentos plus minus in membranis descriptum; in quo vocibus Latinis (sed Gothicismum interdum olentibus ac litera semi-Gothica scriptis), respondent, charactere Africano, Arabica, figuris vocalium omnibus accurate ut plurimum ornata.'

which subsequent scholars were to forget and which has only been reconfirmed recently: that it was compiled not for students of Arabic but for students of Latin.[11] Furnished with this knowledge he made an intelligent use of a work whose very nature could be misleading for a Westerner, especially for one who was just embarking on the study of Arabic, and he managed to distinguish between the choices of Arabic words offered the Arabic-speaking reader and to reverse the lexicon for the benefit of European students. He also, on occasion, gave the correct form of words mistranscribed, and the correct meaning of words mistranslated, in the glossary. In his printed dictionary he gives غضون (*ghuḍūn*) for 'wrinkles', rather than غصون (*ghuṣūn*) in the glossary, and اعطس (*aʿaṭusu*) as meaning 'I sneeze' rather than 'I snore'. We shall see that on other occasions, however, the glossary led him into error.

Raphelengius's precociously skilful treatment of the glossary should perhaps be connected with the other manuscripts he was given at about the same time by the men responsible for transmitting the glossary to Antwerp, Postel and Masius. From Postel Raphelengius acquired some useful works on Arabic grammar. One was the *Sharḥ taṣrīf al-Zanjānī*, al-Afzarī's commentary to the standard manual on declensions and conjugations, the *Kitāb al-taṣrīf*.[12] The manuscript (UBL MS Or. 246) was copied in Mecca, probably in the sixteenth century, and is already something of a rarity from a bibliographical point of view. The work itself, composed in the late fourteenth century, contains, besides an elucidation, the entire text of the thirteenth-century *Taṣrīf*. The *Taṣrīf* provides a far better analysis of conjugations and declensions than was to be found in any of the few available grammars by European Arabists,[13] and it is to Raphelengius's credit that he could recognize and exploit its merits at such an early stage.

We know for sure that Raphelengius received the *Sharḥ taṣrīf* from Postel. Where Raphelengius's other grammatical manuscript is concerned we have no statement to suggest it was from Postel, but only a concurrence of circumstances which makes it most likely. The manuscript in question, UBL MS Or. 235, is of especial interest on account of its origin. It contains two important works on syntax, *al-Muqaddima al-kāfiyya al-muḥsiba fī 'l-naḥw*

---

11   *Cat.Raph.*, sig. I3ʳ: 'Glossarium Latino-Arabicum quod ante septingentos annos scriptum putabat Scaliger, in pergameno, liber insignis, etiam ad illustrationem linguae Latinae faciens.'

12   *Lex.*, sig. 4*ʳ: 'Grammatica quaedam Arabica elegantissima et nitide scripta Mechae, charactere Asiatico, dono Auctori data a Clarissimo viro Guilielmo Postello. Haec ea est quae annotatis paginis crebro in hoc opere citatur.' On al-Afzarī see Jones, pp. 141, 159; C. Brockelmann, *Geschichte der Arabischen Litteratur I* (Weimar-Berlin, 1898–1902), p. 28; *Supplementband II* (Leiden, 1938), p. 170.

13   See Jones, pp. 133–138.

by the eleventh-century Egyptian grammarian Ibn Bābashādh, and the early fourteenth-century Moroccan *al-Ajurrūmiyya* (followed by a further fragment, a repetition of the first pages of *al-Muḥsiba*).[14] The texts were copied, *al-Ajurrūmiyya* in December 1518 and *al-Muḥsiba* in January 1519, for one of the greatest Hebrew scholars of his day, the former General of the Augustinian Order Egidio da Viterbo. Elected cardinal in 1517, Egidio was nominated papal legate by Leo X in March 1518 for the purpose of discussing an alliance against the Turks with the young King Charles of Spain. Egidio's embassy in Barcelona, where he arrived in June 1518, lasted for a year, and the manuscript owned by Raphelengius is one of several copied at the time for the cardinal, who was subsequently to study Arabic in Rome under the tuition of the Moroccan diplomat and writer of Andalusian origin, Johannes Leo Africanus.[15]

But how did the manuscript reach Raphelengius? The most obvious intermediary was Postel. Postel was in Rome between 1544 and 1549 and the vicar apostolic Filippo Archinto appears to have been in the habit of lending him manuscripts from the collection Egidio da Viterbo had left to the Augustinian Biblioteca Angelica. Neither of the two men were overscrupulous in returning what they had borrowed and there is every reason to suspect that Postel took the manuscript back to France.[16]

Masius, on the other hand, gave Raphelengius a manuscript Qur'an. Raphelengius was to possess various copies. Unfortunately the one he used most frequently, a North African codex copied in the late twelfth century (591 A.H.),[17] is not amongst his surviving manuscripts in the Leiden library. What do survive are some North African fragmentary versions. One, UBL MS

---

14 *Lex.*, sig. 4*v: 'Grammaticae complures aliae Ms. inter quas duae illae quae ex Romana Typographia etiam prodierunt, Kaphia nempe et Giarrumia, sed Africano charactere scriptae.' Cf. *Cat.Raph.*, sig. I3r: 'Grammatica Arabica Mauritanico charactere, in charta.' Raphelengius's ownership of the manuscript is specified on fol. 70v. For Ibn Bābashādh see C. Brockelmann, *Supplementband I* (Leiden, 1937), p. 529, and for *al-Ajurrūmiyya* by Ibn Ajurrūm, Jones, pp. 110–112.

15 R.P.A. Dozy, in *CCO*, vol. 1, p. 28 and 43, misread اجدوبه on fol. 66r and اجدبه on fol. 83v as 'Octavii'. On Egidio da Viterbo's Spanish embassy and his Arabic studies see K.K. Starczewska, *Latin Translation of the Qur'ān (1518/1621) Commissioned by Egidio da Viterbo* (Wiesbaden, 2018), pp. xiv–xxii, xxx–xxxi; G. Levi Della Vida, *Ricerche sulla formazione del più antico fondo dei manoscritti orientali della Biblioteca Vaticana* (Vatican City, 1939), pp. 100–110; G. Signorelli, *Il Card. Egidio da Viterbo, Agostiniano umanista e riformatore 1469–1532* (Florence, 1929), pp. 69–76; for other Arabic manuscripts copied for Egidio at the time see J.W. O'Malley, *Giles of Viterbo on Church and Reform. A Study in Renaissance Thought* (Leiden, 1968), pp. 60, 78, 192, 195.

16 Levi Della Vida, *Ricerche*, pp. 311–312, 321.

17 *Lex.*, sig. 4*r: 'Alcoranus Mahomedicus, cuius varia Auctor habuit exemplaria, inter quae unum charactere Mauritanico in membranis pervetustum, quippe anno Hegirae 591 exaratum.'

Or. 241, dates from the fifteenth century and might have been obtained by the Flemish scholar Nicolaus Clenardus when he was in Spain in the 1530s, or in Morocco, which he reached in 1540. He would have given it to Rutger Rescius, the friend of Erasmus and professor of Greek at the university of Louvain, who would then have passed it on to Masius.[18] Since Masius died in 1573 this must have been one of Raphelengius's very first acquisitions. Like most incipient Arabists, he might have read it alongside the medieval Latin translation of the Qur'an edited by Theodor Bibliander and published in 1543. Two other North African fragments also belonging to Raphelengius (UBL MSS Or. 228 and 251),[19] and, probably dating from the twelfth or early thirteenth century, remain to this day among the earliest Qur'anic manuscripts in the Leiden collection. The North African script in which MS Or. 251 is copied served as a model for the Maghrebi typeface which Raphelengius was to have cut in Leiden and smoke-proof impressions of which appear in the margin and on the flyleaves of the manuscript.[20]

Al-Afzarī's grammatical work and the Qur'an are the Muslim manuscripts to which Raphelengius refers most frequently in his dictionary – to the Qur'an there are well over two hundred references and to the grammar more than fifty. By the end of his life Raphelengius owned another manuscript by a Muslim author, which he also gives as a source for his dictionary but of which we cannot say with any certainty that he possessed it in Antwerp. It is referred to in the dictionary as 'Nomocanon Arabicum, seu Mahomedanorum Corpus Iuris civilis quam canonici'. This is UBL MS Or. 222, *Wiqāyat al-riwāya fī masā'il al-hidāya*, a compendium and elucidation of the famous legal commentaries

---

18   *Cat.Raph.*, sig. I3[r]: 'Ex Alcorano Fragmenta quaedam, seu integrae Azoarae, charactere African. in charta. Exemplar hoc fuit primo Rescii Professoris Graeci Lovan. inde And. Masii, etc.' In the original version of the present article Leid. Cod. Or. 241 is confused with Leid. Cod. Or. 251. This was pointed out by T. Dunkelgrün, 'From Tunis to Leiden across Renaissance Europe: The curious career of a maghribi Qur'an' *Omslag. Bulletin van de Universiteitsbibliotheek Leiden en het Scaliger Instituut* 3 (2009), pp. 7–8; idem, 'The Hebrew library of a Renaissance humanist. Andreas Masius and the bibliography to his *Iosuae Imperatoris Historiae* (1574), with a Latin edition and an annotated English translation' *Studia Rosenthaliana* 42–43 (2010–2011), pp. 197–252, esp. pp. 216–217. See also A. Hamilton, 'The perils of catalogues' *Journal of Islamic Manuscripts* 1 (2010), pp. 31–36, esp. p. 34.

19   *Cat.Raph.*, sig. I3[r], 'Fragmentum Alcorani charactere Africano seu Mauritanico elegantissimo. 4. in membrana.' For the dating of the two Qur'ans, MSS Or. 228 and 251, see T. Nöldeke, *Geschichte des Qorâns* (Göttingen, 1860), p. 346.

20   Cf. E. Braches, 'Raphelengius's Naschi and Maghribi. Some reflections on the origin of Arabic typography in the Low Countries' in *Quaestiones Leidenses. Twelve studies on Leiden University Library and its holdings published on the occasion of the quarter-centenary of the University by Quaerendo* (Leiden, 1975), pp. 24–34, esp. p. 29.

of the twelfth-century Hanafite al-Marghīnānī by his brother Burhānaddīn Ṣadr al-Sharīʿa al-Awwal al-Maḥbūbī. The manuscript, which includes Turkish paraphrases, is remarkable for its provenance: it was found by the Spaniards amongst the spoils of the battle of Lepanto in 1571 and was presented by one of the participants, Don Guillén de San Clemente, in the following year to Don Bernardo de Josa in Rome. Don Bernardo scribbled an enthusiastic description of the episode on the flyleaf.[21]

For other early sources of Raphelengius's dictionary we can turn to material, frequently of a theological nature, much of which was printed. First there are his many Scriptural sources – as long as he was in Antwerp, I suggest, versions and parts of the Old Testament, but not of the New. According to his sons[22] the very first work he read in Arabic was the Judaeo-Arabic paraphrase of the Penateuch by the tenth-century Egyptian rabbi Saadia Gaon contained in the polyglot Pentateuch printed in Istanbul by Eliezer Bekor Gerson Soncino in 1546. The other texts are in Hebrew, Aramaic and Judaeo-Persian. To this work, which Raphelengius also used for studying Persian,[23] there are over ninety references in his dictionary and his life-long interest in it accounts for one striking feature of his *Lexicon Arabico-Latinum*: the Hebrew transliterations of so many Arabic words intended both for beginners who knew Hebrew better than Arabic and for readers of Judaeo-Arabic.[24] First a Hebraist and then an Arabist, Raphelengius also consulted the works of a number of Hebrew philologists in order to establish similarities between Arabic and Hebrew and to provide Hebrew equivalents of Arabic words. He refers over seventy times in his dictionary to these sources, the writings of Abraham ibn Ezra and David Kimhi, and above all Nathan ben Jehiel's *Arukh*, the great lexicon of the

---

21   *Lex.*, sig. 4*ʳ. Cf. *Cat.Raph.*, sig. I3ʳ: 'Nomocanon Mahometanorum Arabicus fol. in charta. Bomb, liber Turcis in conflictu ad Naupactum ereptus.' For al-Maḥbūbī see Brockelmann, *Geschichte*, *1*, p. 377; *Supplementband 1*, p. 646. For manuscripts found on the battlefield see R. Jones, 'Piracy, War and the acquisition of Arabic manuscripts in Renaissance Europe' *Manuscripts of the Middle East* 2 (1987), pp. 96–116; for Lepanto in particular (and a reproduction of the flyleaf of Raphelengius's manuscript), Jones, pp. 34–36. It is here pointed out that the veteran of Lepanto, who gave Josa the manuscript and whom Josa calls Don Guillem de Sanctelimente, is the Catalan Guillén de San Clemente i de Centelles. The identification is the work of S. Hanß, *Die materielle Kultur der Seeschlacht von Lepanto (1571). Materialität, Medialität und die historische Produktion eines Ereignisses* (Würzburg, 2017), pp. 348–349.

22   *Lex.*, sig. 3*ʳ: '… initium fecit ab accurata Pentateuchi Arabici R. Saadiae lectione …'

23   Cf. W.M.C. Juynboll, *Zeventiende-eeuwsche Beoefenaars van het Arabisch in Nederland* (Utrecht, 1931), pp. 44–45.

24   *Lex.*, sig. **ʳ: 'Radices autem plerasque ad certiorem lectionem, et usum tyronum scripturae Arabicae nondum satis assuetorum Hebraicis etiam literis expressit; eadem opera docens quomodo Iudaei suis characteribus Arabica soleant exprimere …'

Talmud and Midrash with words of Latin, Greek, Persian, Aramaic and Arabic origin.[25] So frequent a use of rabbinic sources aroused misgivings in Erpenius.[26] He complained that Raphelengius introduced words alien to classical Arabic, while the impossibility of reproducing all the Arabic characters in Hebrew and the poor quality of the printing of the Istanbul Pentateuch led to serious spelling mistakes.

Another Scriptural source which Raphelengius read immediately after the Pentateuch was the polyglot Psalterium[27] with versions of the Psalms in Hebrew, Greek, Aramaic and Arabic printed in parallel columns in Genoa in 1516 and edited by Agostino Giustiniani, bishop of Nebbio – a work owned by nearly every apprentice of Arabic in the sixteenth century. Either in Antwerp or in Leiden, moreover, Raphelengius procured a manuscript edition of the Pentateuch with a patristic commentary in Arabic but written in Syriac characters. This *karshuni* manuscript, copied in 1528, is also retained in the Leiden Library, MS Or. 230.[28]

Finally there was a work, printed and Christian, which Raphelengius almost certainly owned in Antwerp and which he quotes in his dictionary on over 130 occasions: the Spanish-Arabic *Vocabulista Aravigo en letra castellana* by Pedro de Alcalá printed in Granada in 1505.[29] The *Vocabulista*, like the *Arte para ligeramente saber la lengua araviga* by the same author and published in Granada in the same year, was compiled in order to enable Spanish missionaries to tend the converted Muslims in southern Spain after the fall of Granada. In contrast to the Mozarabic glossary, it was intended for students of Arabic and was based

---

25   *Lex.*, sig. 4*ᵛ: 'Aruch et reliqua Rabbinorum scripta Hebraica, quae cum dubiae fidei in hoc negotio esse sciat, numquam producit absque nomine.'

26   *Lex.*, 'Observationes', p. 1: '... quia non raro Rabbini vocem aliquam hoc aut illud Arabice significare mentiuntur, quo eandem significationem Hebraeae voci maiori cum probabilitate attribuant'.

27   *Lex.*, sig. 3*ʳ: '... quo absoluto [sc. Pentateuchi Arabici lectione], Psalterium Arabicum ex editione Nebiensis arripuit ...'

28   *Cat.Raph.*, sig. I2ᵛ: 'Commentarii ex Patribus in Pentateuchum, Arabice, character Syriacus in charta.' I take this to correspond to two sources mentioned separately in *Lex.*, sig. 3*ᵛ: 'Ibidem [sc. quinque libri Mosis] ex alia versione, Syriaco charactere manuscripti' and 'Commentarii Arabici in eosdem libros, literis quoque Syriacis exarati.'

29   *Lex.*, sig. 4*ʳ: 'Lexicon Granatense anno 1505 Granatae excusum, in quo voces Arabicae quamplurimae Latinis literis expressae Hispanice explicantur.' The work is studied by R. Ricard, 'Remarques sur l'Arte et le Vocabulista de Fr. Pedro de Alcalá' in *Mémorial Henri Basset: Nouvelles études nord-africaines et orientales* (Paris, 1928), pp. 229–236; Schnurrer, pp. 16–18, no. 37; Fück, pp. 29–34; O. Zwartjes, 'More on "Arabic linguistic terminology in Pedro de Alcalá"' *Historiographia Linguistica* 41 (2014), pp. 247–297; and Jones, pp. 101–109 (on the *Arte*). Cf. also the nineteenth-century edition of the Spanish text edited by Paul de Lagarde, *Petri Hispani de lingua arabica libri duo* (Göttingen, 1883).

on Antonio de Nebrija's Spanish-Latin dictionary. Yet it was for those who wished to speak the Arabic dialect of Granada rather than for anyone wishing to read or write classical Arabic. The Arabic words, frequently in dialectal form, are transliterated in the Roman alphabet for Castilians. Consequently the *Vocabulista*, the only printed Arabic dictionary in existence, rich in words and invaluable for the study of the Arabic spoken in Andalusia, only really serves the purpose of a classical lexicographer if the words can be checked against some other source and then be correctly re-transliterated in Arabic. In view of this difficulty it is again to Raphelengius's credit that he managed to exploit the work as much as he did. The provenance of his copy is also of some interest. It was sent to him from Spain by Jan van Bodeghem,[30] whose family had numerous business connections with Plantin's agents since the 1570s.[31] By 1585 Jan van Bodeghem himself was a member of the 'Guardia de arqueros', an honorary bodyguard of Philip II formed by Netherlanders.[32] That he should be mentioned specifically in the introduction to Raphelengius's dictionary could suggest that he, like Postel and Masius, provided Plantin's son-in-law with further Arabic material – perhaps even with the legal compendium seized at Lepanto.

2   Leiden

When Raphelengius arrived in Leiden in 1585[33] he brought with him what, by the standards of the time, was a remarkably rich collection of Arabic books and manuscripts. But within half a dozen years the situation changed. In 1591 the Typographia Medicea, which had been founded in Rome in 1584, began to produce a series of works in Arabic.[34] These expanded immeasurably the field

---

30   *Lex.*, sig. 4*r: 'Quo libro aliquamdiu usus est auctor, humanitate Nob. Viri Ioannis a Bodeghem.'

31   Cf. Jan Poelman's letter of 22 August 1578 to Jan Moretus in *CP*, vol. 8–9, p. 277.

32   A. Morel-Fatio and A. Rodríguez Villa, eds, *Relación del viaje hecho por Felipe II en 1585, a Zaragoza, Barcelona y Valencia, escrita por Henrique Cock* (Madrid, 1876), p. 93. I owe this information to the kindness of F. Robben.

33   For Raphelengius's activities as a printer in Leiden and a good bibliography see K. van Ommen, *'Tous mes livres de langues estrangeres'. Het oosterse legaat van Joseph Justus Scaliger in de Universiteitsbibliotheek Leiden* (Leiden, 2020), pp. 31–36.

34   For the Medici Press see G.E. Saltini, 'Della Stamperia Orientale Medicea e di Giovan Battista Raimondi' *Giornale storico degli archivi toscani* 4 (1860), pp. 257–308; A. Tinto, 'Per una storia della tipografia orientale a Roma nell'età della Controriforma' *Accademie e biblioteche d'Italia* 41 (1973), pp. 280–303; R. Jones, 'The Medici Oriental Press (Rome 1584–1614) and the Impact of its Arabic Publications on Northern Europe' in G.A. Russell, ed.,

in which a lexicographer had to work. The Arabic Gospels appeared in 1591; in 1592 there followed the *Nuzhat al-mushtāq* (a long excerpt from al-Idrīsī's vast work on geography), *al-Ajurrūmiyya*, and another book on syntax, Ibn al-Ḥājib's *Kāfiyya*; Avicenna's *al-Qānūn* came out in 1593, and Naṣīr al-Dīn al-Ṭūsī's Arabic version of Euclid's *Elements* in 1594. Raphelengius hastened to procure some of these publications. Plantin's agent Hans Dresseler obtained the *Nuzhat al-mushtāq* for him at the Frankfurt book fair in the autumn of 1592.[35] Besides the Medici edition of the Gospels, to which I shall be returning, Raphelengius also purchased the other two Medici publications of 1592, *al-Kāfiyya* and *al-Ajurrūmiyya* (which he already owned in manuscript) and Avicenna's *Qānūn*.[36] That he never appears to have had access to the 1594 Euclid proves how difficult it was to obtain on the European market a work printed mainly for distribution in the Ottoman Empire: in England William Bedwell only acquired it some five years after its publication.[37]

The impressive output of the Medici press coincided with the period in which Raphelengius had most time to devote to Arabic. In 1586 he was appointed professor of Hebrew at the university of Leiden and in 1589 he all but retired from the administration of his father-in-law's Leiden branch. Already in 1592 he was engaged in translating the Qur'an.[38] Presumably at about the same time he prepared a draft of the Arabic grammar which he hoped to append to his dictionary.[39] Still more than the Officina Plantiniana

---

The 'Arabick' Interest of the Natural Philosophers in Seventeenth-Century England (Leiden, 1994), pp. 88–108; S. Fani and M. Farina, *Le vie delle lettere. La Tipografia Medicea tra Roma e l'Oriente* (Florence, 2012); Jones, pp. 126–140.

35   Cf. Raphelengius's letter to Ortelius of 6 December 1592 in J.H. Hessels, ed., *Abrahami Ortelii Epistulae* (Cambridge, 1887), pp. 544–545: 'Quoniam, mi Compater honorande, incideram in novam Geographiam Arabicam, specimen dico, quod Francofurto attulit mihi Dresselerius …'

36   See *Lex.*, sig. 4*ʳ: 'Avicennae opera medica Romae excusa in fol.'

37   Hamilton, *William Bedwell*, p. 12. On the Medici press's policy of catering for an Eastern market see R. Jones, 'The Medici Oriental Press (Rome 1584–1614) and Renaissance Arabic Studies' Exhibition Leaflet at SOAS, London, May-June 1983.

38   Cf. his letter to Ortelius of 2 July 1592 in *Ortelii Epistulae*, p. 518.

39   The grammar, or a draft of the grammar, must at one point have been lent to Hugo Grotius. In March [1605] Grotius sent a transcription of it to Frans Raphelengius the Younger. In his accompanying letter he wrote: 'Quod communibus literis et parentis vestri memoriae debeo, id non modo negare sed et differre non possum. Mitto igitur ad vos quicquid ex Grammatica Arabica descripsi. Liber ille quem ego primum inscripsi nihil est aliud quam excerpta Alphabeti Romani. A secundo incipiunt ea quae pater vester clare atque luculenter perscripserat …' (P.C. Mollhuysen, ed., *Briefwisseling van Hugo Grotius, 1, 1597–17 Augustus 1618* (The Hague, 1928), p. 54). This transcription, together with the Medici press texts of *al-Ajurrūmiyya* and the *Kitāb al-taṣrīf*, were copied out by Joost Raphelengius in 1613. Cf. Jones, pp. 137–138. They are now contained amongst the Raphelengius papers

in Antwerp the University of Leiden enabled Raphelengius to encounter other scholars who shared his interest in Arabic, and who, like Carolus Clusius and Justus Lipsius, asked him questions about terminology and provided him with further material.

In 1592 Franciscus Junius was appointed professor of theology. As librarian to the elector palatine in Heidelberg Junius had worked on the Arabic versions of the New Testament collected by Postel. In 1578 he had published a Latin translation of the Arabic Acts of the Apostles and the Epistles to the Corinthians and probably kept a transcription of the Arabic original with him when he was in Leiden. This he seems to have lent to Raphelengius. On 4 November 1592 Raphelengius wrote to his brother-in-law Jan Moretus in Antwerp: 'Je me suis très plus, ayant livres de plus grande importance, a sçavoir les 4 Evangelistes en Arabe que m'a presté Franciscus Junius, et les Actes des Apostres aussi les Epistres de Saint Pol; de sorte qu'ayant tout le nouveau Testament je passe le temps à le consulter et d'en tirer quelque fruict aussi long temps que la santé le permet: me convenant en cette estude, veu que je ne voy autre plaisir en ce monde veu l'inconstance des affaires humaines.'[40]

It is not clear to which editions or manuscripts Raphelengius is referring. The Gospels he was lent by Junius could have been the printed Medici press edition published in the previous year: we know from the introduction to his dictionary that this was one of Raphelengius's sources. But it could equally well have been a manuscript, while the version of Acts and the Epistles was probably, as I suggested, a transcription of the Heidelberg codex (now BAV MS Vat. Ar.23 I, II).[41]

---

in UBL, MS Or. 3041. About the original plan to append Raphelengius's grammar to the dictionary, his sons wrote, *Lex.*, sig. **2ʳ: 'Grammaticam quoque huic operi adiicere in animo habebat Auctor (qua de causa plurima nomina verbalia, participalia, denominativa, diminutiva, augmentativa, localia, instrumentalia, numeralia, pluralia, et faeminina, verbaque polygramma, et infintiva, aliaque similia multa, quae Grammatica paucis et succinctis regulis a primitivis formare docet, compendio, uti supra monuimus, studens, in hoc opere omisit:) in quem finem Grammaticas aliquot Arabicas Arabice scriptas in Latinum transtulerat, et opuscula etiam grammaticalia multa ex iis confecerat; quin ante 20 annos plus minus universam Grammaticam 8 tabulis breviter comprehenderat: verum cum morte abreptus nec eas absolverit, nec aliud aliquod opus perfectum, quod studiosorum desiderio satisfacere possit, reliquerit ...' Much of the material here referred to is amongst the aforesaid papers.

40 MPM, Arch. 92, p. 71.
41 I am most grateful to Henk Jan de Jonge for his advice on this matter. For the manuscript in question see Levi della Vida, *Ricerche*, p. 301; E. Mittler, ed., *Bibliotheca Palatina. Katalog zur Ausstellung vom 8. Juli bis 2. November 1986, Heiliggeistkirche Heidelberg. Textband* (Heidelberg, 1986), p. 418. Raphelengius's sons are of little help. Among his sources they list (*Lex.*, sig. 3*ᵛ): 'Quatuor Evangelia elegantissimo charactere Romae excusa, anno 1591 in folio.'; 'Eadem ex alia translatione calamo descripta: ex quibus in hoc opere voces non

Junius thus seems to have introduced Raphelengius to what, for him at least, was a new field of study, the Arabic recensions of the New Testament. A month later Raphelengius wrote to Abraham Ortelius saying that his son, Frans the Younger, had obtained an 'Arabic New Testament' from England which he was perusing in order to gather further words for his dictionary.[42] What this New Testament was is again obscure, for the only surviving New Testament material amongst Raphelengius's manuscripts are two fragments of the Gospels of Matthew and Mark (UBL, MSS Or. 214 and Or. 218).[43] They both bear the name of Frans the Younger on the title-page. The only complete manuscript of the New Testament which Raphelengius consulted appears to have been the one in the possession of Scaliger who arrived in Leiden in 1593 – UBL, Cod. Or. 217. This was the manuscript, later to serve as the basis for Erpenius's 1616 edition of the New Testament in Arabic, which Raphelengius must have collated with 'another codex' of Acts and the Epistles – very possibly with that same transcription shown him by Junius.[44]

Scaliger's arrival in Leiden in the summer of 1593[45] marked the start of a new, but also of a final, phase in Raphelengius's Arabic studies. Scaliger, more than anyone except Postel and Masius, encouraged and stimulated Raphelengius to increase his knowledge in this field. Mercilessly critical of his colleagues, Scaliger had a genuine esteem for Plantin's son-in-law – and from him he had much to learn: despite Scaliger's inspired vision of how the study of Arabic should develop Raphelengius remained the better Arabist.

---

paucae citantur quas in prioribus illis non invenias. quod et de Pentateucho et Psalterio manuscriptis habendum; ac bene observandum, ne auctoris fides suspecta fiat tanquam falso multa allegantis'; and 'Reliqui libri Novi Foederis omnes, manuscripti.' There is, however, also another possibility, namely that Raphelengius consulted for the Epistles and Acts UBL, MS Acad. 2, a fourteenth-century codex which Raphelengius actually seems to have owned. The case is argued persuasively by Vevian Zaki, 'The "Egyptian Vulgate" in Europe: An investigation into the version that shaped European scholarship on the Arabic Bible' *Collectanea Christiana Orientalia* 18 (2021), pp. 237–259, esp. pp. 247–248, 253–254.

42 *Ortelii Epistulae*, p. 544: 'Iam totus sum in percurrendo Novo Testamento Arabico quod ex Anglia per filium accepi, ut inde novas voces colligam Lexico illustrando.'

43 Cf. *Cat.Raph.*, sig. I3ʳ: 'Evangelia Matthaei, et Marci Arabice fol. illud in membrana, hoc in charta.' No other New Testament manuscripts are mentioned in the catalogue. Cf. C.R. Gregory, *Textkritik des Neuen Testaments* (Leipzig, 1900), p. 586.

44 Cf. Thomas Erpenius, ed., *Novum Testamentum Arabice* (Leiden, 1616), sig. **3ʳ: '... potiorem partem, Acta scilicet Apost. et Epistolas omnes accuratissime cum alio codice contulit Vir de linguis Orientalibus optime meritus Franciscus Raphelengius ...'

45 For Scaliger in Leiden see Van Ommen, *'Tous mes livres'*, pp. 15–50.

Scaliger had probably started to study Arabic in the late 1570s and his interest in it was due in the first place to his work on chronology,[46] but, because of the unbounded extent of his curiosity, he endeavoured to read as widely as possible and to collect manuscripts in a variety of domains. If we compare his Arabic manuscript collection to that of Raphelengius we are struck by the quantity of Scaliger's New Testament material. This was one of the areas in which he had something to offer Raphelengius. When compiling his dictionary, moreover, Raphelengius also seems to have borrowed the many Muslim prayerbooks Scaliger had acquired.[47] A number of these manuscripts had Turkish paraphrases or translations of the prayers and passages from the Qur'an and, like the work retrieved from the spoils of Lepanto, may have been discovered on the bodies of Turkish soldiers.

A close collaboration soon developed between Scaliger and Raphelengius.[48] They lent one another their manuscripts and Scaliger based the Arabic wordlist he was compiling almost entirely on two works belonging to Raphelengius, the Mozarabic glossary and Pedro de Alcalá's *Vocabulista*.[49] Raphelengius died in July 1597 and Scaliger completed the title-page of his 'Thesaurus Linguae Arabicae' in March of the same year. That Raphelengius should have used Scaliger's wordlist so frequently for his own dictionary – he quotes it over 140 times – shows that he had constant access to it as it was being compiled.[50] The two men thus worked simultaneously and with the same material on an identical project. Nevertheless there are some striking differences between the two lexicographical works. Scaliger's is almost twice as long as that of Raphelengius, but, for his printed edition, Raphelengius may have made a practical selection from a far longer manuscript. The difference in alphabetical order is a still more

---

46 For Scaliger and the study of Arabic see Fück, pp. 47–53. On Scaliger's early scholarship see A. Grafton, *Joseph Scaliger. A Study in the History of Classical Scholarship* (Oxford, 1983–1993), vol. 1.

47 See, for example, UBL MSS Or. 256, 257, 259, 260, 263, 264. These seem to correspond to the half dozen prayerbooks listed in the 'Catalogus Librorum Manuscriptorum quos Iosephus Scaliger Bibliothecae Leidensi legavit' in the library catalogues drawn up by Daniel Heinsius and published in 1623, 1636 and 1640.

48 Grafton, *Joseph Scaliger*, vol. 2, p. 387.

49 Attested by the numerous references in UBL, MS Or. 212 to H (Hispanum Glossarium = the Mozarabic glossary) and to G (Vocabularium Granatense Hispano-arabicum = the *Vocabulista*).

50 His sons state as much in their description of the source, *Lex.*, sig. 4*r: 'Thesaurus Arabicus, seu Dictionarium Arabicum Illustris et doctissimi viri Iosephi Scaligeri P.M. ex libris quamplurimis ab ipso collectum, et parenti nostro, qui et suum vicissim illi utendum ad tempus dedit, benevole communicatum. Id nunc ex Auctoris legatione cum innumeris aliis eiusdem praestantissimis libris Orientalibus Bibliotheca Acad. Leidensis possidet et asservat.'

striking feature.[51] Scaliger, like William Bedwell in England, chose the earliest Arabic alphabetical order, the so-called Aramaic, *abjad*, or numerical order, and justified his choice by referring to its resemblance to the Hebrew order and to its use by Avicenna (in the list of medicaments contained in his *Qānūn*) and by Maimonides (in the chapter headings of the *Moreh Nevukhim* of which Scaliger possessed both a Judaeo-Arabic and a Hebrew codex).[52] Raphelengius, on the other hand, followed Postel in preferring the more current order, the *hijāʾ*, based on the shape of the characters and in use to this day. He was not, however, entirely consistent. In accordance with the Hebrew treatment of the ש (*sin*) and the ש (*shin*)[53] he indeed ordered the letters by shape but did not always have separate groups for characters differentiated by diacritical points. The ج (*jūm*) and the خ (*khāʾ*) thus come within the entry of the ح (*ḥāʾ*), the ث (*thāʾ*) under the ت (*tāʾ*), the ذ (*dhāl*) under the د (*dāl*), the ش (*shīn*) under the س (*sīn*), the ض (*ḍād*) under the ص (*ṣād*), the ظ (*ẓāʾ*) under the ط (*ṭāʾ*), and the غ (*ghain*) under the ع (*ʿain*).

The presence of Scaliger in Leiden stimulated Raphelengius, as did a more practical form of activity to which he had to turn his hand in the last years of his life. This was the translation, in and out of Arabic, of official dispatches, contracts and safe-conducts. Unfortunately only one of these seems to have survived, a safe-conduct for the merchants Cornelis de Houtman, Gerard van Beuningen, and their fellow passengers sailing to the Far East and signed by the stadhouder Maurice of Nassau.[54] Raphelengius himself printed the letter in Arabic in 1595 with the types he had had cut shortly before and with which the Officina Plantiniana was to print the Arabic passages in the revised edition

---

51   See above, pp. 67–68.
52   On Bedwell's Arabic-Latin dictionary (CUL, MSS Hh. 5. 1–7) see Hamilton, *William Bedwell*, p. 85–93. Scaliger describes his alphabetical order in the preface to his *Thesaurus Linguae Arabicae* (see above, pp. 67–68) His Judaeo-Arabic codex of the *Moreh Nevukhim* is now UBL, MS Or. Hebr. 96 and his Hebrew codex UBL, MS Or. 4723.
53   *Lex.*, sig. **ʳ: 'Literas affines, quae figuras similes punctisque solum discrepantes nactae sunt […] in unam contrahere classem visum fuit Auctori, cum aliis de causis, tum ut Hebraeos Lexicographos, qui literas ש et ש etsi sono et officio diversissimas coniungere solent, imitaretur …'
54   On this letter, the only known copy of which is at MPM, R. 63. 8 (4) [72], see F. de Nave, ed., *Philologia Arabica. Arabische studiën en drukken in de Nederlanden in de 16de en 17de eeuw* (Antwerpen, 1986), pp. 130–133; H. de Leeuw, 'The first Dutch Indonesian treaty. A rediscovered Arabic translation by Franciscus Raphelengius' *Manuscripts of the Middle East* 4 (1989), pp. 115–122; A. Vrolijk, 'Scaliger and the Dutch expansion in Asia: An Arabic translation for an early voyage to the East Indies (1600)' *Journal of the Warburg and Courtauld Institutes* 78 (2015), pp. 277–309, esp. p. 278. On official translations in and out of Arabic for the States General see Juynboll, *Zeventiende-eeuwsche Beoefenaars*, p. 51.

of Scaliger's *De emendatione temporum*, a type specimen, and numerous other texts including Raphelengius's own dictionary. Raphelengius's sons refer to 'innumerable' official documents in Arabic which provided their father with further words for his lexicon, but at their exact nature we can only guess.[55]

Raphelengius's last years may have been busy but they were also years of sadness and ill health. In the winter of 1594–5 he wrote to his friends lamenting the death of his wife and complaining about an increasing number of ailments. His right hand trembled to such an extent that he could hardly write. He was having trouble with his eyes. He suffered from a hernia and colics so violent that he could neither sit nor lie down and had to be submitted to potent emetics.[56] There is little wonder that he was still dissatisfied with his dictionary when he died. The sight of a rapidly expanding field of texts at the very moment when his own strength was diminishing must have impressed on him the knowledge of how much he still had to do in order to produce a lexicon which would satisfy his ambitions.[57]

Now, after over four hundred years, we are in a better position to assess the degree to which Raphelengius's lexicon really did satisfy his ambitions than were his immediate successors who practised a different type of Arabic lexicography.[58] Certainly, as Erpenius pointed out, the *Lexicon Arabico-Latinum* contained a great many mistakes. There are grammatical errors. برهانان (*burhānān*) is one of several examples of a dual which Raphelengius presents as a plural – the correct plural is براهين (*barāhīn*). There are errors of meaning frequently due to the absence of the correct diacritical point. حدق (*ḥadaqa*) is confused with حذق (*ḥadhiqa*), 'to be skilled'. حراب (*ḥarāb*), given as meaning 'destruction', should be خراب (*kharāb*). 'To depart' should be ظعن (*ẓaʿana*), not طعن

---

55   *Lex.*, sig. 4*ᵛ: 'Epistolae, Contractus, Syngrapha, Salvi conductus, similesque schedae innumerae, ex quibus multa se didicisse plurimaque magni usus vocabula de prompsisse saepe fassus est.'

56   Cf. his letter to Ortelius of 12 August 1594 (*Ortelii Epistulae*, pp. 592–593), his letters to Lipsius in April 1595 (P. Burman, *Sylloge Epistolarum* (Leiden, 1724), vol. 1, p. 197), and Clusius' letter to Lipsius written in March 1594 (*ibid.*, p. 324).

57   It was above all Erpenius who emphasized Raphelengius's dissatisfaction with his dictionary. Of the amount of mistakes he wrote: 'Neque id mirabar, cum scirem Auctorem dum in eius compositionem incumberet, adeo infirma perpetuo affectum fuisse valetudine, ut non modo non studiis, sed ne ipsa quidem luce delectaretur, adque omnia fere momenta TAEDET ANIMAM MEAM VITAE MEAE in ore haberet, quin et summum diem ante obiisse, quam ex voto suo hoc opus perficeret et poliret: unde visum mihi fuit in illa loca paucis ea annotare quae maxime necessaria esse, huiusque linguae studiosis non ingrata fore videbantur, Arabica scilicet versione carentia explicando, manifeste erronea corrigendo, et suspecta pleraque indicando …' (*Lex.*, Observationes, p. 1).

58   For an assessment see Juynboll, *Zeventiende-eeuwsche Beoefenaars*, pp. 42–44.

(ṭaʿana). An injudicious use of Pedro de Alcalá's *Vocabulista* led Raphelengius to introduce certain colloquial or dialectal forms which do not exist in classical Arabic. 'Moment' thus becomes لحده (*laḥda*) instead of لحظه (*laḥẓa*). An equally injudicious use of the Mozarabic glossary was the cause of other errors, خرقه النساء (*kharqat al-nasāʾ*), for example, should be عرق النساء (*ʿirq al-nasāʾ*), 'sciatica'.

If we compare Raphelengius's dictionary to other contemporary efforts in the domain of Arabic lexicography its qualities begin to emerge more clearly.[59] From a practical point of view the use of a more current alphabetical order gives Raphelengius a considerable advantage over Scaliger and Bedwell, who, as we saw, used the archaic Aramaic order. But where the purpose of Raphelengius's dictionary is concerned the work can best be compared to Valentin Schindler's *Lexicon Pentaglotton* which was published in Hanau in 1612 and thus appeared just before Raphelengius's work.

Like Raphelengius's lexicon Valentin Schindler's dictionary was posthumous, the author having died in 1604 after teaching Oriental languages in Helmstedt and Wittenberg. The object of the dictionary, which contained words in Hebrew, both ancient and Talmudic, in Aramaic, in Syriac, and in Arabic, was entirely theological. In his preface the editor, Engelbrecht Engels, emphasized the value of languages for spreading the Gospel, but the real purpose of the work was to help scholars understand the 'true meaning of the Holy Scriptures' by studying Hebrew in association with 'kindred' tongues.[60]

That Arabic should be learnt in order to obtain a superior knowledge of Semitic philology and ultimately of Hebrew was a recurrent claim in apologies of the language from the Renaissance to the eighteenth century,[61] and the majority of students of Arabic were theologians. This was something which Raphelengius, himself a Semitic philologist and a biblical scholar, could not

---

59   On contemporary efforts in Paris cf. G. Duverdier, 'Savary de Brèves et Ibrahim Müteferrika: Deux drogmans culturels à l'origine de l'imprimerie turque' *Bulletin du bibliophile* (Paris, 1987), pp. 322–359, esp. pp. 322–326.
60   Valentin Schindler, *Lexicon Pentaglotton* (Hanau, 1612), sig. **r: 'Hoc vero est, linguas Orientales, quae quidam ad genuinum S. Scripturae sensum eliciendum aliquod afferre possunt adjumentum, Hebraicam inquam et huic cognatas, Chaldaicam, Syriacam, Arabicam, Rabbinicam, et Talmudicam, una et eadem quodammodo opera docere: et simul pluribus in medium adductis exemplis monstrare viam, qua et verus Sacrarum literarum sensus erui, et causae, propter quas interpretes, non Latinus modo, et hoc recentior Germanus, sed et Chaldaei, et Graeci, alicubi fuerint allucinati, investigari possint.'
61   Cf. K.H. Dannenfeldt 'The Renaissance Humanists and the knowledge of Arabic' *Studies in the Renaissance* 2 (1955), pp. 96–117; Hamilton, *William Bedwell*, pp. 80–85; J. Loop, *Johann Heinrich Hottinger. Arabic and Islamic Studies in the Seventeenth Century* (Oxford, 2013), pp. 61–80.

afford to overlook. His dictionary has some hundred and fifty references to the Scriptures, and it was for the benefit of biblical scholars that wordlists in Hebrew and Aramaic and in Greek were appended to the work. The wordlist in Hebrew and Aramaic was to enable readers to look up the Arabic equivalent of certain difficult words in the Old Testament, and especially in the Pentateuch, while the one in Greek was for students of both the Old Testament and the New.

Yet the most extensive of the three wordlists appended to Raphelengius's dictionary is the Latin one. This covers every field – botany, medicine, geography, navigation, commerce – and points to the true ambition, originality, and merit of the lexicon. Raphelengius's sons dedicated it to the memory of Abraham Ortelius, Justus Lipsius, and Carolus Clusius, the three men who, with their questions about Arabic words, both in Antwerp and in Leiden, had constantly encouraged the elder Raphelengius to proceed with his work. Ortelius and Lipsius asked questions about geographical and historical terms, while Clusius asked about botany, medicine, and philosophy.[62] Raphelengius was further encouraged by merchants and navigators[63] for whom he formulated the safe-conducts I referred to earlier and who needed to decipher contracts and make themselves understood in the vast Arabic-speaking areas in which they had to travel.

In view of the variety of requirements which Raphelengius hoped to meet, his dictionary has the unique merit of being a handy work which a merchant might carry on his journeys without any great difficulty. All we know about William Bedwell suggests that he too wanted to assist merchants and navigators, but the mere immensity of the seven folio volumes of his own dictionary explains why he temporarily gave up the idea of publishing it when he arrived in Leiden in 1612 and heard that Raphelengius's work had gone to press, and why it was never printed after his death.[64] There is, to my knowledge, no evidence of how many copies of Raphelengius's dictionary were printed in

---

62 *Lex.*, sig. 3*ʳ: 'Calcar ei addidit desiderium satisfaciendi amicis suis, tribus summis illis in re litteraria viris, quibus postea Lexicon hoc destinavit, et a nobis dedicari voluit. Hi enim dum quotidie familiariter cum illo versabantur, crebras ei de vocibus Arabicis movebant quaestiones: Lipsius quidem et Ortelius de regionum, oppidorum, fluviorum et portuum, itemque officiorum nominibus in historia medii et postremi temporis, chartisque Hispaniae, Siciliae et aliis passim obviis; Clusius autem de herbarum, medicamentorum, ac mineralium aliarumque rerum ad materiam medicam aut philosophicam spectantium appellationibus: quibus omnibus respondere satagebat.'
63 *Ibid.*, 'Nec minus eum stimulavit cupiditas gratificandi mercatoribus quibusdam ipsi familiaribus et longo usu coniunctissimis, qui literas Arabice scriptas, ad tutelam plerunque navium et negotiatorum pertinentes, ut explicaret saepenumero eum rogarunt.'
64 Hamilton, *William Bedwell*, p. 40. Cf. above, p. 227.

1613, but one thousand seems a reasonable guess. The great European libraries nearly all possess at least one copy of it (the Vatican Library now has three, one of which belonged to the Maronite College in Rome), and, in contrast to later dictionaries in more than one volume, there is no indication that the publishers had any difficulty in selling their stock.[65]

A final aspect of Raphelengius's dictionary which should be taken into account is the validity of his main sources – of those two sources he quotes so frequently, the Mozarabic glossary and Pedro de Alcalá's *Vocabulista*. For over two and a half centuries these sources were all but completely rejected by the European lexicographers of Classical Arabic. From the first half of the seventeenth century until the second half of the nineteenth century European Arabists tended to use the great Arabic monolingual lexicons which I shall discuss later. These lexicons, however, were primarily intended for the readers and writers of poetry, and not for a general knowledge of Arabic as it was spoken throughout the Arab world. The first European to endeavour to remedy this situation was the Leiden Arabist R.P.A. Dozy, whose *Supplément aux dictionnaires arabes* appeared in 1881, two years before his death. His object was to study non-classical Arabic and to record words in everyday use. For his purpose Dozy consulted both the Mozarabic glossary, which he had already described in the first volume of the catalogue of Oriental manuscripts in the Leiden library, and the dictionary of Pedro de Alcalá. When he had first looked through the Mozarabic glossary, he admitted in 1875, he had not appreciated its value,[66] but when working on his own supplement he came to realize its true worth. Still more important for him was Pedro de Alcalá's *Vocabulista*.[67] Availing himself of an infinitely wider field of lexicographical material than had been available to Raphelengius, he could re-transliterate the *Vocabulista* in correct Arabic and could fully exploit the information it had to offer on Arabic as it was spoken. Dozy's objectives have been pursued by more recent

---

65   Isaac Casaubon, whose copy of the *Lexicon* is now in the BL, wrote eagerly to Erpenius on 13 June 1613: 'Vidi hic Lexicon Raphelengii, cum tuis Notis. Bene operam posuisti, et quid in eo genere eruditionis posses, luculente ostendisti: sed Grammaticam et Proverbia quando audiemus edita? Ego nullum adhuc exemplar illius Lexici potui hic nancisci. Duo tantum hactenus vidi exemplaria, unum in manibus Eliensis, alterum Oxonii apud Professorem Hebraeum.' (*Cas.Ep.*, p. 537).

66   On his first misgivings and later enthusiasm ('Le Glossaire ... est d'une très grande valeur ...') see Van Koningsveld, *The Latin-Arabic Glossary*, pp. 10–11. On Dozy see also J. Brugman and F. Schröder, *Arabic Studies in the Netherlands* (Leiden, 1979), pp. 36–37; A. Vrolijk and R. van Leeuwen, *Arabic Studies in the Netherlands. A Short History in Portraits, 1580–1950* (Leiden-Boston, 2014), pp. 95–102.

67   In his *Supplément aux dictionnaires arabes* (Leiden, 1881), vol. 1, p. x, he said that, of his Western sources, the *Vocabulista* was 'sans contredit le plus riche de tous.'

lexicographers and Raphelengius can thus be placed at the beginning of a tradition which was neglected in the intervening period but which has proved particularly fruitful since. He owes his place in this tradition to no choice of his own, to the limitations of his material rather than to the abundance of it, but so is sometimes the way of the development of scholarship.

3   Publication

Although Scaliger stated on the title-page of his 'Thesaurus Linguae Arabicae' that he had completed it in 1597, he continued to make certain additions to it in later years,[68] and, occupied though he was with his great *Thesaurus temporum*, we see from his letters to Isaac Casaubon and Etienne Hubert that he sustained his interest in Arabic until his death. Particularly in the letters written to his friends after the turn of the century Scaliger expressed a view of the study of Arabic which seems remarkably modern. He pointed out the dangers of studying it exclusively in association with Hebrew and stressed, rather, the use of Turkish and Persian. Why?

Probably owing to his interest in Turkish as a chronologist – this emerges clearly from his marginalia to Leunclavius's *Annales Sultanorum Othmanidarum* which was published in 1588[69] – Scaliger started collecting Ottoman manuscripts, albeit on a small scale. He lamented that his own knowledge of Turkish was far too limited for him to be able to put them to any use,[70] but he could nevertheless perceive certain features. His manuscripts, as we have seen, included various bilingual Islamic prayer-books, in Arabic and Turkish, which he lent to Raphelengius. More important still, they included an Arabic-Turkish dictionary[71] and a Persian-Turkish dictionary,[72] and it was these works, recently

---

68   For a full list of his sources see his letter to Etienne Hubert of 22 March 1608, *Scal.Cor.*, vol. 7, pp. 468–471. Judging from the manuscript of his *Thesaurus Linguae Arabicae* the additions were of no great significance: perhaps the most significant is the source added in later ink to his preface (fol. 1ᵛ): 'Grammaticarum perceptionum appendix in qua vocabularium Arabopersicum et Araboturcicum.' On the importance of these latter sources see below. When giving his sources Scaliger never seems to include Raphelengius's *Lexicon Arabico-Latinum*.

69   The copy is BL, Or. 70. b. 12.1 thank Anthony Grafton for drawing my attention to it.

70   'Utinam nancisci possem, qui Turcice intelligat, et scribat,' he wrote to Casaubon in January 1602 (*Scal.Cor.*, vol. 4, p. 181).

71   UBL, MS Or. 237.

72   UBL, MS Or. 227, That this and the previous manuscript were acquired after Raphelengius's death is confirmed by the addition to the sources listed in Scaliger's 'Thesaurus Linguae Arabicae'.

compiled and easily available in the Ottoman Empire, which fully revealed to Scaliger, just as they had perhaps done to Guillaume Postel some fifty years earlier,[73] the utility of Turkish, and indeed of Persian, lexicographical material for the study of Arabic. Frequently composed of extracts from the huge monolingual dictionaries produced by the Arabs themselves, the Arabic-Turkish and Arabic-Persian dictionaries, compiled for Turkish- and Persian-speaking students of Arabic and thus for readers studying Arabic as a foreign language, were a reliable guide to vocalization, to meaning, and often to grammar. These were instruments inaccessible to Raphelengius who, despite his use of Scaliger's bilingual prayerbooks and his own legal compendium with a Turkish paraphrase, as well as his efforts to learn Persian,[74] does not seem to have known any Turkish or to have possessed a single Arabic-Turkish or Arabic-Persian dictionary, let alone a monolingual Arabic lexicon.

If Raphelengius's dictionary remained in manuscript for so many years after his death this must to some extent have been owing to Scaliger and to his own reservations about what Raphelengius had accomplished. It was only after Scaliger's death in 1609 that the idea of publishing Raphelengius's work again gained momentum. The men immediately responsible were Raphelengius's two surviving sons, Frans and Joost. Both were competent Arabists. Joost, a botanist and a physician, had travelled widely in the Ottoman Empire, and when he returned to the Low Countries in 1602 he brought with him manuscripts which included one of the more popular Arabic-Turkish dictionaries, the *Mirqāt al-lugha*. Over ten years later, in the autumn of 1613, he went to the trouble of copying out his father's surviving writings on Arabic grammar.[75]

---

73 In 1553 Postel wrote to Masius: 'De Lexico Arabico fere nil solidioris spei concipere debes. Nam nec Jerosolymis, nec Damasci, nec Antiochiae, nec Constantinopoli licuit, praeter quaedam Elgeuhari compendia, reperire, unde coactus quidem sum adferre, sed Arabico-Turchicum et nondum conversum, aut Arabice aliave lingua praeter Turchicam aut Persicam explicatum, hoc autem est ignotum per ignotius.' (J.G. de Chaufepie, *Nouveau Dictionnaire Historique et Critique*, vol. 3 (Amsterdam, 1753), p. 221).

74 For Raphelengius's Persian studies see J.T.P. de Bruyn, *De ontdekking van het Perzisch* (Leiden, 1990), pp. 5–9.

75 On Joost Raphelengius see I. Tierlinck, 'Joost van Ravelingen, botanist en dichter' *Verslagen en Mededelingen der Koninklijke Vlaamsche Academie van Taal- en Letterkunde* (1911), pp. 870–892. His copy of the *Mirqāt al-lugha* came into the hands of Jacob Golius and is now at Oxford, Bodl., MS Marsh 466. I owe this information to Jan Just Witkam who discusses the fate of Golius' private collection of manuscripts in his *Jacob Golius (1596–1667) en zijn handschriften* (Leiden, 1980). Joost's attachment to Arabic is confirmed by Frans the Younger's letter to Balthasar Moretus of 7 June 1618. It contains a description of Joost's death. The last word he entered in his journal was 'bismilla' (MPM, Arch. 92, p. 223). For Joost and Frans as Arabists see also Jones, pp. 137–138, 142–143.

Frans was a classicist by training.[76] As we saw, he had already acquired Arabic manuscripts for his father in the 1590s, and the two brothers were probably responsible for the frequently expert descriptions of Franciscus the Elder's Arabic material in the 1626 sale catalogue.

It is possible that, in preparing their father's lexicon for the press, Frans and Joost were assisted by another Arabist – Raphelengius the Elder's pupil Jan Theunisz. Theunisz was a Mennonite who had acted at various periods in his life as an innkeeper, an interpreter, a bookseller, and a printer, and who was to teach Arabic at the University of Leiden from 1612 to 1613.[77] Shortly after Raphelengius's death Theunisz had been given permission by his eldest son, Christoffel, to copy out his entire lexicon – and the transcription, made before Christoffel's death in 1600, shows how faithful Frans and Joost were to the version left by their father.[78] Far less critical than Scaliger, Theunisz seems to have followed its fortunes closely and enthusiastically, and his combined competence as a printer and as an Arabist, who was to have his work in that domain published by the Officina Plantiniana in Leiden, suggests an involvement in the production of the book.[79]

The *Lexicon Arabico-Latinum* was in the press by the autumn of 1611. In October Thomas Erpenius, who also appears to have kept abreast of the publication from the outset, wrote from Paris to Isaac Casaubon that the younger Raphelengius, probably Frans, had shown him a set page of the lexicon containing part of the letter *bā'*.[80] The work, he told Casaubon, could be greatly

---

[76] On Frans the Younger see L. Voet, *The Golden Compasses. A History and Evaluation of the Printing and Publishing Activities of the Officina Plantiniana at Antwerp* (London-Amsterdam, 1969–72), vol. 1, pp. 172–177.

[77] On Theunisz see H.F. Wijnman, 'Jan Theunisz alias Joannes Antonides (1569–1637), boekverkooper en waard in het Muziekhuis "D'Os in de Bruyloft" te Amsterdam' *Jaarboek Amstelodamum*, 25 (1928), pp. 29–123; idem, 'De Hebraïcus Jan Theunisz. Barbarossius alias Johannes Antonides als lector in het Arabisch aan de Leidse universiteit (1612–1613). Een hoofdstuk Amsterdamse geleerdengeschiedenis' *Studia Rosenthaliana* 2 (1968), pp. 1–29, 149–77; and, more recently, D. van Dalen, 'Johannes Theunisz and 'Abd al-'Azīz: a friendship in Arabic studies in Amsterdam, 1609–1610' *Lias* 43 (2016), pp. 161–189, with interesting information (pp. 181–186) about the Arabic dictionary Theunisz himself was compiling, with meanings in both Latin and Dutch.

[78] Amsterdam University Library, MS III E 23. Cf. Wijnman, 'De Hebraicus Jan Theunisz.', pp. 9–10.

[79] *Ibid.*, p. 10.

[80] 'Raphelengius Leydae patris sui Dictionarium Arabicum excudit: quod sic satis bonum et copiosum futurum est, sed parum elegantibus typis. Vidi folium ejus xviii. continens partem literae ب: si scivissem id eum in animo habuisse, potuisset longe copiosius et infinite accuratius edi: si quidem alterius laborem cum patris sui conjungi passus esset. Fortassis absoluto Dictionario non invite opusculum nostrum Proverbiorum, et Grammaticam

improved by adding an appendix by someone else: he obviously had in mind the Arabic grammar he himself was preparing and which would have suited the original purpose of publishing the dictionary together with Raphelengius's own grammar. Judging from what Raphelengius's sons say in the introduction they at first agreed to this proposition, but then decided to publish Erpenius's grammar separately.[81] They asked him, rather, to append notes 'with which certain obscurities would be elucidated, problems explained, and errors corrected.' The sixty-eight pages of 'Observationes' turned out to be a major advance in European Arabic lexicography, and to the education, qualifications, and sources of the young author we should now turn.

Thomas Erpenius,[82] who was born in 1584, had graduated in 1608 at the University of Leiden where, encouraged by Scaliger, he had studied Hebrew besides theology, classical literature, and philosophy. With a letter from Scaliger he made his way to England and, in December 1608, took Arabic lessons from William Bedwell in the hope, he admitted, of improving his Hebrew. In January 1609 he left England for France where he spent most of the year in the company of Scaliger's friend Casaubon. In Paris Erpenius received further tuition in Arabic, first from the Egyptian Copt Josephus Barbatus or Abudacnus, and then from the learned Moroccan diplomat of Andalusian origin Aḥmad ibn Qāsim al-Ḥajarī. In the astonishingly short time of less than three years he all but completed the work that was to remain the best Arabic grammar in Europe until the nineteenth century, his *Grammatica Arabica* published by Raphelengius's sons immediately after their father's dictionary. Late in 1611 Erpenius left France for Venice from where he hoped to make his way to Istanbul. In this he failed. What he did do, with Scaliger's advice in mind, was to learn Turkish. 'As I once started to learn Arabic in order to improve my understanding of Hebrew,' he wrote to Casaubon on 15 May 1612, 'now I study

---

    meam Arabicam excudet. Nisi grave est, poteris id ei per amicos Leydenses significare: nam a me id non ita convenienter fiat.' (*Cas.Ep.*, p. 663).

81 *Lex.*, sig. **2ʳ: 'Lexicon hoc sine Grammaticae comitatu emittere coacti fuissemus, nisi M. THOMAS ERPENIUS pro suo erga defunctum amore, et studia Arabica promovendi ardore, una cum praestantissimis suis in hoc opus Annotationibus, Grammaticam suam Arabicam, brevem quidem, sed absolutam tamen et accuratam, nobis obtulisset; quam propediem in lucem edere constituimus, separatim quidem, sed eadem tamen qua hoc Lexicon prodit forma, ut cum eo compingi, viceque eius quam Auctor adiicere statuerat, fungi possit.' Erpenius's grammar, published in the same format as the dictionary, could be, and sometimes was, neatly bound together with it. See, for example, the copy belonging to the English Arabist Edward Pococke, Bodl., MS Poc. 407 and the copy in Amsterdam University Library, 1065 C 15.

82 For Erpenius see Jones, pp. 144–165; Vrolijk and Van Leeuwen, *Arabic Studies in the Netherlands*, pp. 31–40, 59; Juynboll, *Zeventiende-eeuwsche Beoefenaars*, pp. 59–118.

Turkish in order to know better Arabic.'[83] And in Venice he found, amidst various Arabic manuscripts, the Arabic-Turkish dictionary which was going to be the main source of his corrections to Raphelengius's lexicon:[84] the dictionary known as *al-Akhtarī*, compiled in 1545 by the Turkish lexicographer Muṣṭafā ben Shamsaddīn al-Qaraḥiṣārī.[85]

Al-Akhtarī was one of the most popular and most widely disseminated works of its kind and, for a European Arabist with no first-hand knowledge of the Arabic lexicographers, it could serve as a convenient by-path to the best of their work. For *al-Akhtarī* is based on the very finest monolingual Arabic lexicons – on the great works of the tenth century, the *Ṣiḥāḥ* by al-Jawharī and the *Mujmal* by Ibn Fāris; on the slightly later *Mughrib* by al-Muṭarrizī and the completion of al-Jawharī, *al-Takmila*, by the thirteenth-century lexicographer from Lahore, al-Ṣaghānī; and on one of the best Arabic-Persian dictionaries, al-Naṭanzī's *Dustūr al-lugha*. *Al-Akhtarī*, moreover, is conveniently arranged according to the first radical of the Arabic words, and although it is not generally vocalized, it describes the plurals and inflections, provides Arabic synonyms, and gives definitions partly in Arabic and partly in Turkish. In Erpenius's manuscript, the last page of which he excitedly ripped out to send to Casaubon, the Arabic words are overlined in blue.[86]

---

[83] 'Ut linguam Hebraeam solidius intelligerem, coepi olim Arabicam discere; ut Arabicam melius, nunc Turcicam.' BL, MS Burney 364, fol. 24ʳ. I am most grateful to Robert Jones for supplying me with a transcription of this letter.

[84] *Ibid.*: 'Item dictionarium Arabico-Turcicum elegantissimum et optimae notae, in quo quatuordecim millia vocum difficiliorum (nam faciliora pleraque, quaeque a positis facile derivari possunt, omittuntur) partim Arabice partim Turcice explicantur …'

[85] The sources of the dictionary are enumerated in the introduction written in Arabic. The work is described in G. Flügel, *Die arabischen, persischen und türkischen Handschriften der kaiserlichen Hofbibliothek zu Wien* (Vienna, 1865), vol. 1, MS 114. For al-Qarahisarī see Brockelmann, *Supplementband II*, p. 630.

[86] In his letter to Casaubon of 15 May 1611 Erpenius continued (fol. 24ʳ): 'Vidi hic alia dictionaria Arabica, bona quoque, sed cum hoc conferenda, tum quod multae voces difficiles in iis omittuntur, quas hoc exhibet, tum quod omnia Turcice explicantur versione inter lineas posita, cum meum pleraque Arabice declaret partim per synonyma, partim circumscriptive, idque textu continuo, cuique voci Arabicae quae explicatur nota alio colore superscripta, eo modo quo vides in hic paucis vocibus quae implent paginam unam, quales integrum opus continet 470. Adiunxi versionem Latinam quo minori molestia omnia intelligas.' Erpenius's manuscript is now CUL, MS Gg. 6.41. In one respect it differs from other manuscripts and from the printed editions of the work (Istanbul 1827, 1840): while the author normally refers to himself as Muṣṭafā ben Shamsaddīn al-Qaraḥiṣarī, in Erpenius's manuscript he calls himself Muṣṭafā ben Aḥmad al-Qaraḥiṣārī. As a result Erpenius refers to him, both in his 'Observationes' and in his letter to Casaubon, as 'Mustapha ben Achmed'.

In the middle of 1612 Erpenius journeyed back to Leiden where he hoped to oust Theunisz and to be appointed professor of Arabic.[87] On his way home he visited some of the great European collections of Arabic manuscripts, in Milan, in Basel, and above all in Heidelberg. Somewhere on his travels, perhaps in Venice, perhaps elsewhere, he saw one of the most important of the monolingual Arabic dictionaries, the *Qāmūs* compiled in the late fourteenth and early fifteenth centuries by the Persian lexicographer al-Fīrūzābādī and generally regarded as the first major advance on the *Ṣiḥāḥ*. In due course he was to acquire a copy, but for the time being he can only have seen one and taken notes from it.[88]

Erpenius was in Leiden in July 1612 and seems to have been given a few months in which to write his supplement to Raphelengius's dictionary. In February 1613 he would inform Casaubon that he had finished it 'hurriedly while the press was running'.[89] Although his many observations include a reference to the *Qāmūs* and comments about the 'Arab lexicographers' his main sources were three Arabic-Turkish dictionaries.[90] The main one was *al-Akhtārī*. Another must have been the untitled Arabic-Turkish vocabulary still among his manuscripts in Cambridge University Library, a brief work of 148 leaves, but vocalized and with the Arabic roots arranged according to the last radical.[91] The third Arabic-Turkish dictionary was in the collection of manuscripts Scaliger had bequeathed to the Leiden library on his death, the *Mirqāt al-lugha*,[92] a common work another copy of which, as we saw, Joost Raphelengius brought back from his travels in the Ottoman Empire. Scaliger's manuscript was copied in 1548. The work was probably compiled in the fifteenth or early sixteenth century and contains words taken from the *Ṣiḥāḥ* and the *Qāmūs* arranged according to the final radical. Like the untitled Cambridge vocabulary it is vocalized.

These were the three works which enabled Erpenius to spot so many mistakes in Raphelengius's dictionary. Erpenius's supplement consequently represents a vital intermediary stage in the study of Arabic in Europe. The future

---

87   The episode is described, and Theunisz's case argued forcefully, in Wijnman, 'De Hebraicus Jan Theunisz.', pp. 155–158.
88   He refers to it on p. xxxix of his 'Observationes'. On the availability of the *Qāmūs* in Europe at the time see Hamilton, *William Bedwell*, pp. 88, 152.
89   'Dictionarium Arab. Raph. jam absolutum est et meae in id castigationes quas festinanter et currente prelo scripsi ...' BL, MS Burney 364, fol. 26ʳ.
90   *Lex.*, 'Observationes', p. 1: 'Afferuntur quoque subinde dictiones quaedam ... quas nec usquam legi, nec in copiosissimis Arabico-Turcicis dictionariis, qualia tria habeo, invenio ...'
91   CUL, MS Gg. 6. 39.
92   Leid. Cod. Or. 237. Erpenius, *Lex.*, 'Observationes', p. xxxvii, refers to 'Auctor Dictionarii 'مرقات اللغه'.

of European Arabic lexicography lay in the discovery and use of the monolingual Arabic lexicons.[93] Erpenius himself, who toyed with, but later abandoned, the idea of producing an Arabic dictionary,[94] later acquired copies of both the *Qāmūs* and the *Ṣiḥāḥ*. He bought the *Qāmūs* through an agent in Istanbul in 1618[95] and the *Ṣiḥāḥ* in the following year,[96] and these works were to be the main sources of the first truly extensive European Arabic dictionaries, Antonio Giggei's dictionary of 1632 and above all Jacob Golius's *Lexicon Arabico-Latinum* of 1653, which, like the *Grammatica Arabica* of Erpenius, Golius's teacher and predecessor as Arabic professor at Leiden, was to remain unsurpassed until the nineteenth century. In 1612 Erpenius could only accede to those Arabic works indirectly, through Turkish excerpts, but by so doing he possessed a means of improving his knowledge of Arabic inaccessible to Raphelengius. Raphelengius's *Lexicon Arabico-Latinum*, as it was published in the first months of 1613, is a unique testimony of this development.

4   Raphelengius's Arabic Manuscripts

The last point I wish to discuss in this article is the fate of Raphelengius's Arabic manuscripts, a collection which, by the standards of the time, was remarkable. Some, if not all, of these manuscripts were lent to Scaliger. Scaliger studied them

---

93   For many years the standard study on the monolingual dictionaries was J.A. Haywood, *Arabic Lexicography: Its History and Its Place in the General History of Lexicography* (Leiden, 1965). For al-Jawharī see pp. 68–76 and Fīrūzābādī pp. 83–91. But see now R. Baalbaki, *The Arabic Lexicographical Tradition from the 2nd/8th to the 12th/18th Century* (Leiden-Boston, 2014). For al-Jawharī see pp. 373–381, and for Fīrūzābādī pp. 391–397.

94   Cf. his letter to Casaubon of 27 May 1614, BL, MS Burney 364, fol. 27[r–v]. After expressing his desire to produce a dictionary he continues (fol. 27[v]): 'Dictionarium malim ab aliis quam a me edi qui tamen tum ex pluribus ipsorum Arabum Dictionariis, tum ex quotidiana lectione, vim immensam vocum Arabicarum accuratissime vocalibus suis ornaturum congessi, et in ordinem redegi.' Evidence of Erpenius's plan to compile a dictionary himself is to be found in UBL, MS Or. 1649, a manuscript to which much has been added by later hands and which is of disappointingly little lexicographical interest, and Bodl., MS Bodl. Or. 347, Erpenius's interleaved copy of Raphelengius's dictionary which later belonged to Golius and which contains numerous manuscript notes by both men.

95   CUL, MS Gg.5.14. The information in E.G. Browne, *A Hand-List of the Muhammadan Manuscripts ... in the Library of the University of Cambridge* (Cambridge, 1900), p. 138, is misleading. Browne gives the year of acquisition as 1609, basing himself on an entry written on the inside of the binding, which he then mixes with the words on the title-page of the manuscript. The statement on the title-page is unequivocal: 'Dictionarium Arabicum omnium que extant praestantissimum KAMUS nuncupatum et Constantinopoli mihi emptum Asperis 10000, id est Ducatis aureis 79, et asperis 10. Anno Christi 1618. Thomas Erpenius.'

96   CUL, MS Dd. 2. 38.

exhaustively, occasionally he even wrote marginalia in them (the Mozarabic glossary is an example), but he never owned them. After Raphelengius's death they remained the property of his sons and heirs, Christoffel, who died in 1600, Frans the Younger, and Joost.

Scaliger died in 1609 leaving some forty Arabic manuscripts to the Leiden library.[97] These are listed by Daniel Heinsius as the only Arabic manuscripts in the library's possession in the catalogue of 1612. They are again listed by Heinsius, but with a more detailed description, in the catalogue of 1623. The very same description is included in the following catalogues of 1636 and 1640 – and this is where we encounter a problem. For on 5 October 1626 the firm of Elzevier in Leiden held a public auction of books belonging to the elder Raphelengius and his sons, and the material put up for sale included Raphelengius's entire collection of Arabic manuscripts as we now know it. Unfortunately there are no records of how much money the university spent at that sale or of what the library bought, but it is very likely that the curators did buy at it.[98] So why does Raphelengius's collection of Arabic manuscripts not appear in the catalogues of 1636 and 1640? To this I can give no certain answer. There would seem to be two possibilities: either the manuscripts were bought by a third party who sold them to the library on a subsequent occasion, or they were indeed bought by the library, were placed in the 'arca Scaligerana',[99] the same bookcase as the manuscripts Scaliger bequeathed, and Heinsius, the compiler of the 1636 and 1640 catalogues, ever more negligent in his office as librarian and ignorant of Arabic, simply failed to include them.

That the latter hypothesis may be correct is suggested by a note stuck onto the flyleaf of MS Or. 222, the manuscript discovered amongst the spoils of Lepanto. On it is scribbled in a contemporary hand *Heinsio uyte de cassa van D. Scaligero Extra catalogum*. And that the manuscripts were lodged at a relatively early stage in the Scaliger case is confirmed by their subsequent fate: they are all included in the catalogue of 1674 compiled by Frederik Spanheim and appear there under 'Manuscripti legati Scaligeriani'. From that time on no distinction was made between the manuscripts that had once belonged to Raphelengius and those that had once belonged to Scaliger, and in 1741, in the three months in which he acted as librarian, David van Royen stuck into all

---

97   For Scaliger's legacy see Van Ommen, *'Tous mes livres'*, pp. 157–175.
98   E. Hulshoff Pol, 'The Library' in Lunsingh Scheurleer and Posthumus Meyjes, eds, *Leiden University in the Seventeenth Century*, p. 430: 'The Curators possibly gave their permission for purchase at the Raphelengius auction ...' The hypothesis is further strengthened by the presence in the library of so many of the books put up for sale.
99   For the 'arca Scaligerana' see Van Ommen, *'Tous mes livres'*, pp. 170–175, and for the Leiden catalogues, pp. 187–211.

the manuscripts, indiscriminately, the slip of paper they now bear with the words 'Ex legato illustris viri Josephi Scaligeri'.[100] True, there are only ten of Raphelengius's Arabic manuscripts, but they include some very remarkable items of as great, if not greater, interest than those collected by Scaliger himself, and are an enduring tribute to the author of the first Arabic-Latin dictionary ever to be published.[101]

Appendix: Raphelengius's Arabic Manuscripts in the Leiden University Library

Each entry is accompanied by the appropriate reference in *Lex.*, *Cat.Raph.*, and *CCO*. The (approximate) date of the manuscript is given together with the titles of works in which it is described or discussed.

MS Or. 214
26 chapters from the Gospel of St Matthew and 9 chapters from the Gospel of St Mark. Late sixteenth century (?). *Lex.*, sig. *3ᵛ, nos 7 and 8; *Cat.Raph.*, sig. I3ʳ, no. 7; *CCO*, vol. 5, p. 80, no. 2371; C.R. Gregory, *Textkritik des Neuen Testaments* (Leipzig, 1900), p. 586, no. 45.

MS Or. 218
Gospel of St Mark. Late sixteenth century (?). Same references as MS Or. 214, except for *CCO*, vol. 5, p. 80, no. 2372; Gregory, *Textkritik*, p. 586, no. 47.

MS Or. 222
Wiqāyat al-riwāyā fī masāʾil al-Hidāya by Burhānaddīn Ṣadr al-Sharīʿa al-Auwal al-Maḥbūbī. Sixteenth century (?). MS discovered amongst the spoils of the battle of Lepanto. *Lex.*, sig. 4*ʳ, no. 13; *Cat.Raph.*, sig. I3ʳ, no. 11; *CCO*, vol. 4, p. 120, no. 1801; R. Jones, 'Piracy, War, and the acquisition of Arabic manuscripts' *Manuscripts of the Middle East* 2 (1987), pp. 100–101; idem, *Learning Arabic in Renaissance Europe (1505–1624)* (Leiden-Boston 2020), pp. 34–36.

MS Or. 228
Qurʾan with fragments from suras 21, 22, 23, 24, 25 and 26. Twelfth century. *Lex.*, sig. 4*ʳ, no. 12; *Cat.Raph.*, sig. I3ʳ, no. 13; *CCO*, vol. 4, p. 1, no. 1609; T. Nöldeke, *Geschichte des Qorâns* (Göttingen, 1860), p. 346.

---

100   P.C. Molhuysen, *Geschiedenis der Universiteits-Bibliotheek te Leiden* (Leiden, 1905), p. 37.
101   The same applies to Raphelengius's Hebrew manuscripts. See the next article.

MS Or. 230
Pentateuch with Patristic commentaries. Karshuni. 1528. *Lex.*, sig. 3*ᵛ, nos 2 and 3; *Cat.Raph.*, sig. I2ᵛ, no. 6; *CCO*, vol. 5, p. 76, no. 2364.

MS Or. 231
Mozarabic Latin-Arabic glossary, c. 1175. *Lex.*, sig. 3*ᵛ, no. 9; *Cat.Raph.*, sig. I3ʳ, no. 9; *CCO*, vol. 1, p. 94, no. 170; C.F. Seybold, *Glossarium Latino-Arabicum* (Berlin, 1900); P.S. van Koningsveld, *The Latin-Arabic Glossary of the Leiden University Library* (Leiden, 1977).

MS Or. 235
1) *al-Muqaddima al-kāfiyya al-muḥsiba fī 'l-naḥw* by Abū 'l-Ḥassan Ṭāhir b. Aḥmad b. Idrīs ibn Bābashādh. 31 January 1519. Copied for Egidio da Viterbo; 2) *al-Ajurrūmiyya* by Abū ʿAlī b. Dāʾūd al-Ṣanhājī ibn Ajurrūm. 12 December 1518. Copied for Egidio da Viterbo; 3) the first pages of 1). *Lex.*, sig. 4*ᵛ, no. 17; *Cat. Raph.*, sig. I3ʳ, no. 10; *CCO*, vol. 1, p. 28, nos 47 and 48; p. 43, no. 73.

MS Or. 241
Qurʾan. Fragments from suras 33 to 37. Fifteenth century. Once in the possession of Rutger Rescius and then of Andreas Masius. *Cat.Raph.*, sig. I3ʳ; *CCO*, vol. 4, p. 4, no. 1629; T. Dunkelgrün, 'From Tunis to Leiden across Renaissance Europe: The curious career of a maghribi Qurʾan', *Omslag. Bulletin van de Universiteitsbibliotheek Leiden en het Scaliger Instituut* 3 (2009), pp. 7–8; *idem*, 'The Hebrew library of a Renaissance humanist. Andreas Masius and the bibliography to his *Iosuae Imperatoris Historiae* (1574), with a Latin edition and an annotated English translation' *Studia Rosenthaliana* 42–43 (2010–11), pp. 197–252, esp. pp. 216–217; A. Hamilton, 'The perils of catalogues' *Journal of Islamic Manuscripts* 1 (2010), pp. 31–36, esp. p. 34.

MS Or. 246
Sharḥ taṣrīf al-Zanjānī by ʿAlī b. Muḥammad b. ʿAlī al-Afzarī. Sixteenth century (?). *Lex.*, sig. 4*ᵛ, no. 16; *Cat.Raph.*, sig. I3ʳ, no. 8; *CCO*, vol. 1, p. 50, no. 808.

MS Or. 251
Qurʾan. Two fragments in different hands from suras 28, 29, 30, 31, 32, 33 and 39. Twelfth or early thirteenth century. *Lex.*, sig. 4*ʳ, no. 12; *Cat.Raph.*, sig. I3ʳ, no. 12; *CCO*, vol. 4, p. 1, no. 1608; T. Nöldeke, *Geschichte des Qorâns*, p. 346; E. Braches, 'Raphelengius's Naschi and Maghribi. Some reflections on the origin of Arabic typography in the Low Countries' in *Quaestiones Leidenses* (Leiden, 1975), p. 29.

MS Acad. 2

The Pauline Epistles and Acts of the Apostles. That this fourteenth-century codex was actually owned by Raphelengius (but was never regarded as part of the Scaliger collection) is argued persuasively by Vevian Zaki, 'The "Egyptian Vulgate" in Europe: An investigation into the version that shaped European scholarship on the Arabic Bible' *Collectanea Christiana Orientalia* 18 (2021), pp. 237–259, esp. pp. 247–248, 253–254.

Acknowledgements

This article first appeared in Marcus de Schepper and Francine de Nave, eds, *Ex Officina Plantiniana. Studia in memoriam Christophori Plantini (ca. 1520–1589)* (Antwerpen: Vereeniging der Antwerpsche Bibliophielen, 1989 = *De Gulden Passer* 66–67 (1988–89)), pp. 557–589. In writing it I was constantly in the debt of Jan Just Witkam. My deepest gratitude is also due to the late Jan Brugman and to Henk-Jan de Jonge for their comments on a first draft of the text, and to the late Ronald Breugelmans, Robert Jones, Francine de Nave, Hans Trapman and Joanna Weinberg for their advice.

CHAPTER 13

Franciscus Raphelengius
The Hebraist and His Manuscripts

Franciscus Raphelengius's greatest contribution to scholarship was his Arabic-Latin lexicon published posthumously in 1613. He has consequently gone down to history as one of the first European Arabists. Yet, like most of his contemporaries who studied Arabic, he began with Hebrew. In a short time he became a Hebraist with an international reputation, and as an editor, as a printer and as a professor he promoted the study of Hebrew with unceasing industry.

Raphelengius learnt Hebrew in Paris in the late 1550s under Jean Mercier.[1] In 1566 Christophe Plantin, for whom he had been working as a proof-corrector in Antwerp since 1564 and whose daughter Margaretha he had married, wrote of his proficiency in Latin, Greek, Hebrew and Aramaic.[2] Soon after he could add Syriac. By 1568 Raphelengius was one of a team of scholars known for their skill in Semitic languages who were engaged in editing the *Biblia Regia*, the Antwerp polyglot Bible, under the supervision of the Spanish theologian Benito Arias Montano.[3] The plan had been conceived by Plantin some years earlier and the editors included Andreas Masius and the two Lefèvre de la Boderie brothers, Guy and Nicolas, both pupils of Guillaume Postel who had probably introduced Raphelengius to the study of Arabic.

Raphelengius's part in the undertaking was considerable. Although he was assisted by his fellow editors he was largely responsible for preparing and emending the Latin translation of the Old Testament made by the Italian

---

1 For biographical details and further literature on Raphelengius see F. de Nave, 'Franciscus I Raphelengius (1539–1597), grondlegger van de Arabische studiën in de Nederlanden' in M. de Schepper and F. de Nave, eds, *Studia in Memoriam Christophori Plantini (ca. 1520–1589)* (Antwerpen, 1989) (= *Gulden Passer* 66–67 (1988–1989)), pp. 523–555. Cf. also L. Voet, *The Golden Compasses. A History and Evaluation of the Printing and Publishing Activities of the Officina Plantiniana at Antwerp* (London-Amsterdam, 1969–1972), vol. 1, pp. 147–151.
2 *CP*, vol. 1, p. 50.
3 For a survey see A. Hamilton, 'In search of the most perfect text: The early modern printed Polyglot Bibles from Alcalá (1510–1520) to Brian Walton (1654–1658)' in E. Cameron, ed., *The New Cambridge History of the Bible, Volume 3. From 1450 to 1750* (Cambridge, 2016), pp. 138–156, esp. pp. 143–147.

Hebraist Sanctes Pagnini and first printed about forty years previously.[4] The translation, exceptionally literal and reliant on some of the Jewish medieval commentaries, frequently conflicted with the Vulgate. Initially it had been welcomed as a major advance in Hebrew studies and approved by the ecclesiastical authorities. In the course of the sixteenth century, however, it was criticized increasingly. The quality of the Latin, the rendering of the Hebrew, and above all the orthodoxy of the translation were called in doubt. Arias Montano insisted on its inclusion in the Polyglot – it appeared in the sixth volume with his introduction – but to publish it at all after the deliberations of the Council of Trent was a bold enterprise and an obstacle in gaining official approval when Plantin completed the Bible's publication in 1572.

Of the various editions of Pagnini's Old Testament since its appearance in 1528 the one in the *Biblia Regia* was the first to be bilingual. In his introduction Arias Montano stressed the importance of the translation for students of Hebrew. Pagnini's Latin was thus printed from right to left above the interlinear Hebrew text. The emendations, printed in italics with Pagnini's version in the margin, were mainly intended to give a more literal or a more accurate rendering of the original and, sometimes, to improve the elegance of the Latin.

Besides the laborious preparation of Pagnini's work Raphelengius made a number of contributions to the critical apparatus in the last two volumes of the Polyglot. He is said to have compiled the Greek glossary.[5] He edited Pagnini's Hebrew grammar and dictionary which were based on the writings of the great rabbinic philologist David Kimhi. The Hebrew dictionary was also issued by Plantin as an independent publication and in the fourth edition, which he himself published in Leiden in 1588, Raphelengius expanded the Aramaic wordlist at the end. Indeed, it was in the field of Aramaic studies that he made his most important mark as a Hebraist. He was extolled by Guy Lefèvre de la Boderie for improving the vocalization of the Targums, the Aramaic paraphrases of the Old Testament printed in the *Biblia Regia* beneath

---

4   Cf. B. Rekers, *Benito Arias Montano (1527–1598)* (London-Leiden, 1972), pp. 45–69. On the significance of the Sanctes Pagnini translation for Hebrew studies see G. Lloyd Jones, *The Discovery of Hebrew in Tudor England: a Third Language* (Manchester, 1982), pp. 40–44. On the Pagnini editions see J. Le Long, C.F. Boerner and A.G. Masch, *Bibliotheca Sacra* (Halle, 1778–1785), vol. 3, pp. 473–489. For Pagnini see A. Morisi Guerra, 'Santi Pagnini traducteur de la Bible' in I. Backus and F. Higman, eds, *Théorie et pratique de l'exégèse: Actes du troisième colloque international sur l'histoire de l'exégèse biblique au XVIe siècle (Genève, 30 août–2 septembre 1988)* (Geneva, 1990), pp. 191–198; B. Gordon and E. Cameron, 'Latin Bibles in the early modern period' in Cameron, ed., *The New Cambridge History of the Bible, Volume 3*, pp. 187–216, esp. pp. 198–200.

5   Voet, *The Golden Compasses*, vol. 1, p. 149.

the Hebrew and the Vulgate.[6] For the critical apparatus he composed the *Variae lectiones et annotatiunculae, quibus Thargum, id est, Chaldaica paraphrasis infinitis in locis illustratur et emendatur*. Here he provided variant readings of words in the Targums taken from two manuscripts brought respectively from Rome by Masius and from Spain by Arias Montano, and from the two standard printed versions, the Venice edition published by Daniel Bomberg in 1518 and the one in the Complutensian Polyglot Bible of 1517 on which the text in the *Biblia Regia* was largely based. In his brief tract, which ended with a list of passages he regarded as redundant, Raphelengius displayed a considerable acquaintance with rabbinic sources and gave indications, clear and critically responsible, of his own preferences.

As a result of his participation in the *Biblia Regia* Raphelengius could also exploit his knowledge of Syriac. The Syriac Bible printed in Hebrew characters by Plantin in 1575 has a seven-page appendix drawn up by Raphelengius, *Variae lectiones ex Novi Testamenti Syrici manuscripto codice Coloniensi*. This appendix contains variants derived from a two-volume Syriac manuscript of the New Testament, the first volume, dating from the twelfth or thirteenth century, with the Gospels and a liturgical section, and the second, dating from the early sixteenth century, with Acts and the Epistles. The codex was acquired by Postel in Constantinople and brought to Venice at the expense of the younger Daniel Bomberg in 1550. Bomberg subsequently sent it from Cologne to Antwerp at Plantin's request. In Antwerp it was used by Guy Lefèvre de la Boderie who collated it with Widmanstadt's 1555 edition when he was preparing his version of the Syriac New Testament for the Polyglot. At the same time Lefèvre de la Boderie edited the liturgical section from the 'codex Coloniensis' for publication by Plantin in 1572, *D. Severi Alexandrini quondam patriarchae de ritibus baptismi, et sacrae synaxis apud Syros Christianos receptis, liber*. That the manuscript should now be in Leiden University Library (MS Or. 1198 a–b) suggests that it may have remained in Raphelengius's possession after the completion of the *Biblia Regia* and that he brought it from Antwerp to Leiden. There is insufficient evidence to establish this with any certainty, however.[7]

---

6 *Biblia Sacra* (Antwerp, 1572), vol. 5, sig. †7ᵛ: 'In quorum omnium impressione, indefesso labore, doctissimi ac diligentissimi correctoris officio functus est Franciscus Raphelengius, Plantini gener, cui, ut ornato multarum linguarum peritia, studiosi omnes acceptum ferre debent, quod nunc habeant universam paraphrasim Chaldaicam, longe emendatiorem quam hactenus prodierat, punctorum affixione ad analogiam librorum Danielis et Esrae ubique revocata.'

7 On the manuscript see CCO, vol. 5, pp. 64–67; C.R. Gregory, *Textkritik des Neuen Testaments* (Leipzig, 1909), pp. 497, 513, no. 67.1 can find no sign of the manuscript either in the auction catalogue of Raphelengius's manuscripts or in any seventeenth century catalogue of the Leiden library. The first time it appears to be mentioned is in the catalogue compiled by the Leiden Arabist Johannes Heyman between 1710 and 1716, UBL, Cod. Or. 1372, VI, fols 2518–2519.

With the *Biblia Regia* Raphelengius made his name as a Hebraist. His scholarly ability and the pains he took in correcting the proofs of the Bible drew the highest praise from Arias Montano, who clearly felt an affection for Raphelengius which all the scholars who knew him seem to have shared. In the preface to the Polyglot the Spanish theologian spoke of him with an enthusiasm he expended on few of his other collaborators, referring to his 'extreme industry', his 'incredible diligence', his perspicacious mind and superior judgement.'[8]

Plantin commented on his son-in-law's learning in a more reserved tone. 'Quant à mes gendres,' he wrote to Philip II's secretary Gabriel de Zayas in 1572, 'le premier n'a oncques rien prins à cueur que la cognoisance des langues latine, grecque, hébraicque, chaldée, syrienne, arabe (èsquelles chaicun qui familièrement confère avec luy afferme qu'il n'y est pas mal versé) et des lectres humaines et à bien, léalement, soigneusement et fidèlement corriger ce qui luy est enchargé sans mesmes se vouloir ostenter, monstrer ou venir en cognoissance de plusiers car il est fort solitaire et assidu aux labeurs qui luy sont commis.'[9] Shy and retiring, Raphelengius showed little interest in the business side of the Officina Plantiniana. He continued to live with his family, in cramped conditions, on his father-in-law's premises. He went on correcting proofs in the company of his two most assiduous colleagues, the translator, etymologist and lexicographer Cornelis Kiliaan, and the poet Bernardus Sellius.[10] Above all, encouraged by a widening circle of scholarly friends, he pursued his own studies, concentrating now on Arabic.

By the time he left Antwerp for Leiden in January 1586 Raphelengius had become one of the most competent Arabists of his day. Arabic, however, was a new subject; Hebrew had an accepted place in the university curriculum. So, within six months of his arrival in Leiden, following the departure of Johannes Drusius for Franeker, he was appointed professor extraordinary of Hebrew, and in February 1587 he was given a full professorship, the first in the subject at the recently founded university. Although he also gave instruction in Arabic his chair remained in Hebrew until his death in 1597.

---

8   *Biblia Sacra*, vol. 1, sig.***1ᵛ: 'Maximam vero partem eorum, quae hic diligenter correcta, exornata, perpolita et elaborata sunt, Francisci Raphelingii, quem sibi generum Plantinus adscivit, summae industriae, incredibili diligentiae, continuae sedulitati, perspicaci ingenio, et praestanti iudicio, acceptam referre debes. Te enim Lector iudicem appello, ut ex operis ipsius magnitudine, praestantia, et dignitate tute aestimes quot et quales fuerint huius viri labores, et quam insignis antiquarum linguarum peritia; qua, meo quidem iudicio, nemini suo iure cedit. Amplissimus enim hic scientiarum, et linguarum Thesaurus se, huius viri ope, et industriae ita ut vides, correctissimum in lucem prodisse, sua raritate et excellentia aperte testatur.'
9   *CP*, vol. 3, p. 244.
10 Cf. A. Hamilton and C.L. Heesakkers, 'Bernardus Sellius Noviomagus (c. 1551–93), proofreader and poet' *Quaerendo* 19 (1989), pp. 163–227, esp. pp. 163–165.

The principal purpose of Raphelengius's move to Leiden was to manage the local branch of the Officina Plantiniana opened by his father-in-law in 1583.[11] In March 1586 he was nominated printer to the university. Here too his interest in Hebrew studies was evident. Even if he was to leave the management of the firm more and more to his sons, he was at least partially responsible for the thirteen books which the Officina published in Hebrew before his death. Together with the single Hebrew publication produced by Plantin in Leiden in 1585 these were the first books to be printed with Hebrew moveable type in the Northern Netherlands. Of exemplary typographical quality, they remained models for later printers.[12]

To say that Raphelengius approached Arabic as a Hebraist is not to do justice to his achievements as a lexicographer. Compared to many of his contemporaries Raphelengius was remarkably sensitive to the independence of Arabic.[13] Yet, because of the works he used to study Arabic, Hebrew intrusions were inevitable. The first book he read in Arabic was the polyglot Pentateuch printed in Hebrew characters in Istanbul by Gerson Soncino in 1546. The texts are in Hebrew, Aramaic, Judaeo-Arabic and Judaeo-Persian, and the effect on Raphelengius of the alphabet can be seen not only in certain mistranscriptions in his lexicon but also in the Persian glossary he compiled from the Pentateuch. It was copied by his colleague in Leiden, Joseph Justus Scaliger,[14] and the Persian is left in Hebrew characters. In his Arabic lexicon, moreover, Raphelengius made frequent use of the Hebrew works of the rabbinic philologists. He refers again and again to David Kimhi, Abraham Ibn Ezra, and, above all, to Nathan ben Jehiel's *Arukh*, in order to establish similarities between Arabic and Hebrew and to provide Hebrew equivalents of Arabic words.

So great a student of Hebrew might be expected to have owned a collection of Hebrew manuscripts as singular as his collection of Arabic ones.[15] Six Hebrew codices are listed in the only reliable indication of what Raphelengius possessed, the sale catalogue of the manuscripts belonging to his heirs and put

---

11 For Raphelengius's activities as a printer in Leiden and a bibliography see K. van Ommen, *'Tous mes livres de langues estrangeres'. Het oosterse legaat van Joseph Justus Scaliger in de Universiteitsbibliotheek Leiden* (Leiden, 2020), pp. 31–36.
12 For an assessment and a full list of Raphelengius's Hebrew publications see L. Fuks and R.G. Fuks-Mansfeld, *Hebrew typography in the Northern Netherlands 1585–1815. Historical Evaluation and Descriptive Bibliography* (Leiden, 1984–87), vol. 1, pp. 11, 12, 15–26.
13 Raphelengius's achievements as an Arabist are discussed above, pp. 229–248.
14 UBL, MS Scal. 57. For Raphelengius's Persian studies see J.T.P. de Bruyn, *De ontdekking van het Perzisch* (Leiden, 1990), pp. 5–9.
15 Discussed above. The Arabic manuscripts are listed on pp. 251–253.

up for auction by Elzevier in Leiden in 1626.[16] Of the six it has been possible to trace three in Leiden University Library.

These Hebrew manuscripts experienced the same fate as Raphelengius's entire Arabic collection.[17] They were undoubtedly all consulted by Scaliger, who arrived in Leiden in the summer of 1593 and died in 1609, leaving his manuscripts to the university. Contrary to the accepted belief, Scaliger never owned the codices collected by Raphelengius. They appear nowhere in the lists Scaliger drew up of his own holdings or in the 1612 catalogue containing a description of his bequest to the Leiden library. After Raphelengius's death in 1597 his collection became the property of his heirs, and it was his two youngest sons, Frans the Younger and Joost, who put it up for sale in 1626. After the auction held by Elzevier on 5 October all the Arabic manuscripts and the three traceable Hebrew ones must have been purchased, directly or indirectly, by Leiden University. The librarian, Daniel Heinsius, probably placed the Raphelengius manuscripts in the bookcase containing the Scaliger bequest, the 'arca Scaligerana',[18] and failed to include them in his catalogues of 1636 and 1640. Over thirty years later Frederik Spanheim the Younger, the compiler of the next catalogue, found the manuscripts in the Scaliger bookcase and assumed they had belonged to him. They thus appear in the catalogue of 1674 under 'Manuscripti legati Scaligeriani'. In 1741 David van Royen, who acted as interim librarian for three months, stuck into them the slip of paper which they still bear with the words 'Ex legato illustris viri Josephi Scaligeri'. Just as Raphelengius's ten Arabic manuscripts include some of the most impressive items Scaliger has been credited with having collected, so Raphelengius's three Hebrew works are among the prize exhibits of the Hebrew 'Manuscripti Scaligeriani'.

Perhaps the most intriguing of the Raphelengius Hebrew codices is MS Scal. Hebr. 8 (MS Or. 4725), the *Psalterium Hebraycum*, a Hebrew Psalter with fine illuminated initials and Latin glosses which has been studied by G.I. Lieftinck.[19]

---

16   *Catalogus Variorum Librorum e Bibliothecis Francisci Raphelengii Hebraeae linguae quondam Professoris & Academiae Leidensis Typographi, ejusque filiorum* ... (Leiden, 1626).
17   See above for their fate.
18   For the 'arca' see Van Ommen, 'Tous mes livres', pp. 170–175, and for the Leiden catalogues pp. 187–211.
19   G.I. Lieftinck, 'The "Psalterium Hebraycum" from St Augustine's Canterbury rediscovered in the Scaliger bequest at Leyden' *Transactions of the Cambridge Bibliographical Society* 2 (1955), pp. 97–107. The account that follows is entirely based on Lieftinck's admirable reconstruction. Understandably, but wrongly, Lieftinck believes that 'the present manuscript is one of the few Hebrew manuscripts of the J.J. Scaliger Bequest and has therefore been preserved in this library since 1609.' The Psalter is the first item mentioned in the manuscript section of the auction catalogue: *Cat.Raph.*, p. 68, no 1, 'Psalterium

It was copied by a Christian[20] in England in the middle of the twelfth century and, over the years, it was used as a means of learning Hebrew. By the fourteenth century it was in the library of St Augustine's Abbey in Canterbury after belonging to John of Sturrey, a precentor of St Augustine's. In all likelihood it was removed from the abbey library by that ardent collector Humphrey, duke of Gloucester. After the duke's death in 1447 it found its way, together with a number of Duke Humphrey's other manuscripts, into the library of Henry VI's new foundation, King's College, Cambridge. By the second half of the sixteenth century the manuscript had again changed hands and had been presented to Thomas More's son-in-law William Roper.

How and when Raphelengius acquired the manuscript remains open to speculation. If Lieftinck's hypothesis is correct Raphelengius would have obtained it before his arrival in Antwerp in 1564, possibly during his stay in England in 1562–3. It would then be a unique testimonial of Raphelengius's scarcely documented English visit, even suggesting an acquaintance with Roper. Yet Roper died in 1578, after an honourable career as protonotary of the king's bench all the more remarkable because of his avowed Roman Catholicism. Had Raphelengius received the manuscript directly from Roper this would indeed have been a generous gesture on the part of a man who can hardly have known Plantin's future son-in-law well – certainly less well than his Arabic teacher Guillaume Postel and his fellow editor of the Polyglot Bible Andreas Masius who presented Raphelengius with some of his most precious Arabic manuscripts. So it is conceivable that Raphelengius only received the manuscript after Roper's death, when he was living in Antwerp or even in Leiden. The owners' marks on the first leaf with the names of Raphelengius and his two sons, Frans the Younger and Joost, appear to have been designed by the letter-founder Thomas de Vechter in Leiden and can be dated between 1589 and 1597.

Raphelengius's second Hebrew codex in the Leiden library is MS Scal. Hebr. 2 (MS Or. 4719).[21] It is an immense folio volume, striking for both its size,

---

Hebraicum, cum Annotationibus latinis, in membranis'. Cf. also M. Steinschneider, *Catalogus Codicum Hebraeorum Bibliothecae Lugduno-Batavorum* (Leiden, 1858), p. 349; A. van der Heide, *Hebrew Manuscripts of Leiden University Library* (Leiden, 1977), pp. 4, 9, 62.

20 On the manuscript's non-Jewish authorship and the 'typical Ashkenazi square script' see M. Beit-Arié, *The Only Dated Medieval Hebrew Manuscript Written in England (1189 CE) and the Problem of Pre-expulsion Anglo-Hebrew Manuscripts* (London, 1985), pp. 7–8, 21.

21 *Cat.Raph.*, p. 68, no. 3: 'Volumen magnum in Pergameno, in fol. majore, continens varios Tractatus Medicos Averrhois, vel Rhasis & Avicennae; item excerpta Ali & Rhazi ex Galeno & Hippocrate, &c. omnia Hebraice. Item Galeni Commentarium in Aphorismos Hippocratis, Arabice, sed charactere Hebraeo.' This largely accurate description is

425 × 293 mm., and its content. The manuscript, which Raphelengius must have obtained in about 1580[22] when he was still in Antwerp, dates from the second half of the fourteenth century and was compiled in Spain. It contains twenty medical treatises which have been described and discussed by Moritz Steinschneider.[23] The majority of the works are Hebrew translations of Arabic texts – treatises by, and commentaries on, some of the greatest scholars and physicians, Avicenna, Averroes, Rhazes, 'Ali ben Riḍwān and Maimonides. The rarest pieces, however, are Hebrew versions of Arabic translations of the Greek physicians Hippocrates and Galen. The Greek had been translated into Arabic by Ḥunayn ben Isḥāq in the ninth century and the Hebrew renderings were made by Natan Hamati in the early thirteenth century and Kalonymos ben Kalonymos a hundred years later. Of the Galenic works four were only known in this particular manuscript.[24] It consequently aroused the interest of the Leiden medical faculty. Under the supervision of Pieter Pauw, the professor of anatomy, Raphelengius undertook the translation of Galen's treatise on clysters and colics.[25] To his Latin version of Kalonymos ben Kalonymos' Hebrew he added aphorisms by Maimonides taken from the same manuscript. *Cl. Galeni pergameni de clysteribus et colica liber: A Iohannito a Graeca in Arabicam, et inde a Kalonymo in Hebraeam linguam, translatus* was published by the Officina Plantiniana in Leiden in 1591 and affectionately dedicated to the editor's son

---

incorrect in stating that Galen's commentary on the aphorisms of Hippocrates is in Arabic. Like many of the other texts this one too (no. 8) was translated from Greek into Arabic by Honain ben Isḥāq and from Arabic into Hebrew by Natan Hamati. Van der Heide, *Hebrew Manuscripts*, pp. 3, 10, 49, bases his assumption that Scaliger owned the codex on summary descriptions in the surviving lists of Scaliger's manuscripts (MSS Dupuy and Vulcanius which he publishes on pp. 20–23). The reference in MS Dupuy is far too fragmentary to permit any identification: 'Liber ... Ingens et luculentum Volumen'. The two references in MS Vulcanius, 'Hebraicus codex Medicus, Ms.' and 'Liber Medicinae alius Hebr., MS' apply to MSS Scal. Hebr. 11 and 15 respectively. These two manuscripts from the library of the French ambassador in Istanbul and Venice, Jean Hurault de Boistailler, definitely belonged to Scaliger.

22 Cf. Raphelengius's preface to *Cl. Galeni Pergameni De Clysteribus et Colica Liber* (Leiden, 1591), p. 3: 'Incidit in manus meas, anni sunt circiter decem, Juste fili, volumen Tractatuum Medicorum Hebraea lingua in membrana manu scriptum.'

23 There is a detailed and useful description in Steinschneider, *Catalogus*, pp. 311–341. The manuscript is also discussed in *idem, Die hebräischen Uebersetzungen des Mittelalters und die Juden als Dolmetscher. Ein Beitrag zur Literaturgeschichte des Mittelalters, meist nach handschriftlichen Quellen* (Berlin, 1893), pp. 652, 653, 659, 663, 676, 677, 683, 699, 700, 711, 728, 733, 734, 748, 775.

24 Nos 15, 16, 17 and 18. Cf. Steinschneider, *Die hebräischen Uebersetzungen*, pp. 652–653, 663.

25 No. 16. Cf. Steinschneider, *Die hebräischen Uebersetzungen*, p. 653. Pauw's collaboration is described in the preface to *Cl. Galeni Pergameni De Clysteribus et Colica* Liber, p. 4.

Joost. The text was subsequently incorporated in the 1625 Venetian edition of Galen's works.

The third Hebrew manuscript in Leiden belonging to Raphelengius is a thick quarto volume measuring 180 × 115 mm. and consisting of some 860 leaves. Its identity has defeated all the cataloguers of the Leiden manuscripts but is clearly stated in the 1626 auction catalogue.[26] MS Scal. Hebr. 16 (MS Or. 4733) is basically a copy of Sanctes Pagnini's Aramaic dictionary, the *Enchiridion expositionis vocabulorum Haruch, Thargum, Midrascim, Berescith, Scemoth, Vaicra, Midbar Rabba, et multorum aliorum librorum* published in Rome in 1523. Compared to the printed edition the manuscript lacks the epistle dedicatory and the list of abbreviations at the end. Otherwise it contains Pagnini's text but with numerous additions, and it is written in at least two unidentified hands. There is no indication of when Raphelengius acquired it. We know of his admiration for the Italian Hebraist, some of whose writings he edited for the Polyglot Bible, and we know that Raphelengius had learnt Aramaic by 1566. To do so he may well have used the Pagnini manuscript.

There remain three Hebrew codices in the auction catalogue which do not appear to be in any Dutch library. The first is a manuscript of the Mahzor, the Jewish festival prayerbook, but the rite is not specified.[27] Then there is a small folio volume of medical tracts, a common enough type of manuscript of which Scaliger himself owned two.[28] Finally there is a collection of extracts from the Scriptures with an interlinear translation which Benito Arias Montano had used to study Hebrew.[29] This can be regarded as a gift the editor of the *Biblia Regia* may have given to his younger colleague when he was in Antwerp in the late 1560s.

Certainly Raphelengius's collection of Hebrew manuscripts is meagre in comparison to his Arabic one. It can only be a faint reflection of the works he possessed in Hebrew, most of which must have been printed. Nevertheless

---

26 *Cat.Raph.*, p. 69, no. 16: 'Enchiridion Aramaeum sive Lexicon Chaldaicum Santis Pagnini, cum multis additionibus.' The cataloguers cannot have looked at the manuscript very closely. In Steinschneider, *Catalogus*, p. 378, it is described as having over two hundred leaves. In Van der Heide, *Hebrew Manuscripts*, p. 64 the author says it is far longer but does not specify how long. It is, he writes (p. 4), 'a Rabbinic Hebrew dictionary of substantial scope quoting many examples from Rabbinic literature; the author is not known'.
27 *Cat.Raph.*, p. 68, no. 2: 'Liber Magsorim, seu, Preces Anniversariae Iudaeorum Hebraice, in membranis'.
28 *Ibid.*, p. 68, no. 5: 'Volumen chartaceum in parvo fol. continens varios tractatus medicos Hebraice'.
29 *Ibid.*, p. 69, no. 17: 'Varii Scripturae textus Hebraici. Excerpta e Bibliis Hebraice. cum versione interlineari, charactere partim Hispanico, partim Iudaico currenti. Liber exercitii iuvenilis in studiis Hebraicis Ben. Ariae Montani'.

the three codices in Leiden are of rarity and importance. That Raphelengius should have collected the first two of them is to his credit as a scholar. At the same time a study of Raphelengius's Hebrew and Arabic manuscripts shows that at least twelve of the Oriental manuscripts 'ex legato illustris viri Josephi Scaligeri' never belonged to Scaliger and did not enter the Leiden library before 1626. This has consequences for the history of Leiden University and for the history of scholarship in Europe.

Acknowledgements

This article first appeared in *De Gulden Passer* 68 (1990), pp. 105–117. My special thanks are due to Joanna Weinberg. I am also indebted to Jan Just Witkam and to Henk Jan de Jonge.

CHAPTER 14

Abraham Ecchellensis et son 'Nomenclator Arabico-Latinus'

1   Introduction

Si, à la fin de la Renaissance, on connaissait en Europe la tradition grammaticologique du monde arabe[1], on ignorait tout de sa tradition lexicographique. Le premier vocabulaire d'arabe en latin à être publié avec des caractères arabes, le *Lexicon Arabico-Latinum* de Francis Raphelengien, est paru en 1613, mais l'auteur était mort en 1597. Ses sources principales avaient été un glossaire latino-arabe qui datait du xiie siècle, ainsi que le *Vocabulista aravigo en letra castellana* de Pedro de Alcalá, publié à Grenade en 1505[2]. Car il y avait peu de bibliothèques occidentales qui possédaient les oeuvres lexicographiques classiques – le *Ṣiḥāḥ al-lugha* d'al-Jawharī, le *Mujmal* d'Ibn Fāris, le *Mughrib* d'al-Muṭarrizī, le *Takmīla* d'al-Saghānī, et surtout le *Qāmūs* d'al-Fīrūzābādī[3].

La situation change completement au xviie siècle. L'histoire de la lexicologie arabe en Europe devient alors forcément l'histoire de la découverte des dictionnaires arabes monolingues. D'un côté, on commence à acheter, soit dans le monde ottoman, soit à Venise, des vocabulaires arabo-turcs et arabo-persans, qui s'inspirent des dictionnaires monolingues. Et de l'autre, on en collectionne les versions originales.

Ce développement est bien illustré par le cas de Thomas Erpenius, élève de Joseph-Juste Scaliger à Leyde, et ami des fils (et héritiers) de Raphelengien, qui lui demandent de corriger le lexique laissé par leur père et de le préparer pour la presse. Erpenius avait étudié l'arabe en Angleterre, en 1608-1609, avec l'arabisant anglais William Bedwell, et surtout en France, en 1610-1611, avec le copte Barbatus et le diplomate marocain Aḥmad ibn Qāsim al-Ḥajarī. En peu de mois il est parvenu à compiler une grammaire arabe qui ne sera dépassée qu'au xix[e]

---

1 L'étude fondamentale de la connaissance européenne des grammaires arabes reste R. Jones, *Learning Arabic in Renaissance Europe (1505-1624)* (Leyde-Boston, 2020).
2 Voir ci-dessus p. 209, 212.
3 J.A. Haywood, *Arabic Lexicography. Its History and its place in the General History of Lexicography*, 2ème éd. (Leyde, 1965), p. 68-89 ; R. Baalbaki, *The Arabic Lexicographical Tradition from the 2nd/8th to the 12th/18th Century* (Leyde-Boston, 2014). Pour al-Muṭarrizī voir p. 83, al-Jawharī voir p. 373-381, et pour Fīrūzābādī p. 391-397.

siècle. C'est avec cette grammaire que les fils de Raphelengien espèrent publier le vocabulaire de leur père.

Avant de rentrer aux Pays-Bas, où il sera nommé professeur d'arabe à l'université de Leyde, Erpenius essaye de rejoindre le Proche-Orient. À Venise, où il attend en vain un navire pour Constantinople dans le printemps de 1612, il achète un exemplaire d'*al-Akhtarī*, vocabulaire arabo-turc du lexicographe ottoman Mustafā ben Shamsaddīn al-Qarahisārī, datant de 1545 et fondé non seulement sur une bonne partie des dictionnaires monolingues (le *Ṣiḥāh*, le *Mughrib*, le *Mujmal*, et le *Takmīla*) mais aussi sur un des meilleurs dictionnaires arabo-persans, le *Dustūr al-lugha*. Et c'est peut-être à Venise – ou ailleurs au cours d'un voyage qui l'a amené à consulter les grandes collections de manuscrits arabes qui se trouvaient en Europe – qu'Erpenius a pu acheter encore, outre une œuvre mutilée et sans titre, un vocabulaire arabo-turc, le *Mirqāt al-lugha* (tiré du *Qāmūs* et du *Ṣiḥāh*), et à consulter, mais non pas à acheter (ce qu'il ne fera que beaucoup plus tard), un exemplaire du *Qāmūs* lui-même[4].

Grâce à ces découvertes, Erpenius réussit à fournir un appendice de 68 pages au lexique de Raphelengien rempli de corrections. C'était un moment décisif dans l'évolution des vocabulaires arabes en Europe. À Milan, sous l'impulsion du Cardinal Federigo Borromeo, une collection de manuscrits lexicologiques se forme à la fondation de la bibliothèque Ambrosienne, qui permettra à Antonio Giggei de compiler un lexique en quatre volumes tiré en grande partie du *Qāmūs* et du *Ṣiḥāh*, mais aussi d'*al-Akhtarī* et d'autres dictionnaires et commentaires coraniques. Il paraîtra en 1632.

2   Ecchellensis lexicologue

Le manuscrit du 'Nomenclator arabico-latinus', le lexique arabo-latin du maronite Abraham Ecchellensis actuellement à la Bibliothèque nationale de France (MS Arabe 4345), comporte 337 feuillets écrits des deux côtés et presque 7000 mots arabes rangés en ordre alphabétique selon la tradition européenne[5]. Nous n'avons aucun renseignement sur la date exacte de l'oeuvre. Ecchellensis, qui y a travaillé longtemps avant de l'offrir à Pierre Séguier[6], a dû écrire sa dédicace

---

4   Voir ci-dessus p. 251-254.

5   M. Moubarakah, 'Le "Nomenclator Arabico-Latinus" d'Abraham Ecchellensis (Ibrâhîm al-Hâqilânî) (Paris Arabe 4345)' *Parole de l'Orient* 22 (1997), p. 419-439, donne une description du manuscrit.

6   'Nomenclator arabico-latinus', MS Arabe 4345 [dorénavant N], f. 3[r-v] : 'Haec apud me dudum meditanti Arabico-latinus occurrit Nomenclator ab ipsa florescente elaboratus aetate, nunc

au chancelier pendant son deuxième séjour à Paris, entre 1646 et 1651[7], lorsqu'il en était le protégé et l'employé dans sa bibliothèque[8]. Ces dates bien approximatives nous permettent de placer ce lexique entre celui de Giggei et celui, infiniment plus important, de Jacobus Golius, successeur d'Erpenius à la chaire d'arabe à l'université de Leyde. Le *Lexicon Arabico-Latinum* de Golius, daté de 1653, tiré des dictionnaires d'al-Fīrūzābādī, d'al-Jawharī, d'al-Zamakhsharī et d'Ibn Fāris, et d'une quantité de vocabulaires arabo-turcs et arabo-persans, ne sera dépassé, comme la grammaire d'Erpenius, que deux cents ans plus tard.

Les années pendant lesquelles Ecchellensis travaillait à son lexique étaient pour lui des années de recherche plus ou moins intensive dans les fonds arabes et syriaques en Italie et en France[9]. Non seulement il possédait lui-même une collection de livres et de manuscrits[10], mais il a dû aussi se familiariser avec les bibliothèques pendant son premier séjour à Rome, lorsqu'il étudiait au Collège des maronites, entre 1620 et 1625, puis lorsqu'il y enseignait le syriaque et l'arabe et qu'il préparait son doctorat au Collegio Romano – époque où il expertisa la collection de manuscrits arabes offerts à la bibliothèque du Vatican par un autre maronite, Victor Scialac[11]. Nommé professeur d'arabe et de syriaque à Pise par le grand-duc de Toscane de 1633 à 1636, il eut l'occasion de connaître

---

vero auctior, correctiorque redditus, quo nihil profecto inpraesens magis opportunum, aut acommodum mihi obvenire potuisse duxi, quippe qui abunde vernaculas exhibet voces, et meae professionis vocabula suppeditat, quibus, si non pareo, quod fieri nequit, aliquatenus saltem tibi pro tot beneficiis in me collatis rependi possunt gratiae, quas non libenter sed libentissime tibi debeo, et quamdiu vixero fatebor.'

7 Moubarakah, 'Le "Nomenclator Arabico-Latinus"', p. 422, propose la date de 1650.
8 Y. Nexon, *Le chancelier Séguier (1588-1672) : ministre, dévot et mécène au Grand Siècle* (Ceyzérieu, 2015), p. 246-247.
9 P.J.A.N. Rietbergen, 'A Maronite mediator between seventeenth-century Mediterranean cultures: Ibrāhīm Al-Hākilānī, or Abraham Ecchellense (1605-1664) between Christendom and Islam' *Lias* 16 (1989), p. 13-41, en particulier p. 21-31.
10 La collection d'Ecchellensis a été utilisée par Ludovico Marracci à Rome lorsqu'il préparait sa traduction du Coran. Voir Ludovico Marracci, *Prodromus ad Refutationem Alcorani ... in quatuor partes divisus* (Rome, 1691), p. 7. Ecchellensis lui-même nous donne une idée non seulement des livres qu'il possédait, mais aussi des bibliothèques qu'il avait consultées dans son 'Index operum auctorum' à la fin de la deuxième partie de sa réponse à John Selden, *De origine nominis papae, nec non de illius proprietate in Romano Pontifice adeoque de eiusdem primatu contra Ioannem Seldenum Anglum. Pars altera* (Rome, 1660), signature rrr4[v]-xxx2[v]. Mais voir surtout C.A. Nallino, 'Le fonti arabe manoscritte dell'opera di Ludovico Marracci sul Corano' dans sa *Raccolta di scritti e inediti* (Rome, 1939-48), vol. 2, p. 90-134.
11 B. Heyberger, 'Abraham Ecchellensis dans la République des Lettres' dans B. Heyberger, dir., *Orientalisme, science et controverse : Abraham Ecchellensis (1605-1664)* (Tournai, 2010), p. 9-51. Voir aussi P. Rietbergen, *Power and Religion in Baroque Rome. Barberini Cultural Policies* (Leyde-Boston, 2006), p. 296-335.

les bibliothèques de Florence, et à partir de 1636, de continuer ses recherches dans celles de Rome en tant que professeur d'arabe et de syriaque à l'université papale, conseiller de la Propaganda Fide (qui le consultait déjà en 1624), et ami de Lucas Holstenius, le bibliothécaire de Francesco Barberini. En outre, pendant son premier séjour parisien, entre 1640 et 1642, Ecchellensis avait pu consulter la collection royale, et par la suite, à partir de 1646, il examina les manuscrits orientaux dans les collections du Cardinal Mazarin, du chancelier Pierre Séguier et de Gilbert Gaulmin.

Ecchellensis connaissait donc mieux que personne une bonne partie des collections arabes en France et en Italie. Il avait aussi déjà eu des rapports avec la lexicologie à Rome. En 1639, en tant que conseiller de la Propaganda Fide, il fut chargé d'examiner et d'approuver le vocabulaire du franciscain Domenicus Germanus de Silésie au couvent de S. Pietro in Montorio. Vocabulaire de l'italien (et du latin) en arabe (non vocalisé), cette *Fabrica Linguae Arabicae*, publiée à Rome, reste une oeuvre importante. Elle a été corrigée et revue en 1878, et republiée à Jérusalem par les Gardiens de la Terre Sainte avec le titre de *Dizionario italiano-arabo*. Son succès fut tel qu'elle a continué à paraître dans le monde arabe jusqu'à nos jours. Avec un choix de mots arabes très vaste et tout à fait différent des vocabulaires de Giggei et de Golius, le lexique était surtout destiné aux missionnaires, et il reste d'une grande utilité pour la terminologie théologique chrétienne. L'auteur, né à Schnurgast en Silésie en 1588, et devenu franciscain en 1624, avait fait des études à Rome sous l'arabisant Tommaso da Novara (Giovanni Battista Obicini), et avait vécu en Palestine de 1630 jusqu'à 1634 ou 1635[12]. En 1652, après d'autres séjours au Moyen-Orient, il est nommé bibliothécaire à l'Escorial où il complètera une traduction remarquable du Coran, destinée à rester manuscrite[13].

3   Les sources du 'Nomenclator'

Grâce à la richesse de ses connaissances, Ecchellensis était bien placé pour apporter une contribution considérable à la lexicologie arabe en Europe. Mais quelles étaient les sources principales du 'Nomenclator'? À une seule exception près, Ecchellensis n'en parle pas, ni dans sa préface ni dans le texte de son

---

12   G. Graf, *Geschichte der christlichen arabischen Literatur*, vol. 4 (Cité du Vatican, 1951), p. 176-178.

13   Voir T.E. Burman, *Reading the Qurʾān in Latin Christendom, 1140-1560* (Philadelphia, 2007), p. 178-198.

vocabulaire. Nous pouvons faire pourtant des hypothèses, et dans plusieurs cas nous pouvons passer à des certitudes.

Commençons avec ses prédécesseurs en Europe. Comme Giggei, Ecchellensis annonce la subdivision des lettres en nommant les deux premières lettres en latin, ainsi *Te ante Dal*, mais, en suivant le système arabe, il ajoute en arabe فصل التاء بالدال ت د. A-t-il aussi été influencé par Domenicus Germanus de Silésie ? On trouve plusieurs mots en commun. Mais le franciscain travaillait de l'italien vers l'arabe et non pas de l'arabe vers l'italien (ou le latin), et de plus il offrait un choix de mots arabes bien supérieur à celui d'Ecchellensis. D'habitude, ce dernier ne choisissait qu'un mot en arabe (parfois suivi par des phrases et des exemples), tandis que Germanus en donnait au moins deux et souvent plus. Pour 'immortel', par exemple, il fournit trois possibilités[14] en arabe. Il en fait autant pour 'Pâques'[15], et pour 'invisible' il en fournit huit[16]. Mais l'indice le plus significatif de l'influence du franciscain est, comme on le verra, la prédominance de mots chrétiens.

Venons-en maintenant aux sources arabes. La seule qui soit citée spécifiquement par Ecchellensis est le *Kitāb al-amthāl*, une collection de proverbes, attribués à Abū 'Ubayd, que Thomas Erpenius avait publiée à Leyde en 1614, sous le titre de *Proverbiorum Arabicorum centuriae duae, ab anonymo quodam Arabe collectae et explicatae cum interpretatione latina et scholiis*[17]. Des trois références au *Kitāb al-amthāl* dans le 'Nomenclator', pourtant, il n'y en a que deux que l'on retrouve dans la version publiée, ce qui porte à penser qu'Ecchellensis a utilisé un manuscript[18]. Et, effectivement, la troisième citation se trouve dans le MS Arabe 3969 de la BnF[19]. Or ce manuscrit, qui faisait partie de l'ancien fonds de la bibliothèque[20], a été copié à Rome en 1581 par Domenico Sirleto, un converti tunisien qui avait étudié au Collège des Néophytes de 1577 jusqu'à

---

14   Domenicus Germanus de Silesia, *Fabrica Linguae Arabicae* (Rome, 1639), p. 550.
15   *Ibidem*, p. 746.
16   *Ibidem*, p. 623.
17   Fück, p. 61-62. Voir aussi A. Vrolijk, 'The Prince of Arabists and his many errors: Thomas Erpenius's image of Joseph Scaliger and the edition of the *Proverbia arabica* (1614)' *Journal of the Warburg and Courtauld Institutes* 73 (2010), p. 297-325.
18   N, f. 111^v, 146^v et 246^r. Pour la citation à f. 146^v, voir Thomas Erpenius, *Proverbiorum Arabicorum centuriae duae, ab anonymo quodam Arabe collectae et explicatae cum interpretatione latina et scholiis* (Leyde, 1615), p. 40 (Centuria I, prov. LIII) et pour celle à f. 246^r, voir p. 104 (Centuria II, prov. LXII).
19   BnF, MS Arabe 3969, f. 35^r.
20   Baron de Slane, *Catalogue des manuscrits arabes [de la Bibliotheque Nationale]* (Paris, 1883-95), p. 645.

sa mort en 1587[21]. À un moment donné, le manuscrit avait appartenu au melkite alépin Buṭrus Di'b, nommé professeur au Collège royal en 1667[22]. Mais il est très probable qu'avant cela il ait été la propriété d'Ecchellensis, comme un autre manuscrit copié par Sirleto, un vocabulaire arabo-latin qui contient des corrections de sa main et qui est actuellement à la bibliothèque Vaticane[23].

Très souvent le choix de mots d'Ecchellensis semble être un reflet de ses connaissances, lectures et publications hétérogènes[24]. Il y a plusieurs mots scientifiques – plantes, maladies, animaux – qui font penser à une de ses premières publications, la traduction d'ʿAbd al-Raḥmān b. Abū Bakr al-Ṣuyūṭī, *De proprietatibus, ac virtutibus medicis, animalium, plantarum, ac gemmarum, tractatus triplex, auctore Habderrahmano Asiutensis Aegyptio* (Paris, 1647). Dans le texte publié d' al-Ṣuyūṭī, nous retrouvons plusieurs mots – tels que 'hibou' ('bubo') et 'hérisson' ('herinaceus') parmi les animaux[25]. 'noisette' ('avellana, nux pontica') et 'coriandre' ('coriandrum') parmi les plantes[26] – qui reviennent dans le vocabulaire d'Ecchellensis. Mais le 'Nomenclator' contient aussi d'autres termes botaniques, comme le mot arabe, fort peu habituel, pour 'pepus citreus, citrinus', une espèce de concombre, خياره[27], qui font penser à un usage ultérieur de manuscrits. Il y a aussi une terminologie biblique, dont les noms de prophètes et de patriarches de l'Ancien Testament tels que Moïse, David, Abraham, Isaac, Jérémie, et Isaïe, qui nous rappelle que, juste pendant ces années-là, Ecchellensis participait à la préparation de la Bible de Le Jay.

Le 'Nomenclator', pourtant, prend une saveur 'orientale' du fait que certains mots sont suivis par de longues citations en arabe (et sans traduction) qui illustrent leur emploi mais dont la source n'est pas indiquée. D'où

---

21   Giorgio Levi della Vida, *Ricerche sulla formazione del più antico fondo dei manoscritti orientali della Biblioteca Vaticana* (Cité du Vatican, 1939), p. 407-410. Voir aussi Jones, p. 69-70.
22   N. Gemayel, *Les échanges culturels entre les Maronites et l'Europe. Du Collège Maronite de Rome (1584) au Collège de ʿAyn-Warqa (1789)* (Beyrouth, 1984), vol. 1, p. 249, où il est considéré (à tort) comme maronite. Cf. B. Heyberger, 'De l'image religieuse à l'image profane ? L'essor de l'image chez les chrétiens de Syrie et du Liban (XVIIe-XIXe siècle)' dans B. Heyberger, S. Naef (dir.), *La multiplication des images en pays d'Islam* (Istanbul, 2003), p. 38. Le nom peut être Di'b (Dipy chez Gemayel) ou Diyāb.
23   Biblioteca Apostolica Vaticana, MS Vat.Ar. 185. Voir Levi della Vida, *Ricerche*, p. 429-430.
24   Gemayel, *Les échanges culturels*, p. 299-304. Sur la culture scientifique d'Abraham Ecchellensis, voir aussi G. Gobillot, 'Abraham Ecchellensis, philosophe et historien des sciences' dans Heyberger, dir., *Orientalisme*, p. 171-89.
25   N, f. 57ʳ et 261ᵛ. Cf. al-Ṣuyūṭī, *De proprietatibus, ac virtutibus medicis, animalium, plantarum, ac gemmarum, tractatus triplex, auctore Habderrahmano Asiutensis Aegyptio* (Paris, 1647), p. 133-135 et 113-115.
26   N, f. 56ʳ et 59ʳ. Cf. al-Ṣuyūṭī, *De proprietatibus*, p. 140-142 et 11.
27   N, f. 111ᵛ.

viennent-elles ? Nous avons pu constater que la presque totalité de ces citations provient d'une seule source, le *Qāmūs* d'al-Fīrūzābādī.

Lorsqu'Ecchellensis travaillait dans les fonds arabes de France et d'Italie, le *Qāmūs* y était accessible. La bibliothèque du Vatican, par exemple, en possédait un exemplaire acheté en Orient par le missionnaire maltais Leonardo Abel, exemplaire entré dans la bibliothèque papale avec les autres manuscrits de celui-ci peu après 1610, l'année de sa mort[28]. Quelques années plus tard, bien avant 1631, c'est la bibliothèque du Collège des maronites à Rome qui en possédait un exemplaire[29], et encore plus tard nous en retrouvons un autre dans la bibliothèque du Collège des maronites à Ravenne (qu'Ecchellensis consultera)[30]. Le *Qāmūs*, en outre, est cité largement dans d'autres manuscrits copiés par Domenico Sirleto et actuellement à la bibliothèque Vaticane[31].

Quel qu'ait été le manuscrit du *Qāmūs* utilisé par Ecchellensis, les exemples qu'il en tire sont nombreux. Pour le mot استسقى[32], pour حشا[33], pour جري[34], pour غبيه[35], pour عطا[36], pour عصا[37], pour شكا[38], pour رجا[39], pour قطا[40], pour قنا[41], pour رثيه[42], pour قبه[43], pour غنا[44], pour غفا[45], pour غدا[46], nous trouvons des citations directes et plus ou moins longues du dictionnaire monolingue qui avait contribué à la transformation de la lexicologie arabe en Europe. Et pourtant il y a un aspect surprenant. Une grande partie des mots qui viennent du *Qāmūs* terminent avec la même radicale, et il ne faut pas oublier que dans le *Qāmūs*, tout comme dans le *Ṣiḥāḥ*, c'est la dernière radicale selon laquelle sont rangés les mots. Or, l'impression que l'on a est que Ecchellensis n'a consulté qu'une partie de cet immense dictionnaire, probablement le dernier volume.

---

28   Levi della Vida, *Ricerche*, p. 232.
29   Gemayel, *Les échanges culturels*, vol. 1, p. 189.
30   *Ibidem*, vol. 2, p. 972-973.
31   BAV, MSS Vat. Ar. 194, 304, 329-31. Voir Levi Della Vida, *Ricerche*, p. 432.
32   N, f. 26ᵛ. Cf. al-Fīrūzābādī, *Al-Qāmūs al-muḥīṭ* (Beyrouth, 1998), p. 1296.
33   N, f. 93ʳ. Cf. al-Fīrūzābādī, *Al-Qāmūs*, p. 1274.
34   N, f. 79ʳ. Cf. al-Fīrūzābādī, *Al-Qāmūs*, p. 1270.
35   N, f. 221ᵛ. Cf. al-Fīrūzābādī, *Al-Qāmūs*, p. 1316-1317.
36   N, f. 210ʳ. Cf. al-Fīrūzābādī, *Al-Qāmūs*, p. 1312-1313.
37   N, f. 208ᵛ. Cf. al-Fīrūzābādī, *Al-Qāmūs*, p. 1312.
38   N, f. 171ᵛ-172ʳ. Cf. al-Fīrūzābādī, *Al-Qāmūs*, p. 1301.
39   N, f. 129ʳ. Cf. al-Fīrūzābādī, *Al-Qāmūs*, p. 1287.
40   N, f. 257ᵛ-258ʳ. Cf. al-Fīrūzābādī, *Al-Qāmūs*, p. 1325.
41   N, f. 261ᵛ. Cf. al-Fīrūzābādī, *Al-Qāmūs*, p. 1326.
42   N, f. 128ʳ. Cf. al-Fīrūzābādī, *Al-Qāmūs*, p. 1286-1287.
43   N, f. 249ʳ. Cf. al-Fīrūzābādī, *Al-Qāmūs*, p. 1323.
44   N, f. 231ʳ⁻ᵛ. Cf. al-Fīrūzābādī, *Al-Qāmūs*, p. 1319.
45   N, f. 228ᵛ. Cf. al-Fīrūzābādī, *Al-Qāmūs*, p. 1318.
46   N, f. 222ᵛ. Cf. al-Fīrūzābādī, *Al-Qāmūs*, p. 1317.

4   L'organisation du 'Nomenclator'

Si l'on compare le vocabulaire d'Ecchellensis aux vocabulaires européens contemporains, on est frappé par le caractère arbitraire de son organisation. Parfois, Ecchellensis semble ignorer les racines. À partir de Raphelengien, les lexicographes occidentaux ont tous essayé d'observer un système de racines, qui reste toujours en vigueur aujourd'hui. Chez Ecchellensis, pourtant, un mot tel que ابتدا 'commencement', est rangé sous l'*alif* au lieu du *bā*' pour بدأ[47]. Parfois aussi, il ne fait aucune distinction entre l'article ou une préposition et la première lettre du mot en question. Pour des raisons inexplicables السرا ('arridentia, prospera'), est rangé sous l'*alif* au lieu du *sīn*[48], tandis que الذي لا يرى ('invisibilis') et الذي لا يموت ('immortalis') sont aussi sous l'*alif*[49]. D'autre part, Ecchellensis donne souvent les formes grammaticales fondamentales – première personne du singulier, troisième personne du masculin singulier, et troisième personne du masculin duel de l'indicatif de l'acccompli.

A quelques mots près, le lexique est soigneusement vocalisé. Tandis que la vocalisation et l'orthographe correspondent généralement à l'arabe classique, il a été démontré qu'elles ne sont pas toujours correctes[50]. Certaines formes verbales, comme سمع[51], sont doublement vocalisées, et dans d'autres cas la vocalisation est douteuse. En ce qui concerne l'orthographe, la *hamzah* est parfois mal placée, surtout lorsqu'elle apparaît sur l'*alif* initial des formes verbales, et l'on trouve des formes non classiques, par exemple اوله comme unique forme féminine de اول[52], qui rappellent une influence régionale ou dialectale[53].

5   Un vocabulaire chrétien

Un des traits les plus saillants du 'Nomenclator' est un choix presque exclusif de termes chrétiens. Il est bien rare de trouver une terminologie islamique.

---

47   N, f. 7ʳ.
48   N, f. 36ᵛ.
49   N, f. 36ᵛ.
50   Voir les importantes observations linguistiques de Moubarakah, 'Le "Nomenclator Arabico-Latinus"', p. 424-427.
51   N, f. 158ʳ.
52   N, f. 42ᵛ.
53   Un phénomène qui a été relevé dans l'oeuvre linguistique d'autres maronites contemporains par G. Troupeau, 'Réflexions sur la "Grammaire arabe des Maronites"' *Annales de l'Institut de lettres orientales* 7 (1993-1996), p. 187-197.

Sous يكبر كبر Ecchellensis écrit 'Magnificae, illustrare. Mahometani hoc utantur vocabula ad exprimendos conclamationes, et clamores pro victoria parta, aut felici aliquo successu'[54]. Sous مكه nous lisons : 'Meccha, urbs Mahometi pseudoprophetae natalibus infamis'[55]. Mais ce sont des exceptions. D'habitude, des mots dont il existe des significations strictement islamiques, comme زكاه, n'obtiennent que des significations chrétiennes. Dans ce cas-ci, nous avons 'puritas, animi candor, innocentia'[56], mais il n'est pas question d'aumône.

D'autre part, les fêtes chrétiennes, telles que Pâques, القامه وعيد الكبير عيد[57], les sacrements, tel que la confirmation, تثبيت, et des termes plus généraux comme la Trinité, تثليت[58], l'incarnation, تأنس[59], la vertu du Saint-Esprit, تابد روح القدس[60], et des dérivés de بشر, 'evangelizare', 'evangelizari', 'evangelium', 'evangelista'[61], sont tous définis soigneusement. Il n'y a aucune mention du nom du Prophète, mais bien de celui de Jésus[62], 'Jésus Nazarenus'[63], et du Christ[64].

6   Le 'Nomenclator' et le Coran

Malgré le fait que le 'Nomenclator' soit inutilisable pour des lecteurs de textes islamiques, Ecchellensis connaissait très bien les trois principaux traducteurs du Coran – mot, d'ailleurs, qui ne se trouve nulle part dans sa signification islamique dans son vocabulaire[65] – de son époque. Nous avons déjà parlé de ses rapports avec Domenicus Germanus de Silésie. C'était aussi en tant qu'employé

---

54   N, f. 265ʳ. 'Les Mahométans emploient ces mots pour exprimer des cris et des clameurs pour une victoire remportée ou pour un autre heureux succès'.
55   N, f. 303ᵛ. 'La Mecque, ville décriée comme lieu de naissance du pseudoprophète Mahomet'.
56   N, f. 145ʳ.
57   N, f. 219ʳ.
58   N, f. 60ʳ.
59   N, f. 59ʳ.
60   N, f. 59ᵛ.
61   N, f. 51ᵛ.
62   N, f. 219ʳ.
63   N, f. 319ᵛ.
64   N, f. 294ʳ.
65   Comme a observé Aurélien Girard, 'under the root *qara'a*, the derivative *qur'ān* was only presented as a synonym of *qirā'a*, with the Latin translation of *Lectio*, but without any reference to the Qur'an. For *rasūl* (*apostolus*), or *nabī* (*propheta*), no allusion to Islam was made.' (A. Girard, 'Teaching and learning Arabic in Early Modern Rome: shaping a missionary language' dans J. Loop, A. Hamilton, C. Burnett, dir., *The Teaching and Learning of Arabic in Early Modern Europe* (Leyde-Boston, 2017), p. 189-212, surtout p. 209. Voir N, f. 293ʳ.

de la Propaganda Fide à Rome qu'Ecchellensis fréquentait presque journellement Ludovico Marracci, dont la traduction célèbre du Coran sortira longtemps après la mort du maronite mais a duré tant d'années que celui-ci aurait pu en être informé. Et surtout, il semble fort probable qu'Ecchellensis ait participé à la traduction en français du Coran par André Du Ryer. Nous savons que les deux hommes se connaissaient, et qu'ils échangeaient des manuscrits[66]. Or, quoique sa traduction ait bien des défauts, Du Ryer a été le premier traducteur du Coran à indiquer, dans des notes marginales et dans le texte, certaines significations tirées de commentaires islamiques, les *tafsīr*, qui étaient en contraste avec les traductions traditionnelles chrétiennes.

Deux exemples, qui ont été soulignés par David Durand dans ses *Eclaircissemens sur la religion mahométane* publiés en appendice à sa traduction française de la *De religione mohammedica* d'Adriaen Reland[67], suffisent pour nous donner une idée du problème. Le mot *jinn*, qui se trouve dans le titre de la sourate 72 et ailleurs dans le texte du Coran, avait toujours été traduit par 'démon', ce qui permettait aux ennemis de l'islam de dire que le Prophète avait des démons parmi ses adorateurs. C'est ainsi qu'on le trouve dans la traduction médiévale de Robert de Ketton publiée par Bibliander en 1543, et, encore plus récemment, dans le vocabulaire de termes coraniques, le *Dictionarium Arabo-Latinum ex Alcorano et celebrioribus authoribus*, qu'un autre maronite, Gabriel Sionite, avait préparé à Venise avec Victor Scialac et qui a été recopié par l'arabisant français Pierre Duval[68]. Dans sa traduction du Coran, Du Ryer traduit le titre de la sourate 72 comme 'le Chapitre des Démons', mais il ajoute : 'Quelques Mahometans intitulent ce Chapitre des Esprits'[69]. À vrai dire Du Ryer n'était pas le tout premier à envisager une traduction plus nuancée du mot. Chez Giggei on trouve déjà, sous الجنه, la signification 'angeli, daemones'[70]. Ecchellensis, pour sa part, donne pour جنه, جن, جنون la traduction 'spiritus, genius, daemon'[71].

L'autre mot qui suscitait des polémiques était *sallā* (sourate 33:56 : *yusallūna*). La traduction traditionelle était 'prier', et on en concluait que Dieu et les anges priaient pour le Prophète, ce qui était interprété comme blasphématoire.

---

66   A. Hamilton et F. Richard, *André Du Ryer and Oriental Studies in Seventeenth-Century France* (Londres-Oxford, 2004), p. 47, 164, 166.
67   Adriaen Reland, *La religion des mahometans* (La Haye, 1721), p. 117, 132.
68   BnF MS Arabe 4338, p. 129.
69   *L'Alcoran de Mahomet* (Paris, 1647), p. 605.
70   Antonio Giggei, *Thesaurus linguae arabicae* (Milan, 1632), vol. 1, col. 760. Sous الجن, pourtant, on trouve la signification 'Daemones, et praecipue qui hominum consuetudine delectantur.'
71   N, f. 83r.

Encore une fois, Du Ryer traduit la phrase 'Dieu et les anges prient pour le Prophète', mais il ajoute dans une note marginale que dans le *Tafsīr al-Jalālayn* on lit qu'ils 'bénissent le Prophète'[72]. La signification est donc bien différente, et il n'y a plus de blasphème. Sionite et Scialac, pourtant, traduisent يصلي comme 'oravit'[73]. Giggei donne, pour يصلي, 'oravit, preces fundit', et pour صلى الله على ألنبي 'Misertus est Deus prophetae. Propitius illi fuit'[74]. Chez Ecchellensis nous ne trouvons pour صلى que 'orare, preces fundere'[75].

7 Conclusion

Bien qu'il semble que le 'Nomenclator' ait été compilé surtout pour le propre usage de l'auteur, l'élégance extrême du manuscrit pourrait indiquer l'intention de la part d'Ecchellensis de le publier. Mais a-t-on jamais essayé de le faire ? Probablement pas. L'existence du lexique de Giggei et la parution imminente de celui de Golius qui allait dépasser tout ce qui existait en Europe rendaient un tel projet peu opportun. Après la mort de Séguier, dont les armes sont estampillées sur la belle reliure, le vocabulaire est passé dans la bibliothèque du duc de Coislin et de là, en 1732, à celle de Saint-Germain-des-Prés avant d'arriver à la Bibliothèque nationale en 1796. Il est fort peu vraisemblable que l'on ait essayé de l'utiliser, mais il reste un important témoignage des intentions d'Ecchellensis, à cheval sur la culture arabe et la culture européenne.

Nous avons souligné la possibilité d'une influence de la part de Giggei et de Domenicus Germanus de Silésie – dans le premier cas, la subdivision des mots, dans le deuxième, le choix d'une terminologie surtout chrétienne. L'emploi du *Qāmūs* d'al-Fīrūzābādī, d'autre part, est tout à fait différent de l'usage qu'en faisaient les lexicologues européens. Chez Giggei, comme plus tard chez Golius, les exemples contenus dans le grand dictionnaire monolingue ont été assimilés dans le texte latin. Ecchellensis, par contre, ne fait aucun effort ni pour les traduire ni pour les sortir du texte original. Il donne plutôt des citations littérales entières. Pourquoi ? Faut-il penser à un de ces éléments de mystification que nous retrouvons aussi bien chez les orientalistes occidentaux que chez les chrétiens arabophones en Occident ? *De nonnullis orientalium urbibus nec non indigenarum religione ac moribus tractatus brevis*, l'appendice que Gabriel Sionite a ajouté à sa traduction latine d'al-Idrīsī en 1619, peut servir

---

72   *L'Alcoran de Mahomet*, p. 117.
73   BnF MS Arabe 4338, p. 325.
74   Giggei, *Thesaurus*, vol. 2, col. 1368.
75   N, f. 180ᵛ.

d'exemple[76]. Dans le chapitre où il est question de l'islam, Sionite cite un obscur écrivain ottoman, Yaʿqūb ibn Sayyid ʿAlī, pour démontrer sa familiarité avec des sources islamiques. En réalité, il était mal renseigné sur l'islam, mais la présence dans son texte d'un nom musulman servait de pièce à conviction d'une valeur inestimable dans les yeux d'un public qui en savait encore moins que lui. Ecchellensis ne voulait-il pas aussi éblouir ses lecteurs européens en déployant sa connaissance de la littérature arabe avec une série de citations dont il ne donnait jamais la source ?

Remerciements

Cet article est paru dans Bernard Heyberger, dir. *Orientalisme, science et controverse : Abraham Ecchellensis (1605-1664)* [Bibliothèque de l'École des Hautes Études, Sciences Religieuses, vol. 143] (Turnhout : Brepols, 2010), p. 89-98. Nous tenons à remercier le Père Awad Wadi et la Bibliothèque du Centre d'Études Orientales Chrétiennes des Pères Franciscains au Caire.

---

[76] Gabriel Sionite, 'De nonnullis orientalium urbibus nec non indigenarum religione ac moribus tractatus brevis' dans *Geographia Nubiensis ... ex Arabico a Gabriele Sionita et Ioanne Hesronita* (Paris, 1619), p. 44. Voir aussi les éditions indépendantes de l'appendice de Sionite, *Arabia, seu Arabum vicinarumque gentium Orientalium leges, ritus, sacri et profani mores, instituta et historiae* publiées à Amsterdam en 1633 et 1635. Le manuscrit ottoman est un commentaire de la *sharīʿa*, actuellement BnF, MS Arabe 1249.

PART 3

Islam and the Qur'an

CHAPTER 15

The Study of Islam in Early Modern Europe

Islam could be a dangerous subject with which to meddle in early modern Europe. When the first Latin translation of the Qurʾan ever to be printed was published in Basle in 1543 the printer, Johannes Oporinus, was imprisoned, albeit briefly.[1] Over a century later, in England in March 1649, there was a similar occurrence when the English translation of André Du Ryer's French rendering of the Qurʾan appeared in print. The bookseller, John Stephenson, was arrested, copies of the book were seized, and, in the weeks following the actual publication (which was deferred for a month), the project was attacked.[2] In the tolerant Netherlands, where translations of the Qurʾan were so widely owned and read, Daniel Heinsius informed John Selden in 1633 that there was considerable resistance against allowing Thomas Erpenius or Jacobus Golius, the two great professors of Arabic at Leiden University, to translate it.[3] As for Catholic Europe, possession of the Qurʾan or any other work in Arabic had been forbidden by the Spanish Inquisition in 1511. The Qurʾan was soon placed on the indexes – the Qurʾan in any language on the Portuguese index of 1547, the Spanish index of 1551 and the Venetian index in 1554, and the Basle edition specifically on the Roman indexes of 1559 and 1564.[4] When the French translation by André Du Ryer was about to go to press in 1647 Vincent de Paul, one of the leaders of the French missionary movement, and other members of the *conseil de conscience*, the advisory body of the regent Anne of Austria, were strongly opposed to its publication. It had been approved by the chancellor, Pierre Séguier, to whom it was dedicated, but efforts were made to suppress it, the epistle dedicatory to Séguier was removed from most copies, and

---

1 See C. Gilly, *Spanien und der Basler Buchdruck bis 1600. Ein Querschnitt durch die spanische Geistesgeschichte aus der Sicht einer europäischen Buchdruckerstadt* (Basel, 1985), pp. 16–20.
2 Toomer, pp. 200–201.
3 Ibid., p. 201. The hostility was confirmed by Samuel Bochart in a letter to Jacobus Cappellus over thirty years later. See Samuel Bochart, *Geographia Sacra, seu Phaleg et Canaan, cui accedunt variae dissertationes, philologicae, geographicae, theologicae &c.*, 5th edn. (Leiden, 1692), pp. 854–855. I thank Jan Loop for drawing my attention to this passage.
4 J.M. de Bujanda (ed.), *Index de l'Inquisition portugaise 1547, 1551, 1561, 1564, 1581* [= *Index des livres interdits*, vol. 4] (Sherbroke-Geneva, 1995), p. 296; *Index de l'Inquisition espagnole 1551, 1554, 1559* [*Index des livres interdits*, vol. 5] (Sherbroke-Geneva 1984), p. 218; *Index de Venise 1549 – Venise et Milan 1554* [*Index des livres interdits*, vol. 3] (Sherbroke-Geneva 1987), p. 214; *Index de Rome 1557, 1559, 1564* [=*Index des livres interdits*, vol. 8] (Sherbroke-Geneva 1990), pp. 362–364.

© ALASTAIR HAMILTON, 2022 | DOI:10.1163/9789004498204_016

in May 1650, when Séguier was in momentary disgrace, the parliament decreed that the book should be burnt.[5] The translation, however, was little less than a bestseller and was reprinted again and again, while the English version ran through two editions in a year. It showed just how divided opinion was. We shall see, finally, that in Italy it took Ludovico Marracci, a paragon of orthodoxy, a quarter of a century to get his 1698 edition of the Qur'an into print.

To translate the Qur'an could be justified by an age-old ideal: the conversion of the Muslims.[6] A team of Christians with a sound knowledge of Arabic and well-acquainted with Islamic beliefs and sources, might, it was hoped, confute these beliefs to the satisfaction of their Muslim interlocutors and win them over to Christianity. It was this conviction which was behind the early translations of the Qur'an. The translation by Robert of Ketton, finally published in 1543 but made in about 1143, was to serve such a purpose. The later unpublished translation by Marco de Toledo[7] was also intended for the same object, as were the efforts by Denys the Carthusian, Ricoldo da Montecroce, Juan Andrés and Guillaume Postel to translate the whole, or part of, the Qur'an.

The study of Islam in the West, in short, has been so surrounded by prejudice that it is hard to separate the propaganda inspiring most works on the subject from efforts to transmit a true knowledge and understanding of the Muslim faith. The insertion of Islam in an eschatological scheme, the application to it of passages in the Bible seen as prophesying its rise and, more important still, its fall, did little to promote a true familiarity. And yet – and this is the subject of this essay – certain attempts in that direction were made. Prejudiced though their presentation may have been, Islamic sources were gradually gathered, and, despite the missionary tones and an increasingly confessionalised approach in the sixteenth century, by 1700 the foundations had been laid for the positive treatment of Islam which we occasionally encounter in the Enlightenment. The term 'objective' should perhaps be avoided, since few of the known sources of the time can be regarded as such in the modern sense.[8] At best we can say that a familiarisation with Islamic sources, however open

---

5 A. Hamilton and F. Richard, *André Du Ryer and Oriental Studies in Seventeenth-Century France* (London-Oxford, 2004), pp. 54–55; Y. Nexon, *Le chancelier Séguier (1588–1672) : ministre, dévot et mécène au Grand Siècle* (Ceyzérieu, 2015), pp. 386–387, 429–430.

6 R.W. Southern, *Western Views of Islam in the Middle Ages* (Cambridge, Mass. 1978), pp. 34–42; T.E. Burman, *Reading the Qur'ān in Latin Christendom, 1140–1560* (Philadelphia, 2007), pp. 20–35.

7 Finally published by N. Petrus Pons, *Alchoranus Latinus quem transtulit Marcus canonicus Toletanus. Estudio y edición crítica* (Madrid, 2016).

8 For a more impartial assessment of some of the available sources see B. Lewis, 'Gibbon on Muhammad' in his *Islam and the West* (New York, 1993), pp. 85–98.

to criticism in themselves, made it possible to appreciate the point of view of the Muslims.

1 From the Islamic Conquests to the Reformation

The process of acquaintance with Islam may have been slow in the West, but it was relatively swift in the East. The Byzantines were amongst the most immediate victims of the Arab conquests in the Levant in the seventh century, and it was consequently in circles of Syrian Christians that we find the ingredients of some of the derogatory legends concerning the Prophet which it would take Western students of Islam almost a millennium to explode – the story of Zayd and his beautiful wife Zaynab, intending to illustrate the Prophet's lust and hypocrisy; the tale of the dove trained to pick seeds out of the Prophet's ear, supposed to demonstrate his fraudulence; the myth of the Prophet's burial in a magnetically suspended coffin, evidence of magical practices, and many others.

In contrast with later writers from the West the Byzantine theologians had little interest in the conversion of the Muslims to Christianity, but were concerned mainly with proving them to be heretics and forerunners of Antichrist. Nevertheless the Qur'an was translated into Greek, and polemicists such as John of Damascus in the eighth century and Nicetas of Byzantium a hundred years later quoted passages in a generally accurate translation.[9] In the West we have to wait for many centuries – until the twelfth century when Petrus Alfonsi, a converted Jew, devoted a chapter to Islam in his attack on the Jews, and above all when, in the recently conquered city of Toledo, the abbot of Cluny, Peter the Venerable, arranged for the Qur'an and other works about Islam to be translated into Latin in a declared attempt to combat the Muslims with spiritual weapons.[10]

The scholars who assembled in Toledo and contributed to the various parts of the *Corpus Toletanum* were in daily contact with Muslims and had a good understanding of Islam based on *tafsīr*, the Muslim interpretations of the

---

9　M. Ulbricht, 'Al-tarjama al-awwalī l'l-Qur'ān al-Karīm min al-qarn 8/9 m. fī sijjāl Nīkītās al-Bīzanṭī (al-qarn 9 m.) ma'a al-Islām b-ism "tafnīd al-Qur'ān"' *Chronos* 25 (2012), pp. 33–58, esp. pp. 34–37.

10　The development is well described by H. Bobzin, *Der Koran im Zeitalter der Reformation. Studien zur Frühgeschichte der Arabistik und Islamkunde in Europa* (Beirut, 1995), pp. 38–60.

Qur'an, as well as on the *hadīth* or traditions concerning the Prophet.[11] And there is ample evidence that many Islamic concepts which Christians had difficulty not only in accepting, but even in understanding, had been correctly perceived in the Middle Ages. James of Vitry and Ricoldo da Monte Croce, for example, seem to have grasped fully the Islamic idea of one religion in all ages and nations revealed by different prophets at different times, even if Matthew of Paris presented it as a belief in a succession of three religions, Judaism, Christianity, Islam, each one replacing the other – an interpretation which was more comprehensible, and tended to prevail, in the West. In contrast even to Robert of Ketton, moreover, Marco de Toledo perfectly understood the actual sense of the word 'Islam' as meaning surrender.[12]

Such perceptions continue with little interruption. If we look forward to the late fifteenth century we find Juan Andrés, a Muslim convert to Christianity, producing a polemical work against Islam (which has survived) and a translation of the Qur'an (which has disappeared). What is striking about Juan Andrés is not so much the astonishing accuracy of his translation of those passages of the Qur'an which have survived in his polemical work as his familiarity with some of those very sources which were to play such an important part in the study of Islam in the seventeenth century: the *tafsīr* of two major commentators of the late eleventh and early twelfth century, the Spaniard Ibn 'Atīya and the Persian Mutazilite al-Zamakhsharī, the author of *Al-kashshāf 'an haqā'iq al-tanzīl*.[13]

In the fourteenth century, however, the map of the Islamic world was already changing, and the consequences were considerable. The provisions for the teaching of Arabic at the universities of Paris, Oxford, Bologna and Salamanca announced at the Council of Vienne in 1311 and conceived in the same missionary spirit which prompted most analyses of Islam, had remained a dead letter. Islam, previously associated with the great Arabic-speaking transmitters of Greek thought and science, became the religion of the advancing Mongols and of the Turks who were penetrating far deeper into Europe than the Arabs had

---

11   Cf. T.E. Burman, *Reading the Qur'ān in Latin Christendom*, pp. 36–40; U. Cecini, *Alcoranus latinus. Eine sprachliche und kulturwissenschaftliche Analyse der Koranübersetzungen von Robert von Ketton und Marcus von Toledo* (Berlin, 2012), pp. 17–18, 68–70.
12   The best survey still remains N. Daniel, *Islam and the West. The Making of an Image* (rev. ed. Oxford, 1993), pp. 17–45. See also J.V. Tolan, *Saracens. Islam in the Medieval European Imagination* (New York, 2002); idem, *Faces of Muhammad: Western Perceptions of the Prophet of Islam from the Middle Ages to Today* (Princeton, 2019).
13   Bobzin, *Der Koran*, pp. 77–79, 450. Cf. also H. Bobzin, "Bemerkungen zu Juan Andrés und zu seinem Buch *Confusión de la secta mahomatica* (Valencia 1515)" in M. Forstner, ed., *Festschrift für H.-R. Singer* (Frankfurt-am-Main, 1991), pp. 529–548.

ever done. Even if the Turks would be admired in the West for their valour and their piety, neither they nor the Mongols were regarded as the bearers of civilization. Until well into the modern period there was a marked reluctance in the West to credit them with any cultural achievement. In 1621 a man generally acclaimed as an expert, Thomas Erpenius, could still proclaim: 'Nor, indeed, should my hearers think that the Arabs were anything like those who have now gained power over matters in the Orient, the Turks – a tribe of Scythian barbarians who took over power some three centuries ago when that famous kingdom of the Saracens had been broken up. The Turks neither were nor are lovers of learning.'[14]

With the development of humanism in the West, moreover, the growing study of Greek and the attendant discovery of Greek manuscripts, a critical attitude developed to the Arabic translations of the Greek classics which had an adverse effect on the study of the language of the Qur'an and the culture of Islam. Rather than conveyors, the Arabic translators came to be regarded as distorters of the works of the Ancients.[15] Certainly, an interest persisted in Arabic-writing scientists. Western scholars would collect manuscripts, and continue to read the works, of Avicenna and other writers on medicine into the seventeenth century. But the days when the Arab world was seen as the saviour of a great (and European) culture, and when its own achievements in numerous practical domains were recounted admiringly by European visitors, were over.

The Turkish threat led to renewed calls for a crusade and these were again accompanied by missionary endeavours to study Islamic texts which hardly vary in tone from their medieval predecessors. Islam was viewed more than ever in the West as a dark menace.[16] This encouraged the circulation of the anti-Islamic legends concocted by the Byzantines, and when the study of Islam truly resumed in the sixteenth century it was in very different circumstances from those of the Middle Ages.

An important place was held in this development by the Reformation. Islam was drawn into Western interconfessional disputes within a few decades of Luther's break with Rome. The Catholics accused the Protestants of affinities with the Muslims, and vice versa. Praise of Islamic customs and institutions was almost invariably intended as an implicit criticism of the ecclesiastical

---

14 R. Jones, 'Thomas Erpenius (1584–1624) on the Value of the Arabic Language' *Manuscripts of the Middle East* 1 (1986), pp. 15–25, esp. p. 18.
15 F. Klein-Funke, *Die klassische Antike in der Tradition des Islam* (Darmstadt, 1980), pp. 17–52.
16 R.W. Southern, *Western Views of Islam in the Middle Ages* (Cambridge MA, 1978), pp. 67–109.

situation in Europe. The success of the Prophet and the rise and spread of Islam, which had long been interpreted by Christians as a form of divine punishment, were presented as an enduring warning of where religious divisions might lead. Certain Calvinists believed that they could ally themselves with the sultan to destroy Catholicism and subsequently convert the Turks to Christianity.[17] Descriptions of Islam were coloured – and distorted – accordingly.

The medieval eschatological predictions continued, fostered by the great rift in Western Christendom. The standard range of identifications remained: the Prophet seen as Antichrist; the Turk or the Saracen regarded as the 'little horn' of the fourth beast in Daniel 7:8, as one of the kings of the East in Revelation 15:12, or as one of the three heads of the eagle in the apocryphal 2 Esdras. In the end, however, the Muslims would be converted. The words of St Matthew (24:14) continued to echo: 'And this gospel of the kingdom shall be preached in all the world for a witness unto all nations, and then shall the end come'. This passage remained a constant stimulus to missionary activity and, however disappointing its results, resounded into the nineteenth century when members of the clergy saw the spread of the European empires as the necessary condition for converting the Muslims. They applauded the increasing knowledge of Islam which had been acquired since the sixteenth century and at last made it possible to debate with them on an equal footing.[18]

Another factor which affected the study of Islam from the early sixteenth century onwards was the emergence of the Ottoman empire. The new power that swiftly extended its hold over the Arab world, from the eastern borders of Morocco to the western fringes of Persia, was indeed seen as ideologically hostile, but it was also regarded as a potential political ally and an important trading partner.[19] François I of France had hoped to involve the sultan in an alliance against his Habsburg neighbours, and from then on European powers were for ever courting the sultan in efforts to persuade him to attack their enemies or to prevent him from attacking their friends. This led to the more or less permanent diplomatic representation of nations which had previously had little more than a tenuous foothold in the East. The presence of ambassadors and consulates often entailed, in its turn, the attendance of European scholars, acting as chaplains, employed in commercial or diplomatic capacities, or

---

17 Cf. M.E.H.N. Mout, 'Calvinoturcisme in de zeventiende eeuw. Comenius, Leidse oriëntalisten en de Turkse bijbel' *Tijdschrift voor geschiedenis* 91 (1978), pp. 576–607.
18 See A. Hamilton, 'Western attitudes to Islam in the Enlightenment' *Middle Eastern Lectures* 3 (1999), pp. 69–85, esp. pp. 82–83.
19 N. Malcolm, *Useful Enemies. Islam and The Ottoman Empire in Western Political Thought (1450–1750)* (Oxford, 2019), pp. 104–130.

simply dispatched as collectors of antiquities or as the gatherers of scientific information about the area.

Manuscripts were thus collected on an unprecedented scale, and previously unknown material concerning Islam arrived in Europe.[20] As the seventeenth century drew on this material was classified and exploited systematically by students of Islam. Although certain *tafsīr* had been used in the Middle Ages, allusions and quotations tended to be either implicit or unclear. By the late seventeenth century, on the other hand, the *tafsīr* were being quoted extensively, often both in Arabic and in Latin translation. The more popular were recent and easy to obtain in the East. Such was the case of the fifteenth-century *Tafsīr al-Jalālayn* by the Egyptians Jalāl al-Dīn al-Maḥallī and his pupil Jalāl al-Dīn al-Ṣuyūṭī, one of the best loved commentaries in the Islamic world. The relative brevity and clarity of the work made it particularly desirable in Europe. Arabic chronicles, acquired in manuscript in the Levant, were also published in the original and in translation, and gradually modified the strictly Eurocentric view of the Arab conquests, the Crusades, and the advance of the Turks.

2   Parallel Developments: the Protestant North

Despite the somewhat artificial distinction I propose to make between developments in northern and Protestant Europe and those in southern and Catholic Europe the man regarded as the founder of Arabic studies had a foot in both worlds. Guillaume Postel was a French Catholic.[21] He visited the Levant on two occasions, availing himself each time of the presence of a French ambassador. Besides a great many Christian Arabic manuscripts, Postel, who admired the qualities of the Turks, also collected a considerable amount of Islamic material, such as al-Bukhārī's *Ṣaḥīḥ*, one of the best known collections of *ḥadīth*. In 1542–3 he devoted a part of his *De orbis terrae concordia* to a discussion of the Qur'an. Resting on Juan Andrés, he mentions, albeit in a somewhat garbled form, al-Zamakhsharī and Ibn 'Aṭīya. But he also quotes, from manuscripts of his own, Averroes's *Tahāfut al-tahāfut* and the *Tadhkira* of the thirteenth-century Qur'anic interpreter al-Qurṭubī.

Quite apart from the quality of Postel's translation of large sections of the Qur'an, he proved astonishingly sensitive to Islamic terminology and to certain

---

20   S. Mills, *A Commerce of Knowledge. Trade, Religion, and Scholarship between England and the Ottoman Empire, c. 1600–1760* (Oxford, 2020), pp. 65–138.

21   The highly perceptive discussion by H. Bobzin in *Der Koran*, pp. 365–497, has answered the criticisms of Postel as an Arabist made by Fück, pp. 47–53.

distinctions of crucial importance to Muslim thought. One of these is based on a verse in the third sura, *al-'Imrān* (3:7), and concerns the difference between those parts of the Qur'an which are fixed (*muḥkamāt*) and those susceptible of interpretation (*mutashābihat* or, the term Postel prefers, *ghayr muḥkamāt*). To this passage of the utmost significance for the Mutazilites and other 'rational' interpreters of the text we shall return.[22]

The principal objective of *De orbis terrae concordia* was to convert the Muslims to Christianity. In the tradition of Ramon Llull and Nicholas of Cusa, Postel hoped to present the Muslims with certain irrefutable tenets of the Christian faith with which they would inevitably agree. At the same time, however, there was a distinct streak of anti-Protestantism in his work. He was convinced that the Reformation contained the very same seeds of sedition which had once been sown by the Prophet and that the Protestants might well yield to the same persuasive arguments as the Muslims and return to the bosom of the single Church.

Postel spent the last eighteen years of his life, from 1563 to 1581, enclosed as a lunatic in the convent of St Martin des Champs in Paris. Yet his lunacy was generally admitted to be of a harmless nature and he was free to correspond with the leading Orientalists in Europe and to give tuition in Arabic. His pupils included the compiler of the first Arabic-Latin dictionary to be printed, Franciscus Raphelengius, future professor of Hebrew at the University of Leiden, and the chronologist Joseph Justus Scaliger, who also ended his days at Leiden. Both men had remarkable insights into the study of Arabic, and it is more than likely that they owed some of them to their master in Paris.

It was the sight of the direction that Arabic studies in general were taking by the beginning of the seventeenth century that prompted Scaliger to make his discreet but perceptive remarks about the fruitlessness of the missionary ideal – a mere ploy, he said, which increased the suspicions of the Muslims talking to Christians and made reciprocal understanding all the more difficult.[23] Scaliger's interest in Arabic and in Islam was connected with his studies on chronology. One result of a plan of research which began to upset the accepted biblical view of history was the quest for as many historical sources as possible. Although Scaliger's collection of Arabic manuscripts included a

---

22   Guillaume Postel, *De orbis terrae concordia* (Basle, 1544), p. 153, discussed by Bobzin, *Der Koran*, pp. 473–474. Cf. I. Goldziher, *Die Richtungen der islamischen Koranauslegung* (Leiden, 1970), pp. 127–129 on the importance of the passage for the Mutazilites.

23   *Scal.Cor.*, vol. 7, p. 461: 'Sed quo minus voti compotes fiant, qui Arabismi studio isthic resident, multas equidem causas adferre possem. Duae tamen hae praecipuae sunt. Prior, quod barbari illi suspicacissimi sunt, et Christianos putant ea gratia tantum Arabica discere, ut legem Muhammedis discere, et postea confutare possint …'

copy of the *tafsīr* composed by al-Bayḍāwī in the thirteenth century, *Anwār al-tanzīl wa asrār al-ta'wīl* (UBL, MS Or. 83), Scaliger himself does not seem to have made any use of it. But, with his insights not only into the futility of the missionary objective but also into the dangers of studying Arabic in conjunction with Hebrew (as most Europeans tended to do) and into the extreme importance of a good understanding of the Qur'an,[24] he prepared the way for the great Leiden Arabists of the seventeenth century – for Thomas Erpenius, professor of Arabic at Leiden from 1613 to his death in 1624, and Erpenius's pupil and successor Jacobus Golius.

Both men, in their capacity as professor of Arabic, were public figures who had to prepare apologies for their subject. They needed to combat the same popular prejudice which made the publication of the Qur'an so perilous and they needed to attract patrons who might subsidise the acquisition of manuscripts and the publication of sources. In his second oration of 1621 Erpenius consequently referred to the desirability of converting the Muslims.[25] He also demonstrated his own piety in his application of Arabic to biblical studies and his edition of the Arabic New Testament. The actual direction his studies took, however, recalls the dispassionate curiosity of Scaliger. Besides dismissing some of the more fanciful myths about Islam, such as the idea of the Prophet's burial in a magnetically suspended coffin[26] (a myth revived as late as 1601 by William Parry in a description of the Middle East which was highly influential in England, *A New and Large Discourse on the Travels of Sir Anthony Sherley, Knight, by Sea and over Land to the Persian Empire*), Erpenius, at the start of his second oration, provided a surprisingly impartial survey of the rise of Islam. It was based on his reading of the thirteenth-century Coptic historian al-Makīn, a part of whose vast chronicle, *al-Majmuʿ al-mubārak*, he was preparing for the press on the basis of a manuscript acquired in the East by Postel and held at the Elector Palatine's library in Heidelberg.

The importance of the edition, which was published shortly after Erpenius's death by Golius in 1625 with the title *Historia saracenica*, was that it was the

---

24   For Scaliger's attitude see above.
25   Jones, 'Thomas Erpenius (1584–1624) on the Value of the Arabic Language', p. 22: 'Those of you who are candidates in Sacred Theology, consider what it would be to learn this language without the help of which your Sacred Language (and in my judgement you do not deserve to call it yours unless you lay claim to and acquire Arabic) cannot be fully and perfectly understood, or the impious doctrines of the Muhammadans be examined and beneficially refuted.'
26   *Ibid.*, p. 17: 'Our authorities who say that he invaded Syria and captured Damascus are in fact wrong, as are those who maintain that his body was placed in an iron coffin and supported in the sky at Mecca by means of magnetism. In fact he was buried at Medina in the house of his wife, ʿĀʾisha. This was later made a shrine, and that tomb survives to this day.'

first major break in the West with the Byzantine tradition of historiography. Until then most accounts of the Arab conquest circulated in Western Europe were, or were based on, Greek chronicles, and these accounts, usually accompanied by prophecies of the fall of the Ottoman empire, were highly prejudiced. Although al-Makīn himself was a Christian, a Copt who participated in the Coptic cultural renaissance of the thirteenth century, he wrote for a prevalently Muslim readership. Basing himself on the far earlier work of the Persian al-Ṭabarī, al-Makīn, who was to be the main source of the later Muslim historian al-Maqrīzī, dealt with the Prophet and his triumph in a tone of respect.[27]

Erpenius had failed in his efforts to travel to the East. Even if he assembled what, by the standards of the time in Northern Europe, was an impressive collection of Arabic manuscripts, he was necessarily dependent on an agent in Istanbul for their acquisition. Golius, on the other hand, made long visits to the Arab world, availing himself on each occasion of some diplomatic representation.[28] First, in 1622, he went to Morocco. Later, in 1625, he travelled to the Middle East, and stayed first in the Dutch consulate in Aleppo and then in the embassy in Istanbul. This enabled him to assemble a far larger collection of manuscripts than Erpenius, to benefit from the advice of a network of Muslim and other scholars in the Arab world, stretching from Morocco to Syria, and to gather an unprecedented amount of Qurʾanic material.[29] Just as Erpenius had mentioned the missionary objective in his oration, so Golius expressed his desire for a general conversion to Christianity in the introduction to his great Arabic-Latin dictionary of 1653.[30] Yet we may doubt the extent to which the two scholars, so imbued with the spirit of Scaliger, actually believed in it.

---

27   On al-Makīn see G. Graf, *Geschichte der christlichen arabischen Literatur*, vol. 2 (Vatican City, 1947), pp. 348–351.
28   Cf. W.M.C. Juynboll, *Zeventiende-eeuwsche Beoefenaars van het Arabisch in Nederland* (Utrecht, 1931), pp. 119–183; A. Vrolijk and R. van Leeuwen, *Arabic Studies in the Netherlands. A Short History in Portraits, 1580–1950* (Leiden-Boston, 2014), pp. 41–48.
29   Part of the correspondence of the Leiden Arabists was published by M.Th. Houtsma, 'Uit de oostersche correspondentie van Th. Erpenius, Jac. Golius en Lev. Warner. Eene bijdrage tot de geschiedenis van de beoefening der oostersche letteren in Nederland' *Verhandelingen der Koninklijke Academie van Wetenschappen, Afdeling Letterkunde* 17/3 (Amsterdam, 1887).
30   Jacobus Golius, *Lexicon arabico-latinum* (Leiden, 1653), sig. *5ʳ: 'Faxit Deus ter Opt.Max. ut quam linguam tot gentibus extra Christianum orbem, et quasi omnibus literatis, communem esse voluit, ea utrinque interpres et spiritualis commercii instrumentum fiat, qua eaedem gentes orbi Christiano impertiant quicquid bonae mentis et virtutis habent; hic vero illis salutiferam Evangelii lucem ac vim refundat, ut tandem solus dominetur et universis imperet, qui lux mundi et dominus omnium est, Jesus Christus.'

The tradition of research into historical sources launched by Scaliger, Erpenius and Golius, was pursued by Golius's Swiss pupil Johann Heinrich Hottinger. Hottinger, who studied under Matthias Pasor in Groningen in 1639 and under Golius at Leiden in 1640–1, taught first in his native Zürich and then, from 1655 to 1661, in Heidelberg. He had an exceptionally wide knowledge of Arabic sources, fully apparent in his *Promtuarium* of 1658.[31] It also emerged from his most influential work, the *Historia orientalis* first published in Zürich in 1651 (with the Arabic quotations transliterated in Hebrew characters) and reprinted in an expanded version in 1660 (with the Arabic printed in Arabic).

The work has been rightly criticized, both at the time and since. The fiercest contemporary critic was Abraham Ecchellensis or Ibrāhīm al-Ḥāqilānī, a learned Maronite who had taught oriental languages in Pisa, Rome and Paris, and was involved in editing the Paris Polyglot Bible.[32] After his final return to Rome in 1661 he published his confutation of John Selden, *Eutychius patriarchus alexandrinus vindicatus*, the last two hundred pages of which are directed against Hottinger. He deplored Hottinger's ignorance of the Arabic language, advancing an impressive list of mistakes. While stressing his own detestation of the Qur'an,[33] Ecchellensis was particularly critical of Hottinger's treatment of Islam, and scored a good point when he showed that Hottinger had described the legal schools or *madhāhib* as heretical religious sects. Admittedly, even good Arabists, such as Edward Pococke, were to have difficulty translating *madhhab* into Latin, and used the word *secta* for lack of anything better, but Hottinger, in contrast to Pococke, seemed quite unaware of the legal, rather than the religious, significance of the term.[34]

A further drawback of Hottinger's *Historia orientalis* is that, in contrast to the studies produced in Leiden, it is markedly confessional, inspired by an aggressive Calvinism and violent in its anti-Islamicism and anti-Catholicism. This does much to undermine the qualities of the book. And qualities it has,

---

31 On Hottinger see J. Loop, *Johann Heinrich Hottinger. Arabic and Islamic Studies in the Seventeenth Century* (Oxford, 2013).

32 On Ecchellensis see B. Heyberger, 'Abraham Ecchellensis dans la République des Lettres' in B. Heyberger, ed., *Orientalisme, science et cntroverse: Abraham Ecchellensis (1605–1664)* (Turnhout, 2010), pp. 9–51.

33 Abrahamus Ecchellensis, *Eutychius patriarcha alexandrinus vindicatus* (Rome, 1661), vol. 2, p. 382: 'Alcoranus itaque est omnium rerum obscoenarum prostibulum, et cloaca, fabularum colluvies, copiosissima mendaciorum bibliotheca, uno verbo impietatum omnium Epitome, et Breviarium.' For the dispute see Loop, *Johann Heinrich Hottinger*, pp. 95–101.

34 Ecchellensis, *Eutychius*, vol. 2, pp. 378–446. Cf. J.H. Hottinger, *Historia orientalis* (Zürich, 1551), pp. 340–373. For a further discussion see Loop, *Johann Heinrich Hottinger*, pp. 140–145, 202–214.

for besides the chronicle of al-Makīn, Hottinger used the biographical dictionary of Ibn Khallikān (which Golius was the first Western Orientalist to discover), al-Bukhārī's *Ṣaḥīḥ*, and the account of the lives of the prophets by the eleventh-century al-Kisā'ī, an important guide to the Muslim interpretation of the figure of Christ. He drew on a number of the *tafsīr*, on al-Zamakhsharī, and above all on al-Bayḍāwī, giving sizeable excerpts in Arabic followed by a translation. Hottinger was thus a most useful source. Lancelot Addison would rely on him in his life of the Prophet, his *First State of Mahumedism* which came out in 1678, in order to substantiate his claims that he was basing himself chiefly on Arab sources. So did Humphrey Prideaux who made much of al-Bayḍāwī in his best-selling *True Nature of Imposture fully display'd in the Life of Mahomet* of 1697. But Hottinger was also used, as we shall see, by one of the greatest of the Italian Arabists, Ludovico Marracci.

The other eminent Northern European Arabist of the mid-seventeenth century who added to the knowledge of Islam, the Englishman Edward Pococke, was of a superior calibre to Hottinger.[35] Pococke had acquired his training independently of the school of Scaliger. True, he had had his first Arabic lessons from William Bedwell in London, who had also briefly given instruction to Erpenius on Scaliger's recommendation. But although he was to be in correspondence with Dutch scholars such as Hugo Grotius, and met Golius in Syria, Pococke owed his knowledge of Arabic and his approach to Arabic culture to Muslims he met after his appointment in 1629 as chaplain to the English Levant Company in Aleppo.

A member of the clergy, chaplain to the English merchants in Aleppo, a pious supporter of the Anglican church who suffered for his convictions at the time of the Civil War, Pococke would seem to have confirmed his commitment to Christianity, and to its propagation in the Muslim world, with his translation into Arabic of Grotius's *De veritate religionis christianae* and of the Anglican catechism. Yet Pococke, like Golius, remained in touch with his Muslim friends well after his return to England and his appointment as Laudian professor of Arabic at Oxford. His main work in the field of Islamic studies was, by contemporary standards, a model of impartiality.

This was the *Specimen Historiae Arabum*, an edition of a brief text on early Islamic history by Bar Hebraeus, or Abū 'l-Faraj, the thirteenth-century Jacobite historian, like al-Makīn a Christian, but a Christian writing for a Muslim as well

---

35 For Pococke see Toomer, pp. 116–126, 134–16, 145–146, 155–167, 212–226, 271–279; Mills, *A Commerce of Knowledge*, pp. 71–95.

as a Christian readership.[36] Of the various informed works on Islam published in the seventeenth century – it came out in 1650, a year before Hottinger's *Historia* – this was undoubtedly the most popular, quoted and paraphrased throughout the eighteenth century, and reissued by Joseph White, professor of Arabic at Oxford, in 1806. It was not so much the few pages by Bar Hebraeus that made it important – Pococke would follow it up with the complete text of his entire history, the *Historia compendiosa dynastiarum*, in 1663 – as the huge critical apparatus attached by Pococke, based on an unprecedented study of Islamic sources many of which were included in the manuscript collection which he had assembled in the East and which found its way into the Bodleian.

Bar Hebraeus's text provided information about the religions in Arabia at the time of the birth of the Prophet, about the life of the Prophet, the sects into which Islam was soon divided and the legal schools. In his notes Pococke, in the tradition of Erpenius, attacked the anti-Islamic legends. He quoted from a vast variety of poets, philosophers, lexicographers, topographers and historians. These included Ibn Khallikān and the two Ibn al-Athīr brothers writing at the turn of the twelfth and the thirteenth centuries, Majdaddīn, and above all al-Shaybānī, the author of the *Kitāb al-kāmil fī 'l-tārīkh*. He used the Jalālayn, the *tafsīr* of al-Zamakhsharī and al-Bayḍāwī, and provided an unprecedented amount of data on the Mu'tazilites, derived chiefly from his copy of the work on sects, the *Kitāb al-milal wa 'l-niḥal* completed by al-Shahrastānī in 1127 (Bodl., MS Poc. 83).

Pococke may have been extraneous to the direct line of teaching descending from Scaliger, but his *Specimen* was obviously in that tradition. It resulted from a concern with expanding the available sources in order to reach a greater understanding of the events attending the Arab conquests and the spread of Islam. But while this development was taking place in the Protestant North, a parallel but somewhat different process was occurring in the Roman Catholic South of Europe. Admittedly the first seventeenth-century printed edition of the Qur'an in Arabic – the sixteenth-century one had been produced in Italy – was the work of a German Protestant, the Lutheran Abraham Hinckelmann in Hamburg. But, even if his *Al-Coranus*, which came out in 1694, contained a long introduction, it lacked not only a translation but any form of commentary to the actual text that went beyond a few pages which depended on Pococke and on the *Prodromus* of Ludovico Marracci pubished in 1691. It was thus quickly surpassed.

---

36 Cf. Graf, *Geschichte*, vol. 2, pp. 272–281.

3   Parallel Developments: the Catholic South

If we compare the growth of Arabic studies in northern and southern Europe we are inevitably struck by the advantages with which the South started out. When the northern European libraries held hardly a single Arabic text, the southern libraries already had sizeable collections. The Vatican had had a respectable collection of Arabic manuscripts, which included certain Islamic texts, ever since the foundation of the library in the late fifteenth century.[37] Eastern delegates to the Council of Florence had brought codices with them, and envoys to the Eastern churches returned also carrying manuscripts, although mainly Christian ones. The military campaigns of the sixteenth century – Charles v's occupation of Tunis, the battle of Lepanto, and numerous skirmishes – provided manuscripts amongst the loot, and so, in the course of the sixteenth century, the Vatican collection grew. At the same time private collectors, such as Diego Hurtado de Mendoza, assembled Arabic manuscripts, and, in the case of Mendoza, these would swell the huge collection housed in the Escorial.[38] By the early seventeenth century other Italian libraries were competing with the Vatican – the Medici collection in Florence, the collections in Venice, the Ambrosian library in Milan, as well as numerous smaller libraries in Rome itself. On the whole the emphasis tended to be on Christian works, but a large amount of Islamic writings were also included.

Then there was the presence of Arabic-speaking Christians. There had been a constant trickle of Copts, Jacobites and Maronites making their way to Rome throughout the sixteenth century. This increased with the foundation by Gregory XIII of colleges – for the Greeks and the Neophytes in 1577, and, above all, for the Maronites in 1584. The Catholic world could consequently benefit from the arrival of men who, besides a command of Arabic, often had a direct knowledge of Islam. One example was the Maronite Abraham Ecchellensis who criticized Hottinger's *Historia orientalis* so severely.

The intensification of the Catholic interest in Islam in the course of the seventeenth century was due in part to a growing missionary activity. It was connected with the plans, in France, of Charles de Gonzague, Père Joseph and Cardinal Richelieu; the expansion of the Capuchins and the Jesuits in the

---

37   Analysed in some detail by G. Levi della Vida, *Ricerche sulla formazione del più antico fondo dei manoscritti orientali della Biblioteca Vaticana* (Vatican City, 1939). See also A. Hamilton, 'Eastern Churches and Western Scholarship' in A. Grafton, ed., *Rome Reborn: The Vatican Library and Renaissance Culture* (Washington-New Haven-Vatican City, 1993), pp. 225–249, 303.

38   B. Justel Calabozo, *La Real Biblioteca de El Escorial y sus manuscritos árabes* (Madrid, 1978).

Middle East; and the foundation in Rome of the *Congregatio de Propaganda Fide* in 1622. The missionary objective, which was constantly present, was to lead less to a concern with a careful reconstruction of early Arab history than to a proper understanding of the Qur'an essential for combating Islam. It is thus among the Catholics that we find a particularly thorough use of the *tafsīr*.

André Du Ryer, the man who was to familiarize European readers with the *tafsīr*, was the first Orientalist to publish a translation of the whole of the Qur'an in a European vernacular: it appeared in French in 1647. Born in Marcigny in Burgundy as a member of the petty nobility, probably in the last years of the sixteenth century, he attracted the attention of François Savary de Brèves, ambassador first in Istanbul and then in Rome, who held the French consulate in Egypt. Du Ryer was first sent to serve an apprenticeship at the consulate in Alexandria and then, in 1623, was himself appointed consul in Cairo. He was in office until 1626.[39] In 1631 he was chosen as interpreter to the French ambassador to Istanbul, Henri de Gournay de Marcheville, and was subsequently made ambassador extraordinary of the sultan in Paris.[40] Although he had many links with the circles of free-thinking Frenchmen who fully approved of the French alliance with the sultan and were opposed to the tendency of the zealously Catholic *dévots* who would have preferred an agreement with the Habsburgs, Du Ryer was also involved, either directly or indirectly, in the vast missionary movement that irradiated from France. His first protector, Savary de Brèves, had himself published an influential little work on the importance of wooing the Eastern Christians into an alliance against the Muslims.[41] Marcheville was connected with the missionary plans of Père Joseph, joined Charles de Gonzague's crusading militia, and assisted the Capuchins in their endeavours to form missions in Persia and the Ottoman empire. The various works Du Ryer produced – his Turkish grammar (published) and dictionary (unpublished), as well as his Qur'an translation – contained prefaces stressing their importance for missionaries, and he dedicated them to figures such as Richelieu known to favour the conversion of the Muslims.

When Du Ryer was in the Levant he too collected manuscripts. They included the *Tafsīr al-Jalālayn* and the *Tanwīr fī al-tafsīr* of al-Righī al-Tūnisī who died in 1315 (in fact an abridged version of the *Tafsīr al-kabīr* written by Fakhr al-Dīn al-Rāzī a century earlier), the *tafsīr* of al-Bayḍāwī, and the Turkish

---

39　For Du Ryer's life see A. Hamilton and F. Richard, *André Du Ryer and Oriental Studies in Seventeenth-Century France* (London-Oxford, 2004), pp. 21–57. See also A. Hamilton, 'André Du Ryer' *CMR*, vol. 9, pp. 453–65.

40　See above, pp. 94, 99–100.

41　A. Hamilton, 'François Savary de Brèves' *CMR*, vol. 9, pp. 415–22.

tafsīr entitled *Anfs Joahir tafsīr*.[42] These are the works which he names so ostentatiously in the margins of his translation, even if he never explains to the reader what *tafsīr* actually are. He made his translation of the Qur'an on his return to Paris, where he had been appointed royal interpreter and gentleman of the royal chamber.[43] Although his object was to produce a far more literal version than the paraphrase of Robert of Ketton, the result was in fact more literary than literal – a fluent and readable text, which, in accuracy, often falls behind the medieval translations and does not suggest that Du Ryer consulted the manuscript of Marco de Toledo available in Paris.[44] Of the *tafsīr*, on the other hand, he made an important use in revising some of the accepted translations. When he came to 33:56, for example, traditionally translated as the angels 'praying for' the Prophet and interpreted as a sign of blasphemy, Du Ryer pointed out correctly in the margin with a reference to the *Jalālayn*, that the verb *ṣallā* in fact also meant 'to invoke blessings'. Similarly, the word *jinn*, in the title of sura 72 and elsewhere, had been translated traditionally as 'devils', thus implying that the Prophets included devils amongst his followers, but Du Ryer rightly informed his readers that 'some Mahometans' preferred the term 'spirits'.

But Du Ryer was not always entirely reliable. A telling example is his treatment of the important verse in the third sura (3:8) about how the Qur'an should be interpreted, a passage which, as we saw, was discussed by Postel. An acceptable English translation of the text is: 'He [Allah] it is who has sent down to thee the Book; in it there are verses that are decisive in meaning – they are the basis of the Book – and there are others that are susceptible of different interpretations. But those in whose hearts is perversity pursue such thereof as are susceptible of different interpretations, seeking discord and seeking interpretations of it. And none knows its interpretation except Allah and those who are firmly grounded in knowledge …' Du Ryer translates: 'c'est lui qui t'envoie le livre duquel les préceptes sont très-nécessaires; ils sont l'origine et le fondement de la loi, semblable en pureté les uns aux autres, et sans contradiction. Ceux qui en leur coeur inclinent à s'éloigner de la vérité, ensuivent souvent

---

42 Many of the manuscripts belonging to Du Ryer entered the library of Pierre Séguier, Louis XIII's chancellor and Du Ryer's patron, and subsequently that of Séguier's son-in-law, the duc de Coislin. They are now at the BnF.

43 For Du Ryer's Qur'an translation see Hamilton and Richard, *André Du Ryer*, pp. 91–118.

44 M.T. d'Alverny, 'Deux traductions latines du Coran au Moyen Age' *Archives d'histoire doctrinale et littéraire du moyen-âge* 22–23 (1947–1948), pp. 116–20, suggests that Du Ryer might have used a manuscript of Marco de Toledo's translation. Judging from the copy now at the Bibliothèque Mazarine in Paris (MS 780), however, Marco de Toledo was for more accurate both here and elsewhere.

leur inclination désireux de sédition et de savoir l'explication de l'Alcoran; mais personne ne sait son explication que Dieu et ceux qui sont profonds en doctrine.'[45] The contrast between *mutashābihat*, susceptible of different interpretation, and *muḥkamāt*, decisive and fixed in meaning, has been lost.[46] He seems to have overlooked the interpretations of the passage in the *tafsīr*.[47]

Du Ryer's marginal references to the *tafsīr* were interpreted by an uncritical public as signs of his erudition, and he must go down to history as the first scholar to publicize the works in print and thus to draw attention to their relevance. His translation, moreover, was remarkably successful. Not only did it go through numerous editions in France, but it was published, in its turn, in English, Dutch, German and Russian. The English version was reprinted in 1806 as the first translation of the Qur'an to appear in America. Manuscript copies have come to light in Italian,[48] Spanish,[49] and even in Hebrew.[50]

The great step taken in the Roman Catholic world after Du Ryer's translation of the Qur'an was of such magnitude that it must be regarded as a leap. This was the critical edition of the Qur'an – the Arabic text, a Latin translation, and extensive notes – published by Ludovico Marracci in 1698. Marracci, who learnt his Arabic in Rome largely on his own but with the occasional help of Maronites, never set foot in the East. At one time the confessor of the conservative pope

---

45 *L'Alcoran de Mahomet* (La Haye, 1685), p. 39.
46 Cf. the other translations. Robert of Ketton in T. Bibliander, ed., *Machumetis Alcoranum* (Basle, 1550), p. 21: 'Isteque continet verba quaedam firmissima, et infringibilia, quae sunt libri scilicet mater, ac materia: quaedam vero contraria, quae mutantis perversique cordis homines ad controversiam caeteris inferendam, et ad expositionis suae notitiam exequuntur.' N. Petrus Pons, *Alchoranus latinus quem transtulit Marcus canonicus Toletanus*, p. 42: 'Ipse est qui destinauit tibi Librum, in quo sunt miracula manifesta seu fundamentum Libri. Et alia sunt inuoluta. Illi autem in quorum cordibus est scrupulus, imitantur inuoluta querentes tribulacionem et querentes exposicionem. Et non nouit exposicionem eius nisi Deus.' Cf. the translation of Marracci, p. 105: 'Ipse est, qui descendere fecit super te Librum, ex eo sunt aliqui versus sapienter dispositi, ipsi sunt mater Libri: alii vero assimilati illis. Porro illi, in quorum cordibus est declinatio (a veritate) sectabuntur, quod est assimilatum his ob desiderium schismati.'
47 His treatment of the sura also warrants Marracci's criticisms. When comparing Du Ryer's translation with that of Robert of Ketton he admits: 'Haec magis inhaeret verbis, et fidelius exprimit sensus,' but then goes on: 'Sed in hac quoque non raro Auctor caespitat, vel hallucinatur; credo, quia Arabicae ipse linguae ignarus, interpretes non ita peritos, vel fidos invenit ...' (Marracci, p. 7).
48 P.M. Tommasino, *L'Alcorano di Macometto. Storia di un libro del Cinquecento europeo* (Bologna, 2013), p. 40.
49 J.P. Arias Torres, 'Bibliografía sobre las traducciones del Alcorán en el ámbito hispanico' *Trans. Revista de traductología* 11 (2007), pp. 261–272, esp. p. 264.
50 M.M. Weinstein, 'A Hebrew Qur'ān manuscript' *Studies in Bibliography and Booklore* 10 (1972), pp. 19–52, esp. pp. 23–24.

Innocent XI, Marracci, besides his role in the *Sacra Congregatio de Propaganda Fide*, was active in the organization of the Index, took a leading role in the campaign against Miguel de Molinos and the Quietists, and, in his last publication, attacked the Jews.[51] This austere and committed servant of the Church thus had the perfect credentials for undertaking so polemical a task as the translation and editing of the Qurʾan. Nevertheless such was the prejudice against a text prohibited by so many indexes that it took Marracci almost twenty-five years to have his work printed.[52] The lengthy *Prodromus*, which originally appeared in 1691 and preceded his translation, was a confutation of Islam, and his translation and notes to each sura were followed by further confutations. At first at least, Marracci was avowedly working for missionaries, but in fact some of his less guarded statements, such as his admission that Islam might seem more rational than Christianity,[53] as well as his extraordinary use of sources, were to be invaluable instruments in the hands of the eighteenth-century sympathizers with Islam.

Marracci exploited to the full the existing printed sources. He made abundant use of Pococke's *Specimen*; he even plundered Hottinger's *Historia orientalis* for quotations from *tafsīr*. But he worked mainly on manuscripts. Roberto Tottoli, in the course of his inspection of Marracci's papers at his convent in Rome, discovered that he had started with a copy of the *tafsīr* by the tenth-century Spanish commentator Ibn Abī Zamanīn.[54] Then, availing himself also of the growing collections in the Roman libraries, he consulted manuscripts of the *tafsīr* of al-Bayḍāwī, al-Zamakhsharī, al-Hamdānī and, his favourite, the *Tafsīr al-Jalālayn*. This last was the one he quoted most frequently, going

---

51 The standard study of Marracci's sources is still C.A. Nallino, 'Le fonti arabe manoscritte dell'opera di Ludovico Marracci sul Corano' in his *Raccolta di scritti editi e inediti*, vol. 2 (Rome, 1940), pp. 90–134. Besides the work of Roberto Tottoli cited below, we can now add the new biographical information collected in G.L. D'Errico (ed.), *Il Corano e il pontefice. Ludovico Marracci fra cultura islamica e Curia papale* (Rome, 2015).

52 For Marracci's struggles see G. Pizzorusso, 'Ludovico Marracci tra ambiente curiale e cultura orientalista a Roma nel XVII secolo' in D'Errico, *Il Corano e il pontefice*, pp. 91–118, esp. pp. 103–113.

53 Marracci, *Prodromus*, p. 4 (Praefatio): "Habet nirmrum haec superstitio quidquid plausibile, ac probabile in Christiana Religione reperitur, et quae naturae legi, ac lumini consentanea videntur. Mysteria illa fidei nostrae, quae primo aspectu incredibilia, et impossibilia apparent; et praecipue, quae nimis ardua humanae naturae censentur, penitus excludit. Hinc moderni Idolorum cultores, facilius ac promptius Saracenicam, quam Evangelicam legem amplectuntur; et in posterum amplectentur, nisi a Missionariis nostris, his, quae ego meo opere pono, argumentis praeveniantur, ac praemuniantur.'

54 R. Glei and R. Tottoli, *Ludovico Marracci at Work. The Evolution of his Latin Translation of the Qurʾān in the Light of his Newly Discovered Manuscripts, with an Edition and a Comparative Linguistic Analysis of Sura 18* (Wiesbaden, 2016), pp. 15–31.

so far as to insert some of its identifications into his actual translation of the text. To works which had been used by Hottinger and Pococke Marracci added others. He was the first European to use the *tafsīr* of the highly orthodox Ibn Taymiyyah of the thirteenth century and of the eleventh-century al-Thaʿlabī.[55] Marracci's *Alcorani textus universus* can thus be regarded as the richest collection of Islamic sources (which he quotes in Arabic and in Latin translation) to have appeared to that date.

Apart from his failure to capture the poetic element of the Qur'an, the main criticism which a modern student of Islam might make is that Marracci, like his predecessors and indeed many of his successors, seems to have been unaware of the varying ideologies behind the *tafsīr* he quoted. Although he knew about the Mutazilites, and although Pococke had already pointed out that al-Zamakhsharī was a Mutazilite, Marracci never uses the *tafsīr* of al-Zamakhsharī as an illustration of the Mutazilite point of view and leaves uncommented those passages in the Qur'an – on the freedom of will and other matters – which were of particular significance for the movement. He seems also to have overlooked the relationship between the various *tafsīr* – the fact, for example, that al-Bayḍāwī based his own interpretations on al-Zamakhsharī, but tried to purge them of all Mutazilite bias. The study of Islam had undoubtedly progressed in depth thanks to the systematic collection and use of Islamic sources by the seventeenth-century Arabists, but these sources still had to be sifted and assessed, and that would be the work of later scholars.

4   Conclusion

The republication of Pococke's *Specimen* in the early nineteenth-century is one of many indications that, in the field of Islamic history, as in the fields of grammar and lexicography, the achievements of the seventeenth-century Arabists remained unsurpassed for almost three hundred years. Despite the progress marked by the publications of Adriaen Reland in Holland and by Johann Jakob Reiske in Germany, despite the work of scholars such as Simon Ockley, George Sale, Jean Gagnier and others, the eighteenth century was above all a period in which material gathered earlier was studied. 'Le XVIIe et le XIXe inventent, le XVIIIe illustre, accumule et prépare'.[56] The words of Pierre Chaunu certainly hold true where the study of Islam was concerned. Few new Arabic manuscripts entered the European collections. Few new Arabic texts were published.

---

55   For Ibn Taymiyyah see Goldziher, *Richtungen*, pp. 338–40.
56   P. Chaunu, *La civilisation, de l'Europe des lumières* (Paris, 1982), p. 210.

Travellers (or European residents) in the Islamic world did indeed publish accounts of their experiences and thus brought the daily life of Muslims closer to the European imagination – the Russell brothers, with their *Natural History of Aleppo*, are an example[57] – but students of Islam in quest of original sources still relied mainly on the work of Erpenius, Pococke, Hottinger and Marracci. When he published his English translation of the Qur'an George Sale provided a synthesis of developments which had previously been discrete, one southern and one northern. To a translation heavily indebted to Marracci, Sale added a historical introduction which owed much to Pococke.

Acknowledgements

This article was originally published in a collection edited by Jan Assmann *et al.*, *Archiv für Religionsgeschichte* 3 (Munich-Leipzig: K.G. Saur, 2001), pp. 169–182.

---

57   See M.H. van den Boogert, *Aleppo Observed. Ottoman Syria Through the Eyes of Two Scottish Doctors, Alexander and Patrick Russell* (London-Oxford, 2010).

CHAPTER 16

A Lutheran Translator for the Qur'an
A Late Seventeenth-Century Quest

For much of the 1690s Gottfried Wilhelm Leibniz and his circle showed a special concern with the translation of the Qur'an. The eagerness to read the fundamental Islamic text in translation and the search for a translator were by no means new. There had been numerous attempts to produce partial or entire translations from the Arabic in the course of the seventeenth century.[1] But never does the quest for a translator seem to have been so urgent as it was in the last two decades. One of the first signs of this interest can be traced back to 1681, when the professor of history and oriental languages at Altdorf, Johann Christoph Wagenseil, announced that in Rome Ludovico Marracci, the confessor of Pope Innocent XI, was planning a new Latin translation and a confutation of the Qur'an. Wagenseil, a widely travelled man who had accompanied the young Count Ferdinand Ernst von Traun to Italy in the early 1660s and had taken an active part in Italian intellectual life, had received the news from one of the most prominent citizens of the Republic of Letters in southern Europe, the librarian Antonio Magliabechi in Florence.[2] For a decade little more was said about the matter, but in 1691 Marracci at last published the first part of his great work, the *Prodromus ad refutationem Alcorani*. This was due to be followed by a bilingual, Latin and Arabic, edition of the text itself and provoked an animated exchange of views between Leibniz and his friends.

In the summer of 1692 Leibniz in Hanover told Wilhelm Ernst Tentzel in Gotha about Marracci's project.[3] From his *Prodromus* it was obvious not only that he had an exceptional knowledge of Arabic, but that he also had at his

---

[1] For a survey see H. Bobzin, 'Von Venedig nach Kairo: zur Geschichte arabischer Korandrucke (16. bis frühes 20. Jahrhundert)' in E. Hanebutt-Benz, D. Glass and G. Roper, eds, *Sprachen des Nahen Ostens und die Druckrevolution. Eine interkulturelle Begegnung* (Westhofen, 2002), pp. 151–176, esp. pp. 159–163, and below 327–328.

[2] J.C. Wagenseil, *Tela ignea Satanae. Hoc est: Arcani, et horribiles Judaeorum adversus Christum Deum, et Christianam Religionem libri* (Altdorf, 1681), vol. 1, p. 48: 'Parat tamen nunc Romae, novam Alcorani translationem Latinam, ac confutationem illi adjunget P. Marracci, Innocentio XI. qui nunc sedet, Romano Pontifici, a sacris confessionibus, ceu nuper Florentia nunciavit, Vir in tantum praedicandus, in quantum virtus et eruditio aestimari possunt, Antonius Magliabechus'.

[3] G.W. Leibniz, *Allgemeiner politischer und historischer Briefwechsel* (Darmstadt-Leipzig-Berlin, 1923–), vol. 8, p. 370.

disposal an extraordinary range of *tafsīr*, Muslim commentaries on the Qur'an. Marracci claimed to be working for the missionaries, but, Leibniz said to Henri Justel in London in the summer of 1692 and repeated in May of the following year to Johann Reiske, the rector of the Fürstenschule in Wolfenbüttel, his object was in fact to convey to the Christian world the true significance of the Qur'an for the Muslims.[4] In December 1692 Magliabechi informed Leibniz that he had seen the first two pages of Marracci's forthcoming translation, but that the whole work would take well over a year to be completed.[5]

Leibniz could only applaud such a bold endeavour to convert the Muslims to Christianity and to clarify the significance of the text of the Qur'an to a Western readership. But should it really be left to a Catholic? In March 1693 he received a letter from Reiske suggesting Lutheran candidates – Johann Andreas Danz in Jena, Abraham Hinckelmann in Hamburg, and Andreas Acoluthus in Breslau.[6] And there were other German Arabists eager to try their hand, men such as Matthias Friedrich Beck, Sebastian Gottfried Starck and Heinrich Siecke (subsequently anglicised as Henry Sike). What is striking about the late seventeenth century is the sheer number of specimens and editions which came into circulation of a text that had once been considered extremely dangerous and still met with some suspicion. How can this be explained?

1 The Turkish Defeat

In 1683 the Austro-Polish forces defeated the Turks at the gates of Vienna. The victory of the Kahlenberg was followed by the Christian advance deep into Ottoman territory, through Hungary to Serbia. On the one hand the vanquished

---

4 *Ibid.*, p. 373: 'Le livre du P. Maracci confesseur du feu Pape Innocent XI sur l'Alcoran', he wrote to Justel on 29 July (O.S.) 1692, 'vient de paroistre. Ce Pere, qui est d'un autre ordre que de celuy des Jesuites a fort lû les commentaires Arabes de l'Alcoran, et son but est de nous apprendre le veritable sens de ce livre, que nos auteurs chrestiens prenent souvent de travers'. In May 1693 he was still more specific to Reiske (*Ibid.*, vol. 9, p. 426): 'Romae non ipse Alcoranus est editus sed Maracii viri docti et in Arabum lectione versati in Alcoranum animadversiones non tam ex Christianorum praejudiciis, quam ex ipsorum Mahometanorum commentariis sumtae. Vellem tandem prodiret integer cum versione accurata notisque ad illustrandum sensum aptis. Sed pauci sunt opinor inter nostros, qui tale quid possint. Et puto plerumque Arabismum mediocrem esse, etsi inter caecos lusci merito aestimentur. Mihi nullus est ad haec studia aditus quod juveni defuerit occasio'.
5 *Ibid.*, p. 584.
6 *Ibid.*, vol. 9, p. 323: 'De Alcorano Romae typis edito quod mones, erat gratissimum. Hujus versionem ac editionem Germania meditatur expectatque, cum Jenae Prof. Danzius, Hamburgi Pastor Eccles. D. Hinckelmannus et Wratislaviae D. Acoluthus promiserint.'

Turkish armies were a rich source of booty, and the booty included Qur'āns, Qur'ānic commentaries, and a variety of Arabic and Turkish texts for which translators were in demand.[7] On the other the military success was regarded as the final reward for the collaboration between Innocent XI and the Holy Roman Emperor, Leopold I, and their consistent crusading policy. Even if Turkish raids continued on the Italian coast – indeed, even if the war against the Turks continued to rage in the Mediterranean for much of the eighteenth century – the myth of Ottoman invincibility had been dispelled and Western Europeans could approach Islam in a more dispassionate frame of mind.

As the Christians at last entered territory largely populated by Muslims, the Western Churches believed that they should prepare to debate with them and, like their predecessors in Spain, convert them by persuasion. For the citizens of the Republic of Letters, this was a chance to rise above confessional hostility and welcome the imminent spread of the true faith. The Protestant Leibniz had already urged the Catholic king of France, Louis XIV, to embark on a crusade and overrun Egypt in 1672.[8] Over twenty-five years later, even if he was fully prepared to give his due to Ludovico Marracci, Leibniz was attracted by the idea that a German Lutheran, or at any rate a German Protestant, might produce the translation of the Qur-'an which would make such a decisive contribution to the spread of Christianity. The Latin version made by Robert of Ketton in 1143 but first printed in Basle in 1543, after all, had appeared with introductory texts by Melanchthon and by Luther himself.[9] The association of the text with the reformers did much to account for Catholic hostility, and Luther's followers retained something of a proprietorial attitude to it.

The celebratory atmosphere produced by the Christian victories was expressed in a number of works on Islam. Two appeared in 1688. The first was a German translation of André Du Ryer's French version of the Qur'an, made from Jan Hendricksz Glazemaker's Dutch rendering, by the German physician and professional translator Johann Lange from Hamburg. It was included in Everhard Werner Happel's *Thesaurus Exoticorum*, a collection of

---

7   For manuscripts as booty in an earlier period see R. Jones, 'Piracy, war, and the acquisition of Arabic manuscripts in Renaissance Europe' *Manuscripts of the Middle East*, 2 (1987), pp. 96–110. See also Jones, pp. 29–47; Jan Schmidt, 'Between author and library shelf: the intriguing history of some Middle Eastern manuscripts acquired by public collections in the Netherlands prior to 1800' in A. Hamilton, M. van den Boogert and B. Westerweel, eds, *The Republic of Letters and the Levant* (Leiden-Boston, 2005), pp. 27–551, esp. pp. 47–48.
8   Cf. G.W. Leibniz, *De Expeditione Aegyptiaca Ludovico XIV Franciae Regi proponenda*, ed. O. Klop (Hanover, 1864).
9   H. Bobzin, *Der Koran im Zeitalter der Reformation. Studien zur Frühgeschichte der Arabistik und Islamkunde in Europa* (Beirut, 1995), pp. 48–55.

texts on America, Africa and Asia and on Islam, dedicated to Leopold I.[10] The second was a specimen translation of two suras of the Qurʾan by Matthias Friedrich Beck.

Beck, who was born in Kaufbeyern in Swabia, had studied at the University of Jena and, under the tuition of Johann Frischmuth, had perfected his knowledge of Greek and Hebrew and then passed on to Arabic and Persian.[11] To these he would add Syriac, Ethiopic and Turkish, and his competence in Turkish and Persian would be a source of admiration for Leibniz and his friends – in June 1696 Leibniz referred in a letter to Magliabechi to the edition which Beck, 'vir doctissimus', had just published of the *Ephemerides Persarum* of that year.[12] In 1678 Beck took up his post as a Lutheran minister in Augsburg. There he encountered the booty which the Habsburg army brought back from Turkish territory. This included one copy of the Qurʾan, obtained in Buda and belonging to the imperial councillor Octavian August Langenmantel, and two others presented respectively to the Augsburg library by Langenmantel's colleague in the city council Leonhard Weiss and by the Lutheran pastor Anton Reiser. Beck, who also had a manuscript copy of his own, was urged to undertake a translation.[13] Both the subtitle of the specimen he published and the choice of

---

10   *Vollständiges Türckisches Gesetz-Buch, Oder Des Ertz-betriegers Mahomets Alkoran. Welcher vorhin nimmer vollkomen heraus gegeben, noch im Druck aussgefertiget worden. Auss der Arabischen in die Frantzösische Sprach übergesetzt Durch Herrn Du Ryer. Auss dieser aber in die Niederländische Durch J.H. Glasemacker. Und jetzo zum allerersten mahl in die Hoch teutsche Sprache versetzet Durch Johan Lange, Medicinae Candidatum* in E.W. Happel, *Thesaurus Exoticorum. Oder eine mil Ausländische Raritäten und Geschichten Wohlversehene Schatz-Kammer Fürstellend Die Asiatische, Africanische und Americanische Nationes ... Darauff folget eine Umständliche von Türcken Beschreibung: Der Türcken Ankunfft ... Wie auch ihres Propheten Mahomets Lebens-Beschreibung, und sein Verfluchtes Gesetz-Buch oder Alkoran ...* (Hamburg, 1688). Cf. A. Hamilton and F. Richard, *André Du Ryer and Oriental Studies in Seventeenth-Century France* (London-Oxford, 2004), p. 117.

11   See A. Ben Tov, 'Matthias Friedrich Beck' *CMR*, vol. 14, pp. 81–87.

12   Leibniz, *Briefwechsel*, vol. 12, p. 660.

13   Matthias Friedrich Beck, *Specimen Arabicum, hoc est, Bina Capitula Alcorani XXX. de Roma el XLIIX. de Victoria, e IV. Codicibus MSS Arabice descripta, Latine versa, et Notis Animadversionibusque locupletata. His nostris Temporibus, Quibus Imperium Romano-Germanicum Victorias contra Muhammedanos prosequitur, accommodatum Argumentum* (Augsburg, 1688), sig. X3ʳ: 'Dum vero Bellum Hungaricum contra Turcos feliciter hactenus geritur, cui prosperos quoque successus atque exoptatum tandem finem benignissimum Numen concedere velit! & Praedae Muhammedanae, ut in alias Imperii Urbes, ita in nostram quoque Augustam a militibus, ex militia in hyberna reversis, deferuntur, libri verbi gr. schedulae, annuli, vasa, &c. Arabice exarata & inscripta, quorum usum, literarumque inscriptarum sententiam ignorantes, curiosiores possessores mihi (ex eorum opinione harum literarum perito) interpretationem benevole commiserunt ... Ut vero linguam

suras, 30 (*al-Rūm*), translated by Beck as *de Roma*, and 48 (*al-fatḥ*), translated as *de victoria*, reflected the political events.

Three years later, as we saw, Ludovico Marracci published his *Prodromus*. In the preface he referred in emotional terms to the successful efforts of the pope and the emperor to vanquish the Turks.[14] The text of the Qur'an, finally published in Padua in 1698 (and preceded by a reissue of the *Prodromus*), was dedicated to the victorious emperor. In his dedicatory epistle Marracci quoted the Song of Deborah, Judges 5:20: 'From heaven fought the stars, from their courses they fought against Sisera', and he compared the Turkish general, Kara Mustafa Pasha, to Sisera. With Leopold I, he believed, Christianity would at last be carried back to the East and to the vast area of the Byzantine Empire usurped by the Turks.[15]

2   Competing Translators

But what of the various translators or editors of the Qur'an mentioned so frequently in the learned correspondence of the time and followed intently by

---

    Arabicam magis mihi redderent familiarem, et operam meam (si qua durante hoc bello Anti-Turcico deinceps desideretur) in interpretandis hisce literis majorem impendere queam, ipsum Alcoranum (quem propter stilum atque elegantiorem sermonis summis Muhammedani laudibus extollunt) evolvere, legere atque interpretari in animum induxi …'

[14] Marracci, *Prodromus* (Praefatio), p. 6: 'Spero autem sortiturum, hoc potissimum tempore, cum Invictissimi Cesaris Leopoldi, Principumque foederatorum arma, Sanctissimi, semperque Gloriosissimi Pontificis Innocentii XI. opera sociata, atque ejusdem opibus precibusque roborata; Othmannicam Potentiam, unicum prope Mahumetanicae superstitionis columen, ita depresserunt, atque infregerunt; ut omnem prorsus pristinos vires recuperandi spem amiserit; et majora quotidie mala, atque extremam denique perniciem a Caesareis fulminibus timere cogatur'.

[15] Marracci, sig. †3ʳ: 'Pugnaverunt, inquam, pro Te, Invictissime Imperator, de Coelo non tam stellae, quam Angeli, atque ipse Deus exercituum adversus novum Sisaram Mustapham Karam, atque innumeras Barbarorum copias, quarum ipse Dux erat, cum ea felicitate, quae ex tam validis propugnatoribus poterat expectari. Detur mihi asserere, obsidionem illam tam hostibus infaustam, quam Tibi, Tuisque fortunatam fuisse. Non enim solum opulentissimas Vobis ex illis profligatis manubias comparavit: sed gloriosissimos etiam ex iisdem deinde triumphos acquisivit. Ab ea enim die Aquilae Tuae felicissime alas explicantes, ad ipsam prope hostium Regiam pervolarunt; atque in oculos potentissimi Tyranni rostris, atque unguibus insilierunt. Et jam quidem supra Byzantinas Arces triumphatrices apparerent, nisi Imperii Tui tuendi necessitas identidem illas alio revocasset. Sed spero, hac quoque sublata, cursum suum felicius repetent, ut Te, quemadmodum Occidens, ita etiam Oriens Sol Monarcham salutet, ac veneretur; et prorsus auferatur Luna illa infausta, quae oppositu suo Eclypses tam foedas Christianis rebus per tot aetates adduxit'

Leibniz, by Mathurin Veyssière de La Croze, and by other eminent citizens of the Republic of Lettters? How did they proceed after the victory of the Kahlenberg? And why was it that Marracci alone succeeded where so many others failed? The predicament of Beck is instructive. Despite the arrival of booty taken from the Ottoman armies, Augsburg was by no means the ideal place in which to translate the Qur'an. Beck had to rely on his own small library. Judging from the sources he quotes in his preface and notes this included the only complete Latin translation of the Qur'an in print, Bibliander's edition of Robert of Ketton and the various critical and anti-Islamic texts published with it – by Ricoldo da Montecroce, Savonarola, Nicholas of Cusa and others. He also seems to have owned the Italian version of the Qur'an translated by Giovanni Battista Castrodardo and published by Andrea Arrivabene in Venice in 1547 (based, in its turn, on Robert of Ketton's Latin), in addition to Johann Heinrich Hottinger's *Historia orientalis*, Thomas Erpenius's Arabic grammar and Jacobus Golius's Arabic dictionary. Yet not only was Beck unable to inspect any *tafsīr*, but there were no Arabic types available for what was to be a bilingual edition, and Beck had to content himself with transliterating the Arabic in Hebrew characters. These were unfortunate drawbacks for a man who was clearly capable. Beck's Latin translation of the two suras stands up to comparison with Marracci's, but the scantiness of his sources meant that his commentary was far from satisfactory.[16]

Other northern European Arabists seem to have faced difficulties of a similar nature. The first scholar in our period to produce a specimen of a translation of the Qur'an after Beck was Johann Andreas Danz.[17] Danz, who was born close to Gotha in 1654, had long been regarded as particularly gifted. He had been spotted in his youth by the duke of Sachsen-Gotha-Altenberg, Frederick I, and had studied at the duke's expense, proceeding to the University of Wittenberg in 1673. The language on which he worked most was Hebrew. He studied over the years with the assistance of Jews and Jewish converts to Christianity, in Hamburg, Jena, Amsterdam, and Oxford. In 1683 he set out on a mission for the duke and visited Holland and England. In Amsterdam, besides continuing with his Talmudic studies, he learned Persian from a Carmelite missionary; he was welcomed at Cambridge by Ralph Cudworth, Henry More, Isaac Newton, John Spencer and Edmund Castell; and at Oxford he came to know Isaac Abendana, Edward Bernard, and, above all, the greatest Arabist of his

---

16   A. Ben Tov, 'Matthias Friedrich Beck', p. 86, also makes clear 'how entangled anti-Jewish and anti-Muslim polemics' were in Beck's commentary on the suras.

17   See the extensive entry in *Zedlers Universal Lexicon*, vol. 7 (Halle-Leipzig, 1734), cols. 161–162.

day, Edward Pococke. It was with Pococke's encouragement that he decided to learn Arabic, and he did so in London under the tuition of a Syrian visitor. On his way back to Germany he studied rabbinic literature with the younger Jacob Trigland, the professsor of theology at Leiden, and then made his way, via Franeker, Groningen and Hamburg, to Jena where, in 1685, he was appointed professor of Oriental languages. He taught and preached there until his death in 1727.

In about 1690,[18] about five years after his arrival in Jena, Danz produced his specimen translation of the first sura of the Qur'an and 66 verses of the second. The rare fragment is undated and contains the Arabic with a Latin translation at the foot of the page. Danz makes the common mistake of attributing the composition of the second sura, *al-baqara*, to Mecca, rather than to Medina where by far the greater part of it in fact originated.[19] There are certain points, however, at which his translation differs in the choice of terminology from those of his predecessors and successors. He translates *kafirīn* (2:33), usually rendered as 'infideles', as 'apostatas'. In translating 2:35, he puts: 'At Satanas lapsu praecipitante ex eo ambos, fecitque eos ex inde ejici, ubi hactenus fuerant'. The choice of the word 'lapsus' to convey *fa azalhuma al-shaytān* provided an essentially Christian association with the Fall. This might suggest the influence of Hackspan's *Fides et leges Mohammaedis* where, in an introductory note to the verses in question, Hackspan refers to the 'lapsus Adami', but when translating the text itself Hackspan, like other translators such as Ravius and Marracci, was more cautious.[20]

---

18   The date given traditionally is 1692 (Schnurrer, p. 410, no. 375), but Jan Loop has discovered evidence which shows that the translation was made considerably earlier. See Wilhelm Ernst Tentzel, *Monatliche Unterredungen einiger guten Freunde* (Thorn-Leipzig, 1692), p. 917, where Tentzel writes: 'Und hat jener [i.e. Danz] allbereit das vor etlichen Jahren gedruckte Specimen nicht nur allenthalben in Europa, sondern auch gar im Orient herum geschicket.'

19   Johann Andreas Danz [*Koran, Sure 1–2:66*] (Jena, 1692), p. 1 (Bayerische Staatsbibliothek, shelfmark: 4 L.as. 32). I am most grateful to Helga Rebhan for her advice about Danz and for providing me with a photocopy of his text. For Danz's specimen see also Bobzin, 'Von Venedig nach Kairo', pp. 159–160. Marracci, pt. 2, p. 11, makes the same mistake as Danz at the head of the sura, but in a note admits, with a reference to the *Tafsīr al-Jalālayn* (where both towns are mentioned), that some authorities believed it to have been composed in Medina.

20   Danz [*Koran*], p. 7. Theodor Hackspan, *Fides et leges Mohammaedis exhibitae ex Alkorani manuscripto duplici, praemissis institutionibus arabicis* (Altdorf, 1646) sig. L3ᵛ. His translation (sig. L4ʳ) runs: 'Et peccare fecit eos Satanas ab eo, itaque expulit eos de eo quo fuerunt in eo'. Cf. Christian Ravius, *Prima tredecim partium Alcorani Arabico-Latini* (Amsterdam, 1646) sig. A2ᵛ: '... seduxit autem ambos Satan ab eo, et eiecit eos inde, ubi erant domi, tum

It is not easy to tell from so brief a specimen what might have been expected from Danz had he continued, but the use of Christian terms to express Muslim concepts was infelicitous. The translation is highly literal and there is no evidence of any use of the *tafsīr*. If Danz's approach to Hebrew is anything to go by, he would hardly have been better equipped to cope with the Qur'an. For he dominated Hebrew studies in Germany, and his highly dogmatic approach to the language is said to have had an inhibiting effect on any true form of progress.[21] According to Acoluthus his decision to go no further with his translation was due to his discovery of Marracci's plan.[22]

Hopes were also raised by Abraham Hinckelmann, the Lutheran pastor of the St Katharinen-Kirche in Hamburg, who had learnt his Oriental languages as a student at Wittenberg between 1668 and 1672. On the face of it he was admirably equipped. He had, he claimed, a considerable knowledge of the *tafsīr*, and his library in Hamburg was far more extensive than Beck's in Augsburg and probably than Danz's in Jena.[23] He owned just under two hundred Oriental books and manuscripts, some seventy of which were Arabic and over fifty Persian. The fruit of his knowledge and studies was indeed an edition of the entire text of the Qur-'an. It appeared in 1694 but, to the disappointment of his admirers, it was solely in Arabic.

Hinckelmann's excuses were not regarded as convincing. Much of the Qur'an, he said, was perfectly clear and therefore did not need to be translated. The parts that were not clear, on the other hand, were the object of such argument in the Islamic world, and had been submitted to so many often contradictory commentaries, that no translator could hope to give them their due without making superhuman efforts.[24] These Hinckelmann was evidently not

---

diximus, excedite'. Marracci, pt. 2, p. 21 gives: 'Atqui excidere fecit illos Satan ab eo (*id est Paradiso*): ejecitque eos ab eo statu, in quo erant'.

21 W. Gesenius, *Geschichte der hebräischen Sprache und Schrift. Eine philologisch-historische Einleitung in die Sprachlehren und Wörterbücher der hebräischen Sprache* (Leipzig, 1815), p. 123: '… besonders Danz schadete durch seine pedantische Methode einer liberalern Behandlung des hebräischen Sprachstudiums ungemein, und mehr noch, als er selbst, geistlose Schüler und Nachamer, die an dem Buchstaben seiner Regeln klebten. Ueber ein halbes Jahrhundert konnten sich die deutschen Schulen der hebräischen Sprache nicht von seinen lähmenden Fesseln losmachen'.

22 J.D. Wincklerus, *Sylloge anecdotorum* (Leipzig, 1750), p. 298: 'Famae suae consuluit Danzius … ab ejusdem editione abstinens'.

23 It is described by S.G. Starck, *Bibliotheca manuscripta Abrahami Hinckelmanni* (Hamburg, 1695).

24 A. Hinckelmann, *Al-Coranus S. Lex Islamitica Muhammedis, filii Abdallae Pseudoprophetae* (Hamburg, 1694) sigs t1^r–t2^v 'Quare si meo voto res ageretur,' he concludes (sig. t2^r), 'vel hoc solo nomine, mallem nullam unquam totius Corani versionem procudi. Praesertim cum ad maximam libri partem intelligendam exigua opus sit industria: loca autem

prepared to make. He also added that the Qur'an was a dangerous book, to read which entailed great risks.[25] Yet one of the true reasons for his reluctance to provide a translation or a commentary may again be sought in the contents of his library. Although he had at least six copies of the Qur'an, he only owned a single *tafsīr*, the popular *Tafsīr al-Jalālayn*, the standard commentary drawn up in Egypt in the fifteenth century by Jalāl al-Dīn al-Maḥallī and his pupil Jalāl al-Dīn al-Ṣuyūṭī.[26] This work, amply publicised in Du Ryer's French translation of the Qur'an, had many advantages.[27] In contrast to the majority of the *tafsīr* it was relatively brief and simple, and it was readily available in the East. But it was one of many *tafsīr*, and was not sufficient, as Marracci would show, for an extensive commentary.

Hinckelmann died in 1695, the year after his Qur'an appeared, at the age of forty-three, leaving the continuation of his task to the man who helped him see his edition through the press, the far younger Sebastian Gottfried Starck. In his introduction to the Qur'an Hinckelmann lavished on the twenty-six-year-old Starck the praise so characteristic of scholarly intercourse in the Republic of Letters, stressing his integrity of character and his immense (and precocious) erudition.[28]

---

obscuriora nemo nisi vasta jam linguae hujus scientia, & multorum Interpretum loquacitate instructus et defigatus, expedierit'.

25   *Ibid.*, sig. t1ʳ.: 'A versione fateor me multa deterruerunt. Nam ut nihil jam dicam de tanto Interpretum in locis difficilioribus dissensu (cujus praecipua causa frustra quaesitus ordo est:) nihil de molestia in hoc Augiae stabulo, cujus omnes fere anguli nugis & inanibus repetitionibus implentur, superanda afferam: fuerunt certe et alia, quae me ab ista opera partim vi partim consilio poterant retrahere. Inter haec palmarium est, quod Versionem totius libri, toti Arabicae litteraturae fraudi & damno potius, quam usui fore credidi'. If Hinckelmann intended this as a ploy to avoid censorship he was not entirely successful. The copy at the Arcadian Library in London has 'Liber Prohibitus' stamped on the first page. A. Hamilton, *Europe and the Arab World. Five Centuries of Books by European Scholars and Travellers from the Libraries of the Arcadian Group* (Dublin-London-Oxford, 1994), p. 102.

26   Starck, *Bibliotheca manuscripta*, p. 6.

27   For a discussion see Hamilton and Richard, *André Du Ryer*, pp. 96–101.

28   Hinckelmann, *Al-Coranus*, sigs u1ᵛ–2ʳ: 'Atque hi fere sunt, quibus in acceptis ferendum est, quicquid nostra editio habebit laudabile. Unus superest, quem ingratus praeterierim, quod ejus auxilio ita usus sum, ut sine ipso fuisset, succumbere me oneri potuisse fatear. Sebastianus is est Godofredus Starckius Civis noster, homo erectae indolis, et omnis elegantioris litteraturae supra aetatem peritus, a nobis vero benigno fato in societatem operae allectus. Venit is ad nos commendatione ornatus Viri summi Dn Friderici Benedicti Carpzovii Senatoris Lipsiensis, quem tanquam verum suum decus et commune asylum, quotquot hodie recta studia amant, venerantur. Et sane respondit tantae commendationi egregie optimus Starckius cum in aliis rebus omnibus, tum in eruditione Arabica, quam mea exhortatione et ductu tam feliciter brevi admodum tempore ita assecutus est, ut

But was Starck really worthy of Hinckelmann's recommendations? At first he seemed to be. Born in Brand, near Freiburg in Saxony, the son of a preacher, he studied at the Fürstenschule in Meissen before proceeding to the University of Leipzig. He then visited Holstein, met Hinckelmann to whom he had been recommending by the historian Friedrich Benedict Carpzov, and stayed with him in Hamburg for two years, helping him in his work on the Qur'an and describing his Oriental manuscripts. After he had completed that assignment he moved to Berlin on the advice of the scholar and diplomat Ezechiel Spanheim, and in 1696 was instructed to draw up a catalogue of Eastern manuscripts in the electoral library. As he did so he also lectured in Hebrew, Arabic and Greek at the Berlin Gymnasium, of which he was appointed conrector in 1698. In 1705 he completed his catalogue and received the title of royal librarian, and in the same year was given a chair of Oriental languages at the Swedish university at Greifswald. Three years later he was appointed head of the Ritterschule in Brandenburg and, in rapidly declining health, went back to Berlin. He took up his appointment as librarian in 1710 but died shortly after.[29]

Starck was a versatile scholar, whose achievements included his German translation of John Locke's *Some Thoughts concerning Education*. Nevertheless he ended by disappointing his patrons. Soon after his arrival in Berlin to catalogue the manuscripts he entered into conflict with Andreas Acoluthus, who was working unofficially on the same project. Starck regarded Acoluthus as a rival, and slandered him savagely in 1697. This was seen as inadmissible behaviour in the courteous Republic of Letters, and Spanheim, one of the most powerful figures at the electoral court, lost faith in him. And indeed, Starck never justified the praise bestowed on him by Hinckelmann.

In 1698 Starck published his own specimen of the Qur'an, a Latin translation, together with a commentary, of the nineteenth sura, *Maryam*, *Specimen Versionis Coranicae, Adornatum in Caput XIX. Quod inscribitur Caput Mariae*. The translation was by no means perfect, as we can see from his rendering of the third verse, *idh nādā rabbahu nida'an khafīyan*, 'when he called upon the Lord in secret'. Starck translated it as *Quum is invocavit Dominum suum, precando et manifestando desideria sua*, thus entirely omitting the idea of silence and secrecy conveyed by *khafīyan* and captured by Marracci, 'Cum

---

dubitandum non sit, dignum hunc nostrum esse communi Doctorum favore, et habituram olim Ecclesiam in ipso Virum, de quo sibi jure gratuletur. Mihi molestum non foret ambitiosis precibus eum Bonis omnibus commendare, si his quidem egeret, qui sua se virtute, me tacentem satis commendat'.

29 Starck's life is described by K. Tautz, *Die Bibliothekäre der churfürstlichen Bibliothek zu Cölln an der Spree im siebzehnten Jahrhundert* (Leipzig, 1925), pp. 187–191. See also A. Hamilton, 'Sebastian Gottfried Starck' *CMR*, vol. 14, pp. 88–94.

invocavit Dominum suum invocatione occulta'.[30] For his commentary Starck drew almost entirely on the *Tafsīr al-Jalālayn*. The only other Islamic source he used was a work in the electoral library, the world history by Ibn Kathīr, who wrote in Damascus in the fourteenth century.[31] While Starck's notes have the merit of providing an almost complete translation of the comments in the *Tafsīr al-Jalālayn*, they are limited when compared with the commentary to the same sura by Marracci (which appeared in the same year). For Marracci, who also used the *Tafsīr al-Jalālayn*, not only provided quotations from it in Arabic, but added excerpts from the interpretations of the Persian al-Zamakhsharī and the tenth-century Andalusian Ibn Abī Zamanīn, thus giving a far richer impression of the various allusions which the Muslims detected in the text.

Still greater optimism was inspired by Starck's rival, the even more versatile (and older) Andreas Acoluthus from Bernstadt in Silesia. Acoluthus attended the St Elisabeth Gymnasium in Breslau, and then, like Starck, proceeded to the University of Leipzig.[32] There he was taught Oriental languages by a widely respected scholar and theologian, August Pfeiffer. Acoluthus interrupted his studies at Leipzig with a visit to Wittenberg, where he studied theology for a year, but in 1675 he was again in Leipzig. He mastered Turkish and Persian and, thanks to the presence of an Armenian, Jacob de Gregoriis, started to learn Armenian, the language that would most interest him for the rest of his life, and in which he published the book of Obadiah in 1680. Almost certainly encouraged by August Pfeiffer to criticise the Coptic studies of Athanasius Kircher, however, Acoluthus came to the altogether unwarranted conclusion that the language of the ancient Egyptians was in fact Armenian. Leibniz was intrigued by the idea, but soon abandoned it since Acoluthus's arguments were so unconvincing.

In 1676 Acoluthus settled as Lutheran pastor in Breslau, and would there teach Hebrew at the St Elisabeth Gymnasium. His reputation was high. He received invitations to the Universities of Leipzig, Greifswald, Erfurt and Halle, and was even considered by the great Orientalist Franz Mesgnien Meninski, the imperial interpreter in Istanbul and the author of the best Turkish dictionary to date, as a possible candidate for the post of chief interpreter in Vienna. This appointment, however, was strongly opposed by the Jesuits. Acoluthus remained in Breslau and concentrated on his pastoral duties and his studies.

---

30   Marracci, p. 430.
31   S.G. Starck, *Specimen Versionis Coranicae, Adornatum in Caput XIX. Quod inscribitur Caput Mariae* (Cölln, 1698), sig. A3ʳ.
32   Acoluthus's life is described by Tautz, *Die Bibliothekäre*, pp. 215–24. See also A. Hamilton, 'Andreas Acoluthus' *CMR*, vol. 14, pp. 437–444.

From 1696 on he spent his time between Breslau and Berlin, where Spanheim introduced him to the elector of Brandenburg, Frederick III, and where he started on the activity which would provoke the jealousy of Starck, describing the manuscripts in the electoral library, as well as studying the Oriental coins for the librarian Lorenz Beger. The elector rewarded him with an allowance, and he continued to work for the library – and to correspond with Leibniz, Lacroze and other figures in the Republic of Letters – until his death in Breslau in 1704.

Acoluthus seems to have long been one of Leibniz's favourite candidates as a translator of the Qur'an. In November 1697 Leibniz told the Swedish Arabist Gabriel Sparvenfeld that Acoluthus had been working on a translation for twenty years and that he had serious misgivings about Marracci's achievement.[33] And indeed, Acoluthus claimed to have spotted certain errors in the *Prodromus* and had doubts about Marracci's understanding of the text of the Qur'an and the commentaries. The two men had entered into correspondence, and in one of his replies to Marracci Acoluthus, as he proudly explained to Gerhard Wolter Molanus in April 1694, pointed out two of what he regarded as his more serious mistakes but was less insistent than he might have been out of pity for Marracci's great age.[34] Two years later Acoluthus repeated the story to the French orientalist Louis Picques.[35]

---

33   Leibniz, *Briefwechsel*, vol. 14, p. 759: 'Mons. Acoluthus que nous croyons le plus sçavant la dessus ne fait pas trop grand cas du travail du pere Maracci. Il travaille depuis 20 ans sur l'Alcoran et matieres semblables'.

34   G.W. Leibniz, *Collectanea etymologica* (Hanover, 1717), vol. 2, pp. 168–169: 'Quae de P. Marraccio nunciasti, jam ante plures annos ex *Wagenseilii telis igneis Satanae* didici. Sub anni proximi finem Romam ad ipsum litteras dedi de Alcorani editione expiscatorias, simulque speciminis cujusdam expetitorias. Respondit senex ille grandaevus octogesimum tertium aetatis annum jam agens quam humanissime, primumque duernionem operis illius, sub praelo in urbe Patavina adhuc sudantis, transmisit. Legit omnino in Alcoranum Commentatores Muhammedanos, quos hic loci non habemus: num vero ipsos una cum Alcorano semper intellexerit, dubito. In Alcorani certe versione errores observo, inde procul dubio enatos, quod Philologiae orientalis non habeat fundamentalem scientiam; unde saepius oculis caecutit apertis. Annotationibus ad Caput primum subjungit aliquam refutationem, sed admodum jejunam: Muhammedanus enim vel tribus verbis eandem destruere posset. Unde colligere datur Marraccium Theologiae Muhammedanae solidiorem cognitionem non habere. In mea ad ipsius litteras responsione duos satis graves errores in versione commissos, ipsi modeste aperui; nolui enim plurimum ostensione bonum senem minimum confundere. Quomodo eosdem sit excusaturus, praestolor'. For a letter from Marracci to Acoluthus see below pp. 412–413.

35   Wincklerus, *Sylloge anecdotorum*, p. 298: 'Ludovicus Maraccius in editione Alcorano sui adhuc occupatus est. Ex primo istius operis duernione, ab ipso mihi transmisso, cognosco, esse nonnulla, quae limam merentur, ex quibus etiam duo errata insigniora

The appearance of Marracci's edition of the Qur'an in 1698 obliged Acoluthus to distinguish his own project from the Italian publication. In 1701 he published a specimen of what was both an original and a highly ambitious plan: a polyglot edition of the Qur'an, in Arabic, Turkish and Persian, with literal Latin translations of each version. In his specimen Acoluthus got no further than the first sura, and the main text of his *Tetrapla Alcoranica, Sive Specimen Alcorani quadrilinguis, arabici, persici, turcici, latini*, is devoted to his view of the Qur'an, the polemics attending its editions, and the work of his predecessors. If Marracci insisted on the use of his own edition for missionaries, Acoluthus was even more emphatic about the need to convert the Muslims to Christianity. This, however, was to be a Lutheran prerogative, the continuation of a plan originally formed by Christian Ravius and Matthias Wasmuth in 1670 when they envisaged the foundation of an 'Oriental College' as a Protestant answer to the Catholic *Congregatio de Propaganda Fide*. The English and the Danes had contributed to dispatching missionaries to the East, he lamented, so was it not high time that the Germans did so too?[36]

Acoluthus was always critical of his predecessors. When dealing with Marracci he showed how stung he was by earlier Catholic associations between Lutheranism and Islam and the charge that Luther was no better, if not even worse, than Muḥammad.[37] He consequently reproached Marracci, who had died in the previous year, for not having produced a more convincing refutation of Muslim beliefs. He regarded him as particularly unconvincing in his defence of the Trinity, and added that if Marracci were to have any success in converting Muslims, he should dissociate himself from the Roman Catholics, who were not only prepared to justify points of Christian dogma by pointing out that even the Muslims subscribed to them, but who refused to allow

---

(pluribus enim bono seni nolebam esse molestus) ostendi, quae et ipse postea pro erroribus agnovit, subque finem operis se correcturum spopondit'.

36   Andreas Acoluthus, *Tetrapla Alcoranica, Sive Specimen Alcorani quadrilinguis, arabici, persici, turcici, latini: Cujus textus authenticus arabicus ex collatione XXX. Codicum, recensendus, Hujus autem difficillimi sensus, tanquam obserata Satanae Abyssus, Gemina Clave, eaque felicissima, Nimirum Versione Persica, in ipso Oriente rarissima, & Turcica, adhuc rariore, Christianis autem hucusque prorsus ignorata, recludendi, ac Tripilici Latina versione exponendi, Annotationibus etiam Philologico-Theologicis, ex ipsorum Arabum, Persarum, & Turcarum scriniis, genuina ipsorum Mataeologia Sede, nec non ditissimo Coelestis Veritatis Tliesauro, depromendis, Ad Sectae Muammedicae certam Confusionem, Regni Christiani non desperandam Ampliationem, Et Scientiae Orientalis insignem Augmentationem, illustrandi sunt* (Berlin, 1701), pp. 37, 48. I am particularly grateful to J.M. van de Velde for providing me with a photocopy of Acoluthus's text. The work is discussed in Bobzin, 'Von Venedig nach Kairo', pp. 162–163.

37   Ibid., pp. 15–16.

the laity access to the Bible, 'the only basis of our faith'.[38] But Acoluthus was equally severe towards his fellow-Protestants. In a letter to Louis Picques written in May 1696 he had already dismissed Danz as *interpres, sed infelicissimus, Alcorani Jenensis*[39] He attacked Jacobus Golius for not having done enough to spread Christianity in the Islamic world.[40] He had reservations about the work of Johann Zechendorff.[41] He deplored at length Hinckelmann's failure to provide a Latin translation of the Qur'an and demolished his various arguments. Where Hinckelmann's reference to the contradictory nature of Muslim commentaries was concerned, Acoluthus pointed out that this was usually owing to the polyvalent meanings of so many Arabic words.[42] He also dismissed earlier specimen translations of chapters from the Qur'an by Erpenius, Ravius and Beck, as too short and by no means free of mistakes.[43]

It is hard to deduce from Acoluthus's introduction what he would have achieved had he lived longer. He insisted that the great difference between his own plan and the work of Marracci was that he would produce a polyglot edition as opposed to a monolingual one.[44] He also made it clear that the use of a Turkish and a Persian version of the Qur'an would be still more useful for

---

38   Ibid., pp. 39–40: 'Quid? quod etiam ex diverso fonte nostra utriusque Alcorani confutatio sit emanatura. Ut enim nil dicam, in summo Sacrosanctae Trinitatis mysterio contra Muhammedanos vindicando, Marraccium Part.3.c.5 Prodromi Alcorani, justo tepidiorem esse … adeo ut parum absit, ne S. Chrysostomi censuram incurrat, qui Proditorem veritatis eum vocat, qui non sufficienter eam defendit; non video, quomodo Marraccius Muhammedano Alcorani sui … nauseam per refutationem excitare queat, nisi a Consodalibus suis se velit segregare, qui Alcoranum in auxilium doctrinae suae, Scripturae S. non conformi, vocant, et de consensu ejus sibi gratulantur … Quid imo rationem & modum invenire nescio, quo Marraccius Muhammedanum ad amorem S. Scripturae, unici nostrae fidei fundamenti, per trahere velit, nisi eam relinquat Ecclesiam, quae, ut ne duriora dicam, S. Scripturae lectionem Laicis prohibet'. This, too, is reminiscent of Hackspan, *Fides et leges Mohammaedis*, sig. M1r, where Robert Bellarmine is strongly criticised for claiming that the Muslims believe in purgatory.
39   Wincklerus, *Sylloge anecdotorum*, p. 298.
40   Acoluthus, *Tetrapla Alcoranica*, p. 13: 'Imo quoties eximia Clariss. Jacobi Golii studia Arabica mentis oculis aspicio, non potest non in isto Sole haec mihi macula displicere, quod ad Conversionem Muhammedanorum eadem, praesertim in Otio suo, applicare fuerit pigratus'. Cf. p. 38.
41   Ibid., p. 33.
42   Ibid., pp. 7, 40–7.
43   Ibid., p. 46: 'Quod doctissimi illi Viri ad interpretationem Alcorani contulerunt, parum omnino est, si cum reliquis conferas: & optandum foret illorum versiones ab erroribus immunes esse'.
44   Ibid., p. 39: 'Imo vel ipsae Versiones Orientales Alcorani, Persica & Turcica, a me primum producendae, a Marraccianis mea distinguent'.

the clarification of obscure words than the *tafsīr*.⁴⁵ And although Acoluthus knew about the *tafsīr*, and even emphasised the importance of Islamic commentaries, he does not appear to have intended to make much use of them. The only Islamic works he actually mentions are two sixteenth-century Turkish texts on Muslim beliefs, the first *Kırk suʾāl*, attributed to Mevlana Furati, which he obtained with other manuscripts from 'the Turkish war', and the second the sixteenth-century *Vasīyet-nāme* by Birgili Mehmed Efendi.⁴⁶ He appears, on the other hand, to have owned an ample collection of Qurʾans in Arabic – some thirty in all – as well as a Persian translation which had been obtained in Buda and a rare Turkish translation which had once belonged to Meninski in Istanbul.⁴⁷

Acoluthus's friendship with Meninski suggests that, in contrast to earlier Arabists, of whom Beck is one of many examples and who stressed the proximity between Arabic and Hebrew, he was going to follow the advice given by Scaliger almost a century earlier and, like Golius, study Arabic and the other languages of the Islamic world in an Islamic context. Yet his hatred of Islam, stressed on every possible occasion, exceeded in its virulence the dislike expressed by Marracci and might well have acted as an obstacle to an objective presentation of the text of the Qurʾan.

And how sound, finally, was his knowledge of Persian, Turkish and Arabic? Where his Persian is concerned there is little evidence. The language in which he must have had most practice was Turkish, since the articles looted from the Ottomans from which he profited included an Ottoman slave girl presented to him by an imperial officer in 1694. The wife of an imam in Belgrade, she also knew Arabic and furnished both linguistic and religious information to Acoluthus, who emancipated her, had her to stay as a guest with him and his wife, and looked after her with paternal solicitude until she absconded six months after entering his household.⁴⁸ That his Turkish was never perfect, however, emerges from his praise of William Seaman's Turkish translation of

---

45 *Ibid.*, p. 8: 'Dum vero Persica & Turcica Versio illud Eridos pomum saepe sustollunt, vocis genuinam significationem indicantes, ingens certe interpreti adjutorium praestant, vix aliunde sperandum'.
46 *Ibid.*, pp. 8–9. The texts are described, albeit cursorily, in W. Pertsch, *Die Handschriften-Verzeichnisse der Königlichen Bibliothek zu Berlin. Sechster Band. Verzeichniss der Türkischen Handschriften* (Berlin, 1889), pp. 125, 150. Cf. above all J. Schmidt, *Catalogue of Turkish Manuscripts in the Library of Leiden University and Other Collections in the Netherlands*, vol. 2 (Leiden, 2002), pp. 145, 468.
47 Acoluthus, *Tetrapla Alcoranica*, pp. 6–7.
48 Tautz, *Die Bibliothekäre*, pp. 21–22.

the New Testament, a work which even Protestants, such as Golius, admitted was deplorably defective.[49] Acoluthus's statements about Arabic reveal a mixture of pedantry and dogmatism, combined with the stubbornness evident from the manner in which he clung to his theory about Armenian having been the language of the ancient Egyptians. Louis Picques had been struck, not altogether favourably, by Acoluthus's self-confidence and his conviction that he alone could understand the inscriptions on Arab coins.[50] In his Qur'an specimen Acoluthus argued at length about the correct designation of the opening sura and claimed that Hinckelmann, Marracci and others were wrong in translating *sūrat al-fātiḥa* as 'caput aperitrix' or 'caput aperiens' since this made it seem that *al-fātiḥa* was an adjective in the nominative case whereas he thought it was a genitive construction, 'the sura of the opening'.[51] He claimed that the title of the second sura, *sūrat al-baqara*, should not be translated as 'the sura of the cow' but rather as 'the sura of amplitude or greatness', ('amplitudo' or 'magnitudo').[52] He had derived this idea, he informed Picques, from some Muslim captives (who probably included the Turkish slave girl), and he admitted that it was not to be found in any dictionary.[53] Nor, Acoluthus

---

49   Acoluthus, *Tetrapla Alcoranica*, p. 11: 'Clenardi mentem alii post ipsum etiam habuerunt, qui Catecheses vel alios libros in linguam Arabicam; imprimis Clariss. Seamon, Anglus, qui Novum Testamentum in Turcicam linguam eleganter transtulit, eo scopo, ut Turcarum conversioni inserviret'. Cf. Golius's report of the harsh judgement of Seaman's Turkish New Testament by the Armenian Shahin Kandy, M.M. Kleerkooper and W.P. van Stockum, *De boekhandel te Amsterdam, voornamelijk in de 17de eeuw. Biographische en Geschiedkundige Aanteekeningen* (The Hague, 1914–16), vol. 2, p. 1243: 'Belangende nu de twee bladeren mij toegesonden van de Turcsche oversettinge in Engelant gemaect door een Engelsman genaemt Zeeman ende daer te lande gedruct werdende, can den Armener niet anders oordeelen, ofte sal gants vruchteloos bevonden werden, alsoo onder die natien niet sal met eenige last connen gelesen ende mogelijc niet verstaen werden, om dat de natuyre en gebruyc van de taele is geforceert, hoedanige dingen gemeynlijc geenerveert en crachteloos werden'.
50   Wincklerus, *Sylloge anecdotomm*, p. 316: 'Il est vrai, qu'il croit, qu'il est le seul au monde qui en soit capable'.
51   Acoluthus, *Tetrapla alcoranica*, pp. 2–3.
52   *Ibid.*, p. 8.
53   Wincklerus, *Sylloge anecdotorum*, pp. 298–9. Acoluthus's reasoning remains mysterious, but the greatest Arabic lexicographer of the nineteenth century, Edward William Lane, does indeed give one of the various meanings of *baqara* as a troop or large number, obviously derived from a herd of cows. He refers to two monolingual Arabic dictionaries, al-Zamakhsharī's *Asās al-balāgha* and Murtaḍa al-Zabīdī's *Tāj al-'arās*. E.W. Lane, *Arabic-English Lexicon* (Cambridge, 2003), vol. 1, p. 234.

maintained, should the forty-eighth sura, *sūrat al-fatḥ*, be translated as 'the sura of victory' but rather as 'the sura of the decree'.[54]

The various German Arabists recommended to Leibniz as translators or editors of the Qur'an all published at least a specimen of their work on the text, with the exception of Henry Sike, who may well have been the most qualified. Sike, in contrast to the other Lutheran candidates, was born a Calvinist in the Reformed city of Bremen in 1668.[55] He there completed his education by studying mathematics, Hebrew and Greek at the Gymnasium Illustre, after which he seems to have enlisted in the Danish army and to have served briefly in the Levant. By 1693 he was in the Netherlands and matriculated as a student of theology at Leiden. This provided him with an opportunity to consult a far better collection of Oriental manuscripts than anything he could have found in Germany. The chair of Arabic was vacant, so he probably proceeded with the study of the language on his own. Besides acquiring a reputation as a historian and a classical scholar, he soon gained a name as an Orientalist – Gerhard Meier, the professor of mathematics at the Gymnasium Illustre and one of Sike's mentors in Bremen, drew Leibniz's attention to him in September 1695[56] – and he started to prepare an edition of the apocryphal Arabic Infancy Gospel, the manuscript of which he had managed to obtain at the auction of Golius's private manuscript collection in Leiden in October 1696. The Arabic Infancy Gospel is a late work, probably from the fifth or sixth century, and it was while he was engaged in the edition that he also began to work on the Qur'an.

In 1697 Sike left Leiden for Utrecht, where he was welcomed by two German classicists, Johann Georg Graevius and Ludolf Küster, and published his edition of the Infancy Gospel which established his reputation once and for all. Leibniz was delighted by his achievement. He wrote to Thomas Burnett about it in May 1697 and informed Magliabechi and Hiob Ludolf in September.[57] Sparvenfeld invited Sike to Sweden to inspect his own collection of Arabic

---

54 Acoluthus, *Tetrapla alcoranica*, p. 8. There seems to be slightly more justification for this than for his interpretation of *al-baqara*. *Fatḥ* is attested as meaning both 'judged' and 'granted', Lane, *Arabic-English Lexicon*, vol. 1, p. 2328.

55 A. Hamilton, 'Henry Sike (1668–1712). A German Orientalist in Holland and England' *Journal of the Warburg and Courtauld Institutes* 84 (2021), pp. 127–159; L. Forster, 'Henry Sike of Bremen (1669–1712), Regius Professor of Hebrew and Fellow of Trinity' *Transactions of the Cambridge Bibliographical Society* 10 (1991–95), pp. 249–177.

56 Leibniz, *Briefwechsel*, vol. 11, p. 683: 'Plures, deo sit gratia, sunt in Bremensibus nostris, qui amplam doctrinae messem pollicentur, in quibus Tilingius, Wesenfeldius, Muhlius, Schumacherus, quidam Sikius Linguarum orientalium callentissimus'.

57 *Ibid.*, vol. 14, pp. 225, 522, 544–545.

codices, but Sike preferred to remain in Utrecht and continue to work on Byzantine history.[58] He also taught Arabic to Adriaen Reland, who would return to Utrecht in 1701 as professor of Oriental languages, and lent him some of the manuscripts on which Reland would base his *De religione Mohammedica*, one of the first truly enlightened studies on Islam ever to be published.[59]

In 1703 Sike became the travelling companion and interpreter of George Hastings, the eighth earl of Huntingdon, and accompanied him to Vienna and to Italy, and in 1705 he at last accepted the invitation of the classical scholar Richard Bentley and received the regius professorship of Hebrew at Cambridge. Living at Trinity College, with hardly any teaching duties, Sike was free to pursue his studies on Islam and did so mainly at the Bodleian Library in Oxford. Like Leiden, Oxford had one of the finest collections of Oriental manuscripts in Northern Europe, and it was there that Sike planned an edition of the pre-Islamic poets.[60] Yet Sike brought none of his plans to fulfilment. On 20 May 1712, for reasons which remain mysterious, he hanged himself in his rooms at Trinity.

But what of Sike's translation of the Qur'an? He seems to have embarked on it, as we saw, while he was preparing his edition of the Infancy Gospel. Gerhard Meier had already told Leibniz about his plan in May 1696. It would consist of two volumes, the first containing the text and a translation, the second the Arabic commentaries. The first volume, he said, would be published within six weeks.[61] He referred to it again in January 1697,[62] and in November of the same year Hiob Ludolf offered, by way of Leibniz, his own advice and assistance.[63]

---

58   *Ibid.*, vol. 16, p. 493; vol. 17, pp. 230, 329–332, 446, 501.
59   See above, pp. 133–136, 147–148.
60   On 16 August 1706 Bentley wrote to him (C. Wordsworth, ed., *The Correspondence of Richard Bentley DD Master of Trinity College, Cambridge* (London, 1842), vol. 1, p. 244): 'I ... am glad to hear you have met with such reception at Oxford, so well in searching into the Oriental Manuscripts there. I hope, in time, the Publick will have a testimonial of your labours by something in print. The old Arabic Poems, and the Proverbs, will certainly be worth your edition, and bring a great honour to you, as well as benefit to Learning'.
61   Leibniz, *Briefwechsel*, vol. 12, p. 614: 'Praesentium vero occasio mihi subnascitur ex amici quondam discipuli in Arabicis mei conatibus. Alcoranum ille vertendum ex Msris, quae multa possidet, recepit meis hortatibus. Opus constabit duobus voluminibus, quorum prius ipsam versionem proferet, alterum, quod sequetur cum tempore, Commentarios Arabum in Coranum. Prior pars sex intra septimanas perfecta typographo extradetur. Rogat proinde Sikius, ita viro nomen est Bremensi origine ut si quae habeamus; quae praefationem illustrare queant ad Coranum spectantia, ea suppeditemus'.
62   *Ibid.*, vol. 13, p. 492.
63   *Ibid.*, vol. 14, 730: 'Sikium (cujus quidem *Evangelium Infantiae Jesu apocryphum* non vidi), propter ingenium, quod laudas, admiror. Si versionem Alcorani, utique difficillimam, in animo habet, vellem consilio meo uteretur'.

In February 1698 Meier repeated that Sike was working on a vast edition of the Qur'an, containing the Arabic, a Latin translation, and a corpus of commentaries. Despite the warnings of Acoluthus, he was sure of completing it soon.[64] In October Meier once more reported on his progress.[65]

The ensuing silence can perhaps be explained by the appearance of Marracci's edition. Judging from Meier's remarks, Sike had the very same plan, and the publication in Padua would have meant revising it radically if any publisher were to accept it. But how far had Sike in fact got? According to a note in the *Neuer Bücher-Saal der Gelehrter Welt* early in 1714 he had indeed completed it and left the manuscript together with his other papers at his death, thus allowing 'men of learning' to expect their imminent publication.[66] Nearly all Sike's scholarly notes are now at the Bodleian Library, but there is no trace of his Qur'an translation. The nearest his papers come to it is a transcription of excerpts from the *Tafsīr al-Jalālayn*.[67]

One day, in some library, Sike's translation may still come to light, but as it is we can only speculate on its quality. There are various reasons for which we can consider him better qualified than his rivals in Germany. First of all, Sike was never blinded by religious prejudice. If anything he had the reputation of a free-thinker. He had once been suspected of an admiration for Spinoza and he was known to have defined the Qur'an as 'not only the elegantest but the most rational book in the world.'[68] By studying in Leiden and working in Oxford, moreover, Sike had seen a far wider range of Arabic manuscripts than had those of his colleagues who never ventured outside Germany. On the other

---

64 *Ibid.*, vol. 15, 324: 'Parat ille Alcoranum id est versionem cum textu et commentariorum vastum corpus. Monui Acoluthum videlicet existimare impossible esse factu ut pauxillo annorum tempore mysteria libri intelligantur. Sikius e contra existimat non esse tantae molis hoc conamen, putatque se orbi erudito facturum satis'.

65 *Ibid.*, vol. 16, p. 211: 'Sikius strenuus laborat in parando Alcorano et cum Commentariis Arabum prolixis edendo'.

66 *Neuer Bücher-Saal der Gelehrter Welt, oder Ausführliche Nachrichten von allerhand Neuen Büchern und Andern Sachen, so zur neuesten Historie der Gelehrsamkeit gehören. Die XXXV. Oeffnung* (Leipzig, 1714), p. 811: 'Mr Sike, welcher sich, wie bekannt, vor einiger Zeit an seiner Schlaff-Rock-Gürtel gehangen, hat unterschiedliche MSS. hinterlassen, als eine Lateinische Übersetzung des Alcorans und andere Wercke, die in der Orientalischen Gelehrsamkeit viele Nuzten schaffen werden. Dass diese durch den Druck den Gelehrten solten gemein gemacht werden, hat man Hoffnung. Es hat dieser D. Heinrich Siecke sonst wunderliche fata ausgestanden; in der Orientalischen Sprachen hat er seines gleichen nicht'.

67 Bodl. MS Bodl.Or.409.

68 Thomas Hearne, *Remarks and Collections*, ed. C.E. Doble *et al.* (Oxford, 1885–1921), vol. 3, p. 368.

hand nothing would have been so useful to Sike as a rich collection of *tafsīr*, and we have no evidence that he knew any *tafsīr* other than the *Tafsīr al-Jalālayn*.

3 The Key to Success

The key to a successful edition of the Qur'ān was the number and the nature of Arabic manuscripts a scholar might have at his disposal. In the marginal notes to his French translation André Du Ryer had already drawn the attention of the world of learning not only to the *Tafsīr al-Jalālayn* but also to other commentators, such as Fakhr al-Dīn al-Rāzī and, more important still, the Persian Shafiite al-Bayḍawī. Arabists in Protestant Europe, Edward Pococke in England and Johann Heinrich Hottinger in Switzerland, had made still more significant contributions.[69] Nobody, however, could compete with Ludovico Marracci who never set foot outside Italy and learnt his Arabic partly on his own and partly from Arabic-speaking Christians in Rome. His own edition of the Qur'an is a monument to his linguistic capacities, but it is also a monument to the abundance of Islamic texts assembled in the Roman libraries. Thanks to missionaries, travellers in the Middle East, Eastern Christian visitors and the Catholic victors of the Ottoman armies, the colleges, convents and private collections in Rome contained some of the most interesting Qur'anic commentaries in existence. In his *Prodromus* Marracci lists the libraries he consulted. These included the Vatican, the Collegio Urbano de Propaganda Fide, and the Maronite College; the libraries of the Reformed Franciscans at S. Pietro in Montorio, the Discalced Carmelites at S. Pancrazio and the Minor Clerks Regular at S. Lorenzo in Lucina, as well as the private collections of Cardinal Camillo Massimo, Abraham Ecchellensis and Pietro Della Valle.[70] Having started with the tenth-century commentary of Ibn Abī Zamanīn,[71] Marracci quoted, in his translation, above all the *Tafsīr al-Jalālayn*, but also the *tafsīr* of al-Bayḍawī, al-Zamakhsharī, and al-Hamdānī. He was, moreover, the first European to use the commentaries of the eleventh-century al-Thaʿlabī and the highly orthodox Ibn Taymiyyah of the thirteenth century.[72]

---

69 Cf. above pp. 293–295.
70 Marracci, *Prodromus*, p. 7.
71 Roberto Tottoli's important discoveries are treated in R. Glei and R. Tottoli, *Ludovico Marracci at Work. The Evolution of his Latin Translation of the Qur'ān in the Light of his Newly Discovered Manuscripts, with an Edition and a Comparative Linguistic Analysis of Sura 18* (Wiesbaden, 2016), pp. 15–31.
72 Marracci's sources have been studied and identified by Nallino in 'Le fonti arabe manoscritte dell'opera di Ludovico Marracci sul Corano'. See C.A. Nallino, *Raccolta di scritti editi e inediti*, vol. 2 (Rome, 1940), pp. 90–134.

Marracci had another advantage over the German Arabists who hoped to compete with him – longevity. With the exception of Danz, who lived until he was seventy-three, the Germans all died relatively young, and thus gave rise to the rumour that anyone who meddled with the Qur'an would be punished with a premature death.[73] Hinckelmann was forty-three, Starck forty-two, Sike forty-four and Acoluthus fifty. Marracci, on the other hand, was eighty-eight when he died and eighty-six when his Qur'an translation appeared. He alone had had the time necessary to produce the monumental work which Sike had flippantly thought he could complete in a matter of months. And time was something he needed, for his translation took a long time to be published. He had completed it shortly after 1674. Yet it took almost a quarter of a century more to appear. This was because of interminable arguments and changes of mind among the censors[74] and it was a long time before Marracci could gain the full support of Cardinal Gregorio Barbarigo in Padua, the saintly founder of the seminary with whose Arabic types the work would be printed.

Marracci's name was on many lips for much of the 1690s but, even if he corresponded with Acoluthus, he was hardly a citizen of the Republic of Letters. A member of the congregation of the Clerks Regular of the Mother of God and once the confessor of the conservative Innocent XI, Marracci took an active part in the Roman missionary organisation, the *Propaganda Fide*. He had a leading role in the campaign against Miguel de Molinos and the Quietists, and his last publication was a devastating attack on the Jews. Far from being the sort of elegant Latinist so appreciated as a learned correspondent by Leibniz and his circle, Marracci had written much of his work in Italian, and had proved himself an enthusiastic hagiographer of members of the Catholic clergy. However accurate his Qur'an translation, the Latin was generally regarded as stylistically poor.

Nevertheless Marracci's translation of the Qur'an triumphed. David Nerreter's German version of it, which appeared in 1703, immediately superseded Johann Lange's translation of Du Ryer. When George Sale set to translating the Qur'an into English in the early 1730s he drew on Marracci.[75] And however much Marracci stressed his desire to confute the Qur'an and to serve the missionaries, he acknowledged that Islam had certain qualities which

---

73 Tentzel, *Monatliche Unterredungen*, p. 917. Cf. A. Hamilton, *The Forbidden Fruit: the Koran in Early Modern Europe* (London, 2008), p. 3.

74 See G. Pizzorusso, 'Ludovico Marracci tra ambiente curiale e cultura orientalista a Roma nel XVII secolo' in L. D'Errico, ed., *Il Corano e il pontefice. Ludovico Marracci fra cultura islamica e Curia papale* (Rome, 2015), pp. 91–118.

75 See A. Bevilacqua, 'The Qur'an translations of Marracci and Sale' *Journal of the Warburg and Courtauld Institutes* 76 (2013), pp. 93–130.

made it more attractive to the 'modern idolators' than Christianity.[76] Such an idea might have shocked Acoluthus, but it appealed to the thinkers of the Enlightenment, and Reland would quote the passage in support of his more impartial treatment of Islam.[77]

Acknowledgements

This article first appeared in Alastair Hamilton, Maurits H. van den Boogert and Bart Westerweel, eds, *The Republic of Letters and the Levant* [= Intersections 5] (Leiden, 2005), pp. 197–221.

---

[76] Marracci, *Prodromus*, p. 4: 'Habet nimirum haec superstitio quidquid plausibile, ac probabile in Christiana religione reperitur, & quae naturae legi, ac lumini consentanea videntur. Mysteria ilia fidei nostrae, quae primo aspectu incredibile, et impossibile apparent; & praecipue, quae minus ardua humanae naturae censentur, penitus excludit. Hinc moderni Idolorum cultores, facilius ac promptius Saracenicam, quam Evangelicam legem amplectuntur; & in posterum amplectentur, nisi a Missionariis nostris, his, quae ego in meo opere pono, argumentis praeveniantur, ac praemuniantur. Nunquam enim Agarenicum virus haurient, haustum semper evoment; si Mahumeti, Alcoranique imposturas, & Christianae Religionis solidissima fundamenta probe intellexerint.'

[77] Adriaen Reland, *De religione mohammedica libri duo*, 2nd edn. (Utrecht, 1717), sig. ****2^r. Cf. above.

CHAPTER 17

'To Rescue the Honour of the Germans'

Qurʾan Translations by Eighteenth- and Early Nineteenth-Century German Protestants

If we take 1750 as a vantage point and look back at the achievements of German Protestants in the field of Arabic studies over the previous 150 years, certain features emerge. In contrast to the Catholics, who seem to have attached less importance to the study of Arabic at the time,[1] the Protestants of Germany produced some good Arabists in the seventeenth century and one of the very greatest of the eighteenth century. Arabic was studied more widely in the Protestant areas of Germany than in any other European country. There was a constant flow of Oriental manuscripts into German libraries, and there were numerous Muslim prisoners of war in German territory. Not only did more Germans than citizens of any other nation publish translations of suras from the Qurʾan made directly from the Arabic, but more editions of the entire Qurʾan and more university dissertations on aspects of it were published in Germany than anywhere else in the West.

To the Germans these might have seemed grounds for complacency, but some of them should be qualified. The first German Arabist to make his mark was Christian Ravius; yet, even if he was born in Berlin, attended the University of Wittenberg and died as professor of Oriental languages at Frankfurt an der Oder, he spent most of his life outside Germany – in Sweden, Denmark, Holland, England and Turkey – and it was outside Germany that he made his contributions to Arabic studies.[2] Another Arabist, Levinus Warner from Lippe, was brought up in Bremen but arrived at Leiden University in 1638 and studied under the professor of Arabic Jacobus Golius. By the end of 1645 he was in Turkey and, from 1655 to his death ten years later, he acted as the Dutch diplomatic representative in Istanbul. He assembled a rich selection of manuscripts which he left to the Leiden University library, making it the best collection in Northern Europe.[3] The third, Heinrich Siecke, was born in Bremen and, like

---

1   This impression is also suggested by the comments of the Swiss scholar Johann Heinrich Hottinger in the late 1650s and the 1660s. J. Loop, *Johann Heinrich Hottinger. Arabic and Islamic Studies in the Seventeenth Century* (Oxford, 2013), p. 81.
2   Toomer, pp. 83–84, 142–145, 189–200.
3   A. Vrolijk, J. Schmidt and K. Scheper, *Turcksche boucken. De oosterse verzameling van Levinus Warner, Nederlands diplomaat in zeventiende-eeuws Istanbul* (Eindhoven, 2012), pp. 19–176.

Warner, studied in Leiden. He then taught in Utrecht and subsequently moved to Cambridge, where he became known as Henry Sike and prepared a study of the early Arab poets.[4] The greatest Arabist of the mid-eighteenth century, Johann Jacob Reiske, did indeed spend most of his life in Germany. Dissatisfied with the possibilities of improving his Arabic in a German academy, however, he, too, made for Leiden in 1738 and there consulted the manuscripts and carried out the research which would inspire his Arabic studies until his death.[5]

Reiske's comments on the state of Arabic teaching in Germany bring us to the second point. Largely because of the exorbitant number of universities in Germany, a result of the political fragmentation of the country,[6] Arabic was taught more widely than anywhere else in Europe – it was also given in a number of grammar schools[7] – but it was usually studied at theological faculties in strict conjunction with Hebrew, and it was rarely taught very well.[8] Arabic studies in Germany suffered, moreover, from the absence of any centre which might allow the accumulation both of a teaching tradition and of a library. Oxford and Leiden were examples which were never emulated in Germany; and there were no large cities, such as Paris and Rome, where Arabic speakers were welcomed and manuscript collections were at least united in a single area. Nor were the collections of Arabic manuscripts assembled in Germany of particular value to students of Arab culture. No great collectors had travelled from Germany to the Arab world as had Jacobus Golius from Holland, Edward Pococke from England, or Levinus Warner in the service of the Dutch. Ravius had collected manuscripts in Istanbul but the number of his codices, most of which made their way into the electoral library in Berlin where his brother

---

4 L. Forster, 'Henry Sike of Bremen (1669–1712), Regius Professor of Hebrew and Fellow of Trinity' *Transactions of the Cambridge Bibliographical Society* 10 (1991–95), pp. 249–177; A. Hamilton, 'Henry Sike (1668–1712). A German Orientalist in Holland and England' *Journal of the Warburg and Courtauld Institutes* 84 (2021), pp. 127–159. See above, pp. 319–322.
5 Johann Jacob Reiske, *Von ihm selbst aufgesetzte Lebensbeschreibung* (Leipzig, 1783), pp. 8–16.
6 For a survey of the conditions faced by scholars in eighteenth-century Germany see J.J. Sheehan, *German History 1770–1866* (Oxford, 1989), pp. 72–143.
7 See, for example, A. Ben-Tov, 'Johann Zechendorff (1580–1662) and Arabic studies at Zwickau's Latin school' in J. Loop, A. Hamilton and C. Burnett, eds, *The Teaching and Learning of Arabic in Early Modern Europe* (Leiden-Boston, 2017), pp. 57–92.
8 See Fück, pp. 90–97; D. Bourel, 'Der Deutsche Orientalistik im 18. Jahrhundert. Von der Mission zur Wissenschaft' in H.G. Reventlow, W. Sparn and J. Woodbridge, eds, *Historische Kritik und biblischer Kanon in der deutschen Aufklärung* (Wiesbaden, 1988), pp. 113–126; A. Ben-Tov, '*Studia orientalia* im Umfeld protestantischer Universitäten des Alten Reichs um 1700' *Zeitsprünge: Forschungen zur Frühen Neuzeit* 16 (2012), pp. 92–118. For a discussion of Orientalists and theological faculties in the late eighteenth and early nineteenth centuries see S.L. Marchand, *German Orientalism in the Age of Empire. Religion, Race, and Scholarship* (Cambridge, 2009), pp. 86–88.

Johann had been librarian, remained small. However many Arabic manuscripts some of the German collections may have contained – that of Acoluthus is an example – they tended to be top-heavy. The majority of the manuscripts were Qurʾans, mainly looted by soldiers in the imperial armies who were fighting the Ottomans. The soldiers were no Arabists. They preferred the more spectacular codices with illuminations – and these were usually Qurʾans – to others which would have been of use to students but which could seldom be described as attractive objects.[9] Judging from the work of the German Arabists there were relatively few accessible manuscripts of *tafsīr*, the Muslim interpretations of the Qurʾan which were so important in translating the work. Even if Johann Zechendorff, the rector of the Latin school in Zwickau, translated the *tafsīr* of al-Bayḍāwī to suras 101 and 103 in 1646,[10] most prospective translators of the Qurʾan in Germany seem to have been unable to consult the interpretations directly.

The interest aroused by the Qurʾan in Germany was immense. Numerous attempts were made by German scholars to publish translations of individual suras or even the whole of the text. A recent discovery, by Roberto Tottoli at the Dār al-kutub in Cairo, is an edition of the entire text of the Qurʾan, in Arabic and with an interlinear Latin translation, made by Zechendorff in 1632. As Tottoli suggests, it was almost certainly prepared for publication, but no publisher could be found with sufficient equipment.[11] Yet none of these scholars, most of whom died relatively young, published a complete version.[12] Those German versions of the whole of the Qurʾan published in Germany were all

---

9   Jones, pp. 29–47.
10 H. Bobzin, 'Von Venedig nach Kairo: Zur Geschichte Arabischer Korandrucke (16. bis frühes 20. Jahrhundert)' in E. Hanebutt-Benz, D. Glass and G. Roper, eds, *Sprachen des Nahen Ostens und die Druckrevolution. Eine interkulturelle Begegnung* (Westhofen, 2002), pp. 151–176, esp. 157–159, 172–173. For the fate of Zechendorff's al-Bayḍāwī manuscript, a considerable rarity in northern Europe at the time which was acquired for the Zürich library by Johann Heinrich Escher, see Loop, *Johann Heinrich Hottinger*, p. 143.
11 R. Tottoli, 'The Latin translation of the Qurʾān by Johann Zechendorff (1580–1662) discovered in Cairo Dār al-kutub. A preliminary description' *Oriente moderno* 95 (2015), pp. 5–31. On Zechendorff see A. Ben Tov, 'Johann Zechendorff', pp. 57–92.
12 Besides Ravius, Zechendorff and Sike, these translators included Peter Kirsten, Theodor Hackspan, Matthias Wasmuth, Johann Georg Nissel, Henningius Henning, Matthias Friedrich Beck, Johann Andreas Danz, Sebastian Gottfried Starck and, as we shall see, Andreas Acoluthus. For a survey of German editions of the first sura see the dissertation delivered under the aegis of Johann Andreas Michael Nagel, professor of Oriental languages at the University of Altdorf, Jacob Christoph Wilhelm Holste, *Dissertatio inauguralis derima alcorani sura* (Altdorf, 1743). For a more general survey see above; and Ben-Tov, 'Studia Orientalia', pp. 104–111. See also M.W. Hofmann, 'Germany and the Quran' *Journal of Qurʾanic Studies* 2 (2000), pp. 143–147.

based on other translations, if not on translations of translations. Salomon Schweigger's *Al-Koranum Mahumedanum*, published in 1616, was a translation of Giovanni Battista Castrodardo's Italian translation of Robert of Ketton's Latin rendering, which dated from the twelfth century and was first published by Theodor Bibliander in Basel in 1543.[13] Johann Lange's *Vollständiges Türckisches Gesetz-Buch, oder des Ertz-betriegers Mahomets Alkoran*, which came out in 1688, was a German version of Jan Hendricksz Glazemaker's Dutch translation of the French version by André Du Ryer, originally published in Paris in 1647.[14] The pattern continued well into the eighteenth century. David Nerreter's *Neu-eröffnete Mahometanische Moschea* of 1703 was based on Ludovico Marracci's Latin rendering of 1698, while in 1746 Theodor Arnold produced a German version of George Sale's English translation of 1734.[15] In 1721, moreover, Christian Reineccius, the rector of the Gymnasium in Weissenfels, published a revised version of Marracci's Latin in Leipzig, *Mohammedis filii Abdallae pseudo-prophetae Fides Islamitica, i.e. Al-Coranus*. Although Abraham Hinckelmann issued the entire Arabic text of the Qur'an in Hamburg in 1694, *Al-Coranus sive Lex Islamitica Muhammedis*, it was solely in Arabic and without any translation or commentary. No published German translation of the entire text of the Qur'an was made directly from the Arabic.

In 1698 a turning point occurred in the history of translations of the Qur'an in Western Europe. In that year Ludovico Marracci, once the confessor of Pope Innocent XI, at last published, in Padua, his edition of the entire text, in Arabic and with a Latin translation. Dedicated to the Habsburg emperor Leopold I, *Alcorani textus universus* was something of a belated celebration of the Austro-Polish victory over the Turks at the gates of Vienna in 1683. Each sura was accompanied not only by a new confutation but above all by an extensive

---

13 H. Bobzin, *Der Koran im Zeitalter der Reformation: Studien zur Frühgeschichte der Arabistik und Islamkunde in Europa* (Beirut, 1995), pp. 268–272. For Castrodardo see P.M. Tommasino, 'Giovanni Battista Castrodardo Bellunese traduttore dell'Alcorano di Maometto' *Oriente Moderno*, n.s. 80 (2006), pp. 15–40; idem, *L'Alcorano di Macometto. Storia di un libro del Cinquecento europeo* (Bologna, 2013), pp. 141–59. See also I. Binark and H. Eren, *World Bibliography of Translations of the Meanings of the Holy Qur'an. Printed Translations 1515–198* (Istanbul, 1986), pp. 222–223, nos 826/37–829/40.

14 A. Hamilton and F. Richard, *André Du Ryer and Oriental Studies in Seventeenth-Century France* (London-Oxford, 2004), pp. 116–17; Binark and Eren, *World Bibliography*, pp. 218–219, no. 811/22.

15 *Der Koran, Oder insgemein so genannte Alcoran des Mohammeds, unmittelbahr aus dem Arabischen Original in das Englische übersetzt, und mit beygefügten, aus den bewährtesten Commentatoribus genommenen Erklärungs-Noten, wie auch einer vorläuffigen Einleitung versehen von George Sale, Gen ...*, tr. Theodor Arnold (Lemgo, 1746). For Arnold and Nerreter see also Binark and Eren, *World Bibliography*, p. 213, no. 790/1 and p. 219, no. 813/24.

commentary in which Marracci displayed his extraordinary knowledge of the *tafsīr*. He quoted them in Arabic and gave a Latin translation. Although he started with the tenth-century commentary of Ibn Abī Zamanīn, the *tafsīr* he used included the popular fifteenth-century work of Jalāl al-Dīn al-Maḥallī and his pupil Jalāl al-Dīn al-Ṣuyūṭī, known as the '*tafsīr* of the two Jalāls' or *Tafsīr al-Jalālayn*, and those of al-Bayḍāwī, al-Zamakhsharī, al-Hamdānī, al-Thaʿlabī and Ibn Taymiyyah.[16] The richness and variety of his sources are an enduring tribute to the libraries in Rome. No scholar in Germany could compete with such a broad selection. In the text of his translation Marracci inserted excerpts from the *Tafsīr al-Jalālayn* to explain ambivalent or obscure terms or passages.

Already in 1681 a sense of urgency appears to have developed among German Protestant scholars. Johann Christoph Wagenseil, professor of history and Oriental languages at the University of Altdorf, had heard from Antonio Magliabechi in Florence, whom he had met on his travels in Italy, that Marracci was planning a bilingual version of the entire Qurʾan.[17] For a while nothing seemed to come of the plan, but in 1691 Marracci published, in Rome, the first volume of his work which contained his confutation, the *Prodromus ad refutationem Alcorani*. The event was alarming. Marracci was clearly a good Arabist and had at his disposal a formidable number of Islamic sources. From then on, as we see in the correspondence of Leibniz and his friends, scholars in Germany started to search for an Arabist who could compete. Johann Reiske, the rector of the Fürstenschule in Wolfenbüttel, sent Leibniz a list of candidates. These were Johann Andreas Danz, Abraham Hinckelmann and Andreas Acoluthus.[18] And the race was soon joined by others – Matthias Friedrich Beck, Sebastian Gottfried Starck and Heinrich Siecke. The Germans felt that they must surpass Marracci, possibly by tackling the Qurʾan in a different way, and it was here that Andreas Acoluthus came into his own and took his place at the head of a tradition of German Qurʾan translators in the eighteenth century.

---

16   C.A. Nallino, 'Le fonti arabe manoscritte dell'opera di Ludovico Marracci sul Corano' in his *Raccolta di scritti e inediti* (Rome, 1939–48), vol. 2, pp. 90–134; but see now the new discoveries of Roberto Tottoli in R. Glei and R. Tottoli, *Ludovico Marracci at Work. The Evolution of his Latin Translation of the Qurʾān in the Light of his Newly Discovered Manuscripts, with an Edition and a Comparative Linguistic Analysis of Sura 18* (Wiesbaden, 2016). Cf. also A. Bevilacqua, 'The Qurʾan translations of Marracci and Sale' *Journal of the Warburg and Courtauld Institutes* 76 (2013), pp. 93–130, esp. 108–10. For translators' reliance on *tafsīr*, see the discussion in T.E. Burman, *Reading the Qurʾān in Latin Christendom, 1140–1560* (Philadelphia, 2007), pp. 36–59.

17   Johann Christoph Wagenseil, *Tela ignea Satanae. Hoc est: Arcani, et horribiles Judaeorum adversus Christum Deum, et Christianam religionem, libri* (Altdorf, 1681), p. 48.

18   Gottfried Wilhelm Leibniz, *Sämtliche Schriften und Briefe, Erste Reihe. Allgemeiner politischer und historischer Briefwechsel*, vol. 9 (1693) (Berlin, 1975), p. 323.

∴

Andreas Acoluthus, born to a Lutheran family in Bernstadt an der Weide (now Bierutów) in 1654, attended the St Elisabeth Gymnasium in Breslau, the capital of Silesia, before proceeding to the University of Leipzig, where he was taught Oriental languages by August Pfeiffer.[19] He also studied theology at Wittenberg, but returned to Leipzig in 1675. It seems to have been there that he mastered most of the over twenty languages to which he laid claim. They included Arabic, Turkish, Persian, Chinese, Coptic and, thanks to the presence of a native speaker, Jacob de Gregoriis, Armenian.[20] In 1676 Acoluthus settled as a Lutheran pastor in Breslau, where he taught Hebrew at his former school, the St Elisabeth Gymnasium. He declined invitations from the Universities of Leipzig, Greifswald, Erfurt and Halle but, in 1696, agreed to describe the Oriental manuscripts and coins in the electoral collections in Berlin.[21] He died in Breslau in 1704. The virtues which his hagiographer, Karl Heinrich Tromler, saw in his pastoral activity were attended not only by a very considerable obstinacy but also by a certain eccentricity. In the summer of 1693 he believed he had detected Arabic characters on the wings of the locusts which had devastated the local crops – a conclusion, according to his lodger, Adam Bernd, which could only be explained by his having spent so much time immersed in the Qur'an.[22]

Acoluthus had a high reputation in the Republic of Letters. He was in correspondence with Leibniz, Mathurin Veyssière de La Croze, Louis Picques and other scholars of distinction, but a number of his ideas, which were initially greeted with enthusiasm, were later discarded with scepticism. The language on which he concentrated was Armenian – he published the Armenian Book of

---

19   For Acoluthus's life see K. Migoń, 'Der Breslauer Orientalist Andreas Acoluthus (1654–1704). Seine Beziehungen zu Leibniz und zur Akademie in Berlin' *Sitzungsberichte der Leibniz-Sozietät* 53 (2002), pp. 45–58. See also A. Hamilton, 'Andreas Acoluthus' *CMR* vol. 14, *Central and Eastern Europe (1700–1800)* (Leiden-Boston, 2020), pp. 437–444, and above, pp. 312–319.

20   Karl Heinrich Tromler, 'Leben und Schriften des Hern. Andreas Akoluth, weil. Predigers und Professors zu Breßlau, und der Königl. Preuß. Akad. der Wissenschaften Mitglieds' *Neue Beyträge von alten und neuen Theologischen Sachen, Büchern, Urkunden, Controversen, Anmerkungen, Vorschlägen etc.* (Leipzig, 1761), pp. 414–471, esp. pp. 419–425.

21   K. Tautz, *Die Bibliothekäre der Churfürstlichen Bibliothek zu Cölln an der Spree im siebzehnten Jahrhundert* (Leipzig, 1925), pp. 216–218.

22   Adam Bernd, *Eigene Lebens-Beschreibung* (Leipzig, 1738), p. 92. See the discussion in B. Liebrenz, *Arabische, Persische und Türkische Handschriften in Leipzig. Geschichte ihrer Sammlung und Erschließung von den Anfängen bis zu Karl Vollers* (Leipzig, 2008), pp. 13–15.

Obadiah in 1680 – and one of his most remarkable convictions, based on what he saw as a similarity between the hieroglyphs and Armenian capitals, was that the language of the ancient Egyptians was Armenian.[23] At a time when few scholars in the West knew Armenian and none knew the language of the ancient Egyptians this suggestion was, at first, appealing. Leibniz was intrigued by it, but soon found Acoluthus's arguments unconvincing. Nevertheless, he remained among Leibniz's favourite candidates for the translation of the Qur'an, a project on which Acoluthus said he had been working ever since the late 1670s. It was not until 1701, however, that he published a specimen. By then Marracci's translation had appeared, and Acoluthus felt called upon to exhibit a particular originality.

The objective of Acoluthus's *Tetrapla Alcoranica, sive Specimen Alcorani quadrilinguis, Arabici, Persici, Turcici, Latini* was original indeed.[24] On the one hand it was to serve a missionary purpose, preparing German preachers who would benefit from an edition of the sacred text.[25] Acoluthus wished to carry out the plan formed by Christian Ravius and Matthias Wasmuth in 1670 to found an 'Oriental college' which would be the Protestant equivalent of the missionary organisation in Rome, the *Congregatio de Propaganda Fide*.[26] On the other he wanted to edit a polyglot Qur'an in the tradition of the great polyglot Bibles. To the Arabic would be added a Turkish and a Persian version, each accompanied by a Latin translation. In fact Acoluthus got no further than the first sura.

Acoluthus believed that by comparing versions of the Qur'an in the three principal Islamic languages he could do without the *tafsīr*. The variants, he held, would be based on a thorough knowledge of the meaning of the text, and would thus be more reliable and of greater use. They would enable him to make a far more important contribution than Marracci. Acoluthus seems therefore to have dispensed with any form of Qur'anic commentary. The only Islamic works he admits to having consulted were two sixteenth-century Turkish texts on Muslim beliefs: *Kırk su'āl*, attributed to Mevlana Furati,

---

23 See Wilhelm Ernst Tenzel's letter to Leibniz late in 1694. Leibniz, *Briefwechsel*, vol. 10, pp. 616–617. See also A. Hamilton, *The Copts and the West 1439–1822. The European Discovery of the Egyptian Church*, rev. edn (Oxford, 2014), p. 221.
24 See the description of the work in Schnurrer, pp. 414–415, no. 378.
25 Andreas Acoluthus, *Tetrapla Alcoranica, sive Specimen Alcorani quadrilinguis, Arabici, Persici, Turcici, Latini* (Berlin, 1701), pp. 37, 48.
26 Christian Ravius and Matthias Wasmuth, *Literae Circulares Wegen Errichtung eines Collegii Orientalis* (Kiel, 1670).

Acoluthus's copy of which had been pilfered from the Turks, and *Vasīyet-nāme* by Birgili Mehmed Efendi.[27]

Acoluthus also thought he had the edge on both Hinckelmann and Marracci thanks to his own formidable collection of Qur'anic manuscripts, most of which had been looted by officers of the Polish and imperial armies advancing ever deeper into Ottoman territory since the victory of 1683.[28] He owned some forty Qur'anic codices, many of them fragments, which are now in the Leipzig University library. They included the bilingual Arabic-Persian and the bilingual Arabic-Turkish Qur'ans on which his specimen was based.[29] The Arabic-Persian manuscript came from the spoils of Buda, while the rare Arabic-Turkish Qur'an had been given to him by the Orientalist from Lorraine, Franz Mesgnien Meninski, the imperial interpreter in Istanbul who had produced the best Turkish (and Persian) dictionary to date.[30] Meninski, too, clearly held Acoluthus in high esteem and had proposed his appointment as chief interpreter in Vienna. Confessional considerations prevailed, however, and, apparently owing to the opposition of the Jesuits, the proposition came to nothing.[31]

In another respect, too, Acoluthus was convinced of his superiority to Marracci: he had benefited from Ottoman prisoners of war,[32] and, from them, had obtained important information about the meaning of the Qur'an. He had also profited from the presence in his own house of an Ottoman slave girl, given to him by officers returning from the front. The wife of an imam in Belgrade, she was highly educated and knew Arabic, but, despite the paternal solicitude with which she was treated by Acoluthus and his wife (who emancipated her), she absconded six months after her arrival.[33] It may well have been

---

27   Acoluthus, *Tetrapla Alcoranica*, pp. 8–9.
28   *Ibid.*, pp. 5–7.
29   See the supplement on Oriental manuscripts by H.L. Fleischer and F. Delitsch to E.W.R. Naumann, ed., *Catalogus librorum manuscriptorum qui in bibliotheca senatoria civitatis Lipsiensis asservantur* (Grimma, 1838), pp. 357–358, nos 78–79, for the Persian and the Turkish Qur'ans respectively. For a recent survey of Acoluthus and his manuscripts see Liebrenz, Arabische, Persische und Türkische Handschriften, pp. 13–33.
30   Tromler, 'Leben und Schriften', pp. 429–430. Acoluthus had received a copy of the dictionary as a wedding present from his patron Count Christoph Leopold von Schaffgotsch.
31   Tautz, *Die Bibliothekäre*, p. 220.
32   Acoluthus, *Tetrapla Alcoranica*, p. 13; M. Friedrich, 'Türkentaufen. Zur theologischen Problematik und geistlichen Deutung der Konversion von Muslimen im Alten Reich' in *idem*. and A. Schunka, eds, *Orientbewegungen deutscher Protestanten in der Frühen Neuzeit* (Frankfurt a. M., 2012) (= *Zeitsprünge. Forschungen zur Frühen Neuzeit* 16 (2012)), pp. 47–74.
33   Tautz, *Die Bibliothekäre*, pp. 21–22.

from her, or from other prisoners of war (who seem to have been numerous in Breslau),[34] that Acoluthus derived his ideas about the polyvalent meaning of the Qur'an. He insisted, for example, that the title of the second sura, *sūrat al-baqara*, the 'sura of the cow', should be translated as the 'sura of amplitude or greatness' and that the title of the forty-eighth sura, *sūrat al-fatḥ* or the 'sura of victory', should be translated as the 'sura of the decree'. And then there were minor details on which he faulted Marracci and exhibited his own pedantry. The opening sura, *sūrat al-fātiḥa*, should be translated not as the 'opening sura' but as the 'sura of the opening'.[35] In other matters, Acoluthus was remarkably perceptive. He devoted an extensive footnote to the actual beauty of the text of the Qur'an in Arabic.[36] This was clearly a feature which interested him, and his collection of manuscripts includes instructions about how the Qur'an should be recited.

To what extent, we might ask, could a Turkish and a Persian translation of the Qur'an have served Acoluthus's purposes and absolved him of any use of a *tafsīr*? The answer is that the translations themselves, conceived as interpretations, incorporated *tafsīr*.[37] So much is evident even from the brief opening sura published by Acoluthus. While the Persian translation is quite literal, the Turkish version elaborates on 1:6–7, translated by Sale as: 'Direct us in the right way, in the way of those to whom thou hast been gracious; not of those against whom thou art incensed, nor those who go astray.'[38] In the Turkish there is a specific reference to the Jews and the Christians as those who do 'go astray'. This idea is contained in a number of *tafsīr*, including that of al-Bayḍāwī. Ultimately, therefore, Acoluthus would have been using *tafsīr* all the same, but in a different, and possibly less satisfactory, form. Yet Acoluthus was not alone in his high expectations of other Islamic translations. A few years later Antoine Galland in Paris tackled the Qur'an. His version has not survived, but we do have letters giving us a good idea of his intentions, and in one of them, addressed to the Dutch scholar Gijsbertus Cuperus, he, too, stated that he

---

34   O. Spies, 'Schicksale Türkischer Kriegsgefangener in Deutschland nach den Türkenkriegen' in E. Gräf, ed., *Festschrift Werner Caskel. Zum siebzigsten Geburtstag 5. März 1966 gewidmet von Freunden und Schulern* (Leiden, 1968), pp. 316–335, with interesting details about Turkish prisoners in Breslau, p. 332.

35   Acoluthus, *Tetrapla Alcoranica*, pp. 2–3.

36   Ibid., pp. 15–16. J. Loop, 'Divine poetry? Early modern European Orientalists on the beauty of the Koran' *Church History and Religious Culture* 89 (2009), pp. 455–488, esp. pp. 474–475.

37   T. Zadeh, *The Vernacular Qur'an. Translation and the Rise of Persian Exegesis* (Oxford-London, 2012), pp. 263–268.

38   Sale, p. 1.

would use Turkish and Persian translations.[39] Georg Jacob Kehr, we shall see, announced a similar plan.

Acoluthus's was by no means the only grand Qur'an project to be stimulated by Marracci. Another was that of Christian Ludovici, like Acoluthus a pupil of Pfeiffer at the University of Leipzig, where he would himself have a distinguished career as an Orientalist and a theologian. Starting in about 1700, Ludovici elaborated his plan to produce an edition of the Qur'an in Arabic together with a Latin translation, and an abundant lexicon which would also function as a concordance. Only a rough copy of a small part of the project survives in manuscript in the Leipzig University library.[40]

The appearance of Marracci's Qur'an prompted an interest in the history of Qur'an translations. Between April 1703 and June 1704, Johann Michael Lange, professor of theology at the University of Altdorf, presided over three dissertations, the subject of which he had almost certainly dictated himself, and in them clearly staked the Protestant claims to be better entitled to translate the Qur'an than any Roman Catholic.[41] Some years later, between 1715 and 1719, we find a strong interest in the Qur'an taken by the future Hebraist Johann Heinrich Callenberg, who was then studying at the philosophical faculty of Halle. Callenberg was one of a number of German Orientalists who learnt Arabic from Salomon Negri, a Syrian member of the Greek Orthodox Church.[42] Negri paid a couple of prolonged visits to Halle (and Leipzig) before settling in England, where he worked for the Society for Promoting Christian Knowledge and edited an Arabic edition of the Psalter and the New Testament. First with Negri, and then with his successor, another Syrian of the Greek Orthodox faith, Theocharis Dadichi,[43] Callenberg worked his way through the Qur'an.[44] For

---

39   Bevilacqua, 'The Qur'an translations', p. 129.
40   H. Preissler, 'Orientalische Studien in Leipzig vor Reiske' in H.-G. Ebert and T. Hanstein, eds, *Johann Jacob Reiske: Leben und Wirkung. Ein Leipziger Byzantinist und Begründer der Orientalistik im 18. Jahrhundert* (Leipzig, 2005), pp. 29–43, esp. p. 30.
41   *De speciminibus, conatibus variis atque novissimis successibus doctorum quorundam virorum in edendo Alcorano arabico*, by Georg Michael Schnützlein from Weissenburg; *De Alcorani prima inter Europaeos editione Arabica*, by Michael Conrad Ludwig from Wismar; and *De Alcorani versionibus variis, tam orientalibus, quam occidentalibus impressis*, by Johann Conrad Lobherz from Nuremberg. I am most grateful to Asaph Ben-Tov for drawing my attention to these publications.
42   See J.-P. Ghobrial, 'The life and hard times of Solomon Negri: an Arabic teacher in early modern Europe' in Loop et al., eds, *The Teaching and Learning of Arabic*, pp. 310–321.
43   For Dadichi see S. Mills, *A Commerce of Knowledge. Trade, Religion, and Scholarship between England and the Ottoman Empire, c. 1600–1760* (Oxford, 2020), pp. 233–234.
44   C. Bochinger, 'Arabischstudien und Islamkunde im Hallenser Pietismus des 18. Jahrhunderts' in *Annäherung an das Fremde: XXVI. Deutscher Orientalistentag vom 25. bis 29.9.1995 in Leipzig: Vorträge* (Stuttgart, 1998), pp. 47–54, esp. pp. 48–49.

the Arabic he used Hinckelmann's edition, but we can obtain some idea of how he was taught from the manuscript Latin translation of the entire text attributed to Negri and Dadichi which is now in the Rostock University library.[45] The translation, especially when we compare it with Marracci's, is extraordinarily literal: there appear to be hardly any interjections of *tafsīr* in the text. Shortly afterwards another pupil of Salomon Negri, Georg Jacob Kehr, future professor of Oriental languages at Leipzig, announced his intention of publishing excerpts from the Qur'an and of following Acoluthus's example by adding a Turkish and a Persian version, but he never did so.[46] The professor of Greek and Oriental languages at Helmstedt, Johann Gottfried Lakemacher, added an interlinear version in Latin and Arabic of sura 15 to his Arabic grammar of 1718,[47] and published a bilingual version of the first fourteen verses of the second sura in 1721.[48]

The next important date in the history of German translations of the Qur'an is 1746. In that year Theodor Arnold, the son of Gottfried Arnold, the dissident Pietist whose *Unparteyische Kirchen- und Ketzer-Historie* of 1700 was such a significant contribution to the debate about religious toleration, produced his *Der Koran, oder insgemein so genannte Alcoran des Mohammeds*, a German rendering of George Sale's *The Koran, Commonly called The Alcoran of Mohammed* first published in London in 1734. Alexander Bevilacqua has at last shown the full extent to which Sale's translation was indebted to Marracci.[49] Its success in the English-speaking world, however, was due largely to its being in the vernacular and to a stylistic elegance which has guaranteed its survival, and republication, to this day. While Arnold's German translation, criticised though it was, is generally faithful to the English original, there is one striking feature which should arrest our attention. We saw that Marracci always placed his own additions to the Qur'anic text, usually derived from the *Tafsīr al-Jalālayn*, in italics. The German editor of his Latin text, David Nerreter, did so too. Sale followed suit, even if the italics were not always observed in later editions. Arnold, on the other hand, used no italics. The additions thus appear as part of the text. An example is the opening of sura 17, one of the only two references in the Qur'an to what has become known as the miraj or the Prophet's night journey, the legend according to which he was divinely transported from

---

45 Rostock, Universitätsbibliothek MS Orient. 114.
46 Preissler, 'Orientalische Studien', p. 37.
47 Schnurrer, p. 61, no. 89.
48 *Ibid.*, pp. 415–16, no. 379.
49 Bevilacqua, 'The Qur'an translations', pp. 103–107, 112–130. For a further comparison between Sale and Marracci see Z. Elmarsafy, *The Enlightenment Qur'an. The Politics of Translation and the Construction of Islam* (Oxford, 2009), pp. 37–80.

Mecca to Jerusalem and then to the heavens, where he conferred with God. The Qur'anic references, however, are very brief, and there is no specific mention of Mecca or of Jerusalem. The identification of the two towns is to be found in most *tafsīr*, even if there has always been some doubt about whether it is correct.[50] Marracci's translation runs as follows: 'Laus illi, qui transtulit servum suum *Mahumetum* noctu ab Oratorio Haram (*idest a templo Meccano*) ad Oratorium remotissimum *ab eo* (*idest ad templum Jerosolymitanum*).'[51] The passages missing in the original are clearly indicated by italics and brackets. Sale has: 'Praise be unto him who transported his servant by night from the sacred temple *of Mecca* to the farther temple *of Jerusalem*.'[52] The translation is smoother than Marracci's, but the italics are retained. Arnold has: 'Preiß sey Ihm, der seinen Knecht bey Nacht, von dem heiligen Tempel zu Mecca, biß zu dem fernen Tempel in Jerusalem entzücket hat.'[53]

The qualities of the existing translations of the Qur'an soon became the subject of debate. Johann David Michaelis was one of the best known Orientalists in Germany. He had studied Eastern languages with his father at the University of Halle, had taught there briefly himself, and in 1745 had moved to the University of Göttingen, where he lectured at the faculty of philosophy. Michaelis had long been interested in the Qur'an and had toyed with the idea of translating it. In 1754, in the preface to a dissertation defended by a Swedish student at Göttingen, Olaus Domey, he attacked at some length Marracci's translation. It was, he wrote, too literal and made no attempt to capture the poetry of the original.[54] But it was also filled with excerpts from the *tafsīr*, the fruit of superstition added far later and hardly a reflection of what Muḥammad had in mind. Sale's version, he continued, was certainly less prejudiced and more elegant than that of Marracci, but was, in fact, dependent on it. Having spent eighteen months in England and having translated the first part of Richardson's *Clarissa*,[55] Michaelis was among the few Germans in a position to assess the quality of Arnold's rendering of Sale. He assured his readers that it was far from doing justice to the original. Domey's thesis,

---

50   J. Lassner, *Jews, Christians, and the Abode of Islam. Modern Scholarship, Medieval Realities* (Chicago, 2012), pp. 221–223.
51   Marracci, p. 407.
52   Sale, p. 227.
53   *Der Koran*, tr. Arnold, p. 320.
54   Olaus Domey, *Nova versio partis surae II. Corani, cum illustrationibus subiectis: specimen novae versionis totius Corani* (Göttingen, 1754), sig. *1^{r-v}. See Schnurrer, pp. 424–425, no. 386, I.2.
55   F. Gelzer and J. Loop, 'Samuel Richardsons Romane als "heilige Texte"? Die Clarissa-Übersetzung von Johann David Michaelis und ihre Hintergründe' *Scientia Poetica* 10 (2006), pp. 189–223.

probably dictated by Michaelis himself, contained an alternative Latin translation of the first 109 verses of the second sura. Later still, in 1768, the young Justus Friedrich Froriep, another future professor of Oriental languages at Leipzig, produced his own Latin translation of the first two suras of the Qur'an.[56] When it came to comparing the existing translations, he had words of praise for the Latin version of suras 32, 67 and 75 appended by the Dutch scholar Emo Lucius Vriemoet, professor of Oriental languages at Franeker, to his grammar of 1733,[57] and expressed a decided preference for Sale over Marracci and Du Ryer.[58]

By the time the German translation of Sale appeared, the absence of a complete German version made directly from the Arabic was more striking than ever. With the gradual rise of the vernacular in the eighteenth century[59] and the growing interest in Islam, the urgency of making up for the deficiency was pressing. The two men who took up the challenge, David Friedrich Megerlin and Friedrich Eberhard Boysen, seem to have worked more or less simultaneously and altogether independently, each one unaware of the other's existence. Neither was connected with a university, even if they both studied at one. They were thus on the margins of the world of the German academic Arabists.

∴

Relatively little is known about Megerlin. Apparently born in Königsbronn in Württemberg in about 1698,[60] he matriculated at the University of Tübingen in 1716. His description of himself as 'Brackenheimensis' suggests that he might have attended the Latin school in Brackenheim.[61] At Tübingen he received his master's degree in theology in 1718, and, from 1725 to 1729, he acted as *Repetent* (tutor) at the Tübinger Stift, the clerical training college closely tied to the

---

56   Schnurrer, p. 417, no. 383.
57   *Ibid.*, pp. 69–70, no. 101. See below, pp. 391–392.
58   Justus Friederich Froriep, *Corani caput rimum et secundi versus priores* (Leipzig, 1768), pp. v, xi.
59   For the accumulating number of vernacular German grammars and dictionaries see J. Salmons, *A History of German: What the Past Reveals about Today's Language* (Oxford, 2012), pp. 277–278.
60   See the biographical entry by M. Wolfes in *Biographisch-Bibliographisches Kirchenlexikon*, vol. 16 (Hamm, 1999), cols 1043–1047, esp. col. 1043. According to the obituary in the *Schwäbisches Magazin von Gelehrten Sachen auf das Jahr 1778, Zweites Stück* (Stuttgart, 1778), pp. 252–253, on the other hand, his birthplace was Stuttgart. See also A, Hamilton, 'David Friedrich Megerlin' *CMR*, vol. 14, pp. 187–191.
61   A. Bürk and W. Wille, eds, *Die Matrikeln der Universität Tübingen*, vol. 3, *1710–1817* (Tübingen, 1953), p. 26.

university.[62] At the university, where he was probably taught by the professor of Oriental languages, Johann Christian Klemm, Megerlin became a competent Hebraist and must have learnt at least the rudiments of Arabic.[63] He later claimed to have made a speech in Arabic while he was teaching at the Stift in the presence of the renowned Pietist professor of Greek and Oriental languages at the University of Halle, August Hermann Francke.[64] In 1729, the year in which he left the university city, Megerlin published plans for colleges specialised in Oriental languages, the *Tractatus de scriptis et collegiis orientalibus*. They recall the designs of Ravius and Wasmuth revived by Acoluthus and the project of the *Collegium Orientale theologicum* which Francke, assisted by Johann Heinrich Michaelis, had carried out in Halle in 1702.[65] With a preface by the Pietist reformer, professor of theology and chancellor of the University of Tübingen, Christoph Matthäus Pfaff (Klemm's brother-in-law),[66] Megerlin's *Tractatus* had an added *Catalogus edendorum xx. scriptorum philologico-critico-theologicorum* (dedicated to Pfaff) and the *Hexas orientalium collegiorum philologicorum*. The emphasis was on Hebrew and Aramaic, but Megerlin also recommended the publication of an introduction to the Qur'an,[67] which would include a synopsis of Arabic grammar and a Hebrew harmony; suras 1, 12, 14, 20, 61–63, 109–110, 112 and 114,[68] which were also to be used as linguistic exercises, together with confutations; notes on the use of Arabic in the Bible; and an essay on the present state of learning in Turkey. The questions to be asked were whether Muhammad was Antichrist, to what figures in the Bible he might correspond, and when would the Turks be converted to Christianity.

---

62 For the Tübinger Stift and its relations with the university see H.-W. Thümmel, 'Universität und Stadt Tübingen' in H. Decker-Hauff *et al.*, eds, *Beiträge zur Geschichte der Universität Tübingen 1477–1977* (Tübingen, 1977), pp. 33–84, esp. p. 66; and above all J. Hahn and H. Mayer, *Das Evangelische Stift in Tübingen. Geschichte und Gegenwart: Zwischen Weltgeist und Frömmigkeit* (Stuttgart, 1985), pp. 11–45, and, for the *Repetenten* and student life, pp. 41, 103–111, 125–132. Its more illustrious pupils include Hegel, Schelling and Hölderlin.

63 In 1771 he claimed to have known Arabic for some 40 years: Megerlin *tB*, p. 10.

64 *Ibid.*, pp. 34–35.

65 Bourel, 'Der Deutsche Orientalistik', p. 116; Bochinger, 'Arabischstudien', p. 48; J. Sheehan, *The Enlightenment Bible: Translation, Scholarship, Culture* (Princeton, 2005), p. 60.

66 For Pfaff and the situation at the theological faculty in Tübingen see G. Franz, 'Die theologische Zensur im Herzogtum Württemberg in der Konkurrenz von Universität und Regierung' in M. Brecht, ed., *Theologen und Theologie an der Universität Tübingen* (Tübingen, 1977), pp. 123–194, esp. pp. 166–172.

67 David Friedrich Megerlin, *Catalogus edendorum xx. Scriptorum, Philologico-critico-theologicorum* (Tübingen, 1729), p. 24. See also *ibid.*, pp. 19–20, and idem, *Hexas orientalium collegiorum philologicorum* (Tübingen, 1729), p. 13.

68 In his *Hexas orientalium collegiorum philologicorum*, p. 13, he suggests suras 1, 61, and the 25 last ones.

In 1729 Megerlin was appointed rector of the Latin school and second Lutheran pastor of the German church in the enclave belonging to Württemberg, Montbéliard in the Franche-Comté. Megerlin had to leave Montbéliard in 1734 when it was occupied by French troops. He returned to Württemberg and was appointed second preacher in Maulbronn. It would seem to have been when he was in Maulbronn that he received an invitation to St Petersburg, which he declined.[69] In 1736 he was nominated first preacher. Twelve years later he was made dean of the nearby village of Güglingen, but, within two years, he was accused of embezzlement and placed under house arrest. At this point, in April 1749, he fled to Heilbronn, but was again arrested and brought back to Güglingen to be relieved of his ecclesiastical duties. He retired to Laubach, where he described himself as minister and rector in 1766. In Laubach, and in Frankfurt, where he moved later, besides giving French lessons he also gave tuition in Arabic. His pupils included the Swiss Reformed theologian Georg Joachim Zollikofer and Hofmeister Bauer.[70] In 1751 he published a translation from the Rabbinic Hebrew, *Bedenkliche Lehren der zwey vornemsten Jüdischen Rabbinen, Abarbanels und Maimonidis, von dem gesetzlichen Jubel-Jahr und dessen sonderbaren Absichten, wie auch von denen Kennzeichen des Königs Messiä und dem heiligen Verlangen nach ihm*, which included a Latin version of the last two chapters of Maimonides's *Mishneh torah*.

Despite his chequered career in the Evangelical Church, Megerlin was deeply committed to the defence of Protestantism against Catholicism and to the conversion of the Jews to Christianity. In 1755 he dedicated to the landgrave, Wilhelm VIII von Hessen-Kassel, his *Vertheidigung der Protestantischen Religion, gegen die allerneueste Angriffe der Römisch-Catholischen Clerisey*, a vindication of Protestantism against attacks by the Jesuits. In 1766 there appeared, in Hebrew, his edition of the *Sepes Legis* by the Jewish doctor Aser Anselmus Wormsius. The work was a justification of the antiquity of the Masoretic text of the Bible, and Megerlin agreed with the younger Johannes Buxtorf, who regarded the punctuation of the biblical text as having been sent by God to Moses and transmitted to Ezra.[71]

Megerlin's Qur'an translation, *Die türkische Bibel, oder des Korans allererste teutsche Uebersetzung aus der Arabischen Urschrift*, appeared in Frankfurt, published by Johann Gottlieb Garbe and dedicated to the directors and assessors of the Württemberg consistory, in 1772, six years before the author's death

---

69 Megerlin *tB*, p. 15.
70 Ibid., p. 35.
71 David Friedrich Megerlin, ed., *Commendatio novi operis masoretici* (Frankfurt a. M., 1766), p. 7.

in the same city.[72] It had evidently been long in the making. From Montbéliard in 1731 Megerlin had paid a visit to the Swiss Orientalist and theologian Johann Ludwig Frey in Basle, who was himself planning to translate the Qur'an,[73] and discussed with him both Robert of Ketton's rendering and that of Du Ryer.[74] In 1750 he first published a sample of his Qur'an translation in Latin.[75] Five years later he compared Robert of Ketton's version with two manuscripts of the Arabic. One was his own and the other, in the Frankfurt library, had belonged to the Orientalist Hiob Ludolf. He also planned an edition of sura 61 in Arabic and with different translations.[76] There is no evidence, however, that he ever had direct access to a *tafsīr*.

One of Megerlin's main purposes in translating the Qur'an was, he declares repeatedly in the foreword, to provide a German version made directly from the Arabic and to 'rescue the honour of the Germans', 'der Teutschen Ehre also zu retten'.[77] Although he refers to Acoluthus and appears in many respects to have been influenced by him, his objective seems to have been as nationalistic as it was confessional. He gives a list of his predecessors, of those who translated the Qur'an in its entirety and not necessarily directly from the original, and of those who only managed to publish single suras or fragments or who, like Frey in Basel, Lakemacher in Helmstedt and Johann Heinrich Lederlin in Strasbourg, simply planned to do so.[78] Of Du Ryer, whose translation he misdates to 1633, he is critical,[79] complaining both of the absence of a division into verses and of the freedom of the translation, which he attributes to the need to put it into elegant French rather than to any ignorance of the meaning of the Arabic. He does, on the other hand, fully appreciate the importance of Marracci, even if he laments his attacks on Protestantism and Protestants, and maintains, resting on Acoluthus, that his translation contains mistakes and omissions.[80] For Sale he has nothing but praise. He refers to the 'fine English translation' by a man who has made good use of Marracci and who has produced 'a learned masterpiece'.[81]

---

72 Schnurrer, pp. 430–431, no. 386, v; Binark and Eren, *World Bibliography*, p. 219, no. 812/23.
73 Megerlin *tB*, p. 23.
74 Ibid., pp. 12, 14.
75 Ibid., pp. 7, 34.
76 Ibid., p. 11.
77 Ibid., pp. 9–10, 19.
78 Ibid., p. 23.
79 Ibid., pp. 9, 13.
80 Ibid., p. 21.
81 Ibid., pp. 8–9: '[die] schöne Englische Uebersetzung des im Arabischen sehr geschickten Englischen Ritters Sale, der viel Fleiss angewandt und, nach seinem Geständniss, auch des Marracii Uebersetzungen und Anmerkungen, und andere gelehrten Schriften sich

Even if he was to admit that the Qur'an was not entirely without qualities and, quoting the younger Friedrich Spanheim's church history,[82] mentioned the virtues of the Prophet Muḥammad, Megerlin opened his foreword with an attack on the text as the blasphemous work of an impostor. This led him to the question of why it should be translated in the first place. One of his arguments, already advanced by Bibliander in his edition of Robert of Ketton's translation, was that a reading of the Qur'an can only strengthen faith in the Church of Christ. Convinced that the time of superstition was over and that the days were gone when the Qur'an and the Talmud were committed to the flames by the papacy, he praised the advance of Arabic studies, listing the grammars and dictionaries which continued to appear.[83] To read the Qur'an, he wrote, would also induce the reader to pray for the final destruction of Islam and the conversion of the infidel to Christianity.[84] As a sign of the imminence of this event, he referred to the Russian conquests of Islamic territory and appealed to a more united crusade against the Turks.[85]

Megerlin's translation, which tends to follow Marracci and Sale (in Arnold's version), was reviewed by Johann Friedrich Hirt, at the time professor of theology at Jena, in the second volume of his *Orientalische und exegetische Bibliothek*, published in 1772. Clearly flattered by Megerlin's mention of him as the first in a list of illustrious German Arabists, Hirt was benevolent towards 'this fine new German translation of the Qur'an', which, he assured his readers, 'is in many respects superior to earlier German versions' and mainly accurate.[86] His criticisms consist largely in alternative translations, not all of which seem particularly felicitous. One example is the twelfth sura, entitled 'Joseph'. Sura 12:11 is translated by Sale as 'They said *unto Jacob*, O father, why dost thou not entrust Joseph with us, since we are sincere *well-wishers* unto him?'[87] In Arnold's German translation of Sale we have 'Da sprachen sie zu

---

wohl zu nutz gemacht'. See also p. 15: '... biß endlich der Ritter Sale ... den Engelländern ein gelehrtes Meisterstück gelifert hat ...'.

82   The reference is to Friedrich Spanheim, *Opera, quatenus complectuntur Geographiam, Chronologiam, et Historiam Sacram atque ecclesiasticam utriusque temporis* (Leiden, 1701), vol. 1, col. 1209.
83   Megerlin *tB*, pp. 27–28.
84   *Ibid.*, p. 29.
85   *Ibid.*, p. 30.
86   Johann Friedrich Hirt, 'Die Türkische Bibel ...' in *idem*, ed., *Orientalische und exegetische Bibliothek* (Jena, 1772–76), vol. 2, pp. 433–459, esp. pp. 459, 447: 'diese schöne neue deutsche Uebersetzung des Alcorans ... vor den vorigen deutschen Uebersetzungen in vielerley Absicht den Vorzug habe, und daß sie an den allermeisten Orten richtig und treulich gerathen sey'.
87   Sale, p. 188.

Jacob, Vater, warum trauest du uns nicht mit dem Joseph, da wir es so gut mit ihm meinen, und ihm alles Gute wünschen.'[88] Megerlin translates: 'Hernach sprachen sie: o unser Vatter! was hast du vor Ursach: daß du uns Joseph nicht willst anvertrauen, da wir doch gute Gesellschaft mit ihm haben'.[89] Hirt had doubts about this since the Arabic *naṣaḥ* could also mean 'to advise, to warn and to remind', as well as 'to wish somebody well'. In fact very few translators would give these alternative meanings to the word in this context, but Hirt suggested the excessively verbose 'Hernach sprachen sie: Warum wilst du, o lieber Vater! uns den Joseph nicht anvertrauen; da wir doch demselben schon rathen oder ihn errinnern wollen? daß er sich nemlich in Acht nehmen und vor Schaden hüten soll.'[90] Hirt's objections to 12:15 seem more valid.[91] Sale translates: 'And when they had carried him with them, and agreed to set him at the bottom of the well ...'[92] Megerlin gives 'Als sie nun mit ihm giengen: versammleten sie sich, daß sie ihn iezt ins Loch des Brunnens wolten werfen ...',[93] thus, as Hirt points out, misinterpreting the verb *ajmaʿa* (the fourth form of *jamaʿa*), meaning 'to agree'. An even graver error, as Hirt observes, is to be found in Megerlin's translation of 30:8. Sale has: 'Do they not consider within themselves that God hath not created the heavens and the earth, and whatever *is* between them, otherwise than in truth ...'.[94] Megerlin, on the other hand, gives: 'Wie? wollen sie dann nicht mit ihren Seelen betrachten? wie Gott Himmel und Erde, und was zwischen beeden ist, nur allein erschafffen habe, mit Wahrheit ...'.[95] Megerlin's mistake is to have translated *anfusihim* as '[with] their souls' rather than as the reflexive pronoun '[within] themselves'.

While Megerlin was praised with reservations by Hirt, his Qurʾan translation was demolished with singular savagery in the *Allgemeine Deutsche Bibliographie* of 1772 by Johann Jacob Reiske's former pupil Johann Bernhard Köhler, who, at the time, was professor of Oriental languages at Göttingen and who had not been mentioned by Megerlin among the illustrious German Arabists. In order to bear out his judgement, Köhler quoted Megerlin's translation of the first, and a part of the second, sura, followed by a translation of his own. He described Megerlin's version as thoroughly bad, 'von Herzen schlecht gerathen'. The translator, he went on, 'understands neither enough Arabic nor

---

88   *Der Koran*, tr. Arnold, p. 266.
89   Megerlin *tB*, p. 322.
90   Hirt, 'Die Türkische Bibel', pp. 448–49.
91   *Ibid.*, p. 449.
92   Sale, p. 188.
93   Megerlin *tB*, p. 322.
94   Sale, p. 331.
95   Megerlin *tB*, p. 544.

enough German, and German still less'. He has made no attempt to compare earlier editions, such as those of Marracci and Hinckelmann, and there is no sign of any use of a commentary. After Sale's good translation, Köhler continued, pouring scorn on Megerlin's attacks on the Qur'an, the public might have expected a good German version, but Megerlin's can only be regarded as one of the very worst.[96] And, indeed, Megerlin's translation, in a somewhat wooden prose style, does not read well, and no effort seems to have been made to capture the poetic qualities of the original. His main contribution to the reading of the text is, in contrast to Sale, to have inserted the verse numbers. His translation, after being attacked, was soon forgotten.

∴

Another damning review of Megerlin's Qur'an was by the twenty-three-year-old Johann Wolfgang von Goethe in the *Frankfurter gelehrte Anzeigen* of 1772.[97] Goethe dismissed the 'miserable product' and wished that, one day, a German could produce a proper translation. We may wonder what business Goethe had to review a translation of the Qur'an. He did not know a word of Arabic. It was not until some forty-five years later that, enchanted by Persian poetry, he even started to learn the alphabet.[98] And yet the very fact that he should have dared to discuss Megerlin's version and that he reviewed it so harshly indicates some of the deep changes which had taken place in German intellectual circles by the mid-eighteenth century.

There was a growing tendency among the thinkers of the German Enlightenment to admire both Arab culture and Islam. The sources at their disposal

---

96   Johann Bernhard Köhler, 'Der türkische Bibel ...' *Allgemeine Deutsche Bibliothek* 17 (1772), pp. 426–437, esp. pp. 426–427: 'Hr. Prof. Megerlin versteht weder genug Arabisch noch deutsch, und deutsch am wenigsten: an Kritik, die beym Koran fast noch gar nicht gebraucht worden, an Vergleichung ältrer Abschriften, und wenigstens des Hinkelmannischen und Maraccischen Textes, an Einsicht alter arabischer Ausleger und Grammatiker, ist vollends bey dem Manne nicht zu denken ... Hinter solchen dreyen Uebersetzungen [i.e., Du Ryer, Marracci, Sale], wovon insbesondere die Salische, im Ganzen betrachtet, sehr gut ist, durften wir schon eine gute Deutsche erwarten: aber wahrhaftig Hrn. Megerlins seine, gehört in die Klasse der schlechtesten.'
97   *Frankfurter gelehrte Anzeigen* (22 Dec. 1772), p. 811: 'Diese elende Produktion wird kürzer abgefertigt. Wir wünschten, daß einmal eine andere unter morgenländischem Himmel von einem Deutschen verfertigt würde, der mit allem Dichter- und Prophetengefühl in seinem Zelte den Koran läse, und Ahndungsgeist genug hätte, das Ganze zu umfassen. Dann was ist auch jetzo Sale für uns?'
98   A. Polaschegg, *Der andere Orientalismus. Regeln deutsch-morgenländischer Imagination im 19. Jahrhundert* (Berlin, 2005), pp. 331–335; K. Mommsen, *Goethe und der Islam* (Frankfurt a. M., 2001), pp. 127–128. This point is discussed further below, pp. 347, 374.

were accumulating. The great Arabists of the seventeenth century – Thomas Erpenius and Jacobus Golius in Holland, with their edition of al-Makīn, and Edward Pococke in England, with his *Specimen historiae arabum* of 1650 followed by a complete edition of the 'history of dynasties' by the thirteenth-century Jacobte historian Abū 'l-Faraj or Bar Hebraeus – had started to publish the works of the Arab historians;[99] Erpenius, Golius, Pococke, Samuel Clarke, Filippo Guadagnoli, Johann Fabricius and others had discussed the Arab poets and Arabic metrics.[100] Gradually bibliographies of Arabic literature began to come out, starting with Johann Heinrich Hottinger's *Promtuarium: sive, Bibliotheca Orientalis* of 1658.[101] In 1697 there appeared a further major contribution to European knowledge of the Islamic world, the *Bibliothèque orientale*, an encyclopedic work which had been assembled by Barthélemy d'Herbelot but was issued two years after his death by his friend and collaborator Antoine Galland.[102] Successive editions of the *Bibliothèque* appeared in the course of the eighteenth century with additions by the greatest contemporary Orientalists, including Johann Jacob Reiske.

With the Austro-Polish victory over the Turks of 1683 the fear that had once been a feature of so many Western works on Islam began to recede. It gave way to a more impartial approach from which Islamic studies were to benefit.[103] An early attempt in Germany to present Islam in a favourable light is to be found in Gottfried Arnold's *Unparteyische Kirchen- und Ketzer-Historie* of 1699–1700. Drawing mainly on Hottinger's *Historia orientalis*, Pococke's *Specimen* and a number of Byzantine sources, he attributed the triumph of Islam to the situation of the Christian Church at the time, characterised by impurity, idolatry and superstition. He commended the tolerance of the Prophet and much of his teaching, and denounced the medieval myths and misconceptions.[104] The

---

99 A. Vrolijk and R. van Leeuwen, *Arabic Studies in the Netherlands. A Short History in Portraits, 1580–1950* (Leiden-Boston, 2014), pp. 31–48, 62–63.
100 J. Loop, 'Arabic poetry as teaching material in early modern grammars and textbooks' in Loop et al., eds, *The Teaching and Learning of Arabic*, pp. 230–251.
101 Loop, *Hottinger*, pp. 171–176, 201–216.
102 A. Gunny, *Images of Islam in Eighteenth-Century Writings* (London, 1996), pp. 46–54, and, above all, Alexander Bevilacqua, *The Republic of Arabic Letters. Islam and the European Enlightenment* (Cambridge, Mass., 2018), pp. 108–126.
103 Fück, p. 94.
104 Gottfried Arnold, *Unparteyische Kirchen- und Ketzer-Historie, Vom Anfang des Neuen Testaments biß auff das Jahr Christi 1688* (Frankfurt a. M., 1700), vol. 1, pp. 268–270. Writing about the hostility to Islam of the Byzantine sources he says (p. 268): 'Zu solcher feindschafft mag diese bewogen heben / weill Muhammed in seinem Alkoran nicht selten der Christen verderbnüß und gottloses wesen / item, ihre unreinigkeit, aberglauben und abgötterey beschreibet. Worinnen er den ihnen nicht unrecht thut / da ihre eigene

radicalism of Arnold's work made it unpalatable in more orthodox Lutheran circles.[105] Yet Jacob Brucker, despite his aversion to the Prophet Muḥammad and the Qur'an, provided, in the third volume of his *Historia critica philosophiae* of 1742–44, a reassessment of Arab philosophy and science.[106] He ended his survey of the 'philosophia Saracenorum' with a long list of Arabic proverbs and sayings. His conclusion was that even Islam knew a morality the sobriety and beauty of which sometimes surpassed much that had been produced by the scholastic philosophers of the West.[107] And the interest was spreading fast. In 1750 the twenty-one-year-old Gotthold Ephraim Lessing informed his father that he had been asked to edit a Latin translation of d'Herbelot's *Bibliothèque*.[108]

At the same time another movement was afoot, which can be traced back to the 1740s and in which nearly all the German poets, and many of the philosophers, would be involved.[109] The movement can already be seen in existence in 1748, when Friedrich Gottlieb Klopstock started to publish his *Messias*, the

historien ein gleiches bezeugen / und die schrecklichen ärgernüsse gestehen / welche die Namenchristen diesen und andern völckern mit ihren greueln geben.' Commending the Prophet's admiration for Christ, Arnold observes (p. 270): 'Da er nun also von Christo viel gehalten / und ihm etwas übermenschliches und Göttliches zugeschrieben / so wait sich nemlich sein begriff erstrecket / so ist desto eher noch zu verwundern / weil die Christen selber in ihrer lehre ungewiß / verfallen und unrein waren / daß er gleichwol noch so viel erkant / und nicht durch das ärgerliche leben derselben ganz zugestossen worden.' The originality of Arnold's treatment of Islam and his view of it as a natural religion are stressed by E. Seeberg, *Gottfried Arnold: die Wissenschaft und die Mystik seiner Zeit. Studien zur Historiographie und zur Mystik* (Meerane in Sachsen, 1923), pp. 96–98.

105   J.I. Israel, *Radical Enlightenment: Philosophy and the Making of Modernity 1650–1750* (Oxford, 2001), p. 636.
106   J.I. Israel, *Enlightenment Contested: Philosophy, Modernity, and the Emancipation of Man, 1670–1752* (Oxford, 2006), p. 616. The orthodoxy of Brucker, who had studied at the university of Jena where he had been taught Oriental languages by Johann Andreas Danz, one of the many translators of suras from the Qur'an, is stressed by E. François, 'Bruckers Stellung in der Augsburger Konfessionsgeschichte' in W. Schmidt-Biggemann and T. Stammen, eds, *Jacob Brucker (1696–1770). Philosoph und Historiker der europäischen Aufklärung* (Berlin, 1998), pp. 99–109.
107   Jacob Brucker, *Historia critica philosophiae* (Leipzig, 1766–67), vol. 3, p. 240: 'Has ex multis aliis rosas tibi Lector, ex hoc rosario apponere placuit, ut appareat Muhamedanis quoque moralis doctrinae praestantiam non fuisse denegatam, nec tam barbaram Arabum sub Mohammedismo gentem fuisse, ut animum sapientiae moralis praeceptis non excoluerit. Quae tantum abest, ut non pulcherrima multa praeceperit, ut fatendum sit, plus in hoc rosario esse, quod philosophiam sobriam spiret, quam in mille ethicis libellis philosophorum Scholasticorum, vepreta nobis et spinas, non rosaria, exhibentium.'
108   H. Kiesel *et al.*, eds, *Briefe von und an Lessing 1743–1770* (Frankfurt a. M., 1987), pp. 29–30.
109   The matter is also discussed by Sheehan, *The Enlightenment Bible*, pp. 148–60. See the survey in H.-G. Kemper, *Geschichte der deutschen Lyrik*, vol. 2, *Von der Reformation bis zum Sturm und Drang* (Stuttgart, 2004), pp. 140–78.

epic poem which would continue to appear until 1773. Klopstock, who played on the emotions, saw poetry, whether biblical or otherwise, as the work of a visionary whose gifts verged on the prophetic. Such an idea gained even more force with James Macpherson's publication of the Ossianic texts in 1762 and 1763. Extolled by Klopstock, Goethe and Johann Gottfried Herder, they also satisfied the growing taste for the primitive and the sublime, those very features which would be detected in the Qur'an and the poetry of the East. But the more heated debate about 'sacra poesis' was sparked off by the publication in 1753 of the lectures delivered by Robert Lowth at Oxford on the Old Testament. Lowth's statements about Hebrew poetry, and his suggestion that the sheer beauty of the Bible was evidence of its divine origin, induced both Herder and Johann David Michaelis to venture a comparison with the Qur'an and with Arabic poetry in general.[110]

In the mid- and late eighteenth century there was also a steadily greater appreciation of different aspects of Oriental literature. Although Arabic poetry had been discussed, and the verse systems analysed, in the seventeenth century, the first Arabist to study the great Arab poets more consistently was Reiske with his edition of the *Muʿallaqa* of Ṭarafa, published in Leiden in 1742. By the 1770s the movement had got into its stride. It received a strong impulse from the various publications by William Jones, starting with his *Dissertation sur la litérature orientale*, which appeared in London in 1771. Arabic poetry was praised in lectures and publications by the third and last member of the Schultens dynasty of professors of Arabic at Leiden, the urbane Hendrik Albert Schultens.[111] In Germany Johann Gottfried Eichhorn, professor of Oriental languages at Jena[112] (and later at Göttingen) published his *Monumenta antiquissimae historiae Arabum* in 1775 at the age of twenty-three. The continuation of a plan originally conceived far earlier in the century by Albert Schultens in Leiden, the first member of the dynasty,[113] Eichhorn's purpose was to present excerpts from the writings of all the great Arab historians. He started with a version in Latin and Arabic of a part of the work of the ninth-century Iraqi historian Ibn Qutayba. The manuscript Eichhorn used had belonged to Reiske,

---

110 Michaelis's role in the discussion is treated by M.C. Legaspi, *The Death of Scripture and the Rise of Biblical Studies* (New York, 2010), pp. 105–228; see also Polaschegg, *Der andere Orientalismus*, pp. 163–66; and Loop, 'Beauty of the Koran', pp. 482–485. For Herder's interest in Orientalism see Marchand, *German Orientalism*, pp. 43–52.

111 Vrolijk and van Leeuwen, *Arabic Studies in the Netherlands*, pp. 83–85.

112 See S. Heidemann, 'Zwischen Theologie und Philologie: Der Paradigmenwechsel in der Jenaer Orientalistik 1770 bis 1850' *Der Islam. Zeitschrift für Geschichte und Kultur des islamischen Orients* 84 (2007), pp. 140–184, esp. pp. 143–150.

113 Vrolijk and van Leeuwen, *Arabic Studies in the Netherlands*, pp. 72–78.

whose marginal notes he quoted and who had helped him with his Arabic. In 1777 he produced a new edition of William Jones's studies on Persian poetry, *Poeseos asiaticae commentariorum libri sex*, thus introducing Jones to the German public. In fact, however, Eichhorn made his name above all as an Old Testament scholar. A pupil of Johann David Michaelis in Göttingen, a follower of Herder and Johann Salomo Semler, he managed to reconcile the ideas of his teachers and would hold an eminent position in the school of new biblical criticism.[114]

Where the translation of the Qur'an was concerned there seems to have been a widespread assumption that Marracci had, on the whole, provided a perfectly reliable rendering of the meaning of the words. What remained was the poetic style. And nowhere is this more evident than in the attempt made by Goethe in 1771 and 1772 to translate the Qur'an himself.[115] The result is a series of selected fragments from suras 2–6, 10, 13, 17, 20 and 29. At the time, after having been tormented by doubts, Goethe had lost faith in Christianity. In the Prophet Muḥammad he saw a religious leader he could truly admire, and he was drawn by the Qur'an and its emphasis on a single undivided deity whose presence and might could be detected in the natural world. Such was his enthusiasm that he started to write a tragedy about the Prophet. Only fragments have survived, the best known of which is the poem entitled *Mahomets Gesang* dating from 1773.[116] But Goethe, as we saw, knew no Arabic.[117] He was thus entirely reliant for his own translation of the Qur'an on Marracci's Latin and on Arnold's German version of Sale.

The wish expressed by Goethe that another German might come up with a translation superior to that of Megerlin was soon fulfilled. We know nothing of Goethe's own reactions to it. His interest in Islam seems to have remained dormant until, on the orders of Duke Carl August von Sachsen-Weimar and at a time when he was also fascinated by the *Arabian Nights*, he translated Voltaire's *Le fanatisme ou Mahomet le Prophète* in 1799. He did so reluctantly and much to the annoyance of Caroline Herder, the philosopher's widow, who regarded the play as an insult to Islam.[118]

---

114 H.-J. Kraus, *Geschichte der historisch-kritischen Erforschung des Alten Testaments*, 3rd edn (Neukirchen-Vluyn 1982), pp. 133–151; R.P. Lessenich, *Dichtungsgeschmack und Althebräische Bibelpoesie im 18. Jahrhundert. Zur Geschichte der englischen Literaturkritik* (Cologne-Graz, 1967), pp. 21, 119–120.
115 K. Mommsen, *Goethe und der Islam*, pp. 31–47.
116 *Ibid.*, pp. 47–80. See also Elmarsafy, *The Enlightenment Qur'an*, pp. 163–168.
117 See above, p. 343.
118 Mommsen, *Goethe und der Islam*, pp. 80–95.

...

Thanks to his letters to the poet Johann Wilhelm Ludwig Gleim published in 1772 and to his *Eigene Lebensbeschreibung* (Fig. 18), which appeared in 1795 when he was seventy-five, we are remarkably well acquainted with parts of Friedrich Eberhard Boysen's life. Born in 1720 in Halberstadt in Sachsen-Anhalt, which had been part of the kingdom of Prussia since 1701, Boysen learnt the rudiments of Hebrew at the Märtensschule and made further progress in it at the cathedral school, where he also started to study Aramaic and Syriac.[119] He pursued his studies of these languages at the Gymnasium in Magdeburg,[120] received some instruction in Hebrew from Lakemacher,[121] and was in a good position to tackle other Semitic languages when he arrived at the University of Halle, where he matriculated at the theological faculty on 2 May 1737.[122]

For Boysen, Halle was a revelation. For the first time he encountered a world more open than the one he knew from Halberstadt and Magdeburg. He discovered the virtues of the Vulgate, which had been outlawed by the conservative Lutherans of Halberstadt, and of the Septuagint, which was unknown in his hometown.[123] Encouraged to investigate the history of Judaism, he lost no chance of frequenting, and debating with, the chief rabbi of Halberstadt (which had one of the largest Jewish communities in Germany). In Halle he took up lodgings in the house of the university's illustrious professor of theology, Christian Benedikt Michaelis, and there he first met Michaelis's son Johann David, of whom he became a close friend.[124] Together they learnt Ethiopic and Arabic from the older Michaelis, as well as progressing with the study of Hebrew, Syriac and Aramaic. Boysen's approach to Arabic was traditional. He referred to it as a 'dialect' of Hebrew[125] and studied it under Michaelis with the primary objective of elucidating the Bible.[126] The dissertation set by Michaelis

---

119   Friedrich Eberhard Boysen, *Eigene Lebensbeschreibung* (Quedlinburg, 1795), vol. 1, pp. 59, 61. See also A. Hamilton, 'Friedrich Eberhard Boysen' *CMR*, vol. 14, pp. 210–215.
120   Boysen, *Eigene Lebensbeschreibung*, vol. 1, p. 81.
121   Friedrich Eberhard Boysen, *Kritische Erleuterungen des Grundtextes der heiligen Schriften Altes Testaments* (Halle, 1760–64), vol. 1, (sig. 5ʳ).
122   C.L. Preuß, ed., *Matrikel der Martin-Luther-Universität Halle-Wittenberg*, vol. 2 (1730–41) (Halle, 1994), p. 43.
123   Boysen, *Eigene Lebensbeschreibung*, vol. 1, pp. 93, 98–101.
124   *Ibid.*, pp. 90–91.
125   Friedrich Eberhard Boysen, *Beyträge zu einem richtigen System der hebräischen Philologie, gesammlet und nach den Grundsätzen des Hn. Professor Michaelis zu Göttingen* (Leipzig-Chemnitz, 1762), sig. **2ᵛ. Elsewhere, however, he also refers to Hebrew as a dialect (*ibid.*, sig. **1ʳ). Cf. *idem, Eigene Lebensbeschreibung*, vol. 1, p. 83.
126   Boysen, *Eigene Lebensbeschreibung*, vol. 1, p. 124.

FIGURE 18 Engraving of Friedrich Eberhard Boysen by Friedrich Schlüter
FRIEDRICH EBERHARD BOYSEN, *EIGENE LEBENSBESCHREIBUNG*.
ERSTER THEIL (QUEDLINBURG, 1795), FRONTISPIECE

and defended by Boysen on 4 July 1739, *Ritualia quaedam codicis sacri ex Alcorano illustrans*, was on those passages in the Qur'an which illustrated the Jewish rituals described in the Old Testament.

In Halle Boysen developed his interest in the Qur'an. He read it not only with the older Michaelis,[127] but also with the professor of theology, Johann Heinrich Callenberg, and with the professor of antiquity, Johann Heinrich Schulze.[128] He refers to a private lesson by Michaelis on the second sura in which the Arabic grammar published in 1729 by Johann Christian Clodius, professor of Arabic at Leipzig, was used together with that of Lakemacher. It was probably also in Halle that he sealed his friendship with Gleim. Born in Ermsleben, Gleim would settle in Halberstadt in 1747, acquiring the rank of cathedral secretary and canon. One of the foremost poets of his generation, a close friend of Lessing, he was in touch with Klopstock, Herder, Johann Uz, Heinrich Voss, Christoph Martin Wieland and other exponents of the German Enlightenment. The letters he received from Boysen confirm Boysen's literary aspirations, which would play such an important part in his translation of the Qur'an.

After ending his studies at Halle, Boysen worked first as a tutor in Osterburg and was then appointed conrector of the town school in Seehausen. From there he told Gleim about his desire to teach his students Arabic besides Hebrew, for 'Arabic alone can facilitate the study of Hebrew'. But he lamented the lack of resources. Where, he wondered, were the books to be used for teaching? And he regretted that there was not a single copy of the Qur'an in the vicinity.[129] In 1742, however, Boysen moved to Magdeburg, where he acted as preacher. He informed Gleim that his superior, Johann Julius Struve (to whom he was devoted), understood Arabic,[130] and by 1745 he was immersed in the study of the Qur'an. In his autobiography Boysen claims that he could have published his translation almost fifty years earlier, and he proudly quotes Johann David Michaelis's testimony that his Arabic was good enough to do so.[131] 'I wish I had your mind', he wrote to Gleim in April 1745, 'if I wanted to translate the

---

127 *Ibid.*, p. 122.
128 Boysen *K1* sig. a5ʳ.
129 *Briefe vom Herrn Boysen an Herrn Gleim*, vol. 1 (Frankfurt-Leipzig, 1772), p. 17: 'nur durch das Arabische wird das Hebräische den Lernenden leicht ... Wo sind die Bücher, nach welchen der Unterricht gegeben werden muß? Ich glaube, daß in der ganzen alten Mark kaum ein einziges Exemplar vom Koran ist.'
130 *Ibid.*, p. 33.
131 Boysen, *Eigene Lebensbeschreibung*, vol. 1, p. 124.

Qur'an – so ardent and lofty is that poem.'[132] His description of the Qur'an as a poem, 'ein Gedichte', is striking[133] But he was ill-equipped to translate it. Arnold's translation of Sale would only appear in the following year. There is no evidence that Boysen owned a manuscript of the Qur'an at this point, and he admitted to Gleim that he had been unable to acquire the bilingual edition of Marracci. For the Arabic he had to rely on Hinckelmann's version and for a translation he had Reineccius's edition of Marracci's Latin. On the basis of this he listed what he believed were various mistakes in Marracci's Arabic. 'You cannot expect from me', he said at the end of his letter to Gleim, 'a translation of the Qur'an.'[134]

In the years that followed Boysen changed his mind. He refers in the introduction to the second edition of his translation to a Muslim prisoner-of-war held in Magdeburg whom he consulted about the respective meanings of *raḥmān* and *raḥīm*.[135] Boysen remained in Magdeburg until 1760, and it was there that he prepared both his *Kritische Erleuterungen des Grundtextes des heiligen Schriften Neues Testaments aus der syrischen Uebersetzung*, published with a preface by the Orientalist Johann Gottlob Carpzov, and his *Kritische Erleuterungen des Grundtextes des heiligen Schriften Altes Testaments*, the ten parts of which appeared in Halle between 1760 and 1764. Based on the critical principles of Christian Benedikt Michaelis, the book owed a certain amount to the professor of church history at Halle, Johann Simonis, who displayed a similar approach to the Old Testament in his *Lexicon manuale hebraicum et chaldaicum* of 1757 and to whose work Boysen refers, albeit sometimes critically, throughout. Also a follower of Christian Benedikt Michaelis in Halle, Simonis corrected the proofs of Boysen's work.[136] It had, moreover, a preface by one of the most remarkable and humane scholars of his day, Johann Salomo Semler, an intrepid champion of toleration and widely hailed as the father of the new German biblical criticism.[137]

---

132   *Briefe vom Boysen an Gleim*, vol. 1, p. 38: 'Ihren Geist müßte ich haben, wenn ich den Koran übersetzen wollte; so viel Feuer und Hoheit ist in diesem Gedichte.'
133   Loop, 'Beauty of the Koran', pp. 481–482, for a discussion of the views of Boysen and Gleim of the Qur'an as poetry.
134   *Briefe vom Boysen an Gleim*, vol. 1, p. 52: 'Eine Uebersetzung des Korans können Sie von mir nicht erwarten.'
135   Boysen *K2*, p. 39.
136   Boysen, *Eigene Lebensbeschreibung*, vol. 1, sig. b8r.
137   For a survey of Semler's views see Kraus, Geschichte, pp. 104–113; for an excellent discussion of his relationship with orthodox Lutheranism, see R. Bordoli, *L'Illuminismo di Dio: alle origini della mentalità liberale. Religione teologica filosofica e storia in Johann Salomo Semler (1725–1791). Contributo per lo studio delle fonti teologiche, cartesiane e spinoziane dell'Aufklärung* (Florence, 2004), pp. 12–37.

At the time Semler knew Boysen mainly as a correspondent and there is no evidence that they became much closer at a later date. Although, in their early years, they had both, to different degrees, criticised Pietism and turned to orthodox Lutheranism, Boysen can never have shared Semler's growing sympathy for mysticism and his increasingly critical attitude to any visible Church and above all to the Bible, of which he only accepted the parts that could serve as a permanently valid moral guide. Five years younger than Boysen, Semler matriculated at the University of Halle in 1743 and was taught not only by Boysen's own professors but also by the younger Michaelis, who had not yet been appointed in Göttingen. Semler also started to study Arabic. He was disappointed by his teachers. Although he had words of moderate praise for the elder Michaelis, he derived little from the tedious classes of Callenberg, who availed himself of the proximity of his rooms to the university in order to lecture in his dressing gown, and even less from those of Schulze.[138]

The man to whom Semler was closest and by whom he was most influenced was the professor of theology Sigmund Jacob Baumgarten, one of the most admired theologians at the university. It was probably under the influence of Baumgarten, himself a moderate conservative, that Semler first developed a critical attitude toward the Lutheran Church, but, as long as Baumgarten lived, he was cautious in his expression of it.[139] In 1752, with Baumgarten's support, Semler was appointed professor of theology in Halle. Baumgarten died in 1757 and Semler succeeded him as director of the theological seminary. One of Baumgarten's unfinished projects was the translation into German of the vast *Universal History, from the Earliest Account of Time*, which appeared in sixty-five volumes between 1747 and 1768. Its contributors included George Sale, the translator of the Qur'an, who was responsible for the volume on the Prophet Muḥammad, Islam, and Arab history. Semler took over the editorship of this volume, which came out in German in 1759, and provided a long preface. It was here that he first published his views on Islam.[140] Like Ockley and Arnold he was highly critical of the use of Byzantine sources by historians and applauded the greater availability and use of Arabic ones.[141] But with even greater fervour he deplored the standard Western approach to Islam. What right had the

---

138 Johann Salomo Semler, *Lebensbeschreibung* (Halle, 1781–82), vol. 1, pp. 86–88.
139 G. Hornig, *Johann Salomo Semler. Studien zu Leben und Werk der Hallenser Aufklärungstheologen* (Tübingen, 1996), pp. 4–6, 13, 16–18, 23–24, 32–37, 92–95, 116–18, 136–41.
140 G. Bonacina, *Eretici e riformatori d'Arabia. I wahhâbiti in prospettiva europea 1772–1830* (Naples, 2011), pp. 10–11; idem, *The Wahhabis Seen through European Eyes (1772–1830). Deists and Puritans of Islam* (Leiden-Boston, 2011), p. 24.
141 Johann Salomo Semler, 'Vorrede' *Uebersetzung der Algemeinen Welthistorie der Neueren Zeiten die in England durch eine Gesellschaft von Gelehrten ausgefertiget worden. Erster Teil* (Halle, 1759), p. 7.

Church of Rome to cast aspersions on the Prophet Muḥammad when it was itself so prone to fraudulence and fanaticism?[142]

In 1760 Semler's preface to Boysen's work appeared. Semler approved of Boysen's objective of explaining Hebrew words in the Old Testament through equivalent terms in Arabic in view of a common linguistic root and according to a system which had been used felicitously by the rabbis.[143] But it was on Islam that Semler dwelled at greatest length. Although Semler admitted that the Qur'an committed the grossest errors in biblical, Christian and Jewish matters – a fact which he took as proof of the absence of an Arabic translation of the Scriptures at the time[144] – he was delighted by the rise of Islam. It was, he said, a providential gift of God to the Christians. For it was entirely owing to the scientific and philosophical translations into Arabic of the Greeks and to the scientific works produced by the Arabs and the Persians that the world could emerge from a state of total darkness, that the damage done by the Church Fathers and the Vulgate could be combated, and that the Bible could be appreciated for its moral message. It was due to the translation of these works into Latin and their introduction into Europe, moreover, that scholasticism could break free of the stranglehold of the Church. Semler saw a confirmation of his theory in the freedom Christians enjoyed in Islamic lands, where there was no threat of an inquisition or other forms of ecclesiastical oppression.[145]

---

142   Ibid., pp. 8–9: '… so sehr wir auf die sichtbaren Lustigkeiten des Muhammed ungehalten seyn können, so sehr verdienet es der arglistige römische Hof eben von den Zeiten an; und wenn wir über die vielen ernstlichen und fanatischen Anhänger und feierliche Vertheidiger dieser angeblichen Gesandten Gottes betrübt seyn können, so müssen wir gewis einen eben so grossen Haß wider die Möncherey und diese feierlichen Verfechter der römischen Einrichtungen und Bestimmungen der Religion fassen und behalten. Je gewisser wir voraussetzen und behaupten, daß das vernünftige Nachdenken durchaus der wahren Religion wesentlich sey, und nimmermehr davon getrennet werden dürfe: desto gewisser sind wir von solchen christlichen Coranen sicher, als die abendländischen Derwische und Sophi ehedem in so reichen Anzahl, als ie in Orient, mit schelmischer Andacht den armen fast unvernünftigen Christen zu bereitet haben.'
143   Boysen, Eigene Lebensbeschreibung, vol 1, sigs a8ᵛ–b1ʳ, b3ʳ.
144   Ibid., sig. b2ʳ⁻ᵛ.
145   Boysen, Kritische Erleuterungen., sigs b4ᵛ–b6ʳ: 'Ich will nur noch diese algemeine Betrachtung kurz anzeigen: daß die Christen überhaupt die weise göttliche Vorsehungen zu erkennen haben, welche bey der grossen Ausbreitungen der mohammedanischen Religion zugleich den Wachstum und Vortheil der Christlichen so sehr befordert hat. Zu eben den Zeiten lag die ganze morgen- und abendländische Christenheit in den tiefsten Finsternissen; die infamesten Betrügereien und cyklopischen Maasregeln, wie sie Melanchthon oft nent, herrscheten unter den bekanten Namen, der Mirakel, der heiligen Reliquien, der Erscheinungen aus dem Fegefeuer, der klösterlichen Volkommenheit, der Offenbarung durch Engel und Heilige. Alle diese Schändlichkeiten und Dumheiten wurden gleichwol zu dem Inhalt der Bibel gerechnet, und so lange die Vulgate herrschete, und das uneingeschränkte Ansehen der sogenanten Väter: war es unmöglich, den

Although Semler was clearly criticising the medieval Church of Rome, his hatred of dogmatic constrictions soon extended to Lutheranism as his views on religion, and above all on the Bible, grew more radical. Already in 1761, when he was appointed prorector of the university, he was accused of Socinianism and Arianism.[146] In 1776 he would even write an anonymous preface to the third Latin edition of the *Philosophia S. Scripturae interpres* by Spinoza's collaborator Lodewijk Meijer.[147] But for all the suspicions that weighed against him, especially on account of his bold treatment of the Bible, Semler remained devoted to the tradition of Melanchthon; he had no time for deism and always retained his belief in Revelation. Even if he is generally regarded as having deviated from orthodox Lutheranism in the 1760s and 1770s, well before his

> Ungrund dieser Fantaseien und egyptischen Knechtschaft frey einzusehen, und mit dem innern und moralischen Theil der heiligen Schrift wirklich heilsamlich bekant zu werden. Die Juden lagen in eben so dicker Finsternis; ihre rabbinischen Aussprüche, und die Vätersazungen der lateinischen Kirche zumal, hatten einerley Zweck und Grund. Unter der mohammedanischen Oberherrschaft geraten die alten griechischen nützlichen Bücher den Arabern in die Hände; man macht arabische Uebersetzungen von astronomischen, metaphysischen, historischen Schriften; der Verstand bekomt hiervon einen Gegenstand, wodurch er sich aus dem gemeinen Aberglauben heraus arbeitet ... Die sogenanten *passagia* und heilgen Kriege machen, daß die Christen eine ziemliche Kentnis der arabischen Sprache bekommen; sie bringen viele arabische Bücher mit zurück, welche ebenfals ihren Verstand nach und nach beschäftigen, und viel Aberglauben aus der Arzeneigelartheit, Naturkentnis, vertreiben helfen. Die Franziskaner Mißionarien, und einzelne Reisenden tragen manches bey zur weitern Erhaltung dieser Erkentnis; und die lateinischen Uebersetzungen arabischer philosophischen Schriften geben den fleissigen Scholastikern die Gelegenheit, anstatt der Fegfeuernachrichten, die Vernunft zu Rathe zu ziehen, die Aussprüche der heiligen Väter nach allen Seiten zu drehen, und damit den Weg zu banen, zu völliger Beyseitsetzung dieses so schädlichen Ansehens einzeler grossen und kleinen Päbste. Wäre dieser Zusammenhang nicht vom Orient her enstanden, so wurden wir noch unter dem eisernen Joch der monarchischen Decrete, Bullen und Breven seufzen müssen. Ich gebe nur ganz schwache Züge von diesem wundervollen System der göttlichen weisen Regierung, wodurch wir nun den grossen Vortheil einsehen, den die ganze Christenheit davon hat oder haben kan, daß Gott es zugelassen hat, daß die Mohammedaner das sogenante heilige Land unter ihrer Herrschaft haben, und zugleich über so viel tausend morgenländische Christen herrschen, welche wirklich sich viel besser auch leiblich befinden, als andre Christen unter dem Joch gottloser Pfaffen, atheistischer Buben, und heuchlerischer Köpfe gewesen: welches Joch nicht nur eine viel härtere leibliche Knechtschaft zugleich auflegte, und Millionen Christen verbrant, gesäkt, geköpft, und sonst barbarisch hingerichtet hat, da die Christen unter den Mohammedanern ruhig und zufrieden leben dürfen; sondern auch, welches viel unglückseliger ist, uber den Gebrauch unserer leiblichen Sinnen und unsers Verstandes tyrannisiret hat.'

146 Semler, *Lebensbeschreibung*, vol. 1, p. 250.
147 Israel, *Enlightenment Contested*, p. 200.

death in 1791 he adopted positions which suggested a return to orthodoxy but which were in fact combined with the bolder convictions of earlier years.[148]

Semler may have contributed to Boysen's own statements when he wrote his preface to his translation of the Qur'an. Within the Lutheran Church, however, Boysen seems to have held a generally conservative position, endeavouring to defend and sustain the traditional orthodox values which were coming under increasing criticism. This would account for his strong aversion to mysticism, his hatred of the Pietists and his attacks on the anti-Aristotelian writings of the Enlightened philosopher Christian Thomasius.[149] In the preface to his edition of Johann Lorenz von Mosheim's commentary on the Epistle to the Romans, he deplored thinkers such as John Locke, Henry Hammond, Philipp van Limborch, Adriaan van Cattenburg, Oswald Crell and Johann Jakob Wettstein, and expressed his dislike of Socinianism.[150] Yet, orthodox though he was in certain respects,[151] he was also open to discussion with opponents of his views and hardly deserved the savage entry dedicated to him in the *Allgemeine Deutsche Biographie*.[152] One example is his relationship with Count Ludwig von Zinzendorf, the leader of the Herrnhuters,[153] while another is the deep understanding he had for Struve, who had once succumbed to the charms of mysticism in Amsterdam[154] before returning to the Lutheran fold and assuming positions even more conservative than those of Boysen. At the start of the Seven Years War Boysen was a frequent visitor to the captives held in Magdeburg and was there enchanted by his discussions with an Enlightened French officer, who shared the views of Bayle, and with an Austrian officer, whose Catholicism had been strengthened by his education in Rome.[155] He

---

148   Bordoli, *L'Illuminismo di Dio*, pp. 21–22.
149   Boysen, *Eigene Lebensbeschreibung*, vol. 1, pp. 42, 50.
150   Johann Lorenz von Mosheim, *Exegetische Einleitung in den Brief Pauli an die Römer*, ed. Friedrich Eberhard Boysen (Quedlinburg, 1771), sigs c2ʳ–c3ʳ.
151   N. Hope, *German and Scandinavian Protestantism 1700 to 1918* (Oxford, 1995), pp. 101–106, rightly warns against the monolithic image of Lutheran Orthodoxy conveyed by its Pietist enemies. Boysen is an example of how misleading such an image is. Carl Friedrich Bahrdt, for example, expressed some doubt about the extent of Boysen's orthodoxy, *Kirchen- und Ketzer-Almanach aufs Jahr 1781* ([Sulechow], 1781), p. 33: 'In Absicht auf Orthodoxie ist er weder kalt noch warm.'
152   *Allgemeine Deutsche Biographie*, vol. 3 (Leipzig, 1876), pp. 226–27. After deploring his attacks on the Socinians and proponents of the German Enlightenment, however, the author concludes with some justification: 'Bei aller Sprache der Demuth selbstgefällig und von sich eingenommen, wollte er in mancherlei Wissenschaft Vieles als der Erste und Vieles besser als Andere gemacht haben.'
153   Boysen, *Eigene Lebensbeschreibung*, vol. 2, pp. 85–93.
154   Ibid., pp. 13–14.
155   Ibid., pp. 228–238.

could also adopt independent views. He had words of praise for Kant and, more surprisingly, for the 'scharfsichtige' Spinoza.[156] He was fascinated by, and highly partial to, the Jewish community in Halberstadt. In 1772 Boysen had an amicable debate with the Jewish philosopher, also a friend of Gleim, Moses Mendelssohn in Berlin.[157] He boldly denied that the Jewish vocalisation had been sent down by God and was in outspoken disagreement with Albert Schultens about the book of Job having been written in Arabic.[158] And above all there was his friendship with Gleim, who was himself so close to thinkers of the Enlightenment.

In 1760 Boysen moved to Quedlinburg. There he was nominated first court preacher to the princess-abbess of Quedlinburg abbey, Princess Sophia Albertina of Sweden, *Konsistorialrat* and inspector of grammar schools. From Quedlinburg he edited the *Allgemeines historisches Magazin*, which appeared in Halle from 1767 to 1770, and it was while he was there, in 1773 and 1775, that he had the two editions of his Qur'an translation published, also in Halle. He died in Quedlinburg in 1800.

Between the early 1740s, when Boysen maintained that he was already in a position to translate the Qur'an, and the time when he actually did so, certain changes had occurred. He had expanded his library. He made large acquisitions of books and manuscripts during the last four years he spent in Magdeburg,[159] but we have little information about whether these included Oriental works. He kept up his Arabic as well as his Ethiopic.[160] In his preface to the second edition of his translation he lists the authors he read in Arabic[161] and these correspond to the limited number of publications that appeared in the West – Bar Hebraeus, Avicenna, Abū 'l-Fidā', Ibn 'Arabshāh, al-Tughrā'ī and Ibn Zuhayr. The works he quotes in the footnotes of his translation, too, are the standard ones – besides the editions of the Qur'an of Hinckelmann and Marracci, he cites Pococke's *Specimen*, Johann Heinrich Hottinger's *Historia orientalis* and *Bibliotheca orientalis*, Golius's *Lexicon Arabicum-Latinum*, Samuel Bochart's *Geographia sacra* and *Hierozoicon*, Johann David Michaelis's *Beurtheilung der Mittel*, the dissertation on Jewish rituals in the Qur'an which Boysen himself

---

156   *Ibid.*, vol. 1, pp. 56, 60. The positive reference to Spinoza is particularly surprising in view of the standard Lutheran Orthodox aversion to his philosophy. See W. Sparn, *Frömmigkeit, Bildung, Kultur. Theologische Aufsätze, i, Lutherische Orthodoxie und christliche Aufklärung in der Frühen Neuzeit* (Leipzig, 2012), pp. 253–291.
157   Boysen, *Eigene Lebensbeschreibung*, vol. 2, p. 170.
158   Boysen, *Kritische Erleuterungen*, vol. 4, sigs *4ᵛ–*6ᵛ.
159   Boysen, *Eigene Lebensbeschreibung*, vol. 2, pp. 51–52, 94, 298.
160   *Ibid.*, p. 310.
161   Boysen *K2*, p. 37.

had defended but which was dictated by Christian Benedikt Michaelis, and Jean Chardin's *Voyages en Perse*.

When Boysen finally devoted himself to translating the Qur'an his friendship with Gleim played an important part in his progress and in his approach. Boysen's own poetical ambitions appear to have been limited to the pious verses in his *Sammlung einiger geistreicher Lieder*, published in Quedlinburg in 1762. Gleim, on the other hand, was a versatile poet, who owed much of his reputation to his anacreontic lyrics and his verse fables as well as to his martial songs, the *Preussische Kriegslieder*, and his popular ballads. He had met Lessing in Berlin in 1754 and became one of his most assiduous correspondents. Although many of his letters to Lessing announce his own imminent death, he outlived the playwright by over twenty years and died in 1803. It was with one of these letters, dated 4 February 1774,[162] that Gleim sent Lessing a manuscript draft of his *Halladat oder das Rothe Buch*, a long Orientalising poem intended, he said, for the young. Lessing acknowledged it with gratitude,[163] and on 8 February Gleim explained to him the origin of his poem. Ever since his youth, he said, he had wanted to write a 'Bible'. His intentions were confirmed by conversations with Johann David Michaelis in Göttingen and with Boysen in Quedlinburg, who had both spoken about the Qur'an and 'the divine Mahomet' in the same way as Lessing had spoken of 'the divine Homer'.[164] He had recently told Boysen that the Qur'an should be translated into verse. Determined to give him an example of what such a translation might be like, Gleim wrote his *Halladat*.[165] While Lessing expressed his appreciation to Gleim, another of his closest friends to whom he showed the manuscript, Wieland, replied enthusiastically from Weimar.[166]

The poem itself is uneven; much of it suffers from a sentimental morality which is far from the tone of the Qur'an, and the influence of Ossian is evident throughout. Nor does the veneer provided by Orientalising names which, Gleim would assure Wieland, were all of his own devising,[167] add to its quality. Yet there are passages, especially in the second stanza, 'Gott', which do

---

162 H. Kiesel et al., eds, *Briefe von und an Lessing 1770–1776* (Frankfurt a. M., 1988), pp. 617–618.
163 *Ibid.*, pp. 618–620.
164 *Ibid.*, pp. 620–622, esp. p. 621: 'Ich hörte den Hofrat Michaelis zu Göttingen und den Consistorialrat Boysen zu Quedlinburg von dem göttlichen Mahomet sprechen, wie meinen Lessing vom göttlichen Homer.'
165 *Ibid.*, p. 621. The entire episode is discussed by Loop, 'Beauty of the Koran', pp. 481–482, 486.
166 *Wielands Briefwechsel*, vol. 5, *Briefe der Weimarer Zeit* (21 Sep. 1772–31 Dec. 1777), ed. H.W. Seiffert (Berlin, 1983), p. 239.
167 *Ibid.*, p. 241.

indeed capture some of the concision and grandeur of the Islamic text. And there can be no doubt of Gleim's profound familiarity with the Qur'an, since he had helped Boysen to correct the proofs of his version.[168] Boysen, for his part, included two substantial passages from the tenth stanza of the *Halladat* in the preface to the first edition of his translation.

In contrast to Megerlin, Boysen was in touch with the best Arabists in Germany. He bestowed praise on Reiske, 'my late friend', 'mein nun verewigter Freund'. He could only pity the world for the loss of so great a scholar and hope that his widow would be rewarded as she deserved.[169] Reiske himself referred to him in his autobiography, but not as an Arabist. He mentioned him, rather, as a classical scholar who had included some of Reiske's comments on Tacitus in his 'Schulbibliothek'.[170] Well-disposed though he was towards Reiske, Boysen could be petty and acrimonious in his treatment of his predecessors, as we see from his statements about other translators of the Qur'an. This may have been because of his determination to show that he had translated the work directly from the Arabic and, contrary to what Johann David Michaelis said in his long review of his translation in his *Orientalische und exegetische Bibliothek*,[171] owed nothing to anyone else. At first his denial is absolute. He used, he claimed, neither Marracci nor Sale (whose name he spelt, perhaps deliberately, 'Dale'). He was, however, acquainted with the German translation of Sale. He was undoubtedly influenced, as we shall see, by Michaelis, when he dismissed Arnold's version – by someone, he claimed, who clearly knew no English – and he had an equally low opinion of Du Ryer's French Qur'an[172] Nowhere does he make any mention of his rival Megerlin. Like Acoluthus, he taxes Marracci with not having understood, in his *Prodromus*, the variants in the Qur'an which form the basis of every interpretation, 'die der Grund der Auslegung sind',[173] and he goes on to say that both Marracci and Hinckelmann's editions were full of mistakes in the Arabic text and that they never even admitted which version of the Qur'an they were using, the Kufic or the Bassoran one.[174]

---

168 Boysen *K2*, p. 11.
169 *Ibid.*, p. 9; see also p. 17.
170 Reiske, *Lebensbeschreibung*, pp. 71, 115.
171 Johann David Michaelis, 'Der Koran ...', in *idem*, ed., *Orientalische und exegetische Bibliothek* (Frankfurt a. M., 1773–85), vol. 8, pp. 30–98, esp. pp. 53–54.
172 Boysen, *Eigene Lebensbeschreibung*, vol. 1, pp. 124–125.
173 Boysen *K2* (1775), p. 13.
174 *Ibid.*, p. 38. For the manuscript traditions, such as those of Kufa and Bassora, see *The Encyclopaedia of Islam*, ed. C.E. Bosworth, E. van Donzel, B. Lewis and C. Pellat, vol. 5 (Leiden, 1986), pp. 406–409. But for an answer to Boysen's criticism see below pp. 357–358.

Of one thing Boysen was convinced: his was by far the best translation in existence. In his autobiography he quoted various testimonials. Besides Michaelis he referred to Hirt in Jena[175] and to Christoph Wilhelm Lüdeke, a former student at Halle who had acted as preacher to the evangelical community in Izmir and was later appointed to preach in Stockholm. The author of the *Beschreibung des Türkischen Reichs*, Lüdeke stated in 1778 that Boysen's translation was the best to date,[176] and in 1789 compared it favourably with the French translation of Claude-Etienne Savary which had appeared in 1783.[177]

The first edition of Boysen's translation, *Der Koran, oder Das Gesetz für die Muselmänner, durch Mohammed den Sohn Abdall*, appeared in Halle, published by the firm of Gebauer, in 1773.[178] Dedicated to Karl Wilhelm Ferdinand, the crown prince of Braunschweig and Lüneburg, it was preceded by a short preface in which Boysen thanked his teachers at Halle, Michaelis, Callenberg and Schulze, and announced that he had based his translation on six copies of the Qur'an at the university library in Halle as well as on the Arabic texts published by Hinckelmann and Marracci. He also briefly staked his claims as an Arabist. His emphasis, however, was on the poetic qualities of the Qur'an. The Prophet had such a 'fiery wit', such a 'sharpness of mind', and was so moved and inspired by his subject that he was unable to contain it in a uniform and colourless prose. Admitting his inability to convey the 'lofty and fiery drive' or the 'melodical' quality of the original (which had often led to obscurity), Boysen wondered whether it was indeed possible to express these impulses of the Oriental spirit in German.[179] Gleim, he said, had suggested he write his

---

175   Boysen, *Eigene Lebensbeschreibung*, vol. 1, p. 127.
176   Ibid., p. 131. Christoph Wilhelm Lüdeke, *Beschreibung des Türkischen Reichs nach seiner Religions- und Staatsverfassung in der letzten Hälfte des achtzehnten Jahrhunderts* (Leipzig, 1771–89), vol. 2 (1778), p. 45: 'Die beste Uebersetzung des Koran, unmittelbar aus dem Arabischen in das Deutsche, ist bis jetzt die von dem Hrn. F.E. Boysen, Halle 1773, 8.'
177   Lüdeke, *Beschreibung*, vol. 3 (1789), pp. 32–34.
178   Schnurrer, p. 431, no. 386, v; Binark and Eren, *World Bibliography*, pp. 213–14, nos 791/2–793/4.
179   Boysen K1, p. 10: 'Man wird meine Uebersetzung mehr wörtlich als frey finden, und mir, wie ich hoffen darf, bey allen Unvollkommenheiten, die sie haben mag, doch das Zeugniß nicht versagen, daß ich bemüht gewesen bin, den Sinn des Originals, ohn ihm fremde Gedanken beyzumischen, richtig anzugeben. Nur das Melodische, welches die Urschrift im vorzüglichsten Grade hat, und wodurch sie nicht selten dunkel wird, hab ich nicht ausdrücken können. Der Verfasser, der überall feurigen Witz, Scharfsinnigkeit, und eine glückliche Einbildungskraft zeigt, ward durch die lebhaften Vorstellungen seines Gegenstandes, oft dergestalt erhitzt und gerührt, daß er die Vorstellungen und die Ausdrücke in den engen Grenzen einer matten und einförmigen Prose nicht erhalten konte. Und ich gesteh aufrichtig, daß mirs nicht möglich gewesen ist, das lebhafte Gefühl des Dichters, und den hierdurch erweckten erhabenen und feurigen Schwing in meine

translation in verse, but Boysen had preferred a more prosaic version which would illustrate the tenets of Islam and allow the reader to realise 'the great advantages' of Christianity. Muḥammad, he claimed, wanted to introduce a philosophical religion, and he was more interested in charming his followers by way of short and ingenious utterances and bold comparisons than in convincing them by way of proofs and conclusions.[180] In contrast with Megerlin and his predecessors, Boysen had entirely abandoned any appeal to missionary activity. The translation of the text of the Qur'an ended, in both editions, with twelve Muslim prayers taken from *Bi-smi llahi. Muhammedanus precans*, published in 1666 by Henningius Henning from Schleswig Holstein.

In 1775 Gebauer in Halle brought out the second revised and 'improved' edition, *Der Koran, oder Das Gesetz für die Moslemer durch Muhammed den Sohn Abdall*. The preface was entirely different. It was far longer and provided a survey of the genealogy and the life of the Prophet. Above all, it displayed a sympathy for Islam which can only barely be detected in the first version. This enabled Boysen to launch another attack on Marracci. He also turned on the Prophet's hostile English biographer Humphrey Prideaux and those many scholars who had attributed words to the Prophet which he never uttered.[181] Much of the blame for these distortions, he continued, must be laid on the 'wretched' Crusaders, 'die elenden Kreuzfahrer', dominated by fanaticism and religious hatred. Nor was the Prophet better served by Henri de Boulainvilliers, 'more a eulogist than a biographer' ('mehr Lobredner als Biograph'), or by Jean Gagnier's translation of the Prophet's biography by Abū 'l-Fidā', which, although the best text to date, was marred by Gagnier's mistranslation of a great many passages.[182] As for Gagnier's charges of cruelty in his own biography of the Prophet, these, taken not from Abū 'l-Fidā' but from al-Jannābī, were hardly worthy of credence.[183] Boysen also dismissed the legends of the *miraj*, the Prophet's 'night journey' – which Gagnier, resting on an anonymous account in the Bodleian Library, recorded in detail.[184] 'The entire anecdote', wrote Boysen, 'is preserved by a tradition which contains more

---

Sprache zu bringen; ich zweifle auch, daß sich diese Antriebe des orientalischen Geistes in unsre Sprache übertragen lassen.'

180 Ibid., p. 13: 'Muhammed wollte eine philosophische Religion einführen, und es war ihm mehr darum zu thun, seine Parthey durch kurze sinnreiche Aussprüche, und durch kühne Vergleichungen zu belustigen, als ihren Verstand durch Schlüsse und Beweise zu überzeugen.'
181 Boysen *K2*, pp. 13–14.
182 Ibid., p. 17.
183 Ibid., p. 30.
184 The anonymous manuscript used by Gagnier is Bodl., MS Marsh 18.

beauty than truth, and the story itself is interpreted by sensible Arabs in an allegorical sense.'[185]

Boysen presents the Prophet as a hero in terms resembling those used by Edward Gibbon in the last volume of his *Decline and Fall of the Roman Empire* of 1788. If Muḥammad wished for a new monarchy in Arabia he had to dare to introduce a new religion, to be a hero and a preacher at the same time. In one hand he had to carry a divine book and in the other a sword, since civil power has always been connected with spiritual power in Arabia. He had to claim inspirations in order to give his teaching the necessary authority, and he had to announce a moral doctrine more than a religious one, since the majority of men lack a true understanding of religious doctrine and are consequently more swayed by a moral one.[186] Combating the idolatry he encountered in Arabia, the Prophet took what he believed to be the best points from Judaism and Christianity – even if he was unable to gather much understanding of the latter – and managed to introduce a 'philosophical religion', 'eine philosophische Religion', into the peninsula.[187] In words which recall those of John Toland,[188] Boysen credited the Prophet with having established a religion which he believed was composed of the best elements of the religions already in existence.[189] For the Qur'an he had the greatest admiration: 'Why', he asked, 'should we lie and cover with calumnies a book which expresses the deepest reverence for God, which includes some of the most sacred teachings of Christianity, and which has thereby helped the human race in many wild areas to become more refined or at any rate less primitive?'[190]

---

185 Boysen *K2*, p. 27: 'Die gantze Anekdote ist in der Tradition enthalten, die mehr schöne als wahre Sachen in sich hält, und die Erzehlung selbst wird von vernünftigen Arabern, in einem allegorischen Sinne aufgelöst.'

186 *Ibid.*, pp. 22–23: 'Wollt aber Muhammed eine Monarchie in Arabien wagen, so mußte er eine neue Religion wagen, er muste Held und Prediger zugleich seyn, in der einen Hand mußt er ein göttliches Buch, und in der andern ein Schwerd führen, weil fast immer in Arabien die weltliche Gewalt mit der geistlichen verbunden gewesen ist. Er muste Offenbahrungen vorgeben, um seiner Lehre die nöthige Autorität zu verschaffen, und er muste mehr Sittenlehre als Glaubenlehre verkündigen, weil der gröste Theil der Menschen, der von der Natur der Glaubenslehren, nicht die rechten Begriffe hat, mehr von jenen, als von diesen gelenkt wird.'

187 *Ibid.*, p. 35.

188 For example, John Toland, *Works* (London, 1732), p. iii; *idem*, Nazarenus, ed. J. Champion (Oxford, 1999), p. 135.

189 Boysen *K2*, p. 23.

190 *Ibid.*, p. 12: 'Was ist es nöthig zu lügen, und über ein Buch Lästerungen auszuschütten, welches mit der tiefsten Verhehrung von Gott spricht, welches verschiedne heilige Lehren des Christentums begreift, und welches mit dazu geholfen hat, daß das

To what extent can we credit Boysen's claims of independence of Sale and Marracci? Michaelis was sceptical, and Boysen tended to contradict himself in his denial. He frequently proves independent in his actual translations, but the same cannot be said of his references. He quotes what he calls the 'commentators', the 'Ausleger'.[191] Nearly all his citations can be found in Marracci or in Sale or in other European printed sources. One example is his note to 5:6, on the Islamic ablutions, in which he says that al-Ghazālī maintained the necessity of a fourfold ablution.[192] Although Marracci says nothing of it in his notes to the sura, he does indeed mention it in his *Prodromus*.[193] It is discussed at even greater length by Edward Pococke in his *Specimen*.[194] Boysen mentions al-Bayḍāwī in connection with 3:164, a reference to the Prophet's descent from the Quraysh. So does Sale.[195] In a note on the 'seven gates' of hell in 15:43, Boysen provides a long note naming each gate in Arabic.[196] Marracci does not do so, but Sale does, in his 'Preliminary Discourse'.[197] In connection with 4:32 Boysen gives the very same quotation from the *Tafsīr al-Jalālayn* as Marracci.[198] In his note to 65:13 he follows Marracci in quoting al-Zamakhsharī.[199]

Boysen, however, uses one source unknown to Marracci and Sale – someone he calls 'Abu-Muhammed Elhosain, mit dem Zunamen Elkara'. This is Abū Muḥammad al-Ḥusayn b. Masʿūd al-Farrāʾ al-Baghawī, the twelfth-century Persian scholar noted for his *tafsīr Maʿālim al-tanzīl*. Boysen consulted the manuscript of an extract from it in what is now the library of the Franckesche Stiftungen in Halle.[200] Taking the *fāʾ* for a *qāf*, he misread al-Farrāʾ as 'al-Qarāʾ' and transliterated it as 'al-Kara'.[201] The first of Boysen's two references to al-Baghawī concerns 73:5. Sale translates it as 'For we will lay on thee a weighty

---

menschliche Geschlecht in vielen wilden Gegenden verfeinert, wenigstens geschlachteter geworden ist.'

191   Ibid., pp. 56, 588 (al-Zamakhsharī); 68 (al-Bayḍāwī); 79, 547 (al-Jalālayn); 102, 614 (al-Ghazālī); 607–608, 624–625 (al-Baghawī).
192   Ibid., p. 102.
193   Marracci, *Prodromus*, pt. 4, p. 27.
194   Edward Pococke, *Specimen Historiae Arabum* (Oxford, 1650), p. 302.
195   Sale, p. 55.
196   Boysen *K2*, pp. 253–254.
197   Sale, p. 92.
198   Boysen *K2*, p. 79; Marracci, p. 158.
199   Boysen *K2*, p. 588; Marracci, p. 730.
200   Boysen *K2*, p. 10.
201   I am grateful to Arnoud Vrolijk for pointing this out to me. On al-Baghawī (and the Halle manuscript) see C. Brockelmann, *Geschichte der Arabischen Literatur. Erster Supplementband* (Leiden, 1937), pp. 620–622. For a later use of al-Baghawī in Germany see below. The library of the Franckesche Stiftungen was not alone in possessing al-Baghawī. A four-volume copy of the entire work was also to be found in Leiden. It was part of the

word.'²⁰² In his note Boysen says that al-Baghawī understands the verse to refer to the weight of the commandments, the prohibitions and the definitions in the Qur'an, while other interpreters think it refers to the weight and the exalted value of the Qur'anic truths.²⁰³ The second reference is in a note to 81:8–9 translated by Sale as: 'And when the girl who hath been buried alive shall be asked for what crime she was put to death'.²⁰⁴ While the verse is generally taken to refer to the ancient Arab custom of infanticide, Boysen points out that al-Baghawī connects it with the custom of burying alive daughters who had turned to prostitution.²⁰⁵

Like Megerlin, Boysen tactfully placed Hirt in a list of distinguished contemporary Arabists, and Hirt reviewed the translation of the 'berühmte Herr Konsistorialrath Boysen' with an enthusiasm which led him to lower his opinion of Megerlin. He rejoiced in the number of Arabists with whom Germany was graced and insisted that Boysen's translation was infinitely superior to the earlier one – it may not be perfect in all respects but it 'brings honour to its author in Germany', 'bringt ihrem Verfasser in Deutschland Ehre'.²⁰⁶ From compliments Hirt passed on to reservations. He did not share Boysen's high opinion of Islam, feeling that he presented 'an exaggerated and all too favourable' image of the Prophet and described 'this misled man' too favourably.²⁰⁷ Nor did he agree with Boysen's charges against Prideaux.

Boysen's old friend Johann David Michaelis reviewed the translation in the eighth volume of his own *Orientalische und exegetische Bibliothek* in 1775. Michaelis's review of Boysen's Qur'an was one of the best expressions of his approach to Islam and Arabic studies.²⁰⁸ He congratulated Boysen on having provided the satisfactory German translation which the public had so long

        collection formed in Istanbul by Levinus Warner and was already described in the printed catalogue of 1674. See *CCO*, p. 23.
202 Sale, p. 470.
203 Boysen *K2*, p. 608.
204 Sale, p. 482.
205 Boysen *K2*, pp. 624–625.
206 Johann Friedrich Hirt, 'Der Koran …', in *Orientalische und exegetische Bibliothek*, vol. 6, pp. 341–353, esp. pp. 341–342.
207 *Ibid.*, pp. 343–344: 'daß er sich von dem Mohammed einen etwas übertriebenen und allzugünstigen Begriff gemacht, und diesen verkehrten Mann zu vortheilhaft geschildert habe.'
208 Michaelis, 'Der Koran', pp. 30–98. See the discussion in J. Loop, 'Kontroverse Bemühungen um den Orient. Johann Jacob Reiske und die deutsche Orientalistik seiner Zeit' in Ebert and Hanstein, eds, *Johann Jacob Reiske*, pp. 5–85, esp. pp. 75–77; A. Bevilacqua and J. Loop, 'The Qur'an in comparison and the birth of "scriptures"' in J. Loop, ed. *The Qur'an in Western Europe* (London, 2018) [= *Journal of Qur'anic Studies* 20 (2018)], pp. 149–174, esp. pp. 165–167.

awaited. Yet, like Hirt, Michaelis was unable to share Boysen's regard either for Islam or for the Qur'an. Where Islam was concerned Michaelis first described it as a remarkably rational religion the success and spread of which could only be admired, but he then pointed out that it was ill-suited to any form of state. The state Michaelis himself had in mind was what he regarded as its most perfect manifestation – contemporary Prussia. Islam, he wrote, had suffocated the spirit of enquiry. It was fatalistic, it was nationalistic and, rather than recommending obedience to the civic authorities, it preached obedience to the Prophet alone.[209] As for the Qur'an, Michaelis dismissed those who wished for a poetic translation of the text. Although the language of the Qur'an was not always difficult to understand, the work was elliptical and repetitive, and frequently obscure on account of omitted explanations.[210] So what must a translator do? Should he fill in the omissions? If he did so, he would be accused of transforming the original text. Should he leave the apparent breaks in the original? If he did so, no one would read it. Should he try to preserve the original beauty of the text? This was, quite simply, impossible. Any attempt to do so would mean either sacrificing all fidelity to the original or presenting the endless repetitions in a version which could never be regarded as poetry.[211] Were such an attempt to be successful, he continues, were it possible to present the Qur'an as a work of great poetic content, this, too, would give a false impression of a text the poetic qualities of which he, for one, failed to appreciate, and would endow it with a grossly unfair advantage 'in the examination of the truth of religion', 'was die Prüfung der Wahrheit der Religion angehet', in other words, in a comparison with other sacred texts.[212]

Another point Michaelis makes is that it is inadvisable to rely too heavily on the *tafsīr*. The commentaries, certainly, should be known, since they can provide historical information and philological elucidations; but just as Christians read the Bible without the help of commentaries by the Church Fathers, so the Qur'an should be read not to know what the Persians or the Turks make of it, but what Muḥammad himself says in it.[213] The authors of the *tafsīr*, according to Michaelis – and in this he anticipated the far later studies of Friedrich

---

209 Michaelis, 'Der Koran', pp. 34–35.
210 *Ibid.*, p. 40.
211 *Ibid.*, p. 41. For Michaelis's own attitude to translating see Gelzer and Loop, 'Samuel Richardsons Romane', pp. 195–209.
212 Michaelis, 'Der Koran', p. 47. See J. Loop, '"Viel leichter wäre es, Wolffs Werke in Verse zu übersetzen". Aufgeklärte Debatten um eine poetische Übersetzung des Korans' in J.-M. Valentin, ed., *Akten des XI. Internationalen Germanistenkongresses Paris 2005 'Germanistik im Konflikt der Kulturen'*, vol. 3 (Bern, 2007), pp. 257–270, esp. pp. 267–269.
213 Michaelis, 'Der Koran', p. 49.

Schwally[214] and Ignaz Goldziher[215] – are frequently polemical and prejudiced, and can hardly be regarded as arbiters of the truth.[216] Here, Michaelis writes, Reiske disagreed with him. Reiske believed that we should try to understand the Qur'an as it is understood by Muslims. For this purpose, the *tafsīr* were obviously essential.[217]

Michaelis goes on to indicate certain errors in Boysen's translation.[218] In 4:24, for example, which specifies the punishment for female slaves caught in adultery, Boysen applies to them the same punishment as free and married women.[219] The original, however, says that they should receive *half* the punishment of free and married women. Marracci and Sale render this passage correctly[220] and Boysen would have done well to follow them. Another error made by Boysen, Michaelis points out, is to translate Noah's ark, *fulk* in Arabic (11:39), as 'chest', 'Kasten'.[221] Michaelis also deplores the almost total absence of explanatory notes and Boysen's failure to give verse numbers. He then provides his own translation of the first thirty verses of the third sura.

Boysen's translation was received by Köhler, who was no more mentioned in Boysen's preface than he was in Megerlin's, with little enthusiasm. Admitting that it was better than Megerlin's, Köhler was nevertheless hardly satisfied. Boysen was not sufficiently acquainted with the original and translated it without any poetic sensibility. He consequently failed to catch the tone of the Qur'an. He would also have been better advised not to insert the interpretations into the text but to put them in notes.[222] But despite Köhler's strictures, Boysen's Qur'an translation, in contrast to Megerlin's, was destined to be read, albeit in a revised form, well into the nineteenth century.

...

---

214   T. Nöldeke, *Geschichte des Qorāns*, 2nd edn, ed. F. Schwally (Leipzig, 1909–19). See, above all, Nöldeke's supplement to the second volume, pp. 122–219.
215   I. Goldziher, *Die Richtungen der islamischen Koranauslegung: an der Universität Upsala gehaltene Olaus-Petri-Vorlesungen* (Leiden, 1920).
216   Michaelis, 'Der Koran', p. 51.
217   *Ibid.*, p. 53.
218   *Ibid.*, p. 54.
219   Boysen *K2*, p. 78.
220   Marracci, p. 146; Sale, p. 64.
221   Boysen *K2*, p. 212.
222   Johann Bernhard Köhler, 'Der Koran ...' *Allgemeine Deutsche Bibliothek* 24 (1777), pp. 830–847, esp. pp. 830–831.

Johann Jacob Reiske, Köhler's teacher, could claim to be the greatest Arabist of his day.[223] Attributing his decision to study Arabic to a 'whim', 'eine Grille', of his youth,[224] it was, as we saw, his disappointment in the teaching of Arabic at the University of Leipzig that induced him, despite his poverty, to leave Germany for Holland in 1738 at the age of twenty-two in order to study the Arabic manuscripts in the Leiden library. In Holland Reiske spent eight years – by far the most stimulating ones of his life. Although he himself was particularly interested in the Arab historians, he obeyed somewhat reluctantly the professor of Arabic, Albert Schultens, and thus came across the early poets. Later, embittered by his treatment and the victim of his own bad temper, Reiske wrote that he wished either that he had never gone to Holland in the first place or that, having done so, he had remained there for ever.[225] Instead he returned to Germany in 1746, hoping for financial support for his publications and a professorship at his former university or elsewhere. He obtained neither. His publications were mainly issued at his own expense. The extraordinary professorship he was given in Leipzig provided him with hardly any income, and it was not until he was appointed rector of the Nikolaischule, an illustrious grammar school, in 1758, that he could truly earn a living.

The question remains as to what, if anything, Reiske thought of Megerlin and Boysen's translations. His death in 1774 meant that he had little time in which to react to either of them. But we do know what he thought of Qur'an translations in general.[226] In 1757, in the eleventh part of the *Geschichte der königlichen Akademie der schönen Wissenschaften zu Paris*, which he edited, he published an essay entitled 'Gedanken, wie man der arabischen Literatur aufhelfen könne, und solle'. It was partly an autobiographical description of his own involvement with Arabic, partly an assessment of the teaching of Arabic in Germany and partly an admonition to prospective Arabists. After reading Reiske's account of the appalling, and often insoluble, difficulties which the study of Arabic entailed, few scholars can have felt the urge to undertake it, and to those who persevered Reiske issued a warning never to tackle the Qur'an.

---

223 For an assessment of Reiske's achievements as an Arabist see Fück, pp. 108–124. See also J. Loop, 'Johann Jacob Reiske' *CMR*, vol. 14, pp. 192–209.
224 Johann Jacob Reiske, 'Gedanken, wie man der arabischen Literatur aufhelfen könne, und solle' *Geschichte der königlichen Akademie der schönen Wissenschaften zu Paris*, vol. 11 (Leipzig, 1757), p. 155.
225 Reiske, *Lebensbeschreibung*, p. 16.
226 The matter is discussed by Loop, 'Kontroverse Bemühungen', pp. 79–80. See also *idem*, 'Beauty of the Koran', p. 487.

Dismissing the use of Arabic words for the better understanding of Hebrew ones – an intellectually undemanding task if ever there was one, which required no more than the knowledge of the Arabic alphabet and the use of an Arabic dictionary – Reiske dwelt at length on the polyvalence of many Arabic words and consequently on the difficulty of establishing their exact meaning. He had always been critical of Golius as an editor of Arabic texts, and he now demonstrated the inadequacy of his Arabic dictionary, the *Lexicon Arabico-Latinum* of 1653. It was only by extensive reading and by a thorough consultation of Arab lexicographers such as al-Jawharī (on whose monolingual dictionary much – but according to Reiske not enough – of Golius's work was based) that it would ever be possible to grasp the countless associations and shades of meaning that Arabic words had acquired. A contribution to the solution of this problem could be provided, Reiske admitted, by reliable editions of the great Arabic texts, but what of the Qur'an? Possibly because of his aversion to theology, Reiske had no particular liking for it. He described it as a 'bad book, the content of which hardly deserves any respect'.[227] A satisfactory edition, moreover, would be the work of several lifetimes. First, a concordance was needed – but what European scholar had the time or ability to undertake it? Then, it would be necessary to compare the different readings and different manuscripts. Like Acoluthus and others, Reiske reproached Hinckelmann and Marracci with never having indicated which manuscripts they had used, whether those of the Bassoran tradition or those of the Kufic one, and suggested that the Arabic texts of the two published versions should be compared. Above all, however, Reiske recommended the consultation of *tafsīr* – of far more *tafsīr* than had been consulted by Marracci – in order to establish what the Qur'an meant to the Muslims.[228] Here again, what academic would have the time to do this? The task could only be performed by a 'bookworm', working in total seclusion, 'unknown, unadmired, indifferent to fame, and satisfied alone with the inner applause of his own conscience'.[229]

Reiske's complaint about the failure of Hinckelmann and Marracci to say which manuscript they were using for their translation, whether one of the Bassoran or of the Kufic tradition, was, as we saw, repeated by Boysen some years later. It implies that Reiske and Boysen assumed that the two translators

---

227   Reiske, 'Gedanken', p. 189: '... betrachte ich ferner, daß der Alcoran an und für sich ein schlechtes Buch ist, das seines Inhaltens wegen nicht verdienet angesehen zu werden ...'
228   Reiske, 'Gedanken', pp. 192–194.
229   *Ibid.*, p. 193: 'Dazu gehöret ein Bücherwurm, der in einem versteckten Winkel unbekannt, unbewundert, um Ruhm unbekümmert, und mit dem bloßen inner Beyfalls seines Gewissens zufrieden ...'

had been using a single codex. This, however, was quite wrong. Roberto Tottoli has shown that Marracci originally took his text of the Qur'an from the *tafsīr* of Ibn Abī Zamanīn (which, like all *tafsīr*, included the entire Qur'an).[230] Hinckelmann, who had a large collection of Qur'ans, seems to have used various different ones in addition to the *Tafsīr al-Jalālayn*.[231]

∴

Had Reiske's strictures been taken seriously, the entire process of Qur'an translation might have come to a halt. Not only did Megerlin and Boysen proceed undeterred, however, but another development was underway which, ultimately, would triumph. While both Acoluthus and Michaelis had suggested that the Qur'an could be translated without the help of *tafsīr*, the conviction had been growing that it was essential to capture the poetic quality of the text. The importance of doing this had been emphasized by a new French translator, Claude-Etienne Savary, whose *Le Coran, traduit de l'arabe* was first published in 1783. Despite Savary's criticisms of earlier versions – particularly that of Du Ryer – as a translation his was still manifestly dependent on Marracci.[232] Savary's presentation of the text, on the other hand, was far more positive than that of any of his predecessors, and he joined the chorus of scholars insisting on the poetic aspects of the work. One of the German translators to take up the challenge was Johann Christian Wilhelm Augusti. Born in Eschenberga in 1771, Augusti had had a traditional academic education at the University of Jena, where, under the influence of Herder, he embarked on the study of Eastern languages. He himself became extraordinary professor in 1800 and, in

---

230   Glei and Tottoli, *Ludovico Marracci at Work*, pp. 15–40.
231   Roberto Tottoli was kind enough to show me a draft of his paper 'The Qur'an in Europe: textual features of modern age editions with special reference to Abraham Hinckelmann's work' delivered at the International Conference of the German Middle East Studies Association for Contemporary Research and Documentation (DAVO) and the Section of Islamic Studies of the Deutsche Morgenländische Gesellschaft (DMG), Department for History and Culture of the Middle East of Hamburg University, 3–5 October 2019.
232   Claude-Etienne Savary, tr., *Le Coran, traduit de l'arabe, accompagné de notes et précédé d'un abrégé de la vie de Mahomet* ... (Amsterdam, 1786), vol. 1, pp. viii–ix, xi–xii. Savary's translation is discussed in Elmarsafy, *The Enlightenment Qur'an*, pp. 145–148, 150–154. 'Savary', he writes (p. 145), 'oscillated between translating from the Arabic text directly and offering a French translation of Marracci's text'. See also A. Hamilton, 'Claude-Etienne Savary: Orientalism and fraudulence in late eighteenth-century France' *Journal of the Warburg and Courtauld Institutes* 82 (2019), pp. 283–314, where it is argued that Savary was translating entirely from Marracci rather than from the Arabic.

1803, full professor of Oriental languages at Jena. After obtaining a doctorate in theology at the University of Rinteln in 1808, he was appointed professor of theology first in Breslau and, in 1819, in Bonn. By then he was widely recognised not only as a theologian and a biblical scholar, but as a founder of Christian archaeology.[233] An admirer of Johann Jakob Griesbach and his pupil Wilhelm Martin Leberecht De Wette,[234] a follower of Herder, Augusti championed free enquiry into the Bible[235] – a position that aroused the resentment of his more conservative colleagues – but he remained loyal to what he regarded as the basic principles of orthodox Lutheranism, and it was in their name that he performed his archaeological research.[236] He was one of the 'stalwart Lutherans' who owed his appointment (in Bonn) to the highly conservative Prussian minister for church affairs and education, Karl von Altenstein.[237]

Augusti's translation of passages from the Qur'an, *Der kleine Koran oder Uebersetzung der wichtigsten und lehrreichsten Stücke des Koran's mit kurzen Anmerkungen*, was an early work, apparently compiled in Gotha and published by Friedrich Severin in Weissenfels and Leipzig in 1798.[238] It was dedicated to one of Augusti's closest friends, the classical scholar and theologian Johann Georg Christian Höpfner, known for his work on Euripides and Aristophanes. Besides theology, Höpfner had studied classical philology and Oriental languages at Leipzig. Together with Augusti he edited the *Exegetische Handbuch des alten Testaments*, and they shared the same rational approach to the Scriptures. *Der kleine Koran* can hardly be regarded as the fruit of a special interest in Islam or Arab culture, even if Augusti stated that he might, one day, produce an extensive history of Islam together with a critique of the Qur'an.[239]

---

233 M. Teubner, 'Johann Augusti' in S. Heid and M. Dennert, eds, *Personenlexikon zur Christlichen Archäologie. Forscher und Persönlichkeiten vom 16. bis zum 21. Jahrhundert*, vol. 1 (Regensburg, 2012), pp. 98–99.

234 Johann Christian Wilhelm Augusti, *Grundriss einer historisch-kritischen Einleitung in's Alte Testament* (Leipzig, 1827), pp. vi–vii, xi, xxxii.

235 *Ibid.*, p. ix: 'Ich halte historisch-kritische Untersuchungen über den biblischen Kanon, selbst wenn sie noch so frey und rücksichtslos angestellt werden, nicht nur für erlaubt, sondern sogar für so nothwendig, dass mir ohne sie die vollkommene Durchbildung eines künftigen Religions-Lehrers nicht vollendet werden zu können scheinet.'

236 Johann Christian Wilhelm Augusti, *Beiträge zur christlichen Kunst-Geschichte und Liturgik* (Leipzig, 1841–46), vol. 1, p. vii.

237 Hope, *German and Scandinavian Protestantism*, p. 340.

238 Schnurrer, pp. 431–432, no. 386, v; Binark and Eren, *World Bibliography*, p. 229, no. 856/67.

239 Johann Christian Wilhelm Augusti, *Der kleine Koran oder Uebersetzung der wichtigsten und lehrreichsten Stücke des Koran's mit kurzen Anmerkungen* (Weißenfels-Leipzig, 1798), p. 11.

He never seems to have done so. His purpose, he wrote in his preface, was partly to contribute to the knowledge of Islam and partly to provide 'the friends of antiquity, particularly of Eastern poetry' with 'entertaining reading', for, 'in this beautiful garden ... there is the undetected scent of various beautiful flowers.'[240] He said he had 'translated after' Marracci and had consulted Boysen and Sale.[241] Yet both the presentation and the form of his translation showed signs of originality. His presentation, like that of Boysen and Savary, was decidedly sympathetic to the Prophet Muḥammad and to Islam. Not only did he refuse ever to call the Prophet an impostor, but he taxed Marracci, and even Reland and Sale, with trying to find evidence of imposture in the Qurʾan. The Prophet, rather, was the reviver of the religion of the patriarchs.[242] His notes to the text are not only full of approving remarks[243] but they also emphasize points of community with the New Testament.[244] For his biographical account of Muḥammad in his introduction, Augusti drew almost entirely on Gagnier's edition of Abū 'l-Fidāʾ rather than on Gagnier's own biography of the Prophet.

Augusti's translation was one of the first to be published largely in verse. He was, he said, uncertain as to whether to choose poetry or prose since some of the Qurʾan corresponded to verse, while part of it did not. In the end Augusti chose iambics, justifying his choice with the assumption that that was what

---

240 *Ibid.*, p. 6: '... theils, den Freunden des Alterthums, besonders der morgenlandischen Poesie, eine Schrift zur unterhaltenden Lektüre in die Hand zu geben. Denn es düftet in diesem schönen Garten unbemerkt noch manche schöne Blume, so wie überhaupt die Ueberreste der arabischen Dichtkunst noch so manches schöne Gedicht enthalten ...'

241 *Ibid.*, pp. 7–8: 'Ich habe nach der Ausgabe des Maracci (Padua 1698 fol.) übersetzt und dabey auch die englische Uebersetzung von G. Sale (London 1734. 4.) und die deutsche von Boysen (2te Auflage Halle 1775. 8.) benutzt. Ich sah mich aber sehr oft genöthigt, von ihnen abzugehen, weil sie mir den Sinn entweder ganz verfehlt, oder doch sehr matt dargestellt zu haben schienen.'

242 *Ibid.*, p. 50. Augusti returns to this theme in his commentary on the first sura, p. 66.

243 In his note to 2:107, which can be translated as 'such of Our revelations as We abrogate or cause to be forgotten, We bring one better or the like thereof,' Augusti (*ibid.*, p. 93), who, in contrast to modern translations, assumes that the reference is to verses in the Qurʾan, writes, 'Die Ausleger haben bestimmt angegeben, was im Koran abgeschafft sey d.h. was nicht mehr auf die spätern Zeiten passe, was temporell, local, occasional sey. Wäre doch das auch bey der jüdischen und christlichen Offenbarungskunde immer geschehen!' In his note to 2:114, 'Allah will judge betwen them on the Day of Resurrection concerning that wherein they differ,' Augusti comments (p. 96), 'Ein schöner Gedanke: Allah wird am Weltgerichte den Unterschied der Religionen ausgleichen, wird entscheiden, welches das Wahr oder das Falsche in der Religion sey.'

244 In his note to 2:178, 'Righteous is he who giveth his wealth, for love of Him, to kinsfolk and to orphans and the needy and the wayfarer and to those who ask,' Augusti comments (p. 114): 'Die ganze Stelle ist übrigens in Rücksicht ihres Inhalts eine der trefflichsten des Korans,' and he compares it to the Epistle of James 1:27.

the Prophet would have used had he been writing in eighteenth-century Germany.[245] Augusti informed the reader that, by and large, the Qur'an was perfectly easy to understand, but that the frequent ellipses and jumps from one subject to another, together with the 'rhapsodic and aphoristic' style, often made it obscure. The translator had to fill in the gaps to the best of his ability in order to make it readable, and this meant that a translation 'must often be more of a paraphrase and a commentary'.[246]

∙∙∙

Boysen's translation was reissued by Samuel Friedrich Günther Wahl, professor of Oriental languages at Halle,[247] in 1828, in a heavily revised edition.[248] The worst mistakes and mistranscriptions were corrected; Wahl provided a long historical introduction and added numerous footnotes. Above all, however, Wahl, who suppressed Boysen's preface, adopted an entirely different approach to Islam. He was manifestly hostile to the Prophet from the outset.[249]

---

245   *Ibid.*, p. 9. The largest part of his selection is thus in verse: suras 1, 2, 6:1–84, 13, 29:42–70 (which he misnumbers as sura 20), 30, 31:13–35, 52, 53, 55, 78, 81, 82, 84:4–26, 96, 97, 102, 109, 112, 113 and 114). In an appendix, however, he also added suras 3, 12 and 15 in a prose translation.

246   *Ibid.*, pp. 58–59: 'Der Koran ist an und für sich betrachtet nicht schwer, und kann bey einiger Kenntniß der arabischen Sprache leicht verstanden werden. Aber die häufigen Ellypsen, die kühnen Sprünge von einem Gegenstande auf den andern und die rhapsodische und aphoritstische Manier machen ihn oft dunkel. Der Uebersetzer muß die Lücken des Originals ausfüllen so gut er kann, und seinem Koran hie und da ein modernes Gewand leihen, wenn seine Uebersetzung nicht ganz unleserlich werden soll. Aber eben daher kommt es auch, daß die Uebersetzung oft mehr Paraphrase und Commentar seyn muß.' There are points at which Augusti seems to be echoing Michaelis.

247   S. Mangold, *Eine 'weltbürgerliche Wissenschaft': Die deutsche Orientalistik im 19. Jahrhundert* (Stuttgart, 2004), p. 122.

248   Samuel Friedrich Gunter Wahl, ed., *Der Koran oder Das Gesetz der Moslemen durch Muhammed den Sohn Abdallahs. Auf den Grund der vormaligen Verdeutschung F.E. Boysen's von neuem aus dem Arabischen übersetzt* ... (Halle, 1828).

249   Samuel Friedrich Wahl, ed., *Der Koran oder das Gesetz der Moslemen durch Muhammedden Sohn Abdallahs. Auf den Grund der vormaligen Verdeutschung F.E. Boysen's* ... (Halle, 1828), pp. lxxiii–lxxiv: 'Wer in seiner ganzen Lebensgeschichte und Handlungsweise, in dem Geist und Inhalt seines Korans, und in allem dem, was sowohl in dieser Einleitung als in den Anmerkungen zur Uebersetzung ans Licht gerückt ist, den Wollüstling, den dreisten Kühnling, den leichtsinnigen eigennützigen stolzen und hoffärtigen, ruhmsüchtigen, dünkelhaften und anmaaßenden Menschen, den schlauen und listigen Heuchler, Schleicher und scheinheiligen Gleißner, den spitzfindigen Schwätzer, Lügner und Gaukler, den wenigstens im männlichen Alter seit seinem Auftritt als Religionsstifter bloß verstellten, absichtlichen Schwärmer, Mystiker, Fanatiker, den herrschbegierigen und eroberungssüchtigen, verschlagenen und verschmitzten, arglistigen, die Religion nur zum

He described him throughout as a malignant impostor and thus came far closer to Megerlin than to Boysen. Nevertheless, this was the translation used by the Jewish scholar Abraham Geiger, who shocked many of his contemporaries by his objective approach to the Prophet.[250] The strong dislike that Wahl expressed for Islam was not uncommon in nineteenth-century Germany.[251]

In the meantime other German-speaking Orientalists were, like Augusti, endeavouring to give the translated Qur'an a more poetic form and thus gradually to break away from the influence of Marracci. That the most important of these should have been an Austrian points to the process which would gradually revolutionize the study of Arabic in Europe. For Josef von Hammer, later known as Josef von Hammer-Purgstall, attended the Orientalische Akademie in Vienna. This was an interpreters' school – the development of a phenomenon which had originated with the Venetians, was taken up by the French and would soon exist in England, but was only introduced very much later into Germany, with the foundation of the Seminar für Orientalische Sprachen in Berlin in 1887.[252] The teachers concentrated on living Oriental languages, particularly Turkish, but also Persian and Arabic, and Hammer, even if he specialised in Turkish, had mastered all three when he left the school in 1799 at the

---

Deckmantel benutzenden und mißbrauchenden, gegen andre Glaubensbekenner nur scheinbar duldsamen Betrieger, den grausamen und rachgierigen Machtgebiether, und in vielen seiner Aussprüche und Handlungen unverschämten Bösewicht verkennen kann; und es sich versagt, das thörigte, auf Stellen im Koran und Aussprüche und Sagen in der Sunna gestützte Gewäsch aller moslemischen Andächtler von ihres Propheten leiblichen und geistlichen hohen Vorzügen vor allen Menschenkindern, und von dem unendlichen Werthe seiner Religion und Gesetzgebung zu verlachen, dem fehlt es an Durchschauung, oder er ist nicht redlich gesinnt, und es schlägt in seinem Busen ein verkehrtes Herz.'

250 Abraham Geiger, *Was hat Mohammed aus dem Judenthume aufgenommen? Eine von der Königl. Preussischen Rheinuniversität gekrönte Preisschrift* (Bonn, 1833), p. iii. Geiger was one of the first German scholars to make a systematic use of the *tafsīr* of al-Baghawī which had been unwittingly discovered by Boysen. Geiger, however, used an entirely different manuscript, purchased in Cairo by Ludwig Seetzen in 1807 for the ducal library in Gotha. Thanks to Geiger's teacher, Georg Wilhelm Freytag, it was borrowed by the University of Bonn for Geiger, who subsequently made a copy of it: see Geiger, p. iv. Geiger refers to al-Baghawī as 'Elpherar'. See Claude Gilliot, 'Rétrospectives et perspectives. De quelques sources possibles du Coran mecquois (1)' in B. Broeckaert, S. van den Branden and J.-J. Pérennès, eds, *Perspectives on Islamic Culture. Essays in Honour of Emilio G. Platti* (Louvain, 2013), pp. 19–51, esp. p. 23: 'Le commentaire de Bagawi est de loin la source musulmane la plus citée par Geiger après le Coran.' Wahl himself had consulted the Halle manuscript and had at least got the spelling of al-Baghawī's name right: 'Abu-Muhammed Elhhoßein, met den Zunamen Elfara' (*Der Koran*, p. 640).

251 See the interesting discussion in Marchand, *German Orientalism*, pp. 25–27, 151–152, 189, 343–344, 357–360.

252 Fück, pp. 124–129, 135–140; Mangold, *Eine 'weltbürgerliche Wissenschaft'*, pp. 226–250.

age of twenty-five. After various diplomatic missions to the Ottoman Empire and a stay in England, in 1807 he finally settled in Vienna, where he acted as court interpreter but was permitted to carry out his own research.[253] It was just before he arrived in Vienna that he published the first part of his notes on translating the Qur'an together with a brief sample consisting of the first sura, the 112th sura and verses 67–74 of the second sura in the *Neue Teutsche Merkur*, his 'Proben einer metrischen und gereimten Uebersetzung des Corans'. He followed this up with a further sample in the following year of the 82nd sura, and, in 1811, he published his translation of the last forty suras in the second volume of his *Fundgruben des Orients*,[254] the journal he founded with the financial support of Count Wenzeslaus von Rzewusky in 1809 and which also played a crucial part in making Germany – the German contributors included Eichhorn – such an important centre of Arabic studies.

Hammer's translations are preceded by an effusive presentation of the Qur'an as 'a masterpiece of Arabic poetry' the best translation of which must 'reproduce not only the spirit but also the form'.[255] He himself translated his

---

253   For Hammer-Purgtsall as an Arabist see Fück, pp. 158–66; R. Irwin, *For Lust of Knowing. The Orientalists and their Enemies* (London, 2006), pp. 150–152; and, more generally, P.S. Fichtner, *Terror and Toleration. The Habsburg Empire Confronts Islam, 1526–1850* (London, 2008), pp. 129–161.

254   J. von Hammer, 'Die letzten vierzig Suren des Korans' *Fundgruben des Orients* 2 (1811), pp. 26–46. For a selection see Mommsen, *Goethe*, pp. 144–51. See also Binark and Eren, World Bibliography, pp. 231–32, nos 864/75–866/77; Elmarsafy, *The Enlightenment Qur'an*, pp. 169–72 and his comment (p. 172), 'It is important to note here that we are dealing with a new generation of Qur'anic translation; one where sound and form matter as much as, if not more than, content.'

255   Joseph von Hammer, 'Proben einer metrischen und gereimten Uebersetzung des Corans' *Der neue Teutsche Merkur* (1807) Stücke 2, pp. 77–81, esp. pp. 77–79: 'Der Coran ist nicht nur des Islam's Gesetzbuch, sondern auch Meisterwerk arabischer Dichtkunst. Nur durch den höchsten Zauber der Sprache gelang's dem Sohne Abdallah's, sein Wort im Volke gang und gäbe zu erhalten, als Gottes Wort. In den Werken der Dichtkunst spiegelt sich die Gottheit des Genies. Das ist das Göttliche, was die Araber schon vor Muhammed in ihren großen Dichtern verehrten, deren Gedichte mit goldenen Buchstaben geschrieben, an der Caaba als Gegenstände der allgemeinen Verehrung aufgehangen waren ... Die treueste Uebersetzung davon wird die seyn, so nicht nur den Geist, sondern auch die Form wiederzugeben ringt. Nachbildung der Rede durch Gang und Klang ist unerläßliche Bedingung der Uebersetzung eines Dichterwerkes. Der höchste Zauber arabischer Poesie besteht nicht nur in Bild und Bewegung, sondern verzüglich in des Reimes Gleichklang, der für arabisches Ohr wahrer Sirenenton ist. Um also den poetischen Gehalt des Corans so getreu als möglich auszumünzen, muß die Uebersetzung mit dem Originale nicht nur gleichen Schritt, sondern auch gleichen Ton halten; die Endreime der Verse müssen in Reimen übertragen werden, was bisher in keiner der uns bekannten Uebersetzungen geschehen. So nur kann beiläufig die Wirkung hervorgebracht werden, welche der Text auf ein arabisches Ohr nicht verfehlt. So wird uns die Uebersetzung als Spiegel nicht

samples in verse, and it was largely to Hammer that Goethe owed the revival of his interest in Islam. In May 1814 his publisher, Johann Friedrich von Cotta, presented him with a copy of Hammer's translation of the Persian poet Hafiz.[256] With the help of the professor of Oriental languages at Jena, Johann Gottfried Ludwig Kosegarten, who, like an entire generation of German Arabists, had studied under Antoine Isaac Sylvestre de Sacy in Paris at the other illustrious product of the interpreters' schools, the École des langues orientales vivantes, he started to learn the Arabic alphabet in 1817.[257] For the references to, and the use of, the Qur'an in his *West-östlicher Divan*, which appeared between 1814 and 1819, and for the *Noten und Abhandlungen* accompanying it, Goethe drew mainly on Theodor Arnold's translation of Sale, but he also used Hammer.[258]

∴

The first complete translation of the Qur'an after Wahl's revised version of Boysen was by Ludwig Ullmann, like Abraham Geiger one of the very few Jewish students to have been admitted to the University of Bonn. His translation, dedicated to his master, Georg Wilhelm Freytag, was published in Krefeld in 1840 and, with revisions by later scholars, is in print to this day.[259] Yet was it really a step forward? The judgement of Heinrich Leberecht Fleischer was devastating. Fleischer's approach to Arabic, like that of a number of younger Germans – and these included Freytag – had been transformed by the teaching of Sylvestre de Sacy.[260] The review Fleischer gave to Ullmann's *Der Koran* in the *Allgemeine Literatur-Zeitung* of March 1841 was the most extreme condemnation of the eighteenth-century school of German Arabists. He derided the tradition of Michaelis and Eichhorn. Qur'an translations, he said, had reached an unprecedented level with Marracci and, above all, with Sale. After that they had gone into a precipitous decline. Megerlin, Boysen, Savary, Augusti and

---

nur das Bild des Propheten zeigen, sondern auch den Dichterodem aus seinem Munde auffangen.'

256   Mommsen, *Goethe*, p. 128.
257   *Ibid.*, p. 127; Mangold, *Eine 'weltbürgerliche Wissenschaft'*, pp. 123–124.
258   Mommsen, *Goethe*, pp. 142–163.
259   Ludwig Ullmann, tr., *Der Koran. Das heilige Buch des Islam*, ed. L.W. Winter, 15th edn (Munich, 2007).
260   For Fleischer see Fück, pp. 170–172; Irwin, *For Lust of Knowing*, pp. 152–153; and Hans-Georg Ebert, 'Heinrich Leberecht Fleischer: Geist und Vermächtnis' in Hans-Georg Ebert and Thoralf Hanstein, *Heinrich Leberecht Fleischer – Leben und Wirkung. Ein Leipziger Orientalist des 19. Jahrhunderts mit internationaler Ausstrahlung* (Frankfurt a. M., 2013), pp. 19–25 (together with the other contributions to the volume).

Wahl had each lowered the standards.[261] Fleischer had particular contempt for Wahl, who, he said, had in fact made Boysen's translation even worse than it was in the original. The innovations of Sylvestre de Sacy had passed him by. The improvements in the German language had been neglected. All that Wahl and his predecessors had done was to show *what* the Qur'an said, not *how* it said it. 'The Qur'an translator as such', he continued, 'should not paraphrase and not explain' ('Nicht paraphrasiren, nicht erklären soll der Koranübersetzer als solcher').[262] Even Sale went too far in his paraphrases and explanations. Ullmann marked no improvement.[263] He, too, paraphrased to excess, and, he frequently revealed his dependency on Wahl and Boysen, especially when he deviated from Sale.

We may now wonder whether Fleischer's review was entirely fair. It was written with the arrogance of a young man who saw himself as the standard bearer of a new fashion and a new approach which would sweep away everything that had gone before it. And, indeed, with his meticulous catalogues of the Arabic holdings in German libraries, and above all with his editions of al-Bayḍāwī and al-Zamakhsharī, Fleischer was the first German Arabist to carry out some of the plans that Reiske had regarded as all but impossible to fulfil. In his review, however, Fleischer dismissed with a wave of his hand well over a century of scholarship and research, some of which was leading up to the increasingly source critical approach of the nineteenth and twentieth centuries.

Fleischer's review of Ullmann expressed almost as much pessimism as Reiske's comments on Arabic studies and Qur'an translations. Yet one contemporary of Fleischer was both a great Arabist and a great poet, Friedrich

---

261 Heinrich Leberecht Fleischer, 'Orientalische Literatur' *Allgemeine Literatur-Zeitung*, 53 (1841), cols 417–422, and 54 (1841), cols 429–432, esp. 53, col. 417: 'Wir können uns Gluck wünschen, dass namentlich die Arbeit des Letztgenannten [sc. Weil] kein Maasstab für die deutsche Uebersetzungskunst und Sprachgelehrsamkeit unserer Zeit ist. Denn eben unsere Zeit, mit ihren neuen Mustern und Gesetzen in Kunst und Wissenschaft, war spurlos an Wahl vorübergegangen. Für ihn hatte kein Voss den Homer übersetzt und der Sprache Spannkraft gegeben: ihm war sie, auch für den Koran, noch immer der alte, gemächliche Hausrock, unter dem sich Alles in breite Formlosigkeit verlor; für ihn hatte kein de Sacy eine arabische Sprachlehre geschrieben: ihm galten noch die Ueberlieferungen der quodlibetarischen Grammatik und Exegese aus Michaelis und Eichhorns Schule. Daher liess er die Wasserfluthen, in welche Boysen den Kern des Korans verschwemmt hatte, in ihrer ganzen Ausdehnung fortbestehen, ja vermehrte sie noch durch eigenen Zuguss; daher behielt er die von jenem überkommenen Missverständnisse getreulich bei, fügte noch andere hinzu, und meisterte mit dem schlechtesten Erfolge seine gelehrten Vorgänger, deren wirkliche Schwächen durch das Studium der mohammedanischen Koranerklärer zu entdecken er eben so wenig wie Boysen vermochte …'.
262 *Ibid.*, col. 418.
263 *Ibid.*, col. 429.

Rückert, who had once studied with Hammer-Purgstall in Vienna.[264] Fleischer mentioned Rückert dismissively in his review of Ullmann, but he was referring to his translation of the Minor Prophets, the *Hebräische Propheten* published in 1831. Yet it was in his early years, when he was living as a *Privatgelehrter* in Coburg in the early 1820s, that Rückert had first planned to translate parts of the Qur'an into verse.[265] Then, in the winter of 1822–23, he made a thorough study of Marracci and took as his Arabic text Hinckelmann's Hamburg version of 1694. Appointed professor of Oriental languages at the University of Erlangen in 1826, Rückert returned to his original project, now hoping to translate the entire text, in 1836, two years after Gustav Leberecht Flügel, another pupil of Sacy (as well as of Hammer-Purgstall), had issued a new Arabic edition of the Qur'an. Although he never completed his translation, Rückert did indeed approach a publisher, but his efforts came to nothing and, by 1841, he claimed to have lost interest in the undertaking. Nevertheless, he made further overtures to publishers, which were equally unsuccessful. Only in 1888, twenty-two years after his death, was the translation published. The fragmentary version was free, in verse, not bound to any single metre. It is independent of Marracci. Rückert adheres far more closely to the original, avoids paraphrases and catches some of the allusive ambiguities. He stands in the vanguard of the modern translators of the Qur'an.

Acknowledgements

In writing this article, which was first published in the *Journal of the Warburg and Courtauld Institutes* 77 (2014), pp. 173–209, I was indebted throughout to the encouragement of Jan Loop. My special thanks are also due to Jill Kraye and Jenny Boyle for their scrupulous editing and, for their suggestions and bibliographical advice, to Asaph Ben-Tov, Mordechai Feingold, Noel Malcolm, Gerald Toomer and Arnoud Vrolijk.

---

264 On Rückert see Marchand, *German Orientalism*, pp. 138–141; W. Fischer, 'Friedrich Rückert: Meister im Reich der Sprache' in H. Bobzin, ed., *Friedrich Rückert an der Universität Erlangen 1826–1841. Eine Ausstellung des Lehrstuhls für Orientalische Philologie, des Lehrstuhls für Indogermanistik und Indoiranistik und der Universitätsbibliothek 11. Juni–3. Juli 1988* (Erlangen, 1988), pp. 9–23.

265 H. Bobzin, ed., *Der Koran in der Uebersetzung von Friedrich Rückert* (Würzburg, 2001), pp. vii–x, xv–xxxiii for a discussion of Rückert and his translation. See also Binark and Eren, *World Bibliography*, p. 221, nos 822/833–823/834, and p. 234, no. 877/888. For a critical analysis of the translation see M. Radscheit, 'Aktuelle deutsche Koranübersetzungen im Überblick' *CIBEDO* 13 (1999), pp. 124–135, esp. pp. 124–126.

CHAPTER 18

The Qur'an as Chrestomathy in Early Modern Europe

One of the more mystifying aspects of the grammars of ancient and Oriental languages produced in the West during the Renaissance is how students were expected to proceed. They were obviously intended to memorise the tables and there seems to have been an assumption that to advance any further the help of a teacher was essential. But what about the chrestomathies, the texts frequently added to the grammars as linguistic exercises? In his study of early Greek grammars Paul Botley wrote that 'the language was approached through Greek texts that the pupils already knew by heart in their Latin translations: the Greek Scriptures and the liturgy.'[1] In the case of Arabic a similar approach seems to have been adopted, particularly in the late sixteenth and early seventeenth centuries. The Lord's Prayer remained a favourite text, together with Arabic versions of the Psalms. Thanks to the manuscripts which Guillaume Postel had pawned with the elector palatine in Heidelberg, the German authors of early Arabic grammars who frequented the Palatine library – Jacob Christmann, Ruthger Spey and Peter Kirsten – could use the Arabic versions of the Epistles and Acts of the Apostles. Otherwise knowledge of Arabic literature was highly limited, and the most obvious text to choose, the one regarded as the perfect expression of the Arabic language, was the Qur'an.

Postel, who compiled the first proper grammar of classical Arabic to appear in the West, set a precedent.[2] His *Grammatica arabica*, published in about 1538,[3] gave as reading material, in Arabic and Latin, the Lord's Prayer and the *fātiḥa*, the first sura of the Qur'an. To the *fātiḥa* he added his own translation[4] which is striking for the rendering of the Arabic *iyyāka*, often translated as 'thee alone', as 'o vos omnes', 'oh ye all', and *ṣirāṭ*, 'path', as 'punctum', 'point'. Although these translations gave rise to a prolonged debate among scholars

---

1 P. Botley, *Learning Greek in Western Europe, 1396–1529. Grammars, Lexica, and Classroom Texts* (Philadelphia, 2010), p. 75.
2 Jones, pp. 113–120. For Postel's treatment of the first sura see pp. 118–120.
3 Schnurrer, pp. 18–19, no. 38.
4 G. Postel, *Grammatica Arabica* (Paris, c. 1538), sig. E10ʳ: 'In nomine Dei misericordis, pii. Laus Deo, regi seculorum misericordi et pio. Regi diei iudicii: O vos omnes illi serviamus certe adiuvabimur. Dirige nos domine in punctum rectum, in punctum inquam illorum, in quos tibi complacitum est, sine ira adversus eos, et non errabimus.'

and cast doubt on Postel's competence as an Arabist,[5] his version was added by Theodor Bibliander to the medieval Latin translation of Robert of Ketton[6] and another anonymous rendering probably of Mozarabic origin[7] in the edition of the entire text of the Qur'an which appeared in Basle in 1543. Postel, like his successors in the early modern period, provided no more than a translation of the first sura in his grammar. He made no attempt to elucidate any linguistic problem or to explain to students how they should apply to it the knowledge they had acquired from the rest of his *Grammatica arabica*.

Other compilers of Arabic grammars and type specimens in the sixteenth century avoided the Qur'an as a linguistic exercise, preferring, as we saw, biblical texts. Jacob Christmann, in his *Alphabetum arabicum* of 1582, chose the

---

5   The debate started in the eighteenth century with the publication of Jacob Christof Wilhem Hoste's *Dissertatio inauguralis de prima Alcorani sura* (Altdorf, 1743), in which a detailed comparison was made between all the translations of the *fātiḥa* to date. It was revived in the early twentieth century when E. Nestle, 'Geschichtliches zur ersten Sure' *Zeitschrift der Deutschen Morgenländischen Gesellschaft* 60 (1906), p. 246, pointed to Postel's mistranslations and wondered to what they were due. This drew a sharp reply by A. Fischer, 'Miszellen' *Zeitschrift der Deutschen Morgenländischen Gesellschaft* 60 (1906), pp. 245–254, esp. pp. 249–250, who said that they were simply due to Postel's limited knowledge of Arabic which had already been observed by Scaliger. Three years later the debate was resumed by C.F. Seybold, 'Kleine Mitteilungen' *Zeitschrift der Deutschen Morgenländischen Gesellschaft* 63 (1909), pp. 625–626, who suggested that *punctum* was a misprint of *pontem* and that Postel was referring to the bridge to hell stretching from the Temple of the Mount to the Garden of Olives over the valley of Jehosophat, over which all souls will have to pass on their way to the Last Judgement. Fück, p. 41, agrees with Fischer that Postel's translation 'zeigt, daß die arabischen Kentnisse Postels einer soliden Grundlage entbehrten.' In his *De orbis terrae concordia libri quatuor* (Basel, 1544), pp. 157–158, Postel repeats the translation *punctum* and translates *ayāk* as *heus* or 'hail', while in his *De la République des Turcs* (Poitiers, 1560), pp. 50–51, he translates *ayāk* as 'O bons humains' and *al-ṣiraṭ al-mustaqīm* as 'le point ou certitude'. More recently, however, Postel has been reassessed as an Arabist by H. Bobzin, *Der Koran im Zeitalter der Reformation. Studien zur Frühgeschichte der Arabistik und Islamkunde in Europa* (Beirut, 1995), pp. 447–475. Bobzin argues (p. 451) that some Muslim interpreters explain *al-ṣiraṭ al-mustaqīm* as referring to the Qur'an. 'Von hier aus wird auch Postels Textauffassung erklärbar: durch die Gleichsetzung von صراط مستقيم mit قرآن wird den "Weg" auf den einen "Punkt" des Korans reduziert.'

6   T. Bibliander, ed., *Machumetis Saracenorum principis, eiusque successorum vitae, doctrina, ac ipse Alcoran* ... (Basel, 1543), p. 8: 'Misericordi pioque Deo, universitatis creatori, iudicium cuius postrema dies expectat, voto suppliciter nos humiliemus, adorantes ipsum: suaeque manus suffragium, semitaeque donum et dogma, quos nos ad se benevolos, nequaquam hostes et erroneos adduxit, iugiter sentiamus.'

7   *Ibid.*: 'In nomine Dei misericordis, miseratoris. Gratias Deo domino universitatis misericordi, miseratori, iudicii. Te adoramus, in te confidimus: Mitte nos in viam rectam, viam eorum quos elegisti, non eorum quibus iratus es, nec infidelium.' See Bobzin, *Der Koran im Zeitalter der Reformation*, p. 235; M. d'Alverny, 'Deux traductions latines du Coran au moyen-âge' *Archives d'histoire doctrinale et littéraire du moyen-âge* 22–3 (1947–1948), pp. 69–131, esp. p. 101.

Lord's Prayer and the Epistle to the Philippians; in the following year Ruthger Spey preceded his *Compendium grammatices arabicae* with the Epistle to the Galatians, and added the Ten Commandments and the Lord's Prayer; Franciscus Raphelengius gave the text of Psalm 50 in the type specimen he published in 1595; Bartholomeus Radtmann used Psalm 146 in his Arabic grammar of 1590; and Giambattista Raimondi has the texts of the Lord's Prayer, the Hail, Mary, Psalms 112 (113) and 116 (117) and John 1:1–9 in his *Alphabetum arabicum* of 1592. But this approach changed with the author of the best Arabic grammar of his day which was to remain unsurpassed until the nineteenth century – Thomas Erpenius in Leiden. It was not, however, in his Arabic grammar, the *Grammatica arabica* which first appeared in 1613,[8] that he provided any chrestomathy, but in his edition of the twelfth sura of the Qur'an, *Yūsuf*, the *Historia Iosephi Patriarchae*, published in 1617,[9] one of the first products of the new 'Oriental' press he had just set up in Leiden with his own Arabic types. Printed together with his *Alphabetum arabicum*, it was indeed intended for students of Arabic who had used his grammar.

Erpenius had long been interested in the Qur'an. We can follow this concern in his correspondence with Isaac Casaubon.[10] In 1610 he was still trying to procure a copy of the Arabic and Casaubon generously decided to present him with one of his own. Casaubon also seems to have transmitted to him the notes made by Adriaen Willemsz, the former student at Leiden who had joined him in Paris in 1602. These consisted of an index of suras and marginal notes giving variations with respect to another manuscript in the French royal library.[11] Erpenius became aware too of the importance of the *tafsīr*, the Islamic commentaries, and seems to have discovered one at the library of the Sorbonne in 1611.[12] His acquaintance with the Qur'an led him to dismiss out of hand Peter Kirsten, the Arabist and physician from Breslau. Kirsten had given his own translation of the *fātiḥa* not in his Arabic grammar but in the type specimen he published in 1608,[13] but Erpenius claimed that he had not so much as read

8   Schnurrer, pp. 28–9, no. 49; Jones, pp. 146–165.
9   Schnurrer, pp. 30–31, no. 52.
10 For their friendship see above, pp. 62–3, 71–4, 80–84.
11 A. Hamilton and A. Vrolijk, 'Hadrianus Guilielmi Flessingensis. The Brief Career of the Arabist Adriaen Willemsz' *Oriens* 39 (2011), pp. 1–15, esp. p. 5.
12 *Cas.Ep.*, p. 661: 'Sed nihil est Alcoranus absque suo commentario, et libris سنة, qui continent acta, dicta et responsa Muhammedis [...] Commentariorum autem in Alcoranum pars quaedam etiam extat in Bibliotheca Sorbonica, ubi non singulae solum sententiae, sed et verba familiariter explicantur.'
13 P. Kirsten, *Tria Specimina characterum arabicorum* (Breslau, 1608), pp. 9–10: 'In nomine Dei misericordis miserantis. Laus ad Deum Dominum seculorum Misericordem miserantem. Regem diei Judicii. Eho serviamus, et eho adjuvabimur. Deduc nos viam rectam.

the entire text of the Qur'an.[14] Despite his discovery in Paris, Erpenius's subsequent search for *tafsīr* proved vain. His death in 1624 put paid to any further plans to edit parts of the Qur'an.

In the *Historia Iosephi* Erpenius added to the Arabic an interlinear word by word Latin translation. In the margin he gave a more fluent and readable Latin rendering intended to explain the obscurities entailed by a literal version.[15] The bilingual text of the sura is then followed by Robert of Ketton's Latin translation. By far the largest part of the book is devoted to notes which clarify the grammatical forms. Erpenius ends with the *fātiḥa*. In addition to his own interlinear Latin translation[16] he gives Robert of Ketton's Latin version, then Postel's, and finally one he describes as 'closer' to his own but which in fact is the Mozarabic version added by Bibliander. Here too he adds notes explaining both the significance of the Arabic and grammatical points, such as the fact that *maghḍūb* is the passive participle of *ghaḍiba*.[17] The note to 'creaturarum', *ʿālam*, is of particular interest since it raises the question of a Muslim belief in a plurality of worlds suggested by the plural *rabb al-ʿālamīn*, sometimes translated as 'lord of the worlds'. Erpenius points out that it does not refer to worlds in the plural but to the creatures of which the world consists.[18]

Viam [sc. Illorum] quibus delectaris super eos. Sine, [sc. Illis quibus] irasceris, super eos, et non errantes.' But here the interjection 'eho', 'hail!', is a mistaken translation of 'ayāk'.

14   *Ibid.*, p. 662: 'Petrus autem Kirstenius nuper reliquos duos Grammaticae suae libros evulgavit; qui quales sint, vis uno verbo dicam? Non merentur legi. O inscitiam homines et audaciam! Nec نص quidem conjugare scit, nec Alcoranum nunquam legit (quod certo scio) et tamen Grammaticam Arabicam audet edere […] Quater hac aestate Alcoranum perlegi, singula accuratissime expendens; sed semper nova adhuc multa in Grammatica observatu digna occurrerunt […]'

15   T. Erpenius, *Historia Josephi Patriarchae* (Leiden, 1617), sig. D1ᵛ.: 'Cum phrasis Arabica tantopere a Latina distet, ut de verbo ad verbum aut verti vix possit, aut si vertatur, adeo sit dura, et insolens, ut a linguae Arabicae imperitis intelligi plerumque nequeat: visum nobis fuit, interlineari versioni nostrae, aliam Latiniorem Paulo, et phrases Arabicas obscuriores explicantem in margine adijcere: quanquam nec ea apposite, ubique mihi licuit verba singula Arabica singulis Latinis, et aequipollentibus exprimere, ne plane absurda, et non cohaerens oratio videretur.'

16   *Ibid.*, sig. S3ʳ: 'In nomine Dei miseratoris misericordis. Laus Deo domino creaturarum. Miseratori misericordi, regi diei judicii. Te colimus et te invocamus. Dirige nos in viam rectam, viam eorum qui gratiosus es erga eos, sine ira adversus eos, et non errantium.'

17   *Ibid.*, sig. S4ʳ: 'Sumitur مغضوب pro مغضبه vel غضب, id est forma Participij Passivi pro Nomine Verbali, sicuti et alibi, regitque Casum sui Verbi غضب, et regitur a غیر.'

18   *Ibid.*, sig. S3ᵛ: عالم *est mundus, Universum a Deo creatum*, Plurale autem sit, non ad significandam mundorum pluralitatem, sed entium creatarum, ex quibus mundus constat, diversitatem, itaque عالمون est *entia creata omnia, creaturae omnes*. quas lingua Hebraea vocat *exercitus*, itaque رب العالمين idem est quid יהוה צבאות *dominus exercituum*.'

Erpenius opens his explanatory notes with a brief essay on the Qur'an and the terms used – *qur'ān* itself, *sūra*, *āya*. The choice of sura 12 was a sensible one. It contains remarkably few obscurities. If we look at Ludovico Marracci's later translation and explanatory notes (to which I shall return) we see that the quotations from the *tafsīr* of al-Bayḍāwī, al-Zamakhsharī and al-Jalālayn do not illustrate arcane linguistic points but simply expand the more or less obvious meaning of the passage in question. Erpenius limits himself almost entirely to pointing out grammatical constructions. These range from the simple indication of a broken plural, as in the case of *aḥādīth*, the plural of *ḥadīth*,[19] or a comparative (*akthar* as the comparative of *kathīr*),[20] to the indication of the form of the verb – the fourth form of *falaḥa*,[21] for example, or the tenth form of *'aṣama*[22] – to more complex constructions. He occasionally corrects the errors of his predecessors, noting that Postel was wrong in his translation of *iyyāka* in the *fātiḥa*[23] and that Franciscus Raphelengius, the compiler of the first Arabic-Latin dictionary to be published, mistakenly translated *'īr* as 'city' rather than as 'company' or 'band' (12:82).[24] In fact subsequent translators of the Qur'an have translated it as 'caravan'.

Even if Erpenius made no direct use of a *tafsīr* he does at one point refer to an 'ancient interpreter' in connection with 12:32[25] when the women of Potiphar's wife are so overcome by the beauty of Joseph that they cut themselves and bleed. This passage has been interpreted variously. According to one interpretation the bleeding was menstrual. This is what we find in Robert of Ketton.[26] Erpenius dismissed it as totally erroneous. According to the eighteenth-century English translator of the Qur'an George Sale (who also criticizes Erpenius) it was a peculiarity of 'the old Latin translators' who had misunderstood the Arabic *akbarnahu*, usually rendered as 'they exalted him'.[27]

---

19 Ibid., sig. M3ʳ.
20 Ibid., sig. O3ʳ.
21 Ibid., sig. O4ʳ.
22 Ibid., sig. R2ᵛ–3ʳ.
23 Ibid., sig. N4ᵛ.
24 Ibid., sig. R3ʳ.
25 Ibid., sig. P2ʳ: 'locus ita clarus et perspicuus, ut satis mirari nequeam veteris interpretis lapsum, qui haec vertit *et menstruatae sunt*, cujus quidem significationis nullum prorsus apparet vestigium.'
26 Bibliander, ed., *Alcoran*, p. 77.
27 Sale, p. 191: 'The old Latin translators have strangely mistaken the sense of the original word *acbarnaho*, which they render *menstruatae sunt*; and then rebuke Mohammed for the indecency, crying out demurely in the margin, *O foedum et obscoenum prophetam!* Erpenius thinks that there is not the least trace of such a meaning in the word; but he is mistaken: for the verb *cabara* in the fourth conjugation, which is here used, has that

Some *tafsīr*, however, such as that of al-Ṭabarī,[28] which Robert of Ketton may have known, give an ambivalent interpretation of the term.

Although the first edition of Erpenius's *Grammatica arabica* had no chrestomathy, it did contain a brief passage from the Qur'an (44:51–5) as an example of Arabic script.[29] In far later editions, the first of which appeared in 1636, long after Erpenius's death, a chrestomathy was added consisting of the fables of Luqmān which Erpenius had already edited independently, and some Arabic 'adages'. Each text was followed by explanatory notes elucidating the meaning and the grammar. In 1620, on the other hand, Erpenius published a revised version of his grammar, the *Rudimenta Linguae Arabicae*, to which he added, as a linguistic exercise, sura 64 (*al-taghābun*, 'mutual disillusion') in Arabic with an interlinear Latin translation.[30]

Sura 64 has the advantage of relative brevity – it is far shorter than the *sūrat Yūsuf* – and presents few linguistic difficulties. Erpenius's commentary, as in the case of the *sūrat Yūsuf*, is entirely grammatical, but here he not only analyses every single word in the sura, but he also gives the precise reference (page and line) to that part of his grammar which deals with the construction in question.

∴

While Erpenius's grammar was widely regarded as unrivalled in Protestant Europe, the Catholics south of the Alps had started to produce grammars of their own. Although the great missionary organization in Rome, the *Propaganda Fide*, would only be truly established by Pope Gregory XV in 1622, the religious orders had long needed tools with which to instruct their missionaries in Eastern languages.[31] In the first half of the seventeenth century the most important of these were the work of the Clerics Regular Minor,

---

import, tho' the subjoining of the pronoun to it here (which possibly the Latin translators did not observe) absolutely overthrows that interpretation.'

28 Al-Ṭabarī, *Jāmiʿ al-bayān ʿan taʾwīl āya al-Qurʾān* (Cairo, 1979), vol. 6, pp. 4528–9. For the knowledge of al-Ṭabarī among early Latin Qur'an translators see T.E. Burman, *Reading the Qurʾān in Latin Christendom, 1140–1560* (Philadelphia, 2007), pp. 36–59.

29 T. Erpenius, *Grammatica Arabica* (Leiden, 1613), pp. 25–26.

30 See Schnurrer, pp. 32–34, no. 55. The differences between the *Grammatica* and the *Rudimenta* are discussed in Jones, pp. 164–165.

31 See A. Girard, 'Teaching and learning Arabic in early modern Rome: shaping a missionary language' in J. Loop, A. Hamilton and C. Burnett, eds, *The Teaching and Learning of Arabic in Early Modern Europe* (Leiden-Boston, 2017), pp. 189–212, esp. pp. 201, 207–210, for the general reluctance of Catholic Arabists to give examples from, or indeed to have anything to do with, the Qur'an.

also known as the Caracciolini (or Adorno Fathers) – Francesco Martelotto and Filippo Guadagnoli.[32] Martelotto's *Institutiones linguae arabicae*, completed by Guadagnoli, was published posthumously in 1620,[33] and in 1642 there appeared Guadagnoli's *Breves Arabicae linguae institutiones*.[34] This was one of the very first studies of the Arabic language to include a long section on prosody.[35]

By the time he compiled his grammar Guadagnoli had acquired an immense reputation. Professor of Arabic and Syriac at the Collegio della Sapienza in Rome, he was an esteemed collaborator of the *Propaganda Fide*, and had for years been working on the Arabic translation of the Bible which would finally appear in 1671. He was also widely appreciated as an anti-Islamic polemicist. His *Apologia pro christiana religione* was published by the *Propaganda* in 1631 and displayed a sound knowledge of the Qur'an, even if he was misguided by prejudice, ill-informed about Islam, and unreliable in his interpretations (but not in his translations) of the sacred text.[36]

While he drew for the vocabulary of Arabic poetry in his *Breves arabicae linguae institutiones* on the Arabic monolingual dictionary, the *Qāmūs* (which he borrowed from the Vatican library),[37] he derived the rules of Arabic prosody from the thirteenth-century *Qaṣīda al-Khazrajiyya* and a poem by the Egyptian scholar al-Damāmīnī Badraddīn (to whom he refers as Aladinus), who died in 1424.[38] Guadagnoli also quoted a number of passages from the Qur'an, in Arabic and with a Latin translation, as examples. His first is 77:1–4 to illustrate a line of seven syllables, and then 53:1–6 to exemplify the so-called *carmen emissum* which is not limited to one particular metre but mingles lines

---

[32] For the Orientalists in the Order see G. Pizzorusso, 'Filippo Guadagnoli, i Caracciolini e lo studio delle lingue orientali e della controversia con l'Islam a Roma nel XVII secolo' in I. Fosi and G. Pizzorusso, eds, *L'Ordine dei Chierici Regolari Minori (Caracciolini): religione e cultura in età posttridentina* (Casoria, 2010), pp. 245–278.

[33] Schnurrer, pp. 34–35, no. 56.

[34] Schnurrer, pp. 47–48, no. 72. The two grammars are analysed by A. Girard, 'Des manuels de langue entre mission et érudition orientaliste au XVIIe siècle: les grammaires de l'arabe des *Caracciolini*' in Fosi and Pizzorusso, eds, *L'Ordine dei Chierici Regolari Minori*, pp. 279–295.

[35] See J. Loop, 'Arabic poetry as teaching material in early modern grammars and textbooks' in Loop, et al., eds, *The Teaching and Learnig of Arabic*, pp. 230–251, esp. pp. 246–247.

[36] A. Trentini, 'Il Caracciolino Filippo Guadagnoli controversista e islamologo. Un'analisi dei suoi scritti apologetici contro l'Islam' in Fosi and Pizzorusso, eds, *L'Ordine dei Chierici Regolari Minori*, pp. 297–314.

[37] Girard, 'Des manuels de langue', pp. 289–290.

[38] C. Brockelmann, *Geschichte der arabischen Literatur, Zweite den Supplementbänden angepasste Auflage*, vol. 2 (Leiden, 1949), pp. 32–33.

of different syllables.³⁹ A little further on he quotes 77:8–12 as an example of octosyllabic lines.⁴⁰ There follow the quotations of 78:39–40 as an example of the first type of *carmen coniunctum*; of 76:17–18 to exemplify lines of ten and eleven syllables, the penultimate syllable of which is long; and of 78:1–4 to illustrate lines of seven and nine syllables.⁴¹ He also quotes 51:1–4 to illustrate repeated cadences and 55:1–7 as an example of quiescent consonants;⁴² 74:1–7, and 52:1–6 for lines of three, four and five syllables;⁴³ and the same verses in sura 55 again as examples of mixed syllables. Still further on he quotes 95:1–3 as an example of lines of seven and five syllables, and 78:40 to illustrate lines of seven and nine syllables.⁴⁴

Guadagnoli's close acquaintance with the Qur'an points to the later translation of the entire text by his pupil and colleague Ludovico Marracci. Guadagnoli's short translations, however, have certain independent features. On occasion he supplies alternative translations of certain words. For 77:8–9 he gives 'quando stellae delebuntur, *seu* obscurabuntur. Et quando caelum scindetur, *seu* aperietur.'⁴⁵ Elsewhere what seems to be an attempt to translate into verse leads to slight mistranslations. 77:1 is usually taken to mean 'emissary winds, one after the other'. Guadagnoli, on the other hand, gives 'Per demissos crines, seu Nuncios probos' probably in order to rhyme with the following line 'et procellosos ventos'.⁴⁶

∴

Like most German Arabists Matthias Wasmuth, professor of Oriental languages and theology at Kiel, was primarily a Hebraist, but, a former student of Jacobus Golius, Erpenius's successor at Leiden, he too published an Arabic grammar in Amsterdam in 1654.⁴⁷ He ended it with the *fātiḥa*, without any

---

39   Filippo Guadagnoli, *Breves Arabicae linguae institutiones* (Rome, 1642), p. 292: 'Secunda species, quae dicitur المنسرح *Carmen emissum*, non constat ex una certa mensura, sed ex pluriuso collectis, prout solent Itali in iis quae vocant *Cantilenas*: seu *Madrigale*. Et modo Versus admittitur septem Syllabarum, modo undecim, modo duodecim, et ut profecto dici posit المنسرح *ad voluntatem emissum quoque*: ut constat per totum fere Alchoranum, Mahumetem Carmina protulisse, prout in buccam caderet [...]'
40   Ibid., p. 293: 'Tertia species quae dicitur الخفيف, constat secundum aliquos ex octo Syllabis, eiusque mensuram faciant فاعلاتن مستفعلن, prout sunt Carmina Alchorani سورةالمرسلات.'
41   Ibid., p. 296.
42   Ibid., pp. 323–324.
43   Ibid., pp. 337–338.
44   Ibid., pp. 339–340.
45   Ibid., p. 297.
46   Ibid., p. 292.
47   Schnurrer, p. 56, no. 80.

FIGURE 19   Jacobus Golius
ICONES LEIDENSES 81, COLLECTION LEIDEN UNIVERSITY

commentary, in Arabic with his own interlinear Latin translation followed by two of the Latin translations in Bibliander's edition, the one by Robert of Ketton and the other anonymous early one.[48] Then, in 1656, thirty years after

---

48   M. Wasmuth, *Grammatica arabica* (Amsterdam, 1654), p. 79. His translation runs: 'In Nomine DEI miseratoris misericordis. Laus Deo domino creaturarum. Miseratori

Erpenius's death, Golius himself produced a new edition of Erpenius's grammar, *Arabicae linguae tyrocinium. Id est Thomae Erpenii Grammatica Arabica*, to which he appended a lengthy chrestomathy of his own.[49] In it Golius introduces Qur'anic texts with a brief essay on the history of the Qur'an, a definition of the terms (*sūra, āya*, etc), and speculations about the meanings of the mysterious letters at the beginning of so many of the suras. There follow sura 31, *Luqmān*, and sura 61, *al-ṣaff*, 'the ranks'. The very last section of the chrestomathy is solely in Arabic and includes sura 32.

In contrast to Erpenius Golius had travelled and lived in the Arabic-speaking world – first in Morocco and then in Syria – before settling in Leiden where he combined a professorship in mathematics with the professorship in Oriental languages.[50] As a result of his travels he had managed to create a network of contacts who would supply him with Arabic, Turkish and Persian manuscripts.[51] He consequently had a large collection at his disposal, part of which was his private property and part of which went to the Leiden University library.

Golius had three of the main *tafsīr*s. He had bought al-Bayḍāwī's *Anwār al-tanzīl wa-asrār al-taʾwīl*, dating from the thirteenth century, for the Leiden library.[52] The others, the *Kashshāf* of the twelfth-century Persian Muʿtazilite al-Zamakhsharī[53] and the fifteenth-century *Tafsīr al-Jalālayn*,[54] were in his private collection. But he also owned a Persian commentary on the Qur'an by the sixteenth-century scholar from Khorasan Ḥusain Wāʿiẓ Kāshifī,[55] which he exploited thoroughly in his treatment of suras 31 and 61.[56] His procedure,

---

misericordi, regi diei judicii. Te colimus et te invocamus. Dirige nos in viam rectam, viam eorum qui gratiosus es erga eos, alienorum ab ira contra eos, et non errantium.' He chose the translation 'lord of the created' rather than 'lord of the worlds'. 'Alienorum ab ira contra eos' makes little sense.

49   Schnurrer, pp. 56–7, no. 81. For details see J. Loop, 'Arabic poetry as teaching material' pp. 246–248.

50   A. Vrolijk and R. van Leeuwen, *Arabic Studies in the Netherlands. A Short History in Portraits, 1580–1950* (Leiden-Boston, 2014), pp. 42–48; W.M.C. Juynboll, *Zeventiende-eeuwsche Beoefenaars van het Arabisch in Nederland* (Utrecht, 1931), pp. 119–183.

51   J. Schmidt, *The Joys of Philology. Studies in Ottoman Literature, History and Orientalism (1500–1923). Volume 2. Orientalists, Travellers and Merchants in the Ottoman Empire, Political Relations between Europe and the Porte* (Istanbul, 2002), pp. 9–74.

52   UBL, MS Or. 83, Or. 120.

53   *Catalogus ... librorum m.ss.quos ... Jacobus Golius ... collegit* (Leiden, 1696), p. 13.

54   Bodl., MS Marsh 429.

55   In fact he owned two, one by Wāʿiẓ Kashifī and the other by al-Isfarāʾīnī, both of which are now in the Bodleian Library, MS Marsh 210 and MSS Marsh 168–169. Cf. *Catalogus*, p. 8.

56   *Grammatica Arabicae linguae tyrocinium. Id est Thomae Erpenii Grammatica Arabica* (Leiden, 1656), p. 183: 'Praefatione hac defunctus (venia digresso detur) nunc eiusdem Corani promissum exhibebo, cum uberiore explicatione: quam fere κατὰ πόδα reddere

however, was different in the two cases. With sura 31, *Luqmān*, he added to his Latin translation, in italics and in Latin, extracts from the Persian commentary.[57] This was a novel technique. Johann Zechendorff, headmaster of the Latin school in Zwickau, had already published the entire *tafsīr* of al-Bayḍāwī to sura 61 in about 1647,[58] but it was presented as a *tafsīr* rather than as the Qurʾanic text with quotations inserted from another source. Golius's Latin translation of sura 31 is printed opposite the Arabic, and the translation is framed by notes which contain references to al-Bayḍāwī and al-Zamakhsharī. Sura 61, on the other hand, has, opposite the Arabic, a Latin translation which does not contain insertions and which is framed by notes referring to al-Jalālayn (and to neither al-Bayḍāwī nor al-Zamakhsharī). It is followed by a Latin translation of the entire text of Kashifī's commentary.[59] The notes to sura 31 are both grammatical[60] and elucidatory.[61] In some cases Golius provides an equivalent in Hebrew or Aramaic. His references to the *tafsīr* are often the same as those of Marracci – in connection with the person of Luqmān (v. 11), for example, where Marracci gives the full text of al-Zamakhsharī.[62]

Not only was Golius innovative in his manner of inserting quotations from *tafsīr* in the text of his translation, a procedure that would be adopted by Marracci. He was also one of the first Western scholars to make use of Persian material. Franciscus Raphelengius had encountered the Judaeo-Persian translation of the Pentateuch by Joseph ben Joseph Tavus when he was working on the Antwerp Polyglot Bible in 1584. He subsequently drew up a Persian-Latin lexicon based on it. It was completed by Joseph Justus Scaliger in Leiden, where Raphelengius had been appointed professor of Hebrew. With the Persian transliterated in Hebrew characters, it remained in manuscript.[63] Also

visum fuit ex Persica paraphrasi, ad nos delata ex Mogolorum regno. Hanc quippe omnium, quas vidisse mihi contigit, maxime perspicuam judico, et praecipuorum interpretum medullam.'

57 Bodl., MS Marsh 210, fols 407ᵛ–412ʳ. For Wāʿiẓ Kashifī see T. Zadeh, *The Vernacular Qurʾan. Translation and the Rise of Persian Exegesis* (Oxford-London, 2012), pp. 573–574.
58 Johann Zechendorff, *Unius atque alterius suratae textus* (Zwickau, 1647).
59 Bodl., MS Marsh 210, fols 544ᵛ–546ʳ.
60 *Grammatica Arabicae*, p. 185. To الكيم in verse 1 we get: 'LHACIMI vel active, pro ALHACIMI, *judicantis*, quid fas et nefas sit; vel passiv. pro ALMOHCEMI, *certi*, aut *firmi* et *solidi*, ubi nihil desit. Beid. Hos.'
61 *Ibid.*, p. 189. To لقمن in verse 11 he gives: '*Locmân* cognomento *ALHACIM Sapiens* celeberrimi in Oriente nominis est, in primis apud Muhammedicas gentes. De quo pro diversis doctorum sententiis multa narrant Zamachsjarus, Beidaveus et Persicus paraphrastes, aliique.'
62 Marracci, pp. 546–547.
63 J.T.P. de Bruijn, *De ontdekking van het Perzisch* (Leiden, 1990), pp. 5–10. See, more generally, P. Babinski, 'Ottoman philology and the origins of Persian studies in Western Europe:

in Leiden, Louis de Dieu published the first Persian grammar in 1639. For his own Arabic dictionary, which appeared in 1653 and which, like Erpenius's grammar, remained unsurpassed until the nineteenth century, Golius used not only the main monolingual Arabic dictionaries but also Arabic-Turkish and Arabic-Persian lexicons.[64] Golius himself prepared the first serviceable Persian-Latin dictionary. It was published posthumously in London by Edmund Castell in 1669, as an appendix to Castell's own *Lexicon heptaglotton*. By using Persian material in his work on the Qur'an Golius also prepared the way for a plan cherished in the first years of the eighteenth century of producing a polyglot edition of the Qur'an in Arabic, Turkish and Persian. Proposed by Andreas Acoluthus in Breslau, Georg Jacob Kehr in Leipzig,[65] and Antoine Galland in Paris,[66] it was never fulfilled.

Erpenius's grammars went through countless editions for the rest of the seventeenth century and throughout the eighteenth, and these editions would include his chrestomathy. Occasionally, however, an editor might add something of his own. Leonard Chappelow, professor of Arabic at Cambridge,[67] produced a new version of the *Rudimenta* in 1730.[68] He included sura 64 together with Erpenius's Latin translation and his notes, but he followed the Arabic text of the sura with a transliteration of his own indicating the pronunciation. Above the transliterated words he gave the number of the section of the grammar where that particular word or grammatical form was discussed.

In 1771 Erpenius's *Grammatica Arabica* was reissued in a German translation, edited by Johann David Michaelis at the University of Göttingen, widely acclaimed as one of the greatest Orientalists in Germany. Michaelis added the chrestomathy which had been appended to the text by Albert Schultens, and this did not include the Qur'an. Nevertheless Michaelis expatiated on the Qur'an in his long preface, saying that he would always choose it as the best introduction to Arabic for beginners and, somewhat surprisingly, adding how

---

the *Gulistān*'s Orientalist readers' *Lias* 46 (2019), pp. 233–315; A. Hamilton, 'Afterword,' *ibid.*, pp. 317–325, esp. pp. 321–324.

64 Erpenius had already used the monolingual dictionaries and Arabic-Turkish ones when he prepared a corrective supplement to Franciscus Raphelengius's Arabic-Latin dictionary, first published together with Erpenius's own *Grammatica Arabica* in 1613. See above, pp. 251–4.

65 See above, p. 335.

66 A. Bevilacqua, 'The Qur'an translations of Marracci and Sale' *Journal of the Warburg and Courtauld Institutes* 76 (2013), pp. 93–130, esp. p. 129.

67 A. Hamilton, 'Chappelow, Leonard' *ODNB*.

68 Schnurrer, p. 86, no. 98.

easy it was and that it was no more necessary to read it with the help of a *tafsīr* than to explain the New Testament from the writings of the Church Fathers.[69]

...

Although Erpenius's grammars were unrivalled for so long, and although they were generally regarded as the standard texts for learning Arabic in northern Europe, other Arabists continued to produce grammars, and these often included suras of the Qur'an in the chrestomathy. One example is the *Nucleus institutionum arabicarum enucleatus, variis linguae ornamentis atque praeceptis dialecti turcicae illustratus* published in Zeitz in 1695 and compiled by the twenty-three-year-old Johann David Schieferdecker.[70] Schieferdecker, from Weissenfels, had studied in Leipzig and had then lectured there in Oriental languages until he was summoned to the town of his birth in 1698 to teach at the local grammar school. His work was an Arabic grammar, to which was appended a Turkish one. The Arabic grammar ends with a chrestomathy consisting of the *fātiḥa* followed by ten Arabic adages. While the adages are simply given in Arabic and in Latin translation, the *fātiḥa* is printed first in Arabic, then comes a Latin translation,[71] and finally a word by word grammatical analysis.[72]

Schieferdecker follows Erpenius's *Rudimenta* in providing the page in the grammar in which the various forms that appear in the sura are treated. But although he added his Turkish grammar to his Arabic one, he treats Arabic as a language to be studied in conjunction with Hebrew, Aramaic and Syriac. He endeavours to give the Hebrew, Aramaic or Syriac equivalent of all the words in the *fātiḥa*, thereby exemplifying a tendency typical of Arabic teachers at German universities where pride of place was invariably given to Hebrew

---

69   *Erpenii Arabische Grammatik, abgekürzt, vollständiger und leichter gemacht, von Johann David Michaelis nebst den Anfang einer Arabischen Chrestomathie, aus Schultens Anhang zur Erpenischen Grammatik* (Göttingen, 1771), pp. X–XIV. For Michaelis's attitude to the Qur'an and his contempt for *tafsīr* see above, pp. 336–7, 364–5.
70   Schnurrer, p. 60, no. 86.
71   J.D. Schieferdecker, *Nucleus institutionum arabicarum enucleatus, variis linguae ornamentis atque praeceptis dialecti turcicae illustratus* (Zeitz, 1695), pp. 178–179: 'Laus Deo, domino creaturarum; miseratori misericordi; Regi diei judicii. Te, *o Deus*, colimus, et te adoramus. Dirige nos in viam rectam, viam *nempe* eorum, erga quos gratiosus es, erga quos non iratus es, et *in viam* non errantium.'
72   Ibid., pp. 176–86.

studies. Arabic was treated as ancillary and its study suffered accordingly.[73] But there is one exception to Schiefermaker's painstaking and exclusively grammatical analysis: when he comes to the last two verses he recommends the French Qur'an translation by André Du Ryer[74] which had first appeared in 1647 and had been treated somewhat dismissively by scholars.[75]

∴

Anybody who introduced a sample translation of the Qur'an into a chrestomathy after 1698 had to reckon with a landmark in the history of Qur'anic translations, for it was in that year that the Italian Arabist Ludovico Marracci at last published his bilingual (Latin and Arabic) edition of the whole of the text in Padua.[76] A preliminary volume, the *Prodromus*, had already appeared, published in Rome by the *Propaganda Fide*, in 1691. There Marracci had displayed a wealth of sources with which no scholar in northern Europe could possibly compete. Thanks largely to the missionaries and the Maronites, the various Roman libraries contained a variety of *tafsīr* to be found nowhere north of the Alps. For Protestant scholars, particularly Lutherans who had developed a somewhat proprietorial attitude to the translation of the Qur'an ever since Luther's involvement in the publication of the Latin translation in Basle in 1543,[77] Marracci's version was regarded on the one hand as by far the most reliable to date and one to which scholars could help themselves, and on the other as a challenge, stimulating scholars to do better.

73   Fück, pp. 90–97; A. Ben-Tov, '*Studia orientalia* im Umfeld protestantischer Universitäten des Alten Reichs um 1700' *Zeitsprünge: Forschungen zur Frühen Neuzeit* 16 (2012), pp. 92–118; and above pp. 206–207.
74   *Ibid.*, p. 186. Du Ryer's translation quoted by Schieferdecker runs: 'Conduy nous au droit chemin; au chemin de ceux que tu as gratifié, contre lesquels tu n'as pas esté courroucé.'
75   A. Hamilton and F. Richard, *André Du Ryer and Oriental Studies in Seventeenth-Century France* (London-Oxford, 2004), pp. 104–108.
76   Marracci's sources were listed and discussed by C.A. Nallino, 'Le fonti arabe manoscritte dell'opera di Ludovico Marracci sul Corano' in his *Raccolta di scritti e inediti*, (Rome 1939–48), vol. 2, pp. 90–134. See now, however, R. Tottoli, 'New light on the translation of the Qur'an of Ludovico Marracci from his manuscripts recently discovered at the Order of the Mother of God in Rome' in A. Rippin and R. Tottoli, eds, *Books and Written Culture of the Islamic World. Studies Presented to Claude Gilliot on the Occasion of His 75th Birthday* (Leiden-Boston, 2015), pp. 91–130 and, above all, R. Glei and R. Tottoli, *Ludovico Marracci at Work. The Evolution of his Latin Translation of the Qur'ān in the Light of his Newly Discovered Manuscripts, with an Edition and a Comparative Linguistic Analysis of Sura 18* (Wiesbaden, 2016).
77   See above, p. 305.

An example of the first case is the twenty-three-year-old Johann Gottfried Lakemacher, professor of Oriental languages at Helmstedt,[78] who, in 1718, issued his *Elementa linguae arabicae*,[79] a brief and superficial work which could in no way hope to compete with Erpenius even if it was given to students of Arabic at Halle together with the grammar by Johann Christian Clodius.[80] The chrestomathy at the end consists of the Arabic version of the first chapter of Genesis taken from the London Polyglot Bible, and the second chapter of Matthew's Gospel. In each case the Arabic has an interlinear Latin transliteration followed by a Latin translation. There then comes sura 15 of the Qur'an, *al-ḥijr*, with an interlinear Latin translation (but no transliteration). The grammar ends with a short grammatical analysis of Genesis 1, but not of any other of the texts. Lakemacher's translation of sura 15 is striking for the omission of the mysterious letters (*alif, lām, rā'* الر) in the first verse. He jumps straight to the second and gives a translation which is almost identical to that of Marracci and includes Marracci's insertions of the *Tafsīr al-Jalālayn* in the Latin text.

If Lakemacher used Marracci's version of the Qur'an as a convenient translation, Emo Lucius Vriemoet saw it as a challenge. Professor of Oriental languages at the University of Franeker, Vriemoet, from Emden, had been deeply influenced by Adriaen Reland and Frans Burman when he was studying at Utrecht, and he owed his reputation to his work on Jewish antiquity.[81] Although the majority of his writings are in the field of Hebrew studies, in 1733 he produced his own Arabic grammar, *Arabismus; Exhibens Grammaticam Arabicam Novam, et Monumenta quaedam Arabica, cum notis miscellaneis et glossario arabico-latino. In usum studiosae iuventutis, omniumque qui vel proprio Marte in hisce studiis se exercere cupiunt*.[82] The *monumenta* included a section from Pococke's edition of Abū 'l-Faraj, a Muslim confession of faith, a polemical tract the manuscript of which was in the Utrecht library, parts of the Old and New Testaments, a *maqāma* of al-Ḥarīrī, various poems, and five suras from the Qur'an – 32, 67, 86, 75 and 90. Suras 86 and 90 are solely in Arabic, while the others have a Latin translation on the opposite page. The chrestomathy ends with a detailed commentary of all the suras (including 86 and 90), but not of any of the other material.

In his notes Vriemoet exhibits a vast learning and a close acquaintance with rabbinic texts. All his quotations from the *Tafsīr al-Jalālayn* are to be found in

---

78   *Allgemeine Deutsche Biographie*, vol. 17, pp. 528–529.
79   Schnurrer, p. 61, no. 89.
80   F.E. Boysen, *Eigene Lebensbeschreibung* (Quedlinburg, 1795), vol. 1, p. 122.
81   J. Nat, *De studie van de oostersche talen in Nederland in de 18e en de 19e eeuw* (Purmerend, 1929), pp. 112–113.
82   Schnurrer, pp. 69–70, no. 101.

Marracci, and we can only conclude that he did not have a copy of the *tafsīr* of his own. He tries to argue with Marracci, but the sole point on which he can be said to have won is the idea that the Muslims believed in a plurality of worlds. This, as we saw, had already been raised by Erpenius, who had pointed out that *al-ʿālamīn* referred to 'creatures' rather than to 'worlds'. Marracci, on the other hand, together with a number of earlier interpreters, assumed that the reference was to more than one world.[83] This idea was challenged at some length, but with no reference to Erpenius, by Reland in the second edition of his *De religione mohammedica*,[84] which Vriemoet duly cited.[85] Elsewhere, however, Vriemoet's criticisms are less felicitous. By and large his translation is close to that of Marracci and, like the later eighteenth-century German translators of the entire Qurʾan, David Friedrich Megerlin and Friedrich Eberhard Boysen,[86] when he deviates from Marracci he does so at his peril. He claims, for example, that Marracci was wrong in translating *al-najm al-thāqib* (86:4) as *stella penetrans*, 'the penetrating star' rather than 'ardent or burning star'.[87] Marracci's translation would be accepted to this day. Similarly he criticizes Marracci for translating 86:11, *ʿalā rajʿihi la-qādirun*, as 'resurrecting the body' rather than as 'resurrecting the soul'.[88] Marracci, however, has again been proved right by later translators. And finally there is Vriemoet's translation of 32:20.[89] He translates the verse 'At vero, qui probi sunt, habitaculum eorum erit ignis' as 'the good will go to hell', whereas the Arabic *alladhīna fasaqū* obviously means 'the wicked'.

∙ ∙ ∙

Together with Golius and Erpenius, Vriemoet was one of the few compilers of a chrestomathy which included learned notes to the Qurʾanic texts chosen. The Qurʾan, certainly, continued to be used by a number of compilers of chrestomathies, but usually without any commentary. In 1776 Johann Wilhelm Friedrich

---

83   Marracci, pp. 2–3.
84   A. Reland, *De religione mohammedica libri duo*, 2nd ed. (Utrecht, 1717), pp. 262–268.
85   E.L. Vriemoet, *Arabismus; Exhibens Grammaticam Arabicam Novam, et Monumenta quaedam Arabica, cum notis miscellaneis et glossario arabico-latino. In usum studiosae iuventutis, omniumque qui vel proprio Marte in hisce studiis se exercere cupiunt* (Franeker, 1733), pp. 176, 185.
86   See above, pp. 339–343, 359–363.
87   Vriemoet, *Arabismus*, p. 172.
88   Ibid., p. 173.
89   Ibid., p. 95.

von Hezel, who was twenty-two years old and had just finished his studies at Jena, and who would end his career as professor of theology at Dorpat, published his *Erleichterte arabische Grammatik, nebst einer kurzen arabischen Chrestomathie*.[90] First published in Jena, it would be reissued posthumously in Leipzig in 1825, the year after Hezel's death, but without the glossary that had been added to the chrestomathy in the original edition. The chrestomathy contained verses 1 to 20 of the second sura of the Qur'an and the entire text of suras 57 and 114, but solely in Arabic, without any commentary or translation. In 1798 (year 6 of the French Republican Calendar), Jean-Joseph Marcel, who had followed Napoleon to Egypt, published in Alexandria his *Exercices de lecture d'arabe littéral, à l'usage de ceux qui commencent l'étude de cette langue*.[91] The work consists of five suras of the Qur'an, 1, 97, 109, 110 and 112. Each line of the Arabic has directly below it a transliteration, and below that a literal French translation. At the end of each sura there is a more fluent version of the translation. But there is no commentary.

The use of the Qur'an for linguistic exercises continued well beyond our period. In early modern Europe, however, it is of particular interest since it allows us to assess not only the degree of interest in the text, but also the various stages in translating it and the more general progress of Oriental studies. From a purely grammatical approach such as that of Erpenius, we see a marked advance with Golius, who drew on the *tafsīr* in order to add interpretations and who also introduced Persian material. Filippo Guadagnoli brings us into the world of Marracci – of the missionaries, the participants in the Arabic translation of the bible, and the staff and consultants of the *Propaganda Fide*. By treating the Qur'an as poetry he foreshadowed developments in the eighteenth century and later.[92] The German grammars of the eighteenth century demonstrate both the overpowering influence of Marracci's translation of the Qur'an, and the predominance of Hebrew studies in the German academies which would in fact inhibit progress in Arabic. By the late eighteenth century, however, as more and more versions of the entire text of the Qur'an appeared in the European vernaculars, chrestomathies ceased to play a significant part in the actual history of Qur'an translations.

---

90 Schnurrer, p. 82, no. 116.
91 *Ibid.*, p. 96, no. 140.
92 J. Loop, 'Divine Poetry? Early modern European orientalists on the beauty of the Koran' *Church History and Religious Culture* 89 (2009), pp. 455–488; see above, pp. 345–346.

Acknowledgements

In writing this article, which was first published in Jan Loop, Alastair Hamilton and Charles Burnett, eds, *The Teaching and Learning of Arabic in Early Modern Europe* (Brill: Leiden/Boston 2017), pp. 213–29, I depended heavily on the help and advice of Jan Loop, Arnoud Vrolijk and Alasdair Watson.

CHAPTER 19

After Marracci

The Reception of Ludovico Marracci's Edition of the Qur'an in Northern Europe from the Late Seventeenth to the Early Nineteenth Century

Ludovico Marracci's (Fig. 20) bilingual edition of the Qur'an, in Arabic and Latin, the *Alcorani textus universus*, appeared in 1698. The publication of his

FIGURE 20 Ludovico Marracci. Portrait held in the Church of Santa Maria in Campitelli, Rione Sant'Angelo, Rome. Painter and date unknown

© ALASTAIR HAMILTON, 2022 | DOI:10.1163/9789004498204_020

Prodromus, or 'Introduction', in 1691, however, had prepared the European world of learning for what was to come. In fact Marracci had started on his translation far earlier, and completed it not very long after 1674. In the intervening years he had to struggle with censorship,[1] with the fluctuating views of the inquisitors, and with the decided aversion to the Qur'an of Pope Innocent XI, whose confessor he was but with whom his relations were uneasy.[2] It was only twenty years after he had originally asked the missionary organisation, the *Congregatio de Propaganda Fide*, of which he was one of the most active members, for permission to publish his Qur'an that the work actually appeared – not in Rome, where the *Propaganda* had issued the *Prodromus*, but in Padua, at the Oriental Press of Cardinal Gregorio Barbarigo. In the meantime Marracci seems to have changed his mind, however slightly, about the purpose of his edition. Initially he had hoped to serve the missionaries and to enable them to carry on an informed debate about Islam with Muslims in the hope of converting them to Christianity. Subsequently he appears to have felt that his edition should serve more as a contribution to learned discussions about Islam in the West.[3] The work was consequently intended largely for scholarly Arabists, but its tone remained firmly anti-Islamic.

The *Alcorani textus universus* gave the Arabic text of the Qur'an, each sura followed by a Latin translation, a commentary and, finally, a long confutation. In his *Prodromus* and in his notes and confutations, Marracci quoted an immense array of *tafsīr* or Muslim commentaries.[4] He gave extensive passages in Arabic, followed by Latin translations, and, since the majority of the texts were only available in Rome, Marracci immediately became a unique source in the rest of Europe. Perhaps the most striking element of the Latin translation is the introduction into the actual text of excerpts from the popular *Tafsīr al-Jalālayn*, the fifteenth-century Egyptian commentary by Jalāl al-Dīn al-Maḥallī and Jalāl al-Dīn al-Ṣuyūṭī. Marracci placed these interventions in italics, sometimes between brackets, so that they should be clearly recognized as different from the text itself. Later printers of his work, and of the

---

1 G. Pizzorusso, 'Ludovico Marracci tra ambiente curiale e cultura orientalista a Roma nel XVII secolo' in G.L. D'Errico, *Il Corano e il pontefice. Ludovico Marracci tra cultura islamica e Curia papale* (Rome, 2015), pp. 91–118, esp. pp. 103–113.
2 F. Bustaffa, 'Confessore e "consigliere". Intorno a padre Marracci e Innocenzo XI' in D'Errico, ed., *Il Corano e il pontefice*, pp. 48–66.
3 Pizzorusso, 'Ludovico Marracci', p. 113.
4 C.A. Nallino, 'Le fonti arabe manoscritte dell'opera di Ludovico Marracci sul Corano' in his *Raccolta di scritti e inediti* (Rome, 1939–48), vol. 2, pp. 90–134; but see now the new discoveries of R. Tottoli in R. Glei and R. Tottoli, *Ludovico Marracci at Work. The Evolution of his Latin Translation of the Qur'ān in the Light of his Newly Discovered Manuscripts, with an Edition and a Comparative Linguistic Analysis of Sura 18* (Wiesbaden, 2016).

translations, were, as we shall see, less scrupulous. Whether the interventions were in italics or not, they did not make for a smooth reading of the Latin version.

In the many years between the moment when Marracci started his translation and the time of publication other efforts had been made elsewhere in Europe to translate the Qur'an. The most active were the Germans who had long been dependent on translations – translations into Latin and other languages, and German translations of the translations.[5] German scholars seem to have found out about Marracci's plan in 1681 when Johann Christoph Wagenseil published the information he had received from Antonio Magliabechi, the scholarly librarian, in Florence.[6] Since so many Arabists had announced similar plans and had either never brought them to fruition or had never succeeded in having them published, this was no great cause for alarm. The appearance of the *Prodromus*, on the other hand, was very alarming indeed. It showed that Marracci was an able Arabist with access to a large variety of sources. He was, moreover, an illustrious representative of the Roman Catholic Church. However much the invisible Republic of Letters might have claimed to be above confessional differences, nobody could deny that Marracci's translation had originally been intended for Roman Catholic missionaries and that he himself, a clerk regular in the Order of the Mother of God, former confessor to the pope, and a member of the *Propaganda Fide* and the Congregation of the Index of prohibited books, deplored Protestantism and was profoundly committed to his Church. German Protestants, who prided themselves on the part played by Luther and Melanchthon in the publication of the very first Latin translation of the Qur'an to appear in print, the version produced by Robert of Ketton in 1143 and edited by Theodor Bibliander in Basle four hundred years later, in 1543,[7] felt that it was their prerogative, rather than a Catholic one, to produce the definitive edition of the Qur'an.[8]

From the outset there were various paths open to Marracci's rivals in the course of the eighteenth and early nineteenth centuries. The first was to produce a better translation. This was far from easy not only because of Marracci's

---

5 See above, pp. 327–328. In 1616 Salomon Schwiegger had published a German translation of the Italian translation of the Latin version of the Qur'an edited by Theodor Bibliander in 1543 and in 1688 Johann Lange published his German translation of the Dutch translation of the French version of the Qur'an produced by André Du Ryer in 1647.
6 Johann Christoph Wagenseil, *Tela ignea Satanae. Hoc est: Arcani, et horribiles Judaeorum adversus Christum Deum, et Christianam religionem, libri* (Altdorf, 1681), p. 48.
7 H. Bobzin, *Der Koran im Zeitalter der Reformation: Studien zur Frühgeschichte der Arabistik und Islamkunde in Europa* (Beirut, 1995), pp. 13–275.
8 See above, pp. 303–324.

own immense competence but also because of the variety of sources at his disposal, hardly any of which could be found outside Rome. Marracci had drawn heavily on the *tafsīr*, but might it not be possible, certain Arabists asked, to dispense with the commentaries and simply to make a literal translation? The second main path was to do something different. One of the most obvious solutions was to publish a translation of the Qur'an in a language other than Latin. George Sale published an English version but this, like many of the other versions produced in the eighteenth century, was based almost entirely on Marracci.[9] Another possibility was to compensate for what many Arabists considered the main shortcoming of Marracci's translation and, in an attempt to convey the poetic qualities of the Qur'an which Marracci was accused of neglecting, to make a translation either in more elegant prose or in verse. And finally, there was the possibility of producing a polyglot edition of the Qur'an, in various Islamic languages, in emulation of the polyglot Bibles which had been appearing in the West since the early sixteenth century. Translations made by Muslims, who were themselves well acquainted with the tradition of *tafsīr*, it was thought, would surely absolve a Western Arabist from having to look any further.[10]

Of all the German scholars who reacted to Marracci, Andreas Acoluthus is unquestionably one of the most original and, in many respects, one of the most interesting.[11] A fully fledged citizen of the Republic of Letters, Acoluthus was in correspondence with Gottfried Wilhelm Leibniz, Mathurin Veyssière de la Croze, Louis Picques, and many other scholars of renown. He was invited to teach at the universities of Leipzig, Erfurt, Greifswald, and Halle, but, although he worked for some years at the electoral library in Berlin, he declined the invitations and remained, albeit somewhat reluctantly, a Lutheran pastor in Breslau where he taught Hebrew at the St Elisabeth Gymnasium. A versatile linguist – he laid claim to over twenty languages which included Persian,

---

9 A. Bevilacqua, 'The Qur'an translations of Marracci and Sale' *Journal of the Warburg and Courtauld Institutes* 76 (2013), pp. 93–130.
10 For Persian translations of the Qur'an and, more generally, Muslim attitudes to the translation of the sacred text into other languages, see T. Zadeh, *The Vernacular Qur'an: Translation and the Rise of Persian Exegesis* (Oxford-London, 2012), pp. 263–268.
11 For Acoluthus's life see see K. Migoń, 'Der Breslauer Orientalist Andreas Acoluthus (1654–1704). Seine Beziehungen zu Leibniz und zur Akademie in Berlin' *Sitzungsberichte der Leibniz-Sozietät* 53 (2002), pp. 45–58. See also A. Hamilton, 'Andreas Acoluthus' *CMR*, vol. 14, pp. 437–444; Carl Heinrich Tromler, 'Leben und Schriften des Hern. Andreas Akoluth, weil. Predigers und Professors zu Breßlau, und der Königl. Preuß. Akad. der Wissenschaften Mitglieds' *Neue Beyträge von alten und neuen Theologischen Sachen, Büchern, Urkunden, Controversen, Anmerkungen, Vorschlägen etc.* (Leipzig, 1761), pp. 414–471, esp. pp. 419–425; and above, pp. 312–319, 329–334.

Turkish, Arabic, Coptic, and Chinese – he excelled in Armenian at a time when hardly anybody in the West knew the language. Acoluthus had many admirers, and the imperial interpreter in Istanbul, Franz Mesgnien Meninski, tried to have him appointed as chief interpreter in Vienna. Such prestige conferred on him an almost oracular status in Protestant Germany.

Acoluthus, who owned a large number of Qur'anic manuscripts which had been looted by the Imperial armies,[12] had started to work on the Qur'an in the late 1670s. A devout Lutheran preacher in a largely Catholic city, he always appears to have had a missionary objective at heart and hoped to revive the project of Christian Ravius and Mathias Wasmuth to found an 'Oriental College' which would be the Protestant equivalent of the *Propaganda Fide* in Rome. The appearance of Marracci's *Prodromus* in 1691 prompted Acoluthus to approach the Italian Arabist directly, and the two men developed an epistolary friendship of which only the fragments of a first letter, published by the antiquarian Wilhelm Ernst Tentzel in his *Monatliche Unterredungen einiger guten Freunde* in December 1695, appear to remain.[13] The letter in question was written in 1694 and was accompanied by a brief specimen of Marracci's translation intended to illustrate 'the method and quality of the work'. It testifies to a modesty and warmth on the part of Marracci by which Acoluthus was charmed, and he awaited the publication of the complete translation with eagerness.

By the time Marracci's translation appeared, in 1698, Acoluthus already had a clear idea of what he would produce himself, the *Tetrapla Alcoranica*, a specimen of which (the opening sura with a long introduction) appeared in 1701. It would be entirely different from Marracci's edition. Instead it would be a polyglot Qur'an, giving versions in Arabic, Turkish, and Persian, with respective Latin translations. This, Acoluthus thought, would circumvent the problem of consulting *tafsīr*, but at the same time it would bring out the polyvalence of the text which, Acoluthus believed, Marracci had failed to convey. In fact Acoluthus's objections to Marracci sometimes testify to his own pedantry and eccentricity rather than to any incompetence on the part of Marracci.[14] Acoluthus claimed, for example, that the opening sura, *al-fātiḥa*, should be translated as 'the Sura of the Opening' rather than as 'The Opening Sura'. He went on to say that the second sura, *sūrat al-baqara*, should not be translated as 'The Sura of the Cow' but as 'the Sura of Amplitude or Greatness', and that the title of the forty-eighth sura, *sūrat al-fatḥ*, should be translated as 'The Sura

---

12 B. Liebrenz, *Arabische, Persische und Türkische Handschriften in Leipzig. Geschichte ihrer Sammlung und Erschließung von den Anfängen bis zu Karl Vollers* (Leipzig, 2008), pp. 13–15.
13 See Appendix below, pp. 412–413.
14 See above, pp. 319, 332–333.

of the Decree' rather than as 'The Sura of Victory' or 'of the Opening', *aperiens* (as Marracci translated it).[15] Acoluthus's source for these ideas is by no means clear, but he claimed to have interviewed a number of Turkish prisoners of war, and in 1693 he had as his guest a female captive who was married to an imam in Belgrade. According to Acoluthus she was highly educated.[16]

In the Introduction to his *Tetrapla Alcoranica*, Acoluthus wrote about Marracci with a courtesy and a respect all the more striking in view of his convinced Protestantism.[17] When it comes to theological criticisms of Marracci, he simply regrets the 'tepidity' of Marracci's anti-Islamic polemic, the relative dearth of biblical references, and, more generally, the weak position of a Catholic whose Church refused to circulate the Scriptures amongst the laity. Acoluthus died two years after the publication of his *Tetrapla Alcoranica* and never seems to have added anything further to his Qur'anic research. Yet his influence remained strong among German Lutheran Orientalists. His idea of producing a polyglot Qur'an, moreover, was shared by other Arabists. Antoine Galland in Paris hoped to produce one, as did Georg Jacob Kehr, who would teach briefly in Leipzig, but the plans came to nothing.[18]

Marracci's Qur'an had an immediate success in Germany. Already in 1703 it was translated into German by David Nerreter, a distinguished churchman who, at the time, was pastor of the Batholomäuskirche in Wöhrd, on the edge of his birthplace Nuremberg. His translation of the text of the Qur'an, *Mahometanische Moschea*, was preceded by a long introduction and a confutation of Islam based on the sixth section of Alexander Ross's *ΠΑΝΣΕΒΕΙΑ: Or, A View of All Religions in the World* (to which he added commentaries of his own). When it came to the actual translation of Marracci Nerreter was eclectic in the use he made of Marracci's vast critical apparatus. Nerreter's notes were far fewer and far shorter, but most of them were derived not from the actual notes which Marracci had appended to the text but from Marracci's own confutations which followed the notes. With his German version of Marracci Nerreter was obviously aiming at a broad lay readership unable to read Marracci in

---

15   Andreas Acoluthus, *Tetrapla Alcoranica, sive Specimen Alcorani quadrilinguis, Arabici, Persici, Turcici, Latini* (Berlin, 1701), p. 8.
16   Acoluthus describes his guest, mentions his plan of a polyglot Qur'an, and states his intention of disproving Athanasius Kircher's (correct) assumption that ancient Egyptian was closely related to Coptic – Acoluthus believed rather that the hieroglyphs were related to Armenian – in a letter to Gottlieb Milich written on 12 July 1693, Forschungsbibliothek Gotha, MS Chart. A 1199, f. 7r. I am most grateful to Asaph Ben-Tov for sending me a transcript of this and other letters.
17   Acoluthus, *Tetrapla Alcoranica*, p. 39.
18   See above, p. 335.

Latin and with no interest in the Arabic text – a very different public from the scholars addressed by Acoluthus.

Acoluthus's criticisms of Marracci may have been eccentric, but he was one of the few Qur'an translators who actually engaged with Marracci. Because of the widespread interest in the text in Germany it was not long before dissertations appeared on the various versions of the Qur'an, and it is here that the oracular status of Acoluthus emerges. Between April 1703 and June 1704 three dissertations came out at the University of Altdorf dictated by the professor of theology Johann Michael Lange. The object was to encourage Protestants to produce a proper translation of the Qur'an. Although the great edition of the Qur'an which Acoluthus was planning to produce went no further than the first sura, Acoluthus was quoted constantly and with reverence – 'doctissimus', 'celeberrimus', 'excellentissimus', 'vir summus'.[19] And Marracci, too, received his due, even if the admiration which his edition aroused was combined with a feeling of resentment.[20] Tribute is paid to the man whose letters had touched Acoluthus so deeply,[21] but Acoluthus's expression of regret about Marracci's occasional lack of caution was also quoted. Marracci, the author concluded, should be praised for his industry, but he was by no means always accurate: 'Laudanda est Marracci industria, etsi non ubique rem tetigerit acu.'[22]

Whatever theological or ideological complaints might be made against Marracci's work, nobody could deny the importance of the material it contained. And this takes us out of the somewhat parochial world of German Lutheran Orientalists and brings us to Adriaen Reland, professor of Oriental languages at the University of Utrecht from 1701 to his death in 1718.[23] Such was Reland's versatility not only in the field of Eastern languages but also as a cartographer, an antiquarian, and a poet, that he was venerated even by the most conservative of his colleagues despite his own sympathies for the philosophy

---

19 [Johann Michael Lange, praeses], Johann Conrad, *Dissertatio historico-philologico-theologica de Alcorani versionibus variis, tam orientalibus, quam occidentalibus* (Altdorf, 1704), pp. 6–7, 10, 20.

20 This is emphasised and discussed by Asaph Ben-Tov in his forthcoming study of German Orientalism.

21 [Johann Michael Lange, praeses], Michael Conrad Ludwig, *Dissertatio historico-philologico-theologica de Alcorani prima inter Europaeos editione Arabica* (Altdorf, 1703), p. 19.

22 [Johann Michael Lange, praeses], Georg Michael Schnützlein, *Dissertatio historico-philologico-theologica, De speciminibus, conatibus variis atque novissimis successibus doctorum quorundam virorum in edendo Alcorano arabico* (Altdorf, 1704), p. 30.

23 See above, pp. 129–136.

of Descartes.[24] His attitude was consequently very different from that of the orthodox Dutch Calvinists and from that of a Catholic such as Marracci. His *De religione mohammedica* can be regarded as one of the best informed discussions of Islam.

Reland's treatment of Marracci is puzzling. *De religione mohammedica* first appeared in 1705, and Marracci was not so much as mentioned. The second edition came out in 1717. It was considerably enlarged with respect to the first, and many of the extensions were simply quotations from Marracci. Was this strange delay in quoting him due to the fact that no copy of Marracci had reached Utrecht by 1705? This is possible – the difficulty that Friederich Eberhard Boysen had in obtaining a copy many years later could be seen as a confirmation[25] – but it is nonetheless surprising since the translation was clearly known and read in many parts of Northern Europe within a year or so of publication. Or had Reland not had time to read it? This, in view of what we know about that diligent but sedentary scholar, would be even more surprising.

At all events, in the 1717 edition Reland fully compensated for his neglect. He now quoted entire pages of Marracci, both from the *Prodromus* and from the *Alcorani textus universus*, with frequency and relish, but making no attempt to conceal Marracci's dislike of Protestantism or his allegiance to Rome. In his preface he quoted Marracci's likening of the Muslims to the Calvinists and Sacramentarians in connection with their rejection of images, and went on to say that even a statement such as that could not diminish his admiration for what Marracci had achieved.[26] He then quoted with full approval Marracci's remarks about the potential attractions of Islam for non-Christians and about the need to know Islam in order to dispute with Muslims. One of the few points on which Reland took Marracci to task was the understanding of the term *al-'ālamīn* in the opening sura of the Qur'an.[27] According to Reland (and certain earlier Arabists such as Thomas Erpenius) it meant 'creatures' rather than 'worlds'. Marracci, on the other hand, also together with a number of earlier interpreters, assumed that it meant more than one world.[28] This was a dangerous interpretation since it opened Islam to the accusation of belief in a plurality of worlds. Nevertheless it is quite clear that Reland regarded Marracci as one of the greatest authorities – if not the very greatest – on the subject of

---

24 See above, and the articles contained in B. Jaski, C. Lange, A. Pytlowany, H.J. van Rinsum, eds, *The Orient in Utrecht. Adriaan Reland (1676–1718), Arabist, Cartographer, Antiquarian and Scholar of Comparative Religion* (Leiden-Boston, 2021).
25 See below, p. 351.
26 Adriaen Reland, *De religione mohammedica libri duo* (Utrecht, 1717), sig. ***r–v.
27 *Ibid.*, pp. 262–268.
28 Marracci, pp. 2–3.

Islam. But their approach was entirely different. Marracci made no secret of his intellectual contempt for non-Christians. Reland, influenced by Descartes, believed that truth, wherever it was, should be investigated, 'veritas ubicunque est indagari debet',[29] and that intelligence was 'equally distributed' amongst mankind, 'bona mens aequaliter distributa est'.[30]

In Germany the success of Marracci's Qur'an continued. In 1718 the twenty-three-year-old Johann Gottfried Lakemacher, professor of Oriental languages at Helmstedt, issued his *Elementa linguae arabicae*. The chrestomathy at the end contains sura 15 of the Qur'an, *al-ḥijr*, with an interlinear Latin translation. It is almost identical to that of Marracci and includes Marracci's insertions of the *Tafsīr al-Jalālayn* in the Latin text.[31] Three years later, in 1721, the biblical scholar Christian Reineccius, rector of the Latin school in Weissenfels, published a revised Latin version of the *Alcorani textus universus – Mohammedis filii Abdallae Pseudo-Prophetae Fides Islamitica*, i.e. *Al-Coranus*. From it Marracci's critical and polemical apparatus was entirely removed. Reineccius, however, quoted Acoluthus with veneration. In a note to the opening of the second sura, *al-baqara*, he referred to Acoluthus's idea of entitling it 'The Sura of Amplitude'.[32] When he came to the forty-eighth sura, *al-fatḥ*, he actually adopted Acoluthus's suggestion that it should be entitled 'The Sura of the Decree', but also gave 'The Opening' as an alternative title.[33] The readership Reineccius seems to have had in mind was slightly different to the readers of Acoluthus. The Latin text of Marracci was intended for the educated – and could be greeted with enthusiasm in view of the difficulty of obtaining the original edition of Marracci – but, as we shall see in the case of Boysen, the absence of the Arabic meant that it was only of limited use to Arabists.

In the Low Countries too Marracci remained popular. In 1733 Emo Lucius Vriemoet, professor of Oriental languages at the University of Franeker, and influenced by Reland when he had been at Utrecht, published *Arabismus; exhibens grammaticam Arabicam novam, et monumenta quaedam Arabica*. The *monumenta* included five suras from the Qur'an – 32, 67, 86, 75, and 90. Suras 86 and 90 are solely in Arabic, while the others also have a Latin translation, and are followed by a detailed commentary. All Vriemoet's quotations

---

29 Reland, *De religione mohammedica*, sig. 3*.
30 Ibid., sig. 4*v. See above pp. 147–148. I am particularly grateful to Jan Just Witkam for pointing out to me some of the discrepancies between the two editions of Reland's *De religione mohammedica*.
31 See above, pp. 396–397.
32 Christian Reineccius, *Mohammedis Filii Abdallae pseudo-prophetae fides islamitica, i.e. Al-Coranus* (Leipzig, 1721), p. 2.
33 Reineccius, *Al-Coranus*, p. 462.

from the *Tafsīr al-Jalālayn* are to be found in Marracci. He tries to argue with Marracci, but the only point on which he can be said to have won is his denial that the Muslims believed in a plurality of worlds – an idea which he may have owed to Reland. By and large his translation is close to that of Marracci and when he strays from Marracci he is liable to make mistakes. He objects to Marracci's translation of *al-najmu 'l-thāqib* (86:3) as 'stella penetrans', 'the penetrating star', and gives instead 'ardent or burning star'.[34] He also criticizes Marracci's interpretation of 86:8, *'alā raj'ihi la-qādirun*, as 'resurrecting the body' and prefers 'resurrecting the soul'.[35] In both cases Marracci, rather than Vriemoet, has been followed by later translators.

Marracci's *Alcorani textus universus* entered a new phase with the publication in 1734 of George Sale's English translation of the Qur'an. Before that the English in search of the Qur'an in the vernacular had had to make do with a translation of André Du Ryer's French version. Latinists could turn to the original Marracci, but this was inaccessible to a large group of literate individuals often impelled by curiosity. These were the readers Sale had in mind. 'In 1698', he wrote in his prefatory address to the reader, 'a Latin translation of the Korân, made by father Lewis Marracci, who had been confessor to pope Innocent XI. was published at Padua, together with the original text, accompanied by explanatory notes and a refutation. This translation of Marracci's, generally speaking, is very exact, but adheres to the Arabic idiom too literally to be easily understood, unless I am much deceived, by those who are not versed in the Mohammedan learning. The notes he has added are indeed of great use, but his refutations, which swell the work to a large volume, are of little or none at all, being often unsatisfactory, and sometimes impertinent. The work, however, with all it's faults, is very valuable, and I should be guilty of great ingratitude, did I not acknowledge myself much obliged therto; but still, being in Latin, it can be of no use to those who understand not that tongue.'[36]

Such a statement does not do full justice to Sale's debt to Marracci. With hardly any volumes of *tafsīr* at his disposal – he did indeed have a copy of al-Bayḍāwī, however – Sale took nearly all his references to Muslim commentaries from Marracci and, as Alexander Bevilacqua has shown,[37] did little more

---

34   E.L. Vriemoet, *Arabismus; Exhibens Grammaticam Arabicam Novam, et Monumenta quaedam Arabica, cum notis miscellaneis et glossario arabico-latino. In ususm studiosae iuventutis, omniumque qui vel proprio Marte in hisce studiis se exercere cupiunt* (Franeker, 1733), p. 172. See above, pp. 391–392.
35   Vriemoet, *Arabismus*, p. 173.
36   Sale, p. vi.
37   Bevilacqua, 'The Qur'an Translations of Marracci and Sale', pp. 103–107, 112–130. See also Z. Elmarsafy, *The Enlightenment Qur'an: The Politics of Translation and the Construction of Islam* (Oxford, 2009), pp. 37–80.

than produce an English version of Marracci's translation. It was, however, written in elegant English, and was quickly acclaimed as by far the best rendering of the Qur'an in existence. Its reputation has persisted through the ages and it is still available in numerous different editions. Translations, too, followed. In 1746 Theodor Arnold turned it into German, and it was through his version that the young Goethe became acquainted with the Qur'an.[38] But, more important still, thanks in part to Sale's 'Preliminary Discourse', Marracci's translation was all but entirely removed from the anti-Islamic discourse of the *Prodromus* and the *Alcorani textus universus* and was now presented in the context of the ever more dispassionate assessments of Islam coming into fashion at the time.

Although there had, in the meanwhile, been other attempts to translate the Qur'an in its entirety quite independently of Marracci, none of these had actually been published. The climate, moreover, was changing. Sale had already emphasized the need to improve on Marracci's style, and there was, by the 1740s, a perceptible tendency to regard the Qur'an as an outstanding example of Eastern poetry which should be treated as such.[39] In 1745, almost a quarter of a century before his own German translation of the Qur'an appeared, Friederich Eberhard Boysen, then a Lutheran preacher in Magdeburg, expressed his misgivings about Marracci in a letter to the poet Johann Wilhelm Ludwig Gleim. Boysen had been unable to obtain a copy of the 1698 edition of Marracci's translation and had had to rely, for the Arabic, on Abraham Hinckelmann's edition (1694), and, for the Latin, on Reineccius's version of Marracci.

Marracci, Boysen complained, had been unable to convey the 'ardour and the grandeur' of the original. The translation was 'too literal' and 'in many places wrong'.[40] He then gives a list of errors. This is of particular interest since many of the mistakes can be blamed on Reineccius. The first concerns the introduction of 'fingentes se fidele' in 4:91. In Marracci's text the entire passage is in italics and indeed, it is a somewhat free paraphrase (but not a translation) of the *Tafsīr al-Jalālayn*.[41] In Reineccius's version, on the other hand, 'se fideles' is in italics, but not 'fingentes'.[42] It thus appears that Marracci thought 'fingentes' was part of the Qur'anic text. The second mistake which struck Boysen was

---

38   K. Mommsen, *Goethe und der Islam* (Frankfurt a. M., 2001), pp. 148, 160, 224; above, p. 347.
39   J. Loop, 'Divine Poetry? Early modern European Orientalists on the beauty of the Koran' *Church History and Religious Culture* 89 (2009), pp. 455–488, esp. pp. 474–475.
40   Friederich Eberhard Boysen, *Briefe vom Herrn Boysen an Herrn Gleim*, vol. 1 (Frankfurt-Leipzig, 1772), pp. 38–52, esp. p. 38. For Boysen see above, pp. 348–365.
41   Jalāl al-Dīn al-Maḥallī and Jalāl al-Dīn al-Suyūṭī, *Tafsīr al-Jalālayn* (Casablanca, 2004), p. 92.
42   Reineccius, *Al-Coranus*, p. 87.

in the translation of 4:156.[43] He could not, he told Gleim, understand the addition of 'malediximus eis' at the end of the verse since it was not in the Arabic. Boysen was right. It was neither in the Arabic nor in Marracci's translation, but had been added quite arbitrarily by Reineccius. 5:22 contained an obvious misprint: 'vos' instead of 'nos';[44] and so did 33:72 where 'non' should be 'nos'.[45] Complaining about the translation of 5:89, Boysen pointed out that 'jurantes' was not in the Arabic text.[46] And indeed, yet again Reineccius had failed to put the word in italics as Marracci, who was quoting the *Tafsīr al-Jalālayn*, had done. The same applies to Boysen's objection to 24:10. In Marracci's translation 'certe detegeret veritatem, & statim puniret perjuros' is in italics, and is taken from the *Tafsīr al-Jalālayn*, but has remained in roman in Reineccius's version.[47] Some of the mistakes, however, can also be blamed on Marracci – or on his printer.[48] At 12:8, on Joseph and his brothers, Marracci introduces the name of Benjamin. This is not in the Qur'an, but is in the *Tafsīr al-Jalālayn*.[49] In 22:36 the camels are described as 'standing on three feet'. This is not in the Qur'an but is indeed in the *Tafsīr al-Jalālayn*,[50] and should have been – but was not – printed in italics by Reineccius. On other occasions Boysen simply disagreed with Marracci's translation. In 5:96, for example, Marracci has added 'the Day of Judgement' while the Qur'an simply uses the term 'being gathered (*ḥashara*) to God'.

One of the most outspoken critics of Marracci was Johann David Michaelis, an Old Testament scholar and Orientalist of distinction, and professor of philosophy at the University of Göttingen. Michaelis believed that it was possible to improve vastly on Marracci's version of the Qur'an and to dispense all but

---

43   *Ibid.*, p. 95.
44   *Ibid.*, p. 101.
45   *Ibid.*, p. 384.
46   *Ibid.*, p. 111.
47   Marracci, p. 481; al-Maḥallī and al-Suyūṭī, *Tafsīr al-Jalālayn*, p. 351; Reineccius, *Al-Coranus*, p. 315.
48   For Marracci's dissatisfaction with the published edition of his translation see Glei and Tottoli, *Ludovico Marracci at Work*, p. 31: 'We know that Marracci himself wrote that the Arabic text finally printed was not the one he used for his translation, but that the Arabic was put together by typographers and correctors in the Seminar, and that he could only revise and correct it (in the proofs). In his *L'ebreo preso con le buone*, posthumously published in Rome in 1701, Marracci even stated that printers and correctors had ruined his work.' See also Nallino, 'Le fonti arabe', pp. 93–94, 130. One of the worse misprints, which remains uncorrected in the list of corrections at the end of the text, was 2:26, Marracci, p. 10, 'calix', chalice, instead of 'culex', 'gnat'. Marracci, however, gives the correct word in his notes.
49   Al-Maḥallī and al-Suyūṭī, *Tafsīr al-Jalālayn*, p. 236, and Reineccius, *Al-Coranus*, p. 209.
50   Al-Maḥallī and al-Suyūṭī, *Tafsīr al-Jalālayn*, p. 336, and Reineccius, *Al-Coranus*, p. 302.

entirely with *tafsīr*. He himself provided a specimen, the first 116 verses of the second sura, published in a thesis defended at Göttingen by a Swedish student, Olaus Domey, in 1754.[51] In his preface Michaelis discussed the translations of Marracci and Sale. He was well aware of the similarity between the two, but declared his own preference for Sale who had the advantage of writing an elegant English which caught some of the stylistic charm of the original. Against Marracci he had two main complaints. The first was his Latin style – 'barbarous', 'rough', 'abrupt', and 'uncultivated' – which made it impossible to understand the beauty attributed to the Arabic. This was greatly aggravated by the insertion of extracts from *tafsīr* in the text. But what use, he wondered, were the *tafsīr* anyhow? They were, after all, no more than the fruit of Muslim superstition and could not possibly be regarded as a key to understanding the Qur'an. Later, in his review of Boysen's translation of the Qur'an in 1775, Michaelis would say that *tafsīr* were no more necessary for understanding the Qur'an than were the Church Fathers for understanding the Bible.[52] He did not deny that something might be learnt from the *tafsīr*, but, apart from having been compiled far later than the Qur'an itself, they were the work of men influenced by their own theological positions. The Qur'an, in short, should be freed from any authority and judged on its own terms with 'the help of logic and philology'. Only then could we establish what the Prophet himself had to say.

Michaelis's attitude is interesting since it suggests a critical approach to the *tafsīr* which would only come into its own some 150 years later. Whether it can be attributed to intuitions on the part of Michaelis or simply to the fact that he had no *tafsīr* at his disposal may never be known, but it brings out the fundamental difference between his approach and that of Marracci. However much his attitude to the purpose of his translation might have changed over the years, Marracci, like many translators who served, or pretended to serve, the missionary movement, had always wanted to convey how the Qur'an was understood by Muslims. For this purpose the *tafsīr* were essential. Michaelis, on the other hand, wanted to go far deeper and establish the true meaning of the Qur'an in itself. Although his treatment of the Bible fluctuated over the years, it is also possible to perceive a similarity between his approach to the Qur'anic commentaries and his approach to the Scriptures. Like an increasing number of scholars in the eighteenth century he turned his back on traditional exegesis and felt that the only valid interpretation must be based on

---

51 [Johann David Michaelis, praeses] Olaus Domey, *Nova versio partis surae II. Corani cum illustrationibus subiectis: specimen novae versionis totius Corani* (Göttingen, 1754), sig. *r.

52 Johann David Michaelis, 'Der Koran ...', in *idem*, ed., *Orientalische und exegetische Bibliothek* (Frankfurt a. M., 1773–85), vol. 8, pp. 30–98, esp. p. 49.

archaeological and philological research.[53] In his abundant notes to his sample translation Michaelis drew comparisons with other passages in the Qur'an and, still more frequently, with passages and terms in the Bible.

The translation Michaelis provided of the first part of the second sura was certainly more elegant, and also more readable, than that of Marracci. It is not interrupted by extracts from the *tafsīr*. Michaelis, throughout, tends to use the present tense rather than the future perfect or the future simple used by Marracci. Where the actual meaning of the words is concerned, however, modern translators might still prefer Marracci. Marracci's translation of *ghayb* (2:3) as 'arcanum' could be deemed preferable to Michaelis's 'mysterium', and Marracci's 'stare faciunt orationem' for *yuqīmūna al-ṣalwa* in the same verse could be preferred to Michaelis's 'peragunt preces'. The same applies to 2:27. Michaelis translates *yufsidūna fī 'l-arḍ* as 'latrocinia exercent in terra', while Marracci gives 'corrumpunt in terra' (which is far closer to the Arabic). Sometimes Michaelis also blames Marracci (and Sale) for failing to observe an important element in the sura. The description of the heavenly rewards for the righteous in 2:25 is seen by Michaelis as a parable, and, as such, a means of vindicating the Prophet from the charge of giving a purely sensual description of paradise. By and large Michaelis has made a perfectly competent translation of a section of the Qur'an which presents few problems, but he never seems to have followed it up. As in the case of so many Arabists who produced no more than specimens, we are left wondering how satisfactory a more extensive translation might have been.

In contrast to Michaelis, the greatest Arabist in Germany, Johann Jacob Reiske, who had little interest in the Qur'an, insisted that if a good translation were ever to be produced, *tafsīr* would be of vital importance – far more *tafsīr*, he added, than had even been quoted by Marracci.[54] But where were the *tafsīr* to be found? Not, it would seem, in Germany. And even if occasional attempts were made to undertake an independent translation of the Qur'an,

---

53 For the consequences of the Lutheran belief in *sola Scriptura* see H.-J. Kraus, *Geschichte der historisch-kritischen Erforschung des Alten Testaments*, 2nd edn (Neukirchen-Vluyn, 1969), pp. 6–43, and for Michaelis, pp. 97–103. For the rejection of patristic authority by a Biblical scholar such as Richard Simon in the late seventeenth century see N. Hardy, *Criticism and Confession; The Bible in the Seventeenth-Century Republic of Letters* (Oxford, 2017), p. 381. For Michaelis see also J. Sheehan, *The Enlightenment Bible: Translation, Scholarship, Culture* (Princeton, 2005), pp. 184–191, 213–217.

54 Johann Jacob Reiske, 'Gedanken, wie man der arabischen Literatur aufhelfen könne, und solle' *Geschichte der königlichen Akdemie der schönen Wissenschaften zu Paris* 11 (Leipzig, 1757), p. 194: 'Von einem Ausleger des Korans erwartet man einen getreuen Auszug aus den arabischen Auslegern, die von Maraccio und Sälen bey weiten noch nicht erschöpfet sind.'

there was a more or less general agreement that the sole accessible source of *tafsīr* was Marracci himself. As ever more emphasis was being attached to the poetic style of the Qur'an it was agreed that the meaning could also be left to Marracci.

In 1772 the first German translation of the Qur'an made directly from the Arabic appeared – *Die türkische Bibel, oder des Korans allererste teutsche Uebersetzung aus der Arabischen Urschrift selbst verfertiget* by David Friedrich Megerlin.[55] In a long introduction Megerlin surveyed earlier translations of the Qur'an. Like so many of his Lutheran predecessors he adulated Acoluthus. He admitted a great esteem for Sale and, by association, for Marracci, and indeed his translation tends to follow the two. Boysen, on the other hand, whose own translation *Der Koran, oder Das Gesetz für die Muselmänner, durch Mohammed den Sohn Abdall*, first appeared in 1773, made a substantial use of the *tafsīr* quoted by Marracci and even managed to add one of his own which Marracci had not known about – the *Ma'ālim al-tanzīl* by the twelfth-century Persian scholar Abū Muḥammad al-Ḥusayn b. Mas'ūd al-Farrā' al-Baghawī.[56] In contrast to Megerlin, whose translation had been severely criticised, Boysen, in his own introduction, expressed a great admiration for the text and a considerable sympathy for Islam.

Such admiration and sympathy were fast becoming a characteristic of young German Arabists who tackled the Qur'an,[57] but this was also a new generation, as Ziad Elmarsafy put it, 'where sound and form matter as much as, if not more than, content.'[58] The insistence on the poetic qualities of the Qur'an was increasingly prominent and the quest for *tafsīr* was abandoned. The English could rest on Sale as the demands for the stylistic and poetic qualities of the Qur'an to be conveyed in translation grew.

The situation in France differed from that in Germany. The French translation of the Qur'an by André Du Ryer had appeared in 1647. It was the first published translation to be made directly from the Arabic since Bibliander produced Robert of Ketton's medieval version in 1543, and the first in a vernacular. The readership at which it was aimed was entirely different from that addressed by Bibliander or by Marracci. Du Ryer's Qur'an was presented as a work of exotic entertainment. It was originally issued in Paris by Antoine de Sommaville, a publisher suspected of libertine sympathies and known for his editions of romances, poetry, and a number of 'Orientalising' plays. This,

---

55 See above, pp. 339–343.
56 See above, pp. 362–363.
57 See above, pp. 343–361.
58 Elmarsafy, *The Enlightenment Qur'an*, p. 172.

and the many later editions in a conveniently small format, make of Du Ryer's Qur'an a precursor of future works of Oriental entertainment such as the *Arabian Nights*.[59] Thanks to Du Ryer's use of the vernacular his Qur'an was immensely popular, running through over ten editions in French between 1647 and 1770.[60]

Du Ryer's Qur'an was published in German, Dutch, English, and Russian translations – some editions of the Dutch translation were even illustrated – and manuscripts are known to have existed in Italian,[61] Spanish,[62] and Hebrew.[63] The omissions and mistranslations, however, raised the suspicions of the more professional Arabists. We thus find that Eusèbe Renaudot, in his *Historia patriarcharum Alexandrinorum Jacobitarum* of 1713, stressed the infinite superiority of Marracci.[64] Some years later David Durand in London prepared a French edition of Reland's *De religione mohammedica* which was vastly expanded with a preface and a commentary of his own. While he was prepared to grant Du Ryer's translation a number of points, he nevertheless followed Reland in preferring Marracci. Marracci's version, however, was too difficult to obtain, he said, and too expensive to be worth buying, even by those who could read Latin.[65]

By the third decade of the eighteenth century, therefore, Latin was regarded as a serious obstacle, as we also see in the case of a populariser such as François-René Turpin and his *Histoire de l'Alcoran* of 1775. 'Marucci [sic]', he writes, 'seems to have explored the Muslim system in depth. But who is the man bold enough to undergo the fatigue of an *in-folio* in which a few interesting facts are concealed in a mass of revolting fables?' And yet, he went on, 'we cannot but praise the author for reacting against those popular traditions that slander the Arab Legislator. A critic without bitterness and without prejudices,

---

59 A. Hamilton and F. Richard, *André Du Ryer and Oriental Studies in Seventeenth-Century France* (London-Oxford, 2004), pp. 50–52.
60 *Ibid.*, pp. 93–118.
61 P.M. Tommasino, *L'Alcorano di Macometto. Storia di un libro del Cinquecento europeo* (Bologna, 2013), p. 40.
62 J.P. Arias Torres, 'Bibliografía sobre las traducciones del Alcorán en el ámbito hispanico' *Trans. Revista de traductología* 11 (2007), pp. 261–272, esp. p. 264.
63 M.M. Weinstein, 'A Hebrew Qur'ān manuscript' *Studies in Bibliography and Booklore* 10 (1972), pp. 19–52, esp. pp. 23–24.
64 Eusèbe Renaudot, *Historia patriarcharum Alexandrinorum Jacobitarum* (Paris, 1713), p. 158.
65 Adriaen Reland, *La religion des Mahometans*, tr. David Durand (The Hague, 1721), p. 1: 'J'ose vous dire, sur la bonne foi de mon Auteur, qu'il n'y en a qu'une de bonne; encore, par malheur pour vous, est-elle en Latin, dans un Livre *in folio* de M. l'Abbé Maracci, assez rare & assez cher pour vous en passer, quand même vous entendriez cette Langue.'

he approves with discernment and censures without malice.'⁶⁶ Although by no means entirely averse to Du Ryer's translation, Turpin accused it of having failed entirely to convey the beauty and the fascination of the original.⁶⁷

Not until 1783 was a new French translation issued by Claude-Etienne Savary. In his Introduction he was particularly critical of his predecessors. Marracci, he wrote, was too literal and his Latin too ugly for his version to be satisfactory, and it was further marred by a hostility to Islam which Savary was very far from sharing.⁶⁸ Nevertheless Savary's own translation owed everything to Marracci.⁶⁹ In Germany Johann Christian Wilhelm Augusti produced his *Der kleine Koran* in 1798. The translation was in iambics, but it was made, he wrote, 'after Marracci'.⁷⁰ And even the far later German translation of the entire Qur'an made by Ludwig Ullmann in 1840 seems, despite all claims to independence, to have been all but entirely dependent on Marracci for the references to the Islamic commentaries.⁷¹

An alteration can be noticed, however, in the verse translation of certain suras by Josef von Hammer, later known as Josef von Hammer-Purgstall, in Austria. In the first decade of the nineteenth century he produced samples which he thought would do justice to the sacred text, and those versions of the suras he translated are both literal and poetic. Only rarely do we have faint echoes of Marracci.⁷² As the great changes in Arabic studies led by Isaac Sylvestre de Sacy in Paris made their way across Europe Marracci could gradually be consigned to history. One of the best German Arabists to return from Sacy's courses in France was Heinrich Leberecht Fleischer. In a review he published in 1841 he demolished not only Ullmann's translation of the Qur'an, but

---

66   François-René Turpin, *Histoire de l'Alcoran* (London, 1775), vol. 1, pp. xx–xxi: 'Marucci semble avoir approfondi le système Musulman. Mais quel est l'home assez intrépide pour essuyer la fatigue d'un *in-folio*, ou quelques faits intéressants sont consignés parmi un amas de fables révoltantes? On doit à l'Auteur l'éloge de s'être élevé contre les Traditions populaires qui calomnient le Législateur Arabe. Critique sans fiel & sans préjugé, il approuve avec discernement, & censure sans malignité.'
67   *Ibid.*, vol. 1, pp. xviii–xix.
68   Claude-Etienne Savary, *Le Coran* (Amsterdam, 1786), vol. 1, pp. xi–xii.
69   A. Hamilton, 'Claude-Etienne Savary: Orientalism and fraudulence in late eighteenth-century France' *Journal of the Warburg and Courtauld Institutes* 82 (2019), pp. 283–314, esp. pp. 305–313.
70   Johann Christian Wilhelm Augusti, *Der kleine Koran oder Uebersetzung der wichtigsten und lehrreichsten Stücke des Koran's mit kurzen Anmerkungen* (Weißenfels-Leipzig, 1798), p. 11.
71   See, for example, Ludwig Ullmann, *Der Koran* (Crefeld, 1840), pp. 10–11, 27, 46, 77, and Marracci, *Alcorani textus universus*, pp. 43–44, 92, 131, 194.
72   J. von Hammer, 'Die letzten vierzig Suren des Korans' *Fundgruben des Orients* 2 (1811), pp. 26–46. See, for example, 100:8, p. 43.

most previous ones – those of Megerlin, Boysen, Savary, Augusti, and Samuel Friedrich Günther Wahl (who had produced a revised edition of Boysen). Qur'an translations, he wrote at the beginning of his review, had reached their zenith with Marracci and Sale. Since then they had declined precipitously.[73]

A new era was opening, and Friedrich Rückert, a great poet as well as a great Orientalist, would continue the initiative of Hammer-Purgstall in making a verse translation independent of Marracci. Yet the enduring success of Sale's version meant that Marracci survived. And even the critical approach to the *tafsīr* in the early twentieth century, exemplified by Friedrich Schwally and Ignaz Goldziher, surely owed a debt to the man who helped to bring the Muslim commentaries to the attention of the European Orientalists.

Appendix: Ludovico Marracci to Andreas Acoluthus, 1694, in *Monatliche Unterredungen einiger guten Freunde*, December 1695, pp. 1,009–1,010

Text

Cum enim octogesimum tertium aetatis meae annum percurram, paucos tantum dies vel menses possum mihi, & quidem cum formidine polliceri. Interim gratulor tibi, quod tam praeclara ingenii & eruditionis, praesertim in tot linguarum peritia, specimina depromas. Ego vero, qui in mortuorum potius quam vivorum censu computandus sum, inerti otio paulatim consumor, atque in Cellula mea, velut in sepulchro, detineor, ut vix pedem extra illam efferre liceat ... Versio mea Alcoranica adhuc gemit sub Torculari, sed spero ante obitum meum esse absolvendam: Illius exemplaria ex Urbe Patavina, ubi imprimitur, petenda erunt; Nescio quot ex illis Em. Card. Barbadicus [sic] mihi dono transmittet. Mitto cum Epistola mea responsoria primum illius Folium, in quo sunt aliqua menda, sed reformatum est atque correctum, iterumque impressum. Ex illo poteris facile agnoscere totius Operis Methodum & Qualitatem. Ego vero non tam peritum me in Idiomate Arabico profiteor, ut translationem meam Alcorani ab omni errore imunem esse persuadeam. Etiam antequam opus hoc aggrederer, me in multis hallucinaturum esse credidi. Non tamen ab incepto desistendum putavi facturus quantum possem, ut non errarem, & si

---

73 Heinrich Leberecht Fleischer, 'Orientalische Literatur' *Allgemeine Literatur-Zeitung* 53 (1841), cols 417–22; 54, 1841, cols 430–432, esp. 53, col. 417: 'Von Marracci (1698) aufsteigend, erreichte die Erklärung des Korans in christlichen Europa ihre bis jetzt höchste Stufe durch Sale (1734); Megerlin (1772), Boysen (1773), Savary (1783), Augusti (1798) und Wahl (1828) führten sie, der eine mehr, die andere weniger, wieder davon herab.'

non perfectum, saltem minus imperfectum attingerem. Nihil enim amplius in rebus humanis mortalibus conceditur. Nimirum, est quodam prodire tenus, si non datur ultra. Doctissimos ex Arabibus Alcorani Expositores adhibui: Si illis ducibus erravi, compati mihi merito omnes debent. Gaudeo nihilominus, quod non nisi post mortem meam errores mei deprehendendi sint: Tunc saeviant omnes in Mortuum quantum libet. Unum scio, Te doctissimum & sapientissimum Virum, partes meas acturum, non quidem ut errata mea tuearis, sed ut benigne excuses, & humaniter corrigas, meque hominem fuisse & non Deum, neque aliquid supra hominem affirmes. Interea si quid mihi per literas respondere placuerit, gratissimum habeo, dummodo literae tuae me vivum reperiant.

Translation
Since I have reached my eighty-third year I can only, with a certain sense of dread, promise myself a few more days or months. In the meantime I congratulate you on displaying such brilliant manifestations of ingenuity and learning, especially in the knowledge of so many languages. I, however, who have to be counted more among the dead than among the living, am slowly being consumed by inert idleness, and am held in my cell as in a tomb, hardly daring to set a foot outside it ... My version of the Qur'an is still groaning on the press, but I hope that it will come out before my death. The copies can be obtained from Padua where the work is printed. I do not know how many His Eminence Cardinal Barbarigo will send me as a gift. I enclose with my reply the first folio in which there are various errors but which, altered and corrected, has been printed again. From this you will easily perceive the method and the quality of the entire work. I do not claim to be so proficient in the Arabic language as to think that my translation of the Qur'an is free from any error. Even before I embarked on this task I thought I would commit many mistakes. I did not, however, think that I should abandon what I had started, but was determined to do what I could in order to avoid blunders and to reach an objective which, if not perfect, was at least less imperfect. Nothing more can be conceded to mortals in human matters. For 'you may advance to a certain point if it is not permitted to you to go further' (Horace, *Ep.* 1:1). I added the most learned commentators of the Qur'an. If I erred under their leadership I deserve everyone's compassion. Nevertheless I am glad that I shall only be charged with my mistakes after I am dead: people may then be as savage as they like. I know one thing: you, most learned and wisest of men, will be on my side, not that you will defend my mistakes but that you will gently forgive me and correct me humanely, affirming that I was a man and not God, nor anything more than a man. In the meantime if you were to answer me with a letter I would be most grateful, provided your letter still finds me alive.

Acknowledgements

This article first appeared in Jan Loop, ed., *The Qur'an in Western Europe* (Centre of Islamic Studies: London 2018 [= *Journal of Qur'anic Studies* 20 (2018)]), pp. 175–192. In writing it I profited greatly from the advice of Asaph Ben-Tov, Charles Burnett, Guido Giglioni, Jan Loop, and Roberto Tottoli.

Index

Abbas, shah of Persia 126
Abel, Leonardo 275
Abendana, Isaac 308
abjad alphabetical order *see* Arabic alphabetical order
Abī Zamanīn 300, 313
Abū 'l-Faraj (Bar Hebraeus) 294–5, 344, 356, 391
Abū 'l-Fidā 356, 360, 370
Abū 'Ubayd 60, 67, 75, 273
Abudacnus *see* Barbatus, Josephus
Abyssinians (*see also* Ethiopians) 37
Acoluthus, Andreas 304, 310, 321, 323–4, 327, 340, 368, 388
    career and achievements 313–15, 329–34
    and Marracci 314, 332–3, 398–401, 412–13
    Tetrapla Alcoranica 315–19, 398–400
Addison, Lancelot, *First State of Mahumedism* 294
Adriaen Willemsz 56–63, 66, 73, 79, 81, 82, 379
Afzarī, al-, *Sharḥ taṣrīf al-Zanjānī* 233, 235, 257
Agathange de Vendôme 154–5, 157–8
Ahizade Hüseyn Efendi 102, 104
Aḥmad al-Manṣūr, ruler of Morocco 8–9, 53, 80
Aḥmad ibn Ismāʿīl 108
Ajurrūmiyya 66, 79
Akhtarī, al- *see* Qaraḥiṣārī, Muṣṭafā ben Shamsaddīn al-, *al-Akhtarī*
Albert VII, archduke of Austria 13, 15, 21–22, 24, 30
Alcalá, Pedro de, *Vocabulista, Arte* 209, 212–14, 237–8, 242, 245, 247, 270
Aldobrandini, Ippolito *see* Clement VIII, pope
Alexander VII, pope 156
Alexander the Great 69
Alexandria, Church of *see* Copts
Allgemeine Deutsche Bibliographie 342
Allgemeine Literatur-Zeitung 374
Allgemeines historisches Magazin 356
Altdorf, academy of 22
    University of 303, 334, 401

Altenstein, Karl von 369
American Presbyterians 174, 183
ʿAmīra, Jirjis 100–101
    Syriac grammar 100
Andreas, Valerius 15
Andrewes, Lancelot, bishop of Chichester, Ely and Winchester 10, 13, 69–70, 74, 219, 221
Anfs Joahir tafsīr 298
Anglicans 127, 174
Angusse, Jacques the Elder 94, 99, 107–108
Angusse, Jacques the Younger 94, 108
Anne of Austria, regent of France 283
Antioch, Church of *see* Jacobites
Antonides, Johannes (Jan Theunisz) 12, 13, 81, 221, 250, 253
Antonio of Portugal, prior of Crato 9, 80
Antony, St 56, 149, 151, 155, 161–3, 169, 179
Apollonius of Perga, *Conica* 93, 137
Appian of Alexandria, *Des guerres des Romains* 48
Apremont, Louise d' 87
Arabian Nights 114, 118, 133, 208, 347, 410
Arabic alphabetical order 67–8, 243
Aramaic, Raphelengius and 260–1
Arcadian Library 48
Archange des Fossés 99
Archinto, Filippo 234
Arianism 354
Arias Montano, Benito 231–2, 259–62, 267
Aristophanes 369
Aristotle and Aristotelianism 140, 145, 355
Armenians 19, 85, 215
    Armenian College in Rome 6
    Armenian studies 313, 330–1, 399
    and eucharistic controversy 111, 115, 117–18, 120, 123, 126
Arminianism 138
Arminius, Jacobus 131
Arnald of Villanova 47
Arnauld, Antoine (*see also* Perpetuité de la foy de l'Eglise catholique touchant l'eucharistie, La)
    De la fréquente communion 112
    and Jansenism 111–114, 118–119, 120, 127

Arnauld, Simon, marquis de Pomponne 113
Arnold, Gottfried 352
   Unparteyische Kirchen- und Ketzer-Historie 335, 344–5
Arnold, Theodor, *Der Koran, oder insgemein so genannte Alcoran des Mohammeds* 328, 335–6, 3421–2, 347, 374
Arrivabene, Andrea 308
Arsāniyūs, bishop 182
Arukh see Nathan ben Jehiel
Aschhausen, Johann Gottfried von, bishop of Würzburg and Bamberg 22
Asquier, Michel d' and Barbatus 24–32
   interpreter and bibliophile 42–9
Assemani, Giuseppe Simonio (Yūsuf ibn Simʿān al-Simʿānī) 160–3
   Bibliotheca orientalis 39
Athanasius, St 151, 158
Aubertin, Edme 111
Augeri, Gaspard 95
Augusti, Johann Christian Wilhelm 368, 372, 374, 412
   Der kleine Koran 369–71, 411
   Exegetische Handbuch des alten Testaments 369
Augustine, St 111
Augustinian Order 127
Augustus, elector of Saxony 17
Averroes 266
   Tahāfut al-tahāfut 289
Avicenna 57, 266, 287, 356
   Qānūn 61, 63, 66–7, 75–6, 239, 243
Ayrton, Frederick 200

Bacon, Francis 145
Bacon, Roger 52
Baedeker, Karl 177
Baghawī, Abū Muḥammad al-Ḥusayn b. Masʿūd al-Farrāʾ al-, *Tafsīr Maʿālim al-tanzīl* 362–3, 372, 409
Bahrdt, Carl Friedrich 355
Baillet, Adrien 107
Bancroft, Richard archbishop of Canterbury 10, 13, 219
Bang, Thomas, *Coelum orientis* 36
Baradaeus, Jacob 35, 39

Barbarigo, Cardinal Gregorio 323, 396
Barbatus, Josephus background and education 3–6
   and Bedwell 8, 10, 12. 13, 18, 20, 31
   in England 10–13
   and Erpenius 9–10, 13, 14, 19, 31, 211
   in Germany and Austria 22–5
   Grammaticae arabicae compendium 18–20, 23–4, 36
   Historia Jacobitarum seu Coptorum 4, 32–40
   in Istanbul 26–32
   in Paris 8–10
   in Rome 6–8
   Speculum hebraicum 17–20
   in the Southern Netherlands 13–22
Barberini, Cardinal Antonio 154
Barberini, Cardinal Francesco 92–3, 272
Bar Hebraeus see Abū ʾl-Faraj
Barker, Oliver 184
Barnes, Joseph 11
Baronius, *De rebus sacris et ecclesiasticis exercitationes* 37, 50, 62, 74, 76, 85
Barrānī, ʿAlī Nidā al- 194, 200
Barthélemy, Antoine (Clot Bey) 195
Basel, Council of 205
Basil, St 117, 122
Bauer, Hofmeister 339
Baumgarten, Sigmund Jacob 352
Bayḍāwī, al- 294–5, 301, 322, 337, 375
   Anwār al-tanzīl wa asrār al-taʾwīl 291, 297, 300, 381, 386–7
Bayle, Pierre 355
Beaugé, Charles 181
Beck, Matthias Friedrich 304, 306–8, 310, 316–17, 327, 329
Becker, Carl Heinrich 184
Bedwell, Wiliam 31, 216–17, 231, 239, 243, 245–6
   and Arabic dictionary 206, 227–8
   and Arabic types 218–28
   and Barbatus 10–13, 18, 20, 31
   D. Iohannis Apostoli et Evangelistae Epistolae 12–13, 18, 221–4
   and Erpenius 8, 269
   in Leiden 218–21
   and *Officina Plantiniana* 20, 218–28
   and Pococke 294

INDEX

Bedwell, Mercy 227
Beger, Lorenz 314
Beiart, Willem 11–12
Bekker, Balthasar 140
Bellarmine, Robert 16
    Institutiones linguae hebraicae 18
Benoît de Dijon 154
Bentinck, Hans Willem, earl of Portland 131
Bentinck, Hendrik 131
Bentley, Richard 320
Berg, Patricia 191, 201
Bernard de Paris, *Vocabolario italiano-turchesco* 109
Bernard, Edward 308
Bernd, Adam 330
Beuningen, Gerard van 243
Bevilacqua, Alexander 335, 404–5
Beyerlinck, Laurentius 18
Bible
    Acts 240–1, 258, 261, 377
    Alexandrian Vulgate 79
    Antwerp Polyglot 77, 212, 226, 232, 259–60, 262, 265, 277, 398
    Arabic Gospels 58, 60, 66, 75, 79
    Colossians 13
    Complutensian Polyglot 261, 398
    1–2 Corinthians 240
    Daniel 288
    Epistles 258, 261, 377
    2 Esdras 288
    Galatians 77, 379
    Genesis 391
    Job 207, 356
    John 65, 379
    1–3 John 12–13, 18, 218–19, 221, 223–4, 379
    Judges 307
    London Polyglot 207, 391, 398
    Mark 241, 256
    Matthew 57, 70, 79, 224, 241, 256, 288
    New Testament 75, 82, 85, 219, 240–2, 246, 291, 318, 334, 351, 389
    Obadiah 313, 330–1
    Old Testament 207, 236, 246, 351
    Paris Polyglot 95, 207, 274, 293, 398
    Pentateuch 257, 263
    Peshitta 78, 95
    Philemon 13, 85
    Philippians 64, 379
    Psalms 20, 32, 65, 67, 237, 264–5, 334, 377, 379
    Revelation 288
    Romans 355
    Samaritan Pentateuch 95, 212, 236–7
    Septuagint 79
    Titus 12–13
    Vulgate 79, 261
Bibliander, Theodore, *De ratione communi omnium linguarum et literarum commentarius* 67–8
    edition of Qur'an 212, 235, 278, 283, 308, 328, 341, 378, 380, 385, 397, 409
Biblioteca Ambrosiana, Milan 296
Biblioteca Angelica, Rome 234
Bichler, Kasper 25
Bidwell, Robin 191
Bignon family 118
Bignon, Jean-Paul 166–7
Bill, John 74
Birgili Mehmed Efendi, *Vasīyet-nāme* 317, 332
Bochart, Samuel, *Geographia sacra* 356
    Hierozoicon 356
Bodeghem, Jan van 238
Bodleian Library 33–4, 144, 360
Bodley, Thomas 10, 11, 24
Boileau, Nicolas 119
Boisschot, Ferdinand de 13
Bomberg, Daniel 261
Bomberg, Daniel the Younger 261
Bonavia, Sante 280
Bonjour, Guillaume 127
Bonn, University of 374
Bonomi, Joseph 171
Borromeo, Cardinal Federigo 214, 270
Bossuet, Jacques Bénigne 119
Bostanci Cafer Paşa 103
Botley, Paul 377
Bouchard, Jean-Jacques 93–4, 101, 109
Bougerel, Jacques 87
Boulainvilliers, Henri de 360
Bouthillier, Claude 97
Bouthillier, Nicolas 113
Bouwmeester, Johannes 137, 146
Boyer, Paul, *Dictionaire, servant de bibliothèque universelle* 47
Boyle, Robert 140, 145

Boysen, Friedrich Eberhard (cont.)
Boysen, Friedrich Eberhard   337, 368, 370, 392
  Der Koran, oder Das Gesetz für die Muselmänner   356–65, 366, 409, 412
  early interest in Qur'an   350–1
  education and career   348–56
  Eigene Lebensbeschreibung   348
  and Gleim   348, 350–1, 357–60, 405–6
  Kritische Erleuterungen des Grundtextes des heiligen Schriften Altes Testaments   351
  Kritische Erleuterungen des Grundtextes des heiligen Schriften NeuesTestaments   351
  and Marracci   351, 358, 360, 362, 405–6, 409
  Ritualia quaedam codicis sacri ex Alcorano illustrans   350
  Sammlung einiger geistreicher Liede   357
  and Semler   351–5
  Wahl's edition of his Qur'an translation   371–2, 374–5
Brabant, States of   15, 16
Brattuti, Vincenzo   30, 45
Bremen   319
Brerewood, Edward   38
  Enquiries   120
Breslau   313–14, 330, 333, 398
Brest-Litovsk , Synod of   28, 120
Brevis orthodoxae fidei professio   84–5
Britannicus   75
British Library   64
British Museum   64, 196
Brucker, Jacob   345
Bruyn, Johannes de   139
Bukhārī, al-, *Ṣaḥīḥ*   289, 294
Burckhardt, Johann Ludwig   191, 196
  Notes on the Bedouin and Wahaby   199
Burley, Francis   13
Burman, Frans the Elder   139, 140, 144, 146
Burman, Frans the Younger   144, 146, 391
Burman, Pieter   144, 146
Burman, Thomas   59–60
Burnett, Thomas   319
Burton, Decimus   170
Burton, James   169–71, 176
Burun   172

Buṭrus Ghālī Pasha   182
Buxtorf, Johannes the Elder   62
  Institutio epistolaris hebraica   18
Buxtorf, Johannes the Younger   339
Byzantine Institute of America in Washington, D.C.   184

Callenberg, Johann Heinrich   334–5, 350, 359
Cambridge University   10, 11, 225, 227–8, 320, 388
Cambridge University Library   228, 253
Cambulat Mustafa Paşa   96, 98
Camden, William   69
Canini, Angelo, *De locis Hebraicis*   17
Capuchins   296–7
Caracciolini (Clerks Regular Minor or Adorno Fathers)   383
Carl August, duke of Sachsen-Weimar   347
Carpzov, Friedrich Benedict   312
Carpzov, Johann Gottlob   351
Cartesians (*see also* Descartes, René)   131
  at Utrecht   137–148
Casanova, Giambattista   115
Casaubon, Isaac and Arabic studies   8, 9, 20, 50–8
  and Adriaen Willemsz   56–63, 66, 73, 79, 81, 82
  and Arabic proverbs   20, 60–61, 77, 80–3
  and Barbatus   8, 9, 70–71, 80, 81
  and Bedwell   69–70, 74, 86, 219, 221
  De libertate ecclesiastica   85
  De rebus sacris   76
  De satyrica Graecorum poesi   76
  edition of Persius, *Satirarum liber*   76
  and Erpenius   62–3, 71–4, 80–84, 86, 224, 247–8, 250–1, 379
  Historiae Augustae scriptores   56, 75–7
  and Mozarabic Latin-Arabic lexicon   77–8
  and Qur'an   59–60, 73, 83–4
  and Scaliger   54–63, 67–8, 71, 77–8, 80–81, 84, 86
Caspari, Karl Paul   211
Cassien de Nantes   254
Castell, Edmund   308
  Lexicon Heptaglotton   206–7, 228, 388
Castrodardo, Giovanni Battista   308, 328

INDEX 419

Cattenburg, Adriaan van 355
Césy, Philippe Harlay, comte de 87, 97–9, 101, 103, 105–107, 109
Chabert, Thomas von 49
Chalcedon, Council of 5, 85, 151, 154, 158
Chappelow, Leonard, *Rudimenta* 308
Chardin, Jean 125
    Voyages en Perse 125–6, 357
Charles II, king of England 125
Charles IV, duke of Lorraine 88
Charles V, Holy Roman Emperor 234, 296
Châtillon, Philiberte de 87–8
Chaunu, Pierre 301
Chester, Greville 173
Christensen, Lauge 69
Christmann, Jacob 70, 86
    Alphabetum arabicum 64–5, 210, 377–9
Chronique de Flandres 47
Chrysostom 117, 122
Cicero 130
Clarke, John 227–8
Clarke, Samuel 344
Claude, Jean and eucharistic controversy 112–116, 120, 122
Clenardus, Nicolaus 209–10, 235
Clement VIII, pope 6, 7, 70
Clement XI, pope 160
Clerks Regular Minor *see* Caracciolini
Clodius, Johann Christian 350, 391
Clot Bey *see* Barthélemy, Antoine
Clusius, Carolus 240, 246
    Exoticarum Libri decem 218
Coccejus, Johannes 138
Coislin, Armand du Cambout, duc de 279
Colbert, Jean Baptiste 38, 47, 114, 127, 216
Collège de la Sainte Famille, Cairo 180
Collège de Louis-le-Grand, Paris 216
College of Fort William, Calcutta 216
Collège Royal 8, 15, 53–4, 71, 274
Collegie der sçavanten 139
Collegio della Sapienza 383
Congregatio de Propaganda Fide see Propaganda Fide
Constantinople, Church of *see* Greek Orthodox
Constantinople, Council of 85
Contares, Cyril 29
Copernicus 138

Coppin, Jean 154–7
    Le Bouclier de l'Europe 156–7
Coptic Museum in Cairo 189
Copts (*see also* St Antony, Monastery of, St Paul, Monastery of) 3–7, 33, 36, 149, 151–215, 292, 296
    Coptic language 4
    Coptic studies 33–4, 36, 85, 160
    and eucharistic controversy 116–117, 119, 124
    and western missions 154–5
Cotta, Johann Friedrich von 374
Covel, John, *Some Account of the Present Greek Church* 122–4, 126
Crell, Oswald 355
Cromer, Evelyn Baring, 1st Earl of 182
Cruciador, Armenian patriarch of Sis 116
Cudworth, Ralph 308
Cuperus, Gijsbertus 333
Cusa, Nicholas of 290, 308
Cyril of Alexandria, St 123, 158
Cyril IV, patriarch of Alexandria 174
Cyril V, patriarch of Alexandria 182

Dadichi, Theocharis 334–5
Damāmīnī Badraddīn, al- 383
Danz, Johann Andreas 304, 308–10, 316, 323, 327, 329
Dayr al-Suryān 158
Della Valle, Pietro 34, 322
Denys the Carthusian 284
De' Pomi, David, *Dittionario novo hebraico* 66
Descartes, René (*see also* Cartesians) 131, 134, 402
    admirers in Holland 137–8, 140, 143, 145
    Discours de la méthode 148
    and Marcheville 93, 107, 109
dévots 88–9, 94
De Wette, Wilhelm Martin Leberecht 369
Di'b, Buṭrus 274
Dietrichstein, Cardinal Franz von 26, 29
Dieu, Louis de 388
Digby, Kenelm 145
Dioscorides 57
Dioscorus, patriarch of Alexandria 154–5, 157
Dobelo, Marco (Murqus al-Duʿābilī al-Kurdī) 74

Dolce far niente in Arabia. George August Wallin and his Travels in the 1840s 201
Dombay, Franz von 49
Domenicus Germanus of Silesia, *Fabrica Linguae Arabicae (Dizionario italiano-arabo)* 272–3, 277, 279
Domey, Olaus 336–7, 407
Dositheos II, patriarch of Jerusalem 117, 127
Dousa, Georgius, *De itinere suo Constantinopolitano* 218
Dozy, R.P.A., *Supplément aux dictionnaires arabes* 214, 247–8
Dresseler, Hans 239
Drusius, Johannes 262
  Apophtegmata Ebraeorum ac Arabum 82–3
Drusius, Johannes, abbot of Parc 15, 21
Du Bellay, Martin, *Mémoires* 48
Dubernat, Guillaume 166
Dunlop Gibson, Margaret 182–3
Du Perron, Cardinal Jacques 70, 85
Dupuy, Christophe 70
Dupuy, Jacques 89, 103
Durand, David, *Eclaircissemens sur la religion mahométane* 278, 410
Du Ryer, André careeer and achievements 94
  L'Alcoran de Mahomet 94, 278–9, 283, 297–8, 305, 311, 322–3, 328, 337, 340, 358, 368, 390–1, 409–11
  and Marcheville 94–5, 99, 100, 107–109, 297–9
  Rudimenta grammatices linguae turcicae 94, 297
  Turkish-Latin dictionary 99, 297
Dustūr al-lugha 270
Dutch States General 14
Duval, Pierre 278
Duvergier de Hauranne, Jean Ambroise *see* Saint-Cyran, Jean Duvergier de Hauranne, abbé de
Dūwayhī family 100

East India Company 198
Ecchellensis, Abraham (Ibrāhīm al-Ḥāqilānī) 119, 293, 296, 322
  Nomenclator arabico-latinus 269–80

Ecole spéciale des langues orientales vivantes 216
Egidio da Viterbo, Cardinal 59, 234
Egyptian Geographical Society in Cairo 177
Eichhorn, Johann Gottfried, *Monumenta antiquissimae historiae Arabum* 346–7, 374
Eidyllia in obitum fulgentissimi Henrici Walliae Principis 11
Elia, Jesuit 161
Elichman, Johannes 108
Elizabeth I, queen of England 80
Ellis, John 36
Elmarsafy, Ziad 409
Elmgren, Sven Gabriel 191
Elzevier 251, 264
Eneman, Michael 133
Engels, Engelbrecht 245
Epitome Alcorani 84
Erasmus 86, 235
Erlangen, University of 376
Ernst I, duke of Saxe-Gotha 38, 125–6
Erpenius, Thomas 8, 14, 20, 24, 129, 302, 316, 344, 379–402
  Arabic New Testament 241
  and Barbatus 9–10, 13, 18, 27, 31, 251, 291–3, 392
  and Bedwell 10, 214, 219, 251
  and Casaubon 62–3, 71–4, 80–84, 86, 250–2, 379–82
  Grammatica arabica 211, 221, 251, 269, 308, 379, 382, 386, 388–90
  and al-Ḥajarī 10, 251
  Historia Iosephi Patriarchae 379–80
  and proverbs 60, 80–2, 273
  and Qur'an 283
  and Raphelengius dictionary 213, 229, 244–5, 251–4, 269–70
  Rudimenta Linguae Arabicae 382
  and Scaliger 9, 62–3, 211, 251, 291
Escher, Johann Heinrich 327
Escorial 296
Essenius, Andreas 138
Esterházy, Miklós 30, 45
Ethiopia, exploration of 152–3
Ethiopians 33, 38

INDEX 421

Ethiopians and eucharistic controversy 119, 125
Ethiopic language 18, 38, 85, 356
missions to 157
and Prester John 152
eucharistic controversy 111–128
Euchologium Sinaiticum 175
Euclid, *Elements* 66, 239
Eugenius IV, pope 5
Euripides 369
Eutyches 157
Evangelicals 174

Fabricius, Johann 344
Fazil Ahmet Pasha Köprülü 47
Fell, John, bishop of Oxford 33–4, 36
Ferdinand I, grand duke of Tuscany (Cardinal Ferdinando de' Medici) 58
Ferdinand II, Holy Roman Emperor 24, 26, 28, 30, 32, 45
Ferdinand II, grand duke of Tuscany 271
Ferdinand III, Holy Roman Emperor 32, 45
Ferdinandus, Philippus 56
Ferrier, Jean 93
Fieschi, Sinibaldo 114
Fīrūzābādī, al-, *Qāmūs* 214, 253–4, 269–71, 275, 383
Flavigny, Valérien de 113
Flaxman, John 171
Fleischer, Heinrich Leberecht 198–200, 374–6, 411–12
Fleuriau d'Armenonville, Thomas Charles 166
Florence, Council of 5, 85, 152, 205
Flügel, Gustav Leberecht 376
Frähn, Christian Martin Joachim 199
Francius, Petrus 129–30
Francke, August Hermann 37, 338
François I, king of France 88, 215, 288
Franeker, University of 391, 403
Frankfurter gelehrte Anzeigen 343
Frederick I, duke of Sachsen-Gotha-Altenberg 308
Frederick III, elector of Brandenburg 314
Frederick V, elector palatine 13
Frederick Augustus III, king of Saxony 185
Frederick Henry of Nassau, prince of Orange 107

Freiburg, University of 185
Frey, Johann Ludwig 340
Freytag, Georg Wilhelm 214, 372
Fribourg, University of 185
Frischmuth, Johann 306
Froriep, Justus Friederich 337
Fugger, Count Johann the Younger 23
Fugger, Johann Jakob 23
Fugger, Markus 23
Furati, Mevlana, *Kirk su'āl* 317, 331–2

Gabriel VIII, patriarch of Alexandria 6, 70
Gabriel, Juan (Johannes Gabriel Terrolensis) 59–60
Gagnier, Jean 301, 360–1, 370
Galen 266
De clysteribus et colica liber 266
Galilei, Galileo 91, 109
Galland, Antoine 208, 388, 400 (see also *Arabian Nights*)
and Jansenists 113–118, 127
and Qur'an 333–4, 388
and Reland 133
Gallaup, François, sieur de Chasteuil 95–6, 99, 100–101, 107
Garbe, Johann Gottlieb 339
Garcin de Tassy, Joseph-Héliodore 128
Garden of Eden 132
Gaspar, head of Armenian Church in Cairo 115
Gassendi, Pierre 140, 145
and Marcheville 87, 90–91, 93–4, 99–100, 103
Gaulmin, Gilbert 272
Gebauer 359–60
Geiger, Abraham 372
Geitlin, Gabriel 193–4, 196
Gennadius I, patriarch of Constantinople 119
Gentius, Georgius 31
George, king of Saxony 185
Georgians and eucharistic controversy 115, 125–6
Gerard of Cremona 206
Gerhard, Johann Ernst 37
Ghazālī, al- 362
Gibbon, Edward, *Decline and Fall of the Roman Empire* 36, 135–6, 138, 152, 361

Giggei, Antonio   214, 227, 254, 270–3, 278–9
Gilles de Loches   154
Giustiniani, Agostino, *Psalterium*   67, 237
Giustiniani, Stefano   98
Glazemaker, Jan Hendriksz   137, 305, 328
Gleim, Johann Wilhelm Ludwig and Boysen
    348, 350–1, 357–60, 405–6
    Halladat oder das Rothe Buch   357–8
    Preussische Kriegslieder   357
Goes, Damião de   120
Goethe, Johann Wolfgang von Goethe   343,
    346, 405
    Mahomets Gesang   347
    West-östlicher Divan   374
Goldziher, Ignaz   365, 412
Golius, Jacobus   31, 33, 129, 198, 208, 283,
    291–4, 316, 318–19, 325, 326, 344, 384–5,
    392–3
    Arabicae linguae tyrocinium   386–8
    and Descartes   93
    and Gassendi   90–1, 100, 109
    Lexicon Arabico-Latinum   214, 254, 271–2,
        279, 308, 356, 366
    and Qur'an   283, 386–8, 392–3
Golius, Pieter   31
Gonzague, Charles, duc de Nevers   89,
    296–7
Göttingen, University of   336, 347, 388, 407
Gournay, Regnaut de   87
Graevius, Johann Georg   146
    his Cartesianism   139–40
    and Reland   130, 142
    and Sike   143–4, 319
Grafton, Anthony   59
Granger, Claude (Claude Tourtechot)
    166–74
Greaves, John   31–2, 226–7
Greek College in Rome   6, 296
Greek Orthodox Church   28, 174
    attitudes to Calvinism and Catholicism
        103–104
    and eucharistic controversy   111, 120–22,
        124–7
Gregoriis, Jacob de   313, 330
Gregorius, Abba   125
Gregory of Nyssa   50, 77
Gregory XIII, pope   3, 6, 160, 215, 296
Gregory XV, pope   153, 205, 382–3
Greiffenklau von Vollrats, Alexander   30–31

Griesbach, Johann Jakob   369
Gronovius, Johann Friederich   132
Grotius, Hugo   73, 140, 221, 239, 294
    De veritate religionis christianae   294
    Syntagma Arateorum   218
Guadagnoli, Filippo   344, 393
    Apologia pro christiana religione   383
    Breves Arabicae linguae institutiones   383
Guevara, Antonio de, *Reloj de principes*   48
    Histoire de Marc Aurel   48
Guez de Balzac, Jean-Louis, *Le Prince*   99
Guy de Perpignana (Guido Terrena), *Summa
    de haeresibus*   120

Hackspan, Theodor   327
    Fides et leges Mohammaedis   309
Hafiz   374
Haga, Cornelis   31, 102–104
Häggman, Sofia   201
Hagop IV, Armenian catholicos   117
Ḥajarī, Aḥmad ibn Qāsim al-   10, 53, 73, 81,
    211, 269
Halberstadt   348, 356
Ḥalīmī   108
Halle, University of   338, 348, 350–2,
    359–60, 362, 371, 391
Halma, François   143
Hamati, Natan   266
Hamdānī, al-   300, 322, 329
Hämeen-Antilla, Jaakko   201
Hammer-Purgstall, Josef von   49, 372–4, 376
    Fundgruben des Orients   373
    Qur'an translations   373–4, 411–12
Hammond, Henry   355
Hand-book for Travellers in Egypt   see
    Murray's Guide to Egypt
Happel, Everhard Werner, *Thesaurus
    Exoticorum*   305–6
Harderwijk, University of, Reland teaches at
    131–2, 140, 145
Ḥarīrī, al-   391
Harvey, William   145
Ḥasanī, al-, *al-Durra 'l-naḥwiyya*   57, 81
Hasevelt, Daniel van   13
Hasevelt, Maria van   13
Havercamp, Sigebert   39
Hay, Robert   171
Hebrew studies   206–7, 213, 393
    Barbatus and   15–20, 23–4

Raphelengius and   236–7, 259–68
Reland and   129–31
Heinsius, Daniel   73, 221, 242, 255, 264, 283
Helmstedt, University of   335, 391, 403
Helsinki, University of   193, 198, 200
Henning, Henningius   327
　　Bi-smi llahi. Muhammedanus precans   360
Henri II, duke of Lorraine   88
Henri III, king of France   53
Henri IV, king of France   53
Henry VI, king of England   265
Henry, prince of Wales   11–12
Hepburn, James   9, 80
Herbelot, Barthélemi d', *Bibliothèque orientale*   127, 344–5
Herder, Caroline   347
Herder, Johann Gottfried   346–7, 368–9
Hermann of Carinthia   206
Hermes Trismegistus   50
Herrnhuters   355
Herwarth zu Hohenburg, Johann Georg   22–4
Hesronita, Joannes (Yūḥannā al-Ḥaṣrūnī)   3, 75
Heydanus, Abraham   139
Heyman, Johannes   261
Hezel, Johann Wilhelm Friedrich von, *Erleichterte arabische Grammatik*   392–3
hijā' order   *see* Arabic alphabetical order
Hinckelmann, Abraham   304, 312, 323, 329
　　Al-Coranus   295, 310–11, 316, 318, 328, 335, 343, 356, 358–9, 367, 376, 405
Hippocrates   266
Hirt, Johann Friedrich   341–2, 359, 363–4
　　Orientalische und exegetische Bibliothek   341
Holste, Jacob Christof Wilhelm, *Dissertatio inauguralis de prima Alcorani sura*   327
Holstenius, Lucas, and Marcheville   90, 92–3, 109, 272
Homer   90, 357, 375
Hooght, Everard van der   130, 140
Höpfner, Johann Georg Christian   369
Hottinger, Johann Heinrich   38
　　Bibliotheca orientalis   356
　　Historia orientalis   293–4, 296, 300, 308, 356
　　Promtuarium   293

Houtman, Cornelis de   243
Hubert, Etienne   248
　　and Barbatus   8
　　and Casaubon   53, 56–7, 62, 70, 73–4, 81, 86
Humphrey, duke of Gloucester   265
Ḥunayn ben Isḥāq   266
Huntingdon, George Hastings, 8th earl of   144, 320
Huntington, Robert   33
Hurault de Boistailler, Jean   266
Hurtado de Mendoza, Diego   296
Husrev Paşa   102
Hutter, Elias   17

Ibn Abī Zamanīn   313
Ibn 'Arabshāh   356
Ibn al-Athīr   293
Ibn 'Aṭīya   286, 289
Ibn Bābashādh, *al-Muqaddima al-kāfiya al-muḥsiba fi'l- naḥw*   233–4, 257
Ibn Ezra, Abraham   236, 263
Ibn al-Fāriḍ   198
Ibn Fāris, *Mujmal*   252, 269
Ibn al-Ḥājib, *Kāfiyya*   210, 239
Ibn Kathīr   313
Ibn Khallikān   294–5
Ibn Qutayba   346
Ibn Taymiyyah   301, 322, 329
Ibn al-Tufail, *Hayy ben Yaqdhân*   137, 146
Ibn Zuhayr   356
Ibrāhīm Pasha   172
Idrīsī, al-, *Kitāb nuzhat al- mushtāq*   59, 66, 75–6, 79–80, 84, 239
Illustrated London News   185
Imrū' al-Qays   144
Innocent XI, pope   135, 147, 299–300, 303, 305, 328, 396
interpreters' schools   42, 48–9, 199, 215, 372–3
Isabella, archduchess of Austria   13
Isfarā'īnī, al-   386
Isma'il, khedive of Egypt   176
Istanbul, Barbatus in   26–32, 35
　　Covel, Smith and Rycaut in   122–4
　　Marcheville in   97–109
　　Nointel and Galland in   113–118

Jacob, Hebrew patriarch 35
Jacobi, Johann Balthasar, *Dissertatio historica de secta Jacobitarum* 36
Jacobite term 151
Jacobites (Church of Antioch) 5, 175, 215, 294, 296
  and eucharistic controversy 119
Jacobites (English) 36
James I, king of England 11, 13
James of Vitry 286
James, Thomas 11
Jannābī, al- 360
Jansenists 107
  and eucharistic controversy 111–20
  French Arabists and 127–128
Jawharī, al-, *Ṣiḥāḥ* 252–4, 269–71, 275, 366
Jena, University of 37, 368–9, 374, 393
Jenisch, Bernhard von 48
Jerome, St, *Life of Paul* 149, 155, 162–3, 167, 189
Jesuits 296–7
  and Copts 153, 157–66, 180
  and Jansenists 111–112, 114
Jībriyān ibn ʿĪsā ibn Abī Ḥujāj 232
Johann Georg I, elector of Saxony 89
Johann Georg Herzog zu Sachsen 185–90
Johann Schweikhard von Kronberg, elector of Mainz 89
John XVI, patriarch of Alexandria 161
John XVII, patriarch of Alexandria 163, 174
John XIX, patriarch of Alexandria 186
John of Damascus 285
John of Segovia 209
John of Seville 206
John of Sturrey 265
Joinville, *Histoire et chronique du ... roy Saint Louis* 48
Jones, William 208
  Dissertation sur la litérature orientale 346
  Poeseos asiaticae commentariorum libri sex 347
Josa, Don Bernardo de 236
Journal des Savants 36
Journal of the Royal Geographical Society 170, 191
Juan Andrés 284, 286, 289
Jullien, Michel 179–81
Junius, Franciscus 240–1

Junius, Franciscus the Younger 33
Justel, Henri 304

Kāfiyya see Ibn al-Ḥājib
Kahlenberg, battle of the 304, 308
Kalonymos ben Kalonymos 266
Kandy, Shahin 318
Kant, Immanuel 356
Kara Mustafa Pasha 307
Karl Wilhelm Ferdinand, crown prince of Braunschweig and Lüneburg 359
Kāshifī, Ḥusain Wāʿiẓ 386–7
Kazazian, Armenian photographer 184–5
Kehr, Georg Jacob 333, 335, 388, 400
Kepler, Johann 24, 91, 109, 145
Khalil Pasha 14
Kiachef, Yūsuf 172
Kiel, University of 384
Kiliaan, Cornelis 262
Kimhi, David 236, 260, 263
King, John bishop of London 10
Kircher, Athanasius 34, 37–8, 46–7, 85, 313
  Prodromus coptus sive aegyptiacus 153
Kirsten, Peter 56–7, 63, 70, 81, 86, 327, 377, 379–80
Kisaʾī, al- 294
Kitāb al-amthāl seu Proverbiorum arabicorum centuriae duae (*see also* proverbs) 60, 81–2, 273
Klemm, Johann Christian 338
Klopstock, Friedrich Gottlieb, *Messias* 345–6
Koch, doctor 172
Köhler, Johann Bernhard 342–3, 365–6
Korrat, Luigi 180
Kosegarten, Johann Gottfried Ludwig 374
Kuefstein, Hans Ludwig von 25, 28
Kurz von Senftenau, Johann Jakob 26–9
Küster, Ludolf 143–4, 319

La Bruyère, Jean de 119
La Canaye de Fresnes, Philippe de 52
Lakemacher, Johann Gottfried 335, 340, 348, 350, 403
  Elementa linguae arabicae 335, 391
Lambeck, Peter 32, 36
Lamsveld, Willem 146
Lane, Edward William 191, 195, 200, 214

INDEX 425

Lane Poole, Sophia   195
Lange, Johann, *Vollständiges Türckisches Gesetz-Buch, oder des Ertz-betriegers Mahomets Alkoran*   305–6, 323, 328, 334, 401
Langenmantel, August   306
Lannoy, Ghillebert de   152
Lapi, interpreter   172
Laud, William, archbishop of Canterbury   31–2
Le Bé, Guillaume   50, 69, 73–4, 219
Le Clerc, Jean   86
Leclerc du Tremblay, Joseph (Père Joseph)   89, 296–7
Lect, Jacques   53
Lederlin, Johann Heinrich   340
Lefèvre de la Boderie, Guy   77, 232, 259–61
    D. Severi Alexandrini ... de ritibus   261
Lefèvre de la Boderie, Nicolas   259
Leibniz, Gottfried Wilhelm   86, 156
    and Qur'an translations   303–4, 306–8, 313–14, 319–20, 323, 329–31
    and Sike   141–3, 319–20, 398
Leiden University   12–14, 30–31, 73, 93, 131, 208, 215, 238, 246, 250, 253, 255–6, 269–71, 319, 366, 371
Leipzig, University of   17, 38, 334–5, 337, 366, 369, 388
Le Jay, Guy Michel   274
Le Mire, Aubert   91
Leo Africanus   234
    De totius Africae descriptione, Descrittione dell'Africa   83–4
Leo X, pope   59, 84, 234
Leopold I, Holy Roman Emperor   32, 45–6, 305–7, 328
Leopold V, archduke of Further Austria   89
Lepanto, battle of   236, 238, 242, 256, 296
Le Pois, Antoine, *Discours sur les medalles [sic] et graveures antiques*   47
Lepsius, Karl Richard   171, 196
Lessing, Gotthold Ephraim   345, 357
Leuker, Esaias   22
Leunclavius, Johannes, *Annales Sultanorum Othmanidarum*   248
Leusden, Johan   131, 138
Levant Company in Aleppo   31, 294
Leydekker, Melchior   131, 138, 142, 146

libertins érudits   88–9
Lieftinck, G.I.   264–5
Ligue   88
Limborch, Philipp van   355
Lincoln College, Oxford   33
Lingelsheim, Georg Michael   70, 76
Lipsius, Justus   15, 240, 246
L'Isle, Arnoult de   8, 53
Livy   46
Llull, Raymond   215, 290
Locke, John   355
    Some Thoughts concerning Education   312
Lodvel, Philip   121
Louis XIII, king of France   60, 888, 94, 96–7, 99, 102–103
Louis XIV, king of France   47, 116, 125–6, 154, 216, 305
Louvain, University of, Barbatus teaches at   3, 15–20, 22
Louvois, François Michel Le Tellier, marquis de   154
Lowth, Robert   346
Lubitsch, Petrus   25
Lucaris, Cyril, patriarch of Constantinople   28, 32, 103–104, 120–22, 124
Lucretius   146
Lüdeke, Christoph Wilhelm, *Beschreibung des Türkischen Reichs*   359
Ludolf, Hiob   37–8, 125, 129, 319–20, 340
Ludovici, Christian   334
Ludwig, Michael Conrad   334
Luillier, François   90, 94, 99–100
Luis, Infant of Portugal, duke of Beja   80
Luqmān   382, 387
Lustrier von Liebenstein, Sebastian   26–7, 29, 44
Luther, Martin   287, 305, 315, 390, 397
Lutherans and Copts   37–9, 174
    and Qur'an   303–24
Luyts, Johannes   131, 138

Maastricht, Pieter van   138, 146
Macpherson, James   346
Macready, William Charles   197
Madame Tussaud's   197
Maderus, Johann Melchior   21
Maes, Engelbert   15

Magdeburg 348, 351, 355
Magliabechi, Antonio 303–4, 306, 319, 327, 397
Maḥallī, Jalāl al-Dīn al- *see Tafsīr al-Jalālayn*
Maḥbūbī, Burhānaddīn Ṣadr al-Sharī'a al-Auwal al-, *Wiqāyat al-riwāya fī masā'il al-hidāya* 235–6, 256
Mahzor 267
Maimonides, *More Nevukhim* 66, 69, 243, 266, 339
Majdaddīn 295
Makīn, al- 113, 294
  al-Majmuʿ al-mubārak 291–2, 344
Malebranche, Nicole 140
Mansfelt, Regnerus van 139
Maqāṣid 108
Maqrīzī, al- 292
Marcel, Jean-Joseph, *Exercices de lecture d'arabe littéral* 393
Marchety, François 99, 107
Marcheville, Henri de Gournay, Comte de 137
  achievements of embassy 107–109
  appointed French ambassador in Istanbul 89
  and Descartes 93, 107, 109
  and Du Ryer 94, 99–100, 107, 297
  family and early career 87–9
  instructions and behaviour as ambassador in Istanbul 96–106
  later life 106–107
  and Peiresc 89–90, 92–6, 99–103, 106–109
  plans to recruit leading European scholars 89–96
Marco de Toledo 284, 298
Marghīnānī, al- 236
Marmont, Marshal Auguste-Frédéric-Louis Visse de , duc de Raguse 171–3
Maronite College in Rome 3, 7, 39, 100, 160, 215, 247, 271, 275
Maronites 3, 60, 84–5, 100–101, 160, 215, 217, 271, 296, 301
Marracci, Ludovico 135, 217, 271, 278, 294, 299–302, 310, 323–4, 372
  and Acoluthus 314–18, 331–333, 398–401, 412–13
  Alcorani textus universus 284, 299, 301, 308, 312–13, 328, 334–7, 340, 343, 347, 351, 356, 358–9, 367 , 381, 384, 390–3, 395–413
  and Boysen 362–3, 365, 405–6
  and Fleischer 374
  in Low Countries 403–4
  and Michaelis 406–8
  and Nerreter 400–401
  Prodromus 295, 300, 303–4, 307, 322, 329, 358, 396–7
  and Reiske 367–8, 408–9
  and Reland 147–8, 402–3
  and Rückert 376
  and Sale 335, 404–5
Marshall, Thomas 33–4
Martelotto, Francesco, *Institutiones linguae arabicae* 383
Martin, James (Jacobus Aretius) 11
Martin, Jean 8, 53–4
Martin, John 171
Masius, Andreas 77, 232–5, 238, 241, 249, 257, 259, 261, 265
Massimo, Camillo 322
Matthew IV, patriarch of Alexandria 115, 126
Matthew of Paris 286
Matthias I, Holy Roman Emperor 21, 24–5, 43, 45
Maurepas, Pontchartrain, Jean-Frédéric Phélypeaux de, comte de 166–7
Maurice of Nassau, prince of Orange, stadhouder 54, 243
Maximilian I, duke of Bavaria 22–3, 30, 89
Maximilian, duke of Saxony 185
Mazarin, Cardinal 272
Mecca 277, 336
  Wallin visits 196
Megerlin, David Friedrich 337–43, 363, 368, 392
  Bedenkliche Lehren 339
  Catalogus edendorum XX. scriptorum philologico-critico-theologicorum 338
  Die türkische Bibel 339–43, 347, 360, 366, 372, 374, 409, 412
  education and career 337–9
  Hexas orientalium collegiorum philologicorum 338
  Tractatus de scriptis et collegiis orientalibus 338
  translates Qur'an 339–42

INDEX 427

Vertheidigung der Protestantischen Religion   339
Meier, Gerhard   141–3, 319–21
Meijer, Lodewijk   354
Melanchthon, Philip   305, 354, 397
Melkites   3, 215
Mémoires d'Olivier de la Marche   47
Mendelssohn, Moses   356
Mercati, Michele, *Degli obelischi di Roma*   47
Merchant Adventurers, Company of   33
Mercier, Jean   259
Mersenne, Marin   93
Mesgnien-Meninski, Franz von   26, 45–6, 48, 313, 317, 332, 399
    Thesaurus linguarum orientalium   46
Meursius, Johannes   221
Meyer, Ludwig   146
Michaelis, Christian Benedikt   348, 350–2, 356, 359
Michaelis, Johann David   336, 346–8, 352, 374, 388–9
    and Boysen   348, 350, 356–9, 362–5
    Beurtheilung der Mittel   356–7
    and *tafsīr*   364–5, 368, 406–8
    Orientalische und exegetische Bibiothek   358
Michaelis, Johann Heinrich   338
Minuti, Théophile   95–6, 100–101, 109
Mirqāt al-lugha   249, 253, 270
Mirza Ismail   193
Moghila, Petrus, *Orthodoxa Confessio Fidei*   121
Molanus, Gerhard Wolter   314
Molinism   111
Molino, Giovanni, *Dittionario della lingua italiana-turchesca*   109
Molinos, Miguel de   300, 323
Moravian Brethren   174
Morcos, Antūn   180
More, Henry   308
More, Thomas   265
Moretus, Jan   240
Moretus, Balthasar   18, 20, 225–6, 249
Mortiz, Bernhard   183–4
Moses of Mardin   3
Mosheim, Johann Lorenz von   8, 355
Motto, Balthasar   105–106

Mozarabic 'Latin-Arabic glossary of the Leiden University Library'   211–12, 232–3, 242, 245, 247, 257
    and Casaubon   77–8
    and Raphelengius   77
    and Scaliger   77–8
Muʿallaqāt   144
Müezzinzade Hafiz Ahmed Paşa grand vizir   99, 102, 104
Mughrib   see Muṭarrizī, al-
Muḥammad ʿAlī   169, 171–2, 195
Muḥammad, Prophet   135, 138, 142, 147, 285–6, 288, 291, 315, 336, 341, 345, 347, 352, 357, 360–1, 364, 370, 407, 410
Muḥammad al-Burtuqalī, ruler of Morocco   84
Mujmal   see Ibn Fāris
Munnicks, Johannes   139
Münster, Sebastian, *Lexicon*   58
Murad IV, Ottoman sultan   26, 87, 97, 99, 101–102, 105–106
Murray's guide to Egypt   176–7
Muṭarrizī, al-, *Mughrib*   213, 252, 269–70
Mutazilite   290, 295, 301

Nābulusī, ʿAbd al-Ghanī al-   198
Nagel, Johann Andreas Michael   327
Napoleon   169, 171–2, 393
Nāṣir al-Dīn al-Ṭūsī   66
Naṭanzī, al-, *Dustūr al-lugha*   252
Nathan ben Jehiel, *Arukh*   236–7, 263
Naudé, Gabriel   100
Nebrija, Antonio de   209, 212, 238
Negri, Salomon   334–5
Nektarios, Greek patriarch of Jerusalem   117
Neophytes, College of in Rome   6–7, 215, 273, 296
Nerreter, David   323, 335, 400–401
    Neu-eröffnete Mahometanische Moschea   328, 400
Nestorians   215
    and eucharistic controversy   113, 118–119
Netchetailov, Vladimir   184
Neuer Bücher-Saal der Gelehrter Welt   321
Newton, Isaac   308
Nicaea, Council of   85
Nicetas of Byzantium   285
Nicolai, Johannes   39–40

Nicole, Pierre (see also *Perpetuité de la foy de l'Eglise catholique touchant l'eucharistie, La*) and eucharistic controversy 111–14, 118–20, 127
Nissel, Johann Georg 327
Nointel, Charles Olier, marquis de 125
  and Jansenists 114–18, 121
Nostiz, Otto von 25
Nouveaux mémoires des missions de la Compagnie de Jésus dans le Levant 166
Núñez, Hernán 209

Obicini, Giovanni Battista (Tommaso da Novara) 272
Ockley, Simon 301, 352
Ogier d'Anglure 151–2
Öhrnberg, Kai 191, 195, 198, 200–1
Okolski, Szymon, *Orbis Polonus* 47
Oley, Barnabas 227
Omar Agha 14
Oporinus, Johannes 283
Oriel College, Oxford 11
Orientalische Akademie, Vienna 42, 48–9, 216, 372
Orléans, Gaston, duc d' 88–9, 94, 107
Ortelius, Jacobus 241, 246
Ossian 346, 357
Ottheinrich, elector palatine 377
Ovid, *Metamorphoses* 47
Oxford University 3–4, 10–14, 21, 31–35, 37, 215, 226, 320

Pagnini, Sanctes 260, 266–7
  Enchiridion expositionis vocabulorum Haruch 267
  Lexicon latino-hebraicum 18, 266
Paisios, Greek patriarch of Alexandria 117
Palva, Heikki 201
Panaiotis, Nicousios 46–7, 116–17, 121
Panizzi, Antonio 64
Parry, James 11
Parry, William, *A New and Large Discourse* 291
Parthenius IV, patriarch of Constantinople 117, 126–7
Pasor, Matthias 293
Pattison, Mark 64
Paul the Hermit, St 149, 151, 155, 161, 163, 167, 169, 179

Pauw, Pieter 266
Peiresc, Nicolas Fabri de 86
  and Coptic manuscripts 153–4
  and Marcheville 89–90, 92–6, 99–103, 106–109
Père Joseph *see* Leclerc du Tremblay, Joseph
Perizonius, Jacobus 139
Perpetuité de la foy de l'Eglise catholique touchant l'eucharistie, La (see also Arnauld, Antoine; Nicole, Pierre) 112, 118–19, 122
Persian studies 94, 108, 248–9, 306, 317
  and Galland 114
  and Golius 386–8
  and Raphelengius 236, 249, 387
  and Reland 132
Persius 83
Peter the Venerable 185
Pétis de la Croix, François the Elder 127
Petit, Samuel 109
Petitpied, Nicolas 113–14
Petri, Nicolaus 3
Petrus Alfonsi 185
Pfaff, Christoph Matthäus 338
Pfeiffer, August 318, 330, 334
Philip II, king of Spain 238, 262
Philipp Christoph von Sötern, elector of Trier 89
Piankoff, Alexandre 184
Picques, Louis 314, 316, 318, 330, 398
Pierre de Bretagne 154
Pierre d'Abbeville 109
Pignon, Pierre-Jean 166
Pihlflyckt, Kirn 191
Plantin, Christophe 18, 65, 77, 212, 231, 239, 259, 261–3, 265
Platin, Margaretha 259
Platt, Miss 173–4
Pococke, Edward 31–2, 144, 146–7, 198, 208, 216–17, 293–5, 300–2, 322, 327
  and Danz 309
  Historia compendiosa dynastiarum 295
  Specimen Historiae Arabum 294–5, 344, 356, 362
Pococke, Edward the Younger 146
Pococke, Richard, *Description of the East* 166–9
politiques 88

INDEX

Polybius 61
Pontanus, Hendrik 145–6
Port-Royal
  des Champs 114
  Paris 111, 113
Postel, Guillaume 52, 64, 67, 70, 207, 210–11, 215, 240, 249, 259
  De orbis terrae concordia 289–90
  Grammatica arabica 66–7, 210, 377–8
  Linguarum characterum differentium alphabetum introductio 270
  and Qur'an 265, 284, 289–90, 298, 377–8, 380–1
  and Raphelengius 212, 232–4, 238, 241, 243
  and Scaliger 54, 290
Preindl, Josef von 49
Presbyterians 174, 183
Prester John 151–2, 157
Prideaux, Humphrey 36, 360, 363
  True Nature of Imposture fully display'd in the Life of Mahomet 294
Propaganda Fide, Congregatio de 109, 153–4, 158, 160, 174, 205, 272, 278, 297, 300, 315, 382–3
Protestant Churches and eucharistic controversy 120–7
proverbs, edition of Arabic (*see also Kitāb al-amthāl seu Proverbiorum arabicorum centuriae duae*) 60–1, 81–3, 273
Ptolemy 90
Puchheim, Johann Rudolf von 28, 30, 104–105
Putenaus, Erycius 15, 21, 37, 91, 109

Qāmūs see Fīrūzābādī, al-
Qaraḥiṣārī, Muṣṭafā ben Shamsaddīn al-, al-Akhtarī 213, 252–3, 270
Qaṣīda al-Khazrajiyya 383
Quatremère, Etienne 128, 193
Quedlinburg 356–7
Questenberg, Gerard von 25
Quietists 300, 323
Quirino, Gacomo 114
Qur'an 144
  and Acoluthus 315–19, 398–400
  Augusti's translation 369–71, 411

Beck's specimen 304, 306–8, 310, 316–17, 327, 329
Bibliander's edition 235, 278, 308
Boysen's translation 356–65, 366, 409, 412
and Callenberg 334–5
Casaubon's copies 59–60, 83–4
Castrodardo's translation 308, 328
Danz's specimen 304, 308–10, 316, 323, 327, 329
Ecchellensis and 278–9
and Erpenius 283
and Fleischer 374–6, 411–12
and Frischmuth 306
and Froriep 337
and Galland 333–4
Glazemaker translates 137, 305, 328
and Golius 283, 386–8, 392–3
Hammer Purgstall's specimens 373–4, 376, 411–12
Hinckelmann's Arabic edition 295, 310–11, 316, 318, 328, 335, 343, 356, 358–9, 367, 376, 405
and Holste 378
and Juan Andrés 284, 286, 289
and Kehr 333, 335, 388, 400
and Köhler 342–3, 365–6
and Lange 305–6, 323, 328, 334
and Leibniz 303–4, 306–8, 313–14, 319–20, 323, 329–31
and Ludovici 334
and Magliabechi 303–4, 306, 319, 327, 397
Marracci's translation 284, 299, 301, 308, 312–13, 328, 334–7, 340, 343, 347, 351, 356, 358–9, 367 , 381, 384, 390–3, 395–413
Megerlin's translation 339–43, 347, 360, 366, 372, 374, 409, 412
and Michaelis 364–5, 368, 406–8
Nerreter's translation 328, 400
and Postel 265, 284, 289–90, 298, 377–8, 380–1
Raphelengius's copies 235, 256–7
Raphelengius plans to translate 239
Reineccius's translation 328, 405–6
and Reiske 366–8

Qur'an (cont.)
    and Reland   134, 147–8
    Robert of Ketton translates   206, 278,
        284, 298, 305, 309, 328, 340–1, 378,
        380–2, 385, 397, 409
    Rückert's translation   375–6, 412
    Sale's translation   301, 323, 328, 333,
        335–7, 340–3, 347, 352, 358, 361–3,
        365, 370, 374–5, 381–2, 398, 404–5,
        407–8
    Savary's translation   359, 368, 374, 411–12
    Schweigger's translation   318
    and Sike   142, 144, 320–2
    Starck's specimen   304, 311–14, 323, 327
    Theodor Arnold's translation   328,
        335–6, 341–2, 347, 374
    translated by Dadichi and Negri   334–5
    translated by Du Ryer   94, 278–9, 283,
        297–8, 305, 311, 322–3, 328, 337, 340,
        358, 368, 390–1, 409–11
    Ullmann's translation   373–6, 411
    Wahl's edition   371–2, 374, 412
    and Zechendorff   316, 327, 386
Qurṭubī, al-, *Tadhkira*   289

Racine, Jean   119
Radtmann, Bartholomeus, *Introductio in
    linguam arabicam*   65, 67–8, 210, 379
Raimondi, Giambattista, *Alphabetum
    arabicum*   65, 210, 379
Ramshausen, Frans Wilhelm von, *Exercitatio
    theologica Ecclesiae Copticae*   37
Ramus, Petrus   140
Raphaël du Mans   115
Raphelengius, Christoffel   221–2, 250, 255
Raphelengius, Franciscus the Elder   66, 68,
    73, 77, 212
    his Arabic manuscripts   256–8
    his Hebrew manuscripts   259–68
    Lexicon Arabico-Latinum   213, 214, 227,
        229–58, 269, 381
    and Postel   212, 232–4, 238, 241, 243, 290
    Specimen characterum arabicorum
        64–5, 379
    *Variae lectiones ex Novi Testamenti Syrici
        manuscripto codice Coloniensi*   261
Raphelengius, Frans the Younger   12, 20, 73,
    213, 218–26, 229, 239–40, 249–51, 255,
    264–5

Raphelengius, Joost   12, 20, 73, 213, 218–26,
    229, 239–40, 249–51, 255, 264–5, 276
Ravenel de Sablonnières, Robert de   87
Ravius, Christian   3, 31, 129, 141, 315–16,
    325–7, 331, 338, 399
Ravius, Johann   327
Rawlinson, Henry   196
Rāzī, Fakhr al-Dīn al-, *Tafsīr al-kabīr*   322
Reformed Franciscans and Copts   158, 163
Regius, Henricus   139–40
Reineccius, Christian   351
    *Mohammedis filii Abdallae pseudo-
        prophetae Fides Islamitica, i.e.
        Al-Coranus*   328, 405–6
Reiser, Anton   306
Reiske, Johann   304, 329
Reiske, Johann Jacob   208, 301, 324, 326, 342,
    344, 346, 358, 365, 370, 375
    and Qur'an   366–8
    *Geschichte der königlichen Akademie ... zu
        Paris*   365–8
Reland, Adriaen   301, 391–2, 401–3
    as a cartographer   133
    De religione mohammedica   133–6, 137–8,
        144, 147–8, 278, 320, 410
    De libertate philosophandi   140
    De symbolo Mohammedico   142
    *De consensu Mohammedanismi et
        Judaismi*   142
    education and early career   129–31
    Galatea   132
    and languages   132–3
    and Marracci   147–8, 402–3
    *Oratio de incremento, quod Philosophia
        cepit hoc saeculo*   145
    *Palestina ex monumentibus veteribus
        illustrata*   133
    and Qur'an   134, 147–8
    and Sike   320
    at Utrecht   132, 137–8, 140–2, 144–9, 391
Reland, Johanna Catharina   132
Reland, Pieter   134
Renaudot, Eusèbe (*see also Perpetuité de
    la foy de l'Eglise catholique touchant
    l'eucharistie, La*)   38–9, 118, 120, 127
    Historia Patriarcharum Alexandrinorum
        37, 119, 410
    Liturgiarum orientalium collectio   119

INDEX

Renaudot, Théophraste 119
Reneri, Hendrik 92, 109
Rescius, Rutger 235, 257
Rhazes 266
Richardson, Samuel, *Clarissa* 335
Richelieu, Cardinal Armand-Jean Du Plessis de 89, 113
Ricoldo da Montecroce 284, 286, 308
Ridolfi, Andrea 114
Riḍwān, ʿAli ben 266
Rīghī al-Tūnisī, al-, *Tanwīr fī al-tafsīr* 297
Rivault de Fleurance, David 60
Rivus, Gerardus 17
Robert of Ketton 206
    Qur'an translation 278, 284, 298, 305, 308, 328, 340–1, 378, 380–2, 385, 397, 409
Robinson, Edward 133
Rödiger, Emil 200
Roëll, Hermann Alexander 146–7
Rogers, Daniel 69
Roper, William 265
Ross, Alexander, *ΠΑΝΣΕΒΕΙΑ: Or, A View of All Religions in the World* 400
Royal Geographical Society 197, 200
Royen, David van 255, 264
Rückert, Friedrich 375–6, 412
    Hebräische Propheten 376
Russell, Alexander and Patrick, *Natural History of Aleppo* 302
Russian Geographical Society 200
Russian Orthodox Church 174–5
Rycaut, Paul 98, 122–3
    Present State of the Greek and Armenian Churches 123
Rzewusky, Count Wenzeslaus von 373

Saadia Gaon 212, 236
Saʿdi, *Danistān* 108
    Gulistan 94, 108–109
Sadleir, Sir Edwin, Bart 36
Ṣaghānī, al-, *al-Takmila* 252, 269
St Antony, Monastery of 6, 149, 154–5, 160–2, 167, 169–71, 173–4, 179–84
St Catherine, Monastery of 174, 182, 196
Saint-Cyran, Jean Duvergier de Hauranne, abbé de 111
St Mary Hall, Oxford 11

St Paul, Monastery of 149–90
St Petersburg, University of 193, 199
Saint-Priest, François-Emmanuel Guignard, comte de 98
Sale, George, *The Koran* 301, 323, 328, 333, 335–7, 340–3, 347, 352, 358, 361–3, 365, 370, 374–5, 381–2, 398, 404–5, 407–8
San Clemente, Don Guillén de 236
Ṣanhājī, Muḥammad ibn Muḥammad ibn Dāwūd al- 66
Sanxay, Elzéar de 115
Sattler, Hubert 196
Sauer, Joseph 186
Saumaise, Claude 108
Savary de Brèves, François 3, 53, 94, 97, 297
Savary, Claude-Etienne, *Le Coran, traduit de l'arabe* 359, 368, 374, 411–12
Savonarola, Girolamo 308
Savorgnan di Brazzà 172
Scaliger, Joseph Justus 221, 224, 227, 241, 245, 250, 263, 266, 267, 293–5
    on Arabic studies 58–9, 129, 207, 211, 212, 241–5
    and Barbatus 6, 8, 9, 18, 20
    and Casaubon 54–63, 67–8, 71, 77–8, 80–81, 84, 86, 224
    De emendatione temporum 67, 207
    and Islam 290–1
    Manilius's, *Astronomicon* 218
    Opuscula 69
    and Raphelengius 211–12, 229, 231, 241–4, 254–6, 264
    'Thesaurus linguae arabicae' 242–3
    Thesaurus temporum 248
Schickard, Wilhelm 91, 109
Schieferdecker, Johann David, *Nucleus institutionum* 389–90
Schilling, Gottfried 181
Schindler, Valentin, *Lexicon Pentaglotton* 206, 245
Schledehaus, August 195
Schmid, Johann Rudolf, Freiherr zum Schwarzenhorn 29–32, 44–5, 103–104
Schmidt, Jonas 39
Schnützlein, Georg Michael 372
Schönborn family 40
Schönborn-Buchheim library 25, 48
Schuler, August 181

Schultens, Albert   346, 356, 366, 388
Schultens, Hendrik Albert   39, 346
Schulze, Johann Heinrich   350, 359
Schurman, Anna Maria van   129
Schwally, Friedrich   364–5, 412
Schweigger, Salomon, *Al-Koranum Mahumedanum*   318
Schweinfurth, Georg August   176–9, 183, 185, 189
Schwenter, Daniel   22
Scialac, Victor (Naṣrallāh Shalaq)   271, 278
Scultetus, Abraham   13, 37
Seaman, William   317–18
Seelen, Johann Heinrich von   39
Seetzen, Ludwig   372
Séguier, Pierre   115, 270–2, 279, 283–4
Selden, John   75, 283, 293
    Eutychius patriarchus alexandrinus vindicatus   293
Sellius, Bernardus   262
Seminar für Orientalische Sprachen, Berlin   372
Semler, Johann Salomo   347, 351–5
Senguerd, Wolferd   131
Senkovski, Ossip Ivanovich   199
Serapion   76
Serrurier, Joseph   146–7
Sève, Colonel Joseph (Sulayman Pasha)   172
Severin, Friedrich   369
Severus of Antioch   154–5
Shāhidī, *Tuhfe-i Shāhidī*   108
Shahrastānī, al-, *Kitāb al-milal wa 'l-niḥal*   295
Sharpe, Samuel, *History of Egypt*   171
Shaw, Norton   200
Shaybānī, al-, *Kitāb al-kāmil fī 'l- tārīkh*.   295
Shirwood, Robert   16
Sicard, Claude   180
    and Copts   157–63, 166–9, 177
Sigismund III, king of Poland   23
Ṣiḥāḥ   *see* Jawharī, al-
Sike, Henry (Heinrich Siecke)   141–2, 320–3, 325–6, 329
    Evangelium Infantiae   142–3, 319
    and Qur'an   304, 319–22
    and Reland   131, 141–5
Simon, Richard   127

Simonis, Johann, *Lexicon manuale hebraicum et chaldaicum*   351
Sionita, Gabriel and Scialac, Victor, *Dictionarium Arabo-Latinum ex Alcorano et celebrioribus authoribus*   278–9
Sionita, Gabriel (Jibrā'īl al-Ṣahyūnī)   3, 75, 278–80
Sirleto, Domenico   273–4
Sixtus V, pope   7
Slade, Matthew   12
Smith Lewis, Agnes   182–3
Smith, Agnes   *see* Smith Lewis, Agnes
Smith, Margaret   *see* Dunlop Gibson, Margaret
Smith, Miles, bishop of Gloucester   13
Smith, Thomas   122–123
Snellius, Willebordus   91
Société de Géographie   196
Socinianism   354–5
Sogaro, François   180
Solingen, Nicolas van   139
Somigli, Teodosio   181
Sommaville, Antoine de   409
Soncino, Eliezer Bekor Gerson   212, 236, 263
Sophia Albertina of Sweden, princess   356
Spanheim, Ezechiel   312
Spanheim, Frederik   255
Spanheim, Frederik the Younger   255, 264, 341
Sparvenfeld, Gabriel   314, 319
Spencer, John   308
    De legibus Hebraeorum   228
Spey, Ruthger   377
    Compendium grammatices arabicae   65–6, 77, 210, 377, 379
Spinoza, Benedictus   143, 146, 321, 354, 356
Spitta, Wilhelm
    Grammatik des arabischen Vulgärdialectes von Aegypten   65–6, 77, 200
Spon, Jacob   118
Starck, Sebastian Gottfried   304, 311–14, 323, 327
    Maryam, Specimen Versionis Coranicae   312–13
Steinschneider, Moritz   266
Stephenson, John   283
Strabo   90

INDEX 433

Strassburg, Paul   102–103
Struve, Johann Julius   350, 355
Strzygowski, Josef   183–4
Stuart, Princess Elizabeth   13
Sulayman Pasha   *see* Sève, Colonel Joseph
Suleyman, shah of Persia   126
Surenhuys, Willem   130, 140
Surūjī, Jirjis Abū Yūsuf al-   175
Suyūṭī, ʿAbd al-Raḥmān b. Abū Bakr al-, *De proprietatibus*   274
Suyūṭī, Jalāl al-Dīn al-   *see Tafsīr al-Jalālayn*
Sylvestre de Sacy, Isaac   128, 374–6, 411
    Grammaire arabe   211
Synnodius   161–2
Syriac studies, Raphelengius and   261
Szőny-Gyarmat   26, 44–5

Ṭabarī, al-   292, 382
Tacitus   358
Tafsīr al-Jalālayn   279, 289, 297–8, 300–1, 311, 313, 321–2, 329, 335, 362, 368, 381, 386, 391, 396, 405–6
Takmila   *see* Ṣaghānī, al-
Talavera, Fernando de   209
Tallemant des Réaux, Gédéon   94, 107
Talleyrand   172
Ṭanṭawī ,Muḥammad ʿAyyād al-   193, 200
Ṭarafa, *Muʿallaqa*   144, 346
Taṣrīf, al-   *see* Zanjānī, al-
Tattam, Henry   173–4
Tavus, Joseph ben Joseph   387
Teelinck, Johan   132
Tempesta, Antonio   58
Tengnagel, Sebastian   24, 26–7, 31, 46–8, 61, 86
Tenzel, Wilhelm Ernst   34, 37, 303
    Monatliche Unterredungen   399, 412–13
Thaʿlabī, al-   301, 322, 329
Theophrastus   60
Theunisz, Jan   *see* Antonides, Joannes
Thijssen-Schoute, Louise   137
Thirty Years War   22, 154
Thomas a Jesu, *De procuranda omnium gentium salute*   20
Thomasius, Christian   355
Thompson, Jaaon   201
Thou, Jacques-Auguste de   53–4
Thugut, Franz Maria de Paula von   48

Tiger, Ambroise de   115
Toland, John   361
Toledo, Pedro de   21, 37
Topal Receb Paşa   102, 104
Torricelli, Evangelista   145
Tottoli, Roberto   327
Tourtechot, Claude   *see* Granger, Claude
Traun, Count Ferdinand Ernst von   303
Tremblay, Joseph Leclerc du   *see* Leclerc du Tremblay, Joseph
Tremellius   77
Trent, Council of   260
Trigland, Jacob   309
Tromler, Karl Heinrich   330
    Abbildung der Jacobitischen oder Coptischen Kirche   40
Tübingen, University of   337–8
Tughrāʾī, al-   356
Tuki, Rafael   160–1
Turkish language, study of, Scaliger and   248–9
    Erpenius and   251–4
Turner, Peter   226
Turpin, François-René, *Histoire de l'Alcoran*   410–11
Twelve Years' Truce   14
Typographia Medicea   6–7, 58–60, 65–6, 77–8, 210, 219, 225, 238–9

Ullmann, Ludwig, *Der Koran*   373–6, 411
ʿUrābī Pasha, Aḥmad   180, 183
Urban VIII, pope   215
Uspensky, Porphyrios   174–6, 179
Utrecht, University of   391
    Arabic studies at   129
    Cartesians at   137–38
    Reland at   132, 137–8, 140–2, 144–9, 401
    Sike at   319–20
Uz, Johann   350

Vallan, Jacobus   139
Varick, Hendrik van, markgrave of Antwerp   17
Vatican Library   5, 34, 39, 274–5, 296, 383
Vattier, Pierre   113, 156
Vechter, Thomas de   265
Veer, Pieter van der   146
Velthuysen, Lambert van   139

Verda von Werdenberg, Johann Baptista   25
Veyssière de La Croze, Mathurin   86, 308, 330, 398
Victoria, queen of England   182
Vienne, Council of   205, 286
Vignozzi da Seano, Fortunato   181
Villari, Giovanni, *Historie universali*   48
Vincent de Paul, St   283
Visocha, Casimir de   114
Vitré, Antoine   95, 286
Vitré, Jr   95
Vitringa, Campegius   146
Voetius, Gisbertus   129, 138–40, 147
    Disputatio de Mohammedanismo   141
Voltaire, *Le fanatisme ou Mahomet le Prophète*   347
Voss, Heinrich   350
Vossius, Gerard   10
Vossius, Isaac   33
Vriemoet, Emo Lucius, *Arabismus*   337, 391–2, 403–4
Vries, Gerard de   131, 138–9, 146
Vulcanius, Bonaventura, *Thesaurus utriusque linguae*   77–8

Wādī al-Naṭrūn   149, 158
Wagenseil, Johann Christoph   303, 329, 397
Wahl, Samuel Friedrich Günther   371–2, 374, 412
Wakefield, Robert   16
Wallin, Georg August   191–201
    'Probe'   199
    'Über die Laute des Arabischen'   200
    'Bemerkungen'   200
Wansleben, Johann Michael   33
    Histoire de l'église d'Alexandrie   37–9, 157
    Voyage fait en Egypte   39
Warner, Levinus   31, 129, 208, 325–6
Wasmuth, Matthias   315, 327, 331, 338, 384–5, 399
Weiss, Leonhard   306
Welser, Marcus   56
Westminster College, Cambridge   183
Wettstein, Johann Jakob   355
Wheeler, George   125
Wheelock, Abraham   227

White, Joseph   295
Whittemore, Thomas   184–5
Widmanstetter, Johann Albrecht   23, 85
Wieland, Christoph Martin   357
Wiggers, Johannes   21
Wilhelm VIII, landgrave of Hessen-Kassel   339
Wilkins, David   34
Wilkinson, John Gardner   169–71, 176–7
William III of Orange, stadhouder of Holland and king of England   131
Witsius, Herman   131, 139, 142
Witt, Johan de   138, 147
Wittichius, Christophorus   139
Wolder, David   17
Wolzogen, Ludwig   139
Wood, Anthony, *Fasti oxonienses*   37
Wormsius Aser Anselmus, *Sepes Legis*   339
Wreszinski, Walter   184
Wright, William   211
Wyche, Sir Paul   98

Ya'qūb, *qummuṣ* of St Antony's monastery   6
Ya'qūb ibn Sayyid 'Alī   280
Yūsuf ibn Abū Dhaqn   *see* Barbatus, Josephus

Zabīdī, Murtaḍa al-, *Tāj al-'arūs*   318
Zamakhsharī, al-   286, 289, 295, 301, 313, 322, 329, 342, 375, 381, 386–7
    Al-kashshāf 'an haqā'iq al-tanzīl   286, 294, 300
    Asās al-balāgha   318
Zampio, Giuseppe Maria   115
Zanjānī, al-, *Taṣrīf*   210
Zayas, Gabriel de   262
Zayd   285
Zaynab   285
Zechendorff, Johannes   316, 327, 386
Zeitschrift für Ägyptische Sprache und Altertumskunde   184
Zeitschrift der Deutschen Morgenländischen Gesellschaft   191, 198–200
Zekeriyyazade Yahya Efendi   99, 102
Zinzendorf, Count Ludwig von   355
Zollikofer, Georg Joachim   339
Zonaras chronicles   47